A HISTORY OF THE UNITED STATES
SINCE THE CIVIL WAR

A HISTORY

OF

THE UNITED STATES

SINCE THE CIVIL WAR

BY

ELLIS PAXSON OBERHOLTZER

IN FIVE VOLUMES

VOLUME III: 1872-78

NEGRO UNIVERSITIES PRESS
NEW YORK

Originally published in 1917-37
by The Macmillan Company, New York

Reprinted 1969 by
Negro Universities Press
A DIVISION OF GREENWOOD PUBLISHING CORP.
NEW YORK

SBN 8371-2644-4

CONTENTS

CHAPTER XVII

THE GREELEY CAMPAIGN

CHAPTER XVIII

THE PANIC OF 1873

CHAPTER XIX

CLEARING AWAY THE WRECK.

CONTENTS vii

CHAPTER XX

ROUT OF THE CARPETBAGGERS

PAGES

CHAPTER XXI

HAYES AND TILDEN

CHAPTER XXII

THE HAYES ADMINISTRATION

CONTENTS

CHAPTER XXIII

ON THE PLAINS AND IN THE MOUNTAINS

CHAPTER XXIV

LETTERS AND ART

A HISTORY OF THE UNITED STATES
SINCE THE CIVIL WAR

A HISTORY OF THE UNITED STATES SINCE THE CIVIL WAR

CHAPTER XVII

THE GREELEY CAMPAIGN

THE early months of 1872 found the Grant men and their opponents in line of battle. The issue was made and it would be taken to the people. Should Grant and the organization which had been formed by the audacious, cunning, and, in very considerable part, venal men, who had found their opportunity in his coming to the first office in the land, continue in place for four years more, or should those who had higher ideals for the public service reclaim the Republican party,[1] or, failing in this, accomplish their estimable objects by a new and separate party movement? The call had been heard in Missouri in 1870 when B. Gratz Brown had been elected governor of that state and Carl Schurz had been sent to the United States Senate. These Missouri Republicans were "Liberals." "Liberals" appeared in other states. Schurz, with great parliamentary and forensic talent,[2] proclaimed the principles of the party at Washington, where he found response in the hearts of several men, among whom the ablest and the purest of mind, was Senator Trumbull of Illinois.

[1] Which one of its sturdiest leaders, Senator Grimes, called "the most corrupt and debauched political party that has ever existed." (Horace White, Life of Lyman Trumbull, p. 341.) Whitelaw Reid wrote John Bigelow at the end of the year 1871 that "the depth of corruption" which the administration had reached was "scarcely suspected as yet even by its enemies."—R. Cortissoz, Life of Reid, vol. i, p. 204.

[2] He spoke, said the New York Nation, with "that powerful and telling rhetoric of which he was the greatest master in America." (Issue of April 18, 1872.) "The one man," said Charles Francis Adams, in 1871, "who seemed to understand our institutions, their spirit, their history, their dangers and their possibilities better than any other citizen was of foreign birth, and his name Carl Schurz."—N. Y. Times, May 9, 1872.

1

Sumner's influence was reduced because of the circumstances which had carried him into a camp hostile to the President, and because of the violence of his antagonism to the administration. Anyhow his history, as well as his present character as a public man, made him an unnatural consort of "Liberals." But the prestige of his name and his distinguished abilities constituted him a power in the land which no one could safely underrate. Senator Fenton of New York, a suave and an effective debater, pitted against Conkling, his colleague, who was yokefellow of Grant; Senator Tipton of Nebraska, who had dissolved his partnership with the Radicals for his own reasons in his own state; and Senator Ferry of Connecticut, who, however, drew back under party pressure when he saw the length to which his defection was carrying him, were also skillful members of the opposition. [1]

Here was a group like that one, with Doolittle at its head, which had left the Republican party to support the measures of President Johnson; like the senators, with Fessenden, Grimes and Trumbull as leaders, who had brought the impeachment proceedings, to naught. All were men who could not be leashed by the Radical leaders of the Grant administration for selfish partisan ends.

The "Liberals" were Western men and they had several ideas which they would engraft upon the national polity. First of all they were in favor of amnesty, in letting by-gones be by-gones on the subject of the war, in so far as this result might be attainable. They were opposed to movements which meant further extension and centralization of Federal power. They had obstructed the passage of the Southern "Force Bills," designed to break up the Ku Klux Klan, through Federal interference, in a field which they, in common with the Democrats, held to be sacred to the states. They protested against the penalties and restrictions which the Radicals were including in the bills in Congress for the return of the Southern

[1] The defection of these and other leaders in the nation and the states is described in some detail in E. D. Ross, The Liberal Republican Movement, pp. 17–33.

states to the Union. They were stout advocates of "civil service reform" to correct the atrocious abuses seen South, North and West in official life. They saw oppression and wrong in the high tariff laws and they demanded lower rates, a cause which had come to be generally known as "revenue reform."

The Grant men, not knowing how deeply such doctrines might have come to infect popular thought at the North, and particularly in the West whence they drew their power, had no intention of being caught without a defense. They extended general amnesty, in 1872, to all but a few of the most prominent of the "rebel" leaders, who in a body were restored to their old privileges as electors, and were again made eligible to public office. Through the management of Speaker Blaine, the tariff was reduced in some degree and the civil service reformers were conciliated by the appointment of George William Curtis to head a civil service commission, which came to include the valuable support of the President and his administration by Harper's Weekly, and of Joseph Medill, as an associate of Curtis on the same board, which might, it was supposed, have some influence upon the course of the Chicago Tribune, a journal of so much authority in the West. The resentment which Collector Thomas Murphy's administration of the custom house in New York City had created, emphasized by the Leet-Stocking exposures, was to be met by the removal of this incompetent officer in favor of General Arthur, another lieutenant, though a more respected one, of Senator Conkling in New York state. Grant himself meantime (though he had foolishly expressed regret at Murphy's departure from office in a letter to that man) made public statements which caused many, as well as Mr. Curtis, to look upon the President with a new trust. It was not without a sense of its expediency that Charles Francis Adams, one whom Grant so little liked, was honored with the appointment as our representative at Geneva for the adjustment of the *Alabama* claims.[1] Also it was with

---

[1] Overtures were made to Adams also by the Grant managers, which would have given him a place on the Republican ticket as the candidate for Vice President in 1872.—Life of C. F. Adams, p. 392.

some hope of attaching to the administration the negroes who might, during the approaching campaign, stray away in the retinue of Sumner that their leader, Frederick Douglass, was given a secretary's post in connection with the San Domingo commission.

So much was done by the Republican leaders in an attempt to meet the Liberal secession, and check a movement which no one of them held in much dread, though he could not measure the lengths which it might reach before that day in November when each man should say his say at the polls.

The Democrats, meanwhile, surveyed the scene attentively. Their defeat as a result of their obstinate course in 1868 had not been without its lessons, and it was the subject of melancholy reflection. Some better way must be taken if the party were to make head against the prevailing current of national sentiment. Already in May, 1871, it was announced that the Copperhead, Vallandigham, at a party convention at Dayton, Ohio, would present a series of resolutions enunciating principles for the Democrats in state and nation, which would mark a "new departure." The resolutions in question called for an acceptance of "the natural and legitimate results of the war," including the Thirteenth, Fourteenth and Fifteenth Amendments. These subjects were to be taken out of the realm of party politics; they were no longer issues before the country The Republicans were invited to join the Democrats in a demand for a return to a "strict construction" of the Constitution and make declarations against the abridgment of the rights of the states; against the usurpations of authority by President and Congress, which were giving an altered character to the government; against the destruction of the principles of local self-government. Republicans were called upon to leave the "Radical party," which was no longer the Republican party, but now only "an administration, or Grant party," representing doctrines which the people should emphatically condemn.[1] Even the currency question, the "Ohio idea," which had been held with so much tenacity in 1868, was put to one side. The

[1] Article on Ohio in Am. Ann. Cyclop. for 1871.

"five twenties" could be paid in gold for anything that the Democrats of Ohio now seemed to care. In June, 1871, the Ohio state convention at Columbus incorporated the principal planks of the Vallandigham platform in its platform. The "new departure" met with the favor of Democrats in other states.

It was clear enough that the party, under Western leadership, whatever had been its mistakes in the past, whatever these mistakes might be in the future, was on the eve of a great change. Such declarations might or might not be sincere. In any case they were evidence of a strategy which was a promise that the Democrats might again make themselves a factor in the winning of elections and the direction of the nation's affairs. To bring so much about it was agreed that their correct course was to pursue a "passive" policy.

The Western Liberals within the Republican party were going forward with the hope that they could make the renomination of Grant seem quite inexpedient in the eyes of the Radical leaders. To name him for a second term, they would have it thought, would spell certain defeat. But the President himself had no intention of being served in such a manner. When John W. Forney and other Radicals had visited Grant to tender him the nomination, in 1868, they declared that he had made his leaving the army conditional upon a promise that he should have the office for eight years.[1] If he had voted for James Buchanan in 1856,[2] and for Douglas, as some said, or Breckinridge, as others alleged, in 1860, now, when he could stand at the head of the party, he was a very stubborn Republican. It was plain that he was a candidate to succeed himself; and it was equally plain that the partisans, who had built up so powerful and so corrupt an organization around him, were bent upon his renomination, so that there might be no interruption of their profitable connections with the state. In April, 1871, Grant appeared at a public reception at Indian-

[1] N. Y. Nation, Feb. 29 and March 7, 1872; N. Y. Tribune, Feb. 27, 1872; A. K. McClure, Old Time Notes of Pa., vol. ii, p. 216.
[2] Cortissoz, Life of Whitelaw Reid, vol. i, p. 208.

apolis, at which time the campaign was formally launched.
On this occasion Senator Morton, one of the most powerful
of the administration leaders, found the opportunity to announce that the party would keep to the "main question."
It was, said Senator Thurman of Ohio, "the same old note
again"—"the same old tune again"—"the same old horrors
of the rebellion"—"the same old wickedness of the instigators
of that rebellion"—"the same old terrible suffering that that
rebellion entailed upon the country." [1]

Assuredly the party would stick to the "main question."
Should the Democrats return to power the Radical Republicans
did not hesitate to declare that they would take away the
pensions of Union soldiers. If not this they would, to a certainty, pension the rebel soldiers as well. The Southern states
which had been held in the Union only by the war would, at
Copperhead and rebel instigation, be allowed to secede in peace.
All that had been achieved would be instantly lost. [2] Scandals,
whether at the South or at the North, could be forgiven, civil
service and revenue reforms could be ignored and left for the
future. These were nothing in comparison with loyalty to the
Union during the late war, gratitude to the soldiers for winning
it, and the protection of the freedmen, to the extent at least
of making certain that they could and would cast their ballots
for the Republican ticket. On this platform the Radicals would
go to the country in 1872, as in 1868, with the hero of Appomattox as their leader.

The Liberals looked on not idly. They were preparing to
proceed in their own way. No one had more reason to know
of the low depths to which the administration of Grant had
fallen than Jacob D. Cox, lately his Secretary of the Interior.
All his honest standards for the public service had been sunk
under the weight of the sordid partisanship which was in
ascendency at Washington. Already in February, 1871,
Senator Schurz, who held the most prominent place in the
direction of the movement, had written to Cox opposing Grant's

[1] Harper's Weekly, Feb. 10, 1872.
[2] Article on U. S. in Am. Ann. Cyclop. for 1871.

renomination. The Republican party was "drifting into great dangers," he said; "a great many things" were "as they ought not to be." An attempt was being made to create the impression that the party could be successful in 1872 only if Grant were the candidate. "Nothing can be more demoralizing," Schurz continued, "than to identify a cause with a person, and nothing can be more dangerous, at the same time, when that person is in a fair way of becoming a heavy load to that cause." [1]

Cox shared Schurz's views, and, joined, in March, 1871, by several other Republicans in Cincinnati, an association[2] was organized and a declaration of principles was adopted, reflecting the change of sentiment, which, it was said, had taken place among the people of the West and Northwest. Such evidences of activity in Ohio Schurz welcomed cordially. He asked Cox to extend the movement throughout the state and into Indiana. He hoped that similar associations might be formed "all over the country," so that the party might be cleared of the "train of officers and office-mongers" pressing upon it like "a great incubus."[3]

Schurz was soon ready to state his views publicly, and he did so to a large audience in Chicago on August 12, and again to another audience at Nashville on September 20, 1871, when he openly declared, his words being carried over the country by telegraph, that he would not "help to re-elect" such a President as Grant had shown himself to be by an endorsement of the usurpations and corruptions which had signalized the administration.[4]

So bold a course drew forth expressions of the liveliest satisfaction from Sumner, especially as to those parts of the address which touched upon the person and policies of Grant. "The more I think of him and his doings," said Sumner, "the more I feel his incompetency and wrongheartedness. I tremble for my country when I contemplate the possibility of this man

[1] Schurz, Speeches, vol. ii, pp. 176–7; cf. ibid., pp. 253, 255.
[2] The Central Republican Association of Hamilton County.
[3] Schurz, Speeches, vol. ii, p. 255.
[4] Ibid., p. 272; cf. Harper's Weekly, Jan. 27, March 9, and Aug. 10, 1872.

being fastened upon us for another four years." What might
be done to avert this disaster?[1] Schurz said that the answer
was an opposite organization. "We must act with energy,"
he said. "I am fully determined not to sit still." [2]

Out of Schurz's Nashville speech came a number of organizations in Tennessee and in other parts of the South.[3] The movement was beginning to wear the appearance of being national.
It was gaining a strength which betokened important results.

Meanwhile Trumbull, next to Schurz, the largest and most
influential of the worthy figures leading the movement, was
similarly concerning himself about the situation. He was still
in the Senate, where his voice was raised for reform. All that
was necessary "to sweep the plunderers from power and purify
the government" was "to organize the better elements" of
the party, he said.[4] The time had come to "reform the Republican organization"; he believed that this could be done "without turning the government over to the Democrats." [5] He
spoke in the Senate on February 23, 1872, condemning those
who would "subordinate the public welfare to party," and
calling upon Republicans to consider the principles which
underlay their organization at its foundation, and its departures
from the course then marked out for it. Evils were at hand,
the country was "reeking with corruption," but the party,
always party, and allegiance to party, supervened to obstruct
the progress of men with good ends in view. Trumbull's speech
was an eloquent plea for an immediate return to higher standards of thought and action concerning public affairs.[6]

An event destined to have great importance upon the course
of events was a journey which Horace Greeley made to the
South in the summer of 1871. He was bound for Houston,
Texas, where he had been invited to deliver an address. But
he had the broader purpose of seeing the South and studying

[1] Schurz, Speeches, vol. ii, p. 309.
[2] Ibid., p. 311.
[3] Ibid., p. 314.
[4] Trumbull to a correspondent, March 8, 1872, in Trumbull Papers,
Library of Congress.
[5] Ibid.
[6] Cong. Globe, 42nd Cong. 2nd sess., app., pp. 82–7.

the conditions which prevailed there. Thousands, by whom
his name had long been sounded forth as enemy or fanatic,
acclaimed him and it soon appeared, from his speech and from
the temper of his writing in the New York Tribune, that he had
come to an understanding of the mischiefs of the "carpetbag
system" of government, and that he was in a frame of mind
to denounce it with the courage that he brought to the discussion of whatever cause he espoused. Violent partisan, as he
had been for many a day and many a year, of the black man as
against the white master, he now was constrained to see what
monstrous evils had come from the Radical policy of putting
the old white element into a posture of subjection to the negroes
and the imported whites who were using the freedmen for
their own ends. He made several addresses in Texas as well as
in other Southern states. Upon his return to New York he
was invited to address the Lincoln Club in that city, on which
occasion he dwelt at length in plain terms upon the situation
as he had found it. The "thieving carpetbaggers" were characterized in his vigorous way as "the greatest obstacles to the
triumph and permanent ascendency of Republican principles
at the South." [1] These men represented the North to Southern
eyes, and they disgraced it. Rascality there was and would
be in a democracy.

> "A tyrant—but our masters then
> Were still at least our countrymen,"

Byron had said. Here, however, was stealing by an alien hand.
The plunder was being carried out of the state in which it was
stolen. With pious faces, concerned as they alleged for the
welfare of the blacks, they exclaimed, "Let us pray." But
the "a" in "pray" was an "e", and, with the apostolic injunc-
tion in mind, they "preyed" without ceasing. [2]

For a long time Greeley and the Tribune had been advocates
of universal amnesty and impartial suffrage. He welcomed
the "new departure" of the Democrats. There should be a
"new departure for all men in all parties." The country was

---

[1] L. D. Ingersoll, Life of Horace Greeley, p. 526.   [2] Ibid., p. 525.

done with the old issues. He summoned it to a new contest—to "a departure from strife to harmony, from destruction to construction, from desolation to peace and plenty." [1]

Here was a new and an influential recruit for the Liberal party. That Greeley had been a boisterous protectionist, while most of the Western Liberals were revenue reformers, made common action seem impossible. [2] As late as on January 29, 1872, he said that he was "likely to be against the bolters," since they were "almost certain to make hostility to protection" one of the planks in their platform, "and that the Tribune can never abide." [3] On March 16 he said again: "The protection of home industry is of more importance, in our view, than the success of any party ticket." [4] But Greeley, like the Western leaders, was placing himself in the position of a man without a party. [5]

Clearly the movement was drifting toward independent nominations. Efforts to bring about a reunion of the Republican factions in Missouri had failed. Co-operation in the country at large in the approaching national campaign was equally difficult. To further their plans the leaders in St. Louis called a meeting which was to be held in Jefferson City on January 24, 1872. When that day came delegates from a large number of counties crowded into the straggling little town, set on the rising banks of the murky Missouri, which serves that state as its capital. Now was said more than before. The platform adopted by the meeting, in addition to containing a statement of principles earlier enunciated by the Liberals, attacked the use of Federal patronage for the control of elections, of which the Grant men had been guilty in Missouri as well as in other states, the "packing" of the Supreme Court in the Radical interest, the Ku Klux legislation, and the general corruptions of the time. The meeting issued a call for an "uprising of

---

[1] L. D. Ingersoll, Life of Greeley, p. 528; cf. Autobiography of A. D. White, vol. i, pp. 161-2; E. D. Ross, The Liberal Republican Movement, pp. 38-9.

[2] Ingersoll, Life of Greeley, pp. 518, 528.

[3] N. Y. Tribune, Jan. 29, 1872.

[4] Ibid., March 16, 1872.   [5] Cf. ibid., Jan. 31, 1872.

honest citizens." All who were in sympathy with Liberal principles were invited to assemble in a national convention to meet at Cincinnati on the first Wednesday in May "to take such action as their convictions of duty and the public exigencies may require." [1]

The call met instant response. This and that committee, mass meeting, association forwarded its reply to the chairman of the Liberal Republican State Committee of Missouri, Colonel William M. Grosvenor, a free trader whom Greeley had often flayed, long, and until recently, editor of the Missouri Democrat.[2] A score of Republicans in New York expressed their concurrence in what had been done. Greeley's name was among the number, a fact which was noted and welcomed by the friends of the movement everywhere. The Chicago Tribune said that he represented "a larger following in the state of New York than any other Republican politician." As the editor of the party's ablest and most powerful organ "he wielded an influence over the popular mind which no other Republican statesman can pretend to rival." [3]

This action was followed, on April 12, by a meeting in Cooper Institute. Crowds were turned away. Schurz and Trumbull in powerful speeches urged upon the country a return to a government founded on constitutional principles, a return to respect for law, to a system of local control in public affairs— as against the advances of the Federal government toward the centralization of power—to honesty in the public service.[4] A declaration of principles was adopted. It was New York's "first response to Cincinnati." It was an answer, said the New York Tribune, "worthy of the noblest cause." [5] The movement gathered force rapidly. The Tribune, the Evening Post, the Nation, in New York; the Springfield Republican, the Chicago Tribune, the Cincinnati Commercial, the Louis-

[1] Article on Missouri in Am. Ann. Cyclop. for 1872; letter of Grosvenor in N. Y. Tribune, Feb. 10, 1872; N. Y. Nation, Feb. 15, 1872.
[2] A paper now acting in the opposite interest and zealous in its defense of the Grant administration.
[3] Chicago Tribune, quoted in N. Y. Tribune, April 2, 1872.
[4] N. Y. Tribune, April 13, 1872; N. Y. Nation, April 18, 1872.
[5] N. Y. Tribune, April 13, 1872.

ville Courier-Journal, the St. Louis Republican, a large number of men, well known in state and national politics, came to the support of the enterprise.

But the zeal of some of the "reformers" was too great to give any assurance of the purity of their motives. The leaders in New York were friends of Reuben E. Fenton; they belonged to a faction which had been beaten at their own game of office-hunting at Washington by Roscoe Conkling.[1] That Grant would no longer recognize them as claimants for Federal offices had made them into Liberals. Curtin, his manager, Alexander K. McClure, and the Liberal leaders in Pennsylvania were drawn into opposition to Grant because all the offices in that state were being given to Simon Cameron. No Radical had been more violent than John W. Forney, the editor of the Philadelphia Press. He had been appointed collector of the port in Philadelphia, which he thought but a small reward for his services. He administered the office incompetently. He now resigned his place to turn his newspaper upon the Cameron "machine." These and many more were "soreheads" —all together, to unfriendly judges, they took on the appearance of an "army of soreheads."[2]

In the field, preparing for the Presidential campaign, there were malcontents of other kinds. With little prospect of finding congenial associations in any one of the older parties some men, in August, 1871, held a National Labor Congress in St. Louis. Though black slavery had been abolished this group found that labor generally was still the chattel of a few capitalists. The "Congress" denounced "banking and moneyed monopolies," railroad, land, manufacturing and "commercial and grain monopolies," which were "speculating to enrich their bloated corporations on human necessities." The cure was fiat money. The "five twenties" should be paid in paper currency. The "Congress" also declared for lower tariffs, prohibition of the importation of coolie labor, the financing of future wars by the capitalists of the country and not by the workingmen,

[1] Cf. Harper's Weekly, Aug. 10, 1872.
[2] Ibid., June 8, 1872.

the conservation of the public domain against the assaults upon it of railway companies, the submission to the people of projects for the annexation of territory, and general amnesty as a means of at once restoring the Union "on the basis of an equality of rights and privileges to all classes and interests." [1]

Out of this St. Louis "Congress" came a national convention at Columbus, Ohio, on Washington's Birthday, 1872. A dozen states sent delegates to the meeting and a platform was adopted expressive of the sentiments of what was called the "Labor Reform Party." It made declarations, similar to those which had been formulated at St. Louis in the previous year, in favor of a modification of the tariff, the exclusion of Chinese labor, an eight-hour day for workingmen in government employ, the abolition of the contract labor system in prisons and other public institutions, the conservation of the public lands for the use of landless settlers, the abolition of currency issued by banks, the payment of the national debt, "in good faith according to the original contract," i.e., in greenbacks, civil service reform and amnesty for participants in the rebellion. David Davis, a justice of the Supreme Court by appointment to that place by Lincoln, whose personal friend he was in Illinois, was nominated for President, while Governor Joel Parker of New Jersey was named for Vice President. Davis was held to be a Republican, Parker was a Democrat. They awaited the development of events.

The negroes, and the whites who were engaged in the interesting occupation of guiding them aright on the subject of their political action, also were not idle. In September, 1871, they held a national convention in St. Louis, in the interest of Grant's renomination, endorsing all of his policies, including the scheme for the annexation of San Domingo.

A Southern negro convention met in Columbia, S. C., in October, 1871. Charles Sumner, not without a reasonable hope that he, for his indomitable exertions for the abolition of slavery and his continued efforts, after the war, to secure civil

[1] Article on the U. S. in Am. Ann. Cyclop. for 1871.

rights to the freedman, would be accepted, in some measure, as a leader of the race, addressed the body in a letter, which but ill concealed his hostility to the Grant administration.[1] The Southern negroes on this occasion made some declarations which were published throughout the country, and called a national convention of colored men, which assembled in New Orleans on April 15, 1872. At this meeting several delegates appeared from the Northern states and Fred Douglass was present to act as chairman. Sumner again sent a letter to the delegates on the subject of "equal rights."[2] But they, while expressing the opinion that it would be "ingratitude, loathed by men and abhorred by God," if they should not acknowledge their "overflowing indebtedness" to him, who for so long had stood alone in the Senate as "the Gibraltar of our cause and the north star of our hopes," contented themselves with this verbal tribute. Douglass himself was a politician of ambitions. He had gone to San Domingo with Grant's commissioners. Upon his return he had been insulted, so Sumner said, by being "thrust back from the dinner table" at the White House, "where his brother commissioners were already seated."[3] But Douglass, on reflection, found that he had not been insulted, and he and his negroes now all together pledged their "unwavering devotion" to the nominee of the Republican party, whoever he might be, and who, as everyone knew, would be Grant. They "sincerely and gratefully endorsed the administration of President U. S. Grant in maintaining our liberties, in protecting us in our privileges, in punishing our enemies." They thanked him for the offices to which he had appointed them, and "earnestly prayed" for the "stimulation" which would come to them from further "recognition of Federal patronage."[4] The Republican party is the "deck," said Douglass on this occasion; "all else is the sea."[5]

[1] Article on U. S. in Am. Ann. Cyclop. for 1871.
[2] Sumner's Works, vol. xv, pp. 68–9.
[3] Article on U. S. in Am. Ann. Cyclop. for 1871.
[4] Ibid., for 1872.
[5] Harper's Weekly, May 25 and June 8, 1872.

The Democrats successfully kept to their resolution to remain "passive," [1] in a confident belief that the division in the Republican party would result to their early and great advantage.[2] The investigations in Congress, particularly as to the management of the New York custom house, proceeded— the charges of dishonesty here and corruption there which were bandied about on all sides were heard with unconcealed delight. The defection of a number of Republican newspapers which had been prominent in the movement for Grant's election in 1868 was full of encouragement. In particular did the implacable hostility to the administration of the New York Tribune, influential as it long had been and as it still was accounted to be, raise the hopes of the Democrats. That paper, since it had made the "new departure," was "a more powerful instrument for the disorganization and defeat of the Republican party," said Harper's Weekly, "than the entire Democratic press of the country combined." [3] In February Greeley, as the member of the Republican National Committee for New York, refused to sign the call for a national convention of his party.[4] He was writing private letters to Democrats urging them, as a means of defeating Grant, to nominate a "Liberal," such as Gratz Brown, Trumbull or Cox.[5]

Just this course did they propose to adopt. The Chicago Times, the most influential Democratic newspaper in the West, said that nine out of ten Democrats would, this year, vote for a Republican.[6] The party, were it to act alone, could not secure one-third part of the whole electoral vote. The only way successfully to combat "imperialism and corruption" was to unite with the disaffected Republicans.[7] More than ever was it made plain, after the election in New Hampshire in March, where a Democratic majority in 1871 was converted

[1] Harper's Weekly, Feb. 17 and March 23, 1872.
[2] They were "as quiet as a cat at a mouse hole," said Harper's Weekly, March 30, 1872.
[3] Harper's Weekly, Jan. 13, 1872.
[4] Ibid., Feb. 10, 1872; N. Y. Tribune, Feb. 20, 1872.
[5] Harper's Weekly, Jan. 13, 1872; N. Y. Tribune, Jan. 1 and 4, 1872.
[6] Quoted in Harper's Weekly, Feb. 17, 1872.
[7] Ibid., April 6, 1872.

into a majority for the Republican candidates,[1] that the only hope of the party lay in junction with interests which could more certainly fire the popular heart.[2]

The Cincinnati convention was to be a mixture of town meeting and barbecue of national proportions.[3] Professional party hacks and honest reformers, Susan B. Anthony and two or three other women who found delight in parading the aisles, mounting the platform and imposing themselves upon the scene in the interest, as they believed, of the enfranchisement of the female sex, George Francis Train, cranks, fools and not a few outright knaves—all were jumbled together. Some were delegates of this or that local organization, while others were present simply in testimony of their personal interest in the proceedings. It was a mass meeting of men from all parts of the Union, including the South. There were those who wished to nominate Charles Francis Adams; others who saw in David Davis a suitable leader of the new party in the coming campaign. There were, too, Gratz Brown men, Trumbull men, Greeley men, Curtin men, Fenton men, a few who would have gladly nominated Sumner, though the movement was unorganized and gained no strength. Chase had his friends and he himself, though his health was faltering and his end was near, had the hope that his ambitions might yet be gratified. Again he would "not refuse the use of his name," [4] though he foresaw that it would "not be much considered" by the convention.[5]

The "Queen City" on the "beautiful river" was then a place of larger relative importance than it has since become by reason of Chicago's rise as a great and wealthy metropolis. But its hospitalities were severely tried. The hotels and boarding houses were filled. Private homes were requisitioned for use. Beds were placed in vacant buildings. Some of the invaders of the city remained in their sleeping cars on the rail-

---

[1] N. Y. Nation, March 14 and 21, 1872.
[2] Harper's Weekly, March 30 and April 6 and 27, 1872.
[3] "Come," said Greeley, "and bring your neighbors and your friends."— Ibid., March 30, 1872.
[4] Cf. Warden, Life of Chase, pp. 728, 729; Hart, S. P. Chase, p. 413.
[5] Letter of April 29, 1872, in N. Y. Tribune of May 3, 1872.

way tracks; others, on the steamboats floating at the docks; many crossed the new suspension bridge and quartered themselves upon the people of Kentucky. The Germans came in "swarms," [1] in testimony of the leadership of Schurz. Out of this chaos of persons was to issue a political party which would supersede the two old parties, and put in Grant's place a high thinking and an enlightened statesman, capable of bringing the nation into better paths.

The worthiest element among the throng had come with the wish to nominate Charles Francis Adams. It was agreed. that he would be a fine exponent of the principles of the new party—of civil service reform, revenue reform, state rights, a return to old constitutional rules and precedents; he would be a dignified and an honorable figure for the contest. If there were to be that fusion with the Democrats, which there must be to insure success for the ticket at the polls, their wishes in the matter ought to be taken into account. Many of their leaders had been brought to view the candidacy of Mr. Adams favorably, among the number August Belmont, chairman of the Democratic National Committee, and Manton Marble, the able editor of the New York World. [2]

But the candidate was an Adams. [3] He was in the midst of the tasks incident to the *Alabama* arbitration. After the "cases" had been presented at Geneva, in the interval of time, during the winter of 1871–72, which would be allowed agents and counsel for preparing their counter statements, he had come home and was occupied with his own affairs. Only a few days before the Cincinnati meeting would convene he had set sail for Europe to resume his duties, and, upon his departure, he despatched a letter, which was not calculated to aid his advocates, to David A. Wells. As Mr. Adams saw the strange company gathering for the work of reform he could not regard them with favor or admiration. He would not "peddle" with any one "for power." If he were to be "negotiated for," if

[1] Cincinnati Commercial, quoted in N. Y. Tribune, April 26, 1872.

[2] Horace White, Life of Trumbull, pp. 373–4; cf. N. Y. World, April 26, 27 and 30 and May 1, 1872.

[3] Cf. Merriam, Life and Times of Samuel Bowles, vol. ii, pp. 180–81.

assurances must be given that he was honest, he asked Wells
to have the friendship to draw him "out of that crowd." While
he did say that he would respond to the call, if it were an "unequivocal one," he made it clear that less than this would cause
him to decline an invitation to lead the movement.[1] The tone
of the letter [2] was considered to be one of "lofty contempt." [3]
It had a coldness, some said a frivolity, that could make him
no new friends.[4]

Those who supported Trumbull for the nomination were
active and intelligent also, and, while most of them were found
in Illinois and the West, the favor accorded him was widely
enough scattered to be national in character. His trusted
advocate and representative on the ground was Horace White,
editor of the Chicago Tribune. Trumbull had been clear from
the first that the convention should be "distinctly Republican."
The movement should be within the party were it to attain
success. He was without selfish ambitions. He would not
go to Cincinnati. He must not be nominated, he wrote White,
unless there was a "decided feeling" among the delegates,
"outside of rings and bargains," that he would be "stronger
than any one else." [5]

The least estimable elements in the cave of Adullam, whose
denizens had issued forth to fall upon Cincinnati,[6] were those
who followed the fortunes of David Davis, the nominee of the
Labor party on a paper money platform. In truckling for the
nomination, though he wore the robes of a justice of the Supreme
Court, his course had met with no more favor than had Chase's
unfortunate dalliance with the politicians in 1868. His was a
"poor man's party," but Davis, its leader, enriched by specula-

---

[1] Article on the U. S. in Am. Ann. Cyclop. for 1872.

[2] Printed, it appears, on the mistaken advice of Bowles.—N. Y. World,
April 29, 1872.

[3] N. Y. Times, April 27, 1872.

[4] N. Y. Tribune, April 27, 1872; Henry Watterson, Marse Henry, vol. i,
pp. 253–4; Merriam, Life and Times of Samuel Bowles, vol, ii, p. 181;
Linn, Horace Greeley, pp. 237–8; Horace White, Life of Trumbull, p. 378.

[5] Letter dated April 24, 1872, in Trumbull Papers in Library of Congress.

[6] "A livelier and more variegated omnium gatherum was never assembled."
—Watterson, Marse Henry, vol. i, p. 242.

tions in land in the expanding city of Chicago, was the wealthiest man, it was said, who had ever sought the Presidency.[1] Moreover, he displayed a willingness to use his money in the interest of his nomination. The "job," as Samuel Bowles called it, was "industriously put up" at Washington, and in New York, Pennsylvania and Illinois. Headquarters at which mortal hunger and thirst might be satisfied, were established in Cincinnati. Free tickets upon the railroads, purchased out of the "fund" which the candidate put at the disposal of his managers, brought delegates from the South, and from other parts of the country; many made the free excursion from Illinois and more were to be had in Chicago on a few hours' notice as the need arose for men "to roar for Davis." [2]

In a peculiar way the convention was the creation of several newspaper editors who were on the scene to direct its movements. Never before, and at no time since, have journalists so largely controlled a national political meeting. The leaders in Missouri owned or edited newspapers, or had done so. Horace White, representing Trumbull, used the great influence of the Chicago Tribune in behalf of the Cincinnati movement. It was aided, too, by Murat Halstead, through the Commercial in Cincinnati, by Henry Watterson, through the Courier-Journal in Louisville, by Samuel Bowles, through the Springfield Republican, while Greeley, the greatest figure of them all, lent the entire strength of the New York Tribune to the cause.[3] Four of this number, White, Bowles, Halstead and Watterson, with differing talents, and, one must think, differing standards of honesty as well, full of youthful enthusiasm, made a kind of four-power pact, and, in allusion to the four

[1] Harper's Weekly said that Davis was worth $3,000,000.—Issue of April 6, 1872.

[2] Cincinnati Commercial, quoted in N. Y. Tribune, May 1, 1872; Schurz, Speeches, vol. ii, p. 371; Watterson, Marse Henry, vol. i, pp. 246–7; Horace White, Life of Trumbull, p. 380; F. G. W., That Convention; E. D. Ross, The Liberal Republican Movement, pp. 86–8; G. W. Julian, Political Recollections, p. 338; Letter of Samuel Bowles in N. Y. Tribune, May 6, 1873. The progress of this manipulation is told from memory by A. K. McClure in Old Time Notes of Pa., chap. lxxxi.

[3] Cf. Merriam, Life and Times of Samuel Bowles, vol. ii, pp. 178, 184; N. Y. Evening Post, May 16, 1872.

fortified towns of northern Italy, which were the support of the
Austrian occupation of that country, were pretentiously called
the "Quadrilateral." They met behind closed doors, often in
association with Schurz, with whom they co-operated, agreed
upon policies and directed public opinion, in so far as they
might, through letters and telegrams to their respective newspapers.

The building in which the convention met, the Cincinnati
Exposition Hall, was immense. It seated 8,000 persons.
Colonel Grosvenor called the assemblage to order at noon on
Wednesday, May 1, soon handing the gavel to Judge Stanley
Matthews, a respectable figure in Ohio, afterward a justice
of the United States Supreme Court, the temporary chairman.
Mob delegations were present from every state in the Union.
Each was ordered to meet and to choose representatives equal
to double the number of votes cast by the state, whence the
men came, in the electoral college.

On Thursday Carl Schurz, clearly, as Horace White wrote
to Trumbull, "the leader and master mind of this great movement," [1] was named for the permanent chairmanship. He
took his place in the center of the spacious stage, designed to
hold the large Cincinnati musical choruses, "amid a perfect
whirlwind of cheers and applause." [2] He brought honor to
the post. His occupying it provided assurance that the action
of the convention from day to day would receive the respectful
consideration of the country. His speech was concluded "in
a storm of enthusiastic acclamation." [3]

The platform presented difficulties which were unusual.
Seldom in a convention have there been so many men of so
many minds which were to be harmonized, if the party were
to present a united front to the foe. But these difficulties were
surmounted by a committee over which Horace White presided.
The platform which it proposed and presented began with a
forceful statement or address to the people, the work of Carl

[1] Schurz, Reminiscences, vol. iii, p. 342.
[2] Schurz, Speeches, vol. ii, pp. 354–61.
[3] Cincinnati corr. N. Y. Tribune, May 3, 1872.

Schurz,[1] after which the "Liberal Republicans of the United States, in national convention assembled," enunciated a number of principles in clear language, mainly as follows: Union, with emancipation and enfranchisement, and no reopening of "the questions settled by the Thirteenth, Fourteenth and Fifteenth Amendments to the Constitution"; universal amnesty; supremacy of civil over military authority, and "state self-government"; a reformed civil service—that service had become "a mere instrument of partisan tyranny and personal ambition, and an object of selfish greed"—it was a "scandal and reproach upon free institutions"; a single term for the Presidency; maintenance of the public credit; a "speedy return to specie payments" in the interest of "commercial morality and honest government"; opposition to all further grants of public land to railroads and other private corporations. Only on the tariff, among the questions which had called the convention into being, was there equivocation. Here was a rock upon which the ship might have been split with a spilling of the entire useful cargo. It was ascertained that the old editor of the Tribune would be content if the tariff were dismissed as a local question. The Pennsylvanians who shared his views accepted the compromise,[2] and, as nothing else was possible, the committee on resolutions, dominated by the revenue reformers, after plaguing itself for a whole night in search of a way out of the difficulty, acceded also. The convention would "remit the discussion of the subject to the people in their Congressional districts, and to the decision of Congress thereon, wholly free of Executive interference or dictation."

So much having been effected, the restless groups which had gathered under the banners of particular candidates urged the convention forward to the nominations. From the first the friends of Adams were in the ascendency in point of numbers, and his strength had increased as a result of private meetings preliminary to the balloting. The Davis "boom," it was ob-

[1] Schurz, Speeches, vol. ii, p. 388.
[2] Cf. N. Y. Tribune, April 30, 1872; Horace White, Life of Trumbull, pp. 381-2.

served with satisfaction, became less and less formidable, because of the activities of the "Quadrilateral." Senator Fenton who had been employed in this behalf returned to Washington. A. K. McClure of Pennsylvania, who had been active in the same interest, was obliged to give his mind to new bargainings.[1] As the Davis bubble burst the advocates of Greeley's nomination, made possible by the convention's evasions on the tariff question, gained assurance, as odd a figure as he presented in a bid for favor as a leader of the new party. Still, however, no one outside of his own immediate circle of friends, entertained a serious thought that he would be the convention's choice. Men laughed when his name was spoken. Some delegates might vote for him, as they would for Chase or Sumner; he might, indeed, secure a large complimentary vote, but his nomination would be "an utterly ludicrous thing which would cover the proceedings with ridicule and contempt." [2]

Meanwhile much had been going on behind the scenes. The "Quadrilateral" had been "interviewing" leaders, manipulating delegations, "engineering" deals. Bowles was the particular advocate of Adams, White, of Trumbull.[3] It was agreed that the choice of the convention should be limited to these candidates, if the managers could bring so much about. Greeley remained in New York and Whitelaw Reid was on the ground with the task, self-imposed or delegated, as the case may have been, of representing his employer's interests. He, casting about for some alliances which would set his plans forward,[4] demanded to know by what right he had been excluded from the little circle by the four journalists.[5] In view of the unquestioned power of the New York Tribune, and,

[1] Cf. Merriam, Life and Times of Samuel Bowles, vol. ii, p. 185; Watterson, Marse Henry, vol. i, pp. 245-7; Horace White, Life of Trumbull, p. 380; A. K. McClure, Old Time Notes of Pa., chap. lxxxi; Horace White in Century Magazine, vol. 85, p. 45. "There was too much Democracy behind him [Davis]," White wrote to Trumbull on May 13, "and too much evidence of a net spread to catch the Presidency."—Trumbull Papers in Library of Congress.
[2] Cincinnati corr. N. Y. Nation, May 9, 1872.
[3] Cf. Horace White, Life of Trumbull, p. 375.
[4] Cf. Schurz, Reminiscences, vol. iii, p. 344.
[5] Watterson, Marse Henry, vol. i. p, 243.

with the tacit feeling that Greeley was a candidate in no way
to be feared, they reluctantly admitted him to their confidences,[1]
and the group of editorial oligarchs, who, in recalling their
performances on this occasion came to regard themselves so
seriously, increased their number to five.

Schurz, and the company of independent editors who stood
at his side, except Reid, were very certain that Adams was to
be the nominee. If the convention had been driven forward
to action on Thursday it is believed that this would have been
the result on the second or third ballot.[2] Adams was the second
choice of nearly all the delegations which were committed to
"favorite sons." [3] The oversetting of the planning and the cal-
culation came out of Missouri, the original home of the movement of which the convention was the fruit, and the motives
of those who were responsible for what was soon to occur were
in no manner the outgrowth of the idealism which, up to this
point, had marked the progress of the cause.

No account had been taken of B. Gratz Brown, governor
of Missouri, put into his place on the same wave of Liberal
feeling which had carried Schurz into the United States Senate,
or of General Francis P. Blair, Democratic candidate for Vice
President in 1868, now Schurz's colleague at Washington, a
place to which he had been chosen by Liberal votes in the legislature, in return for Democratic support for the Liberal state
ticket in 1870. It was not expected that either of the two men
would attend the convention. On Wednesday it was stated
that Brown would not and could not be present, but on Thursday morning rumors were heard that he was on his way to
Cincinnati.

During the campaign of 1870 Brown and Schurz had been
brought into the friendliest contact.[4] But Schurz had thought
that fusion with the Democrats in the legislature, with the end
of sending Blair to the Senate, was too great a price to pay for
their aid in 1870, while Brown had espoused Blair's cause.

[1] Cortissoz, Life of Reid, vol. i, p. 210; White, Life of Trumbull, p. 381.
[2] Watterson, Marse Henry, vol. i, p. 254.
[3] N. Y. Nation, May 8, 1872.
[4] Schurz, Speeches, vol. i, p. 521.

On this subject differences had arisen which widened as the
months passed.[1] Indeed the relations of the two men were now
quite cool, and it was by no means agreeable to Brown, when he
found that Schurz was chairman of the convention, and the
acknowledged leader of a national movement in which he believed that he was as well entitled to play a large part.[2] Blair
on his side had his family's feud with the Adamses to spur him
to activity.[3] Hearing that Colonel Grosvenor, who headed the
Missouri delegation, was co-operating with Schurz to bring
about the nomination of Charles Francis Adams, Blair joined
Brown, his kinsman, and his friend in journalism and in other
enterprises, for the journey.[4] On Thursday night the twain
arrived "fit for stratagems and spoils."

Schurz and the "Quadrilateral" were dumfounded. Grosvenor, after the Adams and Trumbull men had gone to bed,
went through the hotel knocking at their chamber doors, announcing the unwelcome event. The unexpected visitors were
already in secret conference with some of the members of the
Missouri delegation unfolding their plans for the morrow.[5]

Greeley's nomination still seemed so preposterous as to be
impossible. On Friday, the platform out of the way, the convention proceeded to the choice of candidates. The votes of
the delegations were being announced—there were 203 for
Adams, 147 for Greeley, 100 for Trumbull, 95 for Gratz Brown,
92½ for Davis, 62 for Curtin, who was being supported by
most of the Pennsylvanians. But, before the result was officially declared, Brown, with rare effrontery, came to the front
of the hall. He had sent a note to the chairman asking that he
be heard from the platform, and Schurz, with more courtesy
than the situation really demanded, interrupted the proceedings
to grant the request. Brown was already mounting the platform stairs. He had received a number of votes as a nominee

[1] Schurz, Reminiscences, vol. iii, pp. 341, 345.
[2] Cf. N. Y. Nation, May 9, 1872; Horace White, Life of Trumbull,
pp. 385, 389.
[3] Linn, Horace Greeley, p. 242.
[4] Cf. Merriam, Life and Times of Samuel Bowles, vol. ii, p. 186.
[5] White, Life of Trumbull, pp. 382–3. According to some newspaper
accounts Montgomery Blair was also on the ground.

for the Presidency. This was the excuse for him thus publicly to make a statement. He would withdraw his name. So much could have been borne, but, to the amazement of every one, he left the contest, so he averred, in the interest of Horace Greeley, for whom he bespoke the support of the convention.[1]

The assemblage was in a state of tense nervous excitement, and the sight of Brown on the platform trying to start a stampede to Greeley induced scenes of wild confusion. Though the result, which Brown and his clique hoped to achieve, was not to be attained immediately, further intrigue, characteristic of men who were old hands at such work, ensued and his dramatic performance was the beginning of the end.

On the second ballot Brown's support melted, leaving him but two votes, while Curtin's 62 friends all passed to other candidates. Adams gained 30, Trumbull 48, but Greeley's vote was increased by 92 to 239. On the third ballot Adams had 264, Greeley 258 and Trumbull 156. Hope of saving Adams was found in a closer compact with the Trumbull men with whom, from the first, there had been the friendliest relations, but who clung too obstinately, and too long to their idol.[2] On the fourth ballot Adams's vote was 279 and Greeley's 251. On the fifth ballot Adams advanced to 309 and Greeley to 258. By this time the Trumbull vote had fallen to 91 and David Davis's following numbered but 30 delegates. Adams's name was greeted with loud cheering whenever it was mentioned, and even yet it was believed that enough votes could be collected to give him the 358 necessary to a choice. More was expected from Illinois where, however, the Davis and Trumbull parties were equally and bitterly divided in strength, and from other states.

On the sixth ballot 324 votes were cast for Adams. Trumbull had but 19; it was clear that little more could come to Adams from that source. Greeley had 332. The end was near. Delegates hastened to change their votes, and, before the movement

---

[1] The unfairness of this action on Brown's part is clear when it is noted that the convention had determined to dispense with nominating speeches and to take the ballots by a mere calling of the roll of states.

[2] G. W. Julian, Political Recollections, p. 339.

had spent itself, 482 were recorded for Greeley, while but 187 remained faithful to Mr. Adams. Greeley was the nominee for President.

The convention proceeded to choose its candidate for the Vice Presidency. Gratz Brown was nominated for the second place on the ticket by a vote even greater than Greeley's, the Adams and Trumbull men supporting, for the most part, after Trumbull's withdrawal from the contest, George W. Julian of Indiana. The deed was done. The cunning elements had captured the convention and the results which now were seen were an expression of their will.[1]

The flotsam and jetsam which had drifted into Cincinnati upon the tide now scattered back in the various directions whence they had come, and Greeley and Brown were carried to the country as the men under whom the work of regenerating the Republican party should proceed. The convention refused to make either Greeley's or Brown's nominations unanimous. Schurz, in his discomfiture, had forgotten to announce that Greeley was the convention's choice until he was reminded from the floor that he had overlooked his duty in this respect.[2]

The group in Cincinnati, which had been a source of so much strength to the movement, left the scene in disgust. Some of them were soon gathered at the house of Judge J. B. Stallo, with Schurz, who, after a few moments of silence, turned to the piano and poured out his feeling through the keys which he so well knew how to use. Tears came to the eyes of the whole company.[3] General Cox was deeply chagrined. Judge Stanley Matthews, who had occupied the chair until Schurz came to the place, repudiated the ticket.[4] To him it was the

---

[1] "With this act, Brown, as a 'reformer,' " said the New York Nation, "left the stage." (Cincinnati corr. N. Y. Nation, May 9, 1872.) "It was the gambler's last chip," White wrote to Trumbull. Those who had thought Brown a sincere man would now know him for a "trickster," an impression which could "never be changed."—Trumbull Papers in Library of Congress.

[2] Cf. Schurz to Godkin in Schurz, Speeches, vol. ii, p. 447.

[3] Samuel Bowles in N. Y. Times, May 9, 1872; N. Y. Evening Post, May 15, 1872, quoting Cincinnati Commercial; Schurz, Speeches, vol. ii, p. 370.

[4] Schurz, Reminiscences, vol. iii, p. 375; G. W. Julian, Political Recollections, p. 340.

"disgraced and disgraceful convention." [1] General Brinkerhoff "swore the ticket blue." The candidates were named, he
said, by men "as clearly intruders" in the convention "as
Satan was when he presented himself among the children of
light." [2] Judge Hoadley was of the same mind—the nominations were the result of "a corrupt alliance of Tammany[3] and
Frank Blair." He would not support the ticket.[4] Judge
Stallo charged the majority with "fraud and duplicity": the
proceedings of the convention and its nominee for President
were "absurd and iniquitous." [5] He would not vote for Greeley. [6] The Germans instantly called a meeting to voice their
feelings. They would bolt the ticket and fight Greeley to the
"bitter end." [7] Brown was denounced by the rank and file
as a "red-headed, red-bearded scoundrel." [8]

The newspapers spoke in an instant. The New York Evening
Post and the New York Nation, two of the most valuable of
the defenders of the Cincinnati movement, would now retire
from all connection with it. The Post said that the popular
mind had turned toward the convention "for a possible decom-
position and recomposition of political affinities." After
Schurz's speech it was "big with promise," but it had "gone
the way of many a similar assemblage." It had "surrendered
stock and fluke to the wire pullers," it had "struck the
flag of its lofty principles," it had "sunk into commonplace
chicanery, intrigue, bargaining and compromise." Greeley
had been on every side of every public question [9] save one,
"and that was protectionism." "With such a head" as is on

[1] Warden, Life of Chase, p. 732; also N. Y. Tribune, May 18, 1872.
[2] Cincinnati corr. N. Y. World, May 4, 1872.
[3] Tammany Republicans of New York under the leadership of Senator Fenton.
[4] N. Y. Times, Aug. 24, 1872.
[5] Cincinnati Commercial, quoted in N. Y. Times, July 1, 1872.
[6] N. Y. Times, Sept. 17, 1872.
[7] Cincinnati corr. N. Y. World, May 4, 1872.
[8] Ibid.
[9] "Like the intoxicated indivijual who coodent get into bed coz the room waz whirlin round, and who determined finally to lay still and wait till the bed come round to him, all thet any question hez got to do is to stay still and Horris is certin to come round to it"—P. V. Nasby quoted in F. G. W., That Convention, p. 163.

Greeley's shoulders, the Post continued, "the affairs of the nation could not, under his direction, be wisely administered; with such manners as his, they could not be administered with common decorum; with such associates as he has taken to his bosom they could not be administered with common integrity."[1] "A greater degree of incredulity and disappointment" had not been felt since the news of the first battle of Bull Run, said the Nation. The nominations had been "effected by a trick of a more than usually barefaced kind." [2]

The New York Times had been calling the party "a combination of malcontents and guerrillas"; [3] it was a "little faction of grumble and fuss." [4] "Nobody in his senses believes," it remarked now, "that so eminently shrewd and practical a people as this would ever place such a man as Horace Greeley at the head of their government. If any one man could send a great nation to the dogs that man is Mr. Greeley. There is no department of business he would not disorganize and unsettle." [5]

It was "probably the only nomination for President ever made which was received by a good humored laugh," said Harper's Weekly.[6] No Liberal Republican in recalling "the origin of the movement could think of the results without mortification or amusement," said the New York Nation.[7] By the nomination, declared the Atlantic Monthly, the whole country had been set "on a broad grin." [8] This idea was very generally uttered in the press. If there were one quality indispensable in a President, it was "sound judgment," Harper's Weekly continued. "If there is one public man who is wholly destitute of it, it is Horace Greeley." [9]

[1] N. Y. Evening Post, May 4, 1872; cf. ibid., May 7, 1872.
[2] N. Y. Nation, May 9, 1872.
[3] Issue of March 2, 1872.
[4] April 9, 1872.
[5] May 4, 1872.
[6] Issue of May 18, 1872. When Trumbull in the Senate heard the news of Greeley's nomination he said: "If the country can stand the first outburst of mirth the nomination will call forth it may prove a strong ticket." —Washington corr. N. Y. Herald, May 4, 1872.
[7] Issue of May 9, 1872.
[8] Issue of July, 1872.
[9] Harper's Weekly, May 18, 1872.

To the New York World, speaking for that responsible element in the Democratic party which had been led to expect from the action at Cincinnati some propitiation of the feeling in that party, the result brought "intense astonishment and disappointment." Greeley was "the most conspicuous and heated opponent of the Democratic party that could be found in the whole country." [1] He was the man "above all others" whom it did not want, and whose "possible selection never entered into its calculations, when it was disposed to look with favor on the Cincinnati movement." [2]

The opportunity was gone. Once in 1866 some of the same forces, with at least a part of the same objects in view—the conciliation of the sections of the nation which had been so bitterly at variance with each other—had met in Philadelphia. Their exertions were brought to naught by Andrew Johnson's mad harangues as he "swung around the circle." In 1868, again, the better side of the national nature might have been reached if the Democrats had made Chase their candidate for the Presidency. That hope was dispelled through the mean activities of the Democratic politicians in New York and the paper money men from Ohio. Now, in 1872, a project marked for a yet finer destiny was wrecked by Republican politicians from New York, and by Frank Blair and Gratz Brown.

The "old curiosity" was at his desk in the Tribune office when the amazing news of his nomination reached New York. Reporters, mail clerks, office boys, pressmen, and then a crowd from the street, which had been intent upon reading the announcements on the bulletin boards, made their way in and called upon him for a speech. He withstood the demand but shook hands with his visitors.[3] A salute of 100 guns was fired at the City Hall in New York, at Albany, at Syracuse. Men in all parts of the Union, Chase and Trumbull among the number, telegraphed him pledging him their support.[4] Greeley campaign clubs were formed. The candidate soon escaped the

[1] N. Y. World, May 4, 1872.
[2] Ibid., May 5, 1872.
[3] N. Y. Tribune and N. Y. Sun, May 4, 1872.
[4] N. Y. Tribune, May 4, 1872.

city, taking refuge at his farm, where he was seen chopping
wood for the newspaper correspondents who were waiting to
carry to the ends of the land the, to him, pleasant accounts
of his axe, his trees, his cows and his crops.[1]

The editors of the "Quadrilateral" were so bewildered by
what had befallen them that they had the greatest difficulty
in choosing their courses. They must decide at once [2] and not
knowing what other road to take, since they all together were
so deeply involved in the movement, they determined to support the candidate with as much grace as they could command.
The Cincinnati Commercial said that the nomination had
been made by "the least responsible and reputable elements
of the convention." [3] Bowles had just written of the "perver-
sity of temper" of Greeley and his "openness to flattery." [4]
But the editor of the Springfield Republican put down the
rebellion within him and faced his tasks. No reading between
the lines in the editorials of the Chicago Tribune was necessary
to make clear the views of Horace White.[5]

Greeley was now 61 years old. Advancing from farm boy
to printer and editor, he was essentially a "self-made" product
of the age. Uneducated as he had been and as he remained, in
any true sense, he had acquired a vast amount of superficial
information about the widest variety of subjects. He wrote
with great ease and much power. With simple natural enthusiasm and the warmest sympathies for his fellow man he
set out to extirpate negro slavery, the greatest evil of the age,
and he did not weary of the struggle until his object was
achieved. His readers came to include not merely the anti-
slavery men of New York, New England and Pennsylvania,
but the zone of his influence covered the Western Reserve and
went farther west, as the settlement of the Mississippi Valley

[1] N. Y. Times, May 7, 1872.
[2] Horace White, Life of Trumbull, p. 384.
[3] Quoted in N. Y. Tribune, May 7, 1872.
[4] Letter of May 4 in Cincinnati Commercial, quoted in N. Y. Tribune,
May 6, 1872.
[5] The opinions of these and many other papers on the Greeley nominations are conveniently gathered together in the N. Y. Tribune, May 6, 7,
8, 9, 10 and 11, 1872.

by Eastern families of Abolitionist sentiments was extended. In a day when hamlets were scattered, when local newspapers were few, when telegraph and postal facilities were yet but poorly developed there was a field for weekly editions of metropolitan journals. The Weekly Tribune gained a very large circulation in the West where it was many men's "political Bible." [1]

In view of his services in behalf of the absorbing national cause which had been won, Greeley's influence, at the end of the war, was immense. But it began to be seen, before the contest was yet finished, that his counsel was often not valuable. He was deficient in good judgment about other men. He was given to sudden changes of course. He was a zealous and an insistent advocate of causes, but no one whom a nation could confidently employ in the development and execution of practicable policies. [2] The power of scolding and irritating, which had been enjoyed by his associates when it was used against the South, became an offense when it was directed against them. His "playing the rôle of infallibility" [3] made his leadership ungrateful to them.

In appearance, in his office, on the streets, or even on a platform, where he spoke with facility and very impressively, he was consciously and affectedly grotesque. His round, babylike face, surrounded to his ears by neck whiskers, his old clothes, the trousers often stuck in his boot-tops, his rumpled white coat, the pockets bulging with newspapers, and his white hat were as well known about as was his indecipherable handwriting. He had published his "American Conflict," a history of the Rebellion, and a work upon the tariff, concerning which he probably knew as little as any one of the many ignorant men who have entered this inviting field of economic discussion, and his "Recollections." A wiseacre on agricultural subjects in the Tribune, he some years since had bought himself a small farm on Chappaqua Creek, a few miles above White Plains,

---

[1] Cf. Rhodes, Historical Essays, p. 267.
[2] Cf. Ogden, Life of E. L. Godkin, vol. i, p. 168.
[3] W. R. Thayer, Life of John Hay, vol. i, p. 173.

beyond the northern limits of New York City,[1] where he
practiced the art with as little pecuniary ability as he brought
to other pursuits. His observations, "What I Know about
Farming," further advertised him as a writer as well as a tiller
of the soil.

Few men were more easily duped. Confiding he may have
been, or broadly sympathetic, or generous, perhaps, in his
dealings with his fellow men. It was what would pass in others
for shiftlessness. He would give away what rightfully belonged
to himself and to his family,[2] join in speculations that he had
no talent for and dissipate that which, by his labors as a writer
and a lecturer, he was entitled to receive and keep.[3]

His outreaching philanthropy, or, else the unsettlement of
his mind, or both, drew him to all kinds of social experiments.
He was the principal representative in journalism of that mental
attitude which had brought forth Brook Farm, which distinguished many a group of men and women in New England
and in the southeastern counties of Pennsylvania. Much
of his receptiveness to new ideas he gained from Mrs. Greeley,
who never allowed any "reform" to escape his notice. His
home was the refuge of women who were serving peculiar
ends. It became a laboratory for experimentation in the
theories of Dr. Sylvester Graham, and Greeley was made into
a vegetarian, an enemy of tea and coffee and an eater of bread
from unbolted flour.[4] He embraced Fourierism, as none of
his rivals in journalism allowed him to forget.[5] He stopped
to see what there was in "spiritualism." Temperance by prohibition laws, religion, free of creed and dogma, prison reform,
the abolition of capital punishment, liberal divorce laws, and
practically all the "isms" of the time, which were travelling
at the heels of Abolition, crowded in upon him to warm his
heart, when they did not move his mind, and much of what
he came to feel he carried into his newspaper, regardless of the

[1] Greeley, Recollections of a Busy Life, p. 295.
[2] Linn, Horace Greeley, p. 107; Ingersoll, Life of Greeley, pp. 561–2.
[3] Autobiography of A. D. White, vol. i, p. 160.
[4] Linn, Horace Greeley, pp. 86–7.
[5] Ibid., pp. 79–86.

predilections of his readers as to the causes which he espoused. It was thus that Greeley and the Tribune were made to stand in the sight of the nation for a soft philosophy.[1]

At the hour of beginning the war, that he, perhaps, more than any other one person had brought to the nation's doors, it was a horror of bloodshed, as much as the journalist's love of saying the sensational thing, of doing the spectacular deed, which led him to advocate letting the South peacefully leave the Union; [2] which then soon led him to demand an immediate advance upon Richmond, so that hostilities should be ended quickly; which later led him, now and again, to disturb Lincoln with proposals for various negotiations for a premature armistice.[3] It was a mixture of charitableness of heart and the showman's instinct, part pity and part Dutch courage, which took him to Richmond to enter his name on Jefferson Davis's bail bond.

But, with this femininity of feeling, this strangely made man mixed a hard and vulgar strength. In his unequal battle with slavery Greeley had not always succeeded in keeping himself in a calm mood. His excitement grew as the heat of the contest increased and his language was often rough and vituperative. When he quarrelled with some one who crossed his path he was an ugly adversary. His "You lie! You villain! You lie!" so frequent a retort to an opponent in a controversy that it became famous, was not hurled about in any meaningless way.[4] It was brute strength which now and again leaped forth to ruffle the surface of this "benign being." He would lay an enemy flat (this enemy being absent), stand on the fallen form and run his iron into the victim day after day with relentless fury.

The position of the editor makes for a despotic temper. He can rave and fulminate at a foe from behind his own doors to

[1] Linn, Horace Greeley, pp. 89–91.

[2] Ibid., pp. 184–7.

[3] Ibid., pp. 190–98, 202–10; cf. Harper's Weekly, May 18, 1872. Garrison said that he was "the worst of all counsellors, the most unsteady of all leaders, the most pliant of all compromisers in times of great public emergency."—Linn, op. cit., p. 171.

[4] Harper's Weekly, June 6, 1872.

the extent of the vocabulary, put the writing into print and send it out over the land. He can use the answer, if and when it shall be received, as he likes. Greeley, without restraint from any hand, developed the editorial character in an unusual degree, and his assurance of righteousness increased as the years multiplied over his head.

For long he had been possessed of a belief that he was created for a larger place in the world than any which he had thus far come to hold, for more honors, for greater distinction. He was the most widely known journalist in the country, if not in the world. He was not content. He had been the self-chosen, the free, the untiring adviser of Presidents, Congresses, Supreme Courts, of popes and potentates: he could not understand, why, if he had wisdom to give to others day by day in such volume and variety, he should not be fitted to occupy some high position in the ranks of his country's men of state. In a word he itched for public office,[1] and it was as much on this account as for want of the ability to choose wisely between men that he so often formed associations with dishonest politicians. Some came his way in the hope of using him for the attainment of their improper ends: he made harmful alliances with others with a view to his personal advancement in politics. They were such entanglements as these which had brought him into close relations with the Fentonites in New York, which now discredited his nomination and which would, during his campaign, make him seem to many eyes no reformer at all.

His hunger for office was bound up with a desire for notice and praise. His vanity took peculiar forms. He was bent upon seeming to be a kind of exemplar, as well as the hero, of the American common people. With this end in view did he wear white hats, white coats and stick his trousers into his boots. There were men to say that they had seen him go up small alleys, then deliberately raise his pantaloons and tuck them into the leather, so that he might present the figure which would serve his uses when he should return to the street. He

[1] Linn, Horace Greeley, p. 172; Cortissoz, Life of Whitelaw Reid, vol. i, p. 200.

would time his appearance at a public meeting after it was
organized so that his coming in would be remarked, and he
might receive a round of applause.[1] Greeley had begun to
pose. In the sight of many he was merely an old effigy. He
thought of himself, it appears, as another Franklin, a kind of
democratic sage whom the populace would run after, and listen
to and acclaim.[2]

Godkin wrote to Schurz about the "wretched mess." He
said that "no man of standing and character" could take the
stump for the nominee "without putting his whole future in
peril." It was conceded by "every man of sobriety and thought-
fulness" that his election would be "a national calamity of the
first magnitude." Did Schurz know "what a conceited, ignorant, half cracked, obstinate old creature" Greeley really was?[3]

William Cullen Bryant wrote that Greeley's "associates"
were of "the worst sort." If he should be elected his administration could not be else than "shamefully corrupt." There
is, Bryant continued, "no extravagance into which that man,
through the infirmity of his judgment, may not be betrayed."[4]
"I should at any time beforehand have said," Bryant remarked
again, "that the thing [the nomination of Greeley] was utterly
impossible, that it could not be done by men in their senses."[5]

Parke Godwin wrote to Schurz of Greeley's "utter unfitness for
the Presidency." He was "a charlatan from top to bottom,
and the smallest kind of a charlatan, for no other motive than
a weak and puerile vanity."[6] Bowles declared that Gratz
Brown's conduct had been "infamous."[7] Schurz's disgust

[1] Harper's Weekly, June 1, 1872, and August 3, 1872.
[2] Cf. Linn, op. cit., p. 95; N. Y. Tribune, May 18, 1872.
[3] Schurz, Speeches, vol. ii, p. 376.
[4] Horace White, Life of Trumbull, p. 386.
[5] Godwin, Life of Bryant, vol. ii, p. 323.
[6] Horace White, Life of Trumbull, p. 393. "Probably the most unfit
man for President, except Train, that has ever been mentioned," said
John Sherman, writing to his brother, General Sherman. (Sherman
Letters, p. 399.) "Capricious, conceited, peculiarly open to flattery and
prejudice, bold in opinion, but timid in action," said the Atlantic Monthly,
however much he might be esteemed there was something in his character
which made it "impossible not to laugh at him."—Atlantic Monthly,
August, 1872.
[7] Schurz, Speeches, vol. ii, p. 368.

was greater than any man's. Had he not, in his speech to the convention, upon taking his place as the presiding officer, condemned "the tricky manipulations" by which political bodies were so often controlled? They were to be despised as "unworthy" of the cause.[1] Precisely that spirit which he had denounced had entered the house of Reform. He did not overlook Brown's part in what had been done, but the principal object of his resentment was Frank Blair. "He," said Schurz, "was the evil genius whose very touch was destruction." He made the convention "the slaughter house of the most splendid opportunities of our times." [2]

But Schurz was left not without hope of finding a way to repair the disaster. He would now state the case candidly and lay it before Greeley in the thought that the nominee might, perhaps, see the futility of leading a contest which must result in his defeat, and the repudiation by the country of the common cause. As soon as he was again in Washington, on May 6, he wrote at length to the old editor of the Tribune. The proceedings at Cincinnati, he said, had "in some very important respects disappointed the expectations of many earnest friends of the national reform movement." He then told Greeley what Frank Blair and Gratz Brown had done. It had been said in the newspapers that they would come to the convention to effect an arrangement "between your and Brown's friends." They did come. It was unbelievable, but in the convention "the piece was enacted in literal accordance with the program announced; trade and delivery appeared in the open light of day." In its "present shape," Schurz continued, the movement could "no longer appeal to that higher moral sense which we hoped to have evoked in the hearts and minds of the people. Its freshness and flavor are gone and we have come down to the ordinary level of a campaign of politicians." He was not ready to state what his own course would be. His paper, the Westliche Post in St. Louis, was supporting Greeley, but, in so

[1] Schurz, Reminiscences, vol. iii, p. 343.
[2] Schurz, Speeches, vol. ii, p. 449; cf. ibid., p. 369; Frank W. Bird in Sumner Papers, quoted in Horace White, Life of Trumbull, p. 385.

far as he was informed, this was the only German journal which was doing so.[1] The whole body of German voters were disheartened. So were the "revenue reformers" and other elements which had been attracted to the movement. It was with a grief he could not express, that he saw a cause, which he had "so laboriously worked for, a movement so hopefully begun . . . stripped of its moral power."[2]

Greeley, to whom words came as water comes from a faucet, courteously but perversely replied. He personally had had nothing to do with any bargain or sale. If there had been trading he personally knew nothing of it and had had no part in it.[3] If the Germans did not approve of his candidacy it was because he was a total abstinence man; they thought that he would restrict them in the use of beer. The "revenue reformers" were "free traders"; Greeley made light of their opposition— it was expected. He entirely disagreed with Schurz's opinion of the new party's prospects. They would carry Illinois, New York, New Hampshire—all of the South and nearly all of New England. His majority in New York would be 50,000. The outlook in the Northwest he believed to be good also. He even had the hope of carrying Pennsylvania. New York and the fifteen ex-slave states alone would give him nearly half the whole vote of the electoral colleges.[4]

Schurz asked Greeley to study the situation and to delay his action. Greeley knew of no reason for delay; he would "accept unconditionally" at once.[5] He was writing letters and making statements. It was difficult to impose silence upon him, but his adjutants—Reid, Horace White, Samuel Bowles— demanded it.[6] Moreover he was still in his place as the editor of the Tribune. It was on May 15 that he printed a "card" at the head of the editorial page of that paper withdrawing

<hr/>

[1] Cf. N. Y. Times, May 20, 1872.
[2] Schurz, Speeches, vol. ii, pp. 361–8; cf. ibid., p. 369 and Reminiscences, vol. iii, pp. 348–9; White, Life of Trumbull, p. 391; G. W. Julian, Political Recollections, p. 339.
[3] But see A. K. McClure, Old Time Notes of Pa., chap. lxxxi.
[4] Schurz, Reminiscences, vol. iii, pp. 350–51, and Speeches, vol. ii, p. 377.
[5] Schurz, Reminiscences, vol. iii, p. 351.
[6] Cortissoz, Life of Reid, vol. i, pp. 312–4; Schurz, Speeches, vol. ii, p. 382.

"absolutely" from its conduct—it had ceased to be a "party organ"—"henceforth, until further notice," he would "exercise no control or supervision over its columns;"[1] five days more, the 20th of May, when he wrote a letter to Schurz and the other officers of the convention accepting the nomination. He had waited, he said, to learn "how the work of your convention was received in all parts of our great country, and judge whether that work was approved and ratified by the mass of our fellow citizens." The "response" had come through "telegrams, letters and the comments of journalists, independent of official patronage and indifferent to the smiles or frowns of power," and the "number and character of these unconstrained, unpurchased, unsolicited utterances" satisfied him that the Cincinnati movement had "received the stamp of public approval and been hailed by a majority of our countrymen as the harbinger of a better day for the republic."[2]

Greeley epitomized and paraphrased the platform, giving it his endorsement throughout. He found in its "propositions" the "basis of a true and beneficent national reconstruction— of a new departure from jealousies, strifes and hates, which have no longer adequate motive, or even plausible pretext, into an atmosphere of peace, fraternity and mutual good will" and, with some of the rhetoric, which he so well knew how to summon for his use, passed on to the words accepting the nomination. This he did "in the confident trust that the masses of our countrymen, North and South, are eager to clasp hands across the bloody chasm which has too long divided them, forgetting that they have been enemies in the joyful consciousness that they are, and must henceforth remain brethren."[3]

In a little while the regular Republican party leaders were ready for their convention, their "renomination convention,"

[1] N. Y. Tribune, May 15, 1872.

[2] The letter, the Boston Evening Transcript said, was full of "egotism and effrontery." (N. Y. Tribune, May 24, 1872.) "The sly old gentleman," the New York Evening Post said, had first felt the "pulse of the people." Having been "uproariously approved by all the toy drums and tin pans of the universe" he was no longer in doubt, etc.—Quoted in ibid., May 23, 1872.

[3] Article on U. S. in Am. Ann. Cyclop. for 1872.

as the New York Tribune called it, in Philadelphia. The "officeholders" were "in council." They met in the Academy of Music on the 5th and 6th days of June. The convention passed under the permanent chairmanship of Thomas Settle of North Carolina,[1] to emphasize the sectional issue which the leaders wished to keep before the country for their advantage on election day. Here was no "new departure." Nor did any appear in the platform. With a flourish of trumpets about the party's suppression of a "gigantic rebellion," its emancipation of four million slaves, its establishment of "universal suffrage," its "unparalleled magnanimity" toward the South in hanging none who deserved to feel the halter around their necks, its reduction of taxation and of the debt, and its "glorious record" generally, which had brought "peace and plenty" throughout the land, a belief was expressed that the people would not entrust the government "to any party or combination of men, composed, chiefly, of those who resisted every step of this beneficial progress." The party had "accepted, with grand courage, the solemn duties of the times." The resolutions were in the same key. The laws must be enforced, including the "recent amendments" to the Constitution; the civil service must be kept pure and honest; public land must no longer be given away; industries must be protected in the interest of higher wages and national prosperity; the soldiers, "whose valor saved the Union," must be pensioned—it was a "sacred debt"; the Irish must be defended against British efforts to punish them as Fenians; franking privileges should be abolished and the rates of postage reduced; the public credit should be maintained; women, if they wished "additional rights," should be treated "with respectful consideration"; unconstitutional measures should be disapproved; the growth of peace and fraternal feeling was cause for rejoicing; commerce and shipbuilding should be encouraged, and so on. "The

[1] Known to no one ("a Mr. Settle," the New York World called him— Issue of June 6, 1872), a North Carolina turncoat who had been rewarded by an appointment as minister to Peru and had lately come home for a nomination for Congress, to which he hoped soon to be elected by the carpetbag-negro party of his native state.

modest patriotism, the earnest purpose, the sound judgment, the practical wisdom, the incorruptible integrity and the illustrious services of Ulysses S. Grant" having "commended him to the heart of the American people," the Republican party, with him at its head, would "start upon a new march to victory."

In a long time so much adjectival pomp, mingled with plain buncombe, had not been written into a party platform.[1] Nothing meant anything of bearing upon the situation, or of worth to the country, except the past three years of the Grant administration, and about that scarcely a true word was said.

Except in one particular the business of the convention was plotted and planned beforehand, and it was on this account a perfunctory event.[2] "That man of whom Greeley had said 'he never has been beaten and never will be,' Ulysses S. Grant,"[3] was named by acclamation, as every one knew that he would be. The uproar which followed this action was protracted; when it showed signs of failing it was renewed. Now for the first time in a Republican national convention were there full delegations from the Southern states, many of them composed in large part of negroes who were much coddled[4] by the aspiring white tacticians, bent upon using them for selfish purposes. Only in the nomination of a candidate for Vice President was there an appearance of free action of the delegates. In this, too, there was management which soon disposed of the pretensions of Mr. Colfax. A man of more friends had seldom appeared in our public life, than the "Great Smiler"; few ever had had success so notable in steering a course which would save him from prejudices and enmities. But some of his advocates had discerned in him a possible figure for the Presidency[5] and, a little seized by the fascination of the prospect, he had given it out that he would not be a candidate for renomination.[6] Then, when he had seen that the tide was not setting in his

[1] Cf. N. Y. Nation, June 13, 1872.
[2] Ibid.
[3] Following the words of the leader of the New York delegation, as it cast its vote in the convention.—Harper's Weekly, June 22, 1872.
[4] A. D. White, Autobiography, vol. i, p. 172; N. Y. Nation, June 13, 1872.
[5] Cf. remarks of Indianapolis Journal in N. Y. Tribune, Feb. 8, 1872.
[6] Cf. Hollister, Life of Colfax, pp. 355, 358–64, 367.

direction, that Grant would be renominated and the Reform movement would free itself of the party machinery he made some gestures indicating a desire to hold his place.[1] But it was too late.[2] Grant was ready to see disloyalty in Colfax's course. The politicians behind the President had made other plans.[3] It seemed to them expedient to offset the disaffection of Sumner with the nomination of his colleague, Henry Wilson, who had been asked to accept the place, who had accepted and who now, at their instigation, refused to retire.[4] If one senator from Massachusetts had left the party, it must be made clear that the other, nearly as irreconcilable and pronounced a representative of the Abolitionist sentiment of New England, remained true to the Republican legend and the Republican name.[5] Thus it came about that, while Colfax's friends resisted what was proposed in the case with as much power as they could command, the "Natick cobbler," risen from the shoemaker's bench to a high position in our national politics, was nominated on the first ballot, after some of the Southern delegates had changed their votes, for the Vice Presidency.

The Grant men, with their black allies, went home in the confident assurance that all would be well with their ticket. On June 10 their candidate accepted the nomination. If he were chosen for another term he promised "the same zeal and devotion to the good of the whole people for the future" as he had "shown in the past." His experience, he said, modestly enough, might guide him "in avoiding mistakes inevitable with novices in all professions and in all occupations." He had a desire "to see a speedy healing of all bitterness of feeling between sections, parties and races of citizens," and he subscribed himself "very respectfully," etc.

The union of sentiment and enthusiasm of purpose which Greeley beheld during the weeks following the nomination were

[1] Cf. Hollister, Life of Colfax, pp. 366, 367–72; N. Y. Nation, June 13, 1872.

[2] Hollister, op. cit., pp. 373–5.

[3] Ibid., pp. 371–2.

[4] Letter of Wilson in N. Y. Tribune, Feb. 19, 1872.

[5] N. Y. Nation, June 13, 1872.

not so perfect as to delude other men. Schurz was importuned to speak in endorsement of the ticket. He told Colonel Grosvenor that he would not do so. "The words would stick in my throat," he said. The weeks following the convention in Cincinnati were, for him, "among the unhappiest periods of time" he had ever passed through.[1] He could not think of the subject "without a pang."[2] What could be done? The New York Evening Post, which from the first had taken the most open measures to discredit the Greeley nomination, proposed a meeting of "notables."[3] Godkin of the New York Nation had the same ends in view.[4] On May 30 a considerable number of men, prominent for their interest in revenue reform, who felt that they had been "betrayed" at Cincinnati, met, pursuant to call, at Steinway Hall in New York. William Cullen Bryant occupied the chair. There were near a hundred vice presidents. Speeches were made, resolutions were adopted, condemning the Cincinnati convention, and a committee of ten appointed to put themselves into communication with congenial minds in all parts of the country, with a view to securing the nomination of a candidate who would "adequately represent" their principles.[5]

The work proceeded. A larger, a more general and representative conference was called to meet at the Fifth Avenue Hotel in New York on June 20. The invitation, which was sent to about 200 men, bore the names of Schurz, Cox, Bryant, David A. Wells, Oswald Ottendorfer of the New York Staats-Zeitung and Jacob Brinkerhoff of Ohio. It was to be a consultation of "gentlemen who are opposed to the present administration and its continuance in office," and who might deem it "necessary that all the elements of the opposition should be united for a common effort at the coming Presidential election."[6]

The meeting was secret, but much concerning it came out at

[1] Schurz, Speeches, vol. ii, p. 381.
[2] Ibid., p. 369; Schurz, Reminiscences, vol. iii, p. 346.
[3] Schurz, Speeches, vol. ii, p. 378.
[4] Trumbull Papers.
[5] N. Y. Evening Post, May 30 and 31, 1872.
[6] Cf. Schurz to Grosvenor in Schurz, Speeches, vol. ii, pp. 379–80; Letters and Memorials of Tilden, vol. i, pp. 305–306.

once. Ex-Governor Cox presided.[1] Bryant and General John A. Dix acted as vice presidents. Among others in attendance were Schurz, Trumbull, Edward Atkinson, Watterson, Horace White, Colonel Grosvenor, Parke Godwin, E. L. Godkin, Judge Stallo of Cincinnati, Senator Rice of Arkansas, ex-Governor Randolph of New Jersey, Hiram Barney, Isaac H. Bromley, General George W. Cass, ex-Senator Fowler of Tennessee, Governor Walker of Virginia, ex-Governor English of Connecticut, ex-Senator Lafayette Foster of Connecticut, Daniel P. Goodloe of North Carolina, B. H. Hill of Georgia, and A. H. H. Stuart of Virginia. All expressed their views with complete freedom. They agreed that Greeley's nomination had been a mistake. They were unanimous in their expression of a "dislike," if not a "loathing" for him. Many went farther; they likened him to a "dose of medicine," to an "emetic."[2] Like Jacob of old they awoke at Cincinnati to find that for their nuptial night they had been given "the weak-eyed old maid, Leah, instead of the young and blooming Rachel."[3] They would not accept such a candidate.

Parke Godwin offered resolutions. He would put in nomination Charles Francis Adams for President[4] and William S. Groesbeck of Ohio, who had made so fine an impression as one of Andrew Johnson's counsel during the impeachment trial, for Vice President.[5] Schurz, while now giving further expression to his disappointment, believed that another ticket would but increase "confusion." He was so deeply convinced of the necessity of defeating Grant that he was ready to use any instrument for the purpose.[6] Trumbull spoke in the same

[1] The recollection of Horace White seems to have been at fault. White who says that Bryant presided and fell asleep in the chair probably had another meeting in mind.—Life of Trumbull, p. 391.

[2] Cf. N. Y. Evening Post, June 21, 1872; J. B. Stallo in Cincinnati. Volksfreund, quoted in N. Y. Times, July 1, 1872.

[3] A figure of speech attributed to Horace White in N. Y. World, June 21, 1872.

[4] Adams himself had written from Europe, when he received news of Greeley's nomination, that "success with such a candidate is out of the question."—Life of C. F. Adams, p. 392.

[5] Resolutions printed in N. Y. Evening Post, June 21, 1872.

[6] Schurz, Speeches, vol. ii, pp. 384–5; N. Y. Nation, June 27, 1872; Lloyd, Life of H. D. Lloyd, p. 35.

sense,[1] as did several others, including Colonel Grosvenor,
Horace White, Henry Watterson, Senator Rice and ex-Governor
English.[2]

The conference ended, therefore, without taking that action
which a number of those present desired it to take, and some
of the anti-Greeley men, led by Judge Stallo, not more than
twenty-five in all, held a meeting next day. Governor Cox,
who was present for a time, seems to have discouraged the
movement,[3] but before adjourning, they adopted an excellent
platform, in which the action of the Cincinnati convention
was repudiated, and recommended the voters of the country
to support William S. Groesbeck for President and Frederick
Law Olmsted of New York, a high-minded publicist, for Vice
President.[4] It was a waste of time and effort, "a feeble by-
play," as the St. Louis Republican said, that would not be heard
"in the tremendous clangor and tumult of the real contest."[5]

So much as this the wisest knew full well. If they could not
follow Greeley the reformers could better draw in their forces,
save their strength and bide their hour. By an economy of
their resources they, in another year, under more favorable
conditions, might make their power felt in the land.[6]

Now what would be done by the Democrats who had postponed their meeting date until the 9th of July so that they
could survey the whole field, both backward and forward, for
what guidance they could gain in their predicament? It would
be a hard surrender, if they were to subdue all their antipathies
and predilections, cast away their principles, forget their
history, and accept the Liberal Republican platform and the
Cincinnati ticket. So much might have been compassed in

---

[1] White, Life of Trumbull, pp. 391–2. White had urged Trumbull to
attend the meeting. "Of course," he said "there is nothing to be done
now but to go for Greeley, and go strong." But another conference might,
he thought, bring Godkin, Wells and others back into line.—Trumbull
Papers in Library of Congress.
[2] N. Y. Evening Post, June 21, 1872.
[3] Cf. N. Y. Tribune, June 22, 1872.
[4] N. Y. Evening Post June 22, 1872; N. Y. Nation, June 27, 1872.
[5] Quoted in N. Y. Tribune, July 1, 1872.
[6] N. Y. Nation, Sept. 19, 1872.

relation to any candidate except Greeley. Adams, or Trumbull, or David Davis, or any one of half a dozen men who had been suggested as possible nominees of the new party, could have been taken, if not with enthusiasm, at any rate without positive and open humiliation. But Greeley was a man who was known for nothing so much as his systematic, untiring and often gross assaults upon the Democratic party as a party and upon all Democrats as individuals for a long period of years. His peculiarly mad and vituperative animadversions were not verbal, and, therefore, like politicians' words, to be forgotten, even denied upon a convenient occasion—his were set down day by day in print in the files of a widely read and freely cited newspaper. Nothing would have seemed so nearly impossible a few years, a few months since as that Greeley, who had called all Democrats "traitors," "rebels," "copperheads," "slave-holders," "slave-whippers" and infinitely worse names, who had confused them with theft and corruption, with filth and drunkenness, with every known form of vulgarity and sin,[1] should become the candidate of that party for the Presidency of the United States.[2]

It was argued that Greeley had undergone a sincere and complete change of heart—at any rate on the subject of Democrats in so far as they were settled in the South, and yet even so much as this was hard to believe, for it was only yesterday that he had roughly justified the Ku Klux laws,[3] against which the entire body of Southern white men protested with their whole might. Could it be that one had been or could be brought to see value in the other?

The New York World in the East and the Chicago Times in the West, leaders of the Democratic press, did all that lay in their way to prevent the party from giving its endorsement to Greeley, whatever the changes which may have come over

[1] Cf. Harper's Weekly, July 27 and Aug. 3 and 10, 1872.
[2] It seems not to have been Greeley but Dr. Dwight who said "that though all Democrats are not horse thieves all horse thieves are Democrats." But Greeley had expressed the same thought in even plainer words.—N. Y. Nation, March 28, 1872.
[3] Cf. Harper's Weekly, July 20, 1872.

his spirit.[1] They were supported by the Detroit Free Press,
the New York Staats-Zeitung, the Boston Post, the Hartford
Times, the Pittsburgh Post, the Washington Patriot and a
few other journals of influence in the communities in which
they appeared.[2] It would be as "self-stultifying" for the Democrats to nominate Greeley, said the New York World, as for
the Republicans to make Alexander H. Stephens or Robert
Toombs their candidate for President.[3] Even Charles Sumner
would be less objectionable than Greeley. Whatever else
Sumner had done he had not "abused and vilified every leading
and representative Democrat by wholesale personal defama-
tion."[4] Greeley could not be nominated by the Democratic
party, the World said again, because he was "the very furthest
from representing its principles." Even if there were no other
reason for rejecting him "the license and wantonness of his
brutal, unretracted slanders would be sufficient."[5] There are,
the World continued, "hundreds of thousands of true and tried
Democrats who will stiffly refuse to vote for Mr. Greeley,
whether he is endorsed at Baltimore or not."[6] "The elevation
of the Chappaqua philosopher to the Presidency would be a
public calamity," said the Chicago Times.[7] His nomination
would "terminate the organic existence of the Democratic
party"; it would be "the disbandment of the party."[8]

Party spokesmen, like Senator Bayard of Delaware, and one
whom his friends knew affectionately as "the Tall Sycamore
of the Wabash," Representative Voorhees of Indiana, were
heard in and out of Congress in uncompromising opposition to
the proposed course. Better be defeated with a "straight-
out" Democrat, they said, than be successful with Greeley.[9]

[1] N. Y. Nation, May 30 and June 20, 1872.
[2] N. Y. World, July 1, 1872.
[3] Ibid., May 13, 1872.
[4] Ibid., May 17, 1872; cf. Letters and Memorials of S. J. Tilden, vol. i,
p. 306.
[5] N. Y. World, May 17, 1872.
[6] Ibid., May 29, 1872.
[7] Quoted in N. Y. Tribune, May 18, 1872.
[8] Quoted in ibid., June 25, 1872.
[9] Baltimore corr. Phila. Ledger, July 8, 1872.

It had no more occurred to him, Voorhees declared, that the men who had nominated Greeley would have "the brazen audacity to expect Democrats to support him, than it did that the disciples of the Christian religion would turn away from their faith for an hour and worship Mahomet as the prophet of God." If the "madness and folly of the hour should consummate his nomination" the editor of the Tribune would not receive more than fifty per cent of the Democratic votes of the United States.[1] Greeley was an "older and a far abler Republican than Grant," Voorhees said again. He had been a "violent Republican when Grant was a Buchanan Democrat in St. Louis." [2] To put forth such a man as the party candidate would be "disgraceful suicide." He was "the most odious man to the Democratic party in the United States." [3]

August Belmont, chairman of the Democratic National Committee, said that Greeley was "the most objectionable person" who could have been chosen. The nomination was "one of those stupendous mistakes which it is difficult even to comprehend." But it was a condition which confronted the party and they must deal with it. Belmont would "willingly vote" for his "deadliest enemy," if, by doing this, he could defeat Grant.[4] He was falling into line. Hendricks of Indiana, Seymour,[5] George H. Pendleton, Garrett Davis, Doolittle, Tilden [6] and other leaders had been brought to view the situation as inevitable, and, therefore, were accepting it.[7] The Cincinnati Enquirer and many Democratic newspapers followed the same course.[8] The South, in its helplessness, found in Greeley hope for relief from the intolerable burdens imposed upon it by Republican rule. The younger men welcomed the

---

[1] Speech in Terre Haute in N. Y. Tribune, May 27, 1872.
[2] N. Y. Tribune, May 27, 1872.
[3] Letter in N. Y. Tribune, May 21, 1872.
[4] Letter quoted in N. Y. Tribune, June 8, 1872.
[5] Letters and Memorials of Tilden, vol. i, p. 311.
[6] Ibid., p. 310.
[7] Cf. Cincinnati Commercial, quoted in N. Y. Tribune, May 6, 1872; N. Y. Tribune, May 7, 21 and 30, 1872; N. Y. Sun, May 30, 1872; N. Y. Times, May 9, 1872.
[8] Cf. N. Y. Nation, May 30, 1872; Cincinnati Enquirer, quoted in N. Y. Tribune, May 4, 1872.

candidate's words of sympathy and his promises of milder
policies for want of sign of hope on any other side. All but
Toombs,[1] Jubal Early, Alexander H. Stephens, Henry A. Wise
and a few of the men of the old régime, who found it impossible
to forget Greeley's long and mad campaign against the South
for its slavery, to whom his name and the name of his paper
continued to be anathema itself, still gave expression to other
views.[2]

The way opened in no other direction. McClellan in 1864,
on a platform declaring the war to be a failure, had been a
stupidity. The refusal to accept Chase's leadership in 1868,
giving the nomination instead to a man who was wholly averse
to receiving it and going to the country on a platform calling
for a repudiation of the national debt, was another folly. The
futility of such management had been borne in upon the leaders,
and, with a man like the Copperhead, Vallandigham, sounding
the call for a "new departure," there was the most impressive
confession of the need of a complete change of tactics, if the
party were soon to resume its old position as a force in American
politics. Moreover the Democracy had been, for the time,
irreparably damaged by the Tammany frauds recently exposed
in New York City. These frightful scandals had taken the
courage out of and had destroyed the influence of that group
of men in the East who had so long dictated the party's course.[3]
Thus it was that most of the leaders, whatever the absurdity
of the projected alliance, prepared themselves for the business
in hand. Their eyes could be blindfolded, their ears and noses
could be stopped. They had never recognized Greeley as a
Democrat before, but he must be "swallowed" now. Governor
Vance of North Carolina expressed the general feeling on the
point. "If the Baltimore convention puts Greeley in our hymn
book," he said, "we will sing him through, if it kills us." [4]

The delegates came to Baltimore—ex-Confederates from the
South, Copperheads from the North and West prominently

[1] Cf. Phillips, Life of Toombs, p. 267.
[2] Cf. N. Y. Tribune, July 15, 1872.
[3] Cf. N. Y. World, Nov. 7, 1872.
[4] N. Y. Tribune, July 1, 1872; N. Y. Nation, July 4, 1872.

numbered among the host—for their ungrateful tasks. The
meetings were held in Ford's Theater. Belmont as chairman
of the National Committee, made the speech of welcome. There
was some method in choosing ex-Senator Doolittle of Wisconsin
as the permanent chairman. His being in the place recalled
the Republican defection which had marked the struggle between Congress and Andrew Johnson; he had presided over the
"Arm and Arm" convention in Philadelphia in 1866. He made
an eloquent speech which was received with loud cheering and
long continued applause. No time was lost in finishing the
work in hand. There were 732 delegates—670 of them voted
to adopt the Cincinnati resolutions, heedless of Bayard's plea
in opposition to taking "cut and dried, without mastication
or digestion," a platform which had been framed by another
body of men.[1]

It was Greeley everywhere. The man who had so long be-
labored all Democrats in the plainest Anglo-Saxon speech,
grinned at them from the fans with which they raised a com-
forting breeze around their perspiring forms in the sultry hall
in which the convention met. There he was, printed on paper,
his neck whiskers and his sparse locks in wool surrounding
the picture, as the delegates stirred the wilting air. He was
nominated for President by 686 votes, while Gratz Brown
received 713 votes for Vice President. Those who refused to
follow the leaders cast their ballots for Senator Bayard and
Jeremiah S. Black. Soon all was done. The convention was
organized at noon on July 9; the next day, at 1.39 P. M., it had
finished its labors and adjourned *sine die*.

Again in many places guns were fired. Flags were unfurled,
fireworks lighted the evening skies, campaign clubs paraded
the streets. Greeley was serenaded in New York. A committee,
headed by Mr. Doolittle, was appointed to visit him, for the
purpose of apprising him officially of what had been done.
They met him on July 12 at the Fifth Avenue Hotel, where
they drew from him a brief speech, in which he accepted the
nomination "gratefully" and in "the spirit" in which it had

[1] N. Y. Tribune, July 11, 1872.

been made. The situation was anomalous—this he would not
conceal. But "I feel certain that time, and in the good Providence of that time," he said, "an opportunity will be afforded
me to show that, while you, in making this nomination, are
not less Democratic but rather more Democratic than you
would have been in taking an opposite course, I am no less
thoroughly and earnestly Republican than ever I was." He
invited his guests to come out to his farm—they could "take
the 8.15 train."

A number of the committeemen, some delegates to the convention who were returning home by way of New York, reinforced by several Democrats resident in and near the city,
betook themselves to Chappaqua the next day. Their host
asked them to "take a drink," which, after walking for some
distance through the wood, they found, to their disappointment, was water from a spring. After luncheon they sat on
the grass and listened to him expound the issues, as he stood
on the seat of a kitchen chair.[1]

It was July 18 when Greeley addressed a formal letter to the
committee. He recognized a truth when he said that the convention would have found it easier to endorse any one of the
other candidates prominently mentioned for the nomination
at Baltimore. In the reaffirmation by the convention of the
principles set forth in the Liberal platform he found deep satisfaction. There was assurance now that Democracy was not
"henceforth to stand for one thing and Republicanism for
another." "I hail this," he declared, "as a genuine new departure from outworn feuds and meaningless contentions in
the direction of progress and reform. Whether," he added,
"I shall be found worthy to bear the standard of the great
Liberal movement, which the American people have inaugurated, is to be determined not by words but by deeds. With
me, if I steadily advance, over me, if I falter, its grand array
moves on to achieve for our country her glorious beneficent
destiny."[2] Greeley was now in the "hymn book" and the

[1] N. Y. Tribune, July 15, 1872.
[2] Article on U. S. in Am. Ann. Cyclop. for 1872.

Democrats, as Vance had said, were face to face with the task of "singing him through" if it killed them.

Laggards, "holdbacks" as Greeley called them, came in.[1] What had been done caused Senator Bayard "astonishment and disappointment." A while ago any man would have laughed at such a condition of affairs "as absurd and impossible."[2] Bayard had "steadily and openly" opposed the nomination, but he would support Greeley to defeat Grant.[3] Senator Thurman would do the same in obedience to "the will of the party."[4] The people of the South, Vance said again, were "trying to get out of hell fire." They would strike hands with anybody who promised to help them. Horace Greeley had been a "good hand at freeing niggers." Now he might "free the white folks at the South."[5] They did not know whither Greeley might lead them, said Governor Whyte of Maryland; but they did know Grant, and no change away from him, whatever it was, could be for the "worse." The Baltimore convention had given Greeley a "shower bath" which had washed all the Radicalism out of him.[6] Andrew Johnson, "on the principle of universal pressure of circumstances beyond human control," which limited the choice to two men, gave his adhesion to the ticket.[7] Jeremiah S. Black, who had said that he would not be "dragooned or bullied" into the support of the nominee,[8] now yielded with an expression of "much sorrow." They might see no good in either candidate; they must take that one which seemed "least bad."[9] Voorhees, abating nothing, asking to be excused for nothing, making no concealment of his "deep regret" at what had been done, now found the Democratic party, even with Greeley, "infinitely preferable" to that portion of the Republican party which acknowledged

[1] Life of J. Glancy Jones, vol. ii, p. 153.
[2] N. Y. Tribune, July 13, 1872.
[3] Harper's Weekly, Aug. 3, 1872.
[4] Ibid.; cf. Letters and Memorials of Tilden, vol. i, p. 311.
[5] N. Y. Tribune, July 11, 1872.
[6] Ibid.
[7] Harper's Weekly, Aug 31, 1872.
[8] N. Y. Sun, May 28, 1872.
[9] Harper's Weekly, Aug. 31, 1872.

the leadership of Grant.[1] Reverdy Johnson would support
Greeley to defeat Grant,[2] so would Groesbeck.[3]

The Democratic newspapers ate their "boiled crow," which
was so many men's portion during this campaign. The New
York World, which a few days before the Baltimore convention
met was still calling Greeley's nomination "preposterous,"[4]
was driven in at last. It was supporting Greeley, though much,
Harper's Weekly said, "as a man supports an aching head."[5]

Some still remained unmoved. The "Bourbons," or
"Straight-out" Democrats, who could not follow the fusion
leaders, had kept their forces together in Baltimore while the
convention was in session. When they were overborne they,
in spite of the deprecation of their action by the principal
party leaders, issued a public address,[6] and called a meeting at
Louisville for September 3. At that place at that time speeches
were made condemning the "sale" of the Democratic party
to "old Hod," who was, one said, nothing at all but a white
hat and a white coat.[7] A long letter from Charles O'Conor
of New York, whom the faction wished to name for the first
place on another ticket, was read. He endorsed the movement
but expressed "an unalterable resolve to remain in private
station."[8] In spite of these protestations he was nominated
for the Presidency, while John Quincy Adams of Massachusetts
was named for Vice President. O'Conor again declined the
honor.[9] David Davis and Joel Parker, the nominees of the
Labor Reformers, after seeing that they were not to have the
endorsement of the Cincinnati convention, withdrew, one on
June 24, the other on June 28. Mr. Groesbeck and Mr. Olmsted,
who had been put upon a ticket by some of the irreconcilables
attending the Fifth Avenue Conference, were submerged in the

[1] N. Y. Tribune, July 19, 1872.
[2] Ibid., July 20, 1872.
[3] Ibid., July 30, 1872.
[4] Quoted in ibid., July 2, 1872.
[5] Harper's Weekly, Aug. 10, 1872. The Chicago Times seems never to
have accepted Greeley.—N. Y. Tribune, Oct. 10, 1872.
[6] Letters and Memorials of Tilden, vol. i, p. 311.
[7] N. Y. Tribune, Sep. 4, 1872.   [8] Ibid.
[9] Ibid., Sep. 13, 1872.

trample and rush of the contest. The issue was clearly drawn between the Republican nominee, "who never was a Republican," as General Sherman observed, and Greeley, the Democratic nominee, "who never was a Democrat." [1]

Schurz finally entered the campaign in a speech for Greeley to an audience in a large and crowded hall in St. Louis on July 22.[2] Other addresses, in which he emphasized the principles underlying the canvass, followed this one. Sumner could not long conceal his preferences. Some had said that he would preside at Cincinnati.[3] His discontent was open, his aim being always directed by vindictiveness at Grant, though he remained a Republican, as he said, and "one of the straitest of the sect." [4] On May 31, the Friday before the meeting of the Republican convention in Philadelphia, he rose in the Senate and in a labored oration for a period of four hours arraigned the President for his sins in detail.[5] Sumner hoped that his voice would still be heard in the land, and that he could persuade the Republican party to commit its fortunes to another leader. But the harangue, because of its extravagance, could be of no advantage to the movement which its author had at heart. His advice having made no impression upon the Philadelphia convention, he openly espoused the Liberal cause. He sent a letter to the negroes urging them to vote for Greeley.[6] Taken to task for his course by Speaker Blaine he wrote to "repel with indignation" the charges and imputations of that partisan.[7] It had been his intention to speak at Faneuil Hall in Boston, in answer to an invitation

[1] The Sherman Letters, p. 337.

[2] Schurz, Speeches, vol. ii, pp. 392 et seq.; Harper's Weekly, Aug. 10, 1872; N. Y. Tribune, July 23, 1872.

[3] E. D. Ross, The Liberal Republican Movement, p. 115, where references are given.

[4] Sumner's Works, vol. xv, p. 83; Harper's Weekly, June 22, 1872; N. Y. Nation, March 21, 1872.

[5] Sumner's Works, vol. xv, pp. 83–171; Pierce, Memoir of Sumner, vol. iv, pp. 523–30: Horace White, Life of Trumbull, pp. 387–8; Harper's Weekly, June 22, 1872; N. Y. Nation, June, 6, 1872.

[6] Sumner's Works, vol. xv, pp. 175–95; Pierce, Memoir of Sumner, vol. iv, p. 531; Harper's Weekly, Aug. 17, 1872.

[7] Sumner's Works, vol. xv, pp. 196–201.

of the Liberal Republican Committee of Massachusetts, but the address went to the printers for use in the campaign without delivery,[1] on account of an attack of ill health which sent him abroad early in September. He did not return home until after the election.

It was to be a campaign of personalities and not much else. Hardly ever had been seen a Presidential canvass in which so little attention was bestowed upon policies and ideas.[2] In 1868 it had been Grant and the Union against rebellion and against rebels. It was again to be this [3] in so far as the Republican tacticians could keep the country to the theme,[4] but they soon were concentrating their fire upon Greeley's shambling form, his irresolute mind, his glaring inconsistencies, the damaging associations which he had contracted in leading the Democrats as well as the reformers, the selfish wish for power which his course seemed to betray. The Republican weapon was ridicule, and not any can more mortally wound the man at whom it is aimed in our American democracy.

It was "Old Horace," "Old Honesty," "Old Honest Horace," "Our Uncle Horace," "the Honest Old Farmer," "Old White Coat," "Old White Hat," "Old Tree Chopper," "the Sage of Chappaqua." [5] Even the campaign clubs, which were formed to forward the canvass, and marched about in white hats and white coats, developed none of the enthusiasm that radiated from the movements of the "Wide Awakes" of Lincoln and Grant's "Tanners."

It was strange enough to see Beauregard, Wade Hampton, Fitzhugh Lee, Governor Vance, Braxton Bragg, Raphael

[1] Sumner's Works, vol. xv, pp. 211–54.

[2] "We designed it to be campaign of ideas and it became a campaign of personalities."—Schurz to Horace White in Schurz, Speeches, vol. ii, p. 444; cf. N. Y. Nation, April 25, 1872; N. Y. Tribune, May 18, 1872.

[3] "Pressing the Democrats with their old iniquities."—Atlantic Monthly, Sep., 1872.

[4] Cf. Conkling's speech at Cooper Institute when he said—"The result is safe because it rests with the same generation which was given by Providence to see through the darkness of the Rebellion, and that generation cannot be blind now."—Harper's Weekly, Aug. 10, 1872.

[5] Harper's Weekly, June 1 and 29, 1872, the inventions principally of the N. Y. Sun.

Semmes and other "rebel" chiefs [1] "declaring" for Greeley; to see men who had worn the gray Confederate uniform, and who had labored for the destruction of the Union, in Greeley clubs, at Greeley ratification meetings in all parts of the South; to see the leaders of the Tammany Society in New York City, lately convicted and condemned in courts of law, cheering for the old editor of the Tribune.[2] Never before had such a "miscellaneous coalition"[3] made its appearance in American politics. It was more than amusing for the enemy, more than confounding for the friend—there was something pitiful in the sight for all men, as the Republican press from day to day hunted out and reprinted from the pages of Greeley's newspaper [4] what he had earlier said of those whose cause he now led—

"When the rebellious traitors are overwhelmed in the field, and scattered like leaves before an angry wind, it must not be to return to peaceful and contented homes. They must find poverty at their firesides and see privation in the anxious eyes of mothers and the rags of children." [5]

"The brain, the heart, the soul of the present Democratic party is the rebel element at the South, with its Northern allies and sympathizers. It is rebel at the core today. . . . Whatever chastisement may be deserved by our national sins we must hope that this disgrace and humiliation shall be spared us." [6]

"The essential articles of the Democratic creed are 'love rum and hate niggers.' The less one learns and knows the more certain he is to vote the regular ticket from A to Izzard." [7]

"All do know that there are several hundred thousand mulattoes in this country, and we presume that no one has any serious doubt that the fathers of at least nine-tenths of them are white Democrats." [8]

[1] Harper's Weekly, July 6 and 20, 1872.
[2] Cf. ibid., Aug. 31, 1872.
[3] Ibid., Sep. 14, 1872.
[4] Cf. C. M. Depew, My Memories of 80 years, p. 93.
[5] N. Y. Tribune, May 1, 1861, quoted in Harper's Weekly, July 27, 1872.
[6] Quoted in Harper's Weekly, July 6, 1872.
[7] Ibid.
[8] N. Y. Tribune, Dec. 10, 1867.

"Everyone who chooses to live by pugilism, or gambling, or harlotry, with nearly every keeper of a tippling house, is politically a Democrat. . . . A purely selfish interest attaches the lewd, ruffianly, criminal and dangerous classes to the Democratic party." [1]

"If there were not a newspaper or a common school in the country the Democratic party would be far stronger than it is." [2]

"Point wherever you please to an election district which you will pronounce morally rotten . . . and that district will be found at nearly, or quite, every election giving a majority for that which styles itself the 'Democratic' party. Take all the haunts of debauchery in the land and you will find nine-tenths of their master spirits active partisans of that same Democracy." [3]

"May it be written on my grave that I was never its [the Democratic party's] follower and lived and died in nothing its debtor." [4]

Max Adeler (Charles Heber Clark) described the "American Battle of Dorking." The people had elected Greeley President of the United States. He was no sooner in the White House when he organized an army of 200,000 men to drive, at the point of the bayonet, the entire population of the seaboard states into the West. Soon they were out on the plains, where multitudes starved to death. Then the President took fright and he directed Congress to vote 700,000 volumes of his book, "What I Know about Farming," for their relief. In his first message to Congress he had said something about rutabagas and beans, but the Czar of Russia, unable to decipher such handwriting as Greeley's, thought it was derogatory reference to him and declared war on America. The President wrote of the potato rot to Bismarck; Emperor William thought Greeley was calling him a "liar" and he opened hostilities. Meanwhile we were in arms against England, the Queen having found the New York Tribune's advocacy of a tariff on pig

---

[1] N. Y. Tribune, Jan. 7, 1868.
[2] Cf. Harper's Weekly, June 29, and Sep. 28, 1872; N. Y. Times, July 18, 1872; N. Y. World, June 6, 1872.
[3] Quoted in Harper's Weekly, Aug. 3, 1872.
[4] N. Y. World, June 6, 1872.

iron to be incendiary. These three enemy powers were joined by Austria, which saw in Greeley's autograph on the fly leaf of a copy of "What I Know about Farming," sent to the Emperor, a caricature of the Imperial Eagle, and by France, which had taken affront when Greeley, who was engaged at the time in writing an editorial, and who, not comprehending French, without turning his head, had mistaken the ambassador for a beggar, and had given that dignitary an order on a haberdasher for a clean shirt, with the advice—"Go West, young man, go West." The foreign host came in, seized Washington, and hanged the President, the cabinet and every member of Congress. So fell the republic—"all the result of blind confidence in a misguided old man who thought himself a philosopher, but who was actually a fool." [1]

The hostility of the New York Times and Harper's Weekly was damning. In Nast's cartoons Greeley was seen in ridiculous guise or humiliating situation, startling in their changes, week by week. The old, lunar, bespectacled face, the short pudgy form, the boots, the white hat and the white coat, a book sticking out of the pocket marked "What I Know about Farming," "What I Know about Liars," "What I Know about Eating my own Words," "What I Know about Clasping Hands over Bloody Chasms," "What I Know about Reform," "What I Know about Bolting," "What I Know about Everything," as it might serve the particular need, a little tag marked "Gratz Brown" pinned always to the coat tail, were set forth for the laughter of the country. Surrounded at one time by the principal "rebels" of the South, at another by the blacklegs of Tammany Hall, pushed into the company, perhaps, by "Whitelie Reid," attired as a little dandy, Greeley could wonder whether he or Tweed had robbed New York City,[2] whether he or Wilkes Booth [3] might deserve the lower place in the history of the republic.

The elongated form of Schurz, a beard and spectacles set

[1] Harper's Weekly, June 29, 1872.
[2] Cf. ibid., Aug. 3, 10 and 31, 1872; Merriam, Life and Times of Samuel Bowles, vol. ii, p. 197.
[3] Cf. Harper's Weekly, Sep. 14, 1872.

on legs, was shown in the most insulting attitudes in association with the vilest figures in American political life. He was now and again urged to take himself back to Germany, if he were not pleased with the institutions of his adopted land.[1] In a similar manner Sumner was depicted with unfeeling barbarity.[2] "Thieves and senators" were associated in "like ignominy," and, however much it amused the masses of the people, it provoked the protests of those who could keep their minds in better discipline amid the bitterness of the hour. [3]

Methods so ribald were unnecessary, as very soon appeared. While the trend of feeling during the summer led politicians to anticipate Greeley's election, this result would seem to have been at no time in the campaign even remotely possible. Nor is there reason to suppose that Adams, if he had been selected to head the opposition to Grant, would have made great progress in this direction,[4] though he should have had the support of a larger number of thoughtful and responsible Republicans, such as those who were included in the constituencies of the New York Evening Post, the New York Nation and the Atlantic Monthly, and should have undoubtedly commanded a more enthusiastic following from the Democratic party. As it was many Democrats would go to the polls with perfunctory steps; many others would not stir from their homes on election day.[5] Under these circumstances for a man like Greeley, well

[1] Cf. Harper's Weekly, Aug. 24, 1872.
[2] Cf. ibid., June 22, and Aug. 17 and 24, 1872.
[3] For Schurz see N. Y. Nation, Feb. 29 and March 7, 1872; J. H. Harper, House of Harper, p. 299; Schurz, Reminiscences, vol. iii, p. 347; Schurz's speech in U. S. Senate, Jan. 8, 1872, in Cong. Globe, 42nd Cong. 2nd sess., pp. 292–3; N. Y. Tribune, Jan. 9, 1872. "Harper's pictorial blackguard has caricatured and libelled him [Schurz] from week to week as if he were a second Tweed or Connolly." (N. Y. Tribune, March 21, 1872.) For Sumner see Pierce, Memoir of Sumner, vol. iv, p. 522; cf. N. Y. Independent, May 8, 1872; Lydia Maria Child in Boston Journal, reprinted in N. Y. Tribune, July 5, 1872. For Greeley see Whitelaw Reid in Century Magazine, vol. 85, p. 44. Similar methods were followed in the West by the Grant newspapers and stump speakers laboring in the Grant cause. Cf. Julian, Political Recollections, pp. 343–4.
[4] For another view see Horace White, Life of Trumbull, pp. 402–403; G. W. Julian, Political Recollections, p. 340.
[5] Cf. A. K. McClure, Old Time Notes of Pa., vol. ii, p. 337; G. W. Julian, Political Recollections, p. 348.

meaning in all his fundamental instincts, as a long life under the
public eye, in a fine kind of public service, had clearly enough
proven, to be caricatured and lampooned, largely on the ground
of his physical peculiarities, was a cruelty that he did not
deserve at the hands of his countrymen.

Greeley had been honestly repelled by the corruptions of
the time. Both Harper's Weekly and the New York Times
had lately come through their contest with the Tammany
Ring with great honor. They had increased their circulation
as newspapers and had won prestige as organs of public opinion.
But the Times was now actually using its influences to block
investigations into rascalities bound up with the Grant administration, as, for example, the Leet-Stocking scandal in
the New York custom house, as vile a thievery as Tweed's.[1]
Thus, too, would it belittle and dismiss as of no moment the
charges concerning the Crédit Mobilier.[2] Both journals took
advantage of their respectable positions to ridicule and disgrace men who, however the Cincinnati movement may have
been turned away from its first purpose, had been put forward
on a platform committed to the extirpation, in a larger field,
of that corruption which had been so usefully exposed in New
York City. Greeley hated evil as they; Schurz, on his side,
hated it more deeply and intelligently than they. It was
particularly unworthy of one of George William Curtis's re-·
finements of conscience, especially as he was to be so soon and
so completely disabused of his temporary confidence in the
Grant administration,[3] to let his "Journal of Civilization"[4]
cover with unjust ridicule men who were in no way his inferiors
in honest purpose and high ambitions for the commonwealth.[5]

[1] Worcester Spy, cited in N. Y. Tribune, Jan. 13, 1872.
[2] N. Y. Times, Sep. 24, 1872. It too plainly showed from day to day,
as it boasted of its gains at the expense of the Tribune, that it was pro-
Grant to increase its circulation. In spite of its great opportunity it was
conducted with far less ability, on its side, than was the Tribune as an
opposition organ during the campaign.
[3] Cary, Life of Curtis, pp. 232–3, 240.
[4] Which had become, some one suggested in the New York Tribune,
June 18, 1872, a "Journal of a Nasty Civilization."
[5] Curtis did protest to Nast about his savage caricatures, but to no avail.
Nast seemed to be a "free lance" directly responsible to the Harpers.

Greeley had another large and benevolent object in view
—the reconciliation and the pacification of the South by
the pursuit of more moderate policies. If he were but a recent
convert to the principle he was sincerely interested in its
triumph.[1] This, too, Harper's Weekly and the Times would
not understand, as they turned their brutal weapons upon the
poor old mortal figure, who, in his heart, a little blindly though
it might be, seems now to have yearned to have some part in
a service of brotherly love.

On the other side Grant was attacked in a like spirit. Personal aspersions aimed at his carriage, his dress, his habits,
his morals, his qualities of person and mind, at the character
of his relations and his wife's relations quartered on the government, his many unworthy associates, the military clique which
surrounded him at the White House, filled the opposition press.[2]

As the campaign proceeded its acerbity increased. The
Tribune, Greeley had said when he withdrew from its management in May, would not be a "party organ." This promise
was forgotten. Lists of names of defaulters who had been
caught and exposed during the past two or three years—
pension officers, internal revenue officers, collectors of the
customs, postmasters, naval paymasters—startling in their
length, were published.[3] Grant's motto was "pleasure before
business"—the absence from Washington of the President and
the members of his cabinet, dates being given, were catalogued.[4]
The New York custom house scandal gave way to other scan-

(J. H. Harper, House of Harper, pp. 302–4.) For influences in the Harper
publishing firm affecting Curtis in this campaign see ibid., pp. 301, 304–6.

[1] Greeley wrote to Bayard Taylor on Aug. 18, 1872: "I feel sure that,
while my election would pacify the country, as it should be pacified, my
nomination and canvass, even though unsuccessful, tends to the same end."
—N. Y. Tribune, Feb. 10, 1873.

[2] Nast in Harper's Weekly was countered by Matt Morgan, an English
cartoonist, in Frank Leslie's Illustrated Newspaper. Leslie had been a
delegate at Cincinnati and was laboring in the Greeley interest. In this
journal Grant was caricatured savagely in order to gain the acclamation
of the Greeley men. See the praise bestowed upon these cartoons in the
New York Tribune as they appeared from week to week; also N. Y. Nation, Nov. 14, 1872.

[3] Cf. N. Y. Tribune, July 27, 1872.

[4] Ibid., July 29, 1872.

dals. Charge followed charge on the subject of Grant's integrity and the personal honesty of the men who were directing his administration.

Much of what was said was founded on too much truth. Dana's New York Sun surpassed every rival in the industry with which it assembled, and the scurrility with which it set such material before the people. But even its Crédit Mobilier exposures, in September,[1] which in a few months, in the hands of Congressional committees, developed great proportions, changed few votes.[2] The Sun, it was said, had originated Greeley's "boom" for the Presidency,[3] but its references to "Dr." Greeley from day to day, in its slattern way,[4] deluded few into thinking that it was sincere in anything connected with the campaign, except its wish to discredit and defeat Grant.[5]

Under cover of the gross abuse which was indulged in, and the acrid feeling which was engendered was an opportunity for the Grant campaign managers to paint the situation in sorry colors in the sight of the railway, banking and financial interests of the country.[6] Rapacious demands were to be made on these interests. A firm in New York, Henry Clews and Company (in London, Clews, Habicht and Company) was given the foreign banking business of the government arising in the State Department, lately taken away from the Barings.[7] The "Navy Account" was transferred by Robeson to Jay Cooke and Company.[8] These advantages, in plain speech, were

[1] Beginning, Sep. 4.
[2] Cf. Horace White, Life of Trumbull, p. 401.
[3] N. Y. World, May 27, 1872; Boston Advertiser, cited in N. Y. Tribune, May 6, 1872; Providence Journal, cited in ibid., May 7, 1872. It was one of Dana's "sensations" for the groundlings with which he established the fortune of his paper. Such a genius for silly journalism, as was Dana's, plus a large infusion of the "old Nick," baffled all comprehension and, very fortunately, defied imitation.
[4] Cf. N. Y. Nation, April 11, 1872; N. Y. Times, April 8, 1872.
[5] Its support was never useful to anyone, nor was it meant to be. Another view in J. H. Wilson, Life of Dana, p. 429.
[6] With these managers it was much as the New York Tribune said it was not—"playing a whole park of artillery to kill a fly."—N. Y. Tribune, Nov. 5, 1872.
[7] Oberholtzer, Jay Cooke, vol. ii, pp. 336, 435–6.
[8] Ibid., pp. 309–10.

sold.[1] Both of these firms were to be assessed, in return, by the
Republican managers. All the corporations and their financial
agencies in Wall Street, which were looking to Washington
for benefits, were importuned to come to the aid of the administration,[2] and their contributions to the national and state committees reached a total never previously approached in a political campaign in America.

Now, as always, the early elections in Vermont and Maine
would be an augury of what was to come in the "October
states," and they, in turn, would clearly foretell the final result
in the country at large in November. Greeley took the stump
and spoke effectively in New England. He was no mean political orator.[3] Crowds assembled to see and hear him wherever
he went. They liked him; he was "genuine"; his speech was
"honest and unaffected"; the grasp of his hand was "hearty
and sincere." He awakened sympathy for himself by expressing it for others; he elicited approbation, which was expressed
in cheers and other spontaneous demonstrations, wherever he
went.[4] A little deceived by what he beheld he still implicitly
believed in his own power over the people and he confidently
anticipated his election. In August he was predicting that he

[1] Cf. N. Y. Nation, April 25, 1872; N. Y. Tribune, Aug. 31, 1872; Oberholtzer, Jay Cooke, vol. ii, p. 357. Clews had demanded both the State
and Navy Department accounts, when they were taken away from the
Barings. Robeson had written to Clews in May, 1871, saying that the
Navy account must be given to Jay Cooke and Company "for the broadest
political as well as financial reasons, looking to the good of the service
abroad as well as to the strengthening of the party and the administration
at home." They were "very powerful friends when actively interested
in the success of the administration, and dangerous enemies in vital localities [including Robeson's state of New Jersey, as he explained] when indifferent or unfriendly." Clews, therefore, was asked to "sacrifice" his
personal feelings "in the interest of the administration and of the country."
(House Mis. Doc., 44th Cong. 1st sess., no. 170, pt. 6, pp. 260–61.) That
Clews lobbied and bargained corruptly for the contract was said later
when his affairs were in the bankruptcy courts, in 1875. Two men then
appeared to say that they had been promised pay, and had received partial
payment for their activities in his behalf.—N. Y. Nation, Jan. 28, Sep. 30,
Oct. 14 and Dec. 16, 1875.
[2] Oberholtzer, Jay Cooke, vol. ii, pp. 352–4, 356–7. Cooke's subscriptions
amounted, in all, to more than $50,000.
[3] A. D. White, Autobiography, vol. i, p. 161.
[4] Boston Post, cited in N. Y. Tribune, Aug. 21, 1872.

would carry New Hampshire, Connecticut, New York and New Jersey. [1]

On September 18 he started for the West. In a private car, sometimes in a special train, accompanied by a number of men friendly to his cause, including Governor Walker of Virginia and ex-Governor Randolph of New Jersey, he proceeded on a journey which attracted national attention. Crowds gathered at the railway stations. At each considerable place he was obliged to halt to acknowledge the salutations of the people. He had got no farther than New Brunswick, N. J., when he was called out to defend the movement which, as he happily said, was "destined to reunite our people in bonds of genuine sympathy, to build up the waste places resulting from the war, and to turn aside and efface its bitter memories." [2] He proceeded through the towns in Pennsylvania on the line of the Pennsylvania Railroad as far as Pittsburgh. "I ask you," he said there, "to take the hand held out to you by your Southern brethren in their adoption of the Cincinnati platform, by those who were our enemies, but are again our fellow countrymen. I ask you to grasp that hand and say—'Brothers, we differed, we fought. The war is ended; let us again be fellow countrymen and forget that we have been enemies.'" [3]

In Cincinnati, where the enthusiasm was expected to reach its greatest height, in acknowledgment of the fact that the platform had been adopted and the candidate nominated in that city, Greeley spoke to immense audiences,—one gathered in the large Exposition Hall, where the convention had met in May. Thence the party proceeded to Louisville and to Indianapolis, there turning back to Dayton and Cleveland. Leaving Cleveland they visited Erie, the towns of the Pennsylvania oil regions and many places in the northern tier of counties in Pennsylvania which had not been touched on the way out. On September 29 the candidate was home again making a speech to a crowd which had gathered to welcome him at the Lincoln Club. Everywhere the receptions had been

---

[1] N. Y. Tribune, Aug. 14, 1872.
[2] Ibid., Sep. 19, 1872.   [3] Ibid., Sep. 20, 1872.

cordial; they contained the proofs, very pleasing to him, of his popularity. Flying banners, cheering people, campaign clubs on horse and on foot in white hats, torchlight parades and fireworks, the music of many bands marked his progress from place to place. Watterson said, after the candidate's visit to Kentucky, that "the situation" had been "revolutionized and reversed." Reid declared Greeley's speeches "perfect"; they were "at once strong, terse, comprehensive, adapted to the plainest understanding, and yet rising at times to true eloquence." [1] But in spite of his activities, in spite of all the evidences of the enthusiasm which his going about among the people evoked, the Republican majorities in Vermont and Maine were large. The Republicans in Pennsylvania, Ohio and Nebraska elected their state tickets in October by substantial majorities. It was but small encouragement which came from Indiana.

November followed soon. Only six of the 37 states favored the Liberal candidates—Missouri, Texas, Georgia, Kentucky, Tennessee and Maryland. [2] Abolitionist as he had been, few of the negroes voted for him—protectionist as he was, he was rejected by Pennsylvania. [3] Greeley had gained not one electoral vote from a Northern state. Grant carried New York by 53,000, Pennsylvania by 137,000, Ohio by 37,000, Illinois by 57,000, Massachusetts by 74,000, Indiana by 22,000, Iowa by 60,000, Michigan by 60,000. It was an overwhelming victory for the Republicans, a crushing defeat for Greeley, in whom hope and pride ran high. He had been "terribly beaten," he wrote his friend, Colonel Tappan of New Hampshire. [4] On one day he had delivered eighteen speeches, on another twenty-two. [5]

[1] Cortissoz, vol. i, p. 222; cf. White, Life of Trumbull, pp. 400–401; C. M. Depew, My Memories of 80 years, p. 94.
[2] In Maryland the plurality was less than 1,000.
[3] N. Y. World, Nov. 7, 1872; Julian, Political Recollections, p. 348. Many men, both Republicans and Democrats, did not go to the polls. "Thousands, perhaps even hundreds of thousands of citizens," said a writer in the Atlantic Monthly, "will abstain from voting at all because they believe both candidates personally unqualified, or disqualified, for the Presidency."—Issue of September, 1872.
[4] Hollister, Life of Colfax, p. 387.
[5] N. Y. Sun, Nov. 28, 1872.

He had been boasting during the campaign, as he successfully came through all his exertions, that he was "as tough as a boiled owl." [1] He could bear "whatever the future" had in store for him.[2] But it was a sore experience. His defeat indicated to him the loss of what was a dear possession—the affection and confidence of the American people. The result had dissipated a great illusion as to his exact place in the estimation of his countrymen.[3] He had been assailed so savagely, he complained to a friend, that he hardly knew whether he was "running for President or the Penitentiary." [4]

But outwardly Greeley made a manly appearance. Two days after the election, on Thursday, November 7, another "card" was printed in the Tribune. He would resume the place as editor of that paper which he had "relinquished on embarking in another line of business" six months since, as if the campaign had been but one of the casual episodes of life.[5]

In this conjuncture the wreck came. Mrs. Greeley was taken dangerously sick before the canvass had ended and he was called from the stump to her bedside. Her death soon followed, a week before election day. It was in such distress that the weight of the electoral reverse fell upon his spirit. The task of fitting himself into his old place in the office of the Tribune was not small or pleasant.[6] That paper had been coming from its presses each day without him, though with damaged fortunes by reason of his political course, which few of his old readers would endorse. The stockholders could blame him—as they did—for the interruption in their dividends.[7] His health broke down. When he wrote to Schurz from the Tribune office a few days after the defeat he was in

[1] Cortissoz, Life of Whitelaw Reid, vol. i, p. 222.
[2] W. B. Parker, Life of J. S. Morrill, pp. 239–40.
[3] N. Y. Nation, Dec. 5, 1872.
[4] Hollister, Life of Colfax, p. 387; cf. C. M. Depew, My Memories of 80 Years, p. 97.
[5] N. Y. Tribune, Nov. 7, 1872.
[6] Cf. Linn, Horace Greeley, p. 256.
[7] Life and Letters of Bayard Taylor, vol. ii, pp. 589, 605. But cf. Reid to Smalley, in Cortissoz, Life of Reid, vol. i, p. 225.

an "agony of emotion." [1] He was "a man of many sorrows," he wrote again.[2] He was "used up." He had "slept little for weeks"; when his eyes were closed they soon opened again.[3] He was taken away to a private asylum at Tarrytown. In a brain fever he became violently delirious, and, in a short while, to the consternation of, and with a shock to, the whole nation, he died on November 29,[4] but little more than three weeks after the decision at the polls.

The circumstances were such that it was more than the death of a man—it seemed a tragic moment in the life of the republic. Enemies who, only a few weeks ago, had so bitterly and ferociously assailed him now found good in his life. They discerned some of the virtues which were, in truth, but little concealed by his uncertain impulses. Republican editors who long had fought at his side saw him again as he used to be. Democrats thought the more of him now that he had made the daring adventure, with their aid, in behalf of a reunited nation to which they might be readmitted in honor and good standing.

The body lay in state for a day in the City Hall in New York City, where it was viewed by thousands of persons drawn from every class of society. Business ceased in New York and Brooklyn, while the *cortége* proceeded through the streets, which at places were so crowded as to be impassable.[5] Grant came, so did Vice President Colfax and Vice President-elect Henry Wilson, the Chief Justice, a number of senators and representatives in Congress, including Lyman Trumbull and Carl Schurz, the governors of several states. Henry Ward Beecher made the address at the church. Congress, state legislatures and city councils adopted resolutions. Bells were tolled, prayers were said, flags drooped, tributes were spoken in pulpit and press the country over. No one had had such a fu-

---

[1] Schurz, Speeches, vol. ii, p. 443.
[2] A. K. McClure, Old Times Notes of Pa., vol. ii, p. 339.
[3] Hollister, Life of Colfax, p. 387.
[4] The whole story is circumstantially related in N. Y. Sun, Nov. 30, 1872, and succeeding issues.
[5] L. D. Ingersoll, Life of Horace Greeley, pp. 551–5.

neral since Lincoln.[1] Men wondered and asked why all this
eulogy should have been reserved for "the dull, cold ear of
death."

Before Greeley was yet dead an unpleasant contest had been
begun for the control of the Tribune. Who should wear his
mantle as editor? Which element of the party—the "regulars,"
supporting Grant, or the "Liberals," should in future direct
the destinies of that powerful organ of opinion? Greeley was
so wanting in financial acumen that he had long since ceased
to hold more than a few shares of the stock of the company.
Samuel Sinclair, the publisher and part owner,[2] offered the
property for sale for a million dollars to interests which would
place Schuyler Colfax in the editorial chair. With Colfax
Sinclair and Greeley had for years maintained warm personal
relations. A contract was on the point of being signed.[3] But
account had not been taken of Whitelaw Reid, the editor in
charge during Greeley's preoccupation with his Presidential
campaign. Whether or not this man had been the large factor
in obtaining Greeley the nomination at Cincinnati that he
accounted himself to be,[4] he anyhow was the only one whose
personal fortunes were to be advanced by the campaign and
the final tragedy. His ambition to supersede the great editor
was well known.[5] It had been gratified temporarily during
the canvass, and was now to be realized in permanency. He
assembled the money to checkmate Sinclair and Colfax,[6] and

[1] N. Y. Tribune, Dec. 4 and 5, 1872; Julian, Political Recollections, p.35.
[2] His wife was a cousin of Greeley.
[3] Hollister , Life of Colfax, pp. 387–8.
[4] Cortissoz, Life of Reid, vol. ii, pp. 215, 218, 224.
[5] Cf. N. Y. Times, Nov. 29 and 30, and Dec. 17 and 19, 1872.
[6] It has been stated that William Orton, president of the Western Union
Telegraph Company, and Jay Gould were involved in this operation.
(Hollister, Life of Colfax, p. 390; cf. N. Y. Times, Dec. 25, 1872; N. Y.
Tribune, Jan. 4 and 6, 1873.) The New York Sun named William Walter
Phelps as Reid's friend in this transaction. (N. Y. Sun, Dec. 24, 1872.)
Jay Cooke had enabled him to buy an interest in the Cincinnati Gazette.
(Oberholtzer, Jay Cooke, vol. i, pp. 480–81.) For other accounts see Cor-
tissoz, Life of Reid, vol. i, pp. 245–8. Bound up with the struggle for
control of the paper was a contest, immediately following Greeley's death,
over his last will, which it was alleged had been made when he was *non
compos.*

made himself master of the Tribune.[1] He could in future do with the great trust as he liked, and his choice did not incline him in the direction of the political and social reforms which the paper, since the first day, had served with so much distinction.[2] He looked about him for a way to leave the company of those men with whom for some time he had been so prominently allied. Then, like Christian's fellow traveller in John Bunyan's story who fell with him into the Slough of Despond, "he gave a desperate struggle or two and got out of the mire on that side of the slough which was next his own house."[3] "Independent journalism" he, in good time, exchanged for the undeviating partisanship which distinguished the newspaper for the rest of his life.

"You knew, as I did," Greeley wrote to a friend after his great defeat, "that we must stop fighting the rebels some time. But it is now settled that we never shall."[4]

[1] Cf. N. Y. Sun, Dec. 12, 20 and 25; N. Y. World, Dec. 22 and 24, 1872; N. Y. Tribune, Dec. 23, 1872.
[2] Merriam, Life and Times of Bowles, vol. ii, p. 184.
[3] Ibid., p. 223.
[4] Hollister, Life of Colfax, p. 387.

CHAPTER XVIII

THE PANIC OF 1873

IT was to be four more years of Grant, "four more years of fraud and corruption,"[1] said the Liberal-Democratic elements which had been borne down by the weight of the Republican victory. Many a one, though the words were not spoken in real confidence, had, during the campaign, cherished and uttered the opinion that Grant would be a better President in his second term than he had proven to be in his first.[2] That a more intelligent comprehension of duty would possess the President, call forth a courage which had distinguished him on the military field, and govern him in his great civil office was a hope entertained on many sides. The uprising which had found expression at Cincinnati, though it had miscarried, was full of admonition, and the discipline of criticism in the four years, to commence on the 4th of March, 1873, by such an opposition as the campaign had revealed, must have some power to check the President in his fatal course of giving the government into the hands of incapable and dishonest persons. In this, it was agreed by his intelligent critics, had he erred thus far—in failure to call high-minded and efficient men, with a talent for statecraft, to influential positions; in a stubborn defense of his chosen agents, though they were proven to be incompetents and knaves; in perverse refusal, in such a case, to dismiss them from the service. His whole training had been in other fields—in accepting the nomination a second time at the hands of the Philadelphia convention he had given fitting expression to some realization of his inexperience. But would the opportunities which he had had for education, and which he may or may not have embraced, yield any gain to the state?

[1] Cf. N. Y. Sun, Nov. 6, 1872.
[2] Greeley was reminded that he had expressed such a view only a few months before he had dissociated himself from the party.

69

The Forty-second Congress came to an end on March 3rd, 1873, amid unusual excitement. It had had a career unlike any Congress which had preceded it. Caught in the tide of its sin, reluctant and uncontrite, it, driven to action, had taken a hand in the business of reproof and punishment. Pursuant to resolutions, in answer to the demands of an outraged popular feeling, or for purposes having to do with party success, inquiry and investigation had proceeded. Prior to and during the Presidential campaign there was, first of all, the investigation instituted by Schurz, supported by Sumner, into information which had reached them to the effect that during the Franco-Prussian war large quantities of arms had been sold to France in a manner suggestive of corruption in the War Department. Though the committee, to which the subject had been referred, exonerated Belknap,[1] it was still believed by many that he had acted in a reckless and an illegal way.[2] The operations of the "syndicate," headed by Jay Cooke, for funding the debt were investigated. The Secretary of the Treasury was exonerated.[3] The Secors and their associate contractors, in the business of building iron clad monitors for the government during the war, had been paid their price, and an additional sum to cover losses, alleged to have been incurred in the prosecution of their work. They had further claims for compensation and, in 1869, Secretary of the Navy Robeson reopened the subject and paid them $93,000 more.[4]

Postmaster General Creswell, in a similar way, had honored the claims of a man named Chorpenning for "extra" services which, in his own view of the matter, he had performed as a mail carrier. Although, even by his own computation, the amount due him was but $176,000, his lobbyists got an award of nearly a half million dollars, which were to be paid them out

[1] House Reports, 42nd Cong. 2nd sess., no. 46.
[2] Schurz, Reminiscences, vol. iii, pp. 336-7.
[3] House Reports, 42nd Cong. 2nd sess., no. 7; Oberholtzer, Jay Cooke, vol. ii, p. 361.
[4] House Reports, 42nd Cong. 2nd sess., no. 80, pp. 13-24; ibid., no. 81, pp. 1-8; House Mis. Doc., 42nd Cong. 2nd sess., no. 201, particularly testimony of Welles and Robeson; N. Y. Nation, April 18 and 25, 1872.

of the Treasury.[1] This case, although it seemed obviously to require inquiry and censure, received none. Congress did, however, in the face of criticism, suspend payment and sent the claimant to other quarters for his redress.[2]

But, surpassing all other infamies, was that one growing out of the Crédit Mobilier, which occupied the Congress in the last weeks of its life. What came out in this investigation by the three committees at work upon it—the maze of "contradictions, untruths and perjuries" of the "wriggling witnesses," [3] as well as the original action which gave rise to these insincerities, was taken to be more than confirmatory of all that underlay the protest which had found expression in the Cincinnati movement.

Worse than all else was the conviction among discerning men that the exposure of sinners brought no repentance. The inquiries, commenced under duress, proceeded with as much polite consideration for the offenders as the circumstances would allow. As much as could be would remain concealed. Investigator and investigated in Congress were in a boat together. It was not the individual fact, exhibiting an immoral performance, but the whole tone of public life which gave the times their disquieting character. It was little that Oakes Ames and James Brooks were censured by the House, that Patterson was marked for reprobation by the Senate. It would have been little if they had been expelled. They were but three men taken out of many for sacrifice in propitiation of an outraged popular feeling.

That there was no sorrow of heart and no penitence of spirit in the body of men who would, at the conclusion of Grant's first term of office, end their two years of national service together was impressively shown by their last act, when, under the cover of the confusion which attends the closing days of a session, they passed the bill increasing their salaries. Fit leader of this brigandage was "Ben" Butler, whose natural

[1] N. Y. Nation, Oct. 10 and 24, 1872.
[2] Ibid., March 19, 1874; House Reports, 43rd Cong. 1st sess., no. 622.
[3] N. Y. Tribune, Feb. 19, 1873.

audacity, enlarged by the courage which he drew from Grant as the President's principal representative on the floor of the House, and as Federal office broker in Massachusetts, if not in a larger field, had raised him to a height of influence that he had not known before.

The scheme in the beginning, was devised for the advantage of the President only. His urgent requirements led to a proposal of his friends to double his salary. It would be made $50,000 instead of $25,000 a year. But many of the Congressmen expressed no enthusiasm for the project, so it was developed to include them among the beneficiaries, when it soon came to wear a new color.[1] While Grant's salary would be doubled, while the Vice President's, each cabinet officer's and each Supreme Court justice's would be increased to $10,000, each senator and representative, now in receipt of $5,000 a year, would henceforward take $8,000 a year from the government for his services. This would mean an increase in the pay of the body which should vote itself the bounty of $1,100,000 annually.[2]

The session would end on March 3rd, at the end of Grant's first term. If there were to be any amelioration of his condition, which his friends had done so much to relieve by contributions from their private fortunes, it must be soon, for the Constitution would forbid all movements in this direction after his second term had commenced. Accordingly, on February 2nd, Butler rose in the House to move an amendment to the general appropriation bill. It was late at night, opportune hour for such a deed. The scheme had undergone some slight modification. Speaker Blaine was to receive $10,000 a year, as much as a cabinet officer. The Congressmen themselves were to have $7,500 a year. Moreover, the provision would be retroactive— the increase would apply to members of the present Forty-second Congress for services during the biennium just past. Each senator and representative would take home with him,

---

[1] Cong. Globe, 42nd Cong. 3rd sess., pp. 1904, 2102; cf. Harper's Weekly, Dec. 13, 1873.

[2] N. Y. Nation, Feb. 13, 1873.

when he should return thither ten days hence, a bonus in "back pay" of $5,000.[1]

The proposal, frank and bold as it was, awakened little remonstrance in debate. It seemed to be and, indeed, was not worse than much that Congress had wound into its daily record during its recent history. Representative Farnsworth denounced it as "a shameless spectacle."[2] This thing, he said, shamed the Crédit Mobilier "and everything else that has taken place in this Congress, or any other."[3] The plea was made that the President could not live on $25,000 a year; but Lincoln had done so. For a part of the time the paper money he had received was worth only forty or fifty cents on the dollar, yet in four years he had contrived to lay by a fortune of $50,000. Everything was found for Grant, except the provisions for his table, and a part of these cost him nothing, since the gardens at the White House and men to work them were contributed by the government.[4]

It was "a raid upon the Treasury," said Edmunds in the Senate. To take two years' back pay was, translating it into English, for Congress to put into its pocket "a million and a half of the money of the people."[5] Those who belonged to the dominant political party, and now supported this proposition, said Representative Hawley of Connecticut, were "digging the grave of that party."[6]

But such words, briefly spoken by a few men, were unheeded. Public service was for millionaires, said Senator Carpenter of Wisconsin; "increase the pay of the members so as to pay the reasonable expenses of living and a fair compensation for the labor we perform, and you open Congress to brains,—reduce the pay and you open it to men of wealth."[7] The cost of living had immensely increased. Simon Cameron declared that, when he first came to Washington, he had boarded at the best place in the city. He was served with canvas-back duck and every luxury in season for $10 a week. His predecessor, James

---

[1] Cong. Globe, 42nd Cong. 3rd sess., pp. 1671–2.

[2] Ibid., p. 1904.	[5] Ibid., p. 2179.
[3] Ibid., p. 2101.	[6] Ibid., p. 1675.
[4] Ibid.	[7] Ibid., p. 2045.

Buchanan, had paid but $9 a week for his meals.[1] In Andrew
Jackson's day, said General Banks, a man could stop at the
leading hotel for one dollar a day for himself and a half dollar
for the keep of his horse.[2] Now senators and representatives
found that they must pay from $45 to $75 a week for the same
accommodations. Their salaries ought to be $10,000—their
services were worth as much as the justices of the Supreme
Court.[3]

Objection to the plan to make the increase cover the activities of the Congress nearing its end was swept away. "If
it is right now," said Senator Carpenter, "it has been right
all these two years for us to have more pay." If it is right to
"raise it" at this time, "it was just as proper to have raised it
five years ago." [4]

The House reduced the salary of the members from $7,500
to $6,500, but, in conference, the higher rate was restored, and
in the last hours, just before adjournment, the report of the
conferees was adopted. Garfield, who, with Butler and Randall,
had a place on the committee as a representative of the House,
expressed regret that he must recommend such a course. But
"compelled to choose between signing the report and running
the risk of bringing on an extra session of Congress," [5] since
the "salary grab" was bound up with the whole question of
appropriations for the ensuing year of government, he had done
so. The Senate concurred by a vote of 36 to 27,[6] the majority
including all the Southern carpetbaggers and scalawags in the
chamber. In the House the final vote was 102 to 96,[7] where
similarly the majority was increased by the Southern members.[8]

If it were not a violation, men said, it was at the least an
evasion of the Constitution. The same President, who was to
sign the bill on March 3, would be in office to enjoy its fruits,

[1] Cong. Globe, 42nd Cong. 3rd sess., p. 2046.
[2] Ibid., p. 1904.   [5] Ibid., p. 2101.
[3] Ibid., p. 2046.   [6] Ibid., p. 2184.
[4] Ibid., p. 2179.   [7] Ibid., p. 2105.
[8] Cf. N. Y. Times, quoted in N. Y. Nation, March 13, 1872. The New
York Tribune said that 62 of the number were men whose terms were
expiring and who, with this act, withdrew from public life.—Issue of
March 6, 1873.

beginning on March 4. It had been designed that no President should exercise the influence of his official position to increase his own salary.[1] But this one had done so. Grant approved the bill at once without a word of regret or protest,[2] and the Congressmen trooped into the sergeant-at-arms' room to receive their portions before proceeding to their respective homes, as he was being sworn into office amid the military pomp and circumstance which became his figure as a President.

Seated in a carriage, drawn by four horses, surrounded by gaily caparisoned cavalrymen, and preceded and followed by bodies of soldiery, he was escorted from the White House to the Capitol. A mass of people crowded the pavements and the Capitol grounds. After Chief Justice Chase had administered the oath, the President, in a voice which only those nearest him could hear, read his inaugural address. At night a multitude of persons, the fashionable and the gross, negroes mingling with the whites, shivered in the penetrating air of an abnormally cold March day at the "Inaugural Ball," held in a huge wooden building, resembling the Mormon Temple at Salt Lake, which had been erected for this use by the citizens of Washington. Grant's second term had commenced amid the idle show, the luxurious vulgarity and the free extravagance which were characteristic of the age.

As Henry Wilson took Colfax's place in the Vice President's chair, sending that once fair idol of the Republican party back to the obscurity of his Indiana home, under the obloquy which had just been put upon his name by the Crédit Mobilier investigation, came Boutwell's chance to take a seat in the Senate from Massachusetts. In league with Butler, who was using all the power of the Grant administration to seize the governorship of Massachusetts, in which design he had failed once and would fail again before he should achieve success, the paltry character who had been Secretary of the Treasury was now to become the colleague of Charles Sumner. Boutwell's friend and assistant, Richardson, no higher in the rank of states-

manship, was appointed to his vacated place. With this exception the cabinet of Grant's first term would, for the time
being, remain unchanged in his second term, and the policies
of the administration, untouched by all the criticism of the
campaign, unimproved by any of its lessons, would develop
as before.

The first disillusionment, if any one could have honestly
cherished illusions as to Grant's course, now that he was for a
second time settled in the Presidential office, came in connection
with the civil service. With all his inept and in many cases
absolutely evil appointments he had made protestations of
concern for this subject. He had deceived at least one man,
George William Curtis, editor of Harper's Weekly and president
of the Civil Service Commission. One of the most indefensible
of the President's perversities was his support of Casey, who
had married his wife's youngest sister, for months involved
in dark conspiracies in the Reconstruction politics of Louisiana.
This man was collector of the port in New Orleans. Grant
had refused point-blank to remove him, and now, in March,
1873, actually reappointed him to his place. Holden, the
North Carolina scalawag, was made postmaster at Raleigh.
A needy preacher, a friend of the President, was commissioned,
at $5,000 a year and travelling expenses, to go abroad as an
"inspector" of United States consulates in all parts of the
world.[1] A politician, named Sharpe, was made surveyor of
the port in New York at the dictation of the Republican
"ring." [2] In the face of Grant's very manifest insincerity, or
want of understanding of the meaning of the "reform," which
the commission was created to advance, Curtis resigned.[3]
Though the President appointed Dorman B. Eaton of New
York,[4] a worthy man, to succeed Curtis, and to cover the
retreat from the high ground on which he was glad to be seen,
his abandonment of the principle as well as the practice of the
"reform," concerning which there had been so many public
expressions, was now frank enough for everyone to understand

[1] N. Y. Nation, Jan. 27, 1876.   [3] Ibid., April 3, 10 and 17, 1873.
[2] Ibid., March 20 and 27, 1873.   [4] Ibid., April 24, 1873.

it.[1] The politicians' hands were on the spoils. The infamies which proceeded in the Southern states, under local Republican management, continued to be supported by Federal patronage. The political leader, wherever he might be, who controlled the party machinery in a city or state, could ask and receive the lucrative offices at the disposal of the President. Never before, and not since, has the scoundrel found so few obstructions standing in the way to keep him from approach to the scene and to the object of his rascalities as in this "coarse and venal régime." [2]

Though the mischiefs at home arising from such a view of the public service were sore and many, it was doubly humiliating when this system of filling Federal offices was extended to the diplomatic and consular service. Men like General Sickles at Madrid, Curtin at St. Petersburg, Jones at Brussels, Shellabarger at Lisbon, the Reverend Cramer, Grant's brother-in-law, at Copenhagen, Washburne at Paris, though the latter had exhibited an unexpected tact amid the difficulties attending the administration of his office during the Franco-Prussian war, were obviously unfitted by nature for their responsibilities. Indeed, the legations and the consulates were in general treated as places of refuge for the personal friends of the President, or for unfortunates of the party, who, left out of office at home by reversals at the polls, or who, on one account or another, desired a trip to Europe, Asia or South America, where they had never been, at public expense. Such methods brought mortification to right thinking Americans who resided or traveled in foreign countries, and lowered the nation in the esteem of other governments.[3] Schenck continued to labor under the disrepute which fairly came to him at London for lending his name to the Utah mining company, whose promoters had set forth to fleece the English aristocracy.[4] He was compiling a treatise to instruct the same aristocracy upon the subject of draw poker, an American game at which he was

[1] Cf. Harper's Weekly, Oct. 25, and Nov. 1, 1873.
[2] N. Y. Nation, Dec. 24, 1874.
[3] Cf. ibid., Jan. 8, 1874.
[4] Cf. ibid., Sep. 25 and Dec. 18, 1873.

accounted proficient.[1] That nothing better could be expected of Grant during his second term was soon made clear, when that old "war horse" of the party, John A. Bingham of Ohio, was appointed to represent us in Japan. Though this man had been involved in the Crédit Mobilier scandal, though he had aided and abetted the "back pay steal," he was thought to be qualified to go forth to fill this important diplomatic position.[2]

In Washington itself the spirit of the day was finding exemplification in many corrupt activities which had for their excuse an entirely worthy ideal, the beautification of the capital city of the republic. The District of Columbia by the act of February 21, 1871, stood under the administrative direction of a governor, appointed by the President. It was in effect a system similar to that in the territories, with a legislative assembly and a delegate in Congress elected by the people. Since many of the white residents of Washington held their citizenship in other parts of the Union, the negroes, as easily herded by the Republican leaders here as in the reconstructed Southern states, were put to the uses of a "Boss," Alexander R. Shepherd, acting nominally in and for a Board of Public Works. By large and costly projects for the laying of pavements, the creation of parks, the extension of the city into the, as yet, rural parts of the District, he was putting burdens upon the taxpayers which they rose to denounce. Jay Cooke, the rich Philadelphia financier, had a branch office in Washington near the Treasury, through which an enormous business in government bonds was done during the war. In charge of it was his brother, Henry D. Cooke, who established close personal relations with Grant, upon that President's coming to the White House. The President's love of wealth and the wealthy had made Cooke's way easy. The favors which were extended at the bank to Grant and his needy kindred did not go unrequited, and, in 1871, Henry Cooke was appointed governor of the District of Columbia.[3]

---

[1] Cf. N. Y. Nation, Dec. 24 and 31, 1874, and Feb. 11 and 18, 1875.
[2] Ibid., June 12, 1873.
[3] Oberholtzer, Jay Cooke, vol. ii, pp. 269-70.

In January, 1872, a large number of citizens of Washington, in petitions and letters, urged Congress to correct the evils which had developed in the new system of government. The Board of Public Works, i. e., Shepherd, had "usurped authority." The terms of the act were being violated, the transactions of the Board were kept secret, debt was being recklessly increased, extravagance was seen on every side.[1] A great volume of testimony was taken, but the committee vindicated Shepherd, except on the point of having made some "mistakes."[2] So the "improvements" proceeded and the resentment of the taxpayers continued and increased.

Governor Cooke was a weak character, and he and the firm of Jay Cooke and Company were soon involved in the large operations which Shepherd had in hand. In the summer of 1873, Jay Cooke, who foresaw what was about to ensue,[3] required his brother's retirement from such associations.[4] The President was afforded as good an opportunity to form an idea of what was being done under the direction of Shepherd, who, it was alleged, was making himself rich and the District bankrupt, yet, when Henry Cooke's resignation was put in Grant's hands, in 1873, Shepherd was appointed to the governorship,[5] action which Grant enforced by a written endorsement of the "Boss."

Meantime an event which would have far-reaching and prolonged effect upon the course of politics, as well as the temper of society, was at hand. It descended upon the country like some great overwhelming tide of the sea. The most natural and necessary of consequences it was, furthermore, as it seems now, in looking back upon the period, a visitation of Providence for the nation's reproof and eventual good. Plainly we could

---

[1] House Reports, 42nd Cong. 2nd sess., no. 72, pp. i–ii.

[2] Ibid., p. xiii. But see the minority report, corroborating the charges of the memorialists and recommending a change in the law.—Ibid., pp. xv–xx.

[3] As he protested against the part some of his partners in London were taking in connection with the Emma mining scheme.—Oberholtzer, Jay Cooke, vol. ii, pp. 290–91.

[4] Ibid., p. 417.

[5] N. Y. Nation, Sep. 18 and 25, 1873.

proceed no farther on the present course. The laws of orderly
conduct had been violated in too many directions; only some
great cataclysm could bring the country to reason. Extravagance must give place to economy and thrift, speculation to
careful industry; roguery must be punished and brought to an
end. New standards, worthier example must be set before the
uprising generation.

On all sides, for many years, discerning men had foreseen
the inevitable result of the reckless riot in which the nation had
been plunged at the end of the war. Railways were being built
for a generation yet unborn. Bonds and stocks, which there
was no money to buy, were for sale on every hand. Credit
had been extended until it was exhausted. New capital, where
it existed, was not to be had for any undertaking. An infinity
of enterprises had contended for public favor—all, no matter
what their intrinsic worth, were now under a suspicion fatal
to any achievement. Confidence in individual and corporate
honesty had been shaken by a series of events calculated to
destroy faith in the best plans and undertakings. The inflated
currency, the artificial means repeatedly employed to maintain
the credit of the government by operations in Wall Street,
instigated by the Treasury Department, the complete failure
of movements toward a resumption of specie payments,
the gold premium and the Gold Room itself, were constant
proof of a derangement in public finance which, if it could not
be corrected, would in the future, as in the past, endanger private finance.

No lesson would be learned; it seemed impossible, by appeal
to history or to reason, to cause those who were entrusted with
the direction of our affairs, if there were, or could have been,
under the conditions which prevailed at this time, any to
wield so great a power, to put the national house in order. The
democracy was running wild after its military triumph. It
was leaping over and breaking down constitutional bounds.
Exultation had turned to a frenzy, which, developing under and
protected by the banners carried by the Republican party in
the war, with many an appeal to the gratitude that its services

in preserving the Union, in freeing the negro from slavery must
evoke, had got beyond all control. Johnson had essayed the
task of checking the popular passion and had failed. Grant
was chosen to further the madness, and put no obstacle in its
path. Congress, Supreme Court, press, people had raised no
barrier to impede its progress. Reckoning day was at hand.

The great shock to the national fabric came through one of
the most potential agencies for the achievement of large ends
which the times had produced. None so little merited the fate
in store for him, since Jay Cooke had stood throughout the
period an honest man. He had been connected with no evil
scheme, his name was untouched by any of the scandals of the
age. Fired by visions of national development, he was carrying
forward, with a fine enthusiam, a great enterprise, the construction of a railroad to extend from Duluth, at the head of
Lake Superior, to Tacoma on Puget Sound, and that road had
reached Bismarck, on the Missouri River, in the Territory of
Dakota. No soldier on a battle field ever fought more manfully
than he to escape the toils in which he found himself as the
months of 1873 wore on. One plan upon another for the raising
of money to complete the railroad had failed. "Pools" "syndi-
cates," popular subscription agencies, advertising campaigns,—
all were tried with but little success. Government subventions
in guaranteed bonds, in addition to the large grants of land
pledged to the company, were sought at Washington. An end
to this prospect was reached with the disclosures affecting the
Crédit Mobilier. After this unfoldment the capital, as well as
the credit, of Cooke's firm was encroached upon to keep the
project in motion. It is true that the loans were intended to
be only temporary, but nothing returned. It had been stipu-
lated in the contract with the company that advances by the
banking house should never be in excess of $500,000. Already
in the summer of 1872, during the excitement attending the
Greeley campaign, when bond sales practically ceased, the
amount which the railroad owed Jay Cooke and Company
was not less than $1,775,000.[1] Protests came from Cooke's

[1] Oberholtzer, Jay Cooke, vol. ii, p. 384.

partners who, unable to share his enthusiasm for the important national work, would detach the firm from the road. It could go its own way, and fail, if it must.

But to this Cooke would not hear. He thought ill of his associates for their want of faith, and but redoubled his energies in the company's behalf. He had not espoused the cause—the construction of this railroad was to him a public cause—without a resolve that it should be made to succeed, and he ordered, in his imperious though kindly way, the entire crew to the tasks which he had set for them when the voyage was begun, Mutiny it may have seemed to the commander, but it was plain enough that they could reach the harbor, which was on Puget Sound, only as a result of some miracle. The times might have improved, but they did not—they grew worse. All who were in contact with the money markets knew the stolid resistance which was offered to any movement in behalf of enterprises calling for fresh drafts upon capital. It was pointed out, and believed, that a new road, even in well settled territory, must pass through five years of operation before it could be relied upon to make a return to those who had invested their money in it. Others, such as the Northern Pacific, would certainly lose their credit—some, like it, already had done so, proof of which was seen in the low prices which their securities commanded—on the way to bankruptcy.[1]

A road in Minnesota, subsidiary to the Northern Pacific, called the St. Paul and Pacific, was in obvious difficulty in 1872. Work upon it ceased. Claims against the Northern Pacific company were paid slowly. Laborers were not receiving their wages. Along the line of the road vouchers were passed from hand to hand and were in use as currency until they could be converted into cash.[2] When work was interrupted for the winter it was freely predicted that it would not be resumed upon the coming of spring.[3] Several times the newspapers had the road in bankruptcy.[4]

---

[1] Phila. Ledger, Sep. 18, 1873; cf. N. Y. Nation, Sep. 24, 1874.
[2] Oberholtzer, Jay Cooke, vol. ii, p. 394.
[3] Ibid., p. 395.
[4] Ibid., p. 410.

Three or four large railroad companies had failed, two or three houses in New York connected with their fortunes had suspended in the summer of 1873. These failures were the text for much homily. There was "no business on the continent already so overdone as railroad building," said the New York Tribune. Loans were made "on wild cat securities to all sorts of third rate railway enterprises in Canada, Kansas, Louisiana and along the frontier of Mexico." Bankers were "loaded to the water's edge with a worthless cargo." It was time for a halt before "another 1857" should be upon the country.[1]

Interest on American railway bonds had been defaulted in England, absolutely closing that market, which long had afforded our promoters little return. The German market was in an even worse position.[2] The quantity of public land given to the companies by the government, much of it "valueless naturally," said the Public Ledger of Philadelphia, was vastly in excess of the number of people who in fifty years would be at hand to take up and cultivate it. So much of it was óffered that it had no salable price.[3] It was alleged that, in the five years past, over $1,700,000,000 had been expended in railway construction in the United States.[4]

Gradually but rapidly Cooke's advances to the Northern Pacific company had been increased until the total sum was alarming. The continual discontent of his associates was manifest. One in particular, Fahnestock, at the head of the firm's New York house, who had come to Cooke as a clerk to enjoy swift advancement, had been, from the beginning, unfavorable to the plan to finance and build the railway. He kept the London partners apprised of the state of affairs. All together appealed to Cooke to withdraw from the connection

[1] N. Y. Tribune, Sep. 16, 1873.
[2] Phila. Ledger, Sep. 18, 1873. "For some years," said Moran in London, "a band of the most unscrupulous speculators have stuffed the banks of England and the Continent with bonds that are utterly worthless, so that no German banker will deal now with an American negotiator until his character is endorsed by a German. The very fact that a scheme for a loan is American makes it distrusted."—Moran's Diary, Sep. 19, 1873, in Library of Congress.
[3] Phila. Ledger, Sep. 18, 1873.
[4] Article on Finances of the U. S. in Am. Ann. Cyclop. for 1873.

which they foresaw must lead to ruin. Nothing availed and the day approached. On Thursday morning, September 18, Fahnestock took the subject into his own hands. As well, as far as available evidence appears, might he have acted a month or six weeks before. He could have waited a while longer. However, so much was now clear—that such conditions could not continue for any considerable period of time, that, though they should become much worse, Cooke himself would not consent either to dissociate his house from the unfortunate railroad or to the confession of failure which would be implied by a suspension of business. Therefore the indomitable head of the firm was not told of the intention of his juniors. The clock had not yet struck eleven; the day had barely commenced when Fahnestock ordered the closing of the doors of Jay Cooke and Company in New York.

When the telegraph bore him the news Jay Cooke, in deep distress, closed the doors of his house in Third Street in Philadelphia. Governor Cooke followed, perforce, at the Washington office and in the First National Bank of Washington.

The moral effect of what was seen was instant. At some times, under some conditions, it might have attracted only casual notice. Not so now. Grant, but a day or two since, had been an overnight guest at "Ogontz," Jay Cooke's "palatial residence" near Philadelphia.[1] Henry Cooke was in the midst of receiving pleasant laudation attending his governorship of the District of Columbia.[2] He was about to be tendered a complimentary dinner at which General Sherman would serve as the presiding officer.[3] It was the failure of "the most enterprising and renowned of American monetary institutions," said one newspaper.[4] The firm's "history was national fame," said another.[5] The Bank of England had not been "more trusted."[6] The "very enterprise" which had "finally dragged

[1] Phila. Inquirer, Sep. 17, 1873.
[2] Ibid., Sep. 16, 1873.
[3] Oberholtzer, Jay Cooke, vol. ii, p. 422.
[4] Phila. Press, Sep. 19, 1873.
[5] Phila. Inquirer, Sep. 19, 1873.
[6] Ibid.

them down," said the New York Tribune, "was of national concern." [1] Disaster had come in carrying forward a work of "imposing importance" for "the common good of the country and of humanity." [2]

When the suspension was announced on the Stock Exchange in New York the scene resembled pandemonium. The brokers, shouting at and jostling one another, were a mob. Anything like orderly procedure ceased. Men rushed in from the streets and crowded the galleries to witness the sight, which the New York Tribune described as "indescribable." [3] Prices fell without regard to worth—the shares of intrinsically valuable properties with the rest. Rumors of other failures filled the air. If this house, which had been godfather to the Northern Pacific, with Cooke's great credit to support it, must suspend, so must other houses that were carrying stocks, in comparison with which "Northern Pacifics" must seem "like 5–20's or British Consols." [4] Men who had money in banks would draw it out. "Runs" were started, long queues of impatient men and women were formed at the cashier's windows even of the most trusted of depositaries. In Philadelphia and Washington similar scenes were enacted. Men fled hither and thither in their excitement, first to verify the unbelievable news and then to safeguard their pecuniary interests. Third Street in Philadelphia, in the vicinity of Cooke's bank, was crowded with men drawn from all directions. Fifteenth Street in Washington was thronged. Government clerks left their posts of duty; a public court was adjourned during a murder trial. Nor was rumor of accumulating ruin without foundation in fact. In Philadelphia the old house of E. W. Clark and Company, established before the Mexican War, whose heads were bound to Mr. Cooke, by the friendliest ties, closed its doors. Before the day was done, several smaller firms in that city, as well as in New York, also suspended.

Night brought no rest to those whose interests and engagements allied them with the stock and money markets. Bankers

[1] N. Y. Tribune, Sep. 19, 1873.   [3] Issue of Sep. 19, 1873.
[2] Phila. Inquirer, Sep. 19, 1873.   [4] Ibid.

and brokers, promoters and speculators in New York adjourned
to the Fifth Avenue Hotel, where, in corridor and rotunda,
conversation and prediction, and bargain and sale continued.
The next day would be Friday—ominous with possibilities
in superstitious minds. Would it be another "Black Friday"?
Upon the commencement of the new day pressure and fall
began at once. Contemplation of the situation overnight,
with the aid of the newspapers, the telegraph and the mails,
multiplied demands which could not be met. Fisk and Hatch,
Cooke's principal agents in New York for the sale of the war
loans, now engaged in financing the Chesapeake and Ohio
Railroad, a new trunk line from the Mississippi Valley to the
Atlantic seaboard,[1] closed their doors. Other firms, a score
in number, followed. A dozen failed in Philadelphia. Brokerage houses and banking institutions, allied with Vanderbilt,
suspended, indicating that he was being sorely pressed. Rumor,
not without reason, extended to the Pennsylvania Railroad,
since its officers, particularly Thomas A. Scott, were so deeply
involved in Western railway schemes.[2]

It was "Black Friday" in very truth. The house of cards
had collapsed. The ruins were seen on every side. Saturday
opened with no cessation of the panic, which by this time had
overtaken the whole financial and mercantile community.
Several national banks and trust companies were included in
the wreck. A "run" upon a solid institution in Philadelphia,
which was the subject of rumors affecting its strength that could
not be allayed, called for cash payments aggregating nearly a
million dollars before the depositors could be reassured. Stocks
which were of established value, "leaders" in the New York
market, fell $30 and $40 a share. Wabash which had been

[1] The fifth, the others being the New York Central, the Erie, the Pennsylvania and the Baltimore and Ohio.—Phila. Ledger, Dec. 12, 1873.
[2] The bonds of his Texas Pacific, "through to the Pacific Ocean," secured by "its equipment, franchises, etc., including upwards of 15,000,000
acres of land donated by the government of the United States to aid in the
construction of the road," of which Scott was president, and J. Edgar
Thomson and Samuel L. Felton, trustees of the mortgage, were not worth
as much as Cooke's Northern Pacific securities.—See advertisement in
Phila. Ledger, Sep. 13, 1873.

selling at 70, was quoted on Saturday, September 20, at 38; St. Paul fell from 51 to 30; Northwestern from 64 to 40; Panama from 117 to 84; Harlem from 130 to 90. Western Union, which had sold a few days since for 92, declined to 54; [1] it was offered now at 45 without meeting a bid;—no buyer would have appeared, it was said, if the price had been reduced to 25.[2] Bonds fell also, though their value none could dispute. The securities of uncompleted railroads which were involved in the fate of the suspended houses had, for the time, practically no salable price. In this conjuncture an unheard of measure was adopted by the officers of the Stock Exchange; all business in it would cease until the public mind could be composed. The decision was announced at ten minutes before twelve o'clock on September 20, amid demoralization affecting the whole membership.[3] The step had been taken, said the vice chairman, "to save the entire 'Street' from utter ruin."

The government would be appealed to, of course, as it had been in every emergency, and a remedy would be sought in a further issue of "greenbacks." In the Treasury were $44,000,000 worth of them which McCulloch had retired, before, denounced as a "contractionist," he was checked in his effort to put the finances of the country on a sounder foundation. The bills, when they were taken in, should have been cancelled and destroyed. But they were not. Boutwell and Richardson insisted upon calling them a "reserve." In the autumn of 1872 some $5,000,000 of the notes had been temporarily released and put into circulation "to move the crops." Their reissue had been contemplated when the subject was before Congress in 1868, and it had been held by most of the senators that such action would be without authority.[4] Accordingly, when Congress convened in December, 1872, Boutwell was brought to book for what had been done. He made the excuse

[1] Financial and Commercial Chronicle, quoted in article on Finances of the United States in Am. Ann. Cyclop. for 1873.
[2] N. Y. Tribune, Sep. 22, 1873.
[3] Phila. Inquirer, Sep. 22, 1823.
[4] See discussion of the point in Cong. Record, 43rd Cong. 1st sess., pp. 2360 et seq.

of absence from the Department,—his assistant Richardson
had acted in the premises.[1] The Senate considered the subject.
It was referred to the Finance Committee, a majority of the
members of which declared, in January, 1873, that Boutwell's
action had been an unlawful exercise of power.[2]

In spite of this opinion a few months since, covering action
in 1872, men said now, in 1873, that the "reserve" should be
drawn upon again. Grant came to New York, so did Richardson. Senator Morton of Indiana, with head and frame like a
giant smith, useful in the war as the governor of his state, but
now no guide to be trusted and followed, though he had usurped
a place at Grant's elbow, had preceded them to the city. They
secured apartments at the Fifth Avenue Hotel, whence they
issued summonses to prominent bankers and financiers whose
counsel might be valuable. Many excitedly demanded, as a
result of conferences with Morton, which had been in progress
for several days,[3] that the "reserve" be put at the disposal of
the New York City banks. They hired Reverdy Johnson to
support Morton and say that so much might properly be done.
Happily other influences prevailed. Grant and his Secretary
of the Treasury declared that such action on their part would
be contrary to law.[4] Instead recourse would be had to a policy
which had been employed with advantage on other occasions.
Government bonds would be purchased at the market price.
Between Saturday, the 20th, and Wednesday, the 24th, some
$13,000,000 in currency was put into circulation by this opera-
tion, through the Sub-Treasury in New York.[5]

But of more practical value in affording relief was the action
of the officers of the principal banks in New York in issuing loan
certificates of a value of $20,000,000, with a promise of further

[1] House Ex. Doc., 42nd Cong. 3rd. sess., no. 26.
[2] Senate Reports, 42nd Cong. 3rd sess., no. 275. A minority opinion
was filed by two Western members of the committee, Wright of Iowa and
Ferry of Michigan.
[3] W. D. Foulke, Life of Morton, vol. ii, pp. 317-8; N. Y. Tribune, Sep. 22,
1873.
[4] Am. Ann. Cyclop. for 1873, p. 284.
[5] Cf. Report of Sec. of Treasury for 1873, p. xv; House Ex. Doc., 43rd
Cong. 1st sess., no. 2.

issues, if they should be needed. These were obtainable in return for government bonds or other good securities, including commercial paper. Another measure was useful,—all large payments made by the banks would be in cheques. These were certified as "good" through the clearing house. Savings banks, to prevent runs, had recourse to their privilege; depositors were reminded that they must give thirty days' notice of their intention of making withdrawals of money committed to the custody of these institutions.[1]

The sedative influence of the closing of the Stock Exchange, together with the measures of relief taken by the government and the bankers, did so much to set opinion and feeling to rights that suspensions, barring the fall, on the 23rd, of the large house of Henry Clews and Company, ceased. The Stock Exchange, after eight days of rest, was, on September 30, reopened, and trading was resumed, timorously, though with returning assurance as the hours passed.

But no one could be in a confident mood. Four banks had closed their doors in Petersburg, Va.,[2] five in Chicago,[3] seven in Louisville.[4] Generally, throughout the country, currency payments were suspended. Playing card and patent medicine manufacturers complained that they could not procure money to buy the revenue stamps which the government required them to affix to the envelopes containing their products.[5] Commerce for a time came to a standstill. The farmers of the West, hauling their grain to the warehouses beside the railroad tracks, could get no money for it. The commission merchants in Chicago could not pay the warehousemen.[6] Ships laden with grain stood in the harbor at New York. They could not proceed to Europe; the owners were unable to buy foreign exchange.[7] The cotton crop in the South could not be moved. The president of the Chamber of Commerce of Charleston telegraphed to the

[1] Am. Ann. Cyclop. for 1873, article on Finances of the United States.
[2] N. Y. Tribune, Sep. 26, 1873.
[3] Ibid., Sep. 27, 1873.
[4] Ibid., Sep. 29, 1873.
[5] Phila. Inquirer, Sep. 30, 1873.
[6] Cf. N. Y. Tribune, Oct. 16, 1873.
[7] Ibid., Sep. 27, 1873.

Secretary of the Treasury for currency for use in South Carolina.[1]

When and where banks violated the general rule and gave out currency it was only in small amounts and for the most necessary purposes. Declining payment cheques were marked "good" and sent on their way. In a number of cities, following New York's example, clearing house certificates were issued. The country had returned, said the New York Times, to a primitive system of barter.[2]

In October further declines in the prices of stocks renewed the tension. There were six failures in New York on the 14th of that month, two more on the following day.[3] Wabash, Northwestern and Western Union fell $9 a share, Rock Island $8 a share. The prices of many stocks were lower in October and November than they had been when the Exchange was closed during the panic. Northwestern, which then had sold for 40, was quoted at $31\frac{1}{2}$ on October 14; St. Paul, which then had fallen to 30, now sold at $21\frac{1}{2}$. The lowest price for Pacific Mail in September had been 31, now it was 25. Ohio and Mississippi had had a further decline from $26\frac{1}{2}$ to $21\frac{1}{2}$, Western Union from $54\frac{1}{4}$ to $43\frac{1}{4}$, Hannibal and St. Joseph from 19 to 15, Union Pacific from 16 to $14\frac{3}{4}$.[4]

The failure of Jay Cooke, and the accompanying and resultant disorders, were of more than transitory meaning. There had been many panics in the stock market. Here was a panic which comprehended the country. Before long it was seen that the whole economic structure had collapsed. It was the end of a far-flung régime of recklessness and extravagance, and the ruin would need to be carefully surveyed to determine what might be saved for future use, in accordance with a more enlightened and a morally better code of conduct.

The promise held out at first that Cooke's firms would soon be reorganized could not be kept. He had failed, as Thurlow

[1] Report of Sec. of Treasury for 1873, p. xiv; Phila. Inquirer, Oct. 2, 1873.
[2] N. Y. Times, Sep. 26, 1873.
[3] N. Y. Tribune, Oct. 15 and 16, 1873.
[4] From tables presented in article on Finances of the U. S. in Am. Ann. Cyclop. for 1873.

Weed observed, "by attempting to carry out a great enterprise fifteen years too soon." [1] No man, without a progress in immigration, settlement and economic development more rapid and steady than any we have known, as Cooke lived to realize, could have built a railroad, capable of paying interest on the money invested in it, through Minnesota, Dakota and Montana to the Pacific coast, in 1872 and 1873. Subscriptions to bond issues, secured by public lands, were for those whose concern for national advancement outran their judgment as lenders of money.

The wreck of the Cooke banks was complete. Henry D. Cooke, late governor of the District of Columbia, appeared in a very unfavorable light. The First National Bank of Washington of which he had been the president was rotten to the core. Many public men, including Grant himself and Speaker Blaine, were numbered among those who had been enjoying the use of its funds in loans. Both of the houses to which the President had inadvisedly, some said corruptly, committed the foreign accounts of the government, Jay Cooke's and Henry Clews's, were now in ruins, thus creating a most unpleasant situation for the administration. [2]

Jay Cooke himself, in adversity as in success, made an heroic figure. The newspaper correspondents found him in the midst of the wreckage in Philadelphia, still sanguine as to the great value of the Northern Pacific Railroad, and eager to serve the creditors, if he should be allowed to do so, in its rehabilitation. The vacations of preachers he made happy by trips to and sojourns on a rocky islet which he owned in Lake Erie. Those at that time at the place came home. Cooke and his family, in his "million dollar" home, fell into simple and inexpensive ways as rapidly as they could. Vacating the great house they, children and grandchildren, were crowded into a little cottage.

Cooke asked that the estate might rest under a trusteeship; he would make payment in full. But some of the creditors were refractory and the law supervened, so that the business went

[1] Life of Thurlow Weed, vol. ii, p. 559.
[2] Cf. N. Y. Tribune, Sep. 25, 1873.

into bankruptcy. It was plain now to what a point his enthusiasm had carried him. The schedule of assets filed with the register in bankruptcy included $6,000,000 of the obligations of the Northern Pacific Railroad Company, while $2,000,000 or $3,000,000 more had been advanced to affiliated enterprises in the Northwest. When the people of America and Europe could not be persuaded to continue to contribute funds for the prosecution of the work the money of depositors, as well as the capital of the firm, had been used to save the railroad.[1]

Before the crash came more than one of Cooke's partners had put away comfortable sums for their future use; he had not done so—all went to his creditors. Few, however bitter their experiences had been, could find it in their hearts to add anything to the distress of so frank and genuine, so really public-spirited and patriotic a man.

So, too, was it with Thomas A. Scott, who had procured himself much trouble and hazarded his financial reputation, as well as that of the Pennsylvania Railroad, with which he was so closely identified, by his enthusiasm concerning the Texas Pacific Railroad. It was to cross the continent, reaching the Pacific Ocean at San Diego. With as clear an eye as Cooke's as to the Northwest Scott foresaw the great potentialities of Texas. He was abroad, hoping to finance the enterprise, the bonds of which could not be sold at home, when the panic came. The road had been completed as far as Dallas. Now it must stop. Notes bearing Scott's name, issued to carry on the work of construction, went to protest.[2] He was so deeply involved that he offered his resignation as vice president of the Pennsylvania Railroad, which, however, was not accepted by his associates,[3] who shared his burdens, and supported him so loyally that in a little while, at J. Edgar Thomson's death, he was advanced to the presidency of the company.

The interest on the bonds of the Northern Pacific and Texas Pacific was being paid, not from earnings on the completed

[1] Cf. N. Y. Tribune, Dec. 26 and 27, 1873; Phila. North American, Sep. 27, 1873.

[2] Phila. Ledger, Nov. 5, 1873.

[3] Ibid., Nov. 8, 1873.

parts of the road, or from sales of the land donated to the company by the government, but from funds obtained from new buyers of bonds,[1] and these were but two of many railroads which had been financed in this dangerous way. Now the coupons could not be paid. Holders, many of them clergymen, small tradesmen, farmers, mechanics, women—all kinds of confiding people of small means—were without the regular and expected receipts from their investment.

Of necessity work ceased upon the lines which were projected into the West. The Vanderbilt and Pennsylvania railroads suspended new construction in the East,—even all but the most necessary repairs. All hands were being dismissed from rolling mill and car building works.

The American Iron and Steel Association held its annual meeting in Philadelphia in November, 1873. Its secretary said that the panic had deranged the whole business of iron making. Prices of many products had declined until they were below the cost of manufacture. At the beginning of November one-third of the furnaces and mills of the country were idle; one-half of them would be so on the first of December. Stocks of pig iron were accumulating with no sales at any price.[2] Six months later it was said that 175,000 men in the iron industry were out of employment.[3]

A large wool house in Philadelphia failed.[4] One of the leading cotton manufacturing establishments was that owned by the Spragues of Providence, who had been accounted very rich men. They, through Senator Sprague, like so many magnates in business and finance, were closely identified with politics. Rumors of their embarrassment were heard on every hand. Their downfall was presaged at the end of October by the suspension of Hoyt, Spragues and Company, their agents in New York, the largest failure since Jay Cooke's.[5]

Other cotton businesses were affected; many mills in New England were closed. Silk, woolen, shoe, cigar and furniture

[1] Phila. Ledger, Sep. 22, 1873.   [4] Phila. Inquirer, Sep. 30, 1873.
[2] N. Y. Tribune, Nov. 21, 1873.   [5] N. Y. Tribune, Oct. 3, 1873.
[3] N. Y. Nation, June 4, 1873.

factories put their employees on half time, when they did not
bring all their operations to an end. The wages of those who
continued at work were lowered. In many places labor must be
paid in scrip which was negotiable only at a discount. Here
and there the workmen, who had been thus unjustly served, as
they believed, organized strikes. The locomotive engineers on
the Pennsylvania Railroad, in December, 1873, resorted to
violence. Engines were disabled, passenger trains were wrecked,
mobs obstructed traffic in Kentucky, Indiana, Illinois and Ohio.
In Ohio the governor was asked to call out the militia to restore
order.[1]

The buying power of the people was generally reduced. Cotton declined twenty per cent, wheat fell about fifteen cents a
bushel, flour fifty cents a barrel. Retail dry goods merchants
"marked down" their prices. Though these reductions reached
twenty-five per cent of what had been asked in September,
before the panic had commenced, stocks still could not be sold.[2]
In teas, sugars and metals the losses of importers were frightful.
The trade in silks, laces, jewelry, silverware and luxuries of all
kinds, which had been so active during the reckless years just
past, practically ceased altogether.

On all sides mercantile houses suspended and went into
bankruptcy. Failures in 1873 reached a total of more than
$228,000,000; they had been $121,000,000 in 1872, and but
$85,000,000 in 1871.[3] In January, 1874, it was computed that
the total amount of railway bonds on which the interest payments had been passed was $386,000,000. Nine months later
the sum had been increased to nearly $500,000,000.[4]

The distress came to affect the people generally. All together, by the closing of factories, by the suspension of work
on railroads and in mines, by the failures in every branch of
business, hundreds of thousands of persons were cast upon
society, and began to look around them for the ways and means
of keeping food on their tables and fires on their hearths during

[1] N. Y. Nation, Jan. 1, 1874.
[2] Harper's Weekly, Nov. 15, 1873.
[3] From Dun's Reports, quoted in Am. Ann. Cyclop. for 1873, p. 291.
[4] Financial Chronicle, quoted in Am. Ann. Cyclop. for 1874, p. 305.

the oncoming winter. Poverty and need assumed pitiful forms and called loudly for alleviation. The out-of-works in factory towns voiced their sufferings and grievances in public meetings. Speakers demanded that government should find employment for the idle. "Internationalists" and other agitators found an opportunity in the state of the times to spread their doctrines. From two platforms in Independence Square in Philadelphia crowds were harangued in English and German by leaders who attacked the social order. The city government must not only find work for the unemployed, it must establish supply depots at which they could procure the necessaries of life at cost.[1] On cold days the poor crowded the railway stations to keep warm. Collections were taken in the churches for the benefit of the needy.[2] Free breakfasts were served in Sunday school rooms. Existing charity associations found their facilities taxed to the utmost. New relief societies were formed. In Philadelphia a policy which had been employed in 1857 was adopted, attracting general admiration. Money and goods were solicited by the ladies of the city; donations were sent to a central hall. Committees were organized in each ward to visit the poor and to examine into the cases which had been brought to the notice of the association.[3] A similar system was successfully employed in Chicago.[4]

On the Pacific coast, leading a life apart from that of the rest of the country, the shock of the panic was not immediately felt. Specie was still in use, but speculation, there, as in the East, was carrying the people to dangerous lengths. California was in the control, economically and politically, of a small oligarchy of men enriched by mines, railroads and other enterprises. Their principal financial organization was the Bank of California. At the head of this powerful institution stood William C. Ralston, who had made himself one of the first of the *novi homines* of every description comprising the upstart civilization which had so lately been established upon the shores of our western ocean. In his youth he had been a shoemaker in Penn-

---

[1] N. Y. Tribune, Nov. 28, 1873.
[2] Ibid., Nov. 25, 1873.
[3] Ibid., Nov. 14, 1873.
[4] Phila. Ledger, Nov. 20, 1873.

sylvania, but he had come to have a "million dollar home," from which he dispensed his munificence as a host. Not so rich as some of his associates on the "slope," one of whom, it was said, enjoyed an income of $10,000 a day, he, nevertheless, was easily able to expend from a quarter to a half million dollars a year in horses, carriages, wines, choice viands, music, balls and other social display, which he mingled judiciously with charities that endeared him to the community. He was involved in speculations as great and perilous as those which had laid low his like in the East. At the end of August, 1875, the Bank of California closed its doors. The next day came the report of Ralston's death at a bathing beach.[1] Other banks suspended, exchanges were closed and a panic, like that which the East had felt two years earlier, overtook legitimate as well as speculative business in San Francisco and the little world of which that city was the center,[2] with results which, being apart from those ensuing upon the disasters on the Atlantic seaboard, may receive discussion in another place.

What had been in progress before the crash in New York, and now what followed it, were making for deep social discontent. The evidences of popular mistrust and resentment were prominently seen among the farmers of the Western and Northwestern states. Mechanics and factory operatives in the East were organized into unions which were growing more powerful. They were fixing a day's work at ten and often at eight hours. Other rules were being imposed upon employers which were new and, it was alleged, irksome.[3] But the relationships between capital and labor in manufacturing and other trades had not been strained. It was that part of the population settled on the agricultural frontier which was ripe for social revolt.

The truth is that much crying up of the West, such as Greeley's, the systematic measures which some state govern-

---

[1] The public admiration for such a spender was expressed in an immense mass meeting which was held in San Francisco after his death to vindicate his memory.—N. Y. Nation, Sep. 16, 1875.

[2] N. Y. Nation, Sep. 2, 9 and 16 and Oct. 7, 1875; Am. Ann. Cyclop. for 1876, p. 103; San Francisco corr. N. Y. Tribune, July 27, 1876.

[3] Cf. Life of Thurlow Weed, vol. ii, p. 513.

ments and many railroad companies had taken to attract
emigrants from Europe and from the Atlantic seaboard into
the states and territories beyond the Mississippi, had so extended the area of cultivation and multiplied the population in that region that it was increasingly difficult for the
farmer, under existing conditions, to gain a subsistence from
the soil.

In 1873 corn in Iowa fetched the industrious man, who had
grown, tended, garnered, husked and shelled it, not more than
ten or fifteen cents a bushel; [1] in Illinois, only twenty or twenty-
five cents.[2] Shipments from Des Moines did not yield enough
in Chicago to pay the freight and elevator charges.[3] Immense
crops were being sold for less than the cost of production.[4] In
the winter time farmers in some parts of Iowa were burning
their corn to keep warm. It was cheaper than coal.[5] The
situation of the wheat farmers, it had been expected, would be
more favorable. Their crop had been small and they entertained the hope of receiving higher prices for it. To their surprise their returns, because of the activity of "rings" which
had been formed by the middlemen, were no greater than
before. Mortgages were put upon farm property; when the
interest was not paid they were foreclosed.

The farmer had been a not inattentive witness of recent
events. If he had not been persuaded to vote for Greeley by a
repetition of all the charges of misgovernment which had rung
up and down the country during the campaign of 1873, he was
well enough informed to understand that much of what was
complained of was founded in truth. The Crédit Mobilier
scandal, the Tweed Ring exposures, such openly scandalous
railway steals as Fisk's and Gould's, the reckless speculation
which had been raging in Wall Street, the infamies attending
"Reconstruction" in the South, the "salary grab" at Washington were not unnoticed by those who lived in unpainted farmhouses on the prairies of the American West, and who were

[1] Western corr. N. Y. Tribune, Sep. 20, 1873.
[2] Ibid., Oct. 18, 1873.
[3] Ibid., Sep. 11, 1873.
[4] Ibid., Nov. 18, 1873.
[5] Ibid., Sep. 11, 1873.

face to face with hard work, which, whatever their exertions, would barely save them from starvation.[1]

Some of the prominent figures in this disreputable age were ostentatiously pious men. The religious press had been used to sell worthless railway securities. Thus were innocent people deceived and robbed of their savings.[2] The editors of two such publications, both of them most unbecomingly allied with the predominant elements in society and politics, would soon give the nation the details of a disgusting private scandal. Theodore Tilton, long of the Independent, accused Henry Ward Beecher, of the Christian Union, pulpit orator and lecturer, known the country over, of seducing Mrs. Tilton. After a thorough airing of the subject, through an investigation conducted by the officers of Beecher's church in Brooklyn,[3] Tilton, demanding $100,000 damages, took Beecher into court. The proceedings were published far and wide and became a topic of national discussion, profoundly to disturb the faith of honest folk, even in those social and spiritual influences which there was right to expect would have remained wholesome and sound.

In a particular way did the farmer feel the hand of the railroad. As he settled farther and farther away from the markets more and more was consumed in freight charges upon his products, more and more was added to the cost of tools, machinery and materials needed for his use. In 1870 Illinois, Iowa, Wisconsin and Minnesota, in the order named, were the leading wheat growing states in the Union. Together they raised more than one-third of the whole American crop. Illinois and Iowa were the largest corn producing states. These grains must be conveyed to the Atlantic seaboard for use in the East or for export—transportation thither was an important factor in

---

[1] Cf. W. M. Grosvenor in Atlantic Monthly, Nov., 1873. The "dangerous classes" were not the communists imported from Europe who were abroad in the land. They were, said the New York Tribune, "Butler and his rabble of blackguard followers, Oakes Ames and his retinue of perjured Congressmen, Tweed and his company of mustached and bejewelled thieves, Fisk and his harlots, Gould and his fellow gamblers."—Issue of Sep. 15, 1873.

[2] N. Y. Nation, Oct. 8 and 22, 1874.

[3] Cf. ibid., Sep. 3, 1874.

determining the price which the farmer would receive for his crop.[1]

Time was, not so long since, when to have a railroad was the hope and ambition of every little prairie settlement. Efforts were made to persuade companies to extend their lines, capital was welcomed to undertakings which were of so much meaning to the farmer. The railroad was the handmaid of his prosperity. Without it he would have been able to seat himself and plant his crops only on the banks of navigable waterways. The interior of the country would have remained an untouched wilderness. The extension of agriculture into the West and the distribution of the farming population over an ever widening area had been due entirely to the fact that a steam locomotive on iron rails was bringing in seed and implements and carrying away the harvests. The farmers in many cases, indeed, had helped to build the roads. Counties and local corporations had subscribed to the companies' bonds.[2]

But the roads had come under new control. They were merged to form "systems," their stock had been "watered," freight and passenger charges were increased to pay the interest on increased stock issues.[3] The owners, living in the East, were in the position of absentee landlords, who, for any reason, and often without reason, are subject to criticism, and at times to grave abuse. The hour had come for a revulsion of feeling on the subject of this great new companion of our westwardly moving civilization, and, however much men in the East blinked it, however much the farmer may have invited ridicule for the ignorant manner in which he tried to state his case and redress his growing wrongs, the subject was one demanding serious consideration.

The railway managers of the time, said Charles Francis Adams, Jr., "stopped at nothing"; any idea of "duty which a railroad corporation owed to the public was wholly lost sight

[1] Cf. Fred E. Haynes, Third Party Movements, p. 51.
[2] N. Y. Tribune, Nov. 18, 1873; cf. Wm. Larrabee, The Railroad Question, p. 329.
[3] Cf. Report of Senate Select Committee, Senate Reports, 43rd Cong. 1st sess., no. 307, pt. 1, pp. 72–5.

of." The companies were "mere private money making enterprises." If "forced to compete, they competed savagely and
without regard to consequences; where they were free from
competition they exacted the uttermost farthing."[1] When
the railway financiers were at peace the rates on the various
trunk lines were fixed in conferences of the agents of the companies.[2] At such times the only competition which existed
came from the Erie Canal. When navigation on that waterway
opened in the spring the companies lowered their rates. When
it was closed by ice they increased their charges again.[3]

On the 30th of December, 1873, it was noted that a bushel
of wheat fetched in New York 45 cents more than in Chicago,
a bushel of corn 35 cents more, the difference being represented
by midwinter charges of railway companies on freight transported between the two cities. A reasonable price for such a
carrier service, it was said, would have been about twelve cents a
bushel.[4]

The companies at other times engaged in "rate wars." In a
recent year, during which their operations were studied, the
freights between New York and Chicago were low at $5 and
high at $37.60 a ton, while the fluctuations in charges between
New York and St. Louis ranged from $7 to $46. At one time
the Erie Railway suddenly announced that it would carry
merchandise from the Atlantic seaboard to Chicago for $2 a
ton; the charge was as suddenly raised to $37.[5]

For short hauls the rate was greater, often much greater
than between distant points. It might be that for carrying
merchandise only a few miles to some small freight shed, set
beside the track in a hamlet, the charge would be higher than on
the same goods carried in the same train of cars to a city hundreds of miles beyond this little place. Those who shipped

---

[1] C. F. Adams, Jr., Railroads, p. 123.
[2] W. M. Grosvenor in Atlantic Monthly, Nov., 1873.
[3] Speech of C. F. Adams, Jr., Feb. 14, 1873, a pamphlet, p. 10; cf. W.
C. Flagg, president of Illinois Farmers' Association in Harper's Weekly,
April 5, 1873; also Harper's Weekly, Aug. 9, 1873.
[4] House Reports, 43rd Cong. 1st sess., no. 28; cf. Senate Reports, 43rd
Cong. 1st sess., no. 307, pp. 16–7.
[5] C. F. Adams, Jr., in North American Review for Jan., 1870, pp. 132–3.

large amounts of goods were given rates, and were accorded other advantages, which were withheld from him whose shipments were small and infrequent. The poor man paid his fare in the passenger coaches of the corporation. Passes for their own and their friends' uses were thrust into the hands of business men of wealth and influence, with the freedom that these privileges were conferred upon lobbyists, politicians and journalists.[1]

Such methods were disorganizing to trade and at variance with the sense of justice of all honest men. Transportation by rail, C. F. Adams, Jr., declared to be "a pure absolute monopoly."[2] So conservative a journal as Harper's Weekly called the railway men of the age "forestallers"[3] and "monopolists."[4] The railway companies, Adams said again, were bringing about conditions which were not to be "tolerated." Their arrogance, their assumption of a position above and outside of the jurisdiction of the government, invited the hostility which was about to descend upon them.[5]

The farmer had another grievance. The public domain was melting away. This was the "people's inheritance." It had been held by the government that it might be partitioned out to settlers in homesteads. But a vast area, larger than the combined extent of a dozen or more of the older Eastern states, had been made over by Congress to rich men, corruptly, as it seemed, in some cases. Good land for the farmer, within reach of markets, was becoming scarce, unless he should buy it from the railroad corporations. Congress had actually transferred to these interests 35,000,000 acres; it had pledged them, on account of lines undertaken to the Pacific coast, 145,000,000 acres more.[6]

The people of the West had complained, said Colonel Grosvenor, and, "complaining in vain," had got "angry."[7] Feeling

---

[1] Cf. C. F. Adams, Jr., Railroads, pp. 124–5, and in North American Review, April, 1875, p. 401.
[2] Speech of Feb. 14, 1873, a pamphlet, p. 10.
[3] Issue of Aug. 9, 1873.
[4] Issue of Aug. 30, 1873.
[5] C. F. Adams, Jr., Railroads, pp. 127–8, 136.
[6] Annual Report of Sec. of Interior for 1873, p. 288; S. J. Buck, The Agrarian Crusade, p. 23; Life of Thurlow Weed, vol. ii, pp. 510–11.
[7] Atlantic Monthly for Nov., 1873.

themselves "helpless" in the case, said Mr. Adams, they had become resentful.[1]

Life in such isolation as was the farmer's and his family's, was, under the best conditions, a dull, sordid round. In the Grange was seen a door of hope through which men and women might enter on equal terms for companionship, entertainment and the improvement of the common lot. Music, lectures, books, picnics, festivals were the promise of this new organization. Thus would women acquire ideas for some beautification of their homes and for a happier family life. Thus would men find an agency for co-operative effort in solving the problems which engaged their care.

It was in 1867 that Oliver H. Kelley, a farmer from Minnesota, acting at the time as a clerk in the Post Office Department at Washington, was imbued with the idea of founding a secret society for the improvement of the lot of the agricultural classes. He spoke to William Saunders,[2] another employee of the government, in the Department of Agriculture, and a few other men, and they together laid their plans for the formation of the National Grange of the Patrons of Husbandry, with a constitution, a ritual and an internal organization suggestive of the Masonic order, or of Odd Fellowship. The soil being the source of "all that constitutes wealth," those who lived near the earth and brought forth its products were to be united, "for mutual instruction and protection," for a lightening of labor and an enlargement of their "views of Creative wisdom and power." The lowest unit would be the local Grange in which there were to be four "degrees"—for men, "Laborer," "Cultivator," "Harvester" and "Husbandman" in turn— for women, "Maid," "Shepherdess," "Gleaner" and "Matron." The head of a local Grange would be called a "Master." All these "Masters" and their wives, called "Matrons," taken together in a state, formed a State Grange. The "Masters" of the State Granges and their wives formed the National

[1] Speech of C. F. Adams, Jr., a pamphlet, loc. cit.; cf. Wm. Larrabee, The Railroad Question, p. 330.

[2] Cf. Washington corr. N. Y. Tribune, Dec. 3, 1873.

Grange, which would meet annually in November. Three higher degrees—"Pomona" (Hope), "Flora" (Charity) and "Ceres" (Faith)—were for women who, in white dresses, added a little pleasant mummery to the meetings.

Kelley, in April, 1868, resigned his government clerkship and commenced a tour of the country for the establishment of local granges, reimbursement for his expenses and a small salary being contingent upon his success as an organizer. The first local body to be formed was at Harrisburg, Pa., the second at Fredonia, N. Y., the third at Columbus, O., and the fourth at Chicago. Before the end of the year, having reached his home in Minnesota, he had organized six more granges in that state. But for the next two years and a half progress was very slow. Kelley remained on his farm with occasional trips to places nearby to lecture upon the subject. But other men in the South, in Iowa and in Missouri interested themselves in the objects of the order. In 1869 39 subordinate granges were established, in 1870 38 and in 1871 125. Thereafter, under the impetus of the social and economic distress which has just been described, the movement spread rapidly. So much did it promise, so much was achieved that 1,105 local organizations were formed in 1872. They were being established at the rate of 60 or 80 in a week in 1873 in Iowa, where it was stated, in September of that year, that the order had 100,000 members.[1] Fifty new branches were organized in Missouri in a week.[2] In the country at large it was said that 36 were formed daily. Thus it came about that 8,400 were established in 1873, and 4,600 in the first two months of 1874; on April 1, 1873, it was believed that the number of members, in all, was not less than 1,500,000. In only three of the states, in only three of the territories had "State Granges" not yet been organized.[3]

To circumvent, in so far as they could, the exactions of the railway companies and the impositions of agricultural machinery makers, the "Grangers," by a system of co-operative action,

[1] N. Y. Tribune, Sep. 20, 1873.
[2] Ibid., Sep. 11, 1873.
[3] Article on Patrons of Husbandry in Am. Ann. Cyclop. for 1873.

would erect elevators and warehouses for the storage of their grain. They would purchase implements, parlor organs, sewing machines, wagons, scales, even groceries and dry goods, in large quantities for cash in the Eastern markets, and, if it were necessary, establish their own manufactories in order to insure lower costs. Both in the sale of their own products and in their purchases, they, in some parts of the West, could, and soon did, in a way creditable to their administrative capacity, eliminate middlemen who had been taking advantage of the farmer's situation, and were demonstrably contributing to the increase of the hardships of his life. In this manner it was stated that, in a few months in 1873, a sum, roughly computed at $3,000,000, had been saved to the farmers of Iowa alone.[1] By boards of arbitration differences arising between members could be adjusted, thus avoiding expensive litigation and appeals to the public courts.

The Granges as such were enjoined to eschew political discussion. But it was clearly stated and well enough understood that the members reserved their right as individuals to seek redress for their ills in political action.[2] They were not slow to make their influence felt in their communities. Before the Grange appeared to claim the interest of the people, there had been Farmers' Clubs, and these clubs were combined for state and regional meetings at which the wrongs suffered by the agricultural classes were vigorously discussed. A Northwestern Farmers' Convention met in Chicago in October, 1873. "Men of great wealth" were "revelling in luxury," they said, while "those who earned the money" were "destitute of the comforts of life."[3]

The object at which the movement was aimed was the railroad and the railway financier, such men as Vanderbilt, Gould, Fisk, Drew and Thomas A. Scott.[4] A "Farmers' War," the

[1] N. Y. Tribune, Oct. 4, 1873. Undoubtedly an overstatement in view of the later failure of the Grange's co-operative movement.—Cf. Haynes, Third Party Movements, pp. 84 et seq.

[2] Cf. declaration of National Grange of Feb., 1874, in Am. Ann. Cyclop. for 1873 in article on Patrons of Husbandry.

[3] N. Y. Tribune, Oct. 24, 1873.

[4] Cf. Grosvenor in Atlantic Monthly for Nov., 1873.

New York Tribune called it, as that journal day by day presented to its readers the accounts from its Western correspondents of this social and political ebullition. "We want a great many things," said a Western Granger, "but first and foremost we want railways so regulated that we farmers can live." [1] A "despotism" had been created, said one of the speakers at a farmers' convention in Chicago. The producers of wealth in "the fairest and most fertile spots of the new world" were bound "hand and foot." The railway was necessary to the farmer—the farmer was on its side when it was rightly managed. But he was not willing that freight rates should be so high as to pay ten per cent on stock for which the present owners of it had never paid anything, or on stock issued as a dividend. [2] The giving away of public land to private corporations, the building of railroads by government subvention and guarantee must, at once, cease. When, by manipulation, a railroad was made into an agency to distress the people, instead of one to serve their convenience, it should be brought under control. It was a highway, and, as such, it was as clearly and fairly a subject under public jurisdiction as a wagon road. The state should interpose rules for, and set up commissions to supervise, its management. The farmers would foster the construction of canals as competitors of the railroad to end its "monopoly."

Others, in termagant speech and resolution, went to greater lengths. The railroads it was said, at a convention at Springfield, Ill., in April, 1873, defied law, plundered shippers, impoverished the people and corrupted the government. They were as much the enemies of "free institutions and free commerce" as the "feudal barons of the Middle Ages." [3] On all sides in the West they were denounced as "monopolists," "extortioners," "banditti," "tyrants," and "Shylocks." The "people" would rule; if the state courts, if the Supreme Court of the United States stood in their path these symbols of an order of society which had served their day and generation would be swept

---

[1] Harper's Weekly, Aug. 30, 1873.

[2] N. Y. Tribune, Nov. 18, 1873.

[3] Quoted by C. F. Adams, Jr., in North American Review, April, 1875, pp. 405-6.

away.[1] Others came forward to advocate government ownership.[2] At a mass meeting in New York Congress was urged to
build a freight-carrying railroad into the West and to operate
it in competition with the privately owned trunk lines.[3]

The farmers uttered a great amount of balderdash as well as
some plain truth. Wild charges and violent proposals would
inevitably issue from such a source under such provocation.
So much activity on the part of the farming population, both
within and without the Grange, soon led to positive results.
The movement "completely upset the politics of some half
dozen Western states." [4] New parties were formed for political
campaigns; combinations were effected with the old parties in
neighborhoods and in states; candidates were elected to county
offices, to the bench, to legislatures (several of which fell under
the control of the Grange), to Congress.[5] The farmers gave
Wisconsin a governor who, for two years, was a picturesque
figure in the politics of that state, and sent two or three men to
the United States Senate.[6] A refractory chief justice in Illinois
was displaced at the polls in favor of one who would do the
bidding of the Grange.[7]

The movement reached its most striking forms in Illinois,
Minnesota, Iowa and Wisconsin in a series of attempts at law
making as yet untried and new, generally known as "Granger
legislation," with a view to regulating the companies in the
interest of lower charges and the more equitable treatment of
the people whom they served. It was in Illinois that this movement commenced, and as early as in 1869. The legislature of
that state in that year declared that railroads should be limited
to a "just, reasonable and uniform rate, toll and compensation,
for the conveyance, or transportation, of passengers and freight,

[1] Quoted by C. F. Adams, Jr., in North American Review, April, 1875,
pp. 409–13.
[2] Cf. proceedings of Northwestern Farmers' Convention at Decatur,
Ill., N. Y. Tribune, Dec. 17 and 19, 1783.
[3] Harper's Weekly, Aug. 30, 1873. Discussed in Senate Reports, 43rd
Cong. 1st sess., no. 307, pt. 1, pp. 140 et seq.
[4] N. Y. Nation, Jan, 22, 1874.
[5] Cf. Haynes, Third Party Movements, pp. 54–6.
[6] S. J. Buck, The Granger Movement, p. 100.
[7] C. F. Adams, Jr., in North American Review for April, 1875, pp. 412–3.

and no more." [1] A convention in 1870 framed a new constitution for Illinois, one of its provisions directing the legislature to
"pass laws to correct abuses, and prevent unjust discrimination
and extortion in the rates of freight and passenger tariffs on the
different railroads," and enforce such laws by adequate penalties. [2] At its next ensuing session the legislature again turned
its attention to the subject—now in a specific way. The roads
were classified. For the carrying of passengers it was declared
that the maximum fare should be from 2½ to 5½ cents a mile,
varying according to the "class" into which the particular
railroad fell. [3] There should be no "unjust discriminations and
extortions" in freight rates, which should be governed by the
distance over which merchandise was transported, and should
be uniform. Any change of rates in increase of those charged
in 1870 was prohibited. [4] A board of railroad and warehouse
commissioners was established to collect information on the
subject and to enforce the laws. [5]

Such legislation was regarded by the railroad men as socialist
and unconstitutional. It filled the coffers of corporation attorneys. The best legal talent in the land was employed by the
Eastern "magnates" to resist the policy and to bring the
Granger laws to a test in the courts. Lobbies were strengthened
at the state capitals to break down the influence of the farmers—
to repeal statutes of their making, and to forestall the enactment
of new ones conceived in a like spirit.

The supreme court of Illinois, in due time, declared the law
regulating freight rates in that state to be invalid. [6] Another
law, designed to meet the objections that were raised as to the
previous one, was passed in 1873, and the railroad commission
was directed to fix maximum rates, which, if they were exceeded

[1] Session Laws of Ill., for 1869, p. 309.
[2] Art. xi, sec. 15.
[3] Session Laws of Ill. for 1871–72, p. 640.
[4] Ibid., p. 635.
[5] Ibid., p. 618. Cf. Buck, The Agrarian Crusade, p. 48. The Massachusetts board, to exercise a calmer supervision over the railroads, was appointed as a result of the efforts of C. F. Adams, Jr., in 1869.—Acts and
Resolves of General Court of Mass. for 1869, p. 699; C. F. Adams, Jr.,
An Autobiography, pp. 172–3, and Railroads, pp. 138–9.
[6] 67 Ill., p. 11.

by the companies, would be regarded, after January 15, 1874, as
extortionate.[1] Such legislation was confiscation, said the railroad men, their attorneys, and the press which was friendly to
their interests, and the companies for several years, denying the
public right to regulate their business, openly defied the state
authorities.

In 1871 Minnesota made an attempt to fix passenger and
freight rates,[2] putting the subject under the eye of a commissioner.[3] When the matter was taken to the supreme court of
that state the legislature was sustained,[4] and the companies
appealed their case to the Supreme Court of the United States.
Meantime the law was not enforced, and, in 1874, the farmers,
strengthening their hands in the elections, replaced it by
another, following the lines of the act in Illinois.[5] But it remained practically a dead letter, and in the next year, with a
waning of the power of the Farmers' Party, the legislature
abandoned the policy,[6] and the subject was brought under the
supervision of a board of commissioners.[7]

In Iowa, which had elected a Granger legislature in 1873, a
law was passed dividing the railroads of the state into classes
and establishing "reasonable maximum rates of charges for
freight and passengers" for each class.[8] In many respects this
measure was the most elaborately formulated one which the
movement produced, and its terms were so specific that the
companies, while it was in effect, from 1874 to 1878, made an
appearance of conforming to its provisions.[9] It was sustained
by the highest court of the state,[10] as it was by the Supreme Court of the United States.[11] When the law was re-

[1] Session Laws of Ill. for 1873, p. 135.
[2] General Laws of Minn. for 1871, p. 61.
[3] Ibid., p. 56.
[4] 19 Minn., p. 419.
[5] Session Laws of Minn. for 1874, p. 140.
[6] Buck, The Agrarian Crusade, p. 50.
[7] Session Laws of Minn. for 1878, p. 67.
[8] Session Laws of Iowa for 1874, p. 61.
[9] S. J. Buck, The Agrarian Crusade, pp. 50–51; Haynes, Third Party
Movements, pp. 75, 82; Larrabee, The Railroad Question, pp. 332–6.
[10] 20 Iowa, p. 343.
[11] 94 U. S., p. 155.

pealed the subject was committed to the supervision of a commission.[1]

In Wisconsin Granger regulation of the railways had a yet shorter life. A law passed in 1874,[2] called the "Potter Law," which was denounced by the railway men as almost confiscatory in its practical effect, was upheld in the supreme court of the state, in spite of the arguments of skillful counsel for the companies.[3] But in 1875, before it could be put into force, it was modified,[4] and in 1876, in its essential details, altogether repealed.[5]

The course taken by the legislatures, if it had been adopted resentfully, clearly had a considerable amount of foundation in legal as well as in moral right. Many of the special laws chartering railroad companies, which had been passed by the state legislatures, contained provisions, designed in the public interest, concerning the rates which they might collect, and had done so from the first days of railway legislation.[6] When railroads came to be chartered under general laws the case was not quite so plain, and, acting with the assurance which comes from prolonged exercise of unrestricted power, it was forgotten that the companies were subject to supervisory authority. Moreover there were general reservations which were operative, and which the railway man had done well to remember. In the constitution of Wisconsin it was prescribed that all laws creating corporations might at any time be amended or repealed by the legislature;[7] in the constitution of Minnesota, that railways, being common carriers, must transport merchandise "on equal and reasonable terms."[8] Iowa had made over public lands to the companies—these grants were accepted with the condition

[1] Session Laws of Iowa for 1878, p. 67.
[2] Laws of Wis. for 1874, p. 599, chap. 273.
[3] 35 Wis., p. 425.
[4] Laws of Wis. for 1875, pp. 213 and 647.
[5] Ibid., for 1876, p. 119; Buck, op. cit., pp. 51-2.
[6] Cf. B. H. Meyer, Railway Legislation in the United States, pp. 56 et seq.
[7] Art. xi, sec. 1.
[8] Art. x, sec. 4.

that the companies should conform to the rules and regulations of the general assembly.[1]

The enthusiasm of the farmers for their "war" had waned before the cases out of Illinois, Minnesota, Iowa and Wisconsin came to decision in the Federal Supreme Court. A number of these cases had accumulated, and they were the subject of opinions in October, 1876. The issue at bottom was the same in all—whether or not a state might regulate a business which, though public in its nature, is privately owned and directed. The right in question was clearly established by the highest judicial authority of the nation, and a basis was laid for a course now so familiar that we look with surprise upon the violence of the hostility which the attempt to exercise such powers awakened so short a while ago.

Already it had been determined in law that the business of operating railways was of a public nature.[2] More followed. The argument that a charter was a contract, a contention upheld in the Dartmouth College case,[3] and that such regulatory legislation was the impairment of a contract, a point of which much was made by the railroad attorneys, had now been swept aside by the Supreme Court in favor of a view that charters could not be contracts to the extent of preventing the regulation of the chartered companies, unless the terms of the charters were specific in a contrary sense.[4]

The subject reached Congress. Grant, foreseeing the direction of events, in his annual message in December, 1872, recommended the appointment of a commission to assemble information which would "insure equitable and just legislation." The Senate referred the subject to a select committee of seven members, later increased to nine, of which Mr. Windom of

[1] Buck, The Agrarian Crusade, pp. 46-7; cf. Larrabee, The Railroad Question, pp. 330-31. For the positions of the states generally see B. H. Meyer, op. cit., chap. iii.

[2] 16 Wall., p. 678.

[3] Buck, The Agrarian Crusade, p. 46.

[4] 94 U. S., pp. 113-81—Munn v. Illinois; Chicago, Burlington and Quincy Railroad Co. v. Iowa; Peik v. Chicago and Northwestern Railway Co.; Chicago, Milwaukee and St. Paul Railroad Co. v. Ackley; Winona and St. Peter Railroad Co. v. Blake.

Minnesota was the chairman.[1] It began its hearings in the
Fifth Avenue Hotel in New York on September 11, 1873, on
the eve of the panic, continuing them in Buffalo, Chicago,
Cincinnati, New Orleans and other cities until the end of the
year.[2] The comprehensive report of the committee made a
number of recommendations, the only one of them upon which
all the members were agreed relating to the improvement of
natural, and the development of artificial, waterways as com-
peting carrier lines.[3]

Mr. Windom, speaking for the majority, found that the
exercise of a control by Congress of interstate commerce on
railroads was constitutional; it was expedient and desirable
that there should be central and national supervision of the
subject.[4] The House Committee on Railways and Canals, in
January, 1874, declared that interstate railroad commerce
"ought to be, and that, sooner or later, it must be" regulated,
and they asserted their belief also, "that every year's delay
on the part of Congress to inaugurate the work but adds to the
difficulties to be overcome, to the dangers to be averted, and
to the evils to be remedied." [5] A bill establishing an interstate
commerce commission of nine members passed the House in
March, 1874.[6]

The campaign of the farmers against the railroads in 1871,
1872 and 1873, induced as it was in large measure by wrongs
which had been contrived and conditions which had arisen in
the East, had been not without a return influence upon the
East. General Garfield said that the Grangers had precipitated
the collapse of the Northern Pacific Railroad,—they had brought
on the panic.[7] The intemperate assaults upon the railroads in
farmers' conventions and farmer-controlled legislatures had
affected the sale of railway bonds. Public subscriptions fell

[1] Cong. Globe, 42nd Cong. 3rd sess., pp. 206, 235.
[2] Senate Reports, 43rd Cong. 1st sess., no. 307, pt. 2.
[3] Cf. McPherson's Handbook for 1874, pp. 193–200; Report, loc. cit.,
pt. 1.
[4] Report, loc. cit., pt. 1, pp. 79 et seq.
[5] House Reports, 43rd Cong. 1st sess., no. 26.
[6] Cong. Record, 43rd Cong. 1st sess., p. 2493.
[7] N. Y. Tribune, Nov. 17, 1873.

away, then entirely ceased. Capital, though it was scarce,
though, on other accounts, its owners were reluctant to commit
it to the hands of railway financiers, was turned from an investment which, it was clear, was to be harassed by the ignorant
and vindictive men whom the farmers were putting into places
of authority in the governments of the Western states.[1]

The Grange movement was merely a transitory protest; it
accomplished little of lasting value in the solution of the railway problem. The "Granger laws" were ill considered and
futile; the commissions created by the organization were made
up of inexperienced and incompetent persons.[2] As the effects
of the panic were prolonged and the farmers were brought to
feel the force of the general depression of business more severely
than they had ever felt the oppressive hand of the "railroad
kings," they became, as could have been expected, the advocates
of new issues of irredeemable paper money. Even now their
influence in this direction was foreshadowed,[3] and it was clear
enough that Grant and the men around him, should they decide
to ally themselves with the inflationists, would find support in
that quarter.

Renewed and continued efforts to secure relief through what
the New York Nation called "tinkering" with the currency [4]
had at once, and still, occupied people and press. The President,
who knew less about financial science than almost any subject
of polity, was almost immediately, following the panic, involved
in a voluble discussion of its causes, and the course which banks,
Treasury Department and Congress should pursue to improve
the situation. It was clear that he and his great office were
being used by some of his adherents for a show of wisdom
which they did not possess. Two letters to merchants and
bankers in New York rapidly followed each other,[5] and these,

[1] N. Y. Tribune, Nov. 17, 1873; Phila. North American, Sep. 23, 1873,
and Boston Advertiser, cited in that place.

[2] Cf. Adams, Railroads, p. 134.

[3] Cf. resolutions of farmers' convention at Decatur, Ill., in December,
1873, in N. Y. Tribune, Dec. 19 and 25, 1873.

[4] Issue of May 28, 1874.

[5] Sep. 28 and Oct. 6, 1873; cf. article on Finances of the U. S. in Am.
Ann. Cyclop. for 1873; McPherson's Handbook for 1874, pp. 134-5.

in turn, were followed by a statement to the Associated Press.[1]

In spite of the fact that, two or three weeks since, they together, in New York, had declared it to be unlawful "thus to employ the public money,"[2] Secretary Richardson was now drawing upon the "reserve" and had increased the outstanding amount of legal tenders,[3] and the President frankly advocated legislation by Congress which would release the entire sum. Except for its "inelasticity," Grant said, the monetary system of the country was "the best" in the world. Silver, which was being mined in the West "in almost unlimited amounts," would soon be on a par in value with greenbacks and the country would be put on a specie basis in spite of itself by the action of natural laws, and so on.[4] Such facile advice concerning difficult questions, with a free use of the personal pronoun "I," and allusions now and again to "you bankers" and "your banks," while it was meant to assist in "restoring confidence," was hardly calculated to have this effect. Most disquieting was it to realize that the President, and those around him, were inclining their minds to plans for inflation by further issues of paper money.[5]

Before the end of November, 1873, Richardson had put out $8,000,000 of the $44,000,000 of greenbacks in the "reserve." The income of the government having been reduced by the panic, and, there being not enough money in the Treasury to meet current expenditures, this was his resource. For his course he did not escape attack. It was "a most flagrant, monstrous violation of the law," said Senator Bayard of Delaware. For the Secretary of the Treasury, "at his own will and pleasure, under circumstances of whose potency he alone is the judge, in his own discretion only," to issue irredeemable paper money, and then recall it, as he may see fit, Bayard found to be a

---

[1] Phila. Ledger, Oct. 13, 1873.
[2] Cf. Report of Sec. of Treasury for 1873, p. xii.
[3] N. Y. Nation, Oct. 9 and 16, 1873.
[4] Article on Finances of the U. S. in Am. Ann. Cyclop. for 1873; Phila. Ledger, Oct. 13, 1873; N. Y. Nation, Oct. 16, 1873.
[5] Cf. N. Y. Tribune, Oct. 13, 1873.

matter for impeachment.[1] The New York Tribune also hinted at impeachment.[2] On December 17 it was stated that Richardson had reissued $17,000,000, making the entire circulation of greenbacks $373,000,000,[3] instead of $356,000,000, the point at which it had stood when McCulloch was stopped in his commendable activities in 1868. In a few weeks more the total reissue was $26,000,000.[4]

Whether the people of the West were inflationist or not their representatives in Congress were ready thus to interpret their sentiments. In the Senate and the House members from the Mississippi Valley states, supported by the adventurers who were contributed to the national legislature by the "reconstructed" South, were advocates of "more money." The country was face to face with an issue of which little had been heard since the "Ohio idea" had been disposed of in the campaign of 1868. Then it was a question of paying the national debt in greenbacks; now it was a question of increasing the volume of legal tender circulation. Congress had no sooner met than the "cheap money" men brought forward their various schemes. With courage and ability the New York Tribune, the New York Evening Post, and the New York Nation again used their instrumental agencies in the dissemination of sound opinion. The newspapers generally came to the support of proper measures,[5] and little progress was made in confusing public sentiment. Business men in Chicago, New York and other cities, held meetings and signed petitions which they sent to Washington.[6] In the Senate Logan of Illinois [7] and Morton of Indiana,[8] both of whom had been wrong on this question in 1868, again exhibited their ignorance, or their cunning as politicians; in the House, Butler, in his characteristic manner, labored in the same in-

---

[1] Cong. Record, 43rd Cong. 1st sess., pp. 2364–5.

[2] N. Y. Tribune, Oct. 9, 1873.

[3] Ibid., Dec. 17, 1873.

[4] Cf. Dunning, Reconstruction, Political and Economic, p. 239.

[5] The proposals of the greenback men were opposed by "the whole body of the respectable press."—N. Y. Nation, March 26, 1874.

[6] Ibid., Jan. 22, March 5 and 26, 1874.

[7] Ibid., Jan. 22, 1874.

[8] W. D. Foulke, Life of Morton, vol. ii, pp. 332–3.

terest—all three, because of their intimate relations with the administration, creating an impression that they spoke for Grant. Boutwell, resting under the aura of his nearly four years in the Treasury Department, was heard from, in and out of the Senate, on the same side of the subject.[1]

The particular proposal which was to claim public attention [2] would validate what Richardson, with Grant's approval, had been doing since the panic, viz. paying out the greenbacks in the "reserve." The amount of inconvertible paper in circulation had been increased from $356,000,000 to $382,000,000. It was proposed now that the entire "reserve" should be reissued, the limit being set at $400,000,000. It was not merely that thereby values would again be unsettled and the speculative spirit fed [3]—worse yet, in a little while a new cry would be raised for "more money," Congress would be besought to issue additional amounts of the same cheap currency. Specie payments, which all citizens of sagacity and honor hoped for, would be put farther and farther into the distance. Schurz [4] and Sherman revealed themselves strongly anti-inflationist, and made speech and rejoinder with effect as the debate proceeded.[5]

Simultaneously the House and the Senate discussed measures bearing upon the question. The House bill came to a vote on March 23, 1874, and it was passed by 168 to 77. In this bill the greenback circulation was fixed at $400,000,000, after two amendments in turn had been rejected—one placing the limit at $356,000,000, where it had been when Grant came to the Presidency, the other at $382,000,000, the amount outstanding as a result of Richardson's reissues—by practically similar majorities.[6]

It was April 6, 1874, when a bill passed the Senate, by a vote of 39 to 24, fixing the circulation at $400,000,000, only one Eastern

[1] Cf. N. Y. Nation, Nov. 6, 1873, Jan. 29 and Feb. 5, 1874.
[2] No less than sixty bills relating to the subject appeared in the Senate.—John Sherman's Recollections, vol. i, p. 490.
[3] Cf. N. Y. Nation, Feb. 19, 1874.
[4] Cf. ibid, March 5, 1874.
[5] Cf. Sherman's Recollections, vol. i, pp. 491–504; N. Y. Nation, Jan. 29, 1874.
[6] Cong. Record, 43rd Cong. 1st sess., pp. 2376–7.

man, Simon Cameron of Pennsylvania, being found, with the
majority from the West and the South, in favor of the bill.[1]
Coming to the House the Senate bill, on April 14, was rushed
through that chamber, with some futile opposition by James A.
Garfield and George F. Hoar, by a vote of 140 to 102, and was
sent to the President.[2]

What Grant was likely to do in this conjuncture no one knew.
He had been talking on the side of inflation. The greenbacks
had been paid out by both Boutwell and Richardson, and his
obstinacy clearly was such, whenever an officer in the enjoyment of his favor was assailed, on whatever account, that he at
once gave that officer increased support. He was advised by
leading newspapers of the country to veto the bill. A committee from Boston visited him in this interest, responsive to
the resolution of a large meeting held in Faneuil Hall,[3] and
they were followed by a similar committee from New York,
carrying a petition which bore the signatures of 2,500 of the
leading business houses in that city, as a result of a meeting in
opposition to inflation held at the home of Cyrus W. Field.
After waiting at the White House, until Grant could finish
a conference with "Ben" Butler, the visitors, led by A. A. Low
and S. B. Chittenden, were allowed to state their case. They
left the President without any assurance that he ascribed value
to their advice, convinced, indeed, that he was likely to sign the
measure against which they had come to protest.[4]

Fortunately other forces were made to operate upon the
President's mind. He was being pressed hard by Morton,[5]
who found, however, that he was being overborne by Conkling.[6]
The veto message followed in a few days, to the great surprise

[1] Cong. Record, 43rd Cong. 1st sess., p. 2835.
[2] Ibid., pp. 3075–8.
[3] McPherson's Handbook for 1874, pp. 135–6.
[4] Ibid., p. 136; N. Y. Nation, April 23 and 30, 1874.
[5] Cf. Morton's letter to Indianapolis Journal, McPherson's Handbook
for 1874, p. 153.
[6] W. D. Foulke, Life of Morton, vol. ii, pp. 333–4; Conkling, Life of
Conkling, pp. 469–72. Boutwell says that Grant actually wrote a message
approving the bill.—Sixty Years in Public Affairs, vol. ii, p. 233; cf. G. F.
Hoar, Autobiography of 70 Years, vol. i, p. 306, and Conkling, Life of
Conkling, p. 470.

and discomfiture of the friends of the "battle-born, blood-sealed" greenback, and amid expressions of the liveliest satisfaction from other men.[1] The nation had been, and still was, eager to give recognition to Grant for anything of value which might accrue from his administration. Here was an act which was a new evidence, many said, of some portion of fundamental common sense, and of his soldier's courage. It was made to rank beside his triumph in the settlement of the *Alabama* claims.

A movement was made in the Senate to pass the bill over the veto, but it failed.[2] Much had been gained. Recovery of trade and industry had been delayed by a fear that the politicians, who, taking up the cause, were committed to inflation, would gain their objects, and that the country in the future, as in the recent past, should have no fixed and certain standard of value. It now seemed clear that the public mind had undergone some improvement of understanding and that, when progress should be made in raising our prostrate trade and industry, it would not be by any "watering" of the currency, but by "economy and hard work." [3]

The President was pleased by the favor which his veto drew from the country. Richardson, of proven incapacity, deeply involved in scandals, to be described in another place, was relieved from duty, early in June, 1874, and Benjamin H. Bristow of Kentucky, a soldier in the Union Army during the war, a lawyer who had been Solicitor General, an office which had just been created and of which he was the first incumbent, came to the tasks of the Department. Such an association strengthened the situation.[4] Very shortly appeared in print a "memorandum," presented by Grant to Senator Jones of Nevada, who had been taking a creditable position in Congress on the money question. In this document, which, as the New York Nation observed, should have been issued on the 4th of June, 1869, instead of the 4th of June, 1874, a plan was devel-

[1] N. Y. Nation, May 7 and 14, 1874, for the attitude of the newspapers.
[2] April 28. Cf. Cong. Record, 43rd Cong. 1st sess., p. 3436.
[3] N. Y. Nation, May 28, 1874.
[4] Cf. ibid., Dec. 10, 1873.

oped for the redemption of the greenbacks and for the resumption of specie payments.[1]

The contention between the inflationists and the hard money men in Congress continued until the last days of the session, when a bill, in the nature of a compromise, formulated in a committee of conference, was passed by the two houses and sent to the President. He signed it on June 20, 1874.[2] In this measure the amount of the "legal tender" circulation was fixed at $382,000,000, thus validating what Richardson had issued and forbidding, for the present at least, the further issues up to $400,000,000, authorized by the bill which Congress had passed and the President had vetoed in April. If the limit were not set where wise men desired that it should be, there was reason for gratitude that some limit had been agreed upon and established.[3]

Confidence was increased by the emphatic and uncompromising language in which Bristow and Grant dealt with the money question when Congress met in December, 1874. The Secretary of the Treasury, in his first report, spoke of the "complicated mischiefs" flowing from "an unstable, or inconvertible currency." He said that "initiatory steps towards the redemption" of the pledges of the government "ought not to be longer postponed." The "era of the war" would not be closed until the period of redemption should be reached. "The history of irredeemable paper currency" repeated itself "whenever and wherever" it was issued. The Secretary urged that Congress fix an early day after which greenbacks would cease to be legal tender. Meantime people and banks should prepare themselves for final resumption. Three years for such preparation, the Secretary thought, would be ample—it might be effected in less time. "The best interests of the government and the people," said the Secretary finally, and "the highest considerations of virtue and morality" demanded that Congress should "undo that state of things" which only "the necessities of war" had

---

[1] Cf. N. Y. Nation, June 11, 1874.
[2] Cf. John Sherman's Recollections, vol. i, p. 508.
[3] Cf. N. Y. Nation, June 25, 1874.

ever justified. The panic had its reason, which was plain enough—it was "the direct and immediate result of that excessive development of speculative enterprises, overtrading and inflation of credit, which invariably follow large issues of inconvertible paper currency." [1]

Grant, addressing himself in the opening words of his message to the "prostration in business and industries, such as has not been witnessed with us for many years," stated it as his firm belief that there could be "no prosperous and permanent revival" until a policy, "with legislation to carry it out," should be adopted "looking to a return to a specie basis." The "debtor and the speculative classes" might think it to their advantage "to make so-called money abundant," at any rate until they could "throw a portion of their burdens upon others." He asked Congress to act at once. "Every delay in preparation for final resumption" partook of "dishonesty." At this session the Congress should devise legislation which would "renew confidence, revive all the industries, start us on a career of prosperity to last for many years, and to save the credit of the nation and of the people." To this "devoutly to be sought for end," he declared, that "steps toward the return to a specie basis" were "the great requisites." [2]

Here was a problem, indeed, for a Congress which at its last session had so abundantly proven its faithlessness on the whole question. It must show a better temper, if it were to do what it was bidden to do by the President. But in the autumn of 1874 the nation had again been consulted about the general course of public affairs, and the response, as will be more fully related in another chapter, was expressive of the pent-up disgust of large classes of the people for the Republican party under its recent leadership. If the Congress, now near the end of its days, did not make some disposition of the currency question that question would be remitted to the Democrats,[3] who, after March 3, 1875, for the first time since the war, would be in control of

[1] Report of Sec. of Treasury, House Ex. Doc., 43rd Cong. 2nd sess., no. 3, pp. x–xvii.

[2] Richardson, Messages and Papers, vol. vii, p. 286.

[3] Cf. Sherman's Recollections, vol. i, p. 520.

the House and in greatly augmented force in the Senate. The lines were drawn, as they had been in the last session. But it was made to appear now that failure of the factions to agree would work the disruption of the party.[1] Accordingly the Republican leaders in the Senate, in a full understanding with the potential factors in the House, held a caucus. Eleven Republican senators were formed into a committee, and were authorized to draft a measure which would conduce to the health and prosperity of the party as a party. By some secret manipulation a bill which should do no more affront than necessary to those who wished to hold fast to the greenback, and, at the same time, meet the demands of the resumptionists, was devised. John Sherman, as chairman of the Finance Committee, was put forward as its sponsor. He alone, on the Republican side, should speak upon the question, and it was agreed that he should make no definite statements as to the meaning of enigmatical provisions which had been written into the bill.[2] In general, it provided for a gradual contraction in the volume of the greenbacks to $300,000,000, with a compensating expansion in the national bank note circulation. The important point gained by the resumptionists was the fixing of a definite date, January 1, 1879, when the redemption of the greenbacks should commence. The law could be repealed before specie payments, four years away, should be resumed, the "cheap money" men argued, as they firmly believed that it would be repealed, while the hard money men, far from content with all the provisions of the measure, welcomed it as the best that could be obtained, with public sentiment what it was at the time.

As the Republican leaders intended, almost no debate in either house accompanied the passage of the bill, fateful as it must have been held to be, if it had been considered as a parliamentary measure rather than a makeshift of the caucus.[3] It was hurried through the Senate within a few hours after it

[1] Cf. Sherman's Recollections, vol. i, p. 509.

[2] Ibid., pp. 510–11.

[3] Cf. Sherman's letter in the Financier, quoted in N. Y. Nation, Jan. 28, 1875.

appeared in printed form on the desks of the members, on December 22, 1874,[1] to receive even less notice in the House, which approved it on January 7, 1875.[2]

The discussion of the question in the last session had been so prolonged, Sherman said, that it had been mentally and physically exhausting to every one.[3] Further debate was needless, and he contented himself with a brief statement, in which nothing was so clear as the fact that the bill must be taken as it was. Any specification of what would be done with the greenbacks after they were retired, whether they would be destroyed, as they should have been when McCulloch had called in $44,000,000 of them, or whether they would be held over the country with a threat of reissue in the manner of Boutwell and Richardson, a point which Schurz [4] and other men of sagacity would clear up, Sherman evaded, in accordance with the instructions which the caucus leaders had given him on the point.[5] To have said yea or nay on this subject would have disturbed the equability, brought about under so much difficulty, of the hostile elements.[6] This and other matters of importance, including the ways and means which must be devised to make resumption at the promised date practically possible, must be left without determination, lest antagonism be awakened and adjournment should be reached without action.

It was "juggling with a plain question which should be honestly treated," said Senator Bayard. The bill would but invite a repetition of those very errors of finance which for so long had played fast and loose with the business of the country.[7] As it stood, without clarification of its meaning, said another

---

[1] Cong. Record, 43rd Cong. 2nd sess., p. 208. Cf. Sherman's Recollections, vol. i, p. 51.

[2] Cong. Record, 43rd Cong. 2nd sess., p. 319. The full proceedings concerning this bill in the House fill only one and a half pages of the Record; in the Senate, but 17 pages.

[3] Ibid., p. 194.

[4] Ibid., p. 195.

[5] Sherman refused to be "catechised." He would leave to the future the consideration of questions "that tend to divide and distract us."—Ibid., p. 196.

[6] Sherman's Recollections, vol. i, p. 510.

[7] Cong. Record, 43rd Cong. 2nd sess., p. 202.

senator, Hamilton of Maryland, it would serve as a mere "bait to the passions and the prejudices of the next Congress." The country would continue to be disturbed by the attempts which would be launched with a view to its repeal.[1]

Some of the defects of the bill were pointed out by the President in a message with which he accompanied it back to Congress, after he had signed it.[2] But it was a time at which, a subject concerning which, as the New York Evening Post said, if you could not get what you wanted, you must make the best of what you could get.[3] As it proved the enactment of this law was a notable step in the history of the country. Industry and trade could and did take heart, if slowly, at sight of action by the government toward a result, which, but for ignorance, party bickering and much demoralization of the representative as well as of the popular mind,[4] should have been attained as Mr. Bristow, and many before him, had observed, soon after the close of the war.

[1] Cong. Record, 43rd Cong. 2nd sess., p. 203.
[2] Ibid., p. 459. Cf. N. Y. Nation, Jan. 21, 1875.
[3] Quoted in N. Y. Nation, Jan. 7, 1875.
[4] Cf. Sherman's Recollections, vol. i, p. 508.

CHAPTER XIX

CLEARING AWAY THE WRECK

THE opportunity for further service to the administration came to Hamilton Fish in connection with the disturbances which continued in Cuba. He was still rather restively performing his duties; he would still have welcomed relief by retirement from the State Department. But the country was to have the advantage of his sagacity and his quiet temper in another critical conjuncture. He had stemmed the strong tide with which Grant moved in favor of our recognition of the insurgents in Cuba who, by methods as barbaric as those employed by Spain in the attempt to repress them, were striving to make the island free, and now faced a crisis which might instantly have involved us in a war with that nation,—by our forbearance to be postponed for yet twenty-five years. One of a considerable number of vessels engaged in the business of carrying men and arms to the "rebels," the *Virginius*, after chase, was captured on October 31, 1873, about six miles off the island of Jamaica by a Spanish gunboat, the *Tornado*. She bore the American flag; some Americans were on board. Undaunted, the Spanish insular authorities conveyed her into Santiago harbor where, in keeping with their character for ferocity, they proceeded to a general shooting of the captain, passengers and crew, whom they had made prisoners, some of the number being citizens of the United States.

The country was aflame at once. The "Free Cuba" men fanned the fires, seeing in the episode a cause for the intervention of this government, which they had so long advocated and had done so much to bring about. Now the President and Congress must act. The flag had been insulted. American citizens had been massacred. Men who cared nothing about Cuba, free or

123

bond, joined in the excitement, which stirred the newspapers and deeply affected all classes of the people.

Our minister at Madrid, General Sickles, immediately upon receipt of the news, visited the President, Castelar, the Spanish government having lately assumed a republican form, from which we had expected much of great value to civilization,[1] and instructions were sent to the Captain General in Cuba to await orders before inflicting penalties upon the prisoners.[2] But the Spanish authorities in Cuba rushed to their bloody work. The order was received too late, or was disregarded to gratify their inhuman propensities,[3] and, in all, in a few days, 53 men were executed.[4]

"Butchery and murder" Secretary Fish called it. Sickles was instructed to "protest, in the name of this government, and of civilization and humanity, against the act as brutal, barbarous and an outrage upon the age." The United States would demand "the most ample reparation of any wrong which may have been committed upon any of its citizens, or upon its flag."[5] "Condemnation, disavowal and deprecation of the act" would not suffice, he said again. There must be "some speedy and signal visitation of punishment on those engaged in this dark deed." Anything else would be a confession by Spain of her impotency with reference to Cuba, and a "virtual abandonment of the control of the island."[6]

It was alleged for Spain that the *Virginius* was seen on the coast of Cuba attempting to land her passengers, including a number of well-known filibusters and recruits for the revolutionary forces, and arms; that she was within Spanish waters when the chase began; that her papers were irregular and were no guaranty of American registry, and of title, therefore, to bear the stars and stripes. Admiral Polo, Spain's minister at Washington, met Secretary Fish; Sickles labored with the minister of state at Madrid, all to no immediate purpose. On

---

[1] Cf. Foreign Relations of U. S., House Ex. Doc., 43rd Cong. 1st sess., pp. 930, 966.
[2] House Ex. Doc., 43rd Cong. 1st sess., no. 30, pp. 15–16.
[3] Ibid., pp. 21–2.   [5] Ibid., p. 21.
[4] Ibid., p. 188.   [6] Ibid., p. 22.

the 14th of November Fish categorically demanded, through
Sickles, the restoration of the *Virginius*, the release and delivery
to the United States of the persons captured, who had not
"already been massacred," the salute of our flag in Santiago
harbor and the "signal punishment" of those who had captured
the steamer and shot her seamen and passengers. Twelve days
were allowed Spain to meet these requirements. At the end of
that time, if she had not complied, Sickles was commanded to
close the legation and to leave Madrid.[1] Meantime, great
activity was displayed in our navy yards and the nation hurriedly adopted measures of war.

To Fish's demands the minister of state made a defiant reply,[2]
and, on the 18th, Sickles was prepared to embark at Valencia
for France with his secretary and the archives of his office.[3]
Popular feeling ran high in Spain as well as in the United States.
The Spanish press indulged in much abuse, a mob assembled in
Madrid, and, but for the police, would have entered and sacked
the legation.[4] Meanwhile the minister of state, acting through
Admiral Polo at Washington, made partial promises to accede
to the American demands and Sickles, on November 19, was
directed to postpone his departure and to await further
instructions.[5] Spain was given a further period of time for
settlement; her decision would be expected by the 26th.[6] She returned with a proposal for arbitration; Fish replied that such a
subject, "being one of national honor," could not be arbitrated.[7]
Sickles, who was eager for a diplomatic rupture, continued his
arrangements for leaving the Spanish capital. In his absence
American interests would be put in the care of the Italian
chargé d'affaires.[8] He had asked for his passports on the 26th,
before a note came from the ministry of state which indicated a
willingness to make the required reclamations. But the negotiations now passed to Washington where, on November 29,
out of the reach of Sickles, whose suspected incompetency for

[1] House Ex. Doc., 43rd Cong. 1st sess., no. 30, pp. 29, 32-3.
[2] Ibid., p. 34.   [6] Ibid., p. 49.
[3] Ibid., p. 45.   [7] Ibid., p. 52.
[4] Ibid., p. 47.   [8] Ibid., p. 50.
[5] Ibid., pp. 48-9.

diplomacy had by this experience been confirmed,[1] a protocol was signed, agreeing to restore to us the *Virginius* and the survivors of the slaughter, to salute the American flag on Christmas Day, unless it should be shown by Spain before that time that the ship had carried it without authority, and to arraign the officers in competent courts and punish them. Reciprocally the United States, if it appeared that the *Virginius* had displayed the flag illegally, would, before Christmas Day, proceed against the vessel, and those who may have been guilty of improper acts in connection with her operations. Questions of indemnity would be left for later determination.[2]

This was the end; the excitement subsided. Fish and Admiral Polo met in Washington on December 8, and agreed that, on the 16th of that month, in the harbor of Bahia Honda, the *Virginius* should be formally delivered up to a war ship of the United States by a Spanish war ship, and that the survivors should be put on board an American naval vessel in the harbor of Santiago, as soon as such vessel could reach that place.[3] On December 18, 102 persons were brought away on the *Juniata* and conveyed to New York. The *Virginius*, in our hands, on her way to New York, ran into a storm and sank off Cape Fear.

Before Christmas Day it was proven by Spain, to the satisfaction of the Attorney General of the United States, that the American papers of the *Virginius* had been obtained by perjury and fraud, wherefore the ceremony of a salute of the flag was dispensed with.[4] Sickles resigned as a result of the entanglements in which the heat of his temper had involved him, and his resignation was accepted.[5]

The school of statesmanship of which Hamilton Fish was a creditable representative was passing into history. With the death of Seward, Chase and Sumner, three of the republic's ties with the past were severed. Each widely different from the

[1] Fuess, Life of Caleb Cushing, vol. ii, pp. 361-2.
[2] Am. Ann. Cyclop. for 1873, pp. 670-71; House Ex. Doc., 43rd Cong. 1st sess., no. 30, pp. 81-2.
[3] House Ex. Doc., 43rd Cong. 1st sess., no. 30, pp. 84-5.
[4] Ibid., pp. 69, 85-145, 208-10; cf. N. Y. Nation, March 18, 1875.
[5] Fuess, Life of Cushing, vol. ii, p. 362.

other two, they were alike valuable for their political capacities
which those who were left upon the scene were not very competent to emulate. Their mantles could descend to rising men,
of whom Blaine and John Sherman were the most prominent
examples, one so devoted to his own welfare and aggrandizement as to seem but a poor heir to eminence, both disposed to
raise party above the state, and too sparingly furnished with
qualities to fit them to adorn the highest places in the annals of
our public life.

Seward had marked his well earned leisure, after retiring from
the State Department in 1869, by a tour of the world and died,
amid the kindly remembrances of his countrymen, in October,
1872, while the Greeley campaign was at its height. Chase
followed in May, 1873, but a few weeks after he had for a second
time administered the oath of office to Grant, to receive just
praise and to be lamented by all discerning men. The illustrious Sumner survived for a few months the indignities put
upon him by Grant and his old associates in the Republican
party, now basking in the light of the President's fame, amid the
pains of the disease which long had afflicted his heroic form, or
until March, 1874.

Who would follow Chase as Chief Justice? To decide so
great a matter was a duty which now faced the President, and
instantly there was curiosity to see how he would discharge it.
On all sides it was said and assumed that Roscoe Conkling,
known as well for his marked arrogance of manner and personal
vanity, as for his fustian on the Republican party "stump"
and his ability as a party manager,[1] would be nominated. Nothing seemed so unfit to be done yet nothing seemed so probable.[2]

First, it is said, the post was offered to Morton of
Indiana, another principal force in directing the movements
of the administration. But Morton who had not accepted the
tender of the English mission, because of the knowledge that
he would be succeeded in the Senate by a Democrat, again was

[1] In the "Senatorial Ring" which directed Grant's movements, he was
"the most magnificent in speech and the most assuming in deportment.—"
N. Y. Nation, Jan. 16, 1873.
[2] Ibid., Oct. 2, 1873.

deterred on the like account.[1] On November 8, 1873, Grant formally invited Conkling to become Chief Justice "in the full belief that no more acceptable appointment could be made." [2] When the senator from New York removed himself as a possibility, for reasons having to do with the successorship to his seat in Congress and his indisposition to leave the fields of forensic battle,[3] and when the excitement over the panic in the stock and money markets, soon to be followed by that aroused by the *Virginius* affair, had in some degree subsided, the President invited his Attorney General, George H. Williams of Oregon, to the place. The response of the country was very unfavorable. Williams's practice had been confined to causes arising in a "frontier state." His conduct, since coming to the Attorney General's office, had exhibited feebleness and partisanship. He was totally without that acquaintance with the law, indeed, without the high personal standards, qualifying him for so eminent a post.[4] Bar associations sent their remonstrances to the President and to the Senate, which was discussing the name with a view to its confirmation,[5] when Grant withdrew it, and nominated Caleb Cushing, who, it had just been announced, was to follow Sickles as minister to Spain.[6]

Here was worse trouble. Cushing, whatever his learning and distinction, and both were quite considerable, was 74 years old, and, more than this, though recently serving the government at Washington in useful capacities, had earlier been an offensive enemy of the Republican party. He had presided over the convention at Charleston in 1860 which had nominated Breckinridge for the Presidency, and later had been known, revengeful men said, as a Copperhead. A letter to Jefferson Davis was produced—he had written it, so it was said—in which he asked

---

[1] W. D. Foulke, Life of O. P. Morton, vol. ii, pp. 339–40.

[2] Conkling, Life of Conkling, pp. 460–61.

[3] Cf. Autobiography of T. C. Platt, pp. 67–8, and N. Y. Nation, Oct. 2, 1873.

[4] N. Y. Nation, Dec. 11 and 25, 1873, and Jan. 1, 1874. Cf. Fuess, Life of Cushing, vol. ii, pp. 364–73. "The eminent unfitness of the nominee for that exalted and responsible position is not debatable."—Letter from a correspondent of J. S. Morrill in Morrill Papers in Library of Congress.

[5] N. Y. Nation, Jan. 8, 1874.

[6] Ibid., Jan. 1, 1874; Fuess, Life of Cushing, vol. ii, p. 363.

the President of the Confederate States to appoint a friend to some position in connection with the rebel government.[1] More was not needed in the country at large, or by the Senate, so Cushing's name was withdrawn, and he was ready to proceed to Madrid,[2] while the President nominated Morrison R. Waite of Toledo, Ohio, another, who like Williams and Cushing, had served the country in the *Alabama* settlement. Though not a "first rate lawyer," though far from being a man of the rank of Chase and most of those who had occupied the great post, the appointment was welcomed as a way out of a situation which, in proportion as it proved the President's want of judgment, brought discredit upon the nation at large. Waite secured the unanimous vote of the senators and was confirmed, amid expressions of satisfaction from law associations and by the press.[3]

The disappointment of those who had supported Grant in 1872, because they could not find it in their consciences and hearts to vote to give over the government to a man like Horace Greeley, and because they had come to feel a hope that Grant's second administration would be an improvement over his first, as a result of four years' experience with his great office, had developed in several Western states, as we have seen, the farmers' protest, illustrated in their success at the elections in 1873. But this was not all. The general tendency of public opinion in the East, as well as the West, was distinctly and increasingly hostile to the President. The Crédit Mobilier disclosures and, more potent yet, the "back pay steal," followed by the panic of 1873 and "hard times," put an onerous weight upon the Republican party.

There were few state platforms that did not contain a plank denouncing the "salary grab." Republican leaders, seeing how grave had been their mistake, vied with the managers of the Democratic party in the denunciation of what they had but lately written into the law of the land. Members who were not returning to Congress pocketed what came to them,

---

[1] N. Y. Nation, Jan. 15, 1874.
[2] Cf. Fuess, Life of Cushing, vol. ii, pp. 364–73.
[3] N. Y. Nation, Jan. 29, 1874.

caring nothing for the result. But those who had a stake in the future as well as some, like Schurz, who, from the first, had opposed the whole movement on conscientious grounds, refused to receive the money. Others who drew it out, frightened by the criticism which their action evoked, returned it to the United States Treasury. Senator Morrill of Vermont presented what he had taken to the treasury of his state, which found such a taint upon the gift that a long controversy about receiving it ensued.[1] Still others sought out useful local charities, to which they forwarded the money to propitiate, if they could, their incensed constituents.[2]

The excitement grew until the "steal" became a principal issue in the electoral campaigns in the autumn of 1873. The most impressive results were seen in New York and Ohio, where Republican majorities in 1872 were converted, in 1873, into Democratic majorities. Ohio elected an old party "war horse," William ("Rise Up") Allen,[3] as its governor.[4]

The turn had come at last in what the New York Nation called "an extremely strong" and, at the same time, an "extremely dirty tide."[5] "Ben" Butler, though he had developed a strength in his latest canvass of the state for the governorship, which gravely reflected upon the political sagacity of the people of Massachusetts, like others, saw clearly enough that the salary bill was a burden far beyond the most adroit politician's power to bear it successfully. First and foremost in the business of passing the act, as he had been, he would now seize the distinction of leading the movement to bring about its repeal in the session which should convene in December, 1873. The party leaders in caucus went about the work in hand at once.

[1] Cf. Morrill Papers in Library of Congress.
[2] Cf. N. Y. Nation, May 1, 1873, and October 2, 1873.
[3] It was demanded that he "rise up" to face this crisis in the party's affairs, and "Rise Up" Allen men called him in the campaign.
[4] Cf. N. Y. Nation, Oct. 23, Nov. 6 and 13, 1873.
[5] Issue of Nov. 6, 1873. Grant's friend E. B. Washburne wrote to Senator Morrill from the American legation in Paris, August 22, 1873— "The truth of the matter is that the people, having for years acquiesced in the most villanous and corrupt legislation by Congress, the members began to believe that they had become so thoroughly debauched that they would submit to any outrage."—Morrill Papers in Library of Congress.

Butler urged that suits at law be instituted to compel those who had taken the money to disgorge it, a plan which was not approved. The nation's body of lawgivers who, at the close of the Forty-second Congress, had voted to take the pay now, at the beginning of the Forty-third Congress, with sufficient hypocrisy and cowardice, engaged in a competition with one another to see which one might the most ostentatiously condemn the act,[1] and before January was ended the House and the Senate had passed and the President had approved the repealer.[2] While the President and the Supreme Court justices were permitted to have the increased sums which had been voted to them in March, the salaries of all the other beneficiaries, including the senators and representatives, were ten months later reduced to the old rates.[3] Needless to say a virtue to which men were compelled in this manner appeased public opinion in only a partial way.

Respect for and confidence in such a parliamentary assembly was not heightened by the investigation of the granting of a subsidy to the Pacific Mail Company. The Washington lobby of this time was a disgrace, as all men knew, but its operations were not seen in so clear a light as when the facts concerning the relations of Congress with the agents of this large steamship line were disclosed in 1874 and 1875. The affairs of a once prosperous corporation were going from bad to worse under unprincipled management, and when it asked for new favors from the government its methods were exposed.[4] It appeared that, in order to secure the subsidy of a half million a year, in

[1] Only about one-third of the senators and less than one-fifth of the representatives returned the money to the Treasury of the United States. In no state in the South, except Maryland, were there members who did so. There were sixteen states which returned nothing, either from senators or representatives.—Morrill Papers, loc. cit.

[2] Votes summarized in McPherson's Handbook for 1874, pp. 20–39.

[3] The 44th Congress, in 1876, passed an act reducing the President's salary to $25,000. But he vetoed the bill on the ground that the incumbent of the office could not live on such a sum of money, and, as the measure was looked upon as partisan and vindictive, his course was generally approved.—Cf. N. Y. Nation, April 20, 1876; Am. Ann. Cyclop. for 1876, p. 172.

[4] Cf. House Reports, 43rd Cong. 1st sess., no. 598; Cortissoz, Life of Whitelaw Reid, vol. i, pp. 314–5.

1872, nearly \$900,000 had been committed to the hands of an agent. Parts of this large sum had been appropriated by the lobbyists for their own uses, while Congressmen and attachés of Congress, including the House postmaster, named King, a politician from Minnesota, who received \$125,000, lawyers and several editors, among them John W. Forney, who got \$25,000, shared in the benefits. An investigation was begun; necessary witnesses fled to Europe and Canada. Although the committee, to which the subject was referred, declared the transaction to be "a reckless robbery of a corporation under the temporary control of speculators," without staining the character of Congress to so great a degree as had been charged, it full well felt the reproach which the exposures conveyed, and asked for judicial investigation of the case and the enactment of measures to cope with the "enormous evil" of lobbying in Washington.[1]

More and many new scandals were coming to light through the friction of the leaders in Congress who, in the battle for positions of advantage, were joined by the opposition press, which uttered charges of maladministration to the discredit of nearly all the departments. The most distinct allegations affected the Treasury Department. Some reforms had been effected in the business of collecting the customs in New York City as a result of the Leet and Stocking disclosures. More would follow. Rates of taxation were high; the temptation to evade the laws had never been so great. Congress, in the interest of enforcement, had adopted unusual measures. As one method of gaining the result Treasury agents and informers were guaranteed a percentage upon the amounts fraudulently withheld from the government, which they should discover and report, a moiety system, as it was termed, the cause of evils now to be published to the country.

[1] House Reports, 43rd Cong. 2nd sess., no. 268, pp. i–xix; N. Y. Nation, Dec. 17 and 24, 1874, Jan. 7, 14, 28 and Feb. 4, 1875. "Our greatest trouble here," said Senator J. S. Morrill to his friend Benedict, April 8, 1876, "is a corrupt lobby." Men who were accepting bribes in the interest of pending measures he said, should have their portraits hung in a "rogue's gallery" to be exhibited for all to see.—Morrill Papers, loc. cit.

In 1873 some proceedings were taken against the prominent firm of Phelps, Dodge and Company in New York.[1] Early in 1874 the same measures were employed in reference to a large importing firm in Boston. A clerk in the employ of Jordan, Marsh and Company of that city had a brother in the service of the United States government; they carried to a Treasury agent a story of fraud which it was alleged had been committed by that firm; its books were seized for examination, and, upon the strength of the complaint, its business was seriously interfered with.[2]

Other firms suffered in a like manner. The zeal of the informers, and of their agents and confederates, grew upon what it fed. The hope of gain led to the invention of methods which amounted to persecution. It appeared that in a period of little more than four years, ending November 1, 1873, the total sum received by the government by these means at Boston and New York was $2,218,897, of which $2,144,015 went to the officers of the two ports and their sleuths. In other words it was costing 100 per cent and much unpleasantness to make the collections. One "special agent" named Jayne, who gained a very unsavory notoriety, accumulated a large fortune by his activities, and a number of other ignorant adventurers had but little less pecuniary success as a result of their operations in this profitable field.[3] The Federal officers who plied such arts in the principal ports of the country were levied on heavily for the expenses of Republican campaigns. The system aroused the protest of chambers of commerce, boards of trade, as well as individual merchants. It was soon to come into the light, where all might see it and join in its condemnation.

Into an appropriation bill which had passed Congress in 1872 a clause had been slipped, not unobserved, since some of the members of the Senate and the House had been ready to expose the trick, permitting the Secretary of the Treasury to employ three persons to aid him in "discovering and collecting" moneys

[1] N. Y. Nation, March 12, 1874.
[2] Ibid., Jan. 8 and Feb. 19, 1874.
[3] Ibid., Feb. 19 and 26, March 19 and April 2, 1874.

unlawfully "withheld" from the United States Treasury.[1]
Boutwell made "contracts," in accordance with the plan of
him who seemed to be the real author of the scheme, no other
than Ben Butler, with John D. Sanborn, a resident of Massachusetts, an old agent of Butler's in commercial speculations in
occupied territory during the war, while that man was in command in the South. Now, in effect, collectors were officially
warned away from a portion of their work by instructions from
Washington. A valuable monopoly was given to Sanborn, and
he and his associates proceeded on their way, farming out the
privilege and developing a conspiracy to defraud both the
Treasury and the taxpayers.[2] Sanborn was to have one-half
of whatever he could recover, and it was made certain that he
should operate in a not too difficult field. Not satisfied with
their large opportunities,[3] he and his agents soon resorted to
blackmail. They threatened rich men in New York and Boston.
Sums of money were demanded; if these were not paid they
set their spies at the doors of those whom they had failed to
mulct.[4]

In two years Sanborn was paid as his share in this business a
sum in excess of $200,000.[5] He was brought to account by
A. W. Tenney, a United States district attorney in Brooklyn,
who proceeded to present the names and describe the offenses of
Sanborn and some of his partners to a grand jury, which indicted them. Richardson, meanwhile, had been asked by
Tenney for information necessary to the prosecution, which
the Secretary of the Treasury withheld, or gave out only with
extreme reluctance,[6] and, though the prosecution came to
nothing,[7] the subject was no longer to be blinked by Congress.
An investigation was instituted by the House. It appeared in
due time that, while the "contract" with Sanborn was made by

[1] N. Y. Nation, March 12 and 19, 1873; House Reports, 43rd Cong.
1st sess., no. 559, p. 1.
[2] N. Y. Nation, March 5, 1874.
[3] Ibid., March 12, 1874.
[4] Ibid., Feb. 19, 1874.
[5] Ibid., March 12, 1874; cf. G. F. Hoar, Autobiography, vol. i, p. 326.
[6] N. Y. Nation, March 12, 1874.
[7] Ibid., April 9, 1874.

Boutwell, it was really Richardson's affair, and that both men in this regard were acting merely as agents of Butler. The defense of Richardson was as remarkable for its evasions as that of any public character who had been caught in the toils of the Crédit Mobilier. His answer to the charges was to the effect that he had signed important papers having to do with the administration of his department without acquainting himself with their contents.[1] He came out of the investigation completely discredited in the sight of the whole country.

The committee made its report in June, through Charles Foster, a Republican representative in Congress from Ohio, who, from the first, had played an honorable and resolute part in forwarding the inquiry.[2] The theory on which the law was enacted had been "completely reversed." Instead of Sanborn and his partners being employed "to assist the proper officers of the government, the proper officers of the government had been made to assist them."[3] They were "marauding upon the public treasury." Richardson and his assistant, and the solicitor of the Treasury were deserving, the committee said, of "severe condemnation" for the manner in which they permitted the law to be administered. Nevertheless, with a view to reflecting not too unfavorably upon them, they and Boutwell were uninfluenced, it was said, by "corrupt motives," so far as appeared in the testimony. The committee recommended that "any system of farming the collection of any portion of the revenues of the government," being "fundamentally wrong," should at once cease. The law under which Sanborn had operated should be repealed;[4] his contracts should be "revoked and annulled."[5]

Clearly Richardson must leave his post, though Grant, as could have been foreseen, clung tenaciously to him.[6] Finally

[1] N. Y. Nation, April 9, 1874.
[2] Ibid., July 2, 1874.
[3] House Reports, 43rd Cong. 1st sess., no. 559, p. 7.
[4] It was repealed in June, 1874.
[5] House Reports, 43rd Cong. 1st sess., no. 559, p. 9.
[6] N. Y. Nation, April 16, May 21 and 28, 1874. Foster's Committee, Senator Hoar says, privately demanded Richardson's removal.—Autobiography, vol. i, p. 328.

he was replaced, early in June, 1874, by Mr. Bristow who, as has been related, brought to the place capacity and a sense of honor calculated to give an improved tone to the Treasury Department, as well as to the entire Grant administration.[1] Richardson, instead of suffering a merited discharge from public service, was appointed by the President to a judgeship in the Court of Claims.

"Boss" Shepherd's management of the affairs of the District of Columbia, which had been exculpated by a committee of Congress in 1872, proceeded under great popular protest. Moved by the petitions of W. W. Corcoran, a banker, and other influential property owners in Washington, a joint select committee of three, Senators Allison, Thurman and William M. Stewart,[2] and several representatives, was appointed for the purpose of making another investigation of the subject, and, on March 5, 1874, the work commenced. The report was made to Congress on the 16th of the following June. The testimony attained an immense bulk [3] without inducing the committee to go so far in their recommendations as the facts might have seemed to warrant.[4] As friendly in its tone as the circumstances would permit, it clearly declared that Shepherd had assumed complete control of the government, and had exercised it in an entirely arbitrary manner.[5]

A system of improvements had been undertaken covering more than 100 miles of streets. The plans called for the completion in "a brief space of time" of what could well have been done only in a period of years. Projects which were to have cost but $6,000,000 were extended until they had come to involve expenditures amounting to three times that sum, and the work was proceeding without legal sanction. True it was

[1] N. Y. Nation, June 4, 1874; H. V. Boynton, North American Review for October, 1876.

[2] Boutwell was originally a member of the committee. His place was shortly taken by Stewart.

[3] Two large volumes of 2,500 pages—Senate Reports, 43rd Cong. 1st sess., no. 453, pt. 2. The report and accompanying material fill nearly 700 pages more—ibid., pt. 1.

[4] Though it was a distinct advance upon the report of 1872. Cf. N. Y. Nation, June 25, 1874.

[5] Senate Reports, 43rd Cong., 1st sess., no. 453, pt. 1, p. 11.

that the capital city of the republic had needed a hand which would lend it a little splendor, but the committee condemned the method by which this result was being brought about. Contracts had been let without opening them to public competition. Some fell into the hands of political favorites who were not expected to perform them, and who, for a consideration, sold them to other men to execute. As the District was practically bankrupt it was recommended by the committee that its debts be funded into a bond or bonds, "payable at a remote period" at a low rate of interest, to be covered by a three per cent tax rate. The work upon the streets would at once be placed under the management of an officer of the engineer corps of the army.[1] The committee also recommended the abolition of the form of government [2] by which Shepherd had risen into power; it had been tried, they said, and it must be accounted "a failure"—until a better could be devised, the affairs of the District might be entrusted to a commission, a suggestion which Congress almost immediately adopted.[3]

The indignation which the exposures induced in the public mind was increased when Grant, who, against protest, had made Shepherd governor in 1873, nominated him to be a member of the commission.[4] Such action was as strongly resented by the Senate as in the country at large and only six senators, half of these Southern carpetbaggers, voted to confirm the nomination.[5]

The accumulation of disgust with all that had recently been seen in our public life, and the multiplying hardships brought upon the country by the "panic," would find full expression in the elections of 1874. The platforms of both parties were denunciations of corruption and extravagance. "Salary grabbers," "ring politicians" and "land monopolists" must be

[1] Senate Reports, 43rd Cong., 1st sess., no. 453, pt. 1, pp. 28-9.
[2] Established by act of Congress of Feb. 21, 1871.
[3] Act of June 20, 1874.
[4] In turn the conduct of this commission, two years later, was made the subject of an investigation on the ground that they were administering their offices in the interest of favorites and friends. See House Mis. Doc., 44th Cong. 1st sess., no. 103; House Reports, 44th Cong. 1st sess., no. 702.
[5] N. Y. Nation, June 25, 1874.

voted out of power. Public thievery must be brought to an end. The recital of "outrages" perpetrated upon the negroes and upon Southern white Republicans, the "midnight assassinations" and the "reigns of terror," in the South, honey in the mouths of the stump speaker and the platform maker, went forward as before, and as it would again in many an electoral campaign. A convention of rascals who were battening on the South, through the agencies of the Republican party, met in Chattanooga to fan the fires of sectional prejudice for election day. They sent out over the country new accounts of the denials which they were suffering and the wrongs which they endured at the hands of the "rebels." [1]

But the reiterations of the services of the Republican party in emancipating and enfranchising the slaves, in suppressing the rebellion and in saving the Union, brought into the canvass in Congress, on the stump and in the press, were heard less patiently than they earlier had been. There were signs of an awakened sense of honor in the people which, displayed and made effective at opportune moments, has more than once been the salvation of our democracy.

The "October states" spoke with emphasis. Ohio remained Democratic by a majority of upwards of 25,000, greatly in excess of that given to Governor Allen in 1873. Indiana elected the candidate of the Democratic party. In the five states of Ohio, Indiana, Iowa, Nebraska and West Virginia, which had elected their representatives in Congress in October, it was said that in districts returning 33 Republicans and 13 Democrats in 1872 there were now, in 1874, 23 Republicans and 23 Democrats.[2] At this rate, when the polling should be finished in November, the Republicans would lose control of at least one branch of Congress.

The political situation in New York was of profound interest to the nation. Here a governor was to be chosen. In 1872 the Republicans had nominated General Dix, a candidate of unusual excellence. He was taken to head the ticket because he had been acting with the Liberals until Greeley's ill-starred

[1] N. Y. Nation, Oct. 22, 1874.   [2] Ibid.

nomination, which he could not endorse. The Republican
managers, in a search for ways and means to meet and certainly
defeat the old editor of the Tribune in his own state, seeing their
opportunity, named and elected Dix. He had proven his
worth.[1] Now he was to be renominated. There would be
no doubt of such a result if the Democrats, as was promised,
should bring forward Samuel J. Tilden as their candidate.
This was precisely the course which, at the state convention
in Syracuse, they elected to pursue, and, as an invitation for the
support of the disintegrating elements of the Liberal party,
with which they had been allied two years before, they placed
on the ticket, with Tilden, as their candidate for lieutenant-
governor, William Dorsheimer, a prominent figure in the
Greeley campaign.

Tilden was a man of acknowledged strength. Now sixty
years of age he was one of the leaders of the bar of New York
and a respectable force in upholding its honor and dignity.
He had been a national figure in the councils of the Democratic
party for many a year. Though he had not been frankly and
zealously active on the Union side, during the war, as he well
could and should have been, in 1874 he was in the full enjoyment of the credit which had come to him in connection with
the exposure of the corruptions of the "Tweed Ring." In this
work, once it was commenced, and it had become publicly
plain that the scandal was one of great proportions, he had been
inflexible. Men asked themselves how he could have been,
as he was for many years, companion of and sage to Tweed and
the Tammany leaders without perceiving what must have been
tolerably clear to him, as it was to others, that they ranked
high among the first rascals of the age. Men pointed to his
political ambitions, which were not short of the Presidency, to
explain a silence to be broken only when self-interest impelled
him to activity. He had taken a pre-eminent place in denouncing Tweed and the rest of the thieves "to save the party,"
not in a fine, large spirit of public service.[2] If leaders should

[1] N. Y. Nation, Sep. 10 and Oct. 1, 1874.
[2] Cf. ibid., Aug. 19, 1875.

not come forward to emphasize the fact that there was a Democratic party, distinct from the Tammany Society, which so long had directed the party's destinies in New York, it might as well cease to exist. Tilden was a "party man," and he had none of the instincts which could ever make him a statesman, if, in reaching such an eminence, he must, on the way, cease to be a Democrat.

Thus had observers and commentators reasoned and spoken. Moreover, Mr. Tilden had some reputation as an heir to the qualities of the "Albany regency." In a matter having to do with "politics" he would dissemble. Nevertheless no one withheld from him a large measure of respect.[1] He had intellectual vigor, he drew to him and had the friendship of worthy people, his career as a lawyer, as well as a man, entitled him to the highest consideration, and his nomination as governor of New York was fairly regarded as a bid by the party for popular support in the approaching election, and a movement on his side, if he should be successful at the polls up to a point where he could be clearly seen by the nation, toward the Presidency two years hence. Such a selection left the Republicans with no doubts as to the need of renominating General Dix, who, however, was defeated. The election was Mr. Tilden's by 50,000 majority, nearly as great as Grant's and Dix's had been in 1872.

The Democratic victory in Massachusetts was no less noteworthy. There a governor was elected by that party by a majority of 7,000. The Republican majority in 1872 had been 74,000. Butler's seat in Congress was taken from him as a rebuke, which was nationally enjoyed, for his effronteries and rascalities. The Democratic candidates for state offices were elected in Pennsylvania[2] by about 5,000 majority. The majority for Grant in 1872 had been 137,000. New Jersey elected a Democratic governor, as did Missouri, a victory which extended to the legislature and presaged the retirement from the Senate of Carl Schurz.

[1] Cf. N. Y. Nation, Sep. 17 and 24, 1874.
[2] No longer, since the adoption of the new state constitution, an "October state."

The Democrats were assured by the "tidal wave" of a majority of about 70 votes in the House, and the division of the party forces in the legislatures of the states was such that, when they should reach the task of choosing senators to seats vacant and to be vacated, the Republican party would have a materially reduced majority in that branch of Congress. [1] The two-thirds majority upon which so much of the arrogance of the Radicals was founded would be broken, and the leaders saw before them not only investigations into maladministration, which their system of government had invited on so many sides, but also a distinct change in public policy, especially in reference to the South. What would be seen in the Capitol at Washington, beginning with the new Forty-fourth Congress, to convene in December, 1875, would importantly affect the elections of 1876, when the party might lose the Presidency itself.

The new Congress was indeed new. In the Senate appeared ex-President Andrew Johnson. He lived only to serve through the extra session of three weeks in March, 1875. [2] It was a sign of revolution that he should return to the scene of national political strife, sent home as he had been amid the execrations of his Radical enemies. From Georgia, General George B. Gordon of the Confederate army had come as a senator to the Forty-third Congress. His opportunity for speech and action on the side of the South was to be increased. Texas sent to the Senate General Samuel B. Maxey, a West Point graduate who had "gone with his state" and rose to high command on the Southern side in the war. From Missouri in Schurz's stead came Confederate General Cockrell.

In the House of Representatives Blaine's brilliant wit and audacious ambitions, exhibited and developed for eight years

[1] Cf. N. Y. Nation, Feb. 11, 1875. Senator Morrill of Vermont had written to the secretary of the Republican committee of his state on June 8, 1874, that the "mission" of the Republican party had not ended. It could "wash and be clean," which the Democratic party had no intention of doing, and, if it had, it could not find enough "soap and water" to do the work. But, on November 4, he concluded that the party had been "smashed." It must get rid of the Butlers, Carpenters and others who had been leading it to ruin.—Morrill Papers in Library of Congress.

[2] Long enough to even some old scores in a speech addressed to his enemies.—Cong. Record, 44th Cong. 1st sess., pp. 121-7.

in the speaker's chair, were now to be actively published from a seat upon the floor. Michael C. Kerr, a Democrat from Indiana, put forward by a caucus, of which L. Q. C. Lamar of Mississippi, an officer in the late vanquished Southern army and in the Confederacy's diplomatic service, was the chairman, was raised to the speakership. That veteran Democratic representative, Samuel J. Randall of Pennsylvania, William M. Morrison of Illinois and "Sunset" Cox of New York, were to be the leaders in preparing and advancing the business of the House. They succeeded to the positions that Butler, Garfield and Dawes had held. Morrison became chairman of the Committee on Ways and Means. In places of Radicals which would see them no more in the House, as in the Senate, were seated high civil officers of the late Confederacy and colonels and brigadiers in the "rebel" army. Alexander H. Stephens, Vice President of the Confederate States, one time Federal prisoner in Fort Warren, had appeared in the Georgia delegation in 1873. He had been re-elected and now became the chairman of a standing committee. From Georgia, too, came Benjamin H. Hill who had been a member of the Confederate Senate. Texas sent John H. Reagan, Postmaster General in Jefferson Davis's cabinet, one of his companions in the southward flight, after Lee's surrender at Appomattox, as well as "rebel" Colonels David B. Culberson and Roger Q. Mills, both of whom were to play prominent parts in this and succeeding Congresses.

From Virginia came General Eppa Hunton, who had sat also in the Forty-third Congress, Colonel George C. Cabell, Major Beverly B. Douglas, John Randolph Tucker and John Goode, Jr., all prominent secessionists. Goode had been a member of the Congress at Richmond. Confederate General Robert B. Vance, brother of Zebulon, who had been refused admittance to a seat in the Senate in 1870, and who did not enter that body until 1879, was a member of the delegation which was sent to Washington by North Carolina, as were Thomas S. Ashe, representative and senator in the "rebel" Congress, and Major Jesse J. Yeates and Colonel A. M. Waddell, of the "rebel" army. General Randall Lee Gibson was the foremost of three or four men, who had worn the "rebel gray," in the Louisiana delegation.

That all of the Southern states had not yet again come into the hands of the old white classes was indicated by the presence in the House of seven negroes.[1] In the Senate the race found a representative in a brilliant orator, Blanche K. Bruce, elected as General Alcorn's associate by the Republican legislature of Mississippi.[2]

Strange sights were these—stranger might be seen. Under the cloak of "loyalty" the Radicals hitherto had gone their way without restraint. Their forces were now reduced to a minority and they must turn their parliamentary skill into a new course. In opposition, no less than when in possession of power, they would principally rely upon the war and what it had brought forth. The daily records of Congress, now and for many years to come, would bristle with the ugly antipathies which hope of party advantage led the Republican politicians to revive, and which were made, through the press, to resound over the country. Of this rebirth of sectional bitterness more need not be said until we reach the campaign of 1876.

The majority would be intimidated in no way by the threat to lay before the country accounts of the record of their party, or of the careers of their leaders on the subject of secession. On January 14, 1876, soon after the members had returned from their Christmas holidays, resolutions were adopted instructing the committees of the House having to do with the appropriation of moneys, the Indians, the army, the navy, the post office, the public lands, claims and foreign affairs to inquire "into any errors, abuses or frauds" in those branches of the public service. The accounts of the expenditures of all the departments were to come under examination for injustice, extravagance and dishonesty.[3]

The new Congress had not commenced the inquiries which

[1] World Almanac for 1875, p. 63.
[2] Cf. A. K. McClure, Recollections of Half a Century, p. 254.
[3] Cong. Record, 44th Cong. 1st sess., p. 414.

led to the exposures in connection with the whiskey tax frauds,
though it forwarded them. Secretary of the Treasury Bristow
had given himself to this service immediately upon the assumption of the duties of his office in 1874, and had made himself
ready for action in 1875. The custom houses had been nests
of iniquity under the management of such collectors as "Tom"
Murphy in New York and Butler's friend, Simmons, in Boston,[1]
while, in independent, extra-legal places, men like Jayne and
Sanborn, with the aid of informers and spies, waxed fat out
of the service. In the best cases, all of the custom houses, under
the prevailing political system, were filled with vulgar and ignorant party "heelers," whose earnings were to be drawn
upon at regular intervals to aid in defraying the cost of electoral
campaigns. When they failed to pay their "assessments"
and to work for the success of the party ticket they were dismissed to make way for more biddable men.[2]

The internal revenue taxes were not collected in a more
honorable way, or by a finer body of civil servants. The distillers, in particular, were making fraudulent returns, and it
clearly appeared in Andrew Johnson's administration that
"rings" were actively engaged in conspiracies to cheat the
Treasury.[3] It was a veritably colossal scheme for the enrich-
ment of organized bands of thieves about which every one knew,
though there was none with the industry, the courage and the
authority to lay bare its intricacies and bring the great scandal
to an end.

The fraud, in the first instance, involved the storekeeper
or gauger, placed by the Commissioner of Internal Revenue at
the distillery. Of such officers there were in the service upwards of 2,300 and the misconduct of a number of them was

[1] Cf. Hoar, Autobiography, vol. ii, p. 2; N. Y. Nation, Feb. 26 and
March 5, 1874.
[2] Cf. contested election case, Abbott v. Frost, House Mis. Doc., 44th
Cong. 1st sess., no. 49.
[3] Johnson Papers; McDonald, Secrets of the Great Whiskey Ring,
revised ed., 1885, p. 32. Some of the men who had a part in this corruption were identified by Butler when he was pursuing the seven recusant
senators after the acquittal of President Johnson. See vol. ii of this work,
p. 145.

well known. Over these men stood higher officials, reaching to party managers, whose purses, in return for "protection," were fattened from the proceeds of the theft. The "Ring" had a "cashier," who received the moneys, perhaps, a half of the tax which the distiller ought to have paid the government, and this sum, being aggregated, was distributed among the conspirators, the amount which came into the coffers of some of the principals reaching a total of several hundred dollars a week. The other half of the tax represented the whiskey maker's share in the corrupt transaction—it was an extra profit on his sales. Such whiskey was called "crooked whiskey."[1] Men with small salaries were disporting themselves in precious stones, riding in fine carriages, living with their vulgar families at expensive hotels, maintaining summer homes.[2]

Whenever a motion was directed against those officers to whom suspicion pointed, the Commissioner at Washington found that notice of what he was about to do had preceded his action.[3] The rogues openly boasted at Washington, at St. Louis, at Saratoga, at Long Branch, that their power was greater than the Secretary of the Treasury's. At need or pleasure they could achieve the removal of the Commissioner of Internal Revenue, or of anyone else who crossed their way.[4]

The principal places at which this thievery throve, in so far as the Department could divine, were St. Louis, Milwaukee and Chicago, and Bristow, with fearless and commendable zeal, gave himself to the task of breaking up the system. He found that he could apply to this use a fund which had been put at the disposal of the Treasury Department for the punishment of counterfeiting and other crimes, and he directed the solicitor of the Treasury, Major Bluford Wilson, to proceed with vigor and celerity. A number of men, entirely detached from

[1] For an account of the arrangements in St. Louis see D. P. Dyer's testimony in House Mis. Doc., 44th Cong. 1st sess., no. 186.
[2] W. M. Grosvenor, quoted in McDonald, Secrets of the Great Whiskey Ring, p. 54.
[3] House Mis. Doc., 44th Cong. 1st sess., no. 186, p. 70; cf. McDonald, Secrets of the Great Whiskey Ring, p. 44.
[4] McDonald, op. cit., pp. 44–5; cf. House Mis. Doc., 44th Cong. 1st sess., no. 186, p. 87.

the internal revenue service, whose movements, therefore, could not be under suspicion, were employed to procure evidence upon which to base prosecutions.[1] The distillers were watched. The barrels were counted as they left the distilleries for the rectifying establishments, and checked against the returns made to the internal revenue office.[2] It was discovered that by duplication, and even triplication, in the use of tax-paid spirit stamps, the greatest frauds had been in progress since 1871. On a smaller scale, in this and other ways, thievery, by collusion between government agents and the liquor men, had been proceeding for a longer time.[3]

During the winter of 1874-75, and the following spring, the work of unearthing the robbers continued.[4] Now and again the detectives, as they pursued their investigations, were set upon and beaten. Bribery was attempted. Every anticipation was realized. Many of the culprits fled to Canada and to Europe. Political influences were invoked to save other men who were involved in the infamy.

The seizure of distilleries commenced in May, 1875, and a large number of cases were made ready for presentation to the Department of Justice, which, upon the retirement of George H. Williams as Attorney General, who, like others around Grant, was too indulgent of the corruptions so damaging to the administration, came under the more honorable direction of Edwards Pierrepoint, an eminent lawyer of New York City.

How gigantic the frauds were plainly appeared. In a period of three or four years a single firm had paid between $50,000 and $75,000 to a group of thieving revenue officers in Milwaukee.[5] In fourteen months five members of a "ring" in St. Louis divided a quarter of a million dollars—each received from $45,000 to $60,000 as his share of the plunder—which meant

[1] H. V. Boynton, North American Review, October, 1876.
[2] For St. Louis see Grosvenor's account in McDonald, op. cit., pp. 47-8.
[3] Cf. McDonald, op. cit., p. 33. There were also frauds in the collection of the tobacco tax.—Ibid., p. 27.
[4] See Bluford Wilson's and Yaryan's testimony, House Mis. Doc., 44th Cong. 1st sess., no. 186; cf. H. V. Boynton, North American Review, October, 1876, pp. 288-92.
[5] House Mis. Doc., 44th Cong. 1st sess., no. 186, p. 147.

that the government was defrauded of a half million dollars, since a similar amount had gone into the coffers of the distillers.[1] In ten months, from July 1, 1874, to May 1, 1875, on such transactions as were discovered and brought to the notice of the Commissioner of Internal Revenue, the government had been cheated out of $1,650,000 in taxes; in two years it was computed that the frauds had reached a total of $4,000,000.[2] All the while large contributions were demanded of, if they were not voluntarily paid by, the thieves for the Republican campaign committees. The revenue officers blackmailed the distillers, the politicians "higher up" blackmailed both the officers and the distillers.[3] The system, in all its intricacies, was such, said a whiskey man in Wisconsin, that he must steal $75,000 from the government to make a profit of $25,000 for himself.[4]

In principle the investigation commended itself to Grant. He, at first, gave his support to Bristow with a certain degree of earnestness, but soon it was made clear that the prosecutions would be far reaching.[5] Some of the men active in the rascality, as in other wrongs which marked this period of our history, had presumed upon their acquaintance with the President, and were relying upon the loyalty which he would show for a friend to save that friend from merited punishment.

The trouble commenced in St. Louis, where John McDonald was supervisor of internal revenue. He seems to have come to know Grant while they were campaigning together in the Mississippi Valley in the first years of the war. He had been speculating in cotton around Memphis and, with a brevet brigadier-generalship, which he had gained before laying off the uniform of a Union soldier, he combined a reputation which little commended him to honest judges of men in Missouri, where he resided. After the war, he, by his own account, was

[1] House Mis. Doc., 44th Cong. 1st sess., no. 186, p. 31.
[2] Report of Com. of Int. Revenue for 1875, pp. xvii–xviii. Much larger totals were named, and doubtless with truth, by other authorities. Cf. House Mis. Doc., 44th Cong. 1st sess., no. 186, p. 473.
[3] Cf. House Mis. Doc., 44th Cong. 1st sess., no. 186, pp. 145, 150.
[4] Ibid., p. 153.
[5] McDonald, Secrets of the Great Whiskey Ring, pp. 141–5.

a claim agent, in the prosecution of which business he was led
to Washington, where he called at the White House to renew
his acquaintance with Grant. The President, though his
citizenship was accredited to Illinois, had interests in and
around St. Louis which quite as closely attached him to Missouri. McDonald was offered a place in the revenue service
there and received the appointment, notwithstanding the
protests of Schurz and the Liberal Republican leaders.[1] Such
action seems to have been regarded as a shrewd flank movement
directed against the opposition to the administration which had
developed in that state, and McDonald soon assumed a position as the President's adviser in reference to Missouri politics,
bringing newspapers to Grant's support, raising campaign
funds and manipulating politicians in the interest of the Republican party.[2] Whether the President knew of the existence
of a "Whiskey Ring," or not, the least talent for comprehension must have made it clear to him, from the first, that the
money poured out of McDonald's cornucopia of plenty was
procured, by some means, from the distillers.

The relations of the two men grew in cordiality. It was soon
remarked that Grant had chosen McDonald, not only as a
supervisor of revenue and a political representative in Missouri,
but also as a personal friend, an attachment to be shared by
his private secretary, General Orville E. Babcock.[3] McDonald
entertained Grant lavishly during his visit to St. Louis in
1874. Many presents came to the White House from this
rich and influential patron—among them a pair of fine horses,
a handsome "buggy," a "buggy" whip, for which the giver
boasted that he had paid $25, and harness embellished with
"gold breast plates" on which Grant's name was engraved—
all sent forward to Washington in a special car in charge of
one of the men employed on the President's Missouri farm.[4]
McDonald was frequently in Washington, where he could be
seen riding with Grant on "the avenue." This friend, it was

[1] McDonald, Secrets of the Great Whiskey Ring, pp. 21–6, 39.
[2] Ibid., pp. 35–6, 41–2.
[3] House Mis. Doc., 44th Cong. 1st sess., no. 186, p. 333.
[4] McDonald, Secrets of the Great Whiskey Ring, pp. 45–6, 96–103, 109.

early discerned by Bristow and his assistants, who were exploring the field, was deeply involved in the scandal which was
about to be disclosed; and worse was in store for the President,
on the subject of one much nearer to his heart, a member of
his own most intimate official household. Bristow and Bluford
Wilson had discovered telegrams, supporting hearsay and
suspicion, current now for some time, seriously implicating
Babcock in the frauds.

In Chicago the investigation brought the "ring" close to
Congressman Farwell and Senator Logan;[1] in Milwaukee to
the doors of Matt Carpenter, the glib and dexterous lawyer,
noted for his cynical apologies for corruption in public life,
in the United States Senate, where he held the seat earlier
occupied by Mr. Doolittle;[2] in San Francisco to Senator Sargent.[3]

It was plain, as soon as the pursuit of the scoundrels was
fairly started, that, through such newspapers, such politicians,
such social connections, as might be brought to the service,
every obstruction which could be put in the path of Mr. Bristow
would be placed there. Since coming to his office, he, by a
variety of activities, in the public behalf, had made enemies
of all the "rings" and combinations which were in existence
for defrauding the government through the Treasury Department.[4] Detectives were set upon him and Major Wilson to
undermine and damage, if possible, their public and private
reputations.[5] Letters were forged, and, for months, a campaign
of falsehood was continued in order to implant in the President's mind a distrust for and antipathy to the accusers of
his private secretary. Grant's and Mrs. Grant's relations in
and around St. Louis, and friends and acquaintances of these
relations who had connections with the conspirators, tried to
make their influences felt at the White House. Casey, the

[1] House Mis. Doc. 44th Cong. 1st sess., no. 186, pp. 372, 412 et seq., 450.
[2] Ibid., pp. 145–322, passim; N. Y. Nation, Jan. 28 and Feb. 11, 1875;
J. S. Black, Essays and Speeches, pp. 209–11.
[3] Cf. Yaryan's testimony, House Mis. Doc., 44th Cong. 1st sess., no. 186.
[4] Boynton, North American Review, October, 1876.
[5] Ibid.

150 BRISTOW'S DIFFICULTIES

brother-in-law in the collector's office in New Orleans, who was
so black a stain upon the history of the administration, appeared
upon the scene to do what he might to impede the course of
justice.

A Presidential campaign impended. Much offered by way
of defense in this direction. It was an attack upon the Republican party,[1] upon the President personally.[2] The investigation
and the prosecutions, coming out of it, were directed by enemies
of the administration. Bristow was a candidate for the Presidential nomination in 1876. Wilson was a "Bristow man."
Grant listened to the tattle of relations, McDonald, the "persecuted" Babcock and another private secretary, Levi Luckey;
letters came to the White House in every mail; Logan and others
called to fill him with suspicion and prejudice,[3] which were so
easily awakened when any one questioned the wisdom of his
purposes or the supremacy of his authority.

A Federal district attorney, named Dyer, was diligently
preparing and trying cases in St. Louis; he was or had been a
Democrat. Ex-Senator John B. Henderson was the "special
assistant" attorney, engaged there in directing the prosecutions[4]
which he did with acknowledged ability and very great effect.
Henderson had been one of the seven "traitors" in the Andrew
Johnson impeachment court in 1868. He was declared to be
an "enemy" of Grant and of the Republican party. The
"lying and plotting" was "scandalous."[5]

Bristow's position was barely tenable, and he had told Grant
as much at Long Branch in August, 1875. The time had come,
he wrote Bluford Wilson, when he "must make a square issue
with the thieves and scoundrels" who had "combined to destroy
him." He would not "turn back"; he would not "stop to
parley with thieves." He had "no ambition to serve and no
purpose to accomplish but the enforcement of the law and an

---

[1] McDonald told Grant that an exposure of the operations of the "Ring"
would reveal "the sources from which its [the Republican party's] life was
derived, and that the party would collapse like a balloon rent by lightning."
—Secrets of the Great Whiskey Ring, p. 144.

[2] House Mis. Doc., 44th Cong. 1st sess., no. 186, pp. 73–4, 115, 124.

[3] Ibid., p 326.   [4] Ibid., p. 361.   [5] Ibid., p. 364.

honest collection of the revenue." [1] He required some statement from the President which would set at rest the reports
that he was acting without authority.[2] This he thought that
he might be given in an endorsement which Grant some days
earlier had put upon a letter from a relation in St. Louis.
Though it had been marked "confidential," Bristow would publish it, and, after some urging, as it seems, on Bristow's part, the
President said that it might be given to the press.[3] One phrase—
"Let no guilty man escape"—soon rang up and down the
country, and became a party slogan for many months to come.[4]
But it was seen and felt by Bristow that Grant had no cordial
or valuable interest in the pursuit of the "guilty." In particular did the determination to punish Babcock, who had been
using his high place to shield the thieves, if he played no worse
part in connection with the operations of the "ring," awaken
a resentment in the President which he took little care to conceal.

In the midst of the excitement Grant, or Babcock for him,
resolved upon another visit to St. Louis. While there, in
September, 1875, though McDonald was under indictment,
Babcock repeatedly conferred with the accused man, and
discussed with him the plight in which they together were
involved, the possibility of dismissing Bristow, and of pardon,
in the worst case, if they should "hear the turn of the bolt"
on their liberties.[5] Grant himself publicly met McDonald
and on the occasion made the man some pledges of his sympathy.[6] Upon the President's return to Washington he was
still less inclined to accord Bristow his hearty support.

The truth is that Babcock had come to have a power over
Grant as great as Rawlins's had been. But, while Rawlins's

[1] House Mis. Doc., 44th Cong. 1st sess., no. 186, p. 363.
[2] Ibid., pp. 357, 486.
[3] Or it was published without his consent.—Cf. ibid., p. 349.
[4] In this endorsement Grant wrote—"Let no guilty man escape, if it
can be avoided. Be specially vigilant, or instruct those engaged in the
prosecutions of fraud to be, against all who insinuate that they have high
influence to protect them. No personal consideration should stand in
the way of performing a public duty."—Ibid., p. 485.
[5] McDonald, Secrets of the Great Whiskey Ring, pp. 201–208.
[6] Ibid., pp. 209–10.

influence had been strengthening, that of Babcock was wholly malign; while one had made him into a hero for the country to admire, the other was allying him for present contemplation and for the view of posterity with corrupt causes and foul men. Quick of intelligence, debonair, ingratiating, with qualities calculated to make him as popular in a ladies' drawing-room as in a soldier's mess,[1] Babcock was liked not only by Grant and the members of Grant's family, but he was also a favorite figure in those circles which in the 1870's answered for "Washington society."[2] To this man all roads led; through him vagabond and thief spoke to the President. It was noted that he was a graduate of West Point. While private secretary he continued to hold his place in the army as a major of the corps of engineers. Since June 1, 1871, he had been commissioner of public buildings and grounds in the District of Columbia,[3] in which post he was associated with "Boss" Shepherd, wherefore Grant's marked indulgence of the "District Ring." For at least a part of the time, since that date, he had also been chief engineer of the government waterworks.[4] Earlier, it will be remembered, he had gone to San Domingo to annex that little black state to the Union. Such a many-sided genius had scarce ever been seen in the White House; a more artful and crafty one had never achieved a free hand to mould the mind of a President of the United States.

If Babcock were a rascal he should be punished, Grant had said, but this friend of his was not a rascal, and his own opinion he put above other men's and the evidence. The President wanted the facts, but he would allow no one to give them to him. In pursuing Babcock, Dyer and Henderson were more than that man's enemies; they had shown themselves to be hostile, Grant said, to him personally. He would have dismissed them both cheerfully. The opportunity with reference

[1] Cf. Morrill Papers, Library of Congress.
[2] By this it is not meant that there was not a permanent group of intelligent, cultivated and socially congenial persons in Washington. They remained while administrations with their official and political glamor passed on.
[3] Ibid., pp., 352, 372.
[4] House Reports, 42nd Cong., 2nd sess. no. 72, p. 628.

to Henderson came in December, 1875. It was brought to
Grant's attention that in a recent speech, while prosecuting
a member of the St. Louis "ring," Henderson had reflected
upon the honor of the President.[1] Instantly he was relieved
from further duty. Attorney General Pierrepont who, at
first, had given unequivocal support to Bristow, now, through
influences centered in the White House, on January 26,
1876, was made to send a letter of instructions to Dyer and
the other district attorneys calculated, so it was held by
many men, including the Committee on the Judiciary of the
House,[2] to arrest the machinery which was moving in the
interest of justice.[3]

Babcock and his minions were allowed to meddle with the
case which was being made up against him. In this he had
Grant's active aid.[4] Defeated at various points in efforts to
turn aside the officers of the Treasury and the Attorney General's
Departments, detectives were used to discover what was the
evidence in hand against the man who stood so amazingly high
in the President's favor, and to abstract, suppress and destroy
papers pointing to his culpability.[5] One of these fellows named
Bell, who seems to have conferred repeatedly with the President, trying in vain to get into the Department of Justice
to spy upon Dyer and steal important documents, was quartered
on the Interior Department. While drawing a salary as an
employee of the Pension Bureau, he was engaged in breaking
down the case against Babcock. When it was found that the
sleuth could or would render no valuable service, indeed had

[1] House Mis. Doc., 44th Cong. 1st sess., no. 186, pp. 5–6, 69–70; Mc-
Donald, op. cit., pp. 223–6.

[2] House Reports, 44th Cong. 1st sess., no. 352.

[3] Clearly calculated to have this effect if there is even a semblance of
truth in McDonald's statement that it was drafted by Babcock's attorney
in St. Louis, who carried it to Washington for Grant, through Pierrepont,
to promulgate. (McDonald, op. cit., pp. 228–41; cf. Pierrepont's, Bluford
Wilson's, Brodhead's and Eaton's testimony in House Mis. Doc., 44th
Cong. 1st sess., no. 186, p. 367.) Certain it is that Babcock, procuring a
copy of the letter, caused its publication.—House Reports, 44th Cong.
1st sess., no. 352, p. 6: cf. H. V. Boynton, North American Review, October,
1876.

[4] House Mis. Doc., 44th Cong. 1st sess., no. 186, p. 367.

[5] Ibid., pp. 11, 75, 117, 136.

turned to the other side, he was dismissed from his sinecure.[1]
A man named Fox, who had been a member of the grand jury
which had indicted Babcock, went to Washington and gave
information to Grant about proceedings in the jury room.[2]
For what he was doing to defeat the ends of justice his son, a
youth not yet of age, who had had a malarial fever and needed
a change of climate, was appointed United States consul at
Brunswick, Germany.[3]

Finally, all else failing, when Babcock saw that he was to
be summoned to St. Louis for his trial, he, as an officer of the
army, asked to be taken before a military court. Grant welcomed this suggestion and earnestly forwarded the plan. The
papers in the case which Dyer had assembled at St. Louis were
demanded. They should be sent to Chicago for the use of the
three generals, Sheridan, Hancock and Terry, whom the President had assigned to the service,[4] and who, beginning December 9, 1875, were to sit on the evidence before a friendly
judge advocate.[5] This proceeding, it was shrewdly supposed,
would supersede and do away with the trial before a civil
tribunal.[6]

But Dyer held on valiantly; he would not surrender papers
which were his for use under another jurisdiction.[7] The inquiry at Chicago was cut short by reason of the progress of
events at St. Louis, where preparation for the civil trial continued. The military court was dissolved and Babcock, in
February, 1876, was brought before a "jury of his peers."
Expensive and cunning counsel had been engaged to defend
him. The court room in St. Louis was crowded, the neighbor-
ing streets were packed with curious men and women. The

[1] Testimony of C. S. Bell, House Reports, 44th Cong., 1st sess., no. 799,
pp. 357 et seq.; also in House Mis. Doc., 44th Cong. 1st sess., no 186.

[2] House Mis. Doc., 44th Cong. 1st sess., no. 186, pp. 40–41.

[3] Testimony of Elias W. Fox in ibid.; McDonald, Secrets of the Great
Whiskey Ring, pp. 215–8, 232.

[4] Testimony of Pierrepont, House Mis. Doc., 44th Cong. 1st sess., no. 186.

[5] Cf. ibid., p. 369; House Ex. Doc., 44th Cong. 1st sess., no. 142.

[6] House Mis. Doc., 44th Cong. 1st sess., no. 186, p. 490.

[7] Dyer's testimony in ibid. A very unfavorable view of Pierrepont's
course at this time is given in Boynton, North American Review, October,
1876.

trial began and proceeded amid expressions of nation-wide interest and solicitude. The now famous defendant made no attempt to deal frankly by those who still hoped that he would be shown to be innocent. Instead of endeavoring to explain away the evidences of his venality he relied upon the trickery of the law to keep them out of the record. Witnesses were suborned[1] to break down truthful testimony. Grant had been sworn before the Chief Justice in Washington. He made a deposition [2] in Babcock's favor which had, as was intended, great influence upon the judge and jury,[3] and the prisoner went free, in spite of the conviction of all who were concerned in the management of the case, a feeling shared by the country at large, that he had been guilty of playing a most opprobrious part in the conspiracy. Without his assistance, and that of other persons close to the administration, the whiskey "rings," in other cities as well as in St. Louis, could not have been formed, and, if formed, they would have been detected and dispersed a long time since.

At the end of the trial Babcock's friends crowded around him in the court room to congratulate him. In the evening he was serenaded at his hotel and stood up in a carriage to make a speech to the mob. Telegrams poured in upon him calling the acquittal a "triumph of justice." He was being persecuted by "rebel influence." "Glory to God!" "God is good!" and other profanations of the name of the Almighty, contained in the messages from his admirers, many of them confederates in his mischiefs, must have caused him to think himself destined for a place in history among the Christian martyrs. [4] Before his return to Washington he visited the jail to make new promises to his friend McDonald bearing upon that transgressor's pardon by the President.

Babcock's instant dismissal as private secretary was expected,

[1] House Mis. Doc., 44th Cong. 1st sess., no. 186, pp. 90–91; McDonald, op. cit., pp. 245–54.
[2] Text in N. Y. Tribune, Feb. 18, 1876, and McDonald, op. cit., pp. 256 et seq.
[3] McDonald, pp. 285–6.
[4] N. Y. Tribune, Feb. 25 and 28, 1876.

but Grant made no motion in this direction. The man carried executive communications to Congress as before. When he appeared in the Senate the Republican leaders gathered in a knot around him to express their satisfaction at his "escape from his enemies," and rich patrons of the Grant administration [1] made up a purse of $25,000 or $30,000 to pay the fees of lawyers and meet other expenses attendant upon the struggle which the President's valued secretary had made to gain his liberty.[2]

But the current against him was running too strong; in a few days he resigned, still, however, to retain his rank in the army, detailed, through the Secretary of War, to duty in connection with the government of the District of Columbia.

What Grant had done with reference to offenders in St. Louis was done also in Chicago, Milwaukee and San Francisco. Men whose wicked courses marked them for prompt and ignominious dismissal were permitted to retire at their leisure, when indeed, so much notice was taken of the storm of popular wrath following the disclosures of their guilt.[3] Often the President delayed the acceptance of their letters of resignation and included in his replies expressions of regret.

Clearly Bristow and Bluford Wilson could remain not much longer at their posts. Immediately upon the acquittal of Babcock, in February, 1876, they were on the point of resigning. Indeed, it is said, that the President had resolved upon Bristow's removal. He had written a letter in which the Secretary of the Treasury was roughly denounced, and which he would give to the press in justification of the course he was about to take.[4] But at this conjuncture statements were laid before him accusing Babcock of being implicated in the "Gold Conspiracy," which had culminated in "Black Friday" in

---

[1] Including men like Zachariah Chandler, Chester A. Arthur, and other Federal office holders, together with Borie of Philadelphia, whose friendship for Grant had already cost him so dear.

[2] N. Y. Tribune, April 17, 1876; McDonald, op. cit., pp. 284, 345.

[3] Cf. House Mis. Doc., 44th Cong. 1st sess., no. 186, pp. 343–4, 487–8.

[4] Boynton, North American Review, Oct., 1876, p. 319; cf. Bluford Wilson's testimony in House Mis. Doc., 44th Cong. 1st sess., no. 186, pp. 343–4, 487–8.

1869,[1] and, of more immediate interest, in a short while, allegations that he had been the instigator of the safe burglary in April, 1874, in the office of the United States attorney of the District of Columbia.

This intrigue enjoyed the glamor of some Oriental romance. A committee of an earlier Congress had been reluctantly induced to investigate the subject.[2] It was clear that in the middle of the night some persons, for reasons of their own, had stolen books or papers from the City Hall in Washington, and then had blown open a fireproof safe to cover the crime; that one or more unknown men had been employed by other men, equally unknown, for the work, and that the conspiracy involved the fame of a respected and prominent citizen of Washington, Columbus Alexander, an outspoken foe of "Boss" Shepherd who had been engaged in the work of exposing the corruptions of the "District Ring." That they had "bungled the job" so that the low plot had miscarried was also clear. But the committee, after a few weeks of inquiry, abandoned it. The matter now fell into the hands of Bluford Wilson and Secretary Bristow of the Treasury Department. Defying the influences around Grant, whom they were to meet in yet closer quarters in their battle with the Whiskey Ring, they boldly cleared the Treasury Department of a "whole division" in New York, which had been implicated in the conspiracy, and, with the assistance of the Department of Justice, ran down the principal culprits, several of whom were arrested and put on trial. The proceedings came to nothing—the jury had been packed, in the interest of the men who were being tried,[3] by the forces which, in the first instance, were seen to be at work in the development of the plot.

But the matter was not to end here. The government, during the war, had been using spies for many purposes.[4] Detec-

---

[1] House Mis. Doc., 44th Cong. 1st sess., no. 186, p. 369.

[2] House Reports, 43rd Cong. 1st sess., no. 785; H. V. Boynton, Am. Law Review, April, 1877.

[3] N. Y. Nation, Dec. 3, 1874. That his sympathies might not be mistaken Grant, or Babcock for him, invited one of the offenders to a reception in the White House.—Ibid.

[4] H. V. Boynton, Am. Law Review, April, 1877.

tives were still in the public service and they were now being
employed by scamps, who had got into high places, to further
their private ends. No honest official, no good citizen, as it
appeared, was safe from espionage. Some of these hired informers had turned against Babcock at St. Louis; another one
now served him in the same manner on the subject of the safe
burglary when the Forty-fourth Congress reopened the investigation. No other than the President's secretary, the same
Babcock, through others, in his alternate capacity as commissioner of public grounds and buildings in the District of Columbia, it was now alleged, had engaged professional criminals to
steal the papers and explode the safe. They had contrived the
plot with the purpose of defaming and fastening a crime upon
an upright man, Mr. Alexander, of taking him into court and
convicting him and imprisoning him, in order to prevent him
from pursuing the leaders of Shepherd's "Ring."

For quite two years the influences closely connected with the
Grant administration had been used to protect the guilty persons. The New York Tribune called it "the most infamous
conspiracy in the criminal annals of the country." [1]   It was
sufficiently evil, indeed, when it reached the very doors of
the White House. The facts were in no kind of doubt [2] and the
grand jury, on April 16, indicted Babcock and a half dozen
other men—the assistant United States district attorney who
had been on trial before, a former chief of the United States
secret service, a government detective, a disreputable New
York lawyer, a professional safe burglar and a villain who had
commended himself to the conspirators through his skill as a
housebreaker and a thief. Babcock was released to await trial
on $10,000 bail, which was provided by his friend "Boss"
Shepherd. [3]

The culprits escaped, thanks again to a packed jury, but the

[1] Issue of April 17, 1876.
[2] H. V. Boynton, loc. cit., April, 1877.
[3] N. Y. Tribune, April 17, 1876; Wilson, Life of C. A. Dana, pp. 434–5;
Letters and Memorials of Tilden, vol. ii, pp. 499–500; H. V. Boynton,
in Am. Law Review, a complete and most valuable account of the conspiracy.

developments, so damaging to the administration and the prospects of the Republican party, whose meeting to nominate candidates for the national campaign directly impended, made further immediate action on the subject of the dismissal of Bristow and Bluford Wilson by Grant not very feasible,[1] and the Secretary of the Treasury and his solicitor remained in office until June 20, 1876, when they quietly left the scene, unhonored by the President, as it appears, in expressions of appreciation for their useful labors, or of regret for their departure from their posts.[2]

Nearly all of the men sentenced to prison for their parts in the whiskey frauds were pardoned before many weeks or months had passed, and Babcock, as the Grant administration drew to its close, had new evidence of the friendly President's continued confidence in him in his appointment as an inspector of lighthouses.

Congress, in an examination into the whiskey frauds, brought before a select committee Attorney General Pierrepont, Secretary Bristow, Bluford Wilson, General Henderson, Senator Logan, Senator Carpenter, and a large number of men acquainted with the facts, further to impress upon the country the extraordinary circumstances attending the thefts, and the attempts which had been made to shield the thieves. Not at any time before in the various exhibitions of Grant's weakness of judgment, the vanity which power had brought to him, the credulity of his nature, if not actual stupidity of his mind, had the nation right to feel itself so deeply humiliated through his being its chief magistrate.[3]

Still more dishonor was being prepared for him through his misplaced trust in the untried, even unknown, man whom, at

[1] House Mis. Doc., 44th Cong. 1st sess., no. 186, p. 369.
[2] Ibid., p. 372. Cf. H. V. Boynton, N. A. Review, Oct., 1876, p. 321.
[3] That Grant had the opportunity to know much of the "Ring's" operations, and that Babcock was closely held to the leaders of it by gifts and payments of money, are made clear by indisputable evidence in the testimony given before Congressional committees, which was informingly supplemented in 1880 by McDonald's Secrets of the Great Whiskey Ring, an historical document, as well as a unique revelation of the mind of a public thief.

Rawlins's death, he had placed at the head of the War Department. Belknap, a small revenue collector in Iowa, it was remembered, had been appointed to a place, concerning which the President, as a military man, should have had the most responsible feelings, because of some favor at one time extended by the appointee to a member of the Grant family. It now appeared that this high officer of the government, sitting at the President's own council table, had been involved in a corruption which, immediately upon its discovery, earned him the contempt of the whole country without regard to party. Prior to 1867 sutlers were appointed by the officers in command; later, by the General of the Army. Since 1870 this power had been exercised by the Secretary of War,[1] to the gross affront, in many cases, of the military commanders in the territory.[2] Post traders these dealers had come to be called, and they enjoyed the exclusive privilege of selling goods upon military reservations to army officers, soldiers, Indians and emigrants. A long time since [3] the farming out of these places had been denounced as a disgrace to our public life,[4] but no one had gained, or used, the evidence to attack the system as it should have been attacked. Now no less a person than the Secretary of War was to be entangled in this wickedness. A House committee had barely commenced to investigate his department— only a week had passed since the ending of Babcock's trial at St. Louis—when it was reported that Belknap had been guilty of malfeasance in office.

Belknap had once told a man who had tendered him $10,000 for a post tradership "that he would kick him down stairs."[5] It would have been better had he resolved to continue in this exemplary course. Now one who had done some kindness to Mrs. Belknap was offered valuable privileges at Fort Sill in Indian Territory. But the trader at that place, already in position, agreed to pay $15,000, if he might continue to hold

[1] House Reports, 44th Cong. 1st sess., no. 799, p. ii.
[2] Cf. J. E. Walker, Campaigns of General Custer, p. 44.
[3] N. Y. Tribune, Feb. 16, 1872.
[4] Cf. Cong. Record, Trial of W. W. Belknap, p. 233.
[5] House Reports, 44th Cong. 1st sess., no. 186, p. 3.

the lucrative office. He actually did pay from $6,000 to $12,000 a year, from and after 1870, throughout all of which time a half of the sum, or about $40,000 in all, was sent by the broker to the Secretary of War, or to some member of the Belknap family.

There was no defense. Belknap, knowing that he faced impeachment proceedings, on the morning of March 2, 1876, sent his resignation to the President, who accepted it at once "with great regret." In a few minutes the communication was presented to the investigating committee and the offender had, so it was supposed, put himself out of the reach of pursuit.[1] Congress would meet at noon. Not to be cheated of fair prey by such a trick the committee unanimously recommended that the House should impeach the man of "high crimes and misdemeanors," and appoint five members to proceed to the bar of the Senate, there, in the name of the "House of Representatives and of all the people of the United States of America," to inform it that charges were in preparation, and requesting it "to take such order in the premises" as might be deemed appropriate. Hiester Clymer, chairman of the committee, declared that it was a record of official corruption and crimes "such as has no parallel in our own history," or, so far as he knew, in that of any other country.[2] After some brief discussion of the point as to jurisdiction with reference to an officer who had ceased to be an officer,—this action had been taken but a few hours since with the manifest purpose of escaping judgment—the House, without a dissenting vote, impeached the Secretary of War,[3] and a committee, entrusted with the duty of announcing the fact, appeared at the bar of the Senate. That body immediately referred the subject to a select committee, of which Senator Edmunds of Vermont was the chairman.[4]

The articles of impeachment were prepared and passed by the House on April 3, and seven members—Scott Lord of New York, J. Proctor Knott of Kentucky, William P. Lynde of

[1] House Report, 44th Cong. 1st sess., no. 186, pp. 1–2, 10–11; Trial of W. W. Belknap, p. 71.
[2] Cong. Record, 44th Cong. 1st sess., p. 1429.
[3] Ibid., p. 1433.   [4] Ibid., p. 1436.

Wisconsin, John A. McMahon of Ohio, **George A. Jenks** of Pennsylvania, Elbridge G. Lapham of New York and George F. Hoar of Massachusetts were appointed managers of the impeachment.[1]

The case followed the course recently taken in the trial of Andrew Johnson, which was fresh in the public mind. On April 5, Chief Justice Waite entered the Senate chamber and the senators were sworn as members of the court. Adjournment was taken until the 17th, when Belknap and his counsel, Jeremiah S. Black, Montgomery Blair and Matt H. Carpenter, appeared to declare that he was a "private citizen of the United States and of the state of Iowa," and, therefore, not within the jurisdiction of the court.[2] After plea, replication, rejoinder, and sur-rejoinder had been filed, and the two sides had been heard, the senators, on May 29, by a vote of 37 to 29, determined that Belknap was "amenable to trial," [3] but it was July 6 before any progress was made with the case. Between that time and August 1, when the vote was taken, the witnesses were called, and managers and counsel wrangled over technical questions as to the introduction of evidence. The division upon the subject of jurisdiction made it entirely clear that no conviction could be secured. Two-thirds of the senators would not find the culprit "guilty."

No one anywhere had the slightest reason to doubt his culpability; no attempt was made to deny the facts. The arguments of his counsel were directed to the question of jurisdiction, and included the allegations that he had fought for his country at Shiloh and with Sherman on the march to the sea, with mawkish allusions to the relations which his wives[4] and

---

[1] Cong. Record, 44t Cong. 1sth sess., pp. 2159–60.

[2] Trial, p. 6.

[3] Ibid., p. 76.

[4] He had married sisters in turn. The truth seemed to be expressed by the New York Nation—"The fall of Mr. Belknap is generally ascribed, and with considerable appearance of truth, to his wife's desire, and doubtless also his own, to live handsomely. She . . . required considerably more money than her husband's income to reach the standard of gentility in the matter of meat, drink, clothing and carriages set up by the people among whom she sought to shine, and she got it out of the sutlers, and they out of the soldiers and settlers on the plains."—Issue of March 16, 1876.

his child held to the contract, and observations concerning the general spirit of the day, which induced the President himself to accept gifts and benefits from almost any one. In particular did Black thrust his keen rapier between the joints of Grant's visor. Was "one measure of justice" to be used for the President and another for this "fallen minister"? "Enormous contributions" were taken from the post traders by the Republican party to forward its cause in electoral campaigns. Was this corruption? General Belknap, he dared to say, had "not acted criminally any more" than other men in the "executive administration." If such be corruption then "all the officers of the government" were "thriving by corruption alone." [1]

Nor could the party associates of the guilty man say aught in extenuation of his infamy. George F. Hoar, one of the managers of the impeachment, always conspicuous as a partisan, declared it a "shameless doctrine" that "the true way by which power should be gained in the republic" was "to bribe the people with the offices created for their service." He asked the Senate not to lay down its high functions "before the sophistries and jeers of the criminal lawyer," alluding to Black and other counsel for Belknap; not "to speculate about the political calculations as to the effect on one party or the other," till it had induced his judges "to connive at the escape of the great public criminal." "Corruption and bribery" should meet "their lawful punishment." [2]

The "great public criminal" did escape. Twelve Republican senators joined the Democrats in voting for conviction, the number including Dawes of Massachusetts, Edmunds and Morrill of Vermont and Sherman of Ohio. But leaders of the administration, like Conkling, Logan and Boutwell, took refuge behind the question of jurisdiction and voted for acquittal.[3] Thus were the records of the country smirched with

[1] Trial, p. 318.
[2] Ibid., p. 63; Hoar, Autobiography of 70 Years, vol. i, pp. 307-9.
[3] Trial, p. 545; cf. ibid., pp. 81 and 356. Morton fell in a committee room and sent word by Sherman that he could not come in to express his opinion in the case.

the story of jobbery by a high officer of the national government, as it seemed, without effect. Yet the proceedings were not in vain. They emphasized the crime and put it in a position where lasting lessons might be drawn from it. The man's name was inscribed on the roll of our principal public scoundrels for succeeding generations to look at and contemplate. He had confessed his guilt, fled from its consequences and won his immunity for the want of a dozen votes.[1]

The conclusion of Belknap's friends, as they argued against his amenability to impeachment, that his punishment should be left to the courts led to his arrest on criminal charges, but, as could have been foreseen, the case was nol. pros.-ed by order of the Attorney General with the approval of the President.[2]

Grant's attitude toward this corruption, as toward Babcock's, was one of indifference, if not of active and open sympathy for the accused man. Those who dared to appear against the Secretary of War he proscribed. General Custer, when he was brought on from the Indian country to testify against Belknap, upon calling at the White House to pay his respects to the President, was left to cool his heels in an ante-room, and was pursued vindictively by official orders meant to humiliate him personally and even to lower his position in the service.[3]

That the President had made so much haste to accept Belknap's resignation, when he had waited for days and weeks before acting upon the cases of thieves involved in the operations of the whiskey "rings," made no pleasing impression upon the public mind.[4] Clearly enough he was playing the game of Belknap and the Republican politicians, who were advising the Secretary of War as to his course in taking himself, if it could be done, out of the reach of the impeaching authority.

[1] Cf. House Reports, 44th Cong. 1st sess., no. 791.
[2] N. Y. Nation, Feb. 15, 1877.
[3] Infra, p. 410.
[4] Grant was "made of such coarse material as to be impervious to public opinion," the New York Nation concluded. (Issue of December 3, 1874.) He was "an ignorant soldier," Mr. Godkin said again, without enough exaggeration to awaken expressions of dissent from the intelligent part of the country, to the attention of which his useful paper came each week, "coarse in his tastes and blunt in his perceptions, fond of money and material enjoyment and of low company."—Issue of March 9, 1876.

Another fact was brought forward. The President and his "trusted companions," as George F. Hoar ironically denominated the evil men gathered around Grant,[1] had had abundant opportunity to know of Belknap's rascality. It was made plain in the trial that the New York Tribune, as long ago as in February, 1872, had published the facts concerning the corruption,[2] including the charges that extortions were laid upon the soldiers by the post trader in the case, because he must pay continuously for the privileges which he enjoyed, that this publication had disturbed the peace of mind of the Secretary of War, if not of other men to whose attention it came, that the commanding officer at Fort Sill, where the facts were common knowledge, corroborated them in official letters to the War Department,[3] that these and other documents, bearing on the case, were accessible to the President and to his advisers, and that the transaction could have been detected and the guilty secretary dismissed four years since. An officer, bold enough to report the facts, was actually cashiered and disabled from making further complaint with, as it appears, the approval of the President.[4] The conviction was compelling that honest men in the army knew it to be useless to bring such conditions to the notice of the Department, or to the President, as commander-in-chief, so long as the atmosphere in Washington was so heavy with malignity, as it was in these unhappy years.

The committee which had discovered Belknap's guilty part in the sale of the Fort Sill tradership meantime proceeded with its investigation unrelentingly, and corruptions were found in other quarters. Although the Indian traderships were in control of the Commissioner of Indian Affairs, attached to the Interior Department, one subject was interlocked with the other, and the inquiry brought to view similar practices in that related field of administration. Brokerage in these valuable offices had developed until it was in no way unusual. Friends and relations, or friends and relations of those friends and relations, of Grant or Mrs. Grant, or of Belknap, or of Babcock, it was

[1] Autobiography, vol. i, p. 308.
[2] Trial, pp. 177, 206-7.
[3] Ibid., p. 178.
[4] Ibid., pp. 306, 312-3.

made to appear, were involved in the sale and enjoyment of
this patronage. One, a General Hedrick, with access to Belknap, was shown to have received no less that $20,750 in con-
nection with five sutlerships; another, a General Rice, was
paid by traders $15,250 for his friendly offices at Washington,
in the same matter. In addition these two men held interests
as partners in the businesses conducted at various posts. Without the investment of a dollar they regularly received shares of
the profits arising from the operation of the monopolies thus
granted to favorites by the War and Interior Departments.[1]

The President's brother, Orvil L. Grant, no more skillful
in any business adventure than he himself had been, asking for
favors, had been told of opportunities that awaited him on the
upper Missouri River. A well-known and competent firm engaged in transportation in that region held several army and
Indian traderships. These privileges were to be taken away
and, with the active support of the administration at Washington, "brother Orvil" in 1874, appeared as a broker for their
sale. In return for his influence in securing the licenses to trade
for men whom he would put in these posts, he, for the investment of no money, became a partner with them and shared
their profits,[2] while he remained in the East, never, except
once, having even visited the country in which the business
was carried on.[3] So far did the machination of these men who
were confusing commerce and politics proceed, that they, so
it was alleged, brought about an extension of the Sioux Indian
reservation. With the ostensible end of suppressing the liquor
traffic that reservation was made to include the east bank of
the Missouri River. Whatever the motive influencing this
action, the effect of the order on this subject was to drive out

[1] House Reports, 44th Cong. 1st sess., no. 799, p. iii; cf. opinion of
minority member of the committee (Ibid., p. xxv) who is obliged to speak
of the "shame and disgrace" of the "great scandal." Hedrick at the
same time was a supervisor of internal revenue at a salary of $3,000 a year
(Ibid., p. iii) and was involved in the whiskey frauds.—House Mis. Doc.,
44th Cong. 1st sess., no. 186, pp. 187, 189.

[2] House Reports, 44th Cong. 1st sess., no. 799, p. viii; House Mis. Doc.
44th. Cong. 1st sess., no. 167, pp. 329–35, 341–44, 348; cf. N. Y. Nation,
Dec. 3, 1874.

[3] House Reports, 44th Cong. 1st sess., no. 799, p. 28.

of business rival traders and increase the profits of the dealers with whom Orvil Grant was confederated.[1] In response to these revelations the President's brother, part and product of the period, displayed no remorse, regretting only, so he declared, that the gain, as a result of his turpitude, had not been larger.[2]

It was the "frauds and wrongs committed against the Indians" by the "heartless scoundrels" who infested the Indian service,[3] which led to the fall of Columbus Delano as Secretary of the Interior. Everyone knew—it was notorious, that the subject was being mismanaged. It was but too plain that the system was fundamentally evil, that white men were now, and had been for long, deriving profit from grants of benefit which were intended for the Indian, but which he did not receive in a prompt or regular way, or in full, if at all. No one person, or group of persons, could be certainly identified for punishment. Mischiefs were so bound up with the really difficult work to be performed in our relations to these "wards" of the government, set out on the plains and in the mountains, as they were, thousands of miles away, that knavery could be not well distinguished from irregular procedure, which was necessitated by conditions and circumstances, and it baffled pursuit.

The business of dealing with the Indians had been and it remained a piece of by-play in the Interior Department. Under Delano's administration as Commissioner of Internal Revenue the whiskey frauds had developed. He had expected to be made Secretary of the Treasury at Richardson's retirement in 1874, when Bristow was appointed to the place.[4] Fortunately so much did not come to pass. It was charged now that he and his son, who was acting as a clerk in the Department,

[1] House Reports, 44th Cong., 1st sess., no. 799, pp. viii–xv.

[2] Testimony of Orvil Grant in ibid.

[3] Words of the House Committee on Indian Affairs in 1873. See House Reports, 42nd Cong. 3rd sess., no. 98; cf. Report of an investigation in 1871, House Reports, 41st Cong. 3rd sess., no. 39. The Department was "whitewashed" by a Congressional committee after another "investigation" in 1874.—House Reports, 44th Cong. 1st sess., no. 778; cf. House Reports, 44th Cong. 1st sess., no. 354, p. 187.

[4] H. V. Boynton, North American Review, Oct., 1876.

were interested in contracts for beef, flour, coffee, sugar and other foods and materials purchased for the Indians.[1] His accusers filled the newspapers with allegations affecting his honor as a public officer. It was clear enough that he had loose ideas concerning public duty, and he and his friends in the "Indian Ring," [2] who, in 1874, had been in close quarters with William Welsh and other Indian philanthropists,[3] were in a little while involved in another spirited controversy. This time their assailant was Professor O. C. Marsh of Yale University, whose scientific interests had taken him to the Sioux Indian country, and who, supported by other witnesses, made damaging charges, founded upon an observation of conditions in and around the Red Cloud Agency, in Nebraska and Dakota, which he sent to the New York Tribune [4] and forwarded to the President.[5]

Professor Marsh alleged that there was rascality in the distribution of the supplies, that the beef cattle, pork, flour, tobacco and other goods, which were issued, were of an inferior quality, that freighters were cheating the government in the price which they charged for conveying material to the agency from Cheyenne.[6] The Indians at Red Cloud, in the winter of 1874–75, were on the verge of starvation. They were reduced for food, an army officer said, to the carcasses of dogs, wolves and ponies, though they would have been abundantly provided for by the government had the supplies been allowed to reach them.[7] The Red Cloud agent was unfitted for his position and should be removed.

Whatever else might be true or untrue, it was certain that at both the Red Cloud and Spotted Tail agencies a most repulsive and degrading practice was followed. The lean beef cattle which were issued to the Indians were driven through files of

[1] N. Y. Nation, April 22, 1875; N. Y. Tribune, April 10, 1876; cf. House Mis. Doc., 44th Cong. 1st sess., no. 167, p. 117.
[2] House Mis. Doc., 44th Cong. 1st sess., no. 167, p. 24.
[3] House Reports, 43rd Cong. 1st sess., no. 778, pp. 275–83.
[4] Report of Red Cloud Commission, p. xii.
[5] Ibid., pp. 1–21; N. Y. Nation, July 22, 1875.
[6] Report of the Red Cloud Commission, p. 2.
[7] N. Y. Nation, May 13, 1875.

mounted savages, who, for their own, and the amusement of the white on-lookers, shot at and chased the poor animals until they were riddled with lead. The cadavers then were skinned, the men taking the hides to the traders for sale, while the squaws carried off the meat and the entrails for food. Such methods of distribution continued to prevail, though the government kept salaried butchers and butchers' assistants at the agencies in order that meat might be supplied "from the block." [1]

While Marsh made specifications and complaints only in reference to one agency he extended his charges to cover the operations of the "Indian Ring" generally.[2] He addressed the President, he said, because of his distrust of the Secretary of the Interior and the Commissioner of Indian Affairs.[3]

Delano came to his own defense; his friends took his part vigorously also.[4] A committee of three members was appointed by the Secretary of the Interior, to which the President added two members (only one of whom gave any attention to the service), and testimony was taken, through the summer of 1875, at New York, Omaha, Cheyenne, Fort Laramie, the Red Cloud Agency and elsewhere, in an effort to quiet the scandal.[5] The investigators were at some pains to exculpate Delano and the Commissioner of Indian Affairs, and to state the conclusion that Marsh had been hasty in many particulars in the formation and the utterance of his judgments. But they found so much amiss that they were constrained to make recommendations under as many as 21 heads looking to a reform of the service, which included the removal "without delay" of the agent at Red Cloud, who was found to be "incompetent and unfit for the position," the censure of several contractors who should not again be permitted to engage in business with the government, and other measures of a more general nature,

[1] Report of Indian Commission for 1875, p. 10.
[2] Report of the Red Cloud Commission, p. 2.
[3] Ibid., p. 1.
[4] N. Y. Nation, April 29, Aug. 5 and 19, Oct. 28, 1875. In great anger one day, while the dispute raged, Delano launched a tirade of abuse at Marsh in the breakfast room of a Washington hotel.—Ibid., Sep. 18, 1875.
[5] Report of Indian Com. for 1875, p. 12.

touching the management of the bureau, confirmatory of much, if not all, that had been said in deprecation of it.[1]

The President, in his familiar manner, attempted to dismiss the outcry as more partisan clamor which it were a form of soldierly fortitude to ignore.[2] But before the commission had published its report Delano, in September, 1875, was dislodged from the service through a "letter of resignation," which Grant had forbearingly held since July 5, because of the "continued persecution which was being unjustly heaped" upon the man by the "public press," with the usual testimonial of good behavior.[3] As a *solatium* for defeat, at the hands of the Michigan legislature, for re-election to the United States Senate, Grant now, after offering the place to his friend J. Russell Jones, just home from a long residence abroad as minister to Belgium,[4] made the venerable Zachariah Chandler, from whom, with his low views of public service there was no reason to hope for an improvement of conditions, Secretary of the Interior.[5]

Responsible persons again recommended the return of the Indian Bureau to the War Department. In 1876 officers of the army generally, of whom advice was sought, urged the House Committee on Military Affairs to this policy.[6] The controversy, in and out of Congress, which the proposal evoked, extended over several years, and may better be described in a place where we shall be more specifically concerned with a discussion of Indian affairs.

The voice of the officers of the army on the subject of the transfer of the Pension Bureau to the War Department was not so clear, but the House Committee on Invalid Pensions recommended it. There were scandals in plenty in the air in connection with this service also. A particularly ugly one appeared

[1] Report of the Red Cloud Commission, pp. xvii, lxxiv–lxxv. Cf. Report of Indian Com. for 1875.
[2] N. Y. Nation, Sep. 30 and Oct. 14, 1875, and March 16, 1876; House Reports, 44th Cong. 1st sess., no. 799, p. 29.
[3] N. Y. Nation, Sep. 30, 1875.
[4] National Cyclop. of Am. Biography, vol. i, 535.
[5] N. Y. Nation, Oct. 28 and Nov. 25, 1875.
[6] House Reports, 44th Cong. 1st sess., no. 354—see especially pp. 100, 107, 113, 146–8, 187–8, 206, 210.

in the Chicago office where an agent had bought his place by
the promise to give a lucrative position to a friend of J. Russell
Jones, who controlled this piece of patronage. Another agent,
having obtained the appointment, sold it on onerous terms to
a young woman, a daughter of a deceased army officer. A
committee of Congress, as well as public opinion in the country
at large, while the investigation proceeded, emphatically condemned "the very low and discreditable tone of opinion,"
which conducted and justified such brokerage in "the procure-
ment of appointments to office."[1]

Already the disbursements on account of soldiers' pensions
had come to be $30,000,000 annually, and they were in course
of swift increase. It cost over four per cent to distribute this
money to its recipients. The Bureau was honeycombed with
"politics." Clerks and other employees were chosen because of
"politics." They were removed because of "politics." Too
many men were on the pay rolls. They shirked their work.
The administration was inefficient and expensive. Fraud was
practiced on the government by the incompetent and often
crafty persons who were permitted to direct the management
of an office entrusted with a great charitable service to the
234,000 persons—the maimed and the wounded, the sick and
the aged, the widow and the orphan—to whom the nation,
in a grateful sense for services rendered in the last and earlier
wars, was dispensing public aid. In the opinion of the committee
of the House, therefore, the administration of this subject
should be given into the hands of the paymaster's department
of the army.[2]

Belknap had scarcely got his head out of the noose in which
he found it on the subject of the sale of post traderships when,
it was alleged, that he had been involved in some apparently
corrupt bargain for the purchase of headstones for soldiers
buried in the national cemeteries. Congress had appropriated
$1,000,000 for this use, and, in 1873, the contract was given out,

[1] House Reports, 44th Cong. 1st sess., no. 796, p. 5; cf. House Mis.
Doc., 44th Cong. 1st sess., nos. 173 and 182.
[2] House Mis. Doc., 44th Cong. 1st sess., no. 93; House Reports, 44th
Cong. 1st sess., no. 678.

not to the lowest bidder, but to some friend of the Secretary
of War, a fellow citizen of Keokuk, Iowa, of little financial
responsibility, by trade a jeweler, with no knowledge of the
marble business.   The awarding of the contract in the first
place, and the manner in which it was allowed to be executed,
was reviewed by a committee of Congress and condemned.[1]
It was a distressing sight to see a Secretary of War playing a
game of this kind over the graves of the men who had laid down
their lives for their country.

More of the same kind of vileness was revealed at every turn
in the progress of the investigation of the conduct of the Navy
Department.   Robeson, during the Greeley campaign, had been
a target of attack, particularly through the New York Sun,
which had led to the examination of his department, and a
statement by the majority of the committee of the House having the subject in hand.   It was a partisan report.   The committee declared that all the charges against Robeson were "malignant and wanton" libels.   Nevertheless it was clear that he had
acted with little attention to the public interest in one particular at least, viz. the approval of the Secor claim.   His ex-
cuses, and those of his friends for him, had been flimsy,[2] and
now that the Democrats were in control of the House, they
would thoroughly explore his public and private life.   The
testimony, and the papers accompanying it, were expanded,
during the weeks in 1876 occupied by the investigation, to fill
three great volumes, and the conditions which were seen to
prevail in the Department were indicative of so much obliquity
of understanding as to correct conduct in public office that the
revelation of them increased the sense of national disgrace.

Welcoming, at the end of the war, the opportunity for a
rest from military preparation, we had drifted into a passive
policy.   This passivity in so far as it concerned the navy was
disquieting because of the rapid progress which was being
made concurrently by foreign nations in the development of their
fleets.   Though the names of 140 vessels appeared on the Naval

---

[1] House Reports, 44th Cong. 1st sess., no. 802, pp. i–vi.
[2] Cf. House Mis. Doc., 42nd Cong. 2nd sess., nos. 80 and 81.

Register in 1876,[1] authorities worthy to be heard said that all but a few of the number would be found to be useless in a trial of strength with the maritime powers of Europe. While they were making their ships of iron ours were of wood; while they were employing steam ours were still using sails—steam was applied only in an auxiliary way.[2] We had but two or three ironclads of value and these were monitors of the type developed during the Civil War, quite inferior to the turret vessels lately added to the European naval fleets.[3] Our iron ships were wanting in modern guns and other equipment, as well as in speed, and could be employed to advantage only in coast defense. We had fallen in a few years from a third to a sixth or eighth rate naval power.[4] When our squadron was collected at Key West, at the time of the *Virginius* excitement, an intelligent American officer who was present said that a single modern English war vessel could have blown all our ships out of the water without doing herself serious harm.[5]

In this country we had never attempted the construction of a first class ship, said Admiral Craven.[6] The navy yards and some private yards, fortunate enough to get the contracts, had been repairing and rebuilding old wooden vessels which were calculated to have little usefulness. For this work, and for the naval establishment generally, we were expending annually from $20,000,000 to $25,000,000.[7]

Goaded to some kind of activity, Congress, in 1873, resolved to build eight new "sloops of war."[8] From time to time members of that body had discussed the question of the cost of vessels constructed in the navy yards as compared with ships completed under contract in private yards. There was, in the first place, a difference in the time of labor, for Congress, taking early

[1] House Mis. Doc., 44th Cong. 1st sess., no. 170, pt. 3, p. 153.
[2] Admiral Pennock in ibid., pt. 8, p. 5.
[3] Ibid., pt. 5, p. 148 and pt. 8, pp. 19, 57.
[4] Ibid., pt. 8, p. 52.
[5] Ibid., p. 93.
[6] Ibid., p. 13.
[7] Ibid., pt. 5, pp. 148, 150, 154, 159; House Reports, 44th Cong. 1st sess., no. 784, p. 4.
[8] Act of February 10, 1873.

notice of the demands of the working man, had fixed eight hours as a day's work for government employees. Private shipbuilders could still command the energies of their men for ten hours.[1] Furthermore there were a number of government yards—these were variously situated and variously equipped —a ship could not be placed in that one qualified to complete it most quickly and economically, for, as soon as its construction was resolved upon politicians engaged in a scramble to bring it to the yards located in their respective neighborhoods. So much was foreordained. Considerations still more unfavorable to the government, in any competition with honest private shipbuilders, were the incompetency and dishonesty which marked the management of the public yards.

It was recommended that several different methods be employed in the construction of the eight new ships in order to determine which might be the best. Politicians and contractors eagerly looked on as the President signed the bill. In reality the "sloops of war" would be not more than small gunboats.[2] They were to be variously rigged; three were to have iron hulls—unarmored and of little value; the other five were to be wholly of wood. Three would be built in New England; three on the Delaware; one in Brooklyn, and one in Norfolk.[3] The iron ships were committed to the hands of private contractors, John Roach, an enterprising shipbuilder at Chester, Pennsylvania[4], being charged with the work upon two of them. The government itself would build three of the vessels in the navy yards at Kittery, Maine, at Brooklyn, and at Norfolk. Still another method would be tried. A private contractor was given the unusual privilege of building one of the ships in the Kittery yard from material owned by the government, and, in accordance with a somewhat similar plan,

[1] House Mis. Doc., 44th Cong. 1st sess., no. 170, pt. 2, p. 4; ibid., pt. 4, p. 11; ibid., pt. 8, p. 67; cf. House Mis. Doc., 42nd Cong. 2nd sess., no. 201, p. 231.
[2] House Mis. Doc., 44th Cong. 1st sess., no. 170, pt. 3, p. 67.
[3] Ibid., pt. 4, p. 11.
[4] Roach was tendered a complimentary dinner at Delmonico's in New York in 1874 for his services to American shipbuilding.—N. Y. Tribune, May 1, 1874; Harper's Weekly, May 30, 1874.

another was put under private contract in the yard at Boston. As could have been foretold experimentation with a variety of systems led to no intelligent conclusions, except to provide further confirmation of what was already well enough known— that the naval administration of the country was in the hands of a low and contemptible type of politician. Contractors having in any way to do with government work, who were ready to tell the truth, and naval commanders in the same situation, were in full agreement on this point.

The Congressional investigation made it quite clear that the various navy yards, like the custom houses, the internal revenue offices and the post-offices were the appanages of the politicians in whose localities they were situated. Indeed, they were colloquially known by the names of the men who controlled the appointment of the shipwrights, foremen, quartermen, calkers, bolt drivers, iron platers, sutlers, and the entire retinue of persons carried upon the pay rolls of the government. Thus Mare Island at San Francisco was "Sargent's Navy Yard," the yard at Norfolk was called for a carpetbagger member of Congress named Platt, and so on.[1] The admiral, or commodore, nominally in command of the yard, was overslaughed by the politician who, acting through Robeson's office at Washington, controlled the patronage. Not one in the service, with the courage to speak out, that did not lament a condition so humiliating to him and so destructive of discipline and efficiency. "Political influence" was overriding "the authorities of the yards," said Commander A. T. Mahan.[2] The commanding officers had been reduced to "mere figureheads," said Admiral Thornton A. Jenkins.[3] "If any private business in the world," were run upon the same plan, said Commander Richard W. Meade, "it would be bankrupt in three months." The system was "infernal."[4] The remedy, Captain W. T. Truxtun observed, was to place the service "entirely outside of and above politics,"[5] which, said Admiral Almy, were "the bane of the navy."[6]

[1] House Mis. Doc., 44th Cong. 1st sess., no. 170, pt. 8, p. 5.
[2] Ibid., p. 122.
[3] Ibid., p. 27.
[4] Ibid., pt. 5, pp. 158, 159.
[5] Ibid., pt. 8, p. 108.
[6] Ibid., p. 5.

Not a man could get into a government shipyard except through "politics." Mechanical efficiency was but small commendation. Useful and experienced shipwrights were dismissed to make places for those who would, it was conceived, aid the party on election days.[1] Organized in gangs under foremen, who were responsible to party managers outside the yards rather than to the commandants, any good result was achieved only under the greatest difficulties. To increase the number of posts preposterous sinecures were created. Men were hired to inspect ships where there were none to be inspected, to move ships where there were none to be moved, to carry drinking water, to open and close the gates in the morning and at the end of the day, to ventilate sheds. There were watchmen and men to watch watchmen. All were held in fear of dismissal if they did not vote, and exert themselves to make others vote, for the nominees of the party which put bread in their mouths.

Everywhere during political campaigns they were "assessed." The foreman took at least one day's wages from members of the working gangs; those in higher positions made larger contributions, in accordance with a fixed scale, to the party treasury.[2]

Prior to critical elections the number of employees would be increased by the local politicians, acting through the authorities at Washington. Suddenly it was found that there was important new work to be done. Instead of giving precinct and district leaders $10 or $50, through the party "executive committee," that committee would put its lieutenants upon the government pay rolls for a week or a fortnight. Five hundred, sometimes a thousand men, would be employed in a navy yard in October with the understanding that they would be discharged in November.[3] At Kittery, when there was need of votes for an election in Maine, men

[1] The artisans into whose midst they came called them "wood butchers."
[2] Cf. Platt v. Goode, House Mis. Doc., 44th Cong. 1st sess., no. 65, p. 178.
[3] House Mis. Doc. 44th Cong. 1st sess., no. 170, pt. 1, p. 105; ibid., pt. 2, pp. 4, 57, 213, 262; ibid., pt. 8, pp. 111, 122; contested election case of Abbott v. Frost, House Mis. Doc., 44th Cong. 1st sess., no. 49, pp. 102 et seq.

were poured into the yard from that state; for an election in New Hampshire they trooped in at Portsmouth. In Philadelphia, Pennsylvanians or New Jerseymen could be used according to the requirements of the occasion. At Norfolk, at work on or standing around a 600-ton ship at which, perhaps, 200 men might be advantageously employed, there were, during the embittered campaign in 1874, in which Platt was endeavoring to hold his seat in Congress, 1,400 or 1,500, many of them his negro adherents.[1] Printers, corn doctors, and sewing machine agents, the newspapers said, were imposed upon the naval officer in nominal command of the yard, as ship carpenters. These "bummers" gathered in groups to tell "stories" and "talk politics." They got in the way of men who were capable of serving, and were trying to serve the government honestly. When persons thus employed could do anything useful it was merely "to stow lumber" and clear up the yards, which consisted, candid observers said, in carrying material from one place to another and then carrying it back again. For want of competent mechanics ships, the keels of which had been laid two and four years since, were still unfinished and were going to pieces in the weather. [2]

The chief naval constructor at Washington, Isaiah Hanscom, visited Boston in person, late in October, 1874, and, in writing, directed Commodore Nichols, the commandant in charge of the yard at Charleston, to approve whatever requisitions for labor were made upon him by the local politicians, since "the administration" desired "the success" of two candidates for Congress in adjacent districts. This done and the purpose served, the commandant was taken to task by Hanscom for his costly management of the yard.[3]

[1] House Mis. Doc., 44th Cong. 1st sess., no. 170, pt. 4, p. 129; Platt *v.* Goode, House Mis. Doc., 44th Cong. 1st sess., no. 65.

[2] House Mis. Doc., 44th Cong. 1st sess., no. 170, pt. 4, pp. 110–11, 129. For the committee's conclusions on this subject see House Reports, 44th Cong. 1st sess., no. 784, pp. 24–37. It was computed that over a million dollars a year of money appropriated to the Navy Department was used in the corruption of elections.

[3] Abbott *v.* Frost, House Mis. Doc., 44th Cong. 1st sess., no. 49, pp. 102–4, 412–5.

Since men could not be employed and kept in place by reason of their proficiency as mechanics, so, of course, they could not be dismissed for "skulking and loafing," [1] or even for infamous offenses. If they were discharged they would find their way back into the yards and their names would be restored to the pay rolls.

Material was purchased at high prices; much of it was of an inferior quality. Inspectors "passed" for a bribe, or in answer to orders from Washington, timber and other supplies which some favorite of the Secretary of the Navy, or of the bureau heads, or of their political friends, held for sale. Of no present use it was left to rot or otherwise deteriorate in value in storage in the yards. Tools belonging to the government were carried out of the gates. Large quantities of lumber disappeared; it could not be traced or recovered. Nearly a million feet credited on the books at the Boston yard were missing, said A. T. Mahan.[2] Material was auctioned off for a song to be repurchased at high prices; good machinery was sold for old iron—it reappeared in government ships built by private contractors. Coal, hemp, live oak, which the regularly deputed authorities condemned as unfit to be received, were, nevertheless, purchased by the government.

Men who had devices of questionable value for sale carried them to the heads of the Department at Washington. These officers bought a machine for bending timber,[3] boiler attachments and guns, against the judgment of experts, for reasons of their own. A contract was made with a man named Halstead for a crude submarine boat, which the sailors derisively called the "intelligent whale," an object of curiosity which lay in the Brooklyn navy yard.[4]

Bills were rendered and paid for extra work upon vessels built under private contract, when they should have been delivered in a complete form at the original price.[5] Men at the Washington navy yard were making walnut sideboards, hat

[1] House Mis. Doc., 44th Cong. 1st sess., no. 170, pt. 2, p. 21.
[2] Ibid., p. 195.
[3] Ibid., pt. 1, p. 59.
[4] Ibid., pt. 5, pp. 158, 395.
[5] Cf. House Reports, 44th Cong. 1st sess., no. 790.

racks, mahogany and rosewood tables and other furniture. Some of these articles, together with a baptismal font, were for Secretary Robeson's account. The font he presented to a church at Long Branch. After he was married it was stated that a number of government employees came to his house to put it in order to receive his bride. The Washington yard repaired a yacht for a club of politicians; the Boston yard remodeled a yacht for Ben Butler; the Brooklyn yard built a conservatory for a brother of the chief naval constructor.[1] At Norfolk cannon were cast to fire salutes at political meetings; billies and clubs were hewn and fashioned for rowdies to strike the heads of other rowdies in party fracases in and around that city.[2]

Even officers subject to court-martial, in a number of instances which were cited, were, after trial and conviction, returned to the service through the devices of their political friends.[3] Men of high rank in the navy, who had entered the service under the impression that it was a profession, filled with an honorable pride in its traditions, looked on helplessly, or turned their eyes away from the scenes which were being enacted around them. What was seen, indeed, was so usual as to call for little remark. It was taken to be a feature of the service, so firmly established that it could not be abolished or changed. Young men, comfortably settled for shore duty, with their families around them, realized that, if they should complain, they would be ordered to sea. Charges would be trumped up against them—they might even be detached from the service.[4] Older men would more wisely say that they were accustomed to receive orders, not to question these orders, or to remonstrate with the Department.[5]

[1] House Mis. Doc., 44th Cong. 1st sess., no. 170, pt. 5, p. 161.
[2] Cf. testimony of many men in Platt v. Goode, House Mis. Doc., 44th Cong. 1st sess., no. 65.
[3] Cf. testimony of Richard W. Meade and Gideon Welles, House Mis. Doc., 44th Cong. 1st sess., no. 170 pt. 5; cf. ibid., pt. 8, p. 110.
[4] Ibid., pt. 1, p. 118.
[5] Any one who will study the volumes of testimony taken by this committee will, I think, feel that this is not more than a conservative summing up of the credible statements of the witnesses.

The truth of the matter, as was guessed and as soon appeared, was that the navy had fallen under the control of a combination of corrupt contractors and politicians. The chief and boldest of these men was Elijah G. Cattell, a brother of ex-Senator Alexander G. Cattell of New Jersey, answerable (together with Mr. Borie) for Robeson's appointment to his position, and his principal supporter in New Jersey and at Washington. They, and some other men in Philadelphia and thereabouts, were known to be in intimate social and political relations with the secretary, and they at once put these relations to commercial account. Under various firm and company names they stood ready to furnish the Department with beef, pork, sugar, molasses, beans, lumber, hemp, wire rope, coal, flour and what not, and although they had nothing of their own to sell, accounted themselves to be in a position to procure contracts at advantageous prices, which they would farm out. Not content with so much as this, though it was a great deal, Elijah Cattell demanded commissions of other men who should make contracts with the government. He alleged that he had such connections at the Department that ship chandlers could not secure favorable consideration for their bids, material would not pass inspection, bills could not be collected promptly, unless he were employed as a broker in the case. The course of the Department toward such as did not choose to employ him created an impression that he had the large influence which he ascribed to himself. He was frequently seen in the offices of the secretary and of the bureau heads in Washington, a fact tending further to confirm his claims. Large dealers in New York and New England gave him a percentage upon all their sales for naval account.[1] So important a shipbuilding plant as Cramps in Philadelphia paid him thousands of dollars for his service, whatever it may have been, in their behalf.[2]

John Roach, who treated Cattell's advances as blackmail,

[1] Cf. testimony of Wm. Matthews and W. C. N. Swift, House Mis. Doc., 44th Cong. 1st sess., no. 170, pt. 5.

[2] Cf. testimony of Theodore and Wm. M. Cramp, House Mis. Doc., 44th Cong. 1st sess., no. 170, pt. 3.

reported them to Robeson, who denied any collusion between
the man and the Department, but strangely failed, though
thus informed of what was being done, to bring it to an end.[1]
Cattell, under examination by the committee, swearing that
he had destroyed most of his papers, or had never had any
on the subject of many of his transactions, admitted that in
two years he had received upwards of $180,000 in commissions
from navy contracts and contractors.[2]

There were others who sought to use the Department in a
similar manner. The President's brother, Orvil Grant, discerned possibilities for gain in this field as well as in post traderships. He and a fellow broker exacted of a man who had
white oak ship knees for sale to the navy two-thirds of the
profit on the transaction, collecting the sum in advance.[3] Orvil
Grant's services were considered valuable enough to a firm in
Baltimore for them to engage him permanently at a monthly
salary in return for a prospect of his procuring them contracts
from the government.[4]

Other men gave their attention to the collection of claims
against the government. Colonel Simeon M. Johnson, an
intimate of Robeson at Washington, was the most successful
of these agents. It was commonly understood that he must
be retained by any one who wished to be accorded a favorable
hearing on this class of subjects in the Department. Following his success in securing the payment of the Secor and the
Governor claims,[5] under circumstances which aroused much
public resentment, he presented other old claims to the Department, payment of which had been declined by Secretary
Welles.[6] On an account, in favor of a man named Hungerford, for property alleged to have been destroyed by General
Sherman in Memphis during the war, Johnson received $75,000

[1] Cf. testimony of Roach, House Mis. Doc., 44th Cong. 1st sess., no. 170, pt. 5.
[2] Cf. testimony of E. G. Cattell, J. P. Warr, Dell Noblit, Jr., and John Noblit, ibid., pt. 3.
[3] Ibid., pt. 5, p. 71.   [4] Ibid., pp. 85 et seq.
[5] Cf. House Mis. Doc., 42nd Cong. 2nd sess., no. 201.
[6] Cf. testimony of Gideon Welles, House Mis. Doc., 44th Cong. 1st sess., no. 170, pt. 5.

from Robeson, a very small part, if any, of which, it was alleged, ever reached the claimant.[1]

Another old war claim of Tilton, Wheelwright and Company, on account of material furnished the government, had been revived. This firm was paid $32,000 by the use of methods which led to the condemnation of Isaiah Hanscom as chief naval constructor by a committee of Congress, and a request for his removal.[2]

But the most compromising of the relations of Robeson with the interests that were prospering at the expense of the navy were those which unfortunately bound him to the Cattells.[3] The presumption, frequently expressed in and since 1872, that he personally must be profiting in some manner through their operations seemed to be not unwarranted. The Cattells were engaged in speculations in which the Secretary of the Navy was also involved. They gave or lent him money. They built him a house at Long Branch, purchased him horses and carriages, managed expensive campaigns with the purpose of making him a United States senator from New Jersey. The committee laboriously examined his bank accounts; he was obliged to use his lawyer's skill to explain his transactions. Though no criminal, or even impeachable offense was brought to his door,[4] it was clear, to the intelligent and the candid, that he was wanting in any correct appreciation of the proprieties of his office. Without abilities or interests qualifying him for the management of the navy, or any pretense to right to appointment to a position so eminent, Robeson had come to be, if he were not at first, the representative of other men.

[1] Cf. testimony of Gideon Welles, House Mis. Doc., 44th Cong. 1st sess., no. 170, pt. 5, pp. 309–30.
[2] House Reports, 44th Cong. 1st sess., no. 788.
[3] For Senator Cattell's relations to Grant and Robeson see H. V. Boynton, North American Review, October, 1876, p. 287.
[4] Impeachment proceedings were suggested by the Committee (House Reports, 44th Cong. 1st sess., no. 784, p. 160) and he was marked for formal censure by Congress in a report of the House Committee on Naval Affairs as a result of a subsequent investigation in 1877–78.—House Reports, 45th Cong. 3rd sess., no. 112, p. 28; cf. House Reports, 45th Cong. 2nd sess., no. 787; House Mis. Doc., 45th Cong. 2nd sess., no. 63; House Mis. Doc., 45th Cong. 3rd sess., no. 21.

He had been an attorney in a small town; he had had no experiences which were large or valuable. Naturally an indolent man, with nothing except what he could earn in his place, any plan by which he could make friends with the masters of our "predatory politics" so that he might become rich, or, perhaps, gain an office which would provide for his future ease, arrested his attention. Thus it was, as Commander George Dewey said, that, during this era, "everything was wrong with the navy." [1]

Corrupt rings were discovered in the administration of the postal service. All seeming not to be well in this Department, Mr. Creswell resigned in June, 1874, and his place was taken by Marshall Jewell, who had been governor of Connecticut, and now, for a year, our minister to Russia. Creswell's conduct of his office was the subject of examination.[2] The inquiries were extended to the Department of Justice, in the use of secret service funds and in other expenditures, under its management by Attorney Generals Akerman and Williams;[6] and to the Government Printing Office which, it was said, through incompetency and extravagance, was wasting a half million dollars annually. The Committee on the Judiciary was instructed to inquire whether the Congressional printer was an officer who might be impeached under the Constitution of the United States.[4] There were new rumors about, and investigations into the sale of cadetships at West Point.[5]

As an outgrowth of the reckless and corrupt operations of "Boss" Shepherd and his "District Ring" came the failure, in 1874, of the Freedman's Savings and Trust Company, usually called the "Freedmen's Bank." During the war military commanders at Norfolk and in Beaufort, S. C., started banks in which the negro troops might deposit their pay. This led to a scheme, closely affiliated with General Howard's

[1] House Mis. Doc., 44th Cong. 1st sess., no. 170, pt. 2, p. 198.
[2] House Reports, 44th Cong. 1st sess., no. 814.
[3] Ibid., no. 800.
[4] Ibid., no. 495.
[5] House Reports, 43rd Cong. 2nd sess., no. 124; House Mis. Doc., 44th Cong. 1st sess., no. 177; George F. Hoar in Trial of W. W. Belknap, p. 63; cf. vol. ii of this work, p. 543.

Freedmen's Bureau, which would extend the advantages of a savings institution to the entire body of "persons lately held in slavery." The bank was chartered by Congress in 1865,[1] and a white man named Alvord organized it. An impressive list of names of well known persons as corporators recommended it, though some of the number, it is said, never knew that they were acting in such a capacity. Others who had lent their favor to the enterprise and had consented to serve as trustees afterward withdrew, and the direction devolved upon the few who remained, the chief of these, in point of reputation in the financial world, being Henry D. Cooke, more lobbyist than banker, but, through his brother, Jay Cooke, and his partnership in Jay Cooke and Company, a figure of prominence in Washington. In a short time more than thirty branches were established in which, at the windows and behind the counters, negroes were seen acting as clerks, tellers and cashiers.

Some $56,000,000 seem to have been intrusted to the company by depositors, and, so long as the money was invested in government bonds, all went well. But in 1870 Congress, through a cunning hand, had been persuaded to amend the charter to the extent of permitting loans to be made on real estate. Here was temptation. While Alvord traversed the South, benevolently preaching thrift to the blacks, the unprincipled men who were gathered around Cooke, preparing the First National Bank of Washington for its disgraceful fall and exploiting the tax and credit systems of the District of Columbia, were speculating with, when they did not steal, the amassed proceeds of the missionary's efforts. Loans were made to a company formed to quarry sandstone in Maryland, shares of which were donated to President Grant, his brother-in-law, General Dent, and other men. A great building for the bank's use, made of this stone, was erected in Washington at a cost of a quarter of a million dollars. Howard's colored university in Washington, Shepherd's paving contractors, real estate "rings" came to the institution and they were befriended. Peculation, forgery and outright thievery in some

[1] Act of March 3, 1865; cf. N. Y. Nation, April 15, 1875.

of the depositary offices marked its brief history. Inspections were a farce. Books were incorrectly kept and were mutilated to conceal robbery and fraud. When the panic of 1873 broke upon the country the bank with difficulty survived. The "runs" upon the various branches were met by the avails from the sale of government bonds which still remained in hand. The white men now found the opportunity to escape and the burden, early in 1874, was put upon Fred Douglass, who, thinking that there was some honor in the presidency of the institution, accepted it, to go down with the wreck in the following July. Then Congress committed the company's affairs to three commissioners and the resulting liquidation, of necessity, bore hard upon thousands of poor colored folk.

A committee of Congress which undertook the investigation of the subject in 1876 called it "a monstrous swindle" in "the guise of philanthropy." No words were spared in condemnation of the men who had thus dealt with the "hard earned and sweat stained savings" of the trusting black people. Even the minority member agreed in every essential regard with his associates. He could not but find what had been done "reprehensible in the highest degree." The managers of the bank had invested the money where it would "inure to their own profit," and, in doing this, had asked for and received no, or little, security for their loans.[1]

The investigations and exposures of the time, following one upon another, came to include Minister Schenck in London. It was clear that he would not be able to escape. Though he had been at his post for five years, his offense in connection with the Emma silver mine in Utah was not forgotten.[2] No dividends had been paid since December, 1872; the high hopes of the investors were dashed to the ground. Recrimination of stockholders, aimed at the promoters and directors of the company at shareholders' meetings and in the press, litigation

---

[1] House Reports, 44th Cong. 1st sess., no. 502; cf. N. Y. Nation, April 15 and Nov. 4, 1875.

[2] Cf. W. J. Stillman, in N. Y. Nation, March 18, 1875.

in the courts, both of England and America, kept the subject in the public mind. For many weeks, in 1876, the House Committee on Foreign Affairs heard the testimony of witnesses. The administration at Washington had promised its support to Schenck, who desired to remain yet a while longer at his post. But when charges most gravely reflecting upon his honor were repeated at the hearings and in the newspapers, Grant and Fish thought better of their plans to defend him, and he was allowed to resign and come home.[1] He himself appeared as a witness before the committee to turn the tide of opinion, if he could. He but partially succeeded. It appeared that though his mistake in connecting his name, while a minister of the United States, to the prospectuses of the company as a director and trustee had been corrected by his retirement from its board of management, he had made a false statement to Mr. Fish when he said that he had paid "dollar for dollar" for the shares standing in his name. He had not done so.[2] His retirement from the management was in a letter which, for the protection of the promoters, he had delayed sending, and, when it was sent, included no candid statement of his reasons for taking the step. Moreover, after leaving the board, he had been speculating in the shares,[3] wherefore the committee recommended that the House of Representatives pass a resolution condemning him for action "ill advised, unfortunate and incompatible with the duties of his official position."[4]

There was a feeling of deep satisfaction when it was announced at Washington that Richard H. Dana, Jr., would take Schenck's place as our representative at the Court of St. James. A high type of the New England man it could have been supposed that the nomination would be confirmed by the Senate promptly and in a cordial and grateful spirit. But, circulating a preposterous charge that Dana had "pirated" some notes of an edition

[1] N. Y. Nation, March 23, 1876.
[2] What Schenck had done amounted to taking a bribe of £10,000 while he was our minister to Great Britain. The only payment he ever made for the stock was in notes.—Moran's Diary, Dec. 20, 1872, and Feb. 17, 1873.
[3] Cf. Moran's Diary.
[4] House Reports, 44th Cong. 1st sess., no. 579, pp. i-xvi, passim.

of Wheaton's treatise on international law, Ben Butler, in whose political retinue the distinguished appointee had never been, organized an opposition and the senators rejected the nomination.[1]

The President then named his Attorney General, Edwards Pierrepont, who, by reason of the duties imposed upon him in connection with the Whiskey Ring prosecutions, had cause to be weary of his office, and he, being confirmed, proceeded to London. Judge Alphonso Taft of Cincinnati, who had been appointed to the place at the head of the War Department, which Belknap had so hastily left, now became Attorney General, while the Grant leader in Pennsylvania, Simon Cameron, who had developed so much choler on the subject of Dana's nomination for the English mission found a place for his son, J. Donald Cameron, a young man little past forty, as Secretary of War.[2]

It was in the midst of these things that a project appeared for the celebration of the one hundredth anniversary of American Independence. It would take the form of a great exposition and it would be held in Philadelphia, the scene of the signing of the Declaration, and the events antecedent to this momentous resolution on the part of Great Britain's American colonies. Plans had been announced, committees had been formed before the panic of 1873. The economic disorders resulting from this crash put almost insurmountable obstacles in the way of the promoters of the public-spirited undertaking. But a few pertinacious men gave of their time and money until success was assured. Women in the quaint dress of their grandames at bazaars, festivals and "tea parties" aroused one community after another to an interest in the enterprise. States supported it, Congress came to its rescue, thus according it a national character. Other nations were addressed and agreed to participate.

As yet there were but few museums; the large department

[1] N. Y. Tribune, April 6, 1876; cf. Diary and Letters of Hayes, vol. iii, p. 318; N. Y. Nation, March 16 and 23, and April 6, 1876.
[2] N. Y. Nation, May 25, 1876.

store with its vast displays of wares was still undeveloped and a temporary exposition of the productions of the country and of the world, gathered together in one place, had in it attractions for the people which it may never have again. International exhibitions there had been in London and Paris and, still more recently, in 1873, in Vienna.[1] But the United States had not yet enlisted its energies in such an enterprise. A beautiful site was chosen in Fairmount Park, overlooking the Schuykill river, and a group of buildings, some 200 in number, one of them, the Main Building, covering 20 acres of ground, were rapidly reared in an enclosure of 236 acres, in pleasing arrangement, to house the machinery, the manufactured goods, the art objects and the materials of whatever kind which were to be assembled for the use.

It was but a poor attempt throughout, in comparison with the expositions which since have been seen. In its architectural lines, in its artistic conception and execution in any regard, it fell far short of the standards later established for such undertakings, but for the very reason that it was a new method of marking a really important national anniversary it riveted the notice of the entire population. Orations were spoken, poems were read, hymn and cantata were sung on the opening day, May 10th, and on the 4th of July. Dom Pedro, Emperor of Brazil, came in testimony of the friendship of the principal sister state in the southern hemisphere of America. As the summer passed into autumn, other distinguished guests graced the occasion with their presence. There was a veritable outpouring of the population to view the wonders which had been brought together in Philadelphia. Hotels, boarding and lodging houses were jammed with visitors. From every part of the Union came rustics and small town people to quarter themselves in the homes of relations and acquaintances who might reside in the city and its neighborhood. Before the exposition was closed, early in October, over nine millions of persons had entered through its various turnstiles, many of them in a

[1] Reports of the commissioners to this exposition published by the government in 1876.

reverent and studious mood, to the improvement, it must be thought, of their minds and the exaltation of their spirits.

Assuredly at no time in our history had we had so little in which to feel a pride from the point of view of any achievement that lay within the field of politics. All that was pernicious to the commonwealth had been associated with the history of our great American experiment in government at the end of its first century of life. One dishonor upon another, one failure upon another had been revealed to the nation, so that the dullest might be filled with shame for our recent past, and with melancholy and doubt with reference to the future. But here was an invitation to look back through the corridors of years at the figures of Washington, Hamilton, Jefferson, Adams, Madison and the founders of the republic, to meditate upon what had been in their minds, to contrast their ideals with those of the Babcocks and McDonalds, the Belknaps, Shepherds and Ben Butlers, and the small, ignorant, vainglorious pretenders to the purple in statesmanship who were now in high places looking on, while these and other knavish men controlled our political life. To some who visited this exposition so much must have been made clear.

Again, there was inspiration in the sight of so many evidences of our material prosperity. The mechanical genius of the country, as well as its natural resources, displayed in the exhibits in Philadelphia, held before the people a vision of future triumphs in the various fields of labor, manufacture, invention, science and the arts. New ideas were gained, old ones enlarged and developed to the national advantage.

And, again, the exposition gave to the masses of the population, so provincial in their outlook, appreciation of the intelligence and capacity of the peoples of foreign lands. Of some of them we were now hearing for the first time. Their products could be inspected, their faces in the foreign buildings were seen. That there was a world beyond New York or Iowa might be understood. The entire nation came through the year 1876 with an enlargement of view in an economical, an industrial, an artistic and an ethnographic sense, as well as with a finer comprehension of American history, and the purpose and design of the government, which had been so laboriously, so hopefully and so sagely founded one hundred years agone.

CHAPTER XX

ROUT OF THE CARPETBAGGERS

It was a hollow trick, as judicious men could see, any longer to disguise the social disorder and political misrule, which disgraced the South, under the name of "Reconstruction." Such conditions were not to be tolerated by the people, and they called, and still call, the struggle to free themselves from the domination of the negroes and those who were using the freedmen for evil ends, "rescuing," or "redeeming" their states. Such, in truth, it was to them, as it will seem to be to the historian of the period which holds this series of events.

Where the negroes were not numerous the work of "redemption" was not long delayed. The carpetbag leaders could not hope, by any activity, to marshal enough blacks to outvote the white inhabitants. Virginia, Tennessee, Georgia, Texas, were the first to escape the toils of negro rule, and they were enjoying a measure of political composure and industrial peace. Virginia had not been restored to the Union until 1870. In that state, from the first, the negro party was a minority party. Brownlow, in Tennessee, seeing his régime at an end, procured himself a seat in the United States Senate. In 1869 that state passed to conservative and Democratic control.

It was in 1870 that Georgia, Bullock failing to get the favor of Congress for his audacious scheme to go forward practically as a dictator, without an election, returned a legislature strongly Democratic in both branches,[1] which, when it met in 1871, so roughly pressed the governor, that, under threat of impeachment, he resigned, and fled the state.[2] At a special election in 1871 a Democrat, James M. Smith, a lawyer of Columbus, who had been a colonel in the Southern army and a member of the Confederate Congress, who had "gone with his state" into

---

[1] C. M. Thompson, Recon. in Ga., pp. 270–71.   [2] Ibid., p. 271.

secession and the war, though it was said, only hesitatingly, was chosen to take the exile's place. Investigation of Bullock and his corrupt despotism was started with a will under the leadership—a welcome task to such a man—of Robert Toombs. It was a sorry record of wrong for which the governor and his cronies in railroad and other thievery were made accountable before the committee was done with them.[1] But it was not until 1876 that Bullock allowed himself to come within the reach of the prosecuting authorities—at too late a day for enough proof to be assembled to procure his conviction, though he underwent arrest and trial for his misdemeanors.[2] Thus were the white people of Georgia released from the preposterous situation of living under the rule of their liberated negro slaves.

Texas, because of its increasingly predominant white population, could not long be kept under Radical control. The schism in the Republican party, due to the rivalries of A. J. Hamilton and Governor Davis, favored the conservatives.[3] The division widened. Davis had proven himself an arbitrary man, and he gained new enemies.[4] Here, as in other parts of the South under Republican management, expenditures, taxes, debt had risen at an unprecedented pace, and popular opposition was easily awakened. A taxpayers' convention met at Austin in September, 1872. Its protests were received by the governor coolly. His answer was another convention of negroes,[5] but the device was of no avail, for at the election the people chose a solidly Democratic delegation in Congress and a Democratic legislature, and the end of negro-carpetbag rule was near at hand. In the following year, 1873, the Democrats nominated for governor Richard Coke, a lawyer of Waco, who had worn the Southern uniform throughout the war and was now a justice of the supreme court of his state, and he was elected by an overwhelming majority. Davis resisted, charging fraud, and Austin

[1] C. M. Thompson, Recon. in Ga., pp. 273–4; article on Georgia in Am. Ann. Cyclop. for 1872.

[2] Ibid., p. 274; I. W. Avery, Hist. of State of Ga., p. 462.

[3] Ramsdell, Recon. in Texas, pp. 301, 303.

[4] Ibid., pp. 304–5.

[5] Ibid., pp. 308–9.

was filled with armed men. Grant, who was appealed to, surveyed developing events from Washington. He had befriended
Davis in the past, but now the popular will was too unmis-
takably plain. If the "verdict of the people" had not been
acquiesced in by the Federal authorities bloodshed would have
certainly ensued. Davis, having been refused the support of the
President,[1] and, seeing that he could do no more, left the scene.
His black militia retired from the public buildings, Coke took
undisputed control of the office to which he had been chosen,
and "reconstruction" passed into history in Texas.

The people of North Carolina, with her credit sunk to the
lowest depths under a weight of theft and extravagance—more
than $27,000,000 had been granted away to railroad com-
panies—[2] found the opportunity at the elections in 1870 to cast
off the men who dishonored that state. Holden, the scalawag
governor, and the carpetbaggers who surrounded him,[3] had
called upon the Federal government for troops—he had pursued
his enemies under martial law in an effort to save himself from
an angry, and, by this time, thoroughly aroused public sentiment. But his struggles were futile; the popular judgment
here, as in Texas, was too hostile. Under the leadership of the
fearless and able editor of the Raleigh Sentinel, Josiah Turner, a
campaign was organized which resulted in a "sweeping conservative victory." [4] The legislature, with a large Democratic
majority, was now ready to impeach and remove Holden from
office,[5] and with him went the carpetbaggers and native rascals,
who were his partners in the mismanagement of the government.
Swepson and Littlefield, the railroad thieves, departed the state
to escape their merited punishments.

"Reconstruction" in North Carolina was now practically
undone. With the aid of the Federal political machinery, in a
campaign of intense excitement, another Republican governor
was elected in 1872,[6] and the state gave Grant a majority over

[1] For Grant's letter of Jan. 12, 1874, see Am. Ann. Cyclop. for 1873, p.
740.
[2] Hamilton, Recon. in N. C., p. 448.
[3] Ibid., p. 343.   [5] Ibid., pp. 537–57.
[4] Ibid., pp. 521–2,   [6] Ibid., p. 589.

Greeley; but the legislature remained conservative.[1] In 1876, when that effective popular orator and adroit campaigner, Zebulon B. Vance, was elected to the governorship, the executive branch of the government also passed out of the hands of the Republicans.

The struggle was to continue for yet a while longer in Alabama, Mississippi, Arkansas, Florida, South Carolina and Louisiana, with South Carolina and Louisiana leading the number in the mad contention of men and parties for the privilege of picking bare the bones of the prostrate Southern states.

But, even where the state governments were again committed to the hands of the native elements, the people were still to be disturbed by electoral contests in districts which were largely inhabited by negroes. Here designing politicians saw the opportunity to win for themselves lucrative local offices, and, now and again, seats in Congress. The Federal administration gave encouragement to this carpetbag and negro minority in the distribution of postmasterships, impost and internal revenue collectorships and other Federal offices, by the activities of the Department of Justice in answer to the terms of the Enforcement Acts and by the use of United States troops.[2] There was at hand, in each state, a Republican party, magnetized by patronage, which threatened to resume the direction of the government, with the sympathy of large bodies of the Northern people, who were animated by lively accounts of the "outrages" perpetrated upon the negroes by their old and cruel masters, not yet ready to give up the "rebellion,"[3] and by contributions of money from the national Republican campaign treasuries.

The response of Congress, and at the North generally, to the movement of the Southern people for "liberation" from such villanies as were put upon them was, as will further appear, a war of opinion—continued Radical enmity on the one side, combating, on the other, a feeling, born of growing disgust for

---

[1] Hamilton, Recon. in N. C., p. 593.
[2] Cf. Charles Nordhoff, The Cotton States, pp. 13–4.
[3] Cf. N. Y. Nation, Oct. 15, 1874.

the hypocrisy of covering public rascality with the mantle of patriotism and philanthropy—out of which came a moderation of sentiment reflected in national policy. The moderates, or Liberals, had had their influence upon the elections of 1874, although the corruptions in the North rather than in the South, had been a principal cause for men in that year to turn from the Republican to the Democratic party.[1] After the "tidal wave" of that year it was clear to the Radicals that whatever partisan measure they might yet wish to include in their program must be hurried forward—it must be made into law before March 4, 1875, when the House would no longer be under Republican management.

The "Enforcement Acts" had been designed primarily to combat the Ku Klux, for which purpose they had been not without value.[2] But their later use was mainly, if not entirely, political and partisan. They were invoked for the "protection" of the black man in voting the Republican ticket. Without such protection for him, President Grant said in his message to Congress in December, 1873, "the whole scheme of colored enfranchisement is worse than mockery and little better than a crime."[3]

This short final session of the Forty-third Congress found the situation in Louisiana, as we shall see, at its most acute conjuncture, with Sheridan, by the President's orders, in command, reaching out with an iron hand beyond the borders of that perturbed commonwealth into Mississippi and Arkansas. Another "Force Bill" was frankly wanted to secure the vote of the Southern states in the approaching Presidential election.[4] It was supported by Grant; his friends originated it and were its obdurate advocates. The battle ground was in the House, where the Democrats successfully filibustered,—at one session (through the night of February 24–25, 1875) for a period of 29 hours—[5] until, when it was passed by a vote of 135 to 109, at

[1] Cf. Mayes, Life of Lamar, p. 204.
[2] Cf. Nordhoff, The Cotton States, p. 80.
[3] Richardson, Messages and Papers, vol. vii, p. 297.
[4] Mayes, Life of Lamar, p. 213; Merriam, Life and Times of Bowles, vol. ii, p. 239.
[5] Mayes, Life of Lamar, p. 214.

midnight on Saturday, February 27,[1] it was too late, under the
rules of the Senate, for that body to act.

The only measure on the Radical program to be made into a
law was the much and long discussed "Supplementary Civil
Rights Bill" for the negroes, sponsored so pertinaciously by
Senator Sumner.[2] On his death bed he had exacted a promise
from Judge Hoar [3] that this project for securing the extension
of Federal guarantees of "equal rights" for the blacks should
not be abandoned by the party. It must be modified; its most
extreme provisions, as, for instance, concerning the intermixture
of the races in the schools,[4] must be abandoned. But it was
adopted to cover the presence of negroes in inns, theatres and
public conveyances and in the jury room by both Houses, and approved by the President,[5] in spite of the plainest assertions that
such action was unconstitutional,[6] a dead letter from the first,
for the negro who was to be favored by it, as well as for the
white man who was to be put under admonishment and penalty,
until he should be rid of his antipathies for another man because of the color of his skin.[7] The only fruit of the law and the
debates attending its passage was a further inflammation of
sectional prejudice and race hate.

The progress out of their troublous bondage of the states,
in which Republican control continued, may be followed in
them in turn to the end.

In Alabama William H. Smith, the Southern lawyer of
"Unionist sympathies," whom the Republicans had put at
the head of the "reconstructed" government, with his carpet-

[1] Many Republicans voted against it, including Dawes, Garfield, Charles
Foster, E. R. Hoar, G. F. Hoar, Kasson, W. W. Phelps, Poland, J. R.
Hawley, H. J. Scudder and Lowndes. For summarized proceedings see
McPherson, Handbook of Politics for 1876, pp. 13–18.

[2] Supplementary to the Act of Apr. 9, 1866.

[3] Pierce, Memoirs and Letters of Sumner, vol. iv, p. 598.

[4] For a view of what this would have meant in the South see Speeches,
Correspondence and Political Papers of Carl Schurz, vol. iii, pp. 90–92.

[5] U. S. Statutes at Large, vol. xviii, p. 335.

[6] Cf. N. Y. Nation, March 4 and April 1 and 8, 1875; also 109 U. S.,
p. 3, in which the Supreme Court, in 1884, declared the law unconstitutional.

[7] Debates and votes summarized in McPherson, Handbook of Politics
for 1876, pp. 3–13.

ALABAMA

197

bag and scalawag associates in the other state offices, and a
Radical legislature, containing many negroes,[1] could not be
reached by the people until 1870. One of the United States
senators, George E. Spencer, who had entered the army as a
sutler of a regiment from Nebraska, though later he had become a soldier, made himself a shrewd and an unscrupulous
influence at the seat of Federal government.[2] He became the
link which bound the Republican organization in Alabama
with the Grant administration. For three years, unhindered,
the plunder of state and county proceeded.[3]

In 1870, when a new governor and a new legislature were
to be elected, the conservatives had cherished the hope of
overturning the perfidious political ring which had laid its
ruthless hand upon the commonwealth. Governor Smith, who
was wanting in authority as a leader and was not cordially
liked even by his own party, was renominated on a ticket,
unfortunately for him, with a negro who was the candidate
for secretary of state. It was an opportunity; the conservatives would oppose Smith with a "white man's candidate," a
Scotchman, settled for some twenty years in northern Alabama,
Robert Burns Lindsay, who won at the polls. But the majority
was so small that a contest was commenced, and Smith, under
Radical advice, protected by United States troops, refused to
yield his place in the state house. His retirement was compassed peaceably by a judicial writ. Though the Democrats,
aided by some anti-radical and independent members, came
into control of the house, the senate, which, by reason of a
subterfuge, continued in place without re-election, remained
Republican, and little of value could be accomplished. Two
years of strife ensued, marked, however, by some amelioration
in the position of the white property-holding inhabitants of
the state, especially in the field of local government.[4]

Again, in 1872, the attempt to entirely free the state from

[1] Fleming, Recon. in Ala., pp. 738-9.
[2] Ibid., p. 737; cf. Fleming, Documentary Hist. of Recon., vol. ii, pp.
131-2.
[3] Fleming, Recon. in Ala., pp. 740-41.
[4] Ibid., pp. 753-4.

the evil forces which oppressed it, could be resumed, but with less opportunity of success, since it was "Presidential year." Grant was to be re-elected over Greeley, a candidate for whom the South could feel only a cool sympathy, if not an emphatic abhorrence. Ku Klux "outrages" were "staged" to support appeals to the Federal government, and the troops which came into the state were so disposed as to serve the interests of the Republican party. Large sums of money were expended to insure a majority in Alabama for Grant,[1] and the Radicals elected their candidate for governor, an unstable character[2] named Lewis. On the face of the returns both houses of the legislature were Democratic. But, Spencer's term in the United States Senate having expired, he wished to be re-elected. The efforts which he had already made to corrupt the fountains of democracy had been large, and he was not willing to yield the prize to another. His adherents were bound to him by payments of money from Republican chests in Alabama and in the North. Some were in possession of lucrative offices which they desired to hold; others had the hope of gaining posts through his activity in their behalf.[3] Separate legislatures were organized, the Democrats in the state capitol building, the Radical minority in the United States court-house at Montgomery. The minority proceeded to re-elect Spencer; the new governor Lewis certified the election and called for Federal troops which were soon upon the ground.[4] Attorney General Williams prepared an artful scheme for a "compromise," which, when the two bodies should be united, would give the Spencer men control of the house. Then a treacherous Radical "broke a pair" which he had made in the senate. A Democratic member was unseated, a Republican claimant was installed in the place, and that chamber also came under Radical control. It would be a stain upon the records of the United States Senate, but Spencer was found to have been legally elected when the contest was transferred to Washing-

[1] Fleming, Recon. in Ala., p. 759.
[2] He had been a member, for a time, of the Confederate Congress.
[3] Fleming, Recon. in Ala., pp. 759–60.
[4] Why the Solid South, pp. 57–8.

ALABAMA 199

ton (though that body refused, until 1885, to reimburse him
for the expense he had incurred in maintaining his title to the
seat), and for six years more he was to be seen in the council
chambers of the republic.[1]

The end was now near. An enormous debt, high taxes,
incompetent and ignorant men in administrative posts, a
corrupt judiciary, riots instigated for political objects, the
arrest of innocent citizens, the free use of Federal troops for
the oppression of the intelligent and property-owning classes
led to a popular rising in 1874. In the undisturbed enjoyment
of power for several years, the Radical leaders had involved
themselves in jealous contention. Scalawag hated carpetbagger; the black man had a diminishing confidence in either
one of the other of the white elements, which had been using
him for the accomplishment of their selfish ends. Negroes
complained that they were given but a small moiety of the
offices. Rewards of any kind which were promised them were
not received. The threats of the coming of the rebel army,
of their re-enslavement, of their suffering other ills, both
general and particular, if they should vote for the Democratic
party, had less and less potency in political campaigns. On
the other hand race "equality," as it was recommended to
the country by the Radicals, who at each session of Congress
discussed Sumner's civil rights bill, was a fearful portent.
There were few who would vote for the Republican candidates
when it was made clear that the imposition upon the South
of such conditions as were contemplated by this measure was
the purpose of the party. Should negro or white man rule
the state? was a question which all could understand.[2] Upon
this issue the result was not doubtful.

The contest brought forward George S. Houston as the
Democratic candidate for governor, a man whose course during
the war had awakened few antipathies in the Republicans,
and, on the "race issue," aided by the revulsion of feeling on

[1] G. S. Taft, Compilation of Senate Election Cases, pp. 556–78; Fleming,
Recon. in Ala., p. 760.
[2] Fleming, Recon. in Ala., p. 779; House Reports, 43rd Cong. 2nd sess.,
no. 262, pp. ii–v; House Ex. Doc., 43rd Cong. 2nd sess., no. 46, p. 7.

the subject of extravagance and venality in the management
of the government, he was elected over Lewis, who had been
renominated for the office by the Radicals. The struggle was
memorable. The inevitable appeals to Washington did not
fail to stir Republicans in the North. Among the least estimable
of a number of entirely unworthy persons then in Congress
from Alabama was Charles Hays, before the war a savage
slave owner, now a scalawag from the "Black Belt." He
wrote a letter to Representative Hawley of Connecticut, in
September, 1874, reciting a number of "outrages" to which
negro and white Republicans had lately been subjected in
Alabama, and, although a correspondent of the New York
Tribune, who was sent to the scene, denounced it as "a tissue
of lies from beginning to end," [1] it was industriously circulated
in the North to serve the purpose for which it had been contrived, and was made the basis for the despatch of troops to
the state by Secretary Belknap, the appointment of deputy
marshals, and the arrest, by order of Attorney General Williams, of many Southern white men under the provisions of
the Enforcement Acts. [2]

Still more would be done. In the spring of 1874 the rivers of
Alabama had overflowed their banks. The floods were not
disastrous, [3] but Congress had charitably made an appropriation of money for the relief of the sufferers. It was summer
time and early fall before the distribution of the bounty was
begun, when it took the form of bacon, which was assigned to
various counties for the use of negroes who would vote the
Republican ticket. In all, about 115 tons, packed in boxes
and hogsheads, were shipped into the state. "Two or three
shoulders" of it were accounted sufficient to keep a black
man from deserting the party of Lincoln and Grant. [4] Much
of it found its way into counties which had no rivers, and which,

[1] N. Y. Tribune, Oct. 7, 8 and 12, 1874.
[2] Fleming, Recon. in Ala., pp. 786–90; House Ex. Dec., 43rd Cong. 2nd
sess., no. 110, p. 3; House Reports, 43rd Cong. 2nd sess., no. 362, pp. lxi.
[3] Why the Solid South, pp. 61–2.
[4] Fleming, Recon. in Ala., p. 785; cf. Charles Nordhoff, The Cotton
States, pp. 13, 87–8.

therefore, could have needed little assistance from the generous hand of Congress on the ground of damage done by the overflow, and in some cases, the fraud detected, the bacon was seized and returned to the government.[1]

Such methods on one side led to the employment of similar measures on the other. Much was at stake. If whites were intimidated by United States marshals and Federal soldiers, so were negroes terrorized. They were barbarously attacked by bodies of Alabama vigilantes, organized as the Ku Klux had been.[2] If blacks were bribed with the bacon of Congress, so were they made to see their duty to the other party by similar means, for, by contributions of citizens of Alabama who were stirred to the need of the greatest sacrifices, of Northern men who had invested capital in the state, and from other sources, a large sum of money had been assembled. Lawyers and all men who could effectively speak from the stump abandoned their accustomed pursuits and entered the campaign. The borders of the state were guarded so that there could be no importation of negroes from Mississippi and Georgia. Polling places were under constant inspection to prevent "repeating," and a fraudulent count and return of the votes.[3] Here and there altercations occurred. A white man shot a negro or the reverse, but, with the exception of a riot at Eufaula in which four men were killed and some 70 or 75 were wounded, the election was held with few infractions of the peace.[4] Houston was successful. There was a majority of 27 Democrats on joint ballot in the legislature, the number of negro members still being about 35. The victory had come; the way was now open for a new constitution, which was adopted in 1875, and a reorganization of the

[1] House Ex. Doc., 43rd Cong. 2nd sess., no. 110; also House Reports, 43rd Cong. 2nd sess., no. 262, majority and minority reports; Fleming, Recon. in Ala., pp. 783-5.

[2] House Ex. Doc., 43rd Cong. 2nd sess., no. 46.

[3] The methods of the Democrats as seen by the Republicans are described in House Reports, 43rd Cong. 2nd sess., no. 262, and Senate Reports, 44th Cong. 2nd sess., no. 704.

[4] The whole subject was investigated by a committee of Congressmen who visited Alabama in the winter of 1874-5 and made majority and minority reports.—House Reports, 43rd Cong. 2nd sess., no. 262.

government in the interest of honesty, economy and good order.

Arkansas had come back into the Union in 1868, and was in complete control of the Radicals, with Powell Clayton, a native of Pennsylvania, later of Kansas, an officer of cavalry in the Union army, since the war the owner of a plantation on the Arkansas River,[1] as its governor. The negroes were not numerous, and the question of their gaining a dominant position over the whites assumed no great importance.[2] It was rather the contentious and turbulent spirit of the people, developed under the impulse of greed for corrupt power, which accounted for the violent factional warfare displayed in Arkansas. Clayton's arbitrary conduct toward his rivals in his own party, and his unyielding attitude toward the old resident white population soon involved him in bitter strife, which extended beyond the boundaries of the state.

In 1870 he had so manipulated the elections that he was in a position to be chosen to the United States Senate.[3] The legislature was organized to do his bidding. He received a large vote for the office, but trouble ensued at once. The lieutenant-governor who would succeed to the governorship, upon Clayton's resignation to go to Washington, was an enemy. That officer was impeached, a movement which came to nothing except to lead in turn to impeachment proceedings directed against Clayton himself,[4] and the chief justice. At length the differences of the tricksters were adjusted, Clayton was again elected United States senator, and, being enabled to leave the governorship in the hands of a friend, he proceeded to Washington,[5] where he must face charges of corruption and maintain his title to his seat, though the Republican majority in the Senate soon took action which made him feel comfortable in it.[6]

[1] J. M. Harrell, Brooks and Baxter War, pp. 47, 50–52, 68.
[2] Clayton, Aftermath of the Civil War, p. 307.
[3] Senate Reports, 43rd Cong. 3rd sess., no. 512; T. S. Staples, Recon. in Ark., pp. 382–4.
[4] Clayton, Aftermath of the Civil War, chap. xv.
[5] Harrell, Brooks and Baxter War, p. 99; Staples, Recon. in Ark, pp. 386–7.
[6] Senate Reports, 42nd Cong. 3rd sess., no. 512; also Taft, Senate Election Cases, pp. 386–422.

In 1872 another governor was to be chosen by the people. The Clayton organization, locally known as "Minstrels," [1] nominated a scalawag, named Elisha Baxter. He had been a slaveholder. Though in its early stages he had had the hope of being a neutral observer of the war, he had taken a post in the quartermaster's department of the Southern army stationed in Arkansas. Later he passed to the other side to serve the Unionists as a wagon master, and in similar capacities, in and around Little Rock, an exhibition of heroism for which he was, for a time, confined by the Confederates in the penitentiary. Baxter had figured prominently in the "rump" government, with which, while the war still continued, it was designed to bring Arkansas back into the Union as a "loyal state" and it was natural that he should now be a Radical. Since he had read law for a little while, Clayton had thought him fit for appointment as a circuit judge. [2]

The other wing of the party, which was a dissatisfied faction, known as "Brindles," or "Brindle Tails," [3] adopted a "reform" platform, espoused the Greeley and Liberal Republican cause, and nominated Joseph Brooks, a rough Methodist preacher, originally from Ohio, who had seen some inconspicuous service in the Union army. [4] The Democrats and conservatives, to whom both tickets were obnoxious, regarded Brooks as the least so, and finally, though reluctantly, gave him their support. [5] Which of the two candidates had received a majority of the ballots at the election could not be clearly ascertained in the light of such frauds as attended the casting and return of the votes, [6]

---

[1] House Reports, 43rd Cong. 1st sess., no. 771, p. 123; Staples, Recon. in Ark., p. 389.

[2] House Reports, 43rd Cong. 1st sess., no. 771, p. 15; Clayton, Aftermath of the Civil War, p. 347.

[3] House Reports, 43rd Cong. 1st sess., no. 771, p. 123; Harrell, Brooks and Baxter War, p. 96; Staples, Recon. in Ark., p. 389.

[4] House Reports, 43rd Cong. 1st sess., no. 771, p. 15. Brooks's powerful voice, was "audible for squares, in its highest cadences, shook the building and thrilled like a lion's roar."—Brooks and Baxter War, p. 112. Cf. Staples, Recon. in Ark., p. 395.

[5] Staples, op. cit., pp. 394–5, 396.

[6] Cf. House Reports, 43rd Cong. 2nd sess., no. 127, pp. 2–3; House Mis. Doc., 43rd Cong. 2nd sess., no. 65, pp. 2–4.

after a canvass of intense bitterness, marked by many vio-
lences, covering the entire state. In one county the disorders
were so grave that the militia was mobilized.[1] Three counties
made no returns—they were suppressed. The votes received
in 48 precincts in other counties were thrown out. Registration books were tampered with and stolen. Ballot boxes were
"stuffed" for one candidate; the tickets bearing the name of the
other were destroyed.[2] Brooks was certainly the choice of
a majority of the people, but it was clear that Baxter was to
be "counted in."[3] When the legislature met, it, too, was
organized in Baxter's interest—his friends were seated, others
found their names excluded from the rolls, and, after much of
this kind of chicanery, the body was ready to canvass the votes.
In conformity with the program, it declared Baxter elected by
some 3,000 majority, and, in January, 1873, he took the oath
of office. No time was lost in electing, as Clayton's colleague
in the United States Senate, another carpetbagger, born in
Vermont, later of Ohio, recently come to Arkansas for some
manœuvres with a railroad company,[4] still barely past thirty
years of age, Stephen W. Dorsey.

Brooks and the "Brindles" refused to recognize the legality
of the canvass, and filled Baxter with so much fear of violent
attempts to dispossess him of the office that he reorganized
the militia and made it ready for action. Denied a hearing in
the legislature, Brooks commenced a long and tedious contest
in the courts. An appeal to the Circuit Court of the United
States was dismissed because of no jurisdiction.[5] A writ of
quo warranto was sought in the supreme court of the state.
This was denied, on the ground that it was the duty of the
legislature to determine the question, and, that it had done

[1] Article on Arkansas in Am. Ann. Cyclop. for 1872.

[2] The "corruption and trickery," cheating and fraud formed an "abhor-
rent mass," said Representative Scudder of New York, a Republican Congressman, in Cong. Record, 43rd Cong. 2nd sess., p. 2087. Cf. Staples,
Recon. in Ark., pp. 396-7.

[3] House Reports, 43rd Cong. 2nd sess., no. 127, pp. 3, 19.

[4] "He built a railroad that was never built."—Senate Ex. Doc., 43rd
Cong. 2nd sess., no. 25, p. 23.

[5] House Ex. Doc., 43rd Cong. 1st sess., no. 229, pp. 16-24; Harrell,
Brooks and Baxter War, p. 171.

so.[1] The faction then instituted a movement for a constitutional convention as a means of ousting the "usurper" and of "reforming" the government.

But what had been unsuccessfully sought in the higher courts was procured in answer to proceedings taken in a lower one, and, in April, 1874, Brooks, armed with such authority, forcibly entered the governor's office in the state house, ejected his rival and assumed "the gubernatorial insignia and paraphernalia."[2] Baxter retired to a college building on the outskirts of the city, from which he soon moved to a hotel near the state house, and convened the legislature. Each appealed to President Grant; each issued addresses to the people; each gathered troops around him. Armed men, horse and foot, came in from all parts of the state. "Brooks' and Baxter's armies" confronted each other in Little Rock; partisans of the two men were in conflict at other places.

Grant, though hard pressed by both contestants and their respective friends,[3] did little except instruct the United States officer in command of a small body of soldiers at the arsenal in Little Rock "to prevent bloodshed." The Federal troops took their posts between the hostile forces. Artillery was set up in the streets. The excitement was immense. The city wore the appearance of some opera bouffe, albeit dangerous military camp.[4] Railroad communication was interrupted; telegraph offices were seized. Business of all kinds ceased. Each side was constantly receiving black as well as white rabble from the country, for increase of its strength, and the struggle bade fair to become what it is sometimes pretentiously called, the "Brooks and Baxter War."

The people of Arkansas had suffered sorely from all the forms of thievery and extravagance which marked the pretended government of the other Southern states during these shameful

---

[1] House Ex. Doc., 43rd Cong. 1st sess., no. 229, pp. 36–41.

[2] Cong. Globe, 43rd Cong. 2nd sess., p. 2088; cf. Harrell, Brooks and Baxter War, p. 203.

[3] Senate Ex. Doc., 43rd Cong. 1st sess., no. 51.

[4] The "armies" were, in appearance, a truly comical assortment of vagabonds.—St. Louis corr. N. Y. Nation, May 7, 1874.

years. There had not been an honest election "since reconstruction." The taxes were six per cent in Little Rock, assessed upon full and even excessive values.[1] Wild lands were confiscated, as was much other property, the owners of which were unable to meet the increased charges laid upon it. Nearly 3,000,000 acres had been forfeited to the state up to the end of 1872.[2] State and county were robbed in turn and together. The chief thieves lived in fine houses in Little Rock, drank champagne and played poker, while their victims, the taxpayers, worked barefoot in the fields in order to gain the meanest necessaries of existence.[3] Immigration, which had started after the war and had promised to bring strength and wealth to the state, entirely ceased.[4] Ruffians, white and black, ran over the country at will.

By this time Baxter and Brooks had changed sides.[5] Clayton and Dorsey, as pretty a pair of carpetbaggers as any Southern state had contributed to the United States Senate, were now · supporting Brooks.[6] Baxter, refusing to follow their advice as to the "railroad steal bill," in which they were interested,[7] and on other subjects,[8] they for some time had been using all their influences against him,[9] while, he, a vain and vindictive man,[10] had installed what they were pleased to call "rebels" [11] in state offices where Radicals had been. Without the favor of the regularly constituted Republican party organization he was identifying his administration with the interests of the old resident parts of the population, ably led by Augustus H.

[1] House Reports, 43rd Cong. 1st sess., no. 771, pp. 107–8.
[2] Article on Arkansas in Am. Ann. Cyclop. for 1875, p. 38.
[3] Nordhoff, The Cotton States, pp. 32–3; Harrell, Brooks and Baxter War, p. 197.
[4] N. Y. Nation, May 7, 1874.
[5] They were "playing the game of double wabble."—Cong. Record, 43rd Cong. 2nd sess., p. 2088; cf. Clayton, Aftermath of the Civil War, pp. 347–8.
[6] Harrell, Brooks and Baxter War, p. 215.
[7] Ibid., p. 175; House Reports, 43rd Cong. 1st sess., no. 771, pp. 119, 149–50.
[8] Staples, Recon. in Ark., pp. 402, 407–8.
[9] House Reports, 43rd Cong. 1st., sess., no. 771, pp. 94–5.
[10] Ibid., p. 32.
[11] House Reports, 43rd Cong. 2nd sess., no. 127, p. 20.

Garland, a lawyer of Little Rock, who had sat in the House and
then in the Senate of the Congress of the Confederacy. The
way was being prepared for the act which would finally release
Arkansas from alien hands.

With the two "armies" facing each other the situation was
too acute to admit of great delay. The authorities at Washington were strenuously endeavoring to bring about an accommodation. But plans agreeable to Brooks were not agreeable to
Baxter, and no progress was made in this direction. At a
place called New Gascony in Jefferson county there was a pitched
battle. Some skirmishing had occurred in Little Rock. A
steamer was fired on in the river twenty miles above that city.
Several men were killed and wounded in this engagement.[1]
Grant was in a difficult position. The recognized wing of the
party which had elected Baxter, through Clayton and Dorsey,
who were in Washington, and who did not scruple now to condemn the man whom earlier, by every variety of fraud, they had
elevated to and held in the place,[2] was favorable to Brooks.
But Baxter had been acting as governor for many months.[3]
The legislature was organized in his behalf and made declarations in his favor.[4]   Attorney General Williams, under some
influence apart from Clayton's and Dorsey's, gave it as his
opinion that Baxter was legally the governor, because the
legislature had declared him to be such. The President "ought
not to go behind that action to look into the state of the vote."
These considerations, together with the knowledge that Baxter
had gained the sympathy of the more responsible elements
of society in Arkansas, which would not much longer patiently
endure such leadership as Brooks's,[5] caused the President to

[1] In all Staples concludes that 200 lives were lost in the "war."—Recon.
in Ark., p. 414.
[2] "These gentlemen [now hunting Republican sympathy in Congress],
and those connected with them were the very men who concocted and
designed and carried out this fraud. . . .   These are the very men who
hatched the conspiracy and carried it to its completion and fulfillment."—
Congressman Poland, Republican, chairman of House Committee on Ark.
Affairs, in Cong. Record, 43rd Cong. 2nd sess., p. 2107.
[3] Cf. House Reports, 43rd Cong. 2nd sess., no. 127, p. 5.
[4] Senate Ex. Doc., 43rd Cong. 1st sess., no. 51, p. 31.
[5] House Reports, 43rd Cong. 1st sess., no. 771, p. 153.

make the only decision which appeared to be possible in the case. On May 15, 1874, he issued a proclamation recognizing Baxter as the rightful incumbent of the office and commanding the forces of Brooks to disband.[1] They promptly did so. Some of Brooks's friends followed him in vacating their offices.[2] By circuitous routes, lest they suffer bodily harm, they left the state, to appear in St. Louis and shortly in Washington, ready to give their accounts of their adventures and persecutions to their partisans in Congress.[3] More impeachments were prepared at Little Rock. Removals and suspensions from office were announced in great numbers.[4] Recalcitrants were dispossessed by the militia, Baxter posting off into the country squads of cavalry for this purpose. Men were arrested for "treason" and incarcerated.[5]

Brooks and his following a while ago had been the advocates of a constitutional convention.[6] Now such a convention was the palladium of the liberties of the Baxterites. Delegates to it were chosen, and it met. The constitution which it adopted was approved by the people. A new governor, the Democratic leader, A. H. Garland, was elected, and Baxter in November, 1874, though he had been chosen for four years, vacated his office, which he was accused by his Radical enemies of doing too compliantly, in order that the new régime might begin. Indeed, it was alleged that he had en-

[1] Richardson, Messages and Papers, vol. vii, pp. 272–3; Baxter's letter of thanks in Senate Ex. Doc. 43rd Cong. 2nd sess., no. 25, pp. 22–3; N. Y. Nation, May 21, 1874.

[2] Staples, Recon. in Ark., pp. 420–21.

[3] The various appeals, addresses and proclamations bearing on this subject are conveniently brought together in article on Arkansas in Am. Ann. Cyclop. for 1874.

[4] House Reports, 43rd Cong. 1st sess., no. 771, p. 36; House Reports, 43rd Cong. 2nd sess., no. 127, p. 31.

[5] House Reports, 43rd Cong. 1st sess., no. 771, pp. 42–5. Fitting revenge for Brooks's promise during the campaign, in 1872, that, if he were elected, he would fill the penitentiary so full of Baxter men that their legs would stick out of the windows.—Ibid., p. 88; Cong. Record, 43rd Cong. 2nd sess., p. 2108.

[6] Cong. Record, 43rd Cong. 2nd sess., p. 2109; House Reports, 43rd Cong. 1st sess., no. 771, p. 151.

tered into a conspiracy to deliver over the state to the Democratic party.[1]

Now a new agitation was commenced by the Radicals, Dramatic appeals to the Republican leaders, deep draughts upon the sympathy of the party which had liberated the slave and saved the Union, supported by many a tale of murder and outlawry directed by "rebels" against the "loyal" people of Arkansas, marked the winter of 1874-75. Clayton, Dorsey, and Brooks moved with all their forces upon Congress and the President.[2] The constitutional convention was declared to have been illegal—the legislature which called it had had no right to act in the premises; the government set up by the new constitution was "revolutionary."

Attempts were made to displace the new governor, Garland, in favor of the Radical lieutenant-governor, who, at Baxter's abdication, was a pretender to the titles and honors of the greater office.[3] Brooks's claims were still pressed also. Congress and the President, under the fourth section of the fourth article of the Constitution of the United States, should intervene on the ground that Arkansas had ceased to have a "republican" form of government.[4]

The Select Committee on the Condition of Affairs in Arkansas, of which Mr. Poland was the chairman, although the House was still under Republican control, on February 6, 1875, halted this movement. The government formed by the new constitution it found to be as "republican" as, and, in many respects, "an improvement," upon that which had preceded it.[5] So much was well, but the President was yet to be heard from. He had directed attention to the condition of affairs in the state in his message to Congress in December, 1874.[6] Now he would

[1] House Reports, 43rd Cong. 2nd sess., no. 127, minority report; Clayton, Aftermath of the Civil War, chap. xvii.

[2] Senate Ex. Doc., 43rd Cong. 2nd sess., no. 25, pp. 77-96; Cong. Record, 43rd Cong. 2nd sess., p. 2107.

[3] See his statements and claims in Senate Ex. Doc., 43rd Cong. 2nd sess., no. 25, pp. 24-77.

[4] The memorial and the arguments are in Senate Mis. Doc., 43rd Cong. 2nd sess., no. 65.

[5] House Reports, 43rd Cong. 2nd sess., no. 127, pp. 15-6.

[6] Richardson, Messages and Papers, vol. vii, p. 298.

say more and in a vigorous style. Though he had announced on May 15, 1874, that Baxter ought, by the citizens of the state, "to be considered as the lawful executive," having been declared "duly elected" by the general assembly,[1] he, on February 8, 1875, two days after the Poland Committee made its report, asserted that Brooks, and not Baxter, had been "lawfully elected." The overthrow of the government by the adoption of the new constitution in 1874 had been accomplished, he said, "by violence, intimidation and revolutionary proceedings." If "permitted to stand" it would be a precedent "dangerous to the stability" of our political institutions.[2] The President who had received the praise of the country, in May, 1874, had been deserted by that rugged common sense which men liked to discern in his character, and he was again in the hands of Dorsey, Clayton and the Arkansas carpet-bag lobby.[3]

But nothing came of the preposterous fustian and threat of the Arkansas men at Washington in spite of their friend, the President.[4] Their somersaults had had too obvious a purpose, and had been made too clearly in public view. To relieve the country, entirely weary of the unworthy dispute, of any further disturbance from this source, if it should be possible, the House on March 2, 1875, by a vote of 147 to 94 adopted the report of Mr. Poland's committee, after a speech from him (the last he was to make before his retirement from a useful political career) and appeals from two or three other Republicans, who could not lend their favor to such performances, declaring to be "inadvisable" any "interference with the existing government" in Arkansas "by any department of the government of the United States."[5]

Mr. Garland, with a Democratic legislature at his hand, appointed a day of thanksgiving for the state's release from its persecutors. He was reforming the election laws, improving

[1] Richardson, Messages and Papers, vol. vii, p. 272.

[2] Ibid., p. 319.

[3] Cf. N. Y. Nation, Feb. 11, 1875; Staples, Recon. in Ark., p. 439.

[4] Except a postmastership at Little Rock for Brooks.—N. Y. Nation, April, 1875.

[5] Cong. Record, 43rd Cong. 2nd sess., pp. 2116-7.

the system of administration, reorganizing the finances and reducing the costs of the government,—it was the end of "reconstructionist" misrule in Arkansas.[1]

In Mississippi, the first civil governor after the reconstruction of the state by Congress, a "rebel" brigadier-general who had gone over to the Republican party, James L. Alcorn, began his administration in 1870. He was identified with the community and should have been able to make the system of government which had been devised for the South as acceptable to the people as it anyhow or anywhere could have been. But he soon resigned to transfer his activities to Washington as the successor of the negro United States Senator, Revels, to be followed in office by the lieutenant-governor, Parsons, a carpetbagger and an ex-Union soldier, who, however, had established *bona fide* residence in the state as a cotton planter, and in some degree enjoyed the respect of the native white population.[2]

Alcorn's colleague at Washington was General Ames, "Ben" Butler's son-in-law, who as the military governor of the state had gained a powerful influence over the new negro voters. The two men now involved themselves in disputes which divided the Republican party in Mississippi. Alcorn, an old resident and the owner of property, would join issue with Ames, a carpetbagger, who owned no property in the state (or had not done so until his situation for politic reasons seemed to require it) and paid no taxes.[3]

Ames gained the nomination for governor in the Republican state convention in 1873 on a ticket containing the names of no less than three negroes, one of them, the nominee for superintendent of education, under indictment for larceny in New York,[4] while Alcorn ran on an independent ticket, being supported by the conservative Republicans and the Democrats, who put forward no candidate of their own. Ames was elected by nearly 20,000 majority over his opponent, and was inducted

[1] House Reports, 43rd Cong. 2nd sess., no. 2, p. 485; Senate Ex. Doc., 43rd Cong. 2nd sess., no. 25, pp. 20–21.
[2] Garner, Recon. in Miss., pp. 280–81, 291.
[3] Ibid., pp. 291–2; Mayes, Life of Lamar, pp. 176–7.
[4] Garner, Recon. in Miss., p. 293; Life of Lamar, p. 258.

into his office in January, 1870, with a legislature which was overwhelmingly Republican in both branches. Half, or nearly half of the members of the house were negroes, one of them being elected speaker.[1]

The groundwork for Ames's great unpopularity with the white conservatives of the state had been prepared while he was military governor, in a time of unusual bitterness of feeling, when upon his own motion, or, by direction from Washington, he had done them so much affront, and his acts now could not but be viewed with the greatest unfriendliness and distrust.[2] He absented himself from the state,[3] and, while beyond its borders, the negro lieutenant-governor, who was an evil spirit and the tool of rogues, presumed to act in his stead. Although Ames himself is not held to have been venal—it is not alleged that he personally profited by jobbery—it is clear that he had almost no knowledge of the principles of civil government, if, indeed, he had the capacity necessary to discharge large engagements of any description.

The debt of Mississippi was trifling, since the constitution forbade the lending of the public credit to railroads and other private enterprises. The field left open for knavish activities of this kind was in the city and county.[4] Thus it was that a crisis in political affairs was reached in Vicksburg. The city had 11,000 inhabitants, including some families of intelligence and wealth. Grants had been made to railroad companies, "improvements" had led to large bond issues. The debt of Vicksburg which had been but $13,000 in 1869 had, by profligate management, been increased, in 1874, to $1,400,000. The people were confronted by a seven per cent tax rate and they formed a "taxpayers' league" to resist such aggressions. The "Ring" was impervious to criticism or protest, as appeared when, in 1874, it nominated an infamous ticket. For mayor its

---

[1] Garner, Recon. in Miss., pp. 294–5.

[2] Ibid., p. 294.

[3] A real carpetbagger he was heard to say that, if he were not an office holder in the state, he would not live in it should he be presented with the whole of it.—House Reports, 43rd Cong. 2nd sess., no. 265, p. xxxvi.

[4] Cf. Nordhoff, The Cotton States, p. 75.

candidate was, indeed, a white man, but one who stood under indictment, it was said, for no less than 23 criminal offenses. For aldermen it put forward one white man, a saloonkeeper who could not write his name, and seven ignorant negroes. Great excitement reigned during the campaign. Armed clubs were formed and paraded the streets. Thoroughly frightened, the negro lieutenant-governor, and Ames, when he returned to Mississippi, telegraphed to Washington for United States troops. But their requests were unheeded and the "People's ticket" was elected.

The whites now were ready to attack the corrupt men who conducted the affairs of Warren county in which Vicksburg is situated. The negroes did not pay one per cent of the taxes, yet the entire collections were disbursed by black men. A "taxpayers' convention" demanded the resignation of the rascals in office. Upon receiving their refusal to comply, the delegates proceeded in a body to the court house, compelling a negro sheriff who was a leader in villany, and others to vacate their places. Ames was appealed to and was asked to visit the scene in person to quell the tumult. He declined, and, instead, ordered negro militiamen to "restore the supremacy of the law," thus adding fuel to the flames. Armed blacks marched in from the country and soon met the organized resistance of the white people. Bloodshed was inevitable. A number of negroes, a few white men were killed—many more were wounded. The Congressional committee which, in due time, visited the scene to investigate the "Vicksburg riots," as this disturbance was called, declared it to have been a "massacre"; it was "wilful, cowardly murder." [1]

The legislature was convened in extraordinary session and Ames, taking the part of the negroes against the whites, although the latter in this controversy included many ex-Union soldiers and Republicans as well as Democrats, sent further calls to Washington for Federal aid. Now there was response. On December 21, 1874, a fortnight after the outbreak, Grant commanded all "disorderly and turbulent persons to disperse

[1] House Reports, 43rd Cong. 2nd sess., no. 265, p. viii.

and retire peaceably to their respective abodes within five days."[1] It was the "Vicksburg riots" in connection with the posture of affairs in Louisiana which, in January, 1875, brought Sheridan to New Orleans. He soon sent troops to Vicksburg to reinstate the deposed black sheriff, action which but delayed, not only in the city but also in the state, the people's final reckoning with their oppressors.[2]

In 1875 the cherished opportunity was at hand. In the elections of that year Congressmen, a state treasurer, members of the legislature and county and local officers were to be chosen. The Democratic party, which, since 1868, had made almost no pretense to activity was now reorganized and a state convention was called to meet in August. In Lucius Quintus Cincinnatus Lamar, a lawyer of intellectual parts and an orator of power, the party had a fine leader. He had been active in politics before the war. He had sat in the Congress of the United States, but had left it in December, 1860, to stump his state for secession. He had been a soldier in the Confederate army, he had served the Southern government in high civil capacities. Now he re-entered public life. While waiting for a return of his law practice, his district, in 1872, re-elected him to the Congress from which he had departed twelve years agone. He was admitted to his seat in December, 1873, to become a leading, useful and popular member of the House of Representatives. An opportunity to conciliate the sections, which he honestly desired, and which, by his parliamentary experience and skill he could effectively use, came to him almost at once upon the death of Charles Sumner. He did not hesitate, and on April 28, 1874, delivered an address to a thronged house, expressive of Southern feeling, with the Massachusetts senator as his theme,[3] which made a profound impression upon his hearers, and, in a little while, through the press, upon the nation at large.[4] He had

---

[1] Richardson, Messages and Papers, vol. vii, p. 323.

[2] Garner, Recon. in Miss., pp. 328–37; Mayes, Life of Lamar, pp. 232 et seq.

[3] Ending with the words—"My countrymen, know one another and you will love one another."

[4] Mayes, Life of Lamar, pp. 183–94.

gained the ear of the North, and, aided by General John B.
Gordon in the Senate, and others recently come to Washington,
was to be of the greatest value to the South in its contest to
regain self-government. In his place in the House he had
spoken with power and effect for Louisiana. He now would not
spare himself in his own state of Mississippi in the struggle
which impended.[1]

The people were to be stirred to action through the newspapers in great open air mass meetings and at barbecues.
Bodies of men, many of them in uniform, some on horse and
others on foot, were organized for the campaign. Every
little town was to be aroused to the need of making an effort
to throw off the burdens of the corrupt Radical government.
Delegates from all parts of the state attended a convention
in the capitol in Jackson in August, which Lamar addressed
for three hours. A "reform" platform was adopted, which,
through his sage influence, avoided a drawing of the "color
line," [2] but he might have saved himself the effort, for black
or white government was the issue which soon claimed the
attention of every mind. As the campaign advanced he appeared before large audiences in all parts of the state. Other
Southern leaders were drawn into the canvass, often to speak
from the platform with him. No measure was overlooked,
no opportunity was neglected, which would further the end in
view. For three months office, shop and field were abandoned,
so absorbing was the contest. Clubs of "White Liners,"
bands of music, the booming of artillery which was dragged
from place to place, the explosion of anvils, flying flags, gal-
loping horsemen, gave an almost military appearance to the
whole countryside.

It was said that to mimic and threaten war was the purpose
of the managers of the campaign. The negroes were to be
frightened and subdued so that they would not dare to vote.
But, if the whites were generally armed and were given to the

[1] Mayes, Life of Lamar, p. 248.
[2] The "white line" as it was called in Mississippi.—Garner, Recon. in
Miss., p. 373.

use of pistols and guns, so were the blacks.[1] Amid such conditions some turbulence was inevitable. A number of political and race riots[2] led Ames to address the Federal government on the subject, again without success. He was once more driven to the use of his black militia.

The governor's appeal, indeed, was not endorsed by all of the Republican leaders of Mississippi. He had implacable enemies who were discrediting him to such a degree that they had persuaded Grant to make them, instead of him, the dispensers of Federal patronage in the state. Ames was told, in effect, that his word was not fit to be taken, that, but for his bungling, there would be no disorder. Further to discredit him Pierrepont, now in the Attorney General's office, sent to Mississippi, a personal friend, a retired business man of New York, named Chase, and this delegate, with the aid of two detectives, after gaining information from independent sources for the Federal administration, made a "treaty of peace" with the Democratic leaders.[3]

The victory of the conservatives was overwhelming and "closed the career of the carpetbagger in Mississippi."[4] Bells were rung; anvils were again filled with powder and exploded; men, rejoicing, marched in torchlight processions; towns were illuminated.

Ames had wished to return to the Senate. He might have done so when Blanche K. Bruce was elected in 1874. But he must resign, if he were to realize his ambition, and, in doing this, he should have left the government with the negro lieutenant-governor, who, from the first, had been the particular bane of his administration.[5] Under such circumstances he has been held deserving of gratitude from the people of Mississippi for staying in his place. In case of Republican success in 1875

[1] Senate Mis. Doc., 44th Cong. 2nd sess., no. 45, pp. 223–4, 226, 234; Senate Reports, 44th Cong. 1st sess., no. 527, p. liv.

[2] Garner, Recon. in Miss., pp. 375–81.

[3] Senate Reports, 44th Cong. 1st sess., no. 527, pp. lxxiii, 2–3, 473–5, 1801 et seq.; Garner, Recon. in Miss., pp. 391, 398, 401; cf. Senate Mis. Doc., 44th Cong. 2nd sess., no. 45, pp. 592–3.

[4] Mayes, Life of Lamar, p. 262.

[5] Garner, Recon. in Miss., p. 407.

it was understood that he should take the seat to be vacated
by General Alcorn, but other things were now to be seen.
The new legislature met in January, 1876, and proceedings
were immediately commenced looking to the impeachment
of the governor, of the lieutenant-governor, who was convicted of bribery in office, and removed, and the negro superintendent of public education, who resigned under charges of
infamous conduct.   Twenty-three articles were needed to
catalogue the misdemeanors of the governor, and, on March
28, 1876, before coming to his trial, he found it convenient to
vacate his place. He would "escape burdens which are com-
pensated by no possibility of public usefulness," he said, and,
with some of the air of martyrdom, left the state.[1] The rest
of the carpetbaggers soon followed him. The legislature effected a thorough reorganization of the government. The
Republicans in 1875 had expended $1,430,000; the Democrats
in 1876 reduced the expenditures to $518,000.[2] Onerous laws
were repealed, taxes were reduced, offices were abolished, new
appointments were made to old offices, quiet returned to the
people, both white and black.

But the Radicals were not disposed to admit their defeat.
The state had been wrested from them by foul means. Ames
had at once declared the new legislature to be an illegal body;
he so denounced it in the message which he addressed to it
when it met. The charge was uttered in the Republican gazettes
of the North, by Republican party leaders in Washington.
Grant repeated it. The state was governed, the President
said in the summer of 1876, by officials "chosen through fraud
and violence, such as would scarcely be credited to savages,
much less to a civilized and Christian people."[3] If he had
believed so much there must be wonder that he did not extend
his favor to Ames, when, in 1875, the governor had asked for
Federal aid, instead of to those office-mongers, Ames's enemies

[1] Mayes, Life of Lamar, pp. 263–4; Garner, Recon. in Miss., p. 402.
[2] Garner, Recon. in Miss., p. 320.
[3] Senate Reports, 44th Cong., 1st sess., no. 527, p. xxxi; Richardson,
Messages and Papers, vol. vii, p. 376; N. Y. Nation, Aug. 10, 1876.

within the Republican party in Mississippi, who impelled, him to adopt another course.

Nothing could be done in the House, which was Democratic, but the Senate was Republican, and a committee, under the chairmanship of Boutwell, was assigned the task of making an investigation of the election, and of proclaiming to the country the irregularities and intimidations which had marked it. In August, 1876, in the midst of the Presidential campaign, the report was made public as a counterweight to the many reports so damaging to the administration which were issued by committees of the House. The questions asked of 162 witnesses and the answers fill two portly volumes. It was clear enough that the negroes had been overawed, if they were not actually terrorized by the general rising of the white people of the state, by the riding about the country of armed men, by the discharge of firearms. Darkies had been told that, if they voted the Republican ticket, they could no longer find employment—they and their families would be left to starve. Some had been forcibly kept from the polls. In one county only four Republican votes had been cast, in another seven, in still another twelve.[1]

But similar methods, where they might be, were used on the other side. Blacks who were ready to vote the Democratic ticket were intimidated. Their lives were not safe if they should but intimate their intention to vote for the Democratic candidates. They were shown papers purporting to be written orders from President Grant directing them to support the Republican party. They were driven about by the carpetbag leaders like cattle, and were as little free, as they were as little qualified, properly to exercise their new privileges respecting the franchise in a community dominated by the Republican party as in one controlled by the Democrats.

The majority of the Boutwell committee found that the evidence which it had brought together constituted "one of the darkest chapters in American history."[2] They made

[1] Garner, Recon. in Miss., pp. 395, 527.
[2] Senate Reports, 44th Cong. 1st sess., no. 527, p. xxviii.

three recommendations: (1) Laws should be passed by Congress for the protection of the rights of citizens. (2) "States in anarchy" should be "denied representation in Congress." (3) If the disorder continued and increased Mississippi should be remanded to "a territorial condition" pending the reconstruction of the government upon a "republican basis."[1]

Unionist and rebel had never fought each other with such bitter antipathy as did the carpetbaggers among themselves in their struggle to gain their malign ends over the prostrate form of Florida. Harrison Reed of Massachusetts and Wisconsin held the governorship against enemies in his own party, who impeached him on charges of bribery and embezzlement and of other high crimes,[2] but he held his post until the end of his term. Then a man named Hart, identified in some degree with the state's interests, occupied the office. But he died in a year, and it came to the hands of the lieutenant-governor, Marcellus L. Stearns of Massachusetts, a soldier who had left an arm on a battle field of the war and had later been an agent of the Freedmen's Bureau. Two carpetbaggers from New York represented the state in the Senate of the United States.

Florida was a mean prize in comparison with some of the other commonwealths which fell a prey to the reconstructionists of the South. By the census of 1870 it contained only 187,748 souls, of whom a half, wanting 4,000, were black folk. In the whole state, from the Georgia line to the coral keys at the Southern end of the peninsula there were at that day not as many white people as there are inhabitants now in the flourishing city of Jacksonville, the gateway each winter for so many travellers into this land of tropic fruits and blowing flowers. As yet its soil was infertile sand, its forests, soon to be valuable to the sawyer, stood for the most part undisturbed in oozing swamps. The growth, for commerce, of the orange, the shaddock, the pineapple, the cultivation of berries and

---

[1] Senate Reports, 44th Cong. 1st sess, no 527, p. xxix.
[2] Article on Fla. in Am. Ann. Cyclop. for 1872; J. Wallace, Carpet Bag Rule in Fla., pp. 160–66, 169–71.

vegetables for dinner tables, set before windows in the north which still looked out upon ice and snow, had scarcely commenced. A few tourists left a few dollars at a few boarding houses on the banks of the St. Johns and the Indian Rivers, but it was a poor promise of the wealth which now is brought into the state, on steamer and in Pullman train, by the whole North's moneyed aristocracy.

It was complained at a taxpayers' convention in Lake City, in 1871, that Florida had no remunerative property except personal property, which had an assessed value of only about $11,000,000. Upon this property fell the whole of the weight which the warring carpetbag factions at Tallahassee pressed upon the bending backs of the people of the state.[1]

While Reed was publicly declaiming about their resources and wealth they were laying plans to free themselves from their alien mastery. The state taxes alone were in excess of $2.50 a year for each man, woman and child, white and black. This was at the rate of about four per cent on the property available for taxation, and computed to be 75 per cent of its gross income. When to this was added the county and local taxes, requiring a total levy of $1,000,000, the rate was eight per cent, an eleventh part of the whole assessed valuation.[2]

But elections, as well as bonds, lands and money, were stolen by the rascals who were using the negro for their purposes, and the overthrow of the corrupt régime was not easily accomplished, especially as Florida had no outstanding popular leaders. The state with its widely scattered population, whole counties having but a score or two of voters, was as useful a "rotten borough" as the Republican party could have desired, and such it continued to be up to and including the year 1876, when it was of critical importance in deciding the Presidential election. In that year, however, during the strife over the canvass of the vote, the governorship came to the Democrats. Thus was brought to the office George F. Drew, Northern of

[1] Article on Fla. in Am. Ann. Cyclop. for 1871.
[2] Davis, Recon. in Fla., p. 598; article on Fla. in Am. Ann. Cyclop. for 1871.

birth, identified with the lumber interests of the state, and with his hand in control, Florida returned to a development under the influence of its own population.

General R. K. Scott, the carpetbagger who served two terms, a period of four years, as governor of South Carolina, was succeeded in 1872 by a scalawag, Franklin J. Moses, Jr. This man, a Jewish lawyer, of no learning and no practice, had distinguished himself by raising the rebel flag over Fort Sumter while he had been the private secretary of Governor Pickens.[1] Now he was enlisted in the ranks of the aliens and native adventurers who, with the aid of the enfranchised negroes, were making the government of South Carolina, as one observer described it, "the worst mockery of the name ever seen on earth." [2] Every variety of public perfidy—embezzlement, bribery, fraud, perjury, theft of this kind and that—had, during the Scott administration, brought the state, as it seemed, to the lowest point of degradation. But, with the coming of Moses to the governorship, still profounder depths were reached. Indeed the open pollution of office by him and his associates—white, mulatto and black—the squandering of the state's resources, the ruin of its credit, the pillage of the taxpayers, surpassed in its infamous flagrancy anything done in this lawless time in any Southern commonwealth.

With a preponderating negro vote nowhere else did the opportunity for the control of the elections promise so great a return for so little effort. South Carolina had riches which invited the thief. More than this she was the head and front of the secession movement, the home of the theory that states might, at their pleasure, leave the Union, the actual beginning point of the attempt to bring so much to realization. Of sympathy for her, whatever might befall her during the war, or now, while she was in the throes of "reconstruction," the North had none. The protests of her leading citizens were but the mutterings of unwhipped "rebels." The "outrages" upon

[1] Reynolds, Recon. in S. C., p. 87.

[2] Atlantic Monthly, February, 1877, p. 178. Called by another "the most ignorant democracy that mankind ever saw invested with the functions of government."—J. S. Pike, The Prostrate State, p. 12.

negroes and "Unionists," accounts of which were assiduously circulated by the thieves, were but further proof of the treason in the hearts of the inhabitants and their unfitness to enjoy the confidence of the country.[1]   Thus it was that a party which was hostile to the people could gain support, or at any rate indulgence at Washington, and in the North generally, for whatever course it might elect to pursue.

Taxpayers' conventions, judicial proceedings and other movements, instituted within the state, were without avail, and the depredations proceeded without restraint.   Nor was remedy to be found by appeal to the Federal government.   The Committee on the Judiciary of the House in 1874 said that "South Carolina is the field where, for the first time in the history of our own country, the capacity of the African race is to be tested."   It was to the negroes, desirous "of proving to the world that they are worthy of the great privileges conferred upon them, after the long night of slavery," that citizens making complaint should look for relief in the confidence of receiving "justice."[2]   South Carolina had become and was to remain a "negro state."[3]

Moses, after serving as speaker of the house of representatives at Columbia, where he was trained to proficiency in every branch of corruption, was not nominated without strong protest from elements in the Radical party, which saw the danger of elevating such a man to a position of so much influence in the government.[4]   But he was successful over all opposition, the white people being so overpowered by the negroes, led

---

[1] Cf. House Reports, 43rd Cong. 1st sess., no. 481, p. 3.

[2] House Reports, 42nd Cong. 1st sess., no. 481, pt. 1, p. 8.   In this case the white people of a Southern state had asked for Federal assistance on the ground that their government had ceased to have a "republican form," and the Democratic minority on the Judiciary Committee urged intervention by Congress on this ground.—Ibid., pts. 2 and 3.

[3] "We have set up in South Carolina," said the New York Nation, "a system of government which converts the majority into a gang of robbers making war on civilization and morality, and have pledged ourselves to prevent the minority from resisting or overthrowing them."—Issue of May 21, 1874.

[4] Reynolds, Recon. in S. C., p. 223; article on S. C. in Am. Ann. Cyclop. for 1872.

by the carpetbaggers and the scalawags, that few of them attended at the polls, and his impious reign began.[1] Money was so openly paid him, and in substantial sums, for the signing of bills, for the granting of pardons and for appointments to office, that he deservedly gained the sobriquets of the "robber governor" and the "great South Carolina thief." [2] He purchased one of the finest houses in Columbia,[3] drove a handsome team of horses through the streets, lived his days in a new and an unfamiliar luxury, in the sight of men who knew him for a knave,[4] until 1874, when such a saturnalia of extravagance and debauchery, even his own party perceived, must be brought to an end.

The debt of South Carolina had, in six years, come to be more that $20,000,000, an increase of about $14,000,000,[5] for which the state had gained not a single public improvement in return.[6] Her bonds were salable only at a great depreciation— in 1873 at from fifteen to forty cents on the dollar.[7] Although John J. Patterson, a carpetbagger from Pennsylvania, who, by an outlay, in 1872, of $60,000, given in bribes to the negroes, the yellow men and the white poltroons in the legislature, had gained a seat in the United States Senate,[8] said, while Moses was governor, that there were "still five years of good stealing" in South Carolina,[9] it was plain that the robber régime would be not much longer tolerated, and that a popular rising was near at hand.

Daniel H. Chamberlain had been allied with the worst of the carpetbag and negro leaders in their mismanagement of the state,[10] but he was a man of a very different type. He

[1] Reynolds, Recon. in S. C., p. 225.

[2] N. Y. Nation, Aug., 6, 1874.

[3] J. S. Pike, The Prostrate State, p. 107.

[4] Reynolds, Recon. in S. C., pp. 226–7; M. L. Avery, Dixie after the War, pp. 355.

[5] Reynolds, Recon. in S. C., p. 238.

[6] D. H. Chamberlain in Atlantic Monthly, April, 1901, p. 477.

[7] Reynolds, Recon. in S. C., p. 239.

[8] Ibid., pp. 220, 472; Why the Solid South, p. 103.

[9] Reynolds, Recon. in S. C. p. 229.

[10] Cf. N. Y. Nation, Oct. 1 and 8, 1874, and April 19, July 12 and Sep. 20, 1877; N. Y. Tribune, Sep. 26, 1874.

was a native of Massachusetts. Graduating at Yale he had later studied law at Harvard. At the end of the war, in which he had served, he settled in South Carolina to engage in cotton planting on the Sea Islands. Not succeeding in this undertaking, he commenced the practice of his profession,[1] and was now ready to lead a reform within his party, and set out of office some of the most reprehensible of the men who had compassed the disgrace of the state. He came forward none too soon. The white people had again called a taxpayers' convention to meet in Columbia in February, 1874. In it all but two of the counties were represented by delegates, some of them leading citizens. They found and declared that the cost of conducting the government in 1873 was $1,896,000; in 1865–66 it had been only $260,-000. The expenditures were increased by every kind of fraud. The printing steals were scandalous. State officers, members of the legislature and clerks made contracts with themselves.[2] They were paid no less than $331,000 in 1873 for work which was said to be worth but $50,000. The whole cost of public printing and the advertisement of the laws, from 1868 to 1874, Chamberlain declared, had been $1,104,000. In three years, embracing the Moses administration, the total was $918,000.[3] The appropriations for public printing in South Carolina for sixty years, from 1800 to 1859, all taken together, had been only $271,180.[4]

The taxes had increased until they consumed more than half of the income of the property selected for the levies. Owners of land were in default; it was confiscated by the state, which, in turn, could not sell it, since there was no one to buy.[5]

Chamberlain's election, in 1874, gave the people an honest governor. A man of wide reading, an eloquent orator, a cultivated gentleman, his abilities were such that he was enabled to make himself a factor of a new kind in the reconstruction

[1] Walter Allen, Governor Chamberlain's Administration, p. 526.
[2] Reynolds, Recon. in S. C., pp. 473–5.
[3] Allen, Chamberlain's Administration, p. 18; Reynolds, Recon. in S. C., p. 268; cf. ibid., p. 474; Fleming, Doc. Hist. of Recon., vol. ii, p. 68.
[4] Reynolds, Recon. in S. C., p. 252.
[5] Cf. N. Y. Nation, May 28, 1874.

politics of the South. His messages arrested attention. He instituted and secured the adoption of some remedial legislation.[1] He vetoed infamous bills.[2] He reduced the expenses of the government and gave the people a measure of relief from the burdens of taxation.[3] But his way was hard; his party in and out of the legislature, used to rich spoils, gave him little support and his achievements fell short of what he would have liked them to be. Praise was bestowed upon him by the people of the state,[4] and his struggle with the nefarious influences which surrounded him caused his name to be pleasantly acclaimed by discriminating men in the North. Especially did his protest against the election by the legislature of the negro Whipper and ex-Governor Moses, as circuit judges, emphasize his courage and integrity.[5] It was a "horrible disaster," he said, a greater "calamity" than any which had yet fallen upon South Carolina, or any other Southern state. He told Grant that Moses was "as infamous a character as ever in any age disgraced and prostituted public position." Whipper, "ignorant of morals, a gambler by open practice, an embezzler of public funds," differed from Moses only in the extent of his opportunities.[6] The governor refused to issue commissions to the two men.

But commendation of Chamberlain in South Carolina was wanting in real sincerity or enthusiasm. He was still associated with perfidious men and seemed often to forward their indecent schemes.[7] He was a carpetbagger; he belonged in Massachusetts. He had the Abolitionist traditions and sentiments which South Carolinians had so long associated with the names and persons of the people of that state, and he revealed himself a negrophile and a partisan.[8] Plainly a man from abroad, come to make

[1] Atlantic Monthly, February, 1877, p. 181.
[2] Cf. Allen, Chamberlain's Administration, pp. 104–5.
[3] Reynolds, Recon. in S. C., pp. 314, 327–8.
[4] Cf. many extracts from the South Carolina newspapers in Allen, Chamberlain's Administration; Why the Solid South, p. 106.
[5] Cf. Porcher, Last Chapter of Recon. in S. C., in Southern Hist. Society Papers, vol. xii, pp. 201–202; Allen, op. cit., pp. 193–219.
[6] Reynolds, Recon. in S. C., pp. 322–3; Allen, op. cit., pp. 228, 232.
[7] Porcher, op. cit., vol. xii, pp. 196–7.
[8] Reynolds, Recon. in S. C., pp. 507–508.

over South Carolina after the Northern pattern, it was impossible to suppose that his administration, however upright and beneficent it might be, could really win popular sympathy.

Nevertheless, when it was seen that he would be a candidate to succeed himself, the resident and taxpaying citizenry were at first disposed to present no opposing name. They might have kept to this resolution. But race conflicts brought in a dividing influence, the gravest of a series occurring in the summer of 1876, when negro militiamen involved themselves in a fracas with a party of whites at Hamburg. The massacre—not without real provocation—which followed, led to acrimonious charges and counter charges calculated to go far in alienating such friends as Chamberlain had made in the state.[1] He appealed to President Grant, called for Federal troops, and soon, in the excited condition of the public mind throughout the country in a "Presidential year," the Democratic party could not resist the temptation to nominate its own candidates.[2] The legislature, anyhow, must be taken out of the hands of the negro party, and, with Mississippi's successful example in the previous year in mind, it was resolved to organize a campaign for the complete "redemption" of the state on the "Mississippi plan."[3] South Carolina had in Wade Hampton, as Mississippi had in Lamar, a leader who stood deservedly high in the popular regard.[4] All signs pointed to him as the Democratic candidate, and he received the nomination for governor. Fitting associates were given him on the state ticket. In the Congressional and legislative districts, and in the counties, citizens of capacity and honor were offered to the people in the stead of the evil men who had been serving in public position.

Unfortunately for Chamberlain on his ticket was the name of a venal negro, the candidate for attorney general, alone enough

---

[1] Reynolds, Recon. in S. C., p. 347; Porcher, op. cit., vol. xii, p. 252; ibid., vol. xiii, p. 82.

[2] Cf. Allen, op. cit., p. 336.

[3] Reynolds, Recon. in S. C., pp. 349–50.

[4] For Chamberlain's good opinion of Hampton see Atlantic Monthly for April, 1901.

to bear him down to defeat.[1] He was consigned to the hard fate
of stumping the state with some of the worst characters whom
the Republican régime had produced, and seemed to, if he did not
actually, ally himself with interests which had done the grossest
affront to the sentiments of all the respectable inhabitants.[2]

Voting had been a form, election a mockery, the "taxpayers"
had said in their convention of 1874,[3] hope had been extin-
guished,[4] but the Democrats of South Carolina, like their
friends in Mississippi in 1875, entered the campaign in a confident and determined mood. Everywhere men in red shirts
were organized into clubs. They were mounted to ride through
the state to arouse the voters. Many were equipped with rifles
and sabres to awe the negroes, who were also armed, and,
laboring under great excitement, were a menace to society.[5]
"Hurrah for Hampton!" was shouted by men, women and
children in the streets of cities, along the country roads, in
field and on plantation. From platforms, embowered in flowers
and evergreens, set often in groves of trees—no hall was large
enough for the use—the candidate spoke in every part of the
state. Young women sang and strewed his way with flowers.[6]
Benjamin H. Hill and General Gordon of Georgia, and many
others came to aid him in his canvass. Great processions of
"Red Shirts," mounted and afoot, accompanied him from
place to place; torchmen lighted his way at night; artillery was
discharged. His tour was a triumphal progress.[7] Meantime
there were smaller meetings. Hundreds of volunteers, many of
whom had never before raised a voice in political matters,
addressed the negroes from cotton bales, cart tails or the steps
of gin houses. All labor ceased as election day drew near.[8]

The dissensions within the Republican party, between the

[1] Reynolds, Recon. in S. C., pp. 367, 372, 510; Porcher, op. cit., vol. xii,
p. 316.
[2] That his rôle throughout was most repugnant to him is certain. See
M. L. Avary, Dixie after the War, pp. 357–60.
[3] Reynolds, Recon. in S. C., p. 253.
[4] Porcher, op. cit., vol. xii, p. 173.
[5] Ibid., p. 177.
[6] Cf. M. L. Avary, Dixie after the War, pp. 360–61.
[7] Atlantic Monthly, Feb., 1877, pp. 183–4.
[8] Reynolds, Recon. in S. C., pp. 355–62.

better men, with hope for its future, and the scoundrels who
had disgraced it; the defection of those for whom Chamberlain
was too virtuous and of others for whom he seemed, as he
associated himself with notorious corruptionists, not good
enough; the winning away from the Radicals of many of the
negroes;[1] the intensive campaigning of the Democrats, and
the resolute leadership of Hampton presaged his success. On
the other side inevitable clashes between the races, in which,
as the canvass progressed, numbers of negroes were killed,
were exaggerated. Whites, too, were slain. The "Red Shirts"
were not for idle parade, for the people were once more filled
with dread of negro risings, and were alert to meet conditions
always so portentous to the South.[2] The news of riot and
insurrection was carried to the North to awaken suspicion of
new "rebellion" in the white people, new sympathy for the
poor folk who had been their slaves.[3] A President, as well as a
governor, was to be elected and the chest of the National Republican Committee was at the command of the leaders, though
Chamberlain's unmitigated castigations of some of the rogues
who surrounded him, had destroyed the confidence felt in him
as a "Republican" by Senator Morton and other Radicals at
Washington.[4]

On the 17th of October, at the governor's request, supported
by Senator Patterson, who had the ear of the President,[5] Grant
issued a proclamation commanding the "rifle clubs"[6] to disband within three days, and Sherman was directed to dispose
troops throughout the state in the interest of public order.[7]

[1] Each white voter was enjoined to get one negro and watch him deposit
his ballot for Hampton, known as the "one man apiece" policy.—Atlantic
Monthly, Feb., 1877, p. 186.

[2] M. L. Avary, Dixie after the War, pp. 360–64.

[3] Reynolds, Recon. in S. C., pp. 374–86; Porcher, op. cit., vol. xii, pp.
318–21 and vol. xiii, pp. 52–3.

[4] Reynolds, Recon in S. C., p. 323; Porcher, op. cit., vol. xii, p. 203;
Allen, Chamberlain's Administration, pp. 229–34.

[5] Porcher, op. cit., vol. xii, p. 312.

[6] Chamberlain said that they numbered at least 213, being a force of
about 13,000 men. Cf. Allen, Chamberlain's Administration, pp. 409–10.

[7] Richardson, Messages and Papers, vol. vii, p. 396; Reynolds, Recon. in
S. C., pp. 386–7; article on S. C. in Am. Ann. Cyclop. for 1876.

Probably 5,000 soldiers in all were stationed at the various county towns, where they were diligently employed in behalf of the Republican party.[1] Hundreds of citizens were arrested under the terms of the Enforcement Acts. It is likely that this appeal to "martial law," as General Hampton called it, was of much more advantage to the Democrats than to the Republicans, for it but solidified the opposition to Chamberlain, and, increased the determination of the people to free themselves once and for all, from alien and negro rule.

In all the churches, on a Sunday prior to election day, prayers were said for the state's deliverance. All varieties of intimidation and fraud were employed on both sides. As a poll of the citizens the result was a farce.[2] The issue was doubtful, the majorities were narrow and there was an opportunity for a contest which was bound up with the Presidential dispute. By excluding the votes of two counties, in which there were charges of fraud, Chamberlain was declared to have been elected by the senate and the house of representatives, which were organized in his interest, to be sworn into office on the 7th day of December. At the same time a Democratic house of representatives, and such senators as chose to attend, upon canvassing the votes, found Hampton to have been the choice of the people, and he qualified for the exercise of his duties, with the support of an overwhelming majority of the respectable and influential people of the state. Finally, by processes to be described in another place, Hampton's position was securely established, and South Carolina passed out from under the weight of a punishment, more poignant and more prolonged, than that which the armies had administered to her during the war.

Under Warmoth, in Louisiana, corruption and extravagance had increased the debt to more than $53,000,000, including guarantees and some other obligations which were later repudiated,[3] and raised the taxes until they pressed with crushing force upon every form of property. Rich Mississippi River

[1] Reynolds, Recon. in S. C., 387.
[2] Atlantic Monthly, Feb., 1877, p. 187.
[3] Lonn, Recon. in La., pp. 83–4, 248.

bottoms could not be made to yield enough to meet the demands of the tax gatherers. Owners would give land to immigrants to be rid of the burden of holding it.[1] Mortgages were wiped out— values were swept away. The citizen lived in hopeless poverty, while the government was used to enrich diabolical men who had seized it. Cities and parishes had a no more honest administration. New Orleans, the richest of the prizes,[2] was loaded with a debt of $20,000,000.[3] Its bonds, like the state's, went begging in the money markets of the country.[4] The year 1872 found Warmoth, who, commencing with nothing, was now in possession of a large fortune,[5] near the end of his extraordinary reign.

The Republican party in Louisiana, was, by this time, divided into factions, which were quarreling so rancorously that the country reverberated with the sound of the conflict. The "custom house ring," called so because it drew its inspiration from Casey, Grant's brother-in-law, who was the United States collector in New Orleans—with Colonel Carter, a scalawag, employed in the custom house, who had become speaker of the house of representatives [6] and Packard, a carpetbagger from Maine, the United States marshal, as other leaders—had involved themselves in a dispute with the governor over the distribution of the plunder taken from the people.[7] They were "reformers," but quite for their own purposes, and they accused Warmoth of all forms of venality and crime. He responded in kind, and, if driven to it, each side could have proven the truth of every allegation. Pinchback, the mulatto lieutenant-governor, headed a third faction, which usually had co-operated with Warmoth.

The relations between the parties were such that general

---

[1] Lonn, Recon. in La., pp. 84–5.
[2] Albert Phelps in Atlantic Monthly, July, 1901, p. 128.
[3] Lonn, Recon. in La., p. 251; cf. J. S. Black, Essays and Speeches, p. 316.
[4] Lonn, Recon. in La., p. 85; House Reports, 43rd Cong. 2nd sess., no. 101, p. 7.
[5] House Reports, 42nd Cong. 2nd sess., no. 92, p. 25; article on La. in Am. Ann. Cyclop. for 1872, p. 473.
[6] Cf. House Reports, 42nd Cong. 2nd sess., no. 92, p. 27.
[7] For reasons for Casey's disaffection see ibid., p. 9.

bloodshed seemed, at times, not far away. One thug assaulted
another. Assassination completed argument. With police,
militiamen, Federal troops, Gatling guns in the streets New
Orleans seemed the home of Mars.

Amid these surroundings conventions and committees of the
helpless citizens met to complain of and protest against such
infamies as they were made to suffer by reason of the governor's
exercising his powers so monstrously, against the activities of
the legislature, "so rank" as this one was "with ignorance and
corruption." [1] A Congressional committee was appointed to
visit the state to report upon the "origin and character of the
difficulties"; but the majority, finding it to be a family quarrel,
made no recommendations for legislation, while the minority,
which scathingly denounced the "organized system of spoliation
and villany," [2] of which the state was the victim, asked merely
for the appointment of honest Federal officers and the opportunity for the people to work their own deliverance through
fair and free elections. [3]

Warmoth, estranged from his old party associates, also
sought protection under the mantle of "reform," and allied
himself with the "Cincinnati movement," which brought
forth Greeley as a Presidential candidate. [4] This confused a
situation already sufficiently complex. Convention followed
convention, conference was added to conference, in 1872, until
finally there were but two tickets in the field—the Democratic
(in fusion with the Warmoth faction) headed by John McEnery,
a native Louisianian, a lawyer who had served in the war on the
Southern side; and the Republican (in fusion with Pinchback)
which offered as its leading candidate William Pitt Kellogg, a
carpetbagger from Vermont and Illinois, an adherent of the
"custom house" wing of the party, Casey's predecessor as
collector of the port at New Orleans and lately a United States
senator.

[1] Am. Ann. Cyclop. for 1872, p. 473.
[2] House Reports, 42nd Cong. 2nd sess., no. 92, p. 8.
[3] Ibid., p. 30. For testimony of this committee see House Mis. Doc.
42nd Cong. 2nd sess., no. 211.
[4] Am. Ann. Cyclop. for 1872, pp. 475, 477; Lonn, Recon. in La., pp.
142-3.

The result was disputed. Each party declared that it had elected its candidate, and proceeded to establish the fact by a manipulation of the returns through three or four rival boards, which essayed to canvass the votes. Warmoth, who was still in the governor's chair, used all his offices in the interest of McEnery. The various courts of Louisiana were appealed to frantically by both sides. In the midst of the melée of suits and counter suits Kellogg, for his security, filed a bill in the United States Circuit Court, where Judge Durell, espousing that man's cause, thinking it the wish of Grant, a supposition in which he went little astray,[1] issued an order, suddenly late at night, for this reason called a "midnight order," in behalf of the claims of the Republicans.[2] Instantly intense excitement ensued. For six weeks Federal troops occupied the state house, and, though public opinion, except that which was the most narrowly partisan, both North and South, denounced the judge's course as the grossest of outrages upon justice, the deed had been done and Kellogg was entrenched in his place.

The contest affected the membership of the legislature, which divided into sympathetic factions, and met in separate halls day by day, amid the most disorderly scenes, both attempting to direct the government. In the body controlled by the "custom house ring" Warmoth's enemies, to get rid of him, impeached him, whereupon Lieutenant-Governor Pinchback presumed to think himself governor and attempted to exercise the prerogatives of the office. Telegrams and letters were flung in great numbers at Grant and the authorities at Washington, a committee was sent to state the case to the President, and he quickly came, as was foreseen, to the support of Pinchback and the Kellogg party.[3] More judicial orders were sought and procured, and the confusion continued while Federal soldiers, militiamen, police and mobs threatened the state with civil war.

---

[1] Cf. N. Y. Nation, Feb. 5, 1874.
[2] Cf. Lonn, Recon. in, La., pp. 192–4.
[3] House Reports, 42nd Cong. 3rd sess., no. 91, pp. 19, 20.

Simultaneously, on January 13, 1873, in different parts of New Orleans, Kellogg and McEnery took the oath of office. The streets were thronged; all business ceased. The legislatures continued to maintain their separate organizations and peace was farther away than ever before. Contesting delegations in Congress appeared at Washington, calling for the judgment of the Senate and the House, Pinchback occupying the unusual position of being a claimant for seats in both chambers of the national legislature.[1]

On January 16, 1873, the Senate referred the whole subject to its new Committee of Privileges and Elections of which Morton, after Sumner had declined the post, had become the chairman. Though but one Democrat, Joshua Hill of Georgia, had a place upon the committee, it did not fail to condemn the course taken by Judge Durell,[2] as well as the conduct of the canvassing boards, especially the so-called "Lynch board" of the "custom house party,"[3] and found in favor of McEnery, if the election were not to be considered entirely void, because of the frauds attending it. But Kellogg had set up and was maintaining a *de facto* government, and Congress might better adopt the alternative of deciding that there was at present no government in Louisiana, and authorize a new election. The committee prepared and submitted a bill with this end in view, and recommended its adoption.[4]

Trumbull dissenting, dwelt upon Grant's implication in the scheme, illegally, through the use of troops, to seat Kellogg in the governor's chair, and advocated a recognition of McEnery; the irregularities, he thought, had not been great enough to invalidate the poll.[5] Hill reached the same conclusion in another way. Morton, also dissenting, in his rôle of leading

---

[1] Cf. Lonn, Recon. in La., pp. 308–12.

[2] "It is impossible to conceive of a more irregular, illegal and in every way inexcusable act on the part of a judge."—Senate Reports, 42nd Cong. 3rd sess., no. 457, p. xvii; cf. ibid., p. xxvii.

[3] "There is nothing in all the comedy of blunders and frauds under consideration more indefensible than the pretended canvass of this board." —Ibid., p. xxvii.

[4] Ibid., pp. xliv, l.

[5] Ibid., pp. liii–lxv.

Radical, though attempting no defense of Judge Durell, came to the support of the Kellogg government.[1]

Grant urged Congress forward in a message sent to it on February 25, 1873. If no other course were laid out for him he made it plain that he would continue to favor Kellogg.[2] In the closing days of the session an angry debate over the subject occupied the Senate, Morton, through his great influence, defeating action of any kind.[3] Thus did Congress fail to embrace an opportunity to compose a trouble, which year by year was to increase constantly in venom and acerbity. The responsibility remained with Grant, and all men knew what he would do.

The people of the state refused to pay their onerous taxes. A "Resisting Association" had been formed during the Warmoth administration; it was now turned against Kellogg, and the government, wanting enforcement measures, was left without financial support.[4] Disorder was inevitable, as the dullest man could have foreseen, and a handle was soon given to the Radicals for the development of a policy, which, necessary though it may have been, in view of the posture in which the state had been left by Congress, increased the asperity of the controversy. At Colfax, in Grant parish, a village in the Red River valley, in the central part of the state, about 350 miles from New Orleans, there were rival parish officers. It was a region where cotton planting flourished and there were two or three blacks for one white man. The negroes were armed by Republican demagogues and, throughout the early days of April, 1873, riot followed riot, until Easter Sunday, April 13, when a party of negroes, who had taken refuge in the court house, were besieged and, refusing to surrender, were killed. Others were burnt to death, after the building had been set on fire. It was a massacre, and was designated as such in the North and in Congress, with exaggeration, where none was

[1] Senate Reports, 42nd Cong. 3rd sess., no 457, pp. lxvii–lxxviii.
[2] Richardson, Messages and Papers, vol. vii, pp. 212–3; cf. Lonn, Recon. in La., p. 240.
[3] W. D. Foulke, Life of Morton, vol. ii, p. 284.
[4] Lonn, Recon. in La., p. 267.

needed, of the barbarities attending it. A House committee, of which Hoar was chairman, when it gave its attention to the subject, found it to be "cold blooded murder"—"without palliation or justification," which would stand for all time as "a foul blot on the page of history." [1] Other riots in the interior of the state ensued, and on May 22, 1873, Grant, Congress having, as he said, "tacitly recognized" the Kellogg government by refusing to take action disturbing it, chose to consider McEnery's partisans "insurgents," ordering them "to disperse and retire to their respective abodes" within twenty days. [2]

McEnery held fast to his office, though counselling against a futile resistance. He could be governor in name only so long as Kellogg had the support of Grant and the Federal troops. The embers were smouldering and would produce new fires.

The campaign of 1874, when the important office of state treasurer was to be filled and a new legislature was to be chosen, was not far distant. The Democrats in that year, making the party coincident with "the white people of Louisiana," denounced Kellogg as a "mere usurper," who had "inflamed the passions and prejudices of the negroes, as a race, against the whites," so that it had become necessary for the latter "to act together in self-defense, and for the preservation of white civilization." [3] The "color line" was being drawn for political purposes. It was plain now that the young men of the state were being enrolled in a new Ku Klux organization. The campaign was not far advanced when it revealed the existence of posses of horsemen, not different from the "White Liners" in Mississippi and the "Red Shirts" in South Carolina, frankly formed for the control of the negroes, made dangerous to society by the "horde of scalawags and carpetbaggers," who "like vultures," for "eight long years" had been "preying" upon the people. [4]

[1] House Reports, 43rd Cong. 2nd sess., no. 261, pp. 13–14.

[2] Richardson, Messages and Papers, vol. vii, pp. 223–4.

[3] Am. Ann. Cyclop. for 1874, p. 477.

[4] Ibid., p. 478. "The crew of godless wretches by whom Louisiana has been almost desolated," Jeremiah S. Black called them. See his Essays and Speeches, p. 308.

Near the end of August, 1874, a race war broke out in Cou-
shatta, in Red River parish, in the Shreveport district, in the
northwestern part of the state, in which several men were
killed. This was the first outrage, to attract national notice,
attributed to the "White Leagues," as the new mounted clubs
were called. The President at Long Branch wrote to Secretary
of War Belknap, who conferred with Attorney General Williams, who, in turn, on September 3, 1874, addressed the United
States marshals and attorneys in Louisiana, ordering them to
act, with the support of the troops, in accordance with the
terms of the Enforcement Laws. The people of the state
answered that the fault was Kellogg's, wno held and exercised
office "in open defiance of law and justice and the opinion of
the civilized world," and who was now devising arbitrary and
oppressive election laws designed to further extend his power.

Such conditions were a standing invitation to a violent
popular rising. On September 14 a great crowd of citizens
assembled in the broad Canal Street in New Orleans to denounce the Republican "usurper," and the odious satrapy
which he had established.[1] A delegation visited him in his
office and demanded his "immediate abdication." McEnery
was not in the city, but a man named Penn, a Warmoth adherent, who had been the candidate for lieutenant-governor
on the McEnery ticket, was present. Proclaiming himself
acting governor of the state, he called upon the men of militia
age to arm and assemble "for the purpose of driving the usurpers from power." Not only Canal Street, but also many of
the thoroughfares leading into it, soon held large numbers of
indignant citizens who raised barricades. The Metropolitan
Police, mostly negroes, under General James Longstreet, commander of the Kellogg militia, and General Badger, were
drawn up for action; but the insurgents were numerous and
desperate, and in a skirmish, in which, on both sides, thirty
or more were killed and many were wounded, at a spot in
Canal Street near the river, which is marked today by a shaft
in affectionate memory of those who here lost their lives in

[1] Article on Louisiana in Am. Ann. Cyclop. for 1874, pp. 479–80.

this attempt to throw off the yoke of the carpetbagger in Louisiana, the defenders were dispersed. On the following day, the 15th of September, the state house was surrendered to the Penn militia, the police laid down their arms and Kellogg found shelter with his friends in the custom house.[1] All state and city property soon fell into possession of the insurgents. Penn was inducted into office as governor and proceeded to reorganize the government. Mass meetings were held in St. Louis, in Mobile and other places to frame and forward congratulatory messages to the city upon the courage which had been displayed in the overthrow of tyranny. The people were also making themselves free of the oppressor in the northern parts of the state.[2]

Such a *coup d'état* would have served well but for Grant. The "usurpers, plunderers and enemies of the people" had been expelled from place. At the North signs of acquiescence, indeed approval, of what had been done were not wanting. "We must say frankly," the New York Nation declared, "that we know of no case of armed resistance to an established government in modern times in which the insurgents had more plainly the right on their side."[3]

Peace would reign, if the President would let the situation alone. This he was not pleased to do. His friends were in the custom house; he had taken a position on the subject; he was a stubborn man, and he would support Kellogg, whatever came. No time was lost. It was on the 15th of September that he issued a proclamation again commanding "turbulent and disorderly persons to disperse" to their homes.[4] More troops and three war ships were ordered to proceed to New Orleans at once, and, there being no other course to pursue, McEnery, who had now arrived upon the scene, and Penn, on the 17th of September, surrendered the capitol and other public buildings, which they and their forces had so recently

[1] Called by the people of New Orleans the "House of Refuge."—Albert Phelps in Atlantic Monthly for July, 1901, p. 127.
[2] Lonn, Recon. in La., pp. 273-4.
[3] Issue of Sep. 24, 1874.
[4] Richardson, Messages and Papers, vol. vii, pp. 276-7.

occupied. Kellogg came from his shelter, and affairs, under the direction of the Federal military authorities, took their accustomed way.

One result came from the battle in Canal Street. A joint committee, composed of leaders of the two parties, Republican and Conservative, was formed and it agreed upon rules to govern the approaching election, thus calming public feeling until November was past. Then hostilities were resumed. It was Christmas time before the returning board had canvassed the votes. Though the Conservatives were conceded some gains they at once protested against the course taken by the board in a number of particulars, with new addresses "to the people of the free states of America." Both President and Congress had failed the "down-trodden people of once fine Louisiana," who would now demand of a higher authority "that the shackles be stricken" from the state, and that the army of the country be "no longer used to keep a horde of adventurers in power." [1] They would reach the ears of their rulers, said Bishop Wilmer, with the voice of their woe. [2]

And such accumulating protest and complaint it befitted no one to dismiss with light speech. An army officer whose duty had taken him over the state said, in December, 1874, that, because of the fraud and corruption, dissatisfaction was so "widespread and deep" that, "sooner or later," there would be "an outbreak of public feeling" attended by "scenes of fearful violence." The Kellogg government could not maintain itself in power for one hour without the protection of Federal troops. It did not have "the confidence or respect of any portion of the community." The army was brought into disparagement among "well disposed people," while it continued to be employed for partisan purposes. General Emory, in command at New Orleans, and General Sherman, at the headquarters of the army, endorsed the report, and asked that it be submitted to the President for his personal reading. [3]

[1] Am. Ann. Cyclop. for 1874, p. 491.
[2] A Defense of La., p. 5.
[3] Senate Ex. Doc., 43rd Cong. 2nd sess., no. 17, pp. 70–75. The officer was Lieutenant-Colonel Henry A. Morrow.

But Grant was minded to take no note of protestants and counsellors. Though the entire country was occupied with the disturbed affairs of Louisiana, and a body of sentiment was forming in the North in no wise sympathetic with him, his answer to all that was said to him on the subject would be a fresh exhibition of military force. Sherman, the General of the Army, who had urged upon the President a consideration of the question, was to be left out of account completely. Instead of pursuing a regular course Grant, in this conjuncture, turned directly to Sheridan, an inferior officer.[1] The name of no commander, except "Ben" Butler's, was so unpleasantly regarded in New Orleans. Sheridan had acted with a kind of brusque bravado, and had shown himself distinctly unfeeling and hostile toward the population, before his removal from command in the district by President Johnson. To send him thither again would be to revive the unhappiest of memories.[2] But he was ordered, at Chicago, to proceed to the South, and, if, in his judgment, the occasion should warrant it, to take the direction of affairs.[3] Thus it was that before the legislature met in January, 1875, Sheridan was in command of the Military Department of the Gulf.[4] He posted troops in and around the state house under General de Trobriand, and, with their active aid, the legislature was organized in the interest of Kellogg and the Republicans.[5]

Sheridan saw in the resistance to law, as he called it, the hand of the White League, and on January 5, 1875, he sent Secretary Belknap a despatch suggesting that Congress pass a bill declaring the "ringleaders" in Louisiana, Mississippi and

[1] "A direct insult to Sherman," the New York Nation called this summary action on Grant's part. (Issue of Jan. 28, 1875; cf. ibid., Feb. 4, 1875.) Sherman himself felt no little resentment because of Grant's course toward him. "The President and Belknap both gradually withdrew from me all the powers which Grant had exercised in the same office," he wrote to John Sherman in a letter in The Sherman Letters, p. 348.

[2] Cf. New Orleans Picayune, Dec. 28, 1874, quoted in Lonn, Recon. in La., p. 292.

[3] Senate Ex. Doc., 43rd Cong. 2nd sess., no. 13, pp. 19–20.

[4] Ibid., pp. 21–2.

[5] Senate Mis. Doc., 43rd Cong. 2nd sess., no. 45.

Arkansas to be "banditti," subject to trial by military commission. This done further action might be left to him.[1]

Sheridan's summary, if not brutal, proceedings, which had the express sanction of the President,[2] and drew him promptly to a defense of them,[3] aroused violent excitement in the country at large as well as in Louisiana. To the revulsion of feeling exhibited by large elements of the people in the North, led by influential newspapers, which had already caused Grant to be seen in an unfavorable light on the subject of his whole Southern policy, was now added new cause for incensement. It was, said the New York Nation, "the most outrageous subversion of parliamentary government by military force yet attempted in this country."[4] It was "the grossest and most notable wrong ever committed against the rights and liberties of a people," said the Philadelphia Inquirer.[5] Oliver Cromwell had driven "the representatives of the English people out of their chamber at the point of the bayonet" in 1653, said the Springfield Republican. Grant was repeating the experiment. Sheridan's soldiers had gone into the state house at New Orleans "on a like illegal, revolutionary, treasonable errand.[6]

In the cabinet both Fish and Bristow denounced Sheridan's conduct[7] and Fish again threatened to resign.[8] Indignant citizens met in Fanueil Hall in Boston, in Cooper Institute in New York, in Cincinnati[9] and other cities. Governors addressed special messages to their legislatures, which adopted resolutions.[10] In Louisiana McEnery, committees of citizens, the New Orleans Cotton Exchange, the press, the clergy (in-

---

[1] Senate Mis. Doc. 43rd Cong. 2nd sess., no. 45, p. 23.
[2] Senate Ex. Doc., 43rd Cong. 2nd sess., no. 13, p. 25.
[3] Message to Senate of Jan. 13, 1875.—Richardson, Messages and Papers, vol. vii, pp. 305–14.
[4] Issue of Jan. 7, 1875; cf. ibid., Jan. 14, 1875.
[5] Issue of Jan. 6, 1875.
[6] Cited in Merriam, Life and Times of Samuel Bowles, vol. ii, pp. 275–6.
[7] N. Y. Nation, Jan. 14, 1875; J. S. Black, Essays and Speeches, p. 319.
[8] Lonn, Recon. in La., p. 299.
[9] For Cincinnati, Mayes, Life of Lamar, p. 208.
[10] Lonn, Recon. in La., pp. 303–307; cf. Senate Mis. Doc., 43rd Cong. 2nd sess., nos. 62 and 63.

cluding the Catholic bishop, the Episcopalian bishop, the Methodist bishop and the Jews) found, and declared to the people of the country, that Sheridan's statements as to social conditions in the state were without foundation in truth, and were calculated merely to serve the interests of the corrupt politicians who were endeavoring to continue their already long reign of wrong.[1] Sheridan, responding, supported by Kellogg, Packard and the evil men in control, pointed anew to the activity of the White League, the anarchy and violence, the infinitude of murders within the state, and the troops remained upon the scene.[2]

The last session of Congress, running through the spring and summer of 1874, had been productive of much animated discussion of the subject of Louisiana, inspired by the claims of the contestants for seats in the Senate and the House, the Republicans fortifying themselves with recitals of the blood curdling murders which had disgraced the state, Morton always leading in a vindictive display of hostility to the white people. Now, after the Republican reverses in the elections in November, the opportunity for the leaders of the party to solve this problem of their own creation would end, it was seen, in March, 1875, so that, even before Sheridan had aggravated the trouble, there was need of action immediately. A committee of seven men was appointed to give its special consideration to the state of the South, and it designated a sub-committee of three members—Charles Foster of Ohio and William Walter Phelps of New Jersey, Republicans, and Clarkson N. Potter, an able lawyer of New York, a Democrat—to proceed to Louisiana. The two Republicans were unfortunate selections from the standpoint of Grant and the Radicals, for both Foster and Phelps were of the fibre, which, in this case at least, would impel them to raise truth above party. In New Orleans they, for eight days, beginning on December 30, 1874, called and interrogated witnesses, and, returning home, they,

[1] Am. Ann. Cyclop. for 1874, p. 499.
[2] The orders, addresses, proclamations, etc., relating to the events of 1874 may be conveniently referred to in the article on Louisiana in ibid.

on January 15, 1875, made a report of their conclusions, which little sustained the pretensions of Kellogg. The disorders in the state, so they said, were induced by a belief among the people that he was governing by usurpation. The legislature had been stolen from the Conservatives; the committee was on the ground at the time and had witnessed Sheridan confirm the Republicans in the possession of it. Their indictment of the venality and oppression of Republican rule was detailed and complete. The condition of the people, as a result of such rule was pictured in sombre colors. Kellogg, they declared, corroborating the view of others, was held in office to promote the ends of corrupt men. The White Leagues were formed simply in self-defense, they said, by the respectable part of the population.[1]

The Radicals, following Morton,[2] were greatly disturbed. The four other members of the special committee of the House would now visit the scene. These were three Republicans— George F. Hoar of Massachusetts, the chairman; William A. Wheeler of New York and William P. Frye of Maine—and a Democrat, S. S. Marshall of Ohio. It was January 22, 1875, when they organized for work at the St. Charles Hotel in New Orleans, each party, Republicans and Conservatives, with counsel, as if it were a great case at law, and, February 23, near the end of the session, when they made their report to the House. That paper was drafted by Hoar, and subscribed to by Wheeler and Frye. It was a minority report, since the two Democrats joined Foster and Phelps, and was principally a recital of outrages and bloodshed. Some of the occurrences which he was obliged to record, said Hoar, were "so cruel and barbarous as to excite astonishment in any people making the least pretense to civilization,"[3] and his descriptions of them justified this sweeping judgment. The White League was condemned in scathing terms. It was "a constant menace to the Republicans of the whole state." [4] The elections might not have been

---

[1] House Reports, 43rd Cong. 2nd sess., no. 101, pp. 1–12. More than 300 pages of testimony follow.
[2] Cf. W. D. Foulke, Life of Morton, vol. ii, p. 296.
[3] House Reports, 43rd Cong. 2nd sess., no. 261, pt. 1, p. 9.
[4] Ibid., p. 18.

fair and free. Irregularities in canvassing the returns were not denied, but the Kellogg government was a fact; it had been recognized by the President, and so on. The report was an unpleasantly partisan and denunciatory piece of political writing.

But Hoar and his associates in the second party of committeemen, which had visited New Orleans, had not returned to Washington without making a notable step toward a composition of the dispute. Mr. Wheeler, a respected figure, of recognized influence in the party, with acknowledged capacity as a pacificator,[1] had taken the initiative in proposing a compromise, known usually, therefore, as the "Wheeler adjustment." The Conservatives, on their side, would, for a time, drop their contention as to McEnery's election, and submit to the government of Kellogg; the Republicans, on their side, would refer to the Congressional committee the subject of the admission or non-admission to seats in the legislature of members, whom the returning board, in 1874, and Sheridan had excluded from the body.

Were the people not to be kept in perpetual contention it was agreed that some settlement, if it were possible, must be arrived at. It has been computed that during the ten years preceding 1876 New Orleans paid in taxes more than the value of the property situated within its limits.[2] The rates, in some instances seven or eight per cent on the appraised valuation,[3] Governor Kellogg himself said, were equal to "confiscation." Business was at a standstill. Shipping, wharves, warehouses in New Orleans were deserted. Dwellings and stores were vacant in every street. Scions of proud families were driving street cars and snipping cloth behind counters in dry goods shops to gain a living.[4] Laborers were idle; their families were begging for bread. In two years the population of the city had decreased 30,000.[5] Nor were happier scenes to be wit-

[1] Hoar, Autobiography, vol. i, p. 243.
[2] Albert Phelps in Atlantic Monthly, July, 1901, pp. 128–9.
[3] Senate Ex. Doc., 43rd Cong. 2nd sess., no. 17, p. 73; House Reports, 43rd Cong. 2nd sess., no. 10., p. 7.
[4] Albert Phelps in Atlantic Monthly, July, 1901, p. 129.
[5] Lonn, op. cit., pp. 340–41, 345.

nessed in the country. "Uncultivated fields, unrepaired fences, roofless and dilapidated dwellings and abandoned houses," an observer said, met the eye at every step.[1] What little could be gained from the land was stolen by the negroes, who had been spoiled for useful work.[2] The pecuniary embarrassment of the people and their consequent depression Bishop Wilmer of Louisiana declared to be "without parallel in any civilized country."[3] Modern history had "no example of equal patience under such misfortunes."[4] To many a high born and accomplished citizen of the state death seemed better than such suffering.[5]

Truly action of some kind could not be postponed. Thus it was that, in spite of much active opposition, after considerable delay looking to better terms, Mr. Wheeler's proposal was accepted by representatives of both parties.[6] Foster and Phelps reluctantly joined their Republican colleagues on the committee to the extent of favoring a recognition of the Kellogg government for the sake of reaching results, which others believed would be "less intolerable than the present distress" of the state.[7] Mr. Hoar's committee then presented its plan, which precipitated more angry discussion in Congress and throughout the country. Many Republicans, as well as the Democrats, viewed the subject as one that could not be compromised. There could be no adjustment of a wrong to the point of recognizing as governor a man who had been seated, and was held in place by fraud. But, on March 1st, the House passed a resolution, recognizing Kellogg and recommending the lower chamber of the Louisiana legislature to admit the adherents of McEnery, who, elected to that body in 1874, had been denied their seats since that time.[8]

[1] Senate Ex. Doc., 43rd Cong. 2nd sess., no. 17, p. 72; cf. J. P. B. Wilmer, A Defense of La., p. 4.
[2] Lonn, p. 346; House Reports, 43rd Cong. 2nd sess., no. 101, p. 7; J. S. Black, Essays and Speeches, p. 317.
[3] Lonn, p. 345.
[4] A Defense of La., p. 10.
[5] Ibid., p. 5; R. H. Wilmer, The Recent Past, p. 187.
[6] McPherson's Handbook for 1876, pp. 200–201.
[7] House Reports, 43rd Cong. 2nd sess., no. 261, p. 3.
[8] Cong. Record, 43rd Cong. 2nd sess., p. 1986. Pursuing the policy of compromise, on the last day of the session, a Kellogg member in the House

While this action marked the proceedings of the House, the Senate practically disposed of the claims of Pinchback. His friend Morton, it was clear, would not be able to muster the necessary votes to seat that pertinacious and egotistical mulatto, whose name by this time had become a household word.[1] At the special session, on March 16, 1875, consideration of this subject, so long and so tediously discussed, was postponed by a vote of 33 to 30.[2] It was March 23, when the Senate, by a vote of 33 to 24, passed a resolution approving the President's course in protecting Kellogg from his enemies, and in "enforcing the laws of the United States" in Louisiana.[3]

Hoar's committee, acting in accordance with the terms of the Wheeler compromise, found in favor of the Conservatives;[4] a new legislature containing the excluded members was convened, Sheridan's having adjourned, and the lower chamber at New Orleans was reorganized under new officers. Some groups and interests remained intractable and continued their opposition, but the adjustment was a *modus vivendi*, which was not without its uses, until the campaign for the election of a President and another governor brought fresh excitements upon the people of the state.

In such a prospect the terms of the compromise were forgotten. The early months of 1876 were occupied in the lower house of the state legislature with futile impeachment proceedings aimed at Governor Kellogg. The Republicans in their party convention, amid the most ruffianly scenes, nominated Packard, the United States marshal at New Orleans, at once the shrewdest as well as one of the most unscrupulous and dangerous

of Representatives of Congress was unseated and a McEnery contestant was allowed by the Republicans to enjoy the empty honor of being sworn in in his stead.—Ibid., p. 2235.

[1] Cf. Lonn, p. 334.

[2] Cong. Record, 44th Cong. 1st sess., p. 91. Pinchback was finally rejected by a vote of 32 to 29 on March 8, 1876, Senator Edmunds of Vermont leading the opposition for a group of independent Republicans.—Ibid., pp. 1557–8; cf. Taft, Senate Election Cases, Senate Mis. Doc., 49th Cong. 1st sess., no. 47, p. 426.

[3] Cong. Record, 44th Cong. 1st sess., p. 148; cf. N. Y. Nation, March 25, 1875.

[4] Cf. McPherson's Handbook for 1876, p. 201.

of their managers,[1] for governor. The Democrats nominated Francis T. Nicholls, a lawyer of ability, a member of a leading Louisiana family, a graduate of West Point, a soldier who had gained the rank of brigadier-general in the Confederate army and bore the marks of grievous wounds, which he had received on battle fields of the war. Under the fearless and incorruptible leadership of General Nicholls the white people girded themselves for a powerful effort to achieve the "liberation" of the state. The canvass proceeded, according to the "Mississippi plan," which was being followed so hopefully throughout these same summer and autumn months of 1876 in South Carolina and Florida. Clubs were formed, great meetings were held. Speakers from without the state were brought in to address the crowds, which assembled at or near all the principal towns. Parades, barbecues, the use of artillery lent picturesqueness and fervor to the campaign. The negroes were to be persuaded to. vote the Democratic ticket, and many of them took their places beside the whites at the Democratic rallies.

Everywhere the national election was made subordinate to the election of the governor and the legislature, and the struggle, to be described in a subsequent connection, took on proportions, which shook the whole structure of the republic, before Louisiana could gain the boon she had striven for so long—the withdrawal of Federal troops, the banishment of the infamous men who had yoked her to them for years, heavy with injustice and wrong, and a return to government by her own people.

[1] Cf. Nordhoff, The Cotton States, pp. 63-4.

CHAPTER XXI

HAYES AND TILDEN

As 1874 and 1875 passed, the imminence of another struggle over the Presidency was borne in upon every mind. The corruptions of the government in the Treasury, Navy, War and Interior Departments, the mishandling of the Southern question, so apparent in the case of Louisiana, the complacency of Grant, as the record of his mistakes was unfolded and his complete failure, as it appeared, to comprehend the weight and gravity of the wrongs which had been done the country by the many evil men who had been making use of his military fame for their own advancement and emolument, called for a "reform movement" more loudly than in 1872. Despite the impropriety, on several accounts, of such a course there were not wanting those who saw in Grant a fit candidate for yet another term. Office holders who were thriving and desired to continue in their places, members of his own and Mrs. Grant's numerous families, of whom so much had long been said, and the President's immediate household at Washington, never so comfortable before, had an ill concealed fondness for suggestions on the subject of a "third term." "Palace cars, fast horses and seaside loiterings," Sumner had said so long ago as in 1872, had had a larger place in Grant's life than duties. The Presidency was a trust, but he had treated it as a plaything and a perquisite. Government under him had become "a species of Cæsarism, or personalism,"[1] usually denominated "Grantism."[2]

[1] Sumner, Works, vol. xv, p. 91.
[2] Ibid., p. 157. Moran, who had so long served us as secretary of legation in London, keeping that office in order, while new and incompetent men in a stream came and passed on, was desirous of promotion as a reward for 21 years of faithful labor. Cyrus W. Field wished him to go to Spain. "But I told him," says Moran, "that Grant would sooner pitchfork one of his own incompetent toadies or needy relatives into such a place, than promote to it a man who had devoted his whole life to diplomatic service, and he agreed with me." (Moran's Diary, Jan. 13, 1874.) Schenck

Such an impression, which more than a few men had gained during his first term, was deepened by observation of, and experience with, his second. In 1874, and before, the New York Herald, in its flippant manner, was busy with its plans for continuing Grant yet longer in office. Other papers, with as little moral responsibility, approved, while others again, thinking it worth while to discuss the subject, opposed it, thus keeping it in the popular mind.[1] The Republicans of Florida said that they were "unqualifiedly favorable" to the President's "renomination and re-election."[2] Southern politicians wrote letters in advocacy of the scheme. Every whiskey thief and corrupt contractor who had thriven, and still wished to poach upon the preserves of the government supported the movement.[3] It was part of a system of flattery of Grant, whose failings were known, and who could be used further, so the authors of it hoped, if they were thus to trumpet him as one without whom the party—the republic, indeed, could not survive.

It was desired during the campaign of 1874 to procure from him a statement declaring his complete opposition to what jesters and too zealous friends proposed. There was "no hope for a leadership" which was "simply personal and revengeful," John W. Forney wrote to Senator Morrill of Vermont, on December 3, 1874. The party would go the way of the old Whig party.[4] The President must learn, said Morrill, "that the country has some interest in the cabinet and the administration of affairs as well as in General Grant." It was strange that he could not "put his foot on the third term matter." It was plain to every one that the scheme would not be "tolerated," yet he would not "break silence."[5] The exigencies of

and Adam Badeau wishing to have Moran's place for another, caused him soon afterward to be tendered a transfer to Washington as a third assistant secretary of state, which he peremptorily declined. A few months later he was sent to Lisbon as our minister to Portugal, which was the doorway out of the public service.

[1] Cf. N. Y. Nation, June 18 and Oct. 8, 1874.
[2] Article on Florida in Am. Ann. Cyclop. for 1875, p. 309.
[3] Cf. McDonald, Secrets of the Great Whiskey Ring, pp. 51, 110–11, 283.
[4] Morrill Papers in Library of Congress.
[5] Ibid.

politics required it. The cries of "Cæsarism" and "imperialism" would damage the party.[1]

The President's friends in the cabinet sought to influence him to make a statement which would quiet the discussion. But they did not know how to approach so great a man, who firmly believed, in the light of his great electoral majorities in 1868 and 1872, that he was a political figure of the first magnitude. It was suggested that Mr. Borie, or, if not he, Tom Murphy, as intimates and companions, might be persuaded to "bell the cat." However, were it done, it was feared that Conkling, the real head and front of the administration, as it seemed, might put himself in the way of the attainment of the desirable end.[2]

The New York Tribune pressed the question upon the President.[3] It was May 29, 1875, before he spoke. Then the statement was drawn from him by the Republican state convention of Pennsylvania, which had adopted a resolution expressive of its unalterable opposition to the "election to the Presidency of any person for a third term."[4] Grant's own party in "the second state in the Union" had noticed the discussion, and he now, in a much too lengthy and rather ill-natured letter to the chairman of the convention, disclaimed the ambition which had been ascribed to him. At the end of his statement, he said that he was not and never had been "a candidate for a renomination." He would not accept it, "if it were tendered, unless it should come under such circumstances as to make it an imperative duty—circumstances," he added, "not likely to arise."[5] It was a belated and, even yet, qualified withdrawal, to which he had been compelled by strong party influences.[6] His administration had brought so much discredit upon the Republican name that new courses must be taken, if there were not to be overwhelming defeat in 1876. The Republicans in

[1] N. Y. Nation, Oct. 22, 1874.
[2] Morrill to Benedict, May 17, 1875, in Morrill Papers, loc. cit.
[3] Cf. Cortissoz, Life of Whitelaw Reid, vol. i, pp. 284, 286, 288, 290, 299; Life of Thurlow Weed, vol. ii, p. 542.
[4] McPherson's Handbook for 1876, p. 155.
[5] Ibid., pp. 154-5.
[6] Cf. N. Y. Nation, June 3, 1875; Cortissoz, Life of Whitelaw Reid, vol. i, pp. 320-21; Stanwood, A History of the Presidency, vol. ii, pp. 360-61.

New York, Ohio and other states, to meet the issue, followed
Pennsylvania with "anti-third term" resolutions.[1]

The elections in the autumn of 1875 were, in general, of no
great moment. They contained little prophecy of what might
be seen in the following year. But they were notable in one
particular. In Ohio, where, for a long time, the two parties had
been evenly balanced, a governor was to be chosen, and, for
an issue, the Democrats, returning to their folly of 1868, of
which it was hoped that they had been cured, chose "rag money."
Two years before, in 1873, they had gone back into their history
and had brought out of retirement a venerable leader, William
Allen. He had been elected by a majority of less than 1,000
votes over his Republican opponent, and he was now, in 1875,
renominated by acclamation. In 1873 the issue had been the
corruptions of the Republican party; in 1875 it was to be the
currency question. Allen and the Democrats would oppose
"contraction" and the return to specie payments, provided for
in the act of Congress of January 14, 1875, a policy, they said,
which threatened the country with "general bankruptcy and
ruin." "Greenbacks" should be the money of the land, for
all purposes and for all time.[2]

The Republicans accepted the issue. That financial policy
should be pursued, they said, which will "ultimately equalize
the purchasing capacity of the coin and paper dollar."[3] As its
leader the convention chose ex-Governor Rutherford Birchard
Hayes. He was a native of the state, descended from New
England sires, a graduate of Kenyon College and of the Harvard
Law School and a lawyer of prominence in Cincinnati, until
the outbreak of the war, when he had entered the military
service with the Union army. He was wounded,[4] rose to a
brevet major-generalship, and, in 1864, was elected to Congress in a campaign, in which he had not participated, since he

---

[1] Cf. N. Y. Nation, June 10, 1875; articles on New York and Ohio in Am.
Ann. Cyclop. for 1875; Life of Thurlow Weed, vol. ii, p. 542.

[2] Article on Ohio in Am. Ann. Cyclop. for 1875, p. 607.

[3] Ibid., p. 606.

[4] "Both legs have the marks of rebel missiles."—Hayes to W. H. Turner
in Diary and Letters of Hayes, vol. iii, pp. 126, 302–303.

had declined to leave the field to engage in a political contest. He was elected governor of Ohio over Thurman in 1867, before the completion of his second term in the House of Representatives at Washington and was re-elected to that office in 1869 over Pendleton, who in that year was the Democratic candidate. Now, in 1875, at a critical conjuncture, General Hayes, against his personal desires, for he was out of sympathy with the extreme policies of the party and saw for what it was, and was repelled by, the corruption, the "Butlerism," as he called it, of the Grant administration,[1] was again brought forward, amid much enthusiasm, to lead the Republican state ticket.[2]

Allen had popularity and strength. He was the uncle of Thurman, lately elected a United States senator, and Ohio was soon in the throes of a noteworthy contest, Hayes taking a high and an unmistakable position on the subject of the currency, while Allen and the men whom he drew to his support, labored with the unintelligent classes in behalf of "inflation and repudiation." Times were "hard"—"more money" was the remedy,[3] and the ears of the farmers, and of men in mines, furnaces and factories, and on the railroads were open to receive the insidious doctrines which any demagogue had to present.[4]

Old Republican politicians feared the result. They urged Hayes to attack the subject with caution lest he alienate votes, but he travelled over the state, speaking in the clearest tones more than fifty times.[5] Attorney General Taft, who had been his rival and whom Hayes had sincerely and generously supported for the nomination, Senator John Sherman, Garfield, with several Republican leaders from other states, took the stump in behalf of the ticket, and for weeks town and countryside rang with the sound of the canvass. General Stewart L. Woodford of New York and Colonel William M. Grosvenor of Mis-

[1] Williams, Life of Hayes, vol. i, pp. 382-3; Diary and Letters of Hayes, vol. i, pp. 269, 271.
[2] Williams, Life of Hayes, vol. i, pp. 384-5.
[3] Ibid., p. 405; Haynes, Third Party Movements, pp. 92-3; J. Q. Howard, Life of Hayes, p. 135.
[4] Cf. Diary and Letters of Hayes, vol. iii, p. 293.
[5] Williams, Life of Hayes, vol. i, p. 406. For Hayes's views on the money question see his Diary and Letters, vol. iii, p. 283.

souri brought to the discussion exact knowledge of the science
of finance, which they ably presented on the platform and
through the press. The Cincinnati Commercial, with Halstead
in charge of its columns, was a powerful influence among newspapers in directing public thought.

Upon the refusal of the legislature of Missouri to re-elect Carl
Schurz to the United States Senate, which had preferred the
Confederate General Cockrell for the place, and the ending of
his term of office in March, 1875, that sterling leader had gone
to Europe. His friends had bidden him Godspeed in New York
at a dinner, over which Evarts had presided.[1] His reception
in Germany was distinguished, and the news of the honors done
him there came back across the sea. He was not out of reach
of his American friends, who still looked to him for further
important exertions in the improvement of our politics. Grosvenor, Charles Francis Adams, Jr., Henry Cabot Lodge, Charles
Nordhoff, Murat Halstead, Whitelaw Reid,[2] as the excitement
of the campaign in Ohio increased, wrote to him urging him to
return. The Germans, whom Schurz had led in 1872, and who
were numerically so important a body of voters in Ohio, must
be brought, if possible, to the support of Hayes. The very
renomination of "old Bill" Allen, Adams wrote, was "a defiance and an insult" to intelligent Americans.[3] It was Schurz's
opportunity to win a hearing and a place for the "Independents"
in the national campaign of the next year.

But in July he still doubted the tactical wisdom of attaching
himself to either side in Ohio, or in any "local contest." [4] In
Switzerland, in August, he changed his plans and resolved to
return home at once.[5] His arrival in New York was marked
by warm greetings and he was soon on the stump.[6] On September 27 he, in the interest of "honest money," addressed a
numerous assemblage, made up in large degree of German-

[1] N. Y. Nation, April 29, 1875; Cortissoz, Life of Reid, vol. i, p. 319;
Reminiscences of Schurz, vol. iii, p. 362.
    [2] Cf. Cortissoz, Life of Reid, vol. i, p. 321.
    [3] Schurz, Speeches, vol. iii, p. 157.
    [4] Ibid., p. 159.
    [5] Ibid., p. 161.
    [6] Diary and Letters of Hayes, vol. iii, p. 293.

Americans, in the Turner Hall in Cincinnati. In taking his
place upon the platform he was not a Republican, he said; he
was establishing no alliances which would bind his judgments
for the election of 1876. It was rather as a Democrat, or at any
rate the companion in arms of Democrats in the "Liberal"
campaign of 1872, that he spoke. His persuasive oratory led
many a voter away from the idols which had been set up for
the worship of the people of Ohio by the inflationists.[1] The
end came on October 12th. "Old Bill Allen's grey and gory
scalp," said C. F. Adams, Jr., was "safely dangling at Schurz's
girdle." He had been the helve which completed "the German
axe necessary to the braining of that aged barbarian."[2] Others
wrote him in acknowledgment of his services in killing the "rag
baby." The majority was not great, little in excess of 5,000.
Hayes was again the governor of the state, and, more than
this, a figure identified with the triumph of a national
principle.

That he would now be a contender of serious pretensions for
the Presidency did not yet appear. But among his friends in
Ohio there were not a few who nourished the idea that he might
be an available man for the Republican nomination, though
he himself, with a modesty other than which his part in politics
hitherto had given him, indeed, no right to display, discouraged
allusion to the future. "The melancholy thing in our public
life," he said sagely, "is the insane desire to get higher." "There
should be," he declared again, "no political hereafter—it is
for us to act well in the present."[3] Very few Republicans in
Ohio were "so completely out of the Hayes movement" as
he was.[4] He was, and he would remain "a mere looker on."[5]
If "management" were needed to yield results his chances
could be "put down at zero."[6]

[1] Schurz, Speeches, vol. iii, pp. 161 et seq.
[2] Ibid., pp. 215–6.
[3] Howard, Life of Hayes, p. 144; cf. Williams, Life of Hayes, vol. i, p. 425.
[4] Diary and Letters of Hayes, vol. iii, p. 316.
[5] Ibid., p. 317.
[6] Ibid. By pursuing such a course Garfield wrote him that he was "gaining strength every day with our most thoughtful people." (Ibid., pp.
318–9.) For Hayes's position as a Presidential candidate in the months

Two men at Washington who had worn their honors in fuller view of the nation, without any of the consciousness of not deserving still more than they enjoyed, were Morton of Indiana and Conkling of New York. Both, plainly enough, were candidates for the succession to Grant, though neither had any high public aim, and neither concerned himself with honesty or morality. They were merely two of the imperious leaders of the Senatorial group which had been so powerful in determining the course of the government during the Grant administrations. Morton was a fearless and an influential man in the national councils whom no one could ignore. His defense, because they were Republicans, of the evil men who were plundering the South awakened the grateful sensibilities of the rascals in that part of the Union, who would appear in person or would send their representatives to the national convention of the party. Their votes, and those of many negroes, he might hope to secure in furtherance of his high ambitions.[1]

Conkling, on the other hand, found his strength in an absolute control, on the spoilsmen's plan, of the Republican party organization in the most populous state of the Union. Though the New York Nation could number him among the "adventurers," come into our politics, "flushed with the fame of county court rooms,"[2] it was his florid forensic talent, fresh from these small triumphs, which had set him forward in public life. He, like Morton, had kept himself in communication with the White House. He had reaped, and was still in a place to claim, many political advantages from the administration, and his close affiliations with Grant, who, in turn, had proffered him, it was said, the English mission, the Secretaryship of State and the Chief Justiceship, all of which he had declined that he might remain in the melée of practical politics, had a wide fame.[3] His flattery of the President in resonant phrase in conversa-

preceding the convention see Williams, Life of Hayes, vol. i, pp. 383, 405, 406, 407, 408, 410, 421–38; Diary and Letters of Hayes, vol. iii, pp. 295, 296, 297, 300–301, 305, 307, 309, 310–12, 316, 320, 322, 323.

[1] Cf. Foulke, Life of Morton, vol. ii, p. 388.

[2] Issue of Sep. 23, 1875.

[3] Conkling, Life and Letters of Conkling, p. 495; Harper's Weekly, March 11, 1876.

tion and in public speech made his way the easier. A haughty, supercilious man, as Blaine had declared him to be, to Conkling's lasting affront,[1] officeholders and other men making use of politics as a means to the lucrative exploitation of the government, allowed him to be their leader, in the knowledge that, while they should be willing to forward his ambitions, he would not disturb their personal plans.

Yet another figure appeared—it had come down the stage with a proud assurance which had captivated many men—no other than Blaine himself. His aspirations to gain the highest prizes had brought him into collision with others as well as Roscoe Conkling. To older men he seemed new and, in some senses, an intruder. He was distinctly a product of the period following the war. A journalist in a little city in the state of Maine, fearless in any presence, his eyes set upon a future in which he should be the guiding genius of national if not international destinies, he had yet been seen only as an able presiding officer in the House of Representatives. His manners were gracious; he was a fascinating orator. Men said that he was "magnetic." At any rate he had the power of drawing others to him, and soon extended his friendships among the people, as some public characters have the power to do, until vast numbers of them spoke his name and were ready to share his own trust in himself as a leader. Not since Clay, said some, not since Schuyler Colfax, said others, had there been a public man with the ability to awaken in the imagination even of those who had not seen him, who might, indeed, never know him, except through hearsay or the newspapers, an admiration which so nearly reached the stage of personal fealty. Especially

[1] On April 30, 1866, while Conkling was still in the House and when Blaine had said in colloquy and retort—"The contempt of that large-minded gentleman is so wilting, his haughty disdain, his grandiloquent swell, his majestic, supereminent, overpowering, turkey-gobbler strut has been so crushing to myself and all the members of this House, that I know it was an act of the greatest temerity for me to venture on a controversy with him." Conkling had been likened to Theodore Tilton, to Winter Davis. "Hyperion to a satyr," Blaine continued, "Thersites to Hercules, mud to marble, dunghill to diamond, a singed cat to a Bengal tiger, a whining puppy to a roaring lion," etc.—Cong. Globe, 39th Cong. 1st sess., p. 2299; cf. Stanwood, Life of Blaine, pp. 71–2.

in the West were his adherents active and numerous, and it
was seen that he would be a factor of importance in the contest
for delegates to the convention.

Blaine now, in January, 1876, in his eagerness to pass his
rivals, precipitated a debate in the House of Representatives,
which was deliberately designed to revive sectional animosity
and move the masses of the Northern people to a fresh contemplation of the atrocities of the war. His course was ad-
judged the more unworthy, because he had lately been acting in
another sense. His enlightenment on the Southern question
had seemed to be beyond that of many of his colleagues in
Congress, and he had been using his office as speaker to bring
about better social relationships in the reunited nation.[1] So
lately as in 1875, a few days before the session of the House
would end, and he should retire as its presiding officer, he had
indicated his want of sympathy with the other Republican
leaders in their design to enact a new "Force Bill." Indeed
he had secretly outlined to Lamar a plan for a filibuster by
the Democrats, and had thereby enabled them to defeat the
measure.[2]

But, convinced of the need of a re-stirring of the crackling
thorns under the pot that held this devil's brew, for the advantage of the party, support for which had been fast slipping
away, and for the improvement of his own fortunes, he soon
undid all that he had been the instrument in doing in an opposite sense. The Democrats had brought forward a general
amnesty bill, similar to the one which Grant, in his message to
Congress in December, 1873, had advocated, and which the
Republicans in the House, Blaine then acquiescing, had presented and had sent to the Senate in the Forty-third Congress.[3]
All who were yet laboring under disabilities imposed upon them
by the Fourteenth Amendment, which Blaine estimated to
number, perhaps, 750 persons,[4] including Jefferson Davis, were

[1] Stanwood, Life of Blaine, pp. 112–5.
[2] Mayes, Life of Lamar, p. 215; cf. Stanwood, Life of Blaine, pp. 117–20.
[3] Cong. Record, 43rd Cong. 1st sess., p. 91; ibid., 44th Cong. 1st sess.,
pp. 328–9.
[4] Ibid., 44th Cong. 1st sess., p. 324; cf. vol. ii of this work, pp. 271–2.

to have their political rights restored to them. In spite of what had then been done Blaine now saw his opportunity, and he embraced it. On January 10, 1876, after some allusions to Toombs, he passed to Davis, whom he held to be responsible, "knowingly, deliberately, guiltily and wilfully," for "the gigantic murders and crimes at Andersonville." The cruelties of that military prison he recited vividly and at length to an excited House and a disorderly gallery.[1] He was frankly baiting the Southern members, who interrupted him as he proceeded, and who prepared responses in a not kindlier spirit. The dead enemy smelt well to Blaine, said "Sunset" Cox, the capable and witty leader of the Democrats, and he found "musk and amber in revenge." His remarks were calculated "to re-inspire wrath and capture the ear of his willing partisans."[2] In the national Centennial year, when there was to be kindness and reunion, the "gentleman from Maine" was "raking up again the embers of dead hates for some bad purpose," which would "never elect him to the Presidency of the United States, if he should live a thousand years."[3]

For the South Benjamin H. Hill of Georgia made the principal defense, and he, as it was, perhaps, hoped that he might do, retorted with attacks upon the Northern management of prisons which had held Confederate captives. Blaine's nimble skill in interlocutory remark was displayed in an unpitying way. His taunts were so savage that they stung Southern members to replies that but spurred him to fresh thrusts. One thing was certain, as Hill said in corroboration of Cox,—"the gentleman from Maine," had, "for an obvious partisan purpose," excited "a bitter sectional discussion," from which his party and he himself, might, it was hoped, be the "beneficiary."[4]

The South might better have remained silent, if its representatives could have contained their resentment.[5] Blaine came out of the encounter, in the sight of his admirers, a redoubtable

[1] Cong. Record, 44th Cong. 1st sess., pp. 324-6.
[2] Ibid., p. 326.
[3] Ibid., p. 329.
[4] Ibid., p. 350.
[5] Mayes, Life of Lamar, pp. 274-5.

antagonist.[1] The passions of boys who, not old enough to take
their parts in the war, were now grown up and were eager to
have it re-fought under their eyes, were easily stirred by such
rhodomontade, and in them it was that Blaine, by "waving
the bloody shirt," was laying the foundations of his political
reputation. So long as such as he were on guard the young
men of the country, especially in the West, where his friends
abounded, assured themselves that there would be no paltering
with "rebels," and the republic would be safe.

In the background, among Presidential candidates, Elihu
Washburne was seen. He was still in Paris. In his bluff
way he had distinguished himself during the Prussian siege as
our minister to France. For some years he had been out of the
brawl of our politics, which, while it had caused him to be half
forgotten, had also made him (so many of his correspondents in
America did not cease to say) the "man of the hour." They
wrote him that Grant did not have in his cabinet "one solitary
man," with the probable exception of Fish, who was "worth
wood-sawyer's wages." He himself, though the original friend
of the President, indulged in free criticism of the administration.
Both before and after the Republican's party's reverses in 1874,
he was frequently mentioned as a suitable successor of Grant.
He was ready to believe that, out of the rancor, which was
certain to develop among the rivals for the nomination, it might
come to him, and he and his adherents awaited the event with
greater hope than the result would have seemed to justify.[2]

In the meantime what were the hopes and prospects of the
Democrats? Easily the most prominent figure in the party was
Samuel J. Tilden, who had been elected governor of New York
in 1874 over General Dix as a protest against "Grantism," on
which issue the New York Tribune had led "independent"
feeling in the state,[3] and was applying himself, in continuation
of his activity in connection with the exposures of the corruptions of the Tammany leaders in New York City, to a discovery

[1] Cf. Gail Hamilton, Life of Blaine, pp. 378–83.
[2] Cf. Washburne Papers in Library of Congress.
[3] Cortissoz, Life of Reid, vol. i, pp. 289–94; Governor Dix to Thurlow
Weed, Nov. 6, 1874, in Life of Thurlow Weed, vol. ii, p. 505.

of frauds in the state administration. The revelations were similarly sensational. The state owned the Erie and other canals and the maladministration of this branch of the public business was of vital interest to the people. Here was a department of government, under the management of a board, which had receipts, in five years, ending on September 30, 1874, of over $15,000,000, while the disbursements exceeded $20,000,000. Other outlays and interest charges brought up the deficit to about $11,000,000.

It was plain that, through collusion between employees of the state and the individuals and companies to whom work upon the canals was entrusted, there had been venality for a long time. Both Republicans and Democrats were in the "ring" and bore forth their respective shares of the plunder.[1] Men were paid for work which they never performed—they were excessively paid for services which they did render. Enemies were punished by withholding from them their just rewards. Through this iniquity politics were demoralized and the credit of the state had been imperilled. Tilden caused an expert engineer to make a survey of the subject,[2] and on March 18, 1875, he was ready to send a special message to the legislature, suggesting various thoroughgoing reforms. His course called forth the warmest expressions of approval from press and people,[3] and measures were adopted, reluctantly enough, since many of the jobbers held seats in the legislature, looking to a better condition of affairs. The governor was authorized to appoint a commission of four members to investigate the whole subject and this body, with John Bigelow at its head, was promptly organized at Albany for its useful service. They made a series of reports to the governor, disclosing frightful rascalities.[4] A number of officers and ex-officers of the state were arrested and arraigned in the criminal courts. Contractors were sued and compelled to disgorge at least a portion of their wrongful gains.

[1] Bigelow, Life of Tilden, vol, i, pp. 258–9.
[2] Ibid., p. 260.
[3] Ibid., p. 261; Letters and Memorials of Tilden, vol. i, pp. 361–70.
[4] Letters and Memorials of Tilden, vol. ii, pp 405 et seq.

The governor was not satisfied. He wished for changes in
the system, to which the "ring's" friends in the legislature
would not agree. "The abuses, perversions of law and morals,
improvidence and waste," which clung around the canal board,
he said, were "the growth of years." It was always "difficult
to carry out reform by instruments that are incurably averse to
reform," as this board was declared to be—he would have
"the debris of the old rotten system" entirely cleared away.[1]

Enough had been done to put Tilden, more clearly than ever,
before the country as a "reformer." The year 1876 was to be a
year in which the immoralities which had come to infect the
national government, under the careless and unseeing eyes of
Grant, would again be set before the people for their condemnation, and the Democrats, if they were to profit by the situation
in which their opponents were so unfortunately involved, must
present a figure who would afford the hope of a better order in
the future. In Tilden a leader of this kind was seen.[2] He was
fresh from his victories. He came from a great and powerful
state, which would exert a decisive influence upon the result
on election day. It was known that he was not now, that for
some years past he would not have been, averse to the leadership of the party which a nomination for the Presidency would
imply. Every prospect favored him, and it came to be regarded
as nearly a certainty that he would be a principal contender for
the honor when the convention should meet. The favor felt
in the West for the "rag money" idea, which had been confirmed by the large vote polled for Allen in Ohio, and which had
its foundations in the economic hardships still felt by the people,
following the panic of 1873, assured Tilden of opposition. His
sentiments were well known. His alliances as an attorney for
capitalists and corporations would have determined his sympathies had he possessed no convictions of his own on such a question. He could not carry the party's banners, if they bore the
words "inflation" and "repudiation"—another must be found,
if cheap money were to provide the impulse for the campaign.

[1] Article on New York in Am. Ann. Cyclop. for 1875, p. 559.
[2] Cf. Bigelow, Life of Tilden, vol. i, pp. 273–4, 283.

The weeks passed and the time for the parties to hold their conventions and make their nominations drew near. That company of virile men, jealous of the country's honor, who had launched the "Liberal Reform" movement in 1872, issued a call in April, 1876, for another meeting of "notables." The conference should be held at the Fifth Avenue Hotel in New York, within walls which had already heard their voices. The call was signed by William Cullen Bryant, ex-President Theodore D. Woolsey of Yale University, ex-Governor Alexander H. Bullock of Massachusetts, Horace White and Carl Schurz. Answers were to be sent to the secretary, Henry Cabot Lodge. The gentlemen invited to this meeting, in protest against "the widespread corruption," which had "disgraced the republic in the eyes of the world," and threatened "to poison the vitality of our institutions," were to consider what might be done "to prevent the national election of the Centennial year from becoming a mere choice of evils." They would aim "to secure the election of men to the highest offices of the republic whose character and ability" would "satisfy the exigencies" of the country's "present situation and protect the honor of the American name."

The movement, in truth, was in the direction of Charles Francis Adams.[1] Its instigators and abettors were, for the most part, the same men who, four years before, had been thwarted in their efforts to bring about his nomination. Woolsey presided and an "address to the American people" was formulated and given to the press. The spoilsman's attitude toward public life was stated and denounced in scathing terms. "We shall support no candidate" who may not meet this requirement, they said; "we shall support no candidate" who may not fulfill that other requirement, and so on, in detail, the platform of the conferees was stated in trenchant words. The known character, the very name of the candidate for the Presidency, to be considered fit for the emergency, must afford "conclusive

---

[1] J. P. Munroe, Life of F. A. Walker, pp. 161-2. For Blaine's scorn of Adams see his letter to Whitelaw Reid in Cortissoz, op. cit., vol. i, pp. 331-2.

evidence of the most uncompromising determination of the American people to make this a pure government once more." [1]

Meantime, the Republican aspirants gathered their forces in the respective states for their nominating convention, which was to meet in Cincinnati on the 14th of June. Blaine by his baiting of the South, so patently for his own profit as it was, and his whole jaunty course as the leader of the opposition in the House, abundantly invited his fate. It was known that he was as ambitious in the making of money as in obtaining high office. His use of the speakership to sell the bonds of the Little Rock and Fort Smith Railroad that he might have the profits accruing from the transactions, were familiar to several men, and, when what he had done became the subject of an investigation by the Committee on the Judiciary of the House, and the "Mulligan letters" appeared, he was in a position which seriously imperilled his fortunes. That he had been acting in a business not in the line of his career, that he was addressing monied men in his public capacity, that he was identified with a property which did not commend itself as an investment to persons of financial sagacity, would be dismissed in some quarters as merely undignified. But, when, under stress, he seized the letters and brought them into the House for exhibition to his colleagues, and, in an impassioned speech in his own defense, flatly contradicted statements which he had earlier made as to his connection with the speculation, until he was entangled in the meshes of truth, half truth and untruth to nearly that extent in which his predecessor in the speaker's chair, Schuyler Colfax, had been, on the subject of the Credit Mobilier,[2] there was a distinct feeling, among such as had attended the Fifth Avenue Conference, that he was not a leader who could well be used by the Republicans in the campaign of 1876.[3]

[1] Schurz, Speeches, vol. iii, pp. 240-48; article on U. S. in Am. Ann. Cyclop, for 1876, pp. 779-80.

[2] See vol. ii of this work, pp. 610-14; Merriam, Life of Bowles, vol. ii, pp. 255-9.

[3] Hayes wrote of Blaine on May 19, 1876: "As a candidate before the people his newly acquired wealth, his schemes for getting the nomination

Adams's name awakening no cordial response in the country, the "Independents," and all Republicans with a finer sense of feeling in regard to the responsibilities of citizenship turned hopefully to Bristow, who was in the midst of his single-handed contest with the Whiskey Ring. The revelations on this subject were opportune. Bristow's attitude toward Babcock and the rascals near Grant, who were parties to the great frauds upon the revenue, made him, naturally, the candidate of the better forces. He had the support of a number of the leading journals, which, in 1876, as in 1872, were to have a weighty influence in directing the course of events. Men, whose names were mentioned with high respect and carried assurance of the worthiest aims and purposes, warmly counselled his nomination. He might not be chosen by the convention, he was at least a figure whose character would attest to the existence of a virtue within the party, which, if it had been flouted during the administrations of Grant, offered hope of a return of some of the attachment to principle, which had been the distinction of Republicanism in 1860 and during the progress of the war.

It was clear, as the delegates assembled at Cincinnati, that Bristow was the "common enemy" of the Blaine, Conkling and Morton factions.[1] But his strength was not great enough, in view of the character of the delegations which had been returned from the South and many of the Western and Northern states, to cause any one to believe that he could be nominated. Then it was, so prophetic men said, that the minds of the delegates would be turned to a compromise candidate such as Hayes, Washburne or Fish.[2]

and his connection with the money interests, depending for success on legislation, will damage him." (Diary and Letters of Hayes, vol. iii, p. 320.) Senator Morrill of Vermont wrote on June 17, 1876: "I know of nothing against the character of Blaine, but he would have pleased me better if he had less to do with those railroad men—he would have pleased me vastly better. A public man ought not to be mixed up with desperate ventures."—To Benedict in Morrill Papers in Library of Congress.

[1] Phila. Ledger, June 13, 1876.

[2] James Freeman Clarke of Massachusetts, in response to a request that he should support Washburne, said that he was for Bristow so long as there was hope of his nomination, and he added—"The man who is most dangerous and represents all the bad principles in the government is Roscoe

On the eve of the meeting of the convention Blaine had been taken sick while on his way to church in Washington,[1] and was writhing on a bed of pain, for several hours in complete unconsciousness, an attack brought on by the excitement under which he was laboring and the great heat of the season. This circumstance, as he convalesced, turned some sympathy to his account, and, as he had, for a certainty, a larger body of delegates than any other one candidate, it was taken for granted by many men, in spite of the transgressions which were laid at his door, that he would be the convention's choice.[2]

The convention met in the large wooden building which had been erected for the National Sængerfest in 1869, and in which Greeley had been nominated by the "Liberals" in 1872. Its proportions were not great enough to admit the many thousands who had come to witness the scene that was to be enᵉcted under its roof. On the second day of the convention, June 15th, the platform was received from the committee on resolutions through General Hawley of Connecticut. The reading of this paper was interrupted by much applause, and loud cheering at points calling for such outbursts of enthusiasm, as in reference to the enforcement of the constitutional amendments for the protection of the negroes, the gratitude which the country owed to Grant for his "immense service in war and in peace," the denunciatory passages aimed at the Democratic party, the protection of "American labor" through tariff laws, the withholding of public funds from sectarian schools, and, more wisely and hopefully, in view of the condition of the popular mind, the redemption of the greenbacks and a return to specie payments.

The presentation of the names of the candidates followed. The "favorite sons" were acclaimed but little, and the response, as the speeches were made in their behalf, did not

Conkling, and we mean to beat him if we can."—Letter of June 14, 1876, in Washburne Papers in Library of Congress; cf. N. Y. Tribune, June 2, 1876.

[1] Gail Hamilton, Life of Blaine, pp. 396, 414-7.
[2] Cf., e.g., Phila. Ledger, June 14, 1876.

greatly prolong the proceedings. Connecticut presented the name of Marshall Jewell, now for several months the respectable occupant of the Postmaster General's office. Governor Hartranft was nominated by the Pennsylvania delegation, held firmly in leash by Cameron. Governor Hayes of Ohio was appropriately presented by ex-Governor Noyes; he was seconded by "Ben" Wade and others. Conkling was nominated by General Woodford of New York. He was recommended to the convention as "a true friend of Grant." While he was accounted more than a "favorite son," it was noted that the bringing forward of his name but little stirred the crowd which filled the great auditorium. On the other hand, Morton, befriended as he was by the negroes, the carpetbaggers and the scalawags, comprising the Southern delegations, whose cause he had represented so blindly at Washington, was the subject of loud and long continued demonstrations of favor. Pinchback, in gratitude for all that the candidate had done to introduce that mulatto to honors and emoluments attending public life at the nation's capitol, seconded the nomination in the name of the "truly loyal people" of Louisiana.

Bristow had for his sponsor General John M. Harlan of his own state of Kentucky, following whom Judge Poland of Vermont, George William Curtis of New York and Richard H. Dana of Massachusetts made speeches for the candidate of the "Independents" and "Reformers." Applause and cheers greeted the mention of his name, and the recital of his deeds.

But it was for Blaine that most of the clamor and turbulence which belong to a political convention were reserved. The friends of this leader, to whom the investigation of his affairs as an agent for the sale of railroad bonds was only a persecution by his enemies, had found a signally gifted orator to make his nomination speech. Colonel Robert G. Ingersoll was a lawyer in Illinois, to which state he had come from New York as a boy of ten years. He had gained his military title with an Illinois regiment during the war. First a Democrat, he became a Republican, and had enjoyed some small distinctions at the hands of the party in his state. For his eloquence he was as yet better known at the bar than on the platform, where, by exasperating the clergy into controversy and retort, he was later to become notorious as the country's principal apostle of atheism. The convention was on its feet, hats and handkerchiefs were waved, men shouted and cheered as Ingersoll appeared for the execution of his task. He was interrupted with great applause as he proceeded with his soaring periods about "the man who had the grandest combination of heart, conscience and brain beneath the flag," the man who had "snatched the mask of Democracy from the face of rebellion," the man who, "like an intellectual athlete," had stood "in the arena of debate and challenged all comers," and who was "still a total stranger to defeat." "Like an armed warrior, like a plumed knight," he had "marched down the halls of the American Congress, and threw his shining lance full and fair against the brazen foreheads of the defamers of his country and the maligners of his honor." For the party to desert him now was "as if an army should desert their general upon the field of battle." For many a year James G. Blaine had been "the bearer of the sacred standard of the Republican party"— "In the name of the great republic, the only republic that ever existed upon this earth; in the name of all her defenders and of all her supporters"; in the name of the dead upon the field of battle, and of those who had "perished in the skeleton clutch of famine at Andersonville and Libby," Illinois— Illinois nominated "that prince of parliamentarians, that leader of leaders, James G. Blaine."[1]

The candidate's own state of Maine followed with its endorsement. The convention wished to proceed to a vote at once, but it was now late in the evening, the hall could not be lighted and adjournment was taken until the next day, the 16th, when the balloting commenced. Blaine's name led all others with 285 votes. He had the entire delegations of Iowa,

<hr/>

[1] Landis and Clare, Life of Blaine, pp. 63–4; A. K. McClure, Recollections of Half a Century, pp. 425–7.

Kansas, Nebraska, Minnesota, Oregon, Wisconsin and the
Western Territories; all but four of the delegates from Illinois,
all but three from California. He was the choice of all the
delegates from Maine, Missouri and Delaware.

Morton had 125 delegates, many of them, as had been foretold, from the South; Bristow 113, Massachusetts adding 17
to Kentucky's 21; Conkling 99, of whom New York contributed 69 (all but George William Curtis), and Hayes 61, of
whom 44 were the delegates from Ohio, solidly attached to
his interests as a candidate.[1] No one had a majority, which
would be 378.

The balloting was continued. In the second call upon the
states Blaine gained 11 votes. On the third and fourth ballots
Bristow slightly improved his position. It was on the fifth
ballot that Hayes made decisive progress, enthusiastic and
effective support coming to him from Michigan where he had
had friends from the first,[2] and from North Carolina. On the
sixth ballot he made further gains, Blaine on this ballot receiving the votes of 308 delegates, the greatest number who at
any time had supported him. He was in a strong position—the
call of the states as it commenced on the seventh ballot indicated a drift toward his standard which might lead to his
nomination—when his opponents hurriedly conferred and turned
the tide to Hayes.

Hayes had been described as a "neutral." [3] He had damaged
his chances by no action or utterance, since the eyes of the
country had been fixed upon him after his re-election to the
governorship of Ohio in 1875. If he were not nominated for
President it was generally conceded that he should have the
second place on the ticket.[4] He himself had been favorable
to the nomination of Bristow.[5] He told an intimate friend
in the convention that he must not be nominated for the Vice

---

[1] Williams, Life of Hayes, vol. i, p. 442.
[2] Ibid., p. 450.
[3] N. Y. Sun, May 9, 1876.
[4] Diary and Letters of Hayes, vol. iii, p. 324.
[5] "I am sure that I prefer him [Bristow] to any other man."—Ibid., p.
309.

Presidency on a ticket with Blaine,[1] but he had made no enemies
even among that man's adherents. In an independent place,
"aloof from bargaining," as he said, he could expect the nomination only in the "contingency" of a union between those who
might look for "availability in the candidate" and those who
stood for "purity and reform in administration." His prospects
would brighten only in case of the need of a "compromise
candidate." [2] This need had now arisen. Bristow telegraphed
from Kentucky, urging his friends to vote for the governor of
Ohio. The Morton forces in Indiana came to his support,[3]
as did the Conkling men from New York, who would now and
always use their energies in opposition to Blaine. On the
seventh ballot, therefore, Hayes's vote was 384 and Blaine's
351.[4] Hayes amid wild uproar, was declared to be the nominee
of the party for the Presidential campaign of 1876.[5] The
result occasioned not a little chagrin to the friends of Blaine,
not a little surprise to the country at large, and, indeed, to the
convention itself, which, until the end, had had the expectation of another choice, though it was far from clear what it
might be.

William A. Wheeler of New York, the respected member of
the House of Representatives who had recently attained some
degree of prominence in connection with the settlement in
Louisiana, was nominated by acclamation for Vice President.[6]

Hayes meantime had remained quietly in the governor's
office in Columbus. If nominated, he wrote in his Diary on the
morning of the day on which the convention made him its
choice, he would "try to do in all things . . . precisely the

[1] Diary and Letters of Hayes, vol. iii, p. 325.
[2] Ibid., pp. 321, 326. Though Washburne and Fish were in the minds
of some of the delegates their candidacy made no progress in the open sight
of the convention, for Fish seems to have received not one vote on any
ballot, and Washburne never more than five.
[3] Foulke, Life of Morton, vol. ii, p. 401.
[4] Cf. Howard, Life of Hayes, pp. 151–4.
[5] Williams, Life of Hayes, vol. i, pp. 450–51.
[6] "I am ashamed to say who is Wheeler?" Hayes wrote to his wife from
the governor's office in Columbus on January 30, 1876, when Sheridan in a
letter had declared his "ticket" to be Hayes and Wheeler.—Diary and
Letters of Hayes, vol. iii, p. 301.

thing that is right—to be natural, discreet, wise, moderate and as firm in the right as it is possible for me to be." [1] In that spirit he waited and received the news from the convention hall. He would make it his "constant effort to deserve" the "confidence" of the "best people," many of whom recently had been dissatisfied with the course of the Republican party, and who hastened now to express their trust in him. [2]

The Democrats would meet in St. Louis on the 27th of June, 1876. The party which, it was predicted, had dug its grave, when it had nominated Horace Greeley in 1872, was now, as it had plainly appeared but two years later, in 1874, stronger than ever. It was, however encumbered by the "Greenbackers," who had proven their power in Ohio in 1875. Thurman and his kinsman, "Rise Up" Allen, in that state, and Hendricks in Indiana, who for tactical reasons, had yielded to the same influences, were aspirants for the Presidential nomination by the Democratic convention. Senator Bayard of Delaware, and a military candidate, if this were desired, General Hancock of Pennsylvania, were also in the field. But Tilden was the pre-eminent figure and it was generally supposed, as it was cordially hoped, that he would be chosen. He was not without his enemies within the party, even in New York, where his course, in connection with the canal and the Tammany frauds, had raised a considerable opposition. [3] These mean forces had been overborne at the Democratic state convention at Utica, and the delegation sent to St. Louis had instructions to vote for the governor and to do their part to make him the party's candidate for President.

A platform which scathingly denounced the Grant administration, and the entire course of the Republican party was adopted. One series of allegations, charges and arraignments upon another, each commencing with the words—"Reform is necessary," comprised this stirring political paper. "Centralism," the carpetbag governments, the delay in resuming specie

[1] Diary and Letters of Hayes, vol. iii, p. 326.
[2] Ibid., p. 328.
[3] Cf. N. Y. Tribune, May 27, 1876.

payments, onerous taxes, high and unjust tariffs, the waste of the public lands, Chinese immigration, extravagance and corruption were attacked in general and in particular, and it may have been, and it did seem to be true, that "all the abuses, wrongs and crimes, the product of sixteen years' ascendency of the Republican party" had created a necessity for a "change of system, a change of administration, a change of parties." The time had come for, and there must be, "a peaceful civil revolution."[1] But in general the phrase was pitched too high, the tone was too strident, the charges were too prolixly described to make the best impression upon the country,[2] which was not unaware of the existence of the evils complained of, and was not unready to adopt remedial measures that might commend themselves to the public judgment.

The "two-thirds rule," some believed, might prevent Tilden's nomination.[3] The whole vote would be 738, and 492 delegates must support a candidate to make him the convention's choice. Hendricks was Tilden's most formidable rival, the "Greenbackers" as well as the Tammany forces, viewing him as the leader best calculated to serve their ends. The voting came on the second day, the 28th, when Tilden had 403½, Hendricks 133½, Hancock 75, Allen 56, with small numbers of votes for other men. The result was foreseen; delegates rapidly came to Tilden, giving him on the second ballot 535 votes, and Pennsylvania, which had been supporting Hancock, and Indiana, which had been the principal sponsor of Hendricks, made the nomination unanimous, amid the tumult marking such meetings at such an hour. On the following day, to satisfy the West and, if possible, secure the electoral vote of a debatable state, at the same time conciliating elements which had been somewhat hostile to Mr. Tilden, Hendricks, though he had expressed an emphatic aversion to the second position, and by telegraph had

[1] Cf. Bigelow, Life of Tilden, vol. i, app. B; McPherson's Handbook of Politics for 1876, pp. 215–6; Stanwood, A History of the Presidency, vol. i, pp. 374–9.

[2] Cf. Williams, Life of Hayes, vol. i, p. 467; Blaine, Twenty Years in Congress, vol. ii, p. 578.

[3] Phila. Ledger, June 27, 1876.

declined the place, was nominated as the candidate for Vice President.

Two new parties had made their appearance in conventions in May. On the 17th of that month a small body of earnest men, calling themselves the Prohibition Reform Party, the principal plank in whose platform was a demand for the prohibition, by statute in the District of Columbia and the Territories, and by a provision in the Federal Constitution for the country generally, of the importation, exportation, manufacture and sale of "alcoholic beverages," met in Cleveland.[1] This party was the expression of a feeling, which was rapidly deepening, in behalf of temperance. Its growth had been signalized in Ohio by the "Crusade," which a number of women had instituted. The saloon was to be abolished. The "Crusaders" entered grog shops and inns, praying with the barkeepers and the bibbers and loafers whom they found there. They picketed the doors of such places and invited men, bent upon entering, to take a pledge to drink no more, and were soon organizing societies over a large part of the country for the promotion of their philanthropic objects in the interest of the mothers and children of the land, upon whom drunkenness bore most cruelly.[2] They, with the aid of men who espoused their cause, had invoked the intervention of city and town councils and the courts, and were ready to strengthen the movement, seen for some years in sporadic and scattered communities, for separate political party organization. At Cleveland a candidate of these elements for President was found in General Green Clay Smith of Kentucky, who had been elected to Congress during the war and afterward had been governor of Montana Territory. At first a lawyer he later had entered the Baptist ministry. Gideon T. Stewart, a founder of the party, an industrious writer and speaker for temperance in Ohio, was nominated for Vice President.

The next day, the 18th of May, the Independent National Convention met in Indianapolis. The men in this assemblage

[1] Stanwood, History of the Presidency, vol. i, pp. 364–5.
[2] Cf. Mother Stewart, Memories of the Crusade.

were "Greenbackers"—their whole purpose was to oppose resumption and give the country paper money. The Greenback national party movement was an outgrowth of conventions held in Indianapolis, Cleveland and Detroit in 1874 and 1875, and it was the legitimate successor of the Labor Reform and the Granger movements.[1] "Greenback clubs" were formed among farmers and workingmen[2] and a few, of charitable instincts and wandering minds, whose names were known to the country in various connections, were drawn in to make speeches and take leading places in the conduct of the new party's affairs. Peter Cooper,[3] the bland philanthropist of New York, now 85 years old, giving his last years and a part of the fortune which he had accumulated in the iron business and other trades, to deeds which seemed to him to be righteous, was nominated for President, while Newton Booth, governor of California, and now a United States senator from that state, whose success in politics had been due to his assaults upon the railway corporations and other expressions and embodiments of wealth, was named for Vice President. Booth declining, the honor fell to Samuel F. Cary of Ohio, once a Congressman and the candidate for lieutenant-governor on the ticket with Allen in 1875, widely known for his aberrations on the money question.[4]

Hayes, on July 8, accepted the nomination tendered him at the hands of the Republicans. His letter was straightforward, terse and comprehensible to the plainest intelligence. It contained the most satisfactory declarations in behalf of civil service reform. With an eye single to the public good he stated his "inflexible purpose" not to be a candidate for re-election. He denounced irredeemable paper money and took positive ground in favor of resumption; he deplored the condition of the Southern states, and gave them hope of respect for their "con-

---

[1] Haynes, Third Party Movements, pp. 105-11; Buck, The Agrarian Crusade, pp. 79-80.

[2] Buck, op. cit., p. 86.

[3] For his views on money see McCulloch, Men and Measures, p. 415.

[4] Haynes, Third Party Movements, pp. 112-14; Stanwood, History of the Presidency, vol. ii, pp. 365-8.

stitutional rights," and early return to local self government, free of Federal interferences.

Tilden issued his letter of acceptance on the last day of July. It was a long essay on the state of the country, the evils to be attacked and the methods by which they might be extirpated. To the average voter's mind it must have seemed a tedious and rather labored writing. While it was sound in its doctrines it wanted directness because of the weight of its verbiage. It was, moreover, destructive—in what would be torn down there was no sign of what would be established in its place, and, however much the sense of the more enlightened parts of the population might be repelled by the venalities of the Grant administration, they could repose but little trust, or hope in the party whose nominee Tilden had become, and whose disloyalties, as well as many stupidities, during the course of and since the war, were fresh in the public mind. His political career thus far, as useful as it had recently been, made it plain that the government, with him at its head, would be a party government; it was equally plain, whatever might be thought of his own intents and purposes, that the organization which he must use for the attainment of his objects was filled with men, who, in a critical hour, had proven themselves wanting in devotion to the Union.

At once on this issue, which only ten years after the war's end could not be eliminated from the canvass, Tilden was at a great disadvantage. He was oppressed, too, by his companion upon the ticket. Hendricks personally was a man of good character, though essentially a politician without any high objects in view.[1] In Congress he was courteous in debate and an effective advocate of the causes which he espoused.[2] He had warm admirers and friends, but, as a candidate for Vice President, he was described by Schurz as "the most objectionable man imaginable."[3] If Tilden should die, and his health was not robust, his successor would represent "exactly opposite"

[1] Rollo Ogden, Life of Godkin, vol. ii, p. 112.
[2] Cf. McCulloch, Men and Measures, p. 73.
[3] Schurz, Speeches, vol. iii, p. 258.

principles. The government would be delivered over to the soft money elements in the party.[1]

On the other side both Hayes and Wheeler were so clear on this subject as to admit of no question about their position, or the position of the party which they were to lead. On March 4, 1876, Hayes wrote to Garfield that the "true contest" would be "between inflation and a sound currency." He would not yield "a hair's breadth." "We can't be," he continued, "on the inflation side of the question."[2] The party, he wrote to Sherman, should be as "sound as coin."[3]

Thus the campaign was begun. It would be a hard fought, likely, a very close contest, and the "Independents," with Schurz at their head, who had met at the Fifth Avenue Hotel, would be factors in deciding it. They had both talent and influence, and it was of interest to discover what course they might adopt. Schurz himself at once gave indications of a preference for Hayes. The hope of seeing Adams or Bristow in the place having vanished, there were suggestions looking to the formation of a third party. Tilden was "too much of a demagogue—too much of a wire puller and machine politician" to be depended upon as "a man of principle."[4] Hayes, on the other side, having been at first regarded as only "a respectable compromise candidate,"[5] presented possibilities to Schurz, which he at once commenced to develop. He was spending the summer in the country near Philadelphia and entered into correspondence with the man whom, by trenchant speeches, he had helped to elect to the governorship of Ohio, but whom he had not met. The "old war issues" should be discarded. The candidate should rise above "the vague and discredited promises of the platform," and make the campaign his own. He should come out for civil service reform "in language bold and ringing"—thus would he "electrify the country" and call to his banner "the best elements

[1] Schurz, Speeches, vol. iii, p. 265; Letters and Memorials of Tilden, vol. ii, p. 439; Bigelow, Life of Tilden, vol. i, p. 306.
[2] Diary and Letters of Hayes, vol. iii, p. 306.
[3] Ibid., p. 308.
[4] Schurz, Speeches, vol. iii, p. 259.
[5] Ibid., p. 258.

of the people from far beyond the lines of party." Then would this become "one of the greatest and most salutary campaigns in our history, a campaign worthy of the Centennial year." [1]

Hayes was not unmindful of Schurz's services in Ohio in 1875; he was prepared to set a value upon them, if they should be enlisted on his side in 1876, and answered promptly and obligingly, which soon led to further epistolary interchanges, in which Schurz went so far as to submit carefully prepared statements on the subjects of civil service reform and the currency, to be included in Hayes's letter of acceptance. He twice visited the candidate in Ohio, who conferred with him as to the declarations which it might be wise to make in the paper,[2] and any comparison of Schurz's suggestions, as they are recorded in his correspondence, and the letter, will reveal the importance of the influence exerted upon Hayes's mind by this indomitable "reformer."[3] When the letter was issued Schurz's satisfaction was very great. He must be for the ticket—he would support it "heartily," and ask others to do so.[4] Hayes Schurz found to be "a man of more than average ability, and decidedly unspoiled as a politician."[5] He was of scrupulous integrity; he had a strong feeling of honor; without artifice and of quiet energy he would uplift the government.[6]

The New York Nation espoused his cause—if coolly, at the same time usefully.[7] The New York Evening Post,[8] Harper's Weekly, the New York Tribune, so closely yoked to Tilden in the campaign for the governorship in 1874 and since,[9] early

[1] Schurz, Speeches, vol. iii, pp. 248–52.
[2] Ibid., p. 258.
[3] Cf. Reminiscences of Schurz, vol. iii, p. 370; Diary and Letters of Hayes, vol. iii, pp. 329–32.
[4] Schurz, Speeches, vol. iii, p. 258.
[5] Ibid., p. 259.
[6] Ibid., p. 267.
[7] Cf. issues of July 13 and 27, 1876; Ogden, Life of Godkin, vol. ii, p. 113.
[8] Cf. Godwin, Life of Bryant, vol. ii, pp. 378–9; Allan Nevins, The Evening Post, pp. 402–5.
[9] On the ground that Hendricks was a soft money man and because of a "bad platform." (Cortissoz, Life of Reid, vol. i, p. 325; Letters and Memorials of Tilden, vol. ii, p. 439.) Whitelaw Reid had suddenly become so complete a Republican that he was ready to support Blaine (Cortissoz,

came to his support, as did the Cincinnati Commercial, the Springfield Republican,[1] and other journals in which there was discerned a responsible concern for the country's welfare.

Upon the best elements in the party in Washington the letter also made a very favorable impression.[2] That Grant himself, as every one knew, had taken it to be almost a personal affront,[3] and had but sparing approval for the ticket, presaged well for the campaign from the standpoint of the "idealists," as Schurz and the "Independents" were called by the Republican press. Schurz told Hayes in July that a considerable number of men had "left the fence" and had come down on the Republican side.[4] Indeed most of those who had taken part in the conference at the Fifth Avenue Hotel did so,[5] though some chose to support Tilden on the ground that, owing his nomination to Conkling and Cameron, Hayes could not be free to give form to his administration, however pure and honorable his own impulses might be.[6] The Adamses turned to Tilden, the Democrats as the weeks passed, making Charles Francis Adams' their candidate for governor of Massachusetts,—as did David A. Wells, Parke Godwin, Oswald Ottendorfer and his New York Staats-Zeitung, George Hoadley and J. B. Stallo of Ohio, and others who had held prominent positions in the reform movement in 1872.[7]

Throughout the campaign Schurz was occupied, in letter and speech, in parrying the accusations that he had betrayed his old friends, and vindicating a course which, in view of his

Life of Reid, vol. i, pp. 337–42), an enthusiasm which was shared by his friend, William Walter Phelps, another young reformer who was about to give up "independence" for "regularity."

[1] Merriam, Life of Bowles, vol. ii, p. 281.

[2] Williams, Life of Hayes, vol. i, pp. 465–6. "Will not what you have said offend some of the machine men?" Hayes was asked. "Well," he replied, "I must offend somebody, I suppose, and I had rather offend them than the men whom this letter will please."—Cortissoz, vol. i, p. 344.

[3] Cf. N. Y. Nation, Aug. 3, 1876; N. Y. Tribune, July 15, 1876; Diary and Letters of Hayes, vol. iii, pp. 334, 336, 394–5.

[4] Schurz, Speeches, vol. iii, p. 260.

[5] Godwin, Life of Bryant, vol. ii, p. 378.

[6] Schurz, Speeches, vol. iii, pp. 281, 287; N. Y. Nation, July 13, 1876; Williams, Life of Hayes, vol. i, p. 472.

[7] Cf. Reminiscences of Schurz, vol. iii, pp. 368–9.

associations in the past, made him seem to some of them false to his principles.[1] He, at the same time, gave Hayes no opportunity to forget his obligations to the "Independents," and the ideas for which they stood. In August he said that, if the election were held then, it would result in the success of Mr. Tilden.[2] The importance of a statement which would serve as a "sequel" to the letter of acceptance was pressed upon the candidate, who must do more to dissociate himself from the Republican party organization and the Grant administration.[3]

Such action seemed to be the more judicious, since Grant had signalized the early weeks of the campaign with further dismissals of men who had played honorable parts in the exposure and the prosecution of the arrant knaves involved in the whiskey frauds. Indeed it seemed only necessary to prove that a man had been a friend of Bristow in these proceedings to secure his removal from office, only necessary to establish the fact that he was an enemy of the worthy Secretary of the Treasury to insure his receiving Executive preferment.[4] The Post Office Department under Marshall Jewell had had creditable direction. All his sympathies had been with Bristow and the honest forces in the administration. He found his way obstructed, told Grant without effect of the situation in which he was placed, resigned,[5] and in July returned to his home in Connecticut, to be replaced by a Republican politician with low views concerning the public service.[6] The "old man," as the conspirators, who were using Grant, familiarly called him, seemed to be possessed of a new determination to make the Republican party an impossible haven for men who were bidden to continue in it, in the hope of seeing it reorganized on the lines along which reformation was promised them by its candidate for the Presidency.

[1] Schurz, Speeches, vol. iii, p. 262.
[2] Ibid., p. 280.
[3] Ibid., pp. 281, 287; N. Y. Nation, July 20, 1876.
[4] Schurz, Speeches, vol. iii, p. 411.
[5] It is said that Mr. Jewell went into a conference with the President without intending to leave his office. When he came out he had resigned.— Article on Jewell in National Cyclop. of Am. Biography, vol. iv.
[6] Cf. N. Y. Nation, July 6, 13 and 20, 1876.

Hayes was not so certain as Schurz of the prospects of defeat.[1]
He was right when he said that the "main interest" with the
"plain people" was not so much "reform" as fear that "a
Democratic victory will bring the Rebellion into power."[2]
Speakers upon the stump, editors in the Republican newspapers were "waving the bloody shirt." The candidate for
Vice President, Mr. Wheeler,[3] Blaine, concealing the chagrin
of his defeat in the convention by a few votes (which were
wanting clearly because of the revelations concerning his
jobbery in railroad bonds, while he had been speaker), Morton,
Edmunds, Sherman, and many another, who took the platform
in Hayes's behalf, ran off easily into a discussion of the Southern
question.[4] Each new "outrage" upon the negro in the South
which, as the campaign proceeded, could be laid at the door
of the Democratic party, was set before the voters of the North
to strengthen them for the contest.[5] The allegations, iterated
and reiterated, that Republican defeat would bring the leaders
of the old Confederacy into power; that Tilden could not con-
struct a government without them;[6] that the negro would
return to his master and that the Southern Republicans would
be at the mercy of the "rifle clubs"; that there would be imposed
upon the people enormous charges, computed at billions of
dollars, to compensate the South for its freed slaves, its sunken
debt and for other "rebel claims," a statement which Tilden,
a few days before the election, was induced to deny in a letter
to the chairman of the Democratic National Committee;[7]

[1] Diary and Letters of Hayes, vol. iii, pp. 359, 360.

[2] Schurz, Speeches, vol. iii, pp. 284–5; Gail Hamilton, Life of Blaine,
p. 422; Merriam, Life of Bowles, vol. ii, pp. 278–9; Diary and Letters of
Hayes, vol. iii, pp. 358, 360. A man so much averse to involving himself
in politics as General Sherman said that "no one should be the President
unless he was with us heart and soul in the Civil War."—The Sherman
Letters, p. 347.

[3] N. Y. Nation, Aug. 31, 1876.

[4] Cf. ibid., Sep. 14, Oct. 5 and 19, 1876; cf. Foulke, Life of Morton,
vol. ii, pp. 415–7.

[5] N. Y. Nation, July 27 and Sep. 21, 1876.

[6] Bigelow, Letters and Memorials of Tilden, vol. ii, p. 485; Recollections
of John Sherman, vol. i, p. 552; Williams, Life of Hayes, vol. i, p. 481.

[7] Tilden's Writings and Speeches, vol. ii, pp. 380–83; Bigelow, Letters
and Memorials of Tilden, vol. ii, pp. 471–3.

that his infirm health gave the country, in the event of his death, the prospect of Hendricks and "soft money"—these allegations were supplemented by asseverations affecting his complicity, for unnumbered years, with Tammany and Tweed, his wealth and his manner of gaining it by bankrupting railroads, for which he was the attorney, and by plucking the stockholders,[1] and his income tax returns. No campaign slander on either side approached that one about Tilden's falsification of the statements of his earnings for the use of the tax agents. It was originated, developed and expanded by the New York Times,[2] the most fervent of the Republican newspapers, to be spread by other gazettes and by the stump orators over the land.[3]

There was little for the Democrats to urge in reply on the subject of the rather obscure Hayes, though assiduous efforts were made to find a seamy side of his life.[4] Their principal discovery was that he was a "Native American," in opposition at heart, therefore, to the foreign born elements, who could muster so many votes, especially in New York City, a charge founded on some letter which had been written for him by a secretary during the progress of the campaign.[5]

Money was freely used by both parties, but, as in the Grant campaigns, the Republicans were the most conspicuous offenders in this respect. They could command the larger sums. They could assess and collect from the great body of Federal office-holders who were the adherents of their party,[6] a work which proceeded under the direction of the chairman of the Republican National Committee, an experienced man in such a connection, Zachariah Chandler, the Secretary of the Interior.

[1] Frequently in Republican newspapers called a "railroad wrecker."—Cf. J. C. Carter, Atlantic Monthly, Oct., 1892.

[2] Supported now by the Tribune.—Cortissoz, Life of Whitelaw Reid, vol. i, pp. 325–6.

[3] Cf. N. Y. Nation, Sep. 28, 1876; Bigelow, Life of Tilden, vol. ii, chap. vii; Letters and Memorials of Tilden, vol. ii, p. 446.

[4] Williams, Life of Hayes, vol. i, pp. 473–8; Diary and Letters of Hayes, vol. iii, pp. 347–71, 353–4, 357.

[5] Williams, Life of Hayes, vol. i, pp. 477, 485; Diary and Letters of Hayes, vol. iii, pp. 364–5; N. Y. Nation, Oct. 5, 1876.

[6] Cong. Record, 44th Cong. 2nd sess., pp. 670–71.

Large sums for partisan uses were taken from the employees
of every bureau and department of the Federal service, a
proceeding against which Schurz protested to Hayes,[1] which
Hayes himself honestly deplored,[2] and from contractors, jobbers
and others having business relations with the government.[3]

Political meetings, marked by the evolutions of marching
clubs, flag raisings, the flinging to the winds of banners, can-
nonading and the blare of brass bands, were held everywhere.
The Democrats, on their side, also made the nights bright with
red fire, marched to the sound of martial music, unfurled flags
at the taverns and from their hickory poles at the cross roads,
and exploded powder. They put their best orators on the
hustings in the interest of their cause in all parts of the republic.

The candidates themselves remained at their homes—Hayes
at Columbus (but for two short visits to the Centennial Exposition in Philadelphia in his capacity as governor of Ohio)[4] quietly
performing his public duties, making no speeches, writing only
brief letters and issuing few statements which bore upon the
course of the contest.[5] Tilden conferred with the managers of
his campaign and observed its course in the governor's office
at Albany and at his house in Gramercy Park in New York City.

The elections in Vermont and Maine, in September, gave no
clue to the probable result—the Republican majorities were
of the usual proportions. October added very little to the
enlightenment of the seers. Then Ohio was carried by the
Republicans, as it was expected that it would be, Indiana, in
accordance with every anticipation, by the Democrats.[6] The

---

[1] Schurz, Speeches, vol. iii, pp. 260–61; cf. N. Y. Nation, July 20, 1876;
Williams, Life of Hayes, vol. i, pp. 471–2.

[2] Williams, Life of Hayes, vol. i, pp. 482–3; Schurz, Speeches, vol. iii, p.
338. If he were defeated Hayes said he hoped that it might be with "clean
hands." He would then still have his "self-respect and an approving
conscience." (Williams, Life of Hayes, vol. i, p. 479; cf. Schurz, Speeches,
vol. iii, p. 286.) If he were in office the "whole assessment business," he
wrote Schurz, would "go up 'hook, line and sinker.'"—Diary and Letters
of Hayes, vol. iii, p. 358.

[3] Cf. Williams, Life of Hayes, vol. i, pp. 479–80; Bigelow, Life of Tilden,
vol. ii, p. 109.

[4] Williams, Life of Hayes, vol. i, pp. 470, 486–8.

[5] Ibid., p. 470.

[6] Cf. ibid., pp. 484–5; Diary and Letters of Hayes, vol. iii, pp. 366–7.

majorities were small in both states. West Virginia was decisively Democratic, leading to the not unfair conclusion that the Republicans could hope for little from the South.[1]

Tuesday, the 7th of November, came and the ballots were cast and counted—in some parts of the Union in an orderly and honest way, in other places, especially in parts of the South, amid exhibitions of chicanery and turbulence. It was seen, early in the night following the election, that the Democrats had polled an immense vote, and that Tilden had, in all probability, been successful. Most candid men in newspaper offices and at campaign headquarters, assembled for the purpose of receiving and compiling the returns, were clear on this point.[2] Hayes, the members of his family and his friends, assembled to hear the news as it was furnished them by telegraph at Columbus, went to bed convinced of his defeat.[3] New York state, with large Democratic majorities in New York City and Brooklyn to neutralize the country vote, had given Tilden an advantage over Hayes of more than 32,000. New Jersey and Connecticut were Democratic. Even the New York Times, which had made itself the leading Republican organ of the country, desponded and practically abandoned hope. An occurrence in the office of that newspaper, it has been frequently stated, with at least a partial basis of truth, was the first in a train of circumstances which robbed Tilden of the fruits of victory.

An inquiry which had been received from Democratic national headquarters concerning the result in Louisiana, South Carolina, Florida, Oregon and California was not without weight in convincing the editors that there was still a chance for Hayes. The first edition of the Times on the morning of the day after the election, which had been issued for country subscribers, declared the choice of the country in doubt. In a later edition all the states which the Times had, an hour or two earlier, held to be in dispute were given to the Republicans,

[1] N. Y. Nation, Oct. 19, 1876.
[2] Cf. Haworth, Hayes-Tilden Disputed Election, pp. 45–6; Williams, Life of Hayes, vol. i, p. 492.
[3] Diary and Letters of Hayes, vol. iii, pp. 375–6.

except Florida, where the result "alone" was said still to be uncertain. There were 369 votes in the electoral colleges—the successful candidate must receive 185. Tilden seemed clearly to have 184 of these. Should Hayes secure Florida and all the rest of the doubtful states he would have the necessary 185 votes.

Impressed with the possibilities of the situation, one of the editors, an enthusiastic partisan, Reid by name, hurried to the Republican headquarters at the Fifth Avenue Hotel, where he met William E. Chandler, a potential politician on the Republican National Committee, who had just returned to the city from a trip to his home in New Hampshire for the purpose of casting his vote. After discussing the subject the two men together proceeded to Zachariah Chandler's room in the same hotel, and, with his approval, they at once despatched telegrams to leaders of the party in the doubtful states who, it was feared, would make their returns for Tilden without full consideration of the grave results which might ensue upon their haste. The election depended upon these leaders; Hayes would be elected, if they could "hold" their states.[1] The next day, November 9, the Times, fortified by knowledge of that in which one of its editors had had a hand, came out boldly in large head lines— "The Battle Won—Governor Hayes Elected President and William A. Wheeler Vice President," etc., etc. Other newspapers made the same claim. Given up as lost on all sides the election was now held to be at least doubtful by every Republican editor and politician in the country. Every available agency was to be used to capture the electoral votes which were needed, and to make them count for Hayes.

The result could not be definitely known, except through the returning boards, which, in the Southern states still held by the carpetbaggers, were strangely constituted. Following the formulation of the plan no time was lost. William E. Chandler at once proceeded to Florida. To each disputed state trusted

[1] Bigelow, Life of Tilden, vol. ii, pp. 8–15; Letters and Memorials of Tilden, vol. ii, pp. 474–81; N. Y. Times, June 15, 1887; cf. A. M. Gibson, A Political Crime, pp. 49–52. For some variations in details of the familiar account see Haworth, op. cit., pp. 46–51.

Republican politicians were sent, with funds at command, to employ counsel, and for other purposes in connection with the contests which were to be instituted. The garrisons of troops which had been increased in the South, prior to the election, were moved to given points for the support of the canvassing boards.[1] The number of pilgrims from the North to the doubtful Southern states increased. Some proceeded thither on their own motion; others were urged forward by President Grant[2] and the party managers. Stanley Matthews, ex-Governor Noyes, John Sherman, General Garfield and Job E. Stevenson of Ohio; Cortlandt Parker, Eugene Hale, John A. Logan, William M. Evarts, John A. Dix, William D. Kelley, E. W. Stoughton, John Coburn, M. S. Quay and others went to New Orleans.[3] John A. Kasson, General Lew Wallace and General Francis C. Barlow joined Chandler in Florida. Abram S. Hewitt, chairman of the Democratic National Committee, also sent to the scene a number of representatives, including several "ex-Republicans," or "new converts," as Hayes called them.[4] Their party included John M. Palmer, Lyman Trumbull, William R. Morrison, Samuel J. Randall, Senator J. E. McDonald of Indiana, Senator John W. Stevenson of Kentucky, William Bigler, A. G. Curtin, J. R. Doolittle, George W. Julian, Henry Watterson, Oswald Ottendorfer, J. B. Stallo of Ohio, F. R. Coudert of New York, James O. Brodhead and Lewis V. Bogy of Missouri, and Professor Sumner of Yale.[5]

These "visiting statesmen," in contact with the local officers who were juggling the votes, exerted no small influence upon the

[1] McPherson's Handbook for 1878, pp. 208-9; Bigelow, Life of Tilden, vol. ii, p. 18.
[2] John Sherman's Recollections, vol. i, p. 554.
[3] Some of these men, led by John Sherman, made a report to the President concerning what they had observed in Louisiana.—Senate Ex. Doc., 44th Cong. 2nd sess., no. 2.
[4] On this account not likely, Hayes thought, to be so amiable of mood or fair in judgment as Democrats older in the faith.—Sherman's Recollections, vol. i, p. 559.
[5] Cf. Senate Ex. Doc., 44th Cong. 2nd sess., no. 2, p. 31. To offset Sherman's report to the President the Democrats made a report to Mr. Hewitt. It, too, was printed. See Senate Mis. Doc., 44th Cong. 2nd sess., no. 14.

result, as it was intended that they should, and foundations were
laid for many a charge of bargaining and jobbery in the interest
of one or the other candidate.[1] That the men, with whom the
fate of Tilden or Hayes rested, were drawn from that class of
predatory politicians in the South whose hands were open to
receive bribes in money, or assurances of continuance in, or of
new appointments to, lucrative office, led to suspicions which
spread over the country, and which were but too well confirmed
in later months, when it was seen how great a number of them
came forward to claim their rewards.[2]

It was soon clear that South Carolina might be eliminated,
since the Republican electors in that state had received a
sufficient, if small majority. To have "gone behind the returns"
would, in all likelihood, have increased the vote for Hayes.
Nevertheless the Democrats continued to claim South Carolina
for Tilden, and resorted to proceedings in the courts. Both the
Republican and Democratic candidates for electors came
together at Columbia on December 6, the date set by Federal
law for the meeting of the colleges in the states, and cast their
votes for Hayes and Wheeler and Tilden and Hendricks, respectively, but it was difficult to perceive on what ground the
Democrats had based their right of acting in the case.[3]

Though Hayes had carried Oregon by an undisputed majority,
as was seen upon the completion of the count, one of the three
Republican electors in that state, it appeared, was the incumbent
of a small postmastership, which circumstance disqualified him
under the terms of the Constitution of the United States. Here
were possibilities for Tilden and, after canvassing the subject
with leaders in the East, a protest was filed with the governor,
who was a Democrat, Grover, by name, and he, upon advice,[4]
refused to certificate the postmaster. The votes cast for one

[1] Bigelow, Life of Tilden, vol. ii, pp. 22-9; A. M. Gibson, A Political
Crime, passim. On the other side see Sherman's Recollections, vol. i, pp.
556-7.
[2] Cf. Bigelow, Life of Tilden, vol. ii, pp. 95-7; Letters and Memorials of
Tilden, vol. ii, pp. 565-7; House Reports, 45th Cong. 3rd sess., no. 140, pp.
21-2, 48-9.
[3] Haworth, Hayes-Tilden Disputed Election, pp. 148-56.
[4] Article on Oregon in Am. Ann. Cyclop. for 1876.

who was ineligible were held to be void, wherefore the leading
Democratic candidate, who had received some 1,000 less, had,
it was said, been elected instead. Disputes ensued, the result
of which was that two separate returns were made to Washington—from one side came three electors for Hayes, from the
other, two for Hayes and one for Tilden,[1] enough, though all
else should fail, to serve the needs of Mr. Tilden.

But it was in Florida and Louisiana that the struggle would
be concentrated. Here it was that the members of the returning
boards, the carpetbag politicians and the "visiting statesmen"
conferred and again conferred, and strove and contended, surrounded by newspaper correspondents, despatched thither by
all the principal gazettes, the links which were to bind the
eager and impatient country, in great anxiety and high excitement, with the actors in the drama.

The votes, as they had been cast and gathered up for counting,
amid much fraud on both sides, as every one knew,[2] were
nearly equal in Florida. In 26 counties the Republicans claimed
a majority of only 45 for Hayes,[3] which they increased by the
canvass of the other counties; the Democrats, a majority for the
lowest Tilden elector of only 93 votes.[4] The board which was to
determine the result was made up of three men. It was distinctly given the power by a state law to "go behind the returns" and reject those that were "false and fraudulent."[5]
A low and disreputable contest was begun in the presence of
William E. Chandler and his companions, and several Democratic "visitors" from the North, including Tilden's friend,
Manton Marble.[6] Money was at hand for discretionary use,
offices were promised to men of easy consciences who were
counting and determining the poll, and, as two of the three
members of the board were Republicans, and Chandler and his
friends were active and skillful, it presented a report which
insured the casting of all of the state's four electoral votes for
Hayes and Wheeler. For the man on the Republican ticket

[1] Cf. Senate Reports, 44th Cong. 2nd sess., no. 678.
[2] Cf. Haworth, Hayes-Tilden Disputed Election, pp. 57–63.
[3] Ibid., p. 68.   [5] Ibid., pp. 66–7.
[4] Ibid., pp. 74, 79.   [6] Ibid., pp. 64–5.

with the smallest majority it was held that 924 more ballots
had been cast than for the most numerously supported Democrat.[1] The Republican governor, Stearns, certified the choice
of the Republicans, and, on December 6, they voted for Hayes
and Wheeler. The Democrats, through the attorney general
of the state, who was a Democrat, had issued certificates to the
four candidates of his party. They met and cast their votes for
Tilden and Hendricks.

The subject now found its way into the state courts, where, in
a partisan tribunal, it was decided that the returning board
could act only in a ministerial, not a judicial, capacity, and
must count the votes as they were presented to it. On a re-
count of the returns for governor, ordered in connection with
this decision, the Democratic candidate, Drew, was found to
have been elected to that office, and he was installed on January 2, 1877. The way opened. The new legislature, Democratic in both branches, now passed an act to authorize a re-
canvass of the vote for Presidential electors. The returning
board, reconstituted because of a change in the political com-
plexion of the state administration, was as Democratic as the
governor and the legislature, and, on January 19, it found and
declared that the Tilden electors in Florida had majorities
ranging from 87 to 90 votes.[2] New certificates were issued and
sent to Washington.

To bring Louisiana to Hayes was a far more difficult task.
An apparent majority of 8,000 or 9,000 votes [3] was to be overcome by the manipulation of the returns, a feat presenting,
however, to the shameless men recently identified with the
management of the politics of that state, no insuperable obstacles. Here again there had been "bulldozing" of the negroes
before the day of the election, fraud in the ballot boxes and on
the tally sheets. The return, whatever it may have been, was
no fair or true expression of public opinion. Experience had
clearly shown that any desired result might be gained through a

[1] Cf. Haworth, Hayes-Tilden Disputed Election, p. 68.
[2] Ibid., p. 79.
[3] My figures are again Mr. Haworth's, op. cit., p. 94.

canvassing board in Louisiana.[1] It was declared to be, and
seems to have been, "for sale to the highest bidder." A specification of the operations and performances of this body, of
which J. Madison Wells was president, acting with a corrupt
scalawag and two negroes, all nominally Republicans, without
one minority party representative upon it, would be but a
repetition of the description of the deceits, frauds and venalities
inseparably associated with carpetbag government in the South
following the war. It is enough to know that, by one device or
another, the returns from so many parishes were rejected or
altered, to the advantage of the Republicans, that the Democratic vote was reduced by more than 13,000. The adjustments
which were effected, so arbitrarily and amid so much evidence
of the rascality of Wells and his associates, which could be
acquiesced in only because of the emphasis put upon the intimidation of the negroes during the campaign and at the polls,
often accompanied by shocking brutalities, converted the
apparent Tilden majority into a majority for the Hayes electors
of 3,437 and upward.[2] The Republican "statesmen" came home
by way of Columbus, to assure Hayes of the entire justice of
what had been done.[3] Governor Kellogg issued certificates to
the Republican electors, while McEnery, the Democratic
pretender to the governorship, conferred a similar authority
upon the Tilden candidates, just in time for the rival and
opposing colleges to meet and cast their votes on the appointed
6th day of December.

Congress had met on December 4, two days before the electors convened in their respective assemblies in the various
capitals of the states. There were contesting and antagonistic
bodies in South Carolina, Florida, Louisiana and Oregon, and,

[1] For a characterization of the members of this one see House Reports,
44th Cong. 2nd sess., no. 156, pt. 1, p. 7; Bigelow, Life of Tilden, vol. ii, p.
39; Haworth, op. cit., pp. 97-8; Henry Watterson, Marse Henry, vol. i,
pp. 298-9. For another view see Sherman's Recollections, vol. i, p. 559;
Williams, Life of Hayes, vol. i, p. 507.

[2] Haworth, pp. 113-4; D. D. Field, The Vote that Made the President,
pp. 4-5. For proceedings of the board see Senate Ex. Doc., 44th Cong.
2nd sess., no. 2.

[3] Williams, Life of Hayes, vol. i, p. 507; Diary and Letters of Hayes,
vol. iii, pp. 384-5; Schurz, Speeches, vol. iii, p. 346.

by the act of 1792 governing the subject, the two houses, on the second Wednesday in February, must meet together to count the votes and declare the result. Nothing had been gained in the weeks which had followed the popular election.

The possibility of such a contingency as had arisen was not out of the public mind. Congress had been engaged in recent months in discussing proposals to amend the Constitution, and for the formulation of rules to govern the Presidential count, including the so-called "22nd joint rule," of doubtful constitutional validity, which had been in force in 1865, 1869 and 1873, by successive action of Congress, and which specified that no vote should be counted except by the concurrence of both houses, now calculated, if it had been ratified for use in 1877, very usefully to serve the Democrats.[1] But all of it had ended in speech making, and there was nothing for the guidance of the country but the provision in the Constitution.

The words were read and re-read: "The president of the Senate shall, in the presence of the Senate and the House of Representatives, open all the certificates, and the votes shall then be counted."[2] But by whom? By the president of the Senate, or by the two houses acting jointly, or by the two houses acting separately? That the president *pro tempore* of the Senate, Mr. Ferry of Michigan, purely a party figure, with no title to remembrance for any service which he would be able to render his country as a statesman, who acted as Vice President, after the death of Henry Wilson, was a Republican, as were a large majority of the members; that the House, to which the subject might have been referred, on the failure of the electoral colleges to make a choice, was Democratic;[3] that on a joint vote of the two chambers there would be a Democratic majority—were considerations which little favored the prospect of an early or a happy outcome of the dispute.

Moreover, to what lengths might those engaged in making the count, whoever they might be, go in the exercise of their

[1] Cf. E. P. Wheeler, Sixty Years of Life, p. 106; Bigelow, Life of Tilden, vol. ii, pp. 57–8.
[2] Constitution of the U. S., art. xii of the amendments.
[3] Ibid.

authority? Must they accept the certificate from the state as
it came to them, or might they examine into the correctness and
legality of the return? It was of the first importance to Tilden
that the course by which the canvassing boards in Florida and
Louisiana had overset what seemed to be Democratic majori-
ities, and had converted them into Republican majorities,
should be open to investigation. Men commenced to discuss
another question. Should no decision be reached before March
4th who would be President? Should Grant continue in the
office, as Caleb Cushing apparently believed that he might,[1] or
should the president of the Senate, as others pretended to
think, exercise executive power until a choice could be made?
Or what other course, any and all of the suggestions being
revolutionary and dangerous, should be pursued at a future
date not far away?

Hot and vindictive passions had increased, and in another
country, inhabited by a people less sane on the subject of their
politics than the Americans,[2] a spark would have precipitated
armed violence. High strung partisans threatened one another—they spoke of shooting men and of cutting their throats;
of raising volunteers, and of marching on Washington. Men
cried "Tilden or Fight," and he was urged to enter the White
House by force if he could not do so peacefully.[3] He had been
elected; if he were deprived of the office, to which he had been
fairly chosen by the people, by such venalities and usurpations
as had been witnessed in Florida and Louisiana, he could properly call upon the country to seat him in his place.

But sound of revolution was scarcely so articulate now as
when Andrew Johnson was in the midst of his contest with
Stanton and the Congress. There was proof in plenty that

[1] Letters and Memorials of Tilden, vol. ii, p. 522.
[2] "Yet not one shot fired, not one man killed, no breaches of the peace,"
said the London Times, quoted in Williams, Life of Hayes, vol. i, p. 512.
[3] Cf. Letters and Memorials of Tilden, vol. ii, pp. 490–91, 524–5;
Haworth, pp. 168–70, 187–8, 194–5; Williams, Life of Hayes, vol. ii, pp.
1–2; D. S. Barry, Forty Years in Washington, pp. 8–9; James Monroe in
Atlantic Monthly, Oct., 1893, p. 524; S. S. Cox, Three Decades, p. 641;
M. H. Northrup in Century Magazine, Oct., 1901; Cong. Record, 44th
Cong. 2nd sess., pp. 379, 380, 382, 633, 807, 947.

many thousands more than a majority had voted for Tilden for
President,[1] but little reason to think that any but a few of these
felt a love for him deep and true enough to make them wish to
pledge their fortunes and their lives to put him in the place.

A more whole-souled, hearty, open-handed man, more
distinguished as a popular leader than as a railroad attorney
and an Albany politician, might have mounted a horse, at least
in a metaphorical sense, and ridden, with an acclaiming crowd
at his stirrups, to the doors of the Capitol. But neither now,
nor at any time in the weeks which followed, did Tilden seem
to be such a character in the sight even of his most devoted
advocates, and the heroics were left for the newspaper reporters,
the letter writers and a few village hotspurs who had never seen
him, and championed his cause merely because, like them, he
was a Democrat. He was in no sense an attractive or eloquent
speaker [2]—he had a feeble voice.[3] When he wrote it was
laboriously, and not in flowing or inspiring measure. He was
doctrinaire,[4] immersed in detail, and was trammelled by his
lawyer's love of accuracy and precedent.[5] He was exacting and
prescriptive as an employer, and, indeed, toward an associate,—
and vain.[6] Given to "wire pulling," secretive, not above a
certain craft attributed to Van Buren, Marcy and their companions, who were reckoned to be his masters in politics,[7] and
unduly ambitious, as many thought, for the Presidency,[8] he
was not trusted or loved as cordially as are some of the fortunate
characters in our public life.

It was agreed that he was the ablest corporation lawyer in

[1] Tilden's plurality over Hayes in the popular vote in the whole country
was upwards of 250,000. The Greenback candidate, Peter Cooper, polled
81,740 votes, the Prohibitionist, General Smith, 9,522 votes.
[2] McCulloch, Men and Measures, p. 414. "I met Samuel J. Tilden for
the first time," writes Moran on July 4, 1873, in London, "and was surprised to see such an ordinary man."—Moran's Diary in Library of Congress.
[3] Bigelow, Life of Tilden, vol. ii, p. 388.
[4] Watterson, Marse Henry, vol. i, p. 274.
[5] Cf. Bigelow, Life of Tilden, vol. ii, pp. 388-9.
[6] J. C. Carter, Atlantic Monthly, Oct., 1892.
[7] John Sherman's Recollections, vol. i, p. 551; D. S. Alexander, Political
History of N. Y., vol. iii, pp. 326-7.
[8] Cf. Williams, Life of Hayes, vol. i, pp. 469-70.

the United States.[1] As such he had grown rich, a quality in a Presidential candidate usually not well calculated to attract popular support. And to his money it was held that he was rather too closely, if not avariciously attached.[2] If he had been loyal to the government during the war, he had been, at many points in its progress, temporizing and reactionary, and, in effect, pro-slavery and pro-Southern, in that he had deprecated the only course of action by which the Union could be saved and slavery could be extirpated.[3] In many ways, therefore, Tilden was a man who could but little stir the nation to any unusual action in his behalf. It would have been, as the sage and candid knew, impossible to send him forward on the crest of a wave of popular enthusiasm and to seat him by main force,[4] and when such suggestions were made, they were met with silence, or, if noticed, were soon buried under a weight of ridicule.[5]

The Democratic House, after electing Samuel J. Randall speaker, to succeed Mr. Kerr, who had died during the recess,[6] had appointed committees—one of 15 members to proceed to Louisiana, one of six members to proceed to Florida, one of nine members to proceed to South Carolina,[7] and still

[1] McCulloch, Men and Measures, p. 411.

[2] Many who held his fate in their hands had an ambition to open "old Tilden's barrel." (Cf. Bigelow, Life of Tilden, vol. ii, pp. 95–7, 145; also ibid., chap. vi.) Chief Justice Waite said that in money matters Tilden was "exacting to the last degree," a miser, in truth. He cited a case in which he (Waite) must pay Tilden $30,000 to get that man's consent to the foreclosure of a mortgage on a railroad. His action was entirely arbitrary and for his own benefit.—Diary and Letters of Hayes, vol. iii, p. 362.

[3] For Tilden's "war record" see Bigelow, Letters and Memorials of Tilden, vol. ii, pp. 453–62. But see the same author's Life of Tilden, vol. i, chap. vii. Cf. McCulloch, Men and Measures, p. 414; Allan Nevins, The Evening Post, pp. 265–6; J. C. Carter, Atlantic Monthly, Oct., 1892; D. S. Alexander, Political Hist. of N. Y., vol. iii, p. 328. He would be, said Evarts, "the phantom of Buchanan's likeness in the Presidential chair."—Cortissoz, Life of Whitelaw Reid, vol. i, p. 326.

[4] Cf. Watterson, Marse Henry, vol. i, p. 314.

[5] As in the case of Henry Watterson's plan to march 100,000 men to Washington as a demonstration in behalf of Tilden. It was laughed out of countenance.—Cf. ibid., pp. 302–4; Northrup, Century Magazine, Oct., 1901; Haworth, p. 189.

[6] Cong. Record, 44th Cong. 2nd sess., p. 6.

[7] By resolution of Dec. 4, 1876.—Cong. Record, 44th Cong. 2nd sess., pp. 11, 16, 17, 45.

another to determine its own "privileges, powers and duties" in connection with the count.[1]

The Senate, on its side, had despatched sub-committees of its Committee on Privileges and Elections, in obedience to a resolution of December 5, 1876,[2] to the Southern states to conduct investigations for the Republicans.

Tilden employed himself [3] studying the precedents; indeed, he compiled a complete history of the electoral counts from the commencement of the government to prove that it was a function of Congress to determine the result, not of the president of the Senate,[4] in whom Hayes and the Republicans put their trust.[5] A copy of the book was placed upon the table of each senator and representative for their information.[6]

Grant took a position in favor of a prompt and peaceful settlement of the controversy, which has been held to be more creditable to him than much of the action marking his career at this period of his life. He denounced "fraudulent counting," and, in a telegram to General Sherman, made it clear that he did not wish the army to be used in influencing the canvassing boards.[7] But he was hostile to Hayes, not only because of the little veiled allusions to his failings as a President, included in the Republican candidate's letter of acceptance of the nomination, but also, because of the prominence given to Schurz in the campaign and the prospect of that man's becoming a force in the administration in case of Republican success.[8]

[1] Cong. Record, 44th Cong. 2nd sess., p. 373; House Reports, 44th Cong. 2nd sess., no. 100, pts. 1, 2 and 3. The minority report, pt. 2, is not without historical value. Also in Cong. Record, 44th Cong. 2nd sess., pp. 856-8. This committee, like the committees which visited the South, called and examined witnesses on the subject of the election. Testimony is in House Mis. Doc., 44th Cong. 2nd sess., no. 42.

[2] Cong. Record, 44th Cong. 2nd sess., p. 40.

[3] Assisted by John Bigelow and Manton Marble. (Watterson, Marse Henry, vol. i, p. 300.) Tilden had left the governor's office at the inauguration of his successor on January 1, 1877.

[4] The Presidential Counts, published by Appleton, 1877; also in Writings and Speeches of Tilden, vol. i, pp. 60, 67-74.

[5] Cf. Williams, Life of Hayes, vol. i, pp. 522, 523.

[6] Writings and Speeches of Tilden, vol. ii, p. 385.

[7] Bigelow, Life of Tilden, vol. ii, p. 19.

[8] Six years since Grant, in conversation with Hayes, had called Schurz "an infidel and atheist," a "rebel" in Germany— "as much a rebel against

Grant was frequently heard to say that Tilden had been elected.[1]
In the interest of some agreement between the angry dis-
putants he now called Abram S. Hewitt, Democratic leader in
the House of Representatives as well as chairman of the Democratic National Committee, to the White House, a conference
which speedily became the subject of widespread discussion.[2]
It seemed clear to Grant, no matter what course might be
taken to effect a settlement of the dispute, that Louisiana
would be found to be for Tilden. Conkling shared with the
President, or, perhaps, had implanted in his mind a distrust
of Hayes, whose campaign had been conducted in the interest of an honesty in public management for which they together had felt too little concern. Though the vote of New
York in the nominating convention had been thrown to Hayes,
in order to check Blaine's ambitions, the man who held it in
his hand accompanied it with few good wishes. Sulky, because
of the rejection of his own claims to the nomination,[3] and
completely at variance with Hayes's public aims, Conkling
had rendered the Republican candidate no valuable assistance during the campaign,[4] an apathy attributed to sick-

his own government as Jeff Davis," and like names. Love for him, by
reason of events in 1872 and since, had not been increased. (Diary and
Letters of Hayes, vol. iii, p. 112.) Grant and Hayes had widely opposite
ideals in public life and each knew this of the other.

[1] Cf. A Political Crime, pp. 24–6, 28–9; G. W. Childs, Recollections of
General Grant, p. 10; Conkling, Life of Conkling, p. 528; Bigelow, Life of
Tilden, vol. ii, p. 60; Letters and Memorials of Tilden, vol. ii, pp. 516–7.
His own pretensions disposed of, as they finally had been by a resolution
of the House of Representatives, condemning a third term as "unwise, un-
patriotic and fraught with peril to our free institutions," by a vote which
was unanimous, except for 18 men, chiefly negroes, and other ardent partisans from the South (Cong. Record, 44th Cong. 1st sess., p. 228; Stanwood, A History of the Presidency, vol. i, p. 361), he must have welcomed
the nomination of either Conkling or Morton. (He was for Conkling then
for Morton, "the ponderous Indianian, whom he hated less than Blaine,"
J. S. Morrill wrote to Benedict, Feb. 27, 1876, in Morrill Papers, Library
of Congress.) If they could not be named he had nourished ambitions for
Washburne or Fish.—J. R. Young, Around the World with General Grant,
vol. ii, p. 275.
[2] Gibson, A Political Crime, pp. 27–8.
[3] Autobiography of T. C. Platt, p. 75.
[4] Though Hayes, upon advice, had written him under date of Aug. 15,
1876, asking him to speak for the ticket in the West.—Diary and Letters
of Hayes, vol. iii, p. 347.

ness,[1] and, now, after the election, was bushwhacking, as he could, to prevent Hayes from reaching the seat which most of the leaders of the party desired him to occupy.[2] Christmas Day was near when each house appointed seven of its members, Edmunds of Vermont, who became a large if not a dominant factor in giving form to what would follow,[3] heading the Senate, and Henry B. Payne of Ohio, the House committee, to evolve some plan of procedure.[4] These men, with the exception of Senator Morton, whose extreme partisanship led him to dissent,[5] after weeks of laborious consideration, agreed upon a bill, which was reported on January 18, 1877.[6] The committees had, so it was said, "applied the utmost practicable study and deliberation to the subject." The plan which they had prepared[7] was, they believed, "the best attainable disposition of the difficult problems and disputed theories arising out of the late election." They asked for speedy action upon their proposal. By the uncertainty of the present situation the country daily was suffering loss in business, in credit, in the morale of the people. More than this—such a condition tended "to bring republican institutions into discredit," and to create doubt as to the success and perpetuity of our form of government.[8]

It was a notable event in the political history of the country when this great matter was taken out of the hands in which

[1] Diary and Letters of Hayes, vol. iii, p. 363.

[2] Cf. Williams, Life of Hayes, vol. i, p. 521, and vol. ii, p. 524; Diary and Letters of Hayes, vol. iii, pp. 384, 390–91; Haworth, p. 221; Hoar, Autobiography of 70 years, vol. ii, p. 44; Conkling, Life of Conkling, p. 528; Cortissoz, Life of Reid, vol. ii, pp. 491, 511–13.

[3] Cong. Record, 44th Cong. 2nd sess., p. 821.

[4] They early caused to be prepared a compilation of more than 800 pages of the debates and proceedings of Congress relating to the counting of the electoral votes at every four-year period since the foundation of the government.—House Mis. Doc., 44th Cong. 2nd sess., no. 13.

[5] Proceedings of Electoral Commission, p. 3.

[6] For report see House Reports, 44th Cong. 2nd sess., no. 108; Cong. Record, 44th Cong. 2nd sess., pp. 713–4, 730–31; Proceedings of Electoral Commission, pp. 4–5.

[7] The processes of the development of the plan in the joint committee are revealed by Mr. Northrup, secretary of the House committee, in Century Magazine, Oct., 1901; cf. S. S. Cox, Three Decades, p. 639.

[8] Proceedings of Electoral Commission, pp. 2–3.

it had been placed by the Constitution, when Congress, in truth, abdicated its powers and transferred and entrusted them to an extra-constitutional tribunal.[1] A commission would arbitrate the dispute. This body was to be composed of five senators (of whom it was understood that three would be Republicans and two Democrats), five members of the House of Representatives (of whom three would be Democrats and two Republicans) and four justices of the Supreme Court, identified in the act as of the first, third, eighth and ninth circuits, which was to say that they should be Miller and Strong, Republicans, and Clifford and Field, Democrats. A fifth justice was to be chosen by his four colleagues in the court, to become the fifteenth member of the commission.[2]

On him the nation's eyes were set. With seven Republicans and seven Democrats he would be the actual arbitrator of the great controversy. It was clearly intended that this man should be Justice David Davis of Illinois. He had been put forward as the candidate for President of the "Labor Reform Party" in 1872, afterward sought the nomination at the hands of the "Liberals" in Cincinnati, and could fairly be regarded as rather loose in his attachments to the Republican organization. While his sympathies in the present dispute were enigmatic it was concluded, after the subject had been carefully canvassed on both sides, that he was likely to favor Tilden.[3] It was with such an understanding, at any rate,

[1] The act begged the question, so much discussed, as to whether the Constitution had vested the two houses at the meeting at which the votes were to be counted with authority to go behind the returns. Congress now gave to the commission "the same powers, if any, now possessed for that purpose by the two houses acting separately or together." To the commission was transferred the indeterminate functions of Congress on the subject—no more and no less.—Cf. Williams, Life of Hayes, vol. i, p. 525.

[2] It was the method of selecting the justices of the Supreme Court upon which the committees so tediously divided. Many proposals were made only to be rejected. It was pretended now, as afterward, though none seems to have believed it, that the justices would rise above partisan feeling. "Would that court be willing," said Hoar, "to go down to history as deciding on a question of such transcendent importance on a party line? Wouldn't their bias against thus appearing in history be infinitely greater than any merely party bias they may happen to feel?"—Northrup in Century Magazine, Oct., 1901.

[3] Cf. Haworth, pp. 201-202, 209; Northrup, Century Magazine, Oct., 1901.

that the Democrats, led in the House by Mr. Hewitt, were furthering the passage of the bill. It was because of such an understanding, on the other hand, that the measure was opposed in Congress by those who were most closely attached to the cause of Hayes.[1]

Grant called upon Conkling to press the bill in the Senate.[2] If the subject were to be taken out of the jurisdiction of the president of the Senate, who had all necessary power in the case, and referred to a commission "you might as well count in Tilden," said ardent Republicans.[3] It was not a "compromise" but a surrender.[4] Hayes himself opposed the submission of the question to the commission. It was, he alleged, the constitutional duty of the president of the Senate to determine and declare the result.[5] Both the New York Times and the New York Tribune desired the defeat of the bill.[6] The Republican press generally was arrayed against it.[7]

Likewise, on the other side, Tilden never favored the compromise, and felt that he was receiving scant consideration by the Democratic leaders at Washington, who were hurrying him forward to what he somehow sensed to be his doom.[8]

But the wishes of the candidates themselves, and their immediate friends, went for nothing. The pressure by the business interests of the country upon both parties for a settlement of the dispute was powerful and could not be ignored.[9]

[1] Cf. Williams, Life of Hayes, vol. ii, p. 521.
[2] Childs, Recollections of Grant, pp. 12–13.
[3] Ibid., pp. 11–12; Gail Hamilton, Life of Blaine, pp. 423–4; Morton in Cong. Record, 44th Cong. 2nd sess., pp. 801, 878, 894; Simon Cameron in ibid., p. 808; Sherman in ibid., pp. 823, 824.
[4] Cong. Record, 44th Cong. 2nd sess., p. 869.
[5] Williams, Life of Hayes, vol. i, pp. 513, 524.
[6] For the Tribune, see Cortissoz, Life of Reid, vol. i, p. 359.
[7] Cf. Morton in Cong. Record, 44th Cong. 2nd sess., p. 879.
[8] Letters and Memorials of Tilden, vol. ii, pp. 530–34; cf. ibid., pp. 549–50, 556; Manton Marble in N. Y. Sun, Aug. 5, 1878; Bigelow, Life of Tilden, vol. ii, pp. 74–82.
[9] See, e.g., petition to Congress signed by the principal banking and mercantile houses in New York in Cong. Record, 2nd sess., p. 406; Haworth, p. 204; Letters and Memorials of Tilden, vol. ii, p. 561; S. S. Cox, Three Decades, pp. 637, 647; Williams, Life of Hayes, vol. ii, p. 520. "The country is agitated," said Grant to Congress. "Its industries are arrested, labor unemployed, capital idle and enterprise paralyzed by reason

The plan was advanced, the Senate passing it, after an all night session, under the leadership of Edmunds,[1] by a vote of 47 to 17, only one Democrat opposing it,[2] on January 25, on the same day on which, by some fate, Davis was unexpectedly elected to Logan's seat as a United States senator from Illinois, through the activities of a small group of "Greenbackers," who had found their way into the legislature of that state, and who compelled the Democrats in that body to the course.[3] Here was a new and an unlooked for complication. The Tilden men were downcast, the friends of Hayes correspondingly elated.[4] "Thunder out of a clear sky," an onlooker said, "could not more thoroughly have startled the Democratic leaders in Washington." [5]

By no chance now could Davis seem to be an "independent." It was assumed that he would decline, even if he were asked to take the place which had been intended for him.[6] The other available justices, as every one knew, were undoubted Republicans. The bill was in the House, pressing for passage. It was in large degree a Democratic measure, and the party leaders seemed to be under an obligation to proceed with it. No other way opened and, on January 26, it was approved by the House by a vote of 191 (all but 30 Democrats) to 86.[7]

of the doubt and anxiety" of the people.—Richardson, Messages and Papers, vol. vii, p. 424.

[1] Cong. Record, 44th Cong. 2nd sess., pp. 821, 823.

[2] Eaton of Connecticut. (Cf. Barry, Forty Years in Washington, p. 11) Blaine (Cf. Gail Hamilton, Life of Blaine, pp. 423–4), a little while before elected to the Senate by the legislature of Maine, Simon Cameron, Morton and Sherman were prominent among the Republicans who voted against the measure.—Cong. Record, 44th Cong. 2nd sess., p. 913.

[3] Haynes, Third Party Movements, p. 119.

[4] James Monroe, Atlantic Monthly, Oct., 1893, p. 529; Clifford, Life of Clifford, p. 316; Williams, Life of Hayes, vol. i, pp. 526–7, 529, 530; Gail Hamilton, Life of Blaine, p. 424; Haworth, p. 219.

[5] Northrup, Century Magazine, Oct., 1901.

[6] Bigelow and others have pretended to believe that Davis's election to the Senate was the result of party bargaining. (Cf. Life of Tilden, vol. ii, p. 64.) Hewitt is said to have shared this opinion. (Haworth, p. 218.) Davis resigned from the bench, though his resignation would not take effect until the 4th day of March next.—Clifford, Life of Clifford, p. 315.

[7] In the opposition were such Republicans as Garfield, Hale, Frye and Kasson, while Mills of Texas and Blackburn of Kentucky were Democrats opposing it.—Cong. Record, 44th Cong. 2nd sess., p. 1050.

Grant signed the bill on January 29,[1] and, on the 31st, the
commission was organized with the following members—Senators Edmunds, Frelinghuysen and Morton, who were Republicans, and Thurman and Bayard, who were Democrats; [2] Representatives Henry B. Payne of Ohio, Eppa Hunton of Virginia
and Josiah G. Abbott of Massachusetts, who were Democrats,
and Garfield and Hoar, who were Republicans,[3] and the four
justices, equally divided in their political sympathies, who
chose Joseph P. Bradley as the fifth member to represent the
Supreme Court. Though a Republican in every sense, as he
had afforded ample proof immediately after Grant had appointed him to the bench, by taking a position in antagonism
to Chase in the legal tender case, Bradley was now considered
to have some conservative leanings. His circuit duties drew
him to the Gulf states, where he was not unpopular with the
old white classes. His attitude toward the negro, the Enforcement acts and the whole subject of Reconstruction, had won
for him a certain approval in the South and among Democrats
generally.[4] Justice Clifford, a pronounced Democrat, was designated in the act, by reason of his seniority,[5] as president of the
commission. These were propitiatory omens, if small ones, for
the party which was to be given the worst of it in the settlement.

Meanwhile the House committees, in Democratic control,
which had visited Louisiana, Florida and South Carolina, were
making their reports, the majority and minority factions differing bitterly, as could have been foretold, as to the conduct
of the elections in those states and the work of the returning
boards.[6] Reports, too, were coming in from the sub-committees

[1] Cong. Record, 44th Cong. 2nd sess., p. 1081; Richardson, Messages and
Papers, vol. vii, pp. 422–4.
[2] Cong. Record, 44th Cong. 2nd sess., pp. 1108–9.
[3] Ibid., pp. 1113–4.
[4] Cf. Atlantic Monthly, Oct., 1893, pp. 529–30.
[5] He had been appointed to the bench by Buchanan in 1858.
[6] For Florida see House Reports, 44th Cong. 2nd sess., no. 143, pt. 1—
minority report, pt. 2—and House Mis. Doc., 44th Cong. 2nd sess., no.
35. For Louisiana see House Reports, 44th Cong. 2nd sess., no. 156, pt.
1—minority report, pt. 2—and House Mis. Doc., 44th Cong. 2nd sess., no.
34. For South Carolina see House Reports, 44th Cong. 2nd sess., no. 175,
and House Mis. Doc., 44th Cong. 2nd sess., no. 31.

of the Senate Committee on Privileges and Elections, appointed
in obedience to Senate resolution of December 5, 1876, offered
by Mr. Edmunds.[1] Senator Howe of Wisconsin was chairman
of the group of senators who had visited and taken testimony
in Louisiana,[2] Senator Cameron of Wisconsin of the committee
which had gone to South Carolina,[3] Senator Sargent of California of the committee which had proceeded to Florida,[4] and
Senator Morton of the committee which had remained in Washington to investigate conditions in Oregon and other states.[5]

Such investigations and reports were without influence upon
the course of the dispute at the time, though they illuminate
the pathways of historical inquiry. Hope of a solution of the
great national problem was seen in another direction. To many
of the leaders of the Democratic party, less attached to Tilden
than to their local and personal interests, it seemed prudent
to accept the situation, as they found it, rather than put themselves in an inextricable position, which would lead directly,
if not to new civil war, certainly to something near akin to this
most unhappy condition. It would be worth more to the Southern people to resume control of their state governments than to
have a Democratic President.[6] If they could secure the retirement from their soil of the Federal troops they would sacrifice much which was accounted of greater importance to
Northern elements in the party. Grant was being badgered by
Packard in Louisiana and by Chamberlain in South Carolina,[7]

[1] Cong. Record, 44th Cong. 2nd sess., pp. 39–40.
[2] This committee published its report in three large volumes. Its findings
were as partisan on the Republican side as the House report was on the
Democratic side. Senators McDonald of Indiana and Saulsbury of Delaware were the minority members of this committee.—Senate Reports,
44th Cong. 2nd sess., no. 701.
[3] Senate Mis. Doc., 44th Cong. 2nd sess., no. 48, another report comprising three volumes.
[4] Senate Reports, 44th Cong. 2nd sess., no. 611.
[5] Senate Mis. Doc., 44th Cong. 2nd sess., no. 44. These reports of 1876
and 1877 were supplemented by investigations of the "Select Committee
on Alleged Frauds in the late Presidential Election," Clarkson N. Potter
of New York, chairman, in 1878–79, in which testimony was taken comprising nearly 3,000 pages.
[6] Cf. Letters and Memorials of Tilden, vol. ii, pp. 465, 536–7.
[7] McPherson's Handbook for 1878, pp. 57–67.

each of whom had been inaugurated as governor, each of whom had his legislature and was supporting himself amid scenes, now for long so familiar in the South, as against an opposing claimant for the office. Florida had gained a Democratic governor by means peculiar to that state, but the fates of General Nicholls in Louisiana and General Hampton in South Carolina were inseparably bound up with the national dispute.

Sentiment in the North, on the subject of the South, had been not a little improved by the recent attitude of the Supreme Court which, after a long course of delay and evasion, again became a distinct voice in the direction of the government. Before Chase's death they had agreed, five votes to four, in the so-called "Slaughter House Cases," [1] upon a construction of the Thirteenth, Fourteenth and Fifteenth Amendments. The whole tendency and purpose of the Radical leaders now for several years had been the Federalization of the government at the expense of the states. It was contended that the exercise of the extra-constitutional war powers, for which a fondness had been acquired by the politicians while they were employed in "saving the Union," might, for their convenience, be continued under peace conditions. Justification for the unusual policy was found in the amendments. It was against this theory that Andrew Johnson had so dauntlessly striven in his ill-starred contest with Congress. The Supreme Court had hestitated, but it now was ready to say that the amendments had no purpose except the protection of the freedom of the negro. State powers had been narrowed and restricted only in this specific regard. The "privileges and immunities," guaranteed by the Federal government to individuals within the states, were only particular rights contemplated by the Constitution. Thus it was declared that the business of slaughtering cattle in New Orleans, which the legislature had converted into a monopoly, could proceed in such manner as the state might dictate, without infringement of any right, privilege or immunity conferred upon citizens of the United States by the

[1] 16 Wall., p. 72.

Fourteenth Amendment.[1] A woman in Illinois wished to practice law in the courts of that state; her rights were infringed, she declared. The Supreme Court held that she was without Federal redress.[2] A whiskey seller in Iowa found that a local prohibition law bore hardly upon him. His United States citizenship gave him no remedy.[3] A woman wished to vote; she found no help in the Fourteenth Amendment, since she had not suffered because of her race, color or previous condition of servitude.

Such an attitude on the part of the court betokened the downfall of the Southern Enforcement acts. These laws were being used, not merely for the protection of the negro,—they were being administered largely, if not pre-eminently, to restrict and punish the white man, especially if he be a Democrat. In 1875, two sections of the act of 1870 were declared unconstitutional.[5] Closely following this decision came another, arising out of a race riot in Louisiana. On this occasion it was clearly stated that the Fourteenth Amendment gave the Federal government no particular duties in guarding the lives of the freedmen. This continued to be a function of the states. The amendment simply meant that the state governments should afford a protection, equal and uniform, to citizens, regardless of color and race. When the states should fail in the performance of their duty they would feel the hand of Federal authority, but in this case only, viz. —in safeguarding the negro with reference to rights which were incidental to citizenship of the United States. If the negroes' rights to assemble or to bear arms were brought into question these rights, being rights appertaining to citizenship of a state, and not of the United States, no redress could be procured through the machinery of government at Washington.[6]

Our public men and the country generally were not unobserv-

[1] 16 Wall., p. 72; cf. N. Y. Nation, April 24, 1873.
[2] Bradwell v. The State, 16 Wall., p. 130.
[3] Bartenmeyer v. Iowa, 18 Wall., p. 129.
[4] Minor v. Happersett, 21 Wall., p. 162.
[5] 92 U. S., p. 214.
[6] U. S. v. Cruikshank, 92 U. S., p. 542. On this subject see Dunning, Reconstruction, Political and Economic, pp. 260–65.

ant of the course of opinion in the Supreme Court, which, though a quieter and slower force than the co-ordinate legislative and executive branches of the government, was, now causing its salutary influence to be felt. President Grant, with a sagacity with which he seemed to be endued for this emergency, had let it be clearly understood that there could be no infractions of the peace, while the protracted dispute over the result of the election of 1876 was in course of settlement,[1] and, at the same time, declined to involve himself, or the troops in the South, in any partisan quarrels. Here were comfort and hope for the tried and weary Southern people, and they found satisfaction in the fact that Hayes, as they were led to believe, though his expressions of sympathy for the negro disturbed them,[2] would afford them relief from their persecutions, if he should be installed as President.

On Thursday, the 1st of February, 1877, the two houses met together to count the votes, in accordance with the terms of the bill, establishing the electoral commission.[3] The joint meeting was held in the hall of the House of Representatives, to the gallery of which tickets of admission were issued from day to day to the number of 1,600, to satisfy at least a part of the great number of persons who thronged Washington to watch the progress of events.[4] Mr. Ferry, the president of the Senate, opened the certificates from the states, proceeding in alphabetical order, and for a time, without question, the votes were counted for Hayes or Tilden, as the case might be. Florida was the first of the disputed states to be reached. Objection was made to the returns, and the subject was at once referred to the commission, sitting in the chamber of the Supreme Court. The decisions of the highest court in Florida and the installa-

[1] McPherson's Handbook for 1878, pp. 57–67; cf. Letters and Memorials of Tilden, vol. ii, p. 560.

[2] Williams, Life of Hayes, vol. i, pp. 488–9, 494–5, 496.

[3] In the interest of a decision prior to March 4th, the date of the joint meeting was set forward from the second Wednesday in February, when it would normally have convened, to the first Thursday of the month.— Cong. Record, 44th Cong. 2nd sess., p. 731.

[4] Barry, Forty Years in Washington, pp. 13–14. Some of these tickets are preserved in the collections of Historical Soc. of Pa.

tion of the Democratic governor, Drew, had resulted in an entirely regular certification of the Tilden electors, except for one fact—the authorization bore a date subsequent to December 6, when the electors everywhere, after performing their duties, had ended their official existence.[1] On that day the Hayes electors in Florida had met, on as regular a certification by the Republican governor, Stearns, and had cast the vote of the state for Hayes and Wheeler. On this point the Democrats alleged that the action of the Hayes electors had been invalid, because their election and certification were involved in fraud, whereupon was raised the vital issue as to whether or not the commission was empowered to go back and investigate the subject, in whole, or in any part, *ab initio*. It was a matter for that body itself to decide, and to it the problem was immediately referred, according to the terms of the act creating it. The Senate retired from the hall of the House of Representatives and each chamber resumed its regular course of legislative procedure, awaiting report of the result of the deliberations of the commission.

Both political parties put forth well known lawyers, holding seats in Congress, as "objectors," who could be heard as such, David Dudley Field, lately come into the House to fill a vacancy in the delegation from New York, for the express purpose of forwarding the case,[2] and J. Randolph Tucker acting for the Democrats—John A. Kasson and George W. McCrary, for the Republicans. In addition there was accomplished counsel, including, for the Democrats, Charles O'Conor, Jeremiah S. Black, George Hoadley, Ashbel Green and William C. Whitney—for the Republicans, William M. Evarts, Stanley Matthews, E. W. Stoughton and Samuel Shellabarger.

After hearing the case stated and argued the commissioners closed their doors and proceeded with their work in secret. The Democrats had found that one of the Republican electors,

[1] Proceedings of Electoral Commission, p. 14.
[2] Although Field had voted for Hayes, Tilden wished Field to be his legal representative in the House. The way opened through the resignation of Smith Ely, who had been elected mayor of New York.—Field, Life of D. D. Field, p. 270.

Humphreys by name, was ineligible, since he was a Federal office-holder, and, on February 7, Justice Bradley had the opportunity to make an appearance of being an impartial judge. He, as the fifteenth commissioner, on February 7th, decided against receiving evidence in addition to the papers delivered to and opened by the president of the Senate, i.e., of "going behind the returns," but he sided with the Democrats in respect of an investigation of the case of Humphreys.[1] On this point, therefore, testimony was taken, but it was soon made to appear to Mr. Commissioner Bradley that the man had surrendered his Federal office prior to election day, in November, 1876, and, on February 9, the commission, by a vote of 8 to 7, found in favor of accepting the Republican return from Florida.[2] Upon objection being offered, the two houses, which had come together to hear the result, separated again, when the Senate, of course, sustained and the House rejected the decision of the commission, which then, in accordance with the terms of the act of January 29, stood unreversed, and the four votes of this state, on February 12, were counted for Hayes and Wheeler.[3]

The case of Louisiana now quickly came to hand. Here was a more perplexing situation. The Republican majority was clearly the product of the state's characteristically and corruptly partisan returning board. Two years had not elapsed since a committee of the House, of which Wheeler, the candidate for Vice President, and Hoar, a commissioner, were members, had investigated this body's rascalities in connection with the elections in 1872 and 1874. Its black and white membership now was practically the same as then, and, though Hoar and Wheeler had dissented from the severely condemnatory report of the majority, which had been inspired by Charles Foster and William Walter Phelps, they had expressed their emphatic disapprobation of the board's view of, and its exercise of its powers.[4]

[1] Proceedings of the Electoral Commission, pp. 138–9.
[2] Ibid., pp. 196–7.
[3] Ibid., p. 203.
[4] House Reports, 43rd Cong. 2nd sess., no. 261, pt. 1, pp. 19–28.

In addition to points affecting the count in Louisiana there were not one, as in Florida, but at least two of the electors, who, contrary to the provision of the Constitution of the United States, held other Federal offices, and four more, who, in violation of the terms of the constitution of Louisiana, held other state offices.[1] Moreover, one of the conflicting certificates now to be laid before the commission had been forged, a fact, however, which was concealed from most of the judges in the case.[2] It seemed not too much to suppose that in such a mass of villanies as lay behind the Hayes return, barring a complete want of the judicial spirit in the commission, would rest a reason for giving the Democrats the one vote, which, added to the 184, securely in their possession, would yield them the Presidency.

John A. Campbell, a justice of the Supreme Court, who had left the bench at the outbreak of the war to engage in secession, now a resident of Louisiana,[3] ex-Senator Lyman Trumbull of Illinois and ex-Senator Matt Carpenter of Wisconsin, who prefaced his speech to the commisssion with a statement that he had voted against Tilden for President and would do so again, if he had the opportunity, and that the accession of the Democratic party to power would be "the greatest calamity that could befall" the country, barring fraud in a determination of the result,[4] skilfully combated the Republican position, Evarts and his associates defending it. As in the case of Florida the lawyers contended that, whatever the methods by which the result had been reached, it was not competent for the present reviewing body to go into evidence *aliunde* the papers submitted to the president of the Senate and to Congress, and that the certification of the canvassing board's work by the governor was conclusive and binding upon the commission. Every offer of proof of the irregularity of the proceedings in Louisiana was declined by the familiar vote of 8 to 7, Com-

[1] Cf. D. D. Field, The Vote that Made the President.
[2] Haworth, pp. 114–6; F. T. Hill, Harper's Magazine, March, 1907; House Reports, 45th Cong. 3rd sess., no. 140, pp. 50–63, 89–91.
[3] For Campbell see his Life by Henry G. Connor.
[4] Proceedings, p. 263.

missioner Bradley, at some cost to his conscience as a judicial officer and the virtual arbitrator, supporting the Rupublicans. It was decided not only that the commission was incompetent to examine the methods by which the returns had been compiled in the state, but also, notwithstanding the course adopted in reference to Humphreys in Florida, that it was incompetent to take testimony *aliunde* the certificates as to the qualifications or eligibility of the persons named as electors.[1] On February 16 it was found that the eight votes of Louisiana were Hayes and Wheeler's.

To the decision the most vigorous objections were made by the Democrats. On the separation of the houses the Senate, on Sherman's motion, by a strict party vote,[2] upheld the commission. In the House of Representatives the situation was, of course, reversed. It was noted with deep interest that two Republicans, Julius H. Seelye, professor in, and soon to be president of, Amherst College, and Henry L. Pierce, both holding seats in the House from Massachusetts, disregarded their party affiliations, and, repelled by the scene, now voted with the Democrats.[3]

Not a little help was coming to the Republicans, as they proceeded, through the discovery of a scandal in connection with the course which adherents of Tilden had chosen to pursue in Oregon. Each day the Republican newspapers were filled with accounts of a corrupt bargain which Colonel W. T. Pelton, a nephew of Mr. Tilden, and acting secretary of the Democratic National Committee, had, so it seemed, been trying to drive in that state in return for the one vote which would

[1] Proceedings, pp. 421-2.
[2] Ibid., p. 440; Cong. Record, 44th Cong. 2nd sess., p. 1683; Mc-Pherson's Handbook for 1868, p. 16. A bolt was organized by Conkling, and he had persuaded a small group of senators to join him in disapproval of the Louisiana decision, in the hope of seating Tilden, but the scheme was frustrated. On authority of George Hoadley in N. Y. Evening Post, cited in Letters and Memorials of Tilden, vol. ii, pp. 511-13. Conkling was an absentee when the vote was taken on the question.— Cong. Record, 44th Cong. 2nd sess., p. 1683; cf. S. S. Cox, Three Decades, p. 656.
[3] Cong. Record, 44th Cong. 2nd sess., p. 1703; McPherson's Handbook for 1878, pp. 16-17.

make his uncle President. The correspondence, which was addressed to Tilden's house in Gramercy Park in New York, indicated that open attempts had been made to purchase the office. The disclosure of such effrontery astounded the country and the moral position of the Democrats, which up to this time had been much better than the Republicans', was at once sensibly shaken.[1]

If all the wrongs which were concealed behind the Louisiana returns were to be accepted and approved it was clear that no more could be expected at later stages of the count. The whole country knew now, if it had not known before, what the end would be, and press, politician and citizen might accommodate themselves to it as amiably or as angrily as they chose. The Democratic editors and the party leaders in Congress, broke out in scathing denunciation of the commission, especially of Justice Bradley,[2] with many a thrust at Davis, the "coward" and "traitor" who had quitted the office of judge in the great case in exchange for six years of comfort and ease in the United States Senate.[3] One Democrat fell upon another in the privacy of his heart, if not in public sight, for having accepted such an arbitration, which was no arbitration,[4] as a means of settlement. Some had been faithless,[5] some rather stupid—all had been in a degree outwitted and honeyfugled, as it seemed, by the Republican managers, first in the Southern states in connection with the operations of the returning boards, particularly in Florida and Louisiana, and then at Washington in the development of the plan for a composition of the great dispute.[6]

[1] Senate Reports, 44th Cong. 2nd sess., no. 678, pp. 9 et seq.; Senate Mis. Doc., 44th Cong. 2nd sess., no. 44; Cong. Record, 44th Cong. 2nd sess., pp. 1653-5; N. Y. Nation, Feb. 22 and March 1, 1877; Haworth, pp. 159-62.
[2] Writings of Bradley, pp. 8-10. Branded by the Democratic newspapers thereafter as "Aliunde Joe."—Barry, Forty Years in Washington, p. 11.
[3] Cf. Bigelow, Life of Tilden, vol. ii, p. 64; Clifford, Life of Clifford, p. 316.
[4] Cf. Haworth, p. 191; Letters and Memorials of Tilden, vol. ii, pp. 482, 536, 549-52, 553-4. Tilden himself laid much of the blame at the doors of Thurman and Bayard.—Bigelow, Life of Tilden, vol. ii, p. 111.
[5] Cf. Bigelow, Life of Tilden, vol. ii, p. 63.
[6] Cf. ibid., p. 74.

Filibustering was now being resorted to by the Democrats
in the joint meetings, and when the houses divided. Parliamentary obstruction would supervene to prolong the proceedings, many believed, beyond the 4th of March. Refractory and revengeful Democratic representatives objected to
receiving the vote of Michigan on the ground that one of the
electors held a Federal office.[1] When Nevada was reached
another obstruction of the same kind was put in the way of
the count.[2] It was, therefore, February 21 before Oregon
was called, where it was known that the eligibility question
would appear in a graver form. After hearing the objectors
and their counsel, and discussing the point uselessly and at
length, George Hoadley leading for Tilden, and Stanley Matthews, for Hayes, the Republicans, on February 23, in Senator
Thurman's home, to which he was confined by illness, and to
which the commission had repaired, gained the one vote which
was in dispute in that state.[3]

More filibustering by representatives in the joint meeting
and in the House ensued in connection with the counting of
the votes of Pennsylvania and Rhode Island, and it was February 26, when less than a week of Grant's term remained, that
the case of South Carolina, where the result, it was charged,
had been gained by the use of armed force through the Federal
troops, was at hand.[4] Senator Thurman having retired from
the commission on account of his sickness, Senator Francis
Kernan of New York was appointed in his stead.[5]

The hour had come for the Democratic counsel, Jeremiah
S. Black and Montgomery Blair, both adepts in vituperative
oratory, to say the last words in the great cause for Tilden,
and for the party which he had led. Black assumed the rôle
of sage, prophet and martyr by turns. His tongue, touched
with bitter irony, he stood at the graveside of the republic.
He had "lost the dignity of an American citizen"; he felt
himself "degraded and humiliated." More now would be

[1] Proceedings, p. 442.
[2] Ibid., p. 446.
[3] Ibid., pp. 38–41.

[4] Ibid., p. 659.
[5] Ibid., pp. 653–4.

vain. Little could be interposed to avert the "horrible calamity" which threatened the country. It would be as well, Black continued, for them to make their prayers to Jupiter or Mars as "bring suit in the court where Rhadamanthus presides." The contemplated seating of Hayes in the President's chair was not only "a shameless swindle"; it was "not merely a fraud, but a fraud detected and exposed." The fowler had set his net—they had been caught—it had been their own fault. But "the waters of truth would rise gradually, and slowly, and surely," when there would be an "overflowing scourge." [1]

Counsel for the Republicans made no reply, the vote of South Carolina was promptly, on the 27th, given to Hayes and Wheeler.[2] The Democrats, who had organized the obstructive movement, during the proceedings connected with the expression of the dissent of the House to earlier decisions, grew more disorderly when the two chambers separated to discuss the case of this state. Speaker Randall was a man of unusual acumen and a presiding officer of talent and authority. The situation called for all his vigor and tact. He resolutely discountenanced the filibustering of some of his colleagues. It was only by the pursuit of an almost despotic course, in which he was supported by the sounder minds of his own party, that he suppressed the roisterers and despatched the business in hand.[3]

South Carolina having been disposed of, objections to receiving the votes of Vermont and Wisconsin, which could only be for the sake of effecting perilous delays, were made, to be very summarily treated by this able parliamentary officer. The end of the count was reached in a night session—it was five minutes past four o'clock on the morning of Friday, March 2, when the president of the Senate was ready to announce the result to the two houses. He hoped that "all demonstrations whatever" would be refrained from by members on the floor and by the galleries, that nothing should "transpire on this occasion to

[1] Proceedings, pp. 695-8.
[2] Ibid., pp. 701-702.
[3] Cox, Three Decades, p. 664; Mayes, Life of Lamar, p. 300; Haworth, pp. 258, 276-8; James Monroe, Atlantic Monthly, Oct., 1893, pp. 533-6.

mar the dignity and moderation" which had characterized the proceedings, "in the main so reputable to the American people and worthy of the respect of the world." [1] Hayes and Wheeler had received 185, Tilden and Hendricks 184 votes. Hayes and Wheeler, therefore, were declared to have been elected President and Vice President of the United States, and the joint meeting of the two houses was dissolved. A few hours later the electoral commission met, concluded its proceedings and its history came to an end.

The House on the same day, by a vote of 136 to 88, adopted a preamble and resolutions, declaring the election of Tilden and Hendricks, who had received 196 votes (including Florida's and Louisiana's) to be President and Vice President,[2] which, however, was of no more force than some statement that it might have made about the weather or the crops.

It was now Friday. At noon on the succeeding Sunday Grant's term would expire. The decision came not a moment too soon, and, bound up with it was a kind of "gentleman's agreement," which had been not without an important influence in bringing the great case to its timely end. Acting with the obstructionists were a number of Southern members, who had had, from the first, a large local object in view. They would have the incoming administration, if it were to be under Hayes's direction, give them assurances as to its Southern policy.[3] The white man should be recognized by the Federal government,—at any rate the authorities at Washington should withdraw the troops and leave the South to itself, without the meddling, which had brought it the many bitter fruits of the system known as "reconstruction." Louisiana should proceed under the governorship of General Nicholls, if the state were to give its electoral votes for Hayes; in South Carolina, Wade Hampton should be governor, if that state were to be counted for Hayes.

As early as on December 1 the editor of the New Orleans Times had visited Hayes at Columbus, conveying, as he al-

---

[1] Proceedings, p. 727.
[2] Cong. Record, 44th Cong. 2nd sess., p. 2227.
[3] Letters and Memorials of Tilden, vol. ii, p. 536; Haworth, pp. 257–8.

leged, the assurances of Lamar and Walthall of Mississippi,
Wade Hampton of South Carolina and other Southern leaders
that the negro, for whose welfare the Republican claimant had
so much honest solicitude, would be humanely and justly treated
in the South, if they might be assisted in their struggles
for good government. In reply Hayes pointed to his letter
of acceptance, saying that, on this subject, it "meant all it
said and all that it implied." [1] Pressed by his friends at Washington for some further declaration of his intentions he declined
giving it. He wrote Sherman on February 15, reiterating what
he had said to the visitor from New Orleans. He authorized
Sherman to say, whenever the question might arise "that you
[Sherman] know that I will stand by the friendly and encouraging words of that letter [the letter of acceptance] and by all
that they imply." [2] On the subject of the use of military power
in the South he told Schurz, on February 4, that "there was to
be an end of all that," except in emergencies which he could
not "think of as possible again." [3]

The subject now appeared in the form of regular negotiations. On the one side were Senator Gordon of Georgia, Representatives Henry Watterson and John Young Brown of
Kentucky and some Democratic Congressmen from Louisiana,
with Lamar standing in the background; on the other, a number
of men who, it was held, could speak for Hayes, including
Charles Foster, Stanley Matthews, James A. Garfield, ex-
Governor Dennison and John Sherman. They met in a series
of conferences, while the work of the electoral commission was
still in progress.[4] The terms of the understanding were finally
formulated, on February 26, in the rooms of Mr. Matthews at
Wormley's Hotel in Washington, on which account it is usually
called the "Wormley Agreement." It was as nearly a pledge
as such an arrangement could be without Hayes being directly

[1] Williams, Life of Hayes, vol. i, p. 505.
[2] Sherman's Recollections, vol. i, pp. 561–2.
[3] Schurz, Speeches, vol. iii, p. 387.
[4] House Mis. Doc., 45th Cong. 3rd sess., no. 31, pt. 1, pp. 875 et seq.;
ibid., pt. 3, pp. 595–633; Reynolds, Recon. in S. C., p. 449; Haworth, pp.
268–72; Watterson, Marse Henry, vol. i, pp. 309–11; T. C. Smith, Life
and Letters of J. A. Garfield. p. 644.

a party to it. Some statements in writing were signed by Matthews and Foster,[1] and on both sides it was taken to be a declaration which would be binding upon the administration. Something, therefore, of that which Mr. Tilden and his friends had lost in the, to them, untoward determination of the dispute accrued to the advantage of their allies in the South, as was promptly proved by the course of events in the few weeks to come.

The bearing of Mr. Tilden and his friends, under all the circumstances, was admirable. While they made no concealment of their belief that they had been the victims of a foul and shameless fraud they saw that "anarchy and civil war" would be the country's fate, if resistance were to be undertaken, and their claims pressed, in spite of the findings of the arbitrary tribunal to which these claims had been not too wisely referred.[2] In bringing about a result so honorable to the nation no small amount of credit attaches to Abram S. Hewitt, a sagacious man of affairs, who took this occasion to retire from his place as chairman of the Democratic National Committee.[3] He did not scruple to say that he preferred four years of Hayes to four years of fratricidal strife—a generation would pass before the country could recover from such chaos as would have resulted from any other course than that which he had chosen to pursue. Lamar, Bayard and Randall were also valuable influences within the Democratic party in favor of a tranquil submission.[4] It was "one of the greatest triumphs of patriotism," said George William Curtis, in the history of the republic.[5]

The Republicans who labored to attain a result by methods so irregular were acting in answer to a conviction, which was

[1] Williams, Life of Hayes, vol. i, pp. 533–4.

[2] Bigelow, Life of Tilden, vol. ii, pp. 111–15.

[3] For a tribute to Hewitt's usefulness see The Education of Henry Adams, p. 294.

[4] Letters and Memorials of Tilden, vol. ii, pp. 549–52, 554; cf. Hoar, Autobiography of 70 Years, vol. ii, p. 41. For Lamar's views see Mayes, Life of Lamar, pp. 297–8; for Randall's see Cong. Record, 44th Cong. 2nd sess., p. 2253. "Mr. Randall will divide the honors of President-making with Justice Bradley."—N. Y. Tribune, March 3, 1877.

[5] Harper's Weekly, June 23, 1888.

widespread in the North, that to give over the government to the Democrats would be, in large degree, a surrender of the gains of the war. To hold the Presidency against a party which had been so unfaithful to the Union was, indeed, in their sight a patriotic act.[1] If the canvassing boards had made up the returns dishonestly, was it not true that thousands of negroes had been intimidated and had been prevented on election day from casting their ballots?[2] It was the old loyal Unionist sentiment of the North mobilized against the "Democratic shotgun at the South."[3]

Those whose eyes were not clouded by partisan feeling, for the most part, viewed the situation with quiet satisfaction. It could be admitted that the work of the commission was a burlesque of justice. But, as Horace White has said, this body was not formed to do justice as between the candidates, but "to save the republic."[4] William Cullen Bryant undoubtedly expressed the sentiments of most men of the highest moral feeling and intelligence. Improper influences had been brought to bear upon the new black voters in the South at and before the elections; the state returning boards had tampered with the count to neutralize the effect of the intimidation practiced upon the negroes.[5] There would have been implication of fraud and fair reason for charges of it, in any case, no matter for which side the commission had rendered its decision. Each party had a "plausible case."[6] To have examined the entire subject *aliunde* the certificates and papers would have led to prolonged investigation, extending beyond the expiration of Grant's

[1] Bigelow, Life of Tilden, vol. ii, p. 106.
[2] Merriam, Life of Bowles, vol. ii, p. 287.
[3] Cf. House Reports, 44th Cong. 2nd sess., no. 100, pt. 3, p. 10.
[4] Life of Trumbull, p. 412.
[5] A justification for the returning boards based, however, on a very extraordinary principle, that a man could be elected to the Presidency or any other office by votes which on any account, were not, but might, under other conditions, have been cast for him.—Cf. D. D. Field, The Vote that Made the President.
[6] Godwin, Life of Bryant, vol. ii, pp. 385-6; cf. Foulke, Life of Morton, vol. ii, p. 477; Williams, Life of Hayes, vol. i, pp. 497, 503, 504; G. W. Curtis in Harper's Weekly, June 23, 1888.

term, still at the end leading to no certain truths,[1] since the whole subject was enshrouded in fraud at its source and at each stage upward, wherever it should have been opened for attack. Meantime the government, the people and all their daily affairs were in dangerous suspense. It is to the lasting credit of both parties [2] that we played the game in a manner befitting our English traditions,—the losers, in general, submitting under defeat in a passive, if sorely wounded dignity; the winners, on their side, taking the victory in a chastened air, with no undue exultation, and that we thus met and passed another crisis in our national history.

[1] Cf. Hoar, Autobiography of 70 Years, vol. i, pp. 371–3. Frelinghuysen said in the Senate—"Congress cannot be a grand returning board to investigate millions of votes, and the authenticated returns from the states are infinitely more likely to approximate to the truth than any investigation by Congress."—Cong. Record, 44th Cong. 2nd sess., p. 803.

[2] Cf. speech of Evarts, quoted in Williams, Life of Hayes, vol. i, p. 535.

CHAPTER XXII

THE HAYES ADMINISTRATION

FOLLOWING the completion of the count, the announcement by the president of the Senate of the election of Hayes found him still in the governor's office in Columbus. He had been torn by conflicting sentiments as the struggle for the title to the seat proceeded. A man of a high sense of honor, with a wife, who greatly influenced his life, of similar standards of feeling and conduct,[1] would come to the Presidency not without questionings as to all which had so recently passed. At first he had doubted whether he had been elected, even after so many claims were made by the Republican managers in his behalf.[2] But he was well convinced that the negroes had been intimidated in the South, and that the poll in a number of states on this account had not been "fair" to the Republicans.[3] He also shared the feeling of men of his party that there had been false registration and ballot box stuffing, to his loss, in New York City and Brooklyn.[4] Whatever was seen on the other side, he required that no fraud, no dishonesty, no improper course should mark any action taken in his interest. Nothing must be done which would not "bear the severest scrutiny."[5] He did not care for "success by intrigues,"[6] as much as he desired, the more he reflected upon it,[7] as his Diary discloses, that the result might be favorable to his pretensions.

[1] Their somewhat unusual relations may be traced in his letters to her which Mr. Williams has included in the Diary and Letters of Hayes.
[2] Williams, Life of Hayes, vol. i, pp. 495–7.
[3] Diary and Letters of Hayes, vol. iii, pp. 377–8, 379, 381, 382, 383.
[4] Ibid., p. 375.
[5] Ibid., p. 382.
[6] Ibid., p. 397.
[7] Williams, Life of Hayes, vol. i, pp. 495, 498, 503–4. Hayes said—"Any man fit to be President, or even a candidate of a great party for the office, would prefer to be counted out by fraud rather than counted in by fraud, of which there is a reasonable suspicion."—Ibid., p. 500. Cf. Sherman's Recollections, vol. i, p. 559.

His and Mrs. Hayes's benevolent interest in the welfare of the colored race [1] was a factor reconciling him to the proceedings,[2] which were turning to his advantage in Florida and Louisiana, and the accounts as to the overreaching of the Democrats to procure an electoral vote in Oregon,[3] including the offers to buy it, which were filling the press, were clearly an offset in his mind to whatever qualms he may have felt on the subject of the methods employed by his friends to procure his ascendency. He had formulated plans for the improvement of the character and purposes of the government, which he dearly desired to realize. The resumption of specie payments and the restoration of a sound currency, the divorce of the civil service from politics, the honest administration of the departments, the proffer of a kindly hand to the whites of the South and their relief from infamous magistrates were ideals standing before him, and he was eager for the opportunities which the great office would provide.[4] Thus it was that he was the more ready to receive the letters from, and to meet and talk with the "visiting statesmen" and other politicians, who, for their own purposes, daily told him of the frightful terrorization of, and the outrages committed upon, the negroes by the Democrats, to prevent these negroes from expressing their will as voters at the polls, and assured him of the entire regularity of all that was being done by the returning boards to bring him safely through the contest.[5] He maintained his dignity and composure,[6] as the dispute proceeded to its settlement, though in the privacy of his heart his hopes rose and fell with the course of the controversy, until it was seen, in February, after the decision of the commission as to Florida, and, still more clearly, after the vote of Louisiana was awarded to him, that he was to come to Washington. Upon the dec-

---

[1] Williams, Life of Hayes, vol. i, pp. 493–4, 508.
[2] Cf. Diary and Letters of Hayes, vol. iii, p. 382.
[3] Williams, Life of Hayes, vol. i, p. 509.
[4] Ibid., pp. 496, 497; Diary and Letters of Hayes, vol. iii, p. 377.
[5] Cf. Williams, Life of Hayes, vol. i, pp. 496–7, 502–3, 504, 507, 538; Diary and Letters of Hayes, vol. iii, p. 381; Sherman's Recollections, vol. i, pp. 558–9.
[6] Williams, Life of Hayes, vol. i, pp. 498–9.

laration of the result he had no doubt of his moral or legal
right to the office, and he entered it with an easy conscience
and an honest heart.[1]

The rancor of the dispute had induced threats of assassination, and one evening in Columbus, while General Hayes was
at supper with his family, a bullet was fired through his
parlor window to lodge in the library wall.[2] It were well,
he was told, to proceed to Washington cautiously, and, if
possible, with secrecy. He was without fear and gave no
care to the injunctions of his friends, though no more advertisement than could be avoided attended his probable
movements, as the day approached for him to leave the office
of governor of Ohio to assume the duties of the Presidency of
the United States. A reception had been tendered him by the
people of Columbus on the night of February 28, and the
next day, Thursday, March 1, two private cars, for the use
of himself, his family and a few intimate friends, were attached
to a train on the Pennsylvania Railroad to bear him east.
He was greeted by crowds at stations along the way. The
result of the count had not yet been announced, and he had
nearly come to Harrisburg in Pennsylvania, before he was to
hear the news which certainly disposed of his suggestion, so
modestly made to the people from the end of his car at Columbus the previous day, that he might, within a week, return to
resume his place "in the governor's office, and as your fellow
citizen." [3] President Grant had asked General Hayes to be
his guest at the White House, but the invitation was declined,
and, met at the station by Senator John Sherman and General
Sherman, on the morning of March 2, the party was driven to
Senator Sherman's house to await the inauguration. After
breakfast Hayes was taken by his host to call upon the President, and then to the Capitol where, in the Vice President's
room, he received many members of the Senate and the House
of Representatives. Grant's term would expire on Sunday
at noon, March 4, but the ceremonies attendant upon the

[1] Williams, Life of Hayes, vol. i, pp. 538–40.
[2] Ibid., vol. ii, p. 2.   [3] Ibid., p. 4.

induction into office of his successor were set for Monday. In order to avert any complications which might arise at so critical a conjuncture, just prior to the state dinner, tendered at the White House on Saturday evening to the President-elect, the Chief Justice, in the presence of President Grant and his son, U. S. Grant, Jr., the little group having withdrawn to the "Red Room," their absence unnoticed by the other members of the company, administered the oath to General Hayes.

The dawn on Monday found all in readiness for the inauguration. Some 30,000 individuals, it is estimated, packed the space in front of the Capitol, awaiting the procession of military bodies and campaign clubs, with their bands of music, and various officers of the government, embodied in which was the open barouche, bearing Grant and Hayes, who, when they reached the scene, dismounted and walked arm in arm into the Senate chamber. When he appeared upon the portico cheers greeted the new President, who had come to his place amid so much convulsion of popular feeling. His reception was warm and hearty on every side,[1] as it had been on the way to the Capitol, and his speech, concerning which, moderately certain of the issue, he had been, for some weeks, taking the advice of his friends, fell upon attentive ears. No words so wholesome had been heard since his letter of acceptance. Tersely and frankly he repeated the pledges of that paper, and left no doubt in the minds of those, in whom correct ideals for public service were not impaired, that a new era in the conduct of the government was about to begin. No other President had laid down for himself so fine a program, or, if he could translate it into performance, would deserve the higher praise of his countrymen.

To the South he again spoke. It was a question there of "government or no government; of social order, and all the peaceful industries and happiness that belong to it, or a return to barbarism." The people of the South, he said again, were entitled to "wise, honest and peaceful self-government." But in gaining this end the rights of the recently emancipated

[1] Williams, Life of Hayes, vol. i, p. 5.

colored people must not be "infringed or assailed." Only "by the united and harmonious efforts of both races" could the evils which afflicted both be removed or remedied. It would be his hope to pursue a policy which would "forever wipe out in our political affairs the color line and the distinction between North and South, to the end that we may have, not merely a united North or a united South, but a united country." [1]

As to the civil service, and the abuses affecting it, his statements were clear. The reform should be "thorough and complete." "He serves his party best who serves his country best," he said.[2] To make the President a better magistrate the Constitution should be amended with a view to limiting that officer to a single term of six years.[3]

On the money question Hayes said that the "only safe paper currency" was one resting upon "a coin basis," and "at all times promptly convertible into coin." He would promote the movement for "an early resumption of specie payments." He alluded to the conflicting claims to the office—to his coming to the Presidency as a result of an arbitration of the questions in dispute concerning the counting of the votes. "It has been reserved for a government of the people, where the right of suffrage is universal," he said, "to give to the world the first example in history of a great nation, in the midst of a struggle of opposing parties for power, hushing its party tumults, to yield the issue of the contest to adjustment according to the forms of law." [4]

---

[1] Richardson, Messages and Papers, vol. vii, pp. 443–4. Cf. Hayes's Diary in Williams, Life of Hayes, vol. ii, p. 12.

[2] Destined to become "one of the permanent political maxims of the race," and thought to have come from the Tenth Book of Homer's Iliad (Pope's translation)—

> "Each single Greek in this conclusive strife,
> Stands on the sharpest edge of death or life.
> Yet, if my years thy kind regard engage,
> Employ thy youth as I employ my age;
> Succeed to these my cares, and rouse the rest;
> He serves me most who serves my country best."

If so Hayes was unconscious of being a borrower.—Williams, Life of Hayes, vol. ii, p. 13.

[3] Richardson, op. cit., vol. vii, pp. 444–5.

[4] Ibid., p. 446.

The address at an end the oath was again administered by
the Chief Justice, Hayes re-entered his carriage and, amid peals
of bells, artillery salutes and the renewed cheers of the crowds
which lined his way, he passed back from the Capitol to the
White House. In the evening the city was illuminated, a
great torchlight procession of campaign clubs, marching to
music, moved through Pennsylvania Avenue, and the new administration had begun.

The reception of Hayes's utterances in the country at large
was very favorable, and went far to conciliate men who had
looked with but little sympathy upon him, and were still
doubting his title to the place. The New York Nation said that
the address was " clear, modest and sensible." [1] Few such documents, said Harper's Weekly, had been superior to this one in
"mingled wisdom, force and moderation of statement." Its
tone was "patriotic in the highest degree." It was "manly and
sincere" and betokened a "new spirit in the conduct of public
affairs." [2] It indicated "in every line an honest devotion
to duty," said the New York Tribune; no one could read it
"without recognizing in it the language of sincerity and courage." [3] The New York Times spoke of its "admirable sentiments"; it was "a plain manly statement of the purposes of a
modest public officer." It would meet "approval throughout
the country." [4] Minister Pierrepont in London wrote that
no message of a President to the people had ever been received
in Europe with "such universal favor." [5]

Upon his cabinet, as well as the inaugural address, Hayes
had expended much thought, while the electoral commission
still discussed his claims and the count proceeded. Indeed,
so early as on January 5th, he was busy with the problems which
might confront him. He might or might not be President—
he must, he wrote in his Diary, "prepare for either event." [6]
On January 17 his mind rested on Evarts for Secretary of
State; Sherman, or, perhaps, a Massachusetts man for Secretary

[1] Issue of March 8, 1877. [4] Issue of March 6, 1877.
[2] Issue of March 24, 1877. [5] Williams, Life of Hayes, vol. ii, p. 15.
[3] Issue of March 6, 1877. [6] Ibid., vol. i, p. 522.

of the Treasury; John M. Harlan of Kentucky for Attorney
General; with George W. McCrary, an able lawyer and a
member of the House of Representatives from Iowa, General
Benjamin Harrison of Indiana, and Settle, the Republican
leader in North Carolina, as other members of the cabinet.[1]
Senator Sherman, Mr. Wheeler, Mr. Schurz, who, at request,
sent a complete list of desirable names, with alternates;[2] William
Henry Smith, a trusted friend; General Jacob D. Cox,[3] and
others were freely consulted in the interest of the selection of
a group of men who might not only give honest and efficient
administration to the departments, but also be representative
of the intelligent sentiment of the people in all parts of the
Union.

In February Hayes had formed the resolution to appoint
no member of the Grant cabinet, "no Presidential candidates,"
and no one, as he said, in order "to 'take care' of anybody."[4]
He wished to honor a Southern Democrat, in emphasis of a
tolerant spirit toward the South, and as a measure likely to
forward his plans for the improvement of relations between the
sections. He had General Joseph E. Johnston in mind, a suggestion which, however, met with so little favor from General
Sherman and others, to whom the idea was broached, that it
must be abandoned.[5] John Sherman was the first member of
the cabinet to be chosen, and, upon the announcement of the
decision of the electoral commission as to the vote of Louisiana,
Hayes, on February 19, wrote tendering the senator from Ohio
the Secretaryship of the Treasury.[6] Upon Sherman's visit to
Columbus, when he accepted the office, he was commissioned to
see Evarts regarding the Secretaryship of State. Schurz, on
February 25, was asked to become the head of the Department
of the Interior.[7] There were yet the War, Navy, Post Office and

[1] Williams, Life of Hayes, vol. ii, p. 17.
[2] Schurz, Speeches, vol. iii, pp. 376–83.
[3] Cf. ibid., pp. 383–4.
[4] Williams, Life of Hayes, vol. ii, p. 18.
[5] Ibid., pp. 18, 20–21.
[6] Ibid., p. 18; cf. Sherman's Recollections, vol. i, p. 56.
[7] Williams, Life of Hayes, vol. ii, p. 19; Schurz, Reminiscences, vol. iii,
pp. 374–5; Schurz, Speeches, vol. iii, p. 403.

Attorney General's departments, the heads of which would not be selected until after General Hayes reached Washington, although Mr. McCrary of Iowa[1] was definitely in mind for one of these positions, and it was hoped that Justin S. Morrill of Vermont might be induced to accept a place. Morrill was "pressed" by Hayes, as well as by Wheeler and others near to the President, to join the administration, but he positively declined to leave his seat in the United States Senate.[2]   A representative of New England, it was thought, had been found in Eugene Hale. He was a son-in-law of Zachariah Chandler and held a seat in the House from Maine,[3] but he, having other objects in view,[4] also declined, and the place was given to General Charles Devens, a justice of the supreme court of Massachusetts, on the warm recommendation of Mr. Hoar[5] and Mr. Wheeler.

Hayes's early design to appoint General Benjamin Harrison of Indiana, defeated in the late election for the governorship of that state, after giving his party gallant leadership, must be abandoned because of Morton's hostility, as was the plan to bestow the honor upon John M. Harlan, on the same account.[6] In deference to Morton's demands John W. Foster might have been appointed, but he was minister to Mexico and could not soon be communicated with on the point, so the choice fell upon Richard W. Thompson, who had presented Morton's name in the Cincinnati convention, an old "war horse" of the Whigs and the Republicans in the West, famous as a political orator.[7] A Southern representative, after a thorough canvass of the subject, was found in David M. Key of Tennessee. He had become a United States senator from that state at the death of Andrew Johnson, a place which he had just ceased to occupy. A Democrat throughout his life he was still this, though he

[1] Cf. Hoar, Autobiography of 70 Years, vol. ii, pp. 8, 10.

[2] Cf. his letter to Benedict, March 11, 1877, in Morrill Papers in Library of Congress.

[3] He had been offered, though he had refused it, the Postmaster Generalship by Grant when Creswell had resigned.—McCulloch Papers in Library of Congress.

[4] Hoar, Autobiography, vol. ii, pp. 7-8.

[5] Ibid., pp. 9, 31-40.

[6] Diary and Letters of Hayes, vol. iii, p. 427.

[7] Williams, Life of Hayes, vol. ii, p. 23.

was regarded as a moderate.[1] He had been a Confederate soldier. He answered the requirements which the President had in mind. Key became Postmaster General, Devens, Attorney General, McCrary, Secretary of War and Thompson, Secretary of the Navy. The cabinet was now complete.

The reception of the names by the country was as cordial as the welcome given to the sentiments which Hayes had so well expressed in his inaugural address.[2] Sherman, it is true, had been a blind party man, and had remained so throughout the dispute over the election of 1876.[3] A truckler for votes, which in his belief he could in this way procure to forward his political ambitions, he had been infirm at times in his adhesion to correct principles of finance.[4] But he had a mastery of the subject which, with Hayes's undeviating support, was soon to enable him to perform the greatest service to the country and to advance his name into the ranks of American statesmen. Moreover, Hayes was under the most weighty obligations to him in connection with the nomination and election,—at first in Ohio, and afterward. Thompson's appointment was made to please the powerful Senator Morton. But in other respects the selections were little influenced by partisan considerations. Evarts, as the New York Nation said, was "plainly marked out" for the Secretaryship of State "by his talents, services and character." He "literally" had "no competitor in the party."[5]

An honest man had come to the Presidency.[6] It was a striking and welcome innovation to witness a cabinet which, as Hayes had promised himself that it should be, was formed for public advantage and not to "take care" of party interests. Mrs.

---

[1] E. E. Sparks, National Development, p. 105.

[2] Cf. Schurz, Reminiscences, vol. iii, p. 275.

[3] Schurz and the Independents had been strong advocates of Bristow for Secretary of the Treasury, and, for all that he had suffered for righteousness's sake (Cf. Bristow to Schurz in Schurz, Speeches, vol. iii, pp. 410–12), he abundantly deserved the appointment. (Reminiscenses of Schurz, vol. iii, pp. 373–4; cf. Schurz, Speeches, vol. iii, pp. 379, 406). All that came to this sterling figure, however, was a "state dinner" at the White House in the winter of 1878.—N. Y. Nation, Feb. 14, 1878.

[4] Cf. N. Y. Nation, March 8, 1877.

[5] Ibid.; N. Y. Herald, March 7, 1877.

[6] Autobiography of A. D. White, vol. i, p. 189.

Hayes, as "mistress of the White House," announced that alcoholic beverages would not be served at her table,[1] a resolution which, at the time, induced nation, if not world wide comment, much of it designed to mark her as a fanatic and to identify her with the temperance "Crusade," though her course was merely a carrying of the simple manners which had marked the conduct of her home in Ohio to a higher and an observed place. It served at the same time as, and was fairly interpreted to be, a protest against a marked grossness which had come to characterize what bore the name of Washington "society."[2]

The President's and Mrs. Hayes's were pure breaths exhaled into the fetid atmosphere which had gathered around Grant, and it was a notice to the entire pack who had feasted and idled at the public cost, who had schemed and stolen so impudently in the public sight for so many years, that they would meet with no favor from the new administration.[3]

The first important task confronting the new President involved the fulfillment of his pledges in regard to the South. None required more courage in view of the temper of the North, still influenced as it was by the memories of the war. But Hayes had stated his policy in his letter of acceptance. He had, dur-

---

[1] Cf. Hoar, Autobiography of 70 Years, vol. ii, pp. 14–5.

[2] Cf. N. Y. Tribune, April 12, 1877. Neither General nor Mrs. Hayes, it is to be observed, were regarded as radicals on the temperance question in Ohio, where the Germans were so important a force in politics, and withheld their votes from candidates who, if elected, it was supposed, might labor for a restriction of their personal rights.—Diary and Letters of Hayes, vol. iii, pp. 368–9.

[3] Hayes was a man who loved his wife and children, said prayers in his house each morning, lunched, whether alone with his family or with guests, on cold meat and tea, and placidly pursued the way of a middle class American of his age. He was a "Victorian" by way of New England and the Western Reserve, who remained unspoiled by any dignity which he gained. He had a high sense of justice and right for himself, for other men and for the state. His courage was equal to any emergency, though he made no show of this or any other of his virtues, which were the simple and homely virtues of the stock from which he sprang. His intellect, if not of the first rank, enabled him to wisely compass any problem which came before him. Mrs. Hayes was a fit consort of such a man. The parade of a matter, which affected her manner of conducting her household on the subject of one detail of it, by the temperance crusaders was as unwelcome to her as to the President.—Cf. Diary and Letters, vol. iii, pp. 616–7; John S. Wise, Recollections of Thirteen Presidents, pp. 137–9.

ing the progress of the electoral dispute, indicated his sentiments to Southern men who had come to him for a confirmation of the impression which they had gained as to his probable attitude toward subjects near to their hearts. His friends, without his being entangled in the negotiation, had made verbal, even written statements, predicated upon his official course. He had restated his views in his inaugural address.

Grant, as has been indicated, had come to see a light. It was clear that the course of the government was about to undergo a radical change, and he had, at the end of his administration, deserted the "Custom House Ring," which Packard, Kellogg and Casey dominated at New Orleans, and which continued to clamor for Federal support, on the ground that they were "loyal to the Union" and "Republican," where all else was disloyalty and wickedness. The most urgent messages were sent to him. The "White League" was in arms; the state house at New Orleans was besieged; the whole city was in terror. Grant was implored to act "for God's sake." [1] These despatches continued to reach the White House, the Attorney General's office and the War Department throughout January. At first ready to "recognize" Packard in his contest with Nicholls for the governorship,[2] the President, on March 1, reached the conclusion that public opinion would no longer support the maintenance of a state government in Louisiana by the use of the military; he would, therefore, "concur in this manifest feeling." [3] His orders to the War Department "to sustain Governor Chamberlain" in South Carolina [4] led to no further activity at Washington in behalf of that man's claims over Wade Hampton's, except a rather meddlesome prohibition of a proposed parade of the "rifle clubs" on Washington's Birthday.[5] Upon the inauguration of Hayes both sides addressed the new President, the conspirators in Louisiana staging new "outrages" in order to direct Northern sympathy to themselves,

[1] Cf. McPherson's Handbook for 1878, p. 62.
[2] Ibid., p. 64.
[3] Ibid., p. 67; Williams, Life of Hayes, vol. ii, pp. 33–4, 35.
[4] McPherson's Handbook for 1878, p. 77.
[5] Ibid., p. 80; Reynolds, Reconstruction in S. C., pp. 440–41.

and to make more difficult the course which he, unless all signs were delusive, was likely to pursue.[1]

Stanley Matthews was still in contact with the subject. He was writing to Packard and Chamberlain, pointing out the impossibility of the government's continuing to support them with troops. They were told in effect, to evoke protests which they immediately gave to the newspapers, that they ought to retire from their offices "for the good of the country."[2] The task was particularly difficult in Louisiana because, if the Hayes electors there could be held to have had honest majorities, so must Packard have been the choice of the people of the state. Indeed, evidence that he was still more clearly entitled to the governor's office than Hayes was to the Presidency was not wanting.[3] Nevertheless, it was plain that both Packard and Chamberlain must be swept aside.[4]

In Hayes's behalf it could be said that he proposed to decide nothing as to the state governments. He would act merely where he might act, and withdraw the United States troops. On this point only was it his duty to intercede. He stood on secure ground and he would develop his policy, as it was his right to do,[5] circumspectly, indeed, but at once.[6] The subject was fully discussed in the cabinet. Delegations of citizens from the two states, representing both sides, were patiently received and heard.

The case of South Carolina, which was simpler than Louisiana's, was the first to win consideration. The supreme court of the state supported Hampton. Practically all the intelli-

---

[1] McPherson's Handbook for 1878, p. 68.

[2] Williams, Life of Hayes, vol. ii, pp. 41–44; Allen, Governor Chamberlain's Administration, pp. 469–71; Reynolds, Recon. in S. C., pp. 451–2.

[3] Williams, Life of Hayes, vol. ii, pp. 38–39.

[4] Cf. Joseph Medill to Richard Smith, ibid., footnote.

[5] Cf. Harper's Weekly, May 19, 1877.

[6] "My policy is trust, peace and to put aside the bayonet," said Hayes. "I do not think the wise policy is to decide contested elections in the states by the use of the national army." (Diary and Letters of Hayes, vol. iii, p. 427.) "The wish is to restore harmony and good feeling between sections and races. . . . We wish to adjust the difficulties in Louisiana and South Carolina so as to make one government out of two in each state."—Ibid., p. 429.

gent forces of society were enlisted in his behalf. His government was organized, and was recognized generally by the people, while Chamberlain's hold upon place and power put him in the position of a mere protestant who was crying "outrage" and "fraud." Hayes began by asking the rival claimants, in letters dated March 23, 1877, to come to Washington.[1] Hampton's trip north approached the proportions of a royal progress.[2] At Richmond he was met by a crowd numbering not less than 5,000 people. Artillery salutes were fired. Though it was two o'clock in the morning when he reached the national capital hundreds of persons awaited his arrival at Willard's Hotel.[3]

Protracted conferences ensued.[4] The contestants visited the President—they discussed their cases with members of the cabinet.[5] The result could have been foretold. Ample notice of Hayes's intentions had been served upon Chamberlain and his coterie of negroes, scalawags and carpetbaggers,[6] superior to them, as everyone knew him to be, and he could have had but little hope of moving Hayes to espouse his waning cause. It was on April 3rd that the President addressed Secretary of War McCrary as to the soldiers whom Grant had stationed in the state house at Columbia. In his opinion there did not exist in South Carolina that "domestic violence" which is contemplated by the Constitution, as ground for the use of Federal military power in a state. Therefore the troops should be removed to "their previous place of encampment." McCrary at once directed Sherman, Sherman directed Hancock, and Hancock directed Ruger, in command on the ground, to make the withdrawal in accordance with the order of the President.[7] It was a day of jubilee in South Carolina,[8] and

[1] Williams, Life of Hayes, vol. ii, p. 50; Allen, Governor Chamberlain's Administration, pp. 472–3.
[2] Williams, Life of Hayes, vol. ii, p. 51; Reynolds, Recon. in S. C., pp. 453–4; Porcher in Southern Historical Society Papers, vol. xiii, p. 85.
[3] N. Y. Tribune, March 29 and 30, 1877.
[4] Allen, Governor Chamberlain's Administration, p. 473.
[5] Reynolds, Recon. in S. C., pp. 454–6.
[6] Williams, Life of Hayes, vol. ii, pp. 42–3.
[7] McPherson's Handbook for 1878, p. 81.
[8] N. Y. Tribune, April 3, 1877.

Hayes's action met with the warm approval of judicious men
in all parts of the country. No more was necessary. Mr.
Chamberlain quietly surrendered his office to General Hampton, issued an address,[1] and returned, after his adventure with
"Reconstruction," to his home in the North.[2]

The obstinate contest between the people of Louisiana and
the carpetbagger-negro cabal which disgraced the name of
the Republican party in that state Hayes proposed to bring
to an end only after despatching a commission to New Orleans.[3]
One more investigation of the subject would be undertaken.
After advances, which were unsuccessful, had been made to
Wheeler, Hoar, Lamar and David Davis,[4] the President appointed for this service Charles B. Lawrence, ex-chief justice
of Illinois, General Joseph R. Hawley of Connecticut, lately
so prominent in the management of the Centennial Exposition in Philadelphia, General John M. Harlan of Kentucky,
ex-Governor and ex-Confederate General John C. Brown of
Tennessee and Wayne MacVeagh of Pennsylvania, son-in-
law of Simon Cameron, appointed by Grant to be minister to
Turkey, but now a Liberal Republican. They represented
all phases of political opinion and, individually, were men of
high character. They bore instructions, forwarded to them by
Secretary Evarts on April 2. While it was made clear that
it was the President's design, in any event, to withdraw the
troops, and to let the state proceed under local influences,
it was desired that there should be some further statement,
justifying the policy which he had resolved upon, from a body
of men in whom the country would repose confidence. The
commission should direct its attention to a removal of the
obstacles which interfered with an acknowledgment of a
"single government," or in any case to the recognition of a
"single legislature as the depository of the representative will
of the people of Louisiana."[5] Great mass meetings were being

[1] Allen, Governor Chamberlain's Administration, pp. 480–82.
[2] For his retrospect see Atlantic Monthly, April, 1901.
[3] Agreed upon with the full approval of the cabinet on March 20.—
Williams, Life of Hayes, vol. ii, p. 45.
[4] Ibid.   [5] McPherson's Handbook for 1878, pp. 70–71.

held in New Orleans in the interest of the retirement of the troops. Petitions bearing the names of all the prominent citizens of that place were coming to the White House. The commissioners were urged to make haste. They departed for Louisiana at once, amid Packard's protests,[1] and met and conferred with that man and Nicholls, and with other leaders of the madly excited parties, members of the antagonistic legislatures, heads of the local governments, and citizens. Knowing what had been done in South Carolina, and with a realization of what was in prospect for them, some of the Packard men left his legislature and joined that of Nicholls, which thus obtained a quorum.[2] Little more needed to be done. The Nicholls legislature met and adopted resolutions commending President Hayes, the Packard legislature of darkies and white roustabouts[3] condemned the President and the commission, which preceded its report with a telegram, on April 20, urging "immediate announcement of the time when the troops would be withdrawn." [4] In a few hours Secretary McCrary issued orders similar to those on the subject of South Carolina of a fortnight earlier. The soldiers were to be removed, said the President, from the positions in which they had been placed by Grant, "to such regular barracks in the vicinity" as might be selected for their occupation.[5] Secretary McCrary fixed the time of the withdrawal at noon on April 24, when they vacated their quarters in New Orleans, were marched to the wharf and left the city, amid the ringing of bells and the discharge of cannon, which but feebly expressed the real joy of the people.[6]

The citadels of corruption, which the Republican party had created and had so long defended in South Carolina and Louisi-

[1] Williams, Life of Hayes, vol. ii, p. 56.
[2] Cf. ibid. It was charged that this result was brought about in large degree by a statement of Wayne MacVeagh—"If there is any member of the legislature who entertains the most lingering idea that troops are going to remain, for God's sake disabuse him of that idea, for they are going to be removed."—McPherson's Handbook for 1878, p. 69.
[3] Williams, Life of Hayes vol. ii, p. 47.
[4] McPherson's Handbook for 1878, p. 73.
[5] Ibid., p. 69.
[6] Cf. N. Y. Tribune, April 30, 1877.

ana, had now fallen. It was one of the bravest acts which any President of the United States had ever performed, since the measure must be taken under the clamorous and vituperative opposition of a large section of his own political party, and since he was, by this act, to put himself, at the very commencement of his administration, in a place apart from very many of those to whom he was allied by the obligations of friendship and of service. Packard, left without the troops to support his pretensions, amid loud complaints, yielded, as he said, "to superior force," and shortly returned to his own state of Maine. Nicholls and Wade Hampton were in undisputed possession of the governments of Louisiana and South Carolina, and were ready to reorganize them in accordance with the needs and desires of the native white population. All the states of the South had now been returned to the care and direction of their citizens, with power of self-determination concerning their local affairs.[1]

There were signs of a better day—a friendlier feeling was evidenced in the South as in the North. In 1877, on Memorial Day, when it was the custom in the North to strew flowers upon the graves of fallen Union soldiers, Hayes was asked to visit Tennessee.[2] Southern generals were invited to speak on the same day in several Northern cities. The "blue and the gray" became the subject of much sentimental allusion, and already, now and again, they were seen to mingle on public occasions.[3] Hayes, after a tour through New England, in the summer of 1877, when his text was "the old harmony

---

[1] At a point, when we are taking leave of the subject of "Reconstruction," these words of the New York Nation may be not inappropriately introduced—"It will be said of the Republican party which is now passing from the stage of events that, while it had the rude and fanatical energy which was needed to suppress the rebellion and extinguish slavery, it had neither the wisdom, nor the skill, nor the foresight to assist the unfortunate communities which the struggle had devastated to build up a new and better civilization on the ruins of the old one, but that it hindered and vexed them in their very first efforts to rise by maxims and expedients borrowed from the arsenals of ruined monarchies and the dreams of sentimental philanthropists."—Issue of Feb. 11, 1875.

[2] Harper's Weekly, June 9, 1877.

[3] E. E. Sparks, National Development, p. 99.

and concord," and "no North, no South," responded to an invitation to visit the ground of the old Confederacy. In the party, beside the President and Mrs. Hayes, were Secretary Evarts and members of his family, Secretaries Schurz and McCrary, Postmaster-General Key, and the governors of Rhode Island and West Virginia. Crossing the Ohio to Louisville, where, on September 17, the tour was begun, Governor Wade Hampton of South Carolina joined the company, and they proceeded to Nashville, Knoxville, Atlanta, Lynchburg and Charlottesville. The country, the President concluded after his return, is "again one and united." [1]

A few weeks later Hayes and members of the cabinet, including Sherman, certain to be less liked in the South than any other in it, at the invitation of the governor of Virginia, visited Richmond.[2] Patriotic utterances from the same platform by leaders of the adversary armies, and by statesmen who had been arrayed on opposing sides of the question which had nearly compassed the destruction of the Union, allayed distrust and built foundations of returning respect and understanding. The President comported himself with dignity, as he held out a cordial hand to the old enemy, now again to be brother and friend. The applause and the cheers which at frequent points greeted his speeches are proof, if no other testimony were at hand, of the success of what one newspaper correspondent, accompanying the party, described as not else than "a triumphal march." [3]

The President had been not unmindful of the negroes, for whom he now, as at first, had a very heartfelt sympathy. He had been at pains to secure from the Southern leaders, when he met them, assurances of their intention to treat the colored people with kindness and justice. It was his conviction that the freedmen would enjoy greater security under the control of the better white classes of the South than if they should continue to be disturbed by the agitators and demagogues,

[1] Diary and Letters of Hayes, vol. iii, p. 443.
[2] Harper's Weekly, Nov. 17, 1877.
[3] Williams, Life of Hayes, vol. ii, pp. 248–53.

who, with selfish political ends in view, had been for the past
ten years, so mischievously misleading them. Time would
tell, he said, whether he was right in this surmise.[1]

The hour had now come for a declaration of war upon the
President by the coterie of arrogant leaders who had been
directing the government since Andrew Johnson's overthrow,
and by James G. Blaine, who, while he co-operated with them
for his own particular ends, stood apart from the men older in
service at Washington. They had made the Republican party
what it was in recent years—they were that party. All together now sounded the tocsin, and, with the assistance of the
corruptionists still in Congress from the Southern states,
led a revolt calculated to make Hayes's way one which it would
be painful, indeed, for him to follow.[2] At once, upon the forwarding to the Senate of the names of the appointees to the
cabinet, signs of disaffection had been seen. Hayes had recognized none of the mighty men except Morton.[3]

Conkling was egotist enough to view himself as the chief of
these dynasts. He had long known that he could expect to
receive no favors—that they would be extended instead to
the "reform" element in the party, with which he was careful
to have no connections, but his friends had not scrupled to
send an emissary to Hayes, in December, 1876, in the interest
of his appointment as Secretary of State and of the carpetbag senators from the South who were full of fear, not
without reason, for their future.[4] Later Conkling had
vainly urged the appointment of his lieutenant, Thomas C.
Platt, now for four years a member of the House of
Representatives, as Postmaster General, a suggestion which
the President declined.[5] Little could have done Conkling

[1] Williams, Life of Hayes, vol. ii, p. 64; cf. ibid., p. 66.
[2] Cf. John S. Wise, Recollection of Thirteen Presidents, p. 136.
[3] And him only because of his services as a "War Governor."—Diary and
Letters of Hayes, vol. iii, p. 427.
[4] Williams, Life of Hayes, vol. i, pp. 514–5.
[5] "Contemptuously," says Platt in his Autobiography, p. 83; cf. Williams,
Life of Hayes, vol. ii, p. 24; Diary and Letters of Hayes, p. 515. For an
account of Platt's rise to power as a politician see early chapters of Gosnell,
Boss Platt and his New York Machine.

greater affront than the choice of Mr. Evarts to be Secretary of State.[1]

Cameron had demanded that his son "Don" should remain at the head of the War Department, where Grant had placed the young man.[2] He himself was proposed by his friends for the English mission.[3] Blaine would have found satisfaction in Hale's appointment; when that young man from Maine had refused the offer, he insisted with expressions of threat, were he not heard with favor, that another adherent, William P. Frye, be taken for a place in the cabinet.[4] That flaming typification of "regularity" in Republicanism, John A. Logan, to whose seat as a United States senator, David Davis had been elected in Illinois, now so poor that a friend must advance $40 to pay a bill which he owed in Chicago, desired an appointment to the cabinet.[5] Ben Butler had withdrawn from his retirement of two years and was again in the House, now, as in the past, the turbulent enemy of all good measures and all good men. Such leaders, used to the exercise of great and untrammelled powers, were, by nature and interest, unappreciative of Hayes's character and hostile to his outlook. They could be relied upon to antagonize his liberal projects at every point, and their unconcealed enmity would be felt at once.

Thompson, McCrary and Devens might be well enough, but Evarts, who was accredited to New York, where he was an enemy of the Conkling "machine"; Key, who was not only a Democrat, but also an "ex-rebel," chosen on these accounts

---

[1] Williams, Life of Hayes, vol. ii, p. 24; Autobiography of Platt, pp. 83, 85. Conkling, Hoar says, never spoke of Hayes "in public or private without a sneer." (Hoar, Autobiography of 70 Years, vol. i, p. 383.) It is to Conkling that the derisive phrase "snivel service reform" has been ascribed.—Cf. Williams, op. cit., vol. ii, p. 17.

[2] Impressive efforts were made, by petitions presented by M. S. Quay and by visits to Hayes, in the interest of young Cameron's retention in office. All the Republican members of the Pennsylvania delegation in Congress called upon the President-elect in a body at Sherman's house immediately upon his arrival in Washington.—N. Y. Tribune, March 5, 1877. Cf. Williams, op. cit., vol. ii, pp. 22, 24.

[3] Hoar, Autobiography of 70 Years, vol. i, p. 383.

[4] Williams, Life of Hayes, vol. ii, p. 221; Hoar, Autobiography of 70 Years, vol. ii, p. 7.

[5] Diary and Letters of Hayes, vol. iii, pp. 433–4.

to further a policy for which the "regulars" could feel no sympathy, since it would damage, if it did not destroy the "Republican party" in the South; and Schurz, the "renegade," worse than any Democrat, who in 1872 had led the "independent" movement, which had been inaugurated to put down just such men as those that were now judging him, and who, at his own pleasure, had returned to the party in 1876, when, as they well enough knew, he had put his mark upon Hayes and would still more indelibly impress his views upon the President—these three men must be opposed and go down for want of the "advice and consent" which the nominations must receive in the Senate.

The leaders were full of their audacious scheme. They had broken Andrew Johnson upon their wheel; they had gained complete possession of the weak and yielding Grant;[1] they would rend Hayes asunder. They might have done so, if the country, especially the South as it was represented in the Senate by men like Lamar, Gordon and Hill,[2] had not so clearly expressed its approval of the nominations. The press, resolutions of public meetings, letters, telegrams, contact with men whom the magnates of the Senate dare not disregard, all operated in the same sense—in commendation of the President's announced policies and the persons he had chosen to assist him in enforcing his program—whereupon the enemy sullenly left off its opposition, and allowed him to organize his government.[3] The Scot in Cameron rose so high that he, unwilling to subject himself to discipline,[4] resigned his seat as a senator from Pennsylvania, and caused his submissive legislature at Harrisburg to elect in his stead his son (who

[1] Cf. Hoar, Autobiography of 70 Years, vol. ii, p. 46.
[2] Diary and Letters of Hayes, vol. iii, p. 427.
[3] N. Y. Nation, March 15, 1877; Williams, Life of Hayes, vol. ii, pp. 24–9. There were 11 Democratic votes against the confirmation of Sherman on the ground that he was an unreasonable partisan, 2 against Key, 2 against Evarts and 1 (Chaffee of Colorado) against Schurz.—Senate Ex. Journal, vol. xxi, pp. 5–7.
[4] He had been chairman of the Committee on Foreign Relations, since Sumner had been driven from the place, and there he must have met Evarts whom he so much disliked.—Williams, Life of Hayes, vol. ii, p. 28.

could not have a place in the cabinet) to carry on the feud with the administration.

The President's policy in relation to the South furnished theme and excuse for much tirade directed against him. It was said that there had been corrupt bargaining—he had promised the South its freedom from soldiers and carpetbaggers, if the Democrats in Congress from that part of the Union would forego their opposition to him in the work of completing the count.[1] But, when pressed to do so, he had merely repeated, and in a quite guarded way, what he had said in his letter of acceptance.[2] Nor had any of his friends in the Wormley Conference done aught which could involve him improperly.[3] He was acting in answer to his convictions, as any one of fair judgment must have seen then, and can clearly comprehend now, with no obligations to discharge, and without regard for his personal advantage, which, if he had had this in mind, lay in a quite different direction.

Blaine had leaped into prominence as a Presidential candidate in the convention of 1876 by "waving the bloody shirt," and he was on his feet at once for further activity of the same kind in furtherance of the ambitions which he entertained in reference to 1880. Kellogg, for his share in perpetuating and defending the wrongs which the Republicans had imposed upon Louisiana, was, upon leaving the governorship, to be sent back to the United States Senate, from which he had been called in 1872 by his friends in the New Orleans custom house for the contest with McEnery. Hayes had been inaugurated on Monday. On Tuesday Blaine espoused the cause of the notorious carpetbagger. He would, by appealing to the country on this issue, make himself the party leader in the Senate, to which he had just come, and checkmate the President, whose well known design it was to do away, in so far as this

[1] Williams, Life of Hayes, vol. ii, pp. 66–7; cf. Chamberlain in Allen, Governor Chamberlain's Administration, p. 520.
[2] Cf. Williams, Life of Hayes, vol. ii, p. 36.
[3] Cf. remarks of Foster and Ellis in House of Representatives in 1878, Cong. Record, 45th Cong. 2nd sess., pp. 1010–11; E. E. Sparks, National Development, p. 98.

might be possible, with prejudice and passion, and to pacify the sections.[1] The orator was effusively congratulated by admirers on the floor and in the gallery, and by the old Radical Republican press. He found occasion to continue his attacks for his own advertisement in the same circles, as Hayes's policy in South Carolina and Louisiana unfolded.[2] The efforts made unofficially by Stanley Matthews to secure the retirement of Packard and Chamberlain in the interest of peace and order in the two states Blaine assailed, with a dashing show of patriotism not lost upon the imaginations of our young Northern fire-eaters. He would not desert "the remnant of the brave men who have borne the flag and the brunt of the battle in the Southern states against persecutions unparallelled in this country." When he should cease "to stand for Southern Union men of both colors," he ejaculated, with a flourish of his trumpets, "may my tongue cleave to the roof of my mouth and my right hand forget its cunning."[3]

The invitation of Hayes to Chamberlain and Hampton to come to Washington to discuss their differences, and the appointment of the Louisiana commission furnished the President's foes with new opportunities for activity. Fortunately for Hayes the senators, their special session at an end, went home on March 17, and he wisely, when, on May 5, he called an extra session of Congress, forebore selecting a date for it to convene earlier than the 15th day of the next October,[4] so that the administration might have a few months in which it would be little disturbed by the imperious and vindictive partisans who found in themselves, and not in the President, the talent and the sagacity necessary for the leadership of the party.[5]

But they were heard from in speech,[6] by letter, and through

[1] Cong. Record, 45th Cong. 1st sess., p. 16; cf. Williams, Life of Hayes, vol. ii, p. 16. An indication of the insincerity of Blaine's course on this subject may, perhaps, be found in Hoar, Autobiography of 70 Years, vol. ii, p. 12.

[2] Williams, Life of Hayes, vol. ii, p. 43.

[3] Cong. Record, 45th Cong. 1st sess., p. 21.

[4] Diary and Letters of Hayes, vol. iii, pp. 428, 429.

[5] Cf. N. Y. Nation, May 17, 1877.

[6] As at Woodstock, Conn., on July 4; cf. E. E. Sparks, National Development, pp. 108–109.

"interviews" in the newspapers.[1] The venerable "Ben" Wade, who had seconded the nomination of Hayes in the Cincinnati convention, had been "deceived, betrayed and humiliated." He was filled with "inexpressible indignation." [2] The old Abolitionists came to the support of the politicians. It were "far better to have Tilden than Hayes with such a policy," said Wendell Phillips; it were "madness" to withdraw the troops from the South. Hereafter there would be no Republican state south of Pennsylvania.[3] The President's Southern policy was a "flagrant betrayal of the trust so confidently committed to his hands," said William Lloyd Garrison. The party should repudiate it. It indicated "a childish credulity, a blindness of vision and an imbecility of judgment equally surprising and deplorable." [4]

Packard and Chamberlain, who had not left their offices without addresses to their constitutents intended for the ear of the country, and other Southern Republicans, still filled the air with charges impugning the faith of the President. Hayes's action, said Chamberlain, was "unconstitutional and revolutionary, subversive of constitutional guarantees and false to every dictate of political honor, public justice and good morals"; it formed the "basest passage" in our political history.[5] Packard, was for driving out of the party moderates like Hayes and the men whom the President had gathered around him. This course only would save it from dissolution and ruin.[6] Blaine, and those who spoke as he, came to be called "Stalwarts."[7]

[1] See., e.g., Blaine in Boston Herald, quoted in N. Y. Nation, April 19, 1877; Williams, Life of Hayes, vol. ii, p. 65.
[2] From a letter to U. H. Painter, a Washington correspondent, in N. Y. Tribune, April 24, 1877.
[3] Gail Hamilton, Life of Blaine, p. 426.
[4] Phila. Inquirer, Oct. 30, 1877.
[5] Allen, Governor Chamberlain's Administration, pp. 519–20; cf. N. Y. Nation, May 24, 1877.
[6] E. E. Sparks, National Development, pp. 99–100.
[7] Probably ascribable to a passage in one of Blaine's own letters. Cf. his communication to the Boston Herald, when, in referring to the attitude of the Boston press toward the President's desertion of Chamberlain, he said that it now no more represented "the stalwart Republican feeling of New England," than this same press had done so, when, in 1851, it had

The Southern problem having been disposed of, the President was at liberty to give his attention to a still more difficult question. Both parties, in their platforms in 1876, had made protestations on the subject of the civil service. The hunt, by the Republican leaders for offices for their henchmen, in nation, state, city and county, degraded American government. So evil had come to be the system of giving out places, large and small, as rewards for party service, instead of for competency, faithfulness or other personal merit, that it was intolerable from the standpoint of all intelligent observers of our politics. Sinecures were created to satisfy the demands of those who, with friends, relations, and retainers, wished, on one account or another, to quarter them on the government. Men were appointed to the salary, Schurz had said one day in the Senate, and not to the office.[1]   It was not better than giving money directly out of the Treasury to Conkling, or Cameron, or Logan, or Butler for him to expend for his own aggrandizement among a corrupted constitutency in New York, Pennsylvania, Illinois or Massachusetts.[2]

In the Federal service every post office, navy yard, custom house, tax office, Indian agency was filled with men who were of but limited use in, if they were not a positive block to, the efficient administration of the government. Held in subjection by threats of dismissal, if they did not vote the Republican party ticket and work for its success at each recurring election, contribute a percentage of their salaries to help meet the costs of political campaigns, this great body of tinklers and cravens, set about in centres over all the land, were, aside from the theft which it was to pay large sums of money to unfit and superfluous

demanded the enforcement of the Fugitive Slave Law.—N. Y. Tribune, April 12, 1877.

[1] January 27, 1871.

[2] A correspondent in New York wrote to Senator J. S. Morrill on Nov. 29, 1874, that the cause of our condition was to be found in political rings and cliques in the states, which were composed, instead of the wisest, best and most influential citizens of those states, of "cunning and unscrupulous persons." "So corrupt are those rings," he continued, "that, as with us in New York, scarcely an honest man is admitted to a state or Federal office." —Morrill Papers, Library of Congress.

persons and the consequent demoralization of the service, a menace, in a larger sense, to our republican institutions.[1]

Nothing had been done by Grant toward a keeping of his promises on the point, as George William Curtis, while chairman of the civil service commission, was ready to testify when he resigned, and, as Dorman B. Eaton learned afterward. Grant's administrations had been in defiance of all the principles looking to the abolishment of this great and growing wrong, and the problem fell to the portion of Hayes. He had said what it was in his mind to do on this point, as well as in reference to the South. He had at his back the law of March 3, 1871, which had been rendered meaningless by Grant, and, as and when he could, he would act in conformity with its provisions, pending further legislation by Congress. By his own example at least he would do what Grant had failed to do—he would, in so far as authority rested with him, and in so far as action along this line was practicable, make efficiency the test for holding public office.[2]

The President early let it be understood that the brother-in-law and other relations, who had brought the repeated charge of nepotism upon Grant, would not lay a discreditable hand upon the new administration.[3] He would dismiss men already in office only for the improvement of the service.[4] Applications for positions need not be addressed to him personally, since the heads of the departments would determine, subject only to his general supervision, how their departments should be organized.[5]

These officers acted without delay. Schurz, as might have been expected, immediately promulgated sound rules for the Interior Department and put them into execution,[6] and others

---

[1] Cf. Letters and Recollections of J. M. Forbes, vol. ii, p. 189.

[2] Cf. Williams, Life of Hayes, vol. ii, p. 74.

[3] Ibid., vol. ii, p. 75; N. Y. Tribune, March 16, 1876. It has been said that Stanley Matthews was a brother-in-law. He was not; he had married a cousin of Mrs. Hayes. Matthews had long been an important figure in politics. He and Hayes were old associates and friends in public life.

[4] At the end of the first year of his administration he said that he had made fewer removals than any other President for the same time since John Quincy Adams.—Williams, Life of Hayes, vol. ii, p. 89.

[5] Ibid., p. 75.

[6] Schurz, Reminiscences, vol. iii, pp. 377–81.

issued orders and adopted measures calculated to fulfill the pledges of the President and of the party platform. Instantly the employees of the government, relieved from fear of reprisals and freed from party constraint generally, with the example of industry under discipline before them, gave it more useful service.[1] Sherman, as a partisan, was far from sharing all the enthusiasm of Hayes and Schurz for the reform,[2] and it was in the Treasury that many of the corruptions of the Grant administration were entrenched.

The New York custom house, a nest of iniquity, as was proven while it stood under the direction of "Tom" Murphy, was only a little better place with another Conkling adherent, Chester A. Arthur, in charge of its affairs. It was resolved to appoint a commission, under the chairmanship of John Jay, to investigate the conduct of this office. Similar commissions were named to institute similar inquiries as to the management of the custom houses at Philadelphia, San Francisco and New Orleans. In each case two private citizens and one officer of the government constituted the investigating body.[3] The disclosures, as could have been anticipated, were appalling from the point of view of every well disposed and intelligent citizen.

The New York office appeared to be the worst only because of the greater magnitude of the business transacted in it—from 70 to 75 per cent of all the taxes paid upon imports coming into the country were collected in that city—[4] and the opportunities, therefore, which were at hand to mulct the government under cover of collecting the revenues, and because the commission conducting the inquiry in this case was composed of men bent upon the discovery of wrong, if it existed, and not upon glozing it over with fair report. Scores of persons whom Conkling and his "machine" had imposed upon the Treasury, it was revealed, rendered little if any useful service. Quite 200 men could be discharged without overburdening with labor any of

[1] Williams, Life of Hayes, vol. ii, pp. 76–7.
[2] Cf. Letters of C. E. Norton, vol. ii, p. 82.
[3] Cf. Sherman's Recollections, vol. ii, p. 673; House Ex. Doc., 45th Cong. 1st sess., no. 8, p. i; N. Y. Nation, June 7, 1877.
[4] House Ex. Doc., 45th Cong. 1st sess., no. 8, p. 16.

the remaining employees. To offices requiring "the skill and experience of experts" men were appointed, "at the request of politicians," without any regard for their fitness to perform the duties of their places. The whole system, calculated as it was "to encourage and perpetuate official ignorance, inefficiency and corruption," was "perverting the powers of government to personal and party ends . . . burdened the country with debt and taxes, and assisted to prostrate the trade and industry of the nation." Assessments upon the salaries of the men for party uses, and the "improper acceptance of gratuities" still further demoralized the service.[1]

It was May 26 when Hayes, apprised of at least some of the findings of Mr. Jay and his associates, ordered that no useless man should be retained, no assessments should be levied upon salaries by party leaders, no officer should be chosen for any reason except his efficiency in the performance of the duties with which he was charged, and his fidelity to duty. The collection of the revenues should be "organized on a strictly business basis."[2] On June 22 he went further. The President restated his rules, in so far as they related to the political activity of government employees. He made his order applicable to every department of the civil service, and he said that he desired it to be understood "by every officer of the general government" that such officer should "conform his conduct" to the "requirements" of that order.[3] It was, "after the rout of the carpetbaggers at the South," said the New York Nation, "the best thing" Mr. Hayes had yet done for politics.[4]

The dismissal of many persons in government employ; the appointment of better ones in their stead, if they were not supernumeraries, kept in place solely for personal or party ends; the reorganization of the service, with proficiency in view, went forward during the summer, amid the sullen, if not angry

[1] House Ex. Doc., 45th Cong. 1st sess., no. 8, pp. 15–16.
[2] Ibid., p. 17; Williams, Life of Hayes, vol. ii, p. 77; Sherman's Recollections, vol. ii, p. 674.
[3] Williams, Life of Hayes, vol. ii, pp. 79–80.
[4] Issue of June 28, 1877.

complaint of the interests affected, and of that part of the
Republican press which saw obliquely through their eyes. The
advocates of the reform persisted with what seemed, to the
politicians of the Conkling and Cameron type, a pestilent
energy. The reformers were sneered at as "doctrinaires and
impracticables." The scheme was Chinese and Prussian, the
latter suggestion containing a thrust at Schurz, whose foreign
birth always made it possible to denounce him and his measures,
when necessity invited it, as "un-American." At the same time,
very fortunately, the policy of the administration elicited the
approval of men and newspapers whose opinions were better
entitled to respect.[1]

But promise was not entirely fulfilled and dissatisfaction continued to be expressed by the civil service "reformers."[2] The
demands of some of the number, actuated as they were by the
best impulses, and protesting as they did against one of the most
vexatious of wrongs, were unreasonable. They were not willing to give due consideration to the exigencies of party government in a democracy, and, in particular, to these exigencies as
they affected our republic at this time in its history. Its condition was not normal; it was rising from disorders brought upon
it by the war. It was much that honest, intelligent, resolute
men, with high standards, were at the head of the government,
if they were not realizing all that their friends urged upon them
and expected of their administration.[3]

It was pointed out that some old party "war horses" were
being appointed to office. Ex-Senator Lot M. Morrill of
Maine had been made collector of customs at Portland, more
by way of pensioning a decrepit politician than in hope of receiving any valuable returns in service in the place. Logan,
in Hayes's pity for his poverty, recalling his services to the
Union in the war, but for an outburst of popular opposition,
would, probably, have been appointed collector of the port at

---

[1] G. W. Curtis was impressed with Hayes's sincerity. See Letters of
Charles Eliot Norton, vol. ii, p. 70.

[2] Cf. Bristow to Schurz in Schurz, Speeches, vol. iii, p. 418; N. Y. Nation,
March 7, 1878; Merriam, Life of Bowles, vol. ii, p. 421.

[3] Cf. Samuel Bowles to Schurz in Schurz, Speeches, vol. iii, p. 414.

Chicago.[1] Boutwell, "out of work," was taken care of. The President's private secretary desired a lucrative consulship—he was sent to Frankfort-on-the-Main.[2] Fred Douglass, to please the negroes, was made marshal of the District of Columbia.[3] The English mission, it was said, had been offered to the Pennsylvania delegation in Congress,[4] the German mission to the Illinois delegation.[5] A lady in reduced circumstances, whom her friends wished to aid, entirely wanting in experience, was made postmistress of Louisville.[6] Men who should have been removed for their obvious incapacity continued in their posts. Grant's old clerks in the White House, masters of wickedness, it was complained, were still in place. General Boynton, and other newspaper correspondents stationed in Washington, would not visit the President's business offices while these men remained.[7] Simmons, Butler's friend, was still collector of customs at Boston.[8] Babcock, than whom none so abundantly deserved incontinent discharge, was on the pay roll of the government at Baltimore, where he was the head of the engineers' department of the Fifth Lighthouse District.[9] Badeau continued to dishonor the foreign service in the consulate general at London, though at the end of the year 1877 he was dropped from the army, and ceased to enjoy pay as a military man in addition to his large receipts as a civil officer.[10]

[1] Diary and Letters of Hayes, vol. ii, pp. 433–4.
[2] Alfred E. Lee, private secretary of Hayes while he had been governor of Ohio.
[3] N. Y. Nation, June 7, 1877.
[4] An unpleasant situation created by Evarts.—Diary and Letters of Hayes, vol. iii, pp. 514–5.
[5] If so, the English mission had first been tendered to others, as, e.g., George William Curtis. (Cary, Life of Curtis, pp. 253–4; Letters of C. E. Norton, vol. ii, pp. 66–8.) The German mission was most suitably bestowed upon a leading man of letters, Bayard Taylor, deeply and sympathetically interested in the people among whom he was to dwell.
[6] N. Y. Nation, June 7, 1877; cf. Diary and Letters of Hayes, vol. iii, p. 436.
[7] Diary and Letters of Hayes, vol. iii, p. 446.
[8] Cf. Hoar, Autobiography of 70 Years, vol. ii, pp. 2–3. Simmons was not removed until 1878.—Cf. Harper's Weekly, March 16, 1878.
[9] N. Y. Tribune, March 16, 1877; cf. N. Y. Nation, June 7, July 12 and Dec. 20, 1877.
[10] Phila. Inquirer, Jan. 2, 1878.

But no such damage to Hayes's prestige on the subject of the civil service came from any source as in connection with his appointments in the South. It was soon made clear that a number of bargains, which had been struck while he was being counted in, were now to be quietly consummated, though not without attracting the attention of the country. "Republicans" who were set aside in the turning over of the Southern state governments to the Democrats must be solaced with new offices.

The honors which were bestowed upon the "visiting statesmen" were viewed jealously, and evoked from Tilden's friends many a hint of corruption. Even the appointment to cabinet places of Evarts and Sherman, who had so actively espoused the cause of Hayes, was held to have been bound up somehow with the settlement of the dispute over the count. Ex-Governor Noyes was appointed minister to France, E. W. Stoughton, minister to Russia, and John A. Kasson, minister to Austria. Stanley Matthews was sent to the United States Senate from Ohio in the place which Sherman had vacated. Lew Wallace was to have gone to Bolivia or Brazil, but, declining,[1] he was appointed governor of New Mexico, where he wrote "Ben Hur."[2] Such a connection as there was a wish to establish between the proceedings at Tallahassee and at New Orleans in relation to the count and the selection of the "pilgrims" for lucrative positions in the administration need not employ retrospective attention. They were not unworthy men; they were, for the most part, as competent as any that could have been named for the places which they were invited to fill. Several of them were clearly marked out by pre-eminent fitness for their offices. They were friends of Hayes before they went South, proceeded thither, perhaps, as such, and that he should choose them for preferment can have led to no fair criticism.

The selection for valuable posts of various carpetbaggers, against whom the movement to improve the Southern situation was directed, and the reward, by appointment to offices

[1] Autobiography of Lew Wallace, vol. ii, pp. 911–12.
[2] Ibid., pp. 921, 923.

of greater or less value, of many of the hewers of wood and drawers of water in the business of making Florida and Louisiana Republican are not so defensible. In the first place Packard, who might have become a dangerous enemy if he had been permitted to proceed with his abuse of the administration, after being set out of the governorship to which he seemed to have been elected in Louisiana, was to be conciliated. He held himself at a high price. At a time when shipping to and from England was largely centred at Liverpool the consulship at that port was considered to be the most lucrative post in the Federal service. The fees, under the prevailing system, which were collected there in a year, it was commonly stated, amounted to a sum larger than the salary of the President of the United States. Lucius Fairchild, appointed to the office by Grant in 1872, was to be relieved and sent to Paris to make way for the vituperative leader of the Republican party in Louisiana, who, it was hoped, might have been satisfied by a mission to some Central or South American state.[1] It was May, 1878,[2] before this daring appointment was gazetted, to be promptly confirmed by the Senate.[3] Chamberlain, who was a gentleman, was left to make his way in the world as best he could in the practice of the law in New York. Stearns, ousted as governor of Florida, received the honor of an appointment as a commissioner of the Hot Springs of Arkansas. Kellogg having got from the negro-carpetbag legislature of Louisiana, before it was disrupted, an election to the United States Senate, was dexterous enough at Washington, aided by Blaine, as we have seen, and other partisans, to gain admission to that body without great delay. All of the members of the Louisiana returning board received places, either for themselves or for members of their families, or both, as did the secretaries and clerks of that infamous body of men.[4]

The number of minor figures in the play, both white and black, who were appointed to various Federal positions in the South,

[1] New York Tribune, April 28, 1877.
[2] Cf. N. Y. Nation, May 9 and 30, 1878.
[3] By a vote of 27 to 23.—Senate Ex. Journal, vol. xxi, p. 326.
[4] Bigelow, Life of Tilden, vol. ii, pp. 54–5.

or were brought to Washington for reward in the departments was large. No less than 47 persons in the legislature of Louisiana, which had been instrumental in advancing Kellogg to Washington, were rewarded with places in the Federal service.[1]

The Democrats did not cease to point to the facts, as they came to public knowledge, in confirmation of what they had said, and continued to believe, was a great political deal. It wore such an appearance. The point of contact with the administration, as could have been foretold, was in the Treasury Department. Sherman had been a leader in Louisiana, he had taken the first place in assuring Hayes of the clearness of the Republican title to the Presidency, and, through the portals of the office of such a partisan, the head of a department which had many favors to bestow, the Southern traders easily entered. All of the 47 men in the Louisiana legislature who took Federal office received Treasury appointments, and all but 16 of the whole number who were connected with the negotiations, which had led to Hayes's securing the electoral votes of Louisiana, and who were appointed to Federal places of any kind, accepted their rewards at the hands of Sherman.[2] It is clear enough that it is at this point that Hayes's record presents its least favorable side to view.

It has been said that he was informed of only a part of what proceeded in the repayment of debts which had been incurred in Florida and Louisiana, that others, and particularly Sherman, acted on their own accounts. But that the President was aware of most of what went on around him in this particular there is no doubt. In August, 1877, in his Diary he was deploring his "mistakes." He had removed men who, perhaps, "ought to have been retained." He had appointed "wrong men."[3] In October he was again complaining to himself of

[1] Bigelow, Life of Tilden, vol. ii, p. 54.

[2] Ibid., p. 54; cf. Schurz, Reminiscences, vol. iii, p. 382. Hayes believed the number of such appointments to be "grossly exaggerated." (Cf. Williams, Life of Hayes, vol. ii, p. 109.) They are classified and totalled in Bigelow, Letters and Memorials of Tilden, vol. ii, pp. 565–7; House Reports, 45th Cong. 3rd sess., no. 140, pp. 21–2, 48–9.

[3] Williams, Life of Hayes, vol. ii, p. 81.

himself. In his "anxiety to complete the great task of pacification" he had neglected to give "due attention" to the civil service. He would endeavor to make amends in the future.[1]

To some impatient idealists on one side, and the politicians on the other, to whom "reform" was, in any case, anathema, it was a patent inconsistency for the President to appoint to office such men as Sherman imposed upon him, and he must certainly have expected to receive criticism for his course from these sources.[2] But, having cleared away the Southern question, he was deeply involved, throughout his administration, in a struggle with the enemies of a sound currency system, which is to be described in a later place. In coping with ignorant forces, which threatened all society with havoc, some measures in small fields, in themselves recognized to be obnoxious, must now and again be taken to gain larger ends.[3] The important public service rendered to the country in achieving the resumption of specie payments, which called for acute management, were it to be successful, in the face of organized and powerful opposition, will outweigh, in any correct appraisement of the administration, the questionable disposition of a few appointments to Federal office.

Grave political problems, the subject of factional strife, were complicated with an attack by mischief-making leaders of the Democratic party upon the President's title to his office,[4] which, too, is to be subsequently discussed, and this movement, until it was frustrated in a way as surprising as it was complete, served, on its side, to make the President's course in reference to civil service reform not so straightforward as he could have liked it to be.

The President was sincerely desirous of a return of the "ancient concord"[5] between North and South, which could not exist while there were dual governments. Every candid man knew

[1] Williams, Life of Hayes, vol. ii, p. 83.
[2] Cf. Schurz, Reminiscences, vol. iii, p. 382.
[3] Cf. Diary of Hayes, entry for May 15, 1891, in Williams, Life of Hayes, vol. ii, p. 109.
[4] Cf. Hoar, Autobiography of 70 Years, vol. ii, pp. 41–4.
[5] Williams, Life of Hayes, vol. ii, p. 81.

that such conditions as prevailed in the South could not indefinitely endure. Every competent and honest reviewer of the period will now say that they were allowed to continue much too long.[1] It was Hayes's task, and one of the most valuable of his services, to bring such an untoward state of affairs to an end. He acted as a Republican, under criticism; neither Tilden, nor any other Democrat, could have done so much, without opposition, which might have reached a violent form.[2]

It was undoubtedly a necessary part of the general work in hand, after suppressing the carpetbag governments, to conciliate some of the leaders of these governments, else dangerous commotion might have recurred. How much more than what it was tactful and expedient to do in this direction was done it is difficult to determine. Whatever his apparent shortcomings the fact remains that Hayes had an honest determination, if he could bring so much about, to make real the theories which he and other untiring and useful men entertained regarding civil service reform.[3] Schurz, at his shoulder,[4] who was setting the country a fine example in the administration of the Interior Department, would not have permitted him to neglect this question,[5] if he himself had wished it out of his sight. That he had not done very ill was proven by the fact that before October 15, when Congress would meet, he was at loggerheads with all the corrupt and arrogant men who led, and who had too long controlled his party.

Republican state conventions adjourned, as in Iowa[6] and Maine, without commending him—by their silence or indirec-

[1] Cf. E. E. Sparks, National Development, p. 101.

[2] It could be said of Hayes, to stop detractors in the North, as it could not have been said of Tilden—"President Hayes from his early manhood had been an anti-slavery man; his life was imperilled on many battlefields in the great cause of liberty," etc. Thus spoke John Sherman to allay Republican disaffection. See his Recollections, vol. i, p. 589.

[3] Cf. N. Y. Nation, July 19, 1877. "I see no leadership in our present politics, worthy of respect but his," said Samuel Bowles.—Merriam, Life of Bowles, vol. ii, pp. 430-31.

[4] Cf. Schurz's speech at the Harvard commencement.—N. Y. Nation, July 5, 1877.

[5] Cf. N. Y. Nation, March 7, 1878; Reminiscences of Schurz, vol. iii, pp. 381-2.

[6] N. Y. Nation, July 5, 1877.

tion they, indeed, expressed a censure of his policies.[1] Pennsylvania gave him only sparing and qualified praise. But the centre of hostility to the administration was in New York. The Jay commission had made its report concerning the custom house in that city, of which for more than five years Arthur had been the administrative head. While Arthur had appointed a commission of his own to investigate the management of the office, had reduced his force, in reply to the President's orders of May and June, 1877, and had made some other changes, which might be taken to be in the interest of better service,[2] it was plain that he was adopting no practical or effective measures with a sincere purpose of dissociating the office from Conkling's New York Republican "machine." Alonzo B. Cornell, who was the naval officer at New York, defiantly continued to act as chairman of the New York Republican state committee, though party activity of this kind, while in government employ, had been distinctly prohibited by the President. In such an attitude he received the encouragement of Conkling who, with "swelling port and indomitable conceit,"[3] inflamed by Evarts's presence in the Cabinet, by Hayes's friendship for George William Curtis and by the denial at the White House of his suggestions and demands, was losing no opportunity personally to emphasize his small respect for, and opposition to, the President.

The wrath of the spoilsmen in New York, their eyes set upon no public question above appointments of collectors, appraisers, gaugers, weighers, and tidewaiters, to whom the party which they arbitrarily controlled, was merely an organization to enable them to reach their hands into the Treasury of the United States, came to loud utterance at the Republican state convention in Rochester in September, 1877. Conkling's lieutenant, Thomas C. Platt, spoke insolently on this occasion. The importance of civil service had been "magnified by demagogues" into "unseemly proportions." "Hungry expectants of office" stood on street corners and shouted "the shibboleth" until they were

---

[1] Cf. Harper's Weekly, Sep. 15, 1877.
[2] House Ex. Doc., 45th Cong. 2nd sess., no. 25, p. 14.
[3] N.Y. Nation, Oct. 4, 1877.

"hoarse and weary." The "Independent" rolled it "as a sweet morsel under his tongue," and daily blurted it in "the face of a nauseated public." [1] The whole subject had been "inaugurated for the sole purpose of disrupting the party" in New York state.[2] The President was denounced on another account. He had made the South "solid." In every Southern state the Republican organization was "demoralized, paralyzed and politically crushed out." [3] Hayes had done for the Democrats "all that Mr. Tilden could have done." [4]

Conkling himself passed up and down the aisles of the convention hall, the Apollo that his admirers found him to be, his "Hyperion curl" rolling down his forehead,[5] "hurling barbed epithets" at the President. Nor did he spare George William Curtis, a delegate seated nearby among foes, who were assembled, indeed, to enjoy their leader's forensic flings at the man who parted his hair "in the middle," the "man milliner," the "dillettante" and "carpet knight of politics," and who did not weary of painting them for what they were in the columns of Harper's Weekly.[6]

Conkling having "scorched" Hayes "unmercifully," [7] his convention having exultingly refused to adopt a resolution which Curtis had offered, commending the administration, the senator from New York was now in that place which Blaine had earlier made an effort to occupy—he was the leader of the enemies of the administration. The Conkling newspapers savagely attacked the President throughout the campaign,[8] and party organs in the country at large followed their example. The election in

[1] Autobiography of Platt, p. 89.
[2] Ibid., pp. 84–5; cf. N. Y. Nation, Oct. 4, 1877.
[3] Autobiography of Platt, p. 91.
[4] Ibid., p. 92.
[5] Ibid., p. 55.
[6] Cf. ibid., pp. 85, 93; Cary, Life of Curtis, pp. 257–8; Depew, Memories of 80 Years, pp. 79–89; Conkling, Life of Conkling, pp. 538–49; D. S. Alexander, Political History of N. Y., vol. iii, pp. 370–77. It was in this speech that Conkling, with all his actor-like and elocutionary grandeur, exclaimed—"When Dr. Johnson said that patriotism was the last refuge of a scoundrel he ignored the enormous possibilities of the word refawr-rm."—Cf. Alexander, loc. cit.
[7] Autobiography of Platt, p. 85.
[8] Ibid., p. 93. .

the President's own state of Ohio in 1877 returned a Democratic majority of some 20,000, Pennsylvania, a Democratic majority of nearly 10,000. In the new House of Representatives, when it assembled for its special session in October, the Democrats would have a majority—small, (it was but 13) but enough to enable them to re-elect Randall over Garfield for speaker, and to control the course of legislation. The Republican majority in the Senate had been reduced until it was precarious. One more vote fell away when Morton died on November 1, 1877, to be succeeded by a Democrat. After Kellogg, Republican, and Butler, Democrat, were seated for Louisiana and South Carolina respectively, on December 1, and James B. Eustis, Democrat, was admitted from Louisiana on December 10, 1877, the balance stood at 38 Republicans and 37 Democrats, with all eyes upon David Davis who played the rôle of an "independent," wavering from side to side on important issues,[1] in which activity he was emulated by two corrupt Southern carpetbaggers, held to be Republicans. If the control of the Senate had not definitely passed from the Republican party, the day was measurably near when it would do so.[2] It was an ill prospect, indeed, which the President faced in the winter of 1877–78.

Sherman put forth his ablest endeavors to keep the insurgents in order,[3] but they were bent upon their own measures. Evarts, Schurz and Key in the cabinet were denounced—they were not Republicans. The administration's Southern policy, and its course in reference to the civil service, which would deprive senators and representatives of control of the patronage, the "Stalwarts" said, were disorganizing the party.[4] Hayes's way was not made the easier when Democrats in Congress declared that he was conducting the government "on the principles of the great Democratic party."[5]

[1] Cf. Hoar, Autobiography of 70 Years, vol. ii, pp. 63–4.
[2] Cf. McPherson's Handbook for 1878, pp. 141–2; N. Y. Nation, Nov. 29, 1877.
[3] Cf. Williams, Life of Hayes, vol. ii, p. 82; N. Y. Nation, Oct. 25, 1877.
[4] Williams, Life of Hayes, vol. ii, pp. 82–3.
[5] Cong. Record, 55th Cong. special sess., p. 127. More commendation than came to him from that side would have been his, but for their duty

The special session was mainly occupied, in the House, with an acrimonious discussion of the currency question, which was now to be pressed into a foremost place as a political issue; in the Senate, by the Southern question, reopened in the debates over the admission of claimants to seats from Louisiana and South Carolina.

The President, in spite of the threatening attitude of his foes, was in no mood to parley with them. The New York post office under General Thomas L. James, though he was an appointee of Grant and enjoyed the favor of Conkling, was being administered in conformity with rules insuring efficient service. It was an example before the eyes of the people of the city,[1] and there was no valid reason why the other Federal offices should not have equally competent direction. The President had received further communications from Mr. Jay's commission of inquiry. On July 4 a second report [2] followed the first, which had been dated May 24. A third report was submitted on July 21.[3] The commission by this time had extended its inquiries to the department of weighers and gaugers. A fourth report, on August 31, covered the conduct of the appraiser's office, where such rascalities throve as could not be patiently described.[4]

At the naval office errors had been discovered in the accounts, indicating a loss to the government of $1,500,000 annually.[5] The provision of law, making it a punishable offense for a customs officer to accept gratuities and bribes, was a dead letter. Fees, indeed, were exacted of merchants, thus greatly increasing the salaries of the men.[6] Favorites who were paying for immunity from taxation, were enabled, by collusion with Conkling's henchmen, installed in influential places, to reap such advantages that honest men, if not driven to abandon their

of iterating and reiterating that he had been seated by fraud and, in occupying the office, was a "usurper."
[1] Cf. Williams, Life of Hayes, pp. 93, 96, 111.
[2] House Ex. Doc., 45th Cong. 1st sess., no. 8, pp. 36–42.
[3] Ibid., pp. 50–53.
[4] Ibid., pp. 58–68.
[5] Ibid., p. 38.
[6] Ibid., p. 39.

business, were obliged to buy of the "smugglers." As an instance in point it was cheaper to obtain silk in the New York market through these agencies than to import it directly.[1] Maladministration had driven trade to other ports, where, however, merchants, in the face of such corruption at New York, were also unable to make fair progress. William Henry Smith, the valued friend of Hayes, whom he had appointed collector of customs at Chicago in the room of J. Russell Jones, home from Belgium, spoilsman and friend of Grant, who, having refused to resign, was dismissed,[2] said that honest merchants in that city keenly felt the competition of interests which were being improperly favored by the Federal authorities at New York.[3]

Generally, and on all sides, the commission found employees who were incompetent as well as supernumerary. Some never made a motion to serve the government. Their exertions ended with "signing their names to the pay rolls and receiving their pay." Many incumbents of responsible places were disqualified by age and by indifference to the gravity of their tasks; others, by simple ignorance and incapacity. Men were installed in positions at the dictation of the party leaders to perform the "delicate duties" of the appraiser's office who were " better fitted to hoe and plow." [4]   Every evil which could enter the civil service through politics flourished unashamed in this place.[5]

In Philadelphia not dissimilar conditions were reported by the committee appointed to inquire into the conduct of the agencies established for the collection of the customs revenues at that port. The naval officer and the port physician resided at Lancaster, a place 70 miles away, where they had their own business and professional interests. The surveyor of the port was the editor of a country newspaper at a town located still farther in the interior of the state; other principal officers,

---

[1] House Ex. Doc., 45th Cong. 1st sess., no. 8, p. 59; cf. ibid., p. 39.
[2] Diary and Letters of Hayes, vol. iii, p. 451.
[3] Williams, Life of Hayes, vol. ii, p. 91.
[4] Ibid., p. 38.
[5] Cf. N. Y. Nation, May 31, Aug. 2 and 23, 1877.

appointed for political reasons, continued to publish papers, keep drug stores, manage inns and butcher cattle in their respective communities, while drawing pay from the government for work which they did not perform, and were unfitted for performing, in Philadelphia.[1]

The situation called aloud for immediate action. The duty could not have been ignored had there been a wish on the part of the President to evade it. He had determined upon the removal of Arthur and Cornell at New York. In September, 1877, they were asked to resign. Arthur was offered the solace of the consulship at Paris, if he would step out of his place. No enticement would move either of the incumbents,[2] and, on October 29, the President sent to the Senate the names of Theodore Roosevelt, a well known merchant in New York,[3] to be collector of the port and L. Bradford Prince to be naval officer. Edwin A. Merritt was nominated to be surveyor of the port to succeed Mr. Sharpe, whose term had expired.[4]

The reading of the names in the Senate was greeted with laughter.[5] They were referred to a committee of which Conkling was the chairman. His pride had been sorely wounded. He acted upon the principle that no one should be appointed to Federal office in the state of New York without his permission, previously secured, a plain statement of the "boss" system of government, which he, and such as he, had been developing to a high state of perfection.[6] The President's action was not so good a joke as it seemed. So deeply disturbed were the spoilsmen by what was seen that, at a gathering of the Republican senators, held on November 10, Conkling and other enemies of the administration strove to read the President out of the party. His friends nobly defended

[1] House Ex. Doc., 45th Cong. 1st sess., no. 8, pp. 84–5.

[2] Sherman's Recollections, vol. ii, pp. 679–82; N. Y. Nation, Sep. 6 and 13 and Dec. 13, 1877.

[3] Father of Theodore Roosevelt, 26th President of the United States.

[4] Senate Ex. Journal, vol. xxi, pp. 98–9. The selections, except Mr. Roosevelt, were not approved by the civil service reformers.—Cf. Harper's Weekly, Nov. 17, 1877.

[5] Phila. Inquirer, Oct. 30, 1877.

[6] Cf. Hayes's Diary and his letter to W. H. Smith in Williams, Life of Hayes, vol. ii, p. 87; also Diary in ibid., pp. 89–91.

him,[1] but the special session was nearly at an end before the nominations had emerged from Conkling's committee, which reported the names of Roosevelt and Prince unfavorably.[2] Merritt, who had been appointed to fill a vacancy, was confirmed.

The President in his first message, which was forwarded early in December, when the regular session convened, restated his views on the subject of civil service reform in the most definite terms, and he asked for the co-operation of Congress in the "better systematizing of such methods and rules of admission to the public service, and of promotion within it," as would tend to establish tests for competency, efficiency and character. He desired Congress to make an appropriation for the purposes of the Civil Service Commission, which for years had been in receipt of no money to defray its expenses, in order that it might resume its usefulness.[3]

Little enough did the leaders care for such advice. Arthur said that the investigation of the Jay commission was neither thorough nor unbiased. He made a vigorous defense of his department, and of his administration of it.[4] The nominations, on December 6, were again sent to the Senate.[5] Conkling and his friends were bent upon Hayes's condign punishment. They appealed to what they called "senatorial courtesy," by which it was meant that no senator should vote to confirm the name of a Federal appointee in a brother senator's state without that brother senator's approval and consent. The names of Roosevelt and Prince were promptly rejected; there were 31 senators opposing, and but 25 to support the President.[6]

Though comment on Conkling's "victory" was accompanied by much remark in the "Stalwart" Republican press, unfavorable to Hayes,[7] there were many worthier newspapers

[1] Phila. Inquirer, Nov. 12, 1877.
[2] Senate Ex. Journal, vol. xxi, p. 144.
[3] Richardson, Messages and Papers of the Presidents, vol. vii, p. 466.
[4] House Ex. Doc., 45th Cong. 2nd sess., no. 25, pp. 7–16.
[5] Senate Ex. Journal, vol. xxi, pp. 159–60.
[6] Ibid., p. 171; Sherman's Recollections vol. ii, p. 682; Williams, Life of Hayes, vol. ii, pp. 87–8.
[7] For Arthur's letter of thanks to Conkling at this time, see Conkling, Life of Conkling, p. 557.

ready to accord him praise. Two of the most violent of the
Republican senators, Howe of Wisconsin and Sargent of California, sought, in April, 1878, to secure the adoption of a resolution by the Republican Congressional caucus, repudiating
the President's civil service order, but this enterprise was
frowned upon by wiser leaders of the party.[1] William
E. Chandler of New Hampshire, thinking no reward whatever too little for his activities in New York on the night after
the election, and his hard service in the ensuing weeks in
Florida, became an offensive foe of the administration in the
press, and as a pamphleteer.[2] But public sentiment was forming in protest against such men and the demoralizing principle
which they had the temerity to defend.

The report of another investigating commission attracted
less attention than Mr. Jay's, but its achievements were
many and noteworthy. Secretary Schurz, as he improved the
tone of his department and abolished "politics" in it, was
not unmindful of all that had so long been said concerning the
management of the Indian Bureau. In June, 1877, he appointed a board, composed of an officer from the Department
of Justice, designated by the Attorney General, an officer
from the army, designated by the Secretary of War and the
chief clerk of the Interior Department, a new incumbent of
the place of distinct worth, to take testimony and ascertain
the facts respecting the conduct of the government touching
its relations with the American aborigine, an activity in which
there were expended of the public moneys some $6,000,000
annually. As they pursued their examinations they were
"hindered in every conceivable way" by the employees under
inspection [3]—the commissioner himself refused to attend as a
witness[4]—but they concluded their work, after a few months of
diligent and intensive inquiry, and made their findings public
in January, 1878. Little rhetoric, and, indeed, no particular

[1] Williams, Life of Hayes, vol. ii, p. 89–91.
[2] Cf. J. H. Wilson, Life of Dana, pp. 444–5; Harper's Weekly, Jan. 12
and 19, 1878.
[3] N. Y. Nation, Jan. 10, 1878.
[4] Report of Board of Inquiry, p. xi.

skill of any kind, were displayed in presenting the alarmingly discreditable facts which had been uncovered by the board. The public, in view of what had so long been said about the dishonesty of Indian agents generally, and of the riches which had been amassed by the "Indian Ring," [1] had been led to expect more startling revelations. A reading of the report will sufficiently attest to the dexterity of these transgressors in masking their operations as well as to their shameless guilt.

There was, it was alleged, no body of instructions or regulations to which officers in the service must conform. The commissioner had left many subjects to the unguided care and sole discretion of the chief clerk. This officer acted in a capricious and arbitrary way to the extent, if not of direct participation in corrupt bargains, of suppressing charges made against those who were accused of culpable acts.[2] His "absolutism," the board of inquiry said, was "unknown to our form of government, or to the laws of the country." [3] An almost total neglect of mercantile usages in awarding contracts, furnishing supplies and directing the business of the bureau was discovered and unqualifiedly condemned.[4] It was the custom to carry on much of the business, though it be of the weightiest importance, involving large expenditures of money, by correspondence marked "personal," which was excluded, therefore, from the files of the office.[5]

The employees of the bureau were of inferior capacity and notable for their incompetency to perform their duties. Bids were manipulated, contractors fulfilled their contracts as they pleased, fraud was practiced in transporting and distributing supplies. The contractors controlled the bureau.[6] Indian agents carried the members of their families on the pay rolls as teachers, physicians, farmers, millers, blacksmiths, car-

---

[1] For example Harper's Weekly said—"The Indian Ring has long been known as one of the most corrupt and ingenious conspiracies in the public service."—Issue of Feb. 2, 1878.

[2] Report of Board of Inquiry, p. v; N. Y. Nation, Jan. 10 and 17, 1878.

[3] Report of Board of Inquiry, p. xxxv.

[4] Ibid., p. xvi.

[5] Ibid., pp. viii, ix.

[6] Ibid., pp. xix–xxiv.

penters, though they knew nothing of the work for which they were paid and rendered no valuable service to the government. Agents used supplies intended for the Indians for their own subsistence, or sold these supplies, and profited in still grosser ways from their posts.[1] Inferior beef cattle, "rotten" bacon, flour "mixed with corn" were furnished to the unhappy wards of the government. By false returns of weights and measures of the material received, by false statements of the number of Indians to be provided for by the government, the contractors were overpaid.

As an agency at the time was organized and conducted it was "simply a license . . . to cheat and swindle the Indians in the name of the United States of America."[2] The board remarked an "accumulation of fortunes" by persons who were in receipt of salaries "that would barely provide for the necessaries of life."[3] The poor people who were plundered had no recourse in law. It was a "reproach to the whole nation." "No bureau or office of the government has afforded more opportunity for downright irregularity and concealment of fraud than has the management of the Indian Bureau and service," the board said again.[4] "Cupidity, inefficiency and the most barefaced dishonesty" had been the cause not only of "sudden fortunes," but also of Indian wars.[5] The board did not pursue its inquiries to the point of fastening corruption upon individuals. But "to uncover and secure the punishment" of the guilty, it declared, was "one of the first duties of those responsible" for this branch of the public service.[6]

Schurz removed the commissioner, who had declined to attend the meetings of the board as a witness, the chief clerk who was so arrogant in the exercise of his powers, some employees who had been accepting presents from contractors,[7]

[1] Report of Board of Inquiry, pp. xxi–xxii, xxv.
[2] Ibid., p. lxii.
[3] Ibid., p. lxiii.
[4] N. Y. Nation, Jan. 24, 1878.
[5] Report of Board of Inquiry, p. lxiv.
[6] Ibid., p. lxv.
[7] N. Y. Nation, Jan. 10, 1878. One of these had been in office for 21 years.—Report of Board of Inquiry, pp. xi–xii.

and reorganized the bureau in a thoroughgoing way. The
dismissed men, supported by the "Indian Ring," now opened
warfare upon Schurz.[1]

But interest in such a subject was eclipsed by the feud between the President and Conkling in New York. Hayes had
no intention of surrendering his position because of the vote of
the Senate. "I am right," he said, "and shall not give up the
contest." [2] Further reports were made public by the Jay commission. The scandal grew until, in midsummer, 1878, after
the adjournment of Congress, the President summarily suspended Arthur and Cornell. Mr. Roosevelt, meanwhile, had
died, and General Merritt, whom the Senate had confirmed
some months earlier as surveyor of the port, was put in Arthur's
place, while Silas W. Burt, Mr. Cornell's deputy, was appointed to Cornell's position as naval officer. Both men at
once entered upon the discharge of their duties, and, under
the direction of the President, reorganized their offices to
the great advantage of the service. The appointments were
in the nature of promotions and, therefore, were made in full
conformity with the spirit of "reform." Hayes, if he had
acted tardily, as not a few believed,[3] nevertheless displayed a
sustained and an admirable courage.

Conkling and his coterie of office mongers made themselves
heard in the angriest and most denunciatory language at once.
Upon the meeting of Congress in December the names were
sent to the Senate to encounter the vindictive opposition of the
"Stalwart" leaders.[4] For two months the discussion was continued until it became a weariness to the country, and the
public mind underwent a revulsion of feeling, as it will in such a
case, quite unfavorable to the man who is on the wrong side of a
question, no matter how secure he may be in his power. On
January 31, 1879, the President forwarded a special message
to the Senate in justification of his course. The officers suspended were, and had been for years, "engaged in the active

[1] N. Y. Nation, Jan. 17, 1878.
[2] Diary and Letters of Hayes, vol. iii, p. 454.
[3] Cf. Williams, Life of Hayes, vol. ii, p. 88.
[4] Senate Ex. Journal, vol. xxi, pp. 378-9.

personal management of the party politics of the city and
state of New York." They had regarded their duties "as of
subordinate importance to their partisan work." The custom
house, which should have been a "business office," had been
"a centre of partisan political management." [1] Sherman used
his influence with senators like W. B. Allison, William Windom,
and Justin S. Morrill, asking them to allay, if they could, the
malignity of Conkling, whose course was doing inestimable
damage to "the party." [2] The issue was drawn, and, after a
prolonged discussion, Stanley Matthews leading for the President against the Conklingites, the nominations, on February
3rd, were confirmed, the vote being 33 to 24 on the collector-
ship,[3] and 31 to 19 on the subject of a successor to Cornell as
naval officer.[4]

The victory was now the President's.[5] He had broken the
power of the senatorial group which for so long had been dic-
tatorially directing the government, and had accomplished,
though it seemed on its face to be but a small matter, covering
the conduct of two rather minor Federal offices, a return to the
principles enunciated in the Constitution. The magnitude of
the achievement he saw very clearly, as is disclosed by the
entries in his Diary. It was a question whether the President
should make the appointments (subject to the "advice and
consent" of the Senate in its plenary capacity) and direct the
government, or whether, on this subject, it should continue
to be controlled by the heads of political "rings" in the states,
who should cause themselves to be elected to the Senate or

[1] Richardson, vol. vii, pp. 511–12; Senate Ex. Journal, vol. xxi. pp.
497–8.

[2] He would have resigned, he subsequently declared, if he had been compelled to act at New York through "unfriendly subordinates."—Sherman's
Recollections, vol. 11, pp. 683–4.

[3] Only 13 Republicans voted in support of Hayes.—Williams, vol. ii,
p. 94.

[4] Senate Ex. Journal, vol. xxi, pp. 502–503; cf. D. S. Alexander, Pol.
Hist. of N. Y., vol. iii, pp. 399 et seq.

[5] To John Jay it was the liberation of the custom service "from the
vicious grip of the immoral factions of office-holders and their retainers
who have made it a scandal to the nation, with such gigantic loss to the
Treasury and immeasurable damage to our commerce, industry and
morals."—Sherman's Recollections, vol. ii, p. 685.

the House of Representatives of Congress. The President had
won through his moral force, "unaided by public opinion," as
he observed, and "opposed in and out of Congress by a large
part of the most powerful men" in his party.[1] Letters were
sent to General Merritt and Mr. Burt—appointments and
removals hereafter were to be made in their offices "on business
principles and by fixed rules," without regard to political
recommendation or influence, and a body of regulations governing the subject were formulated and officially promulgated by
the President to guide the heads of the Federal service in making appointments, promotions and removals in the country
generally as well as in New York, a notable event in the history
of this political reform.[2] If Hayes had had the support of
Congress, if he could have lived up to such an example throughout his administration, if his successors in office had been
minded to follow the rules which he established for his action,
the triumph would have been not less than an important
revolution in the political system of the United States.

Blaine, in pursuit of his rising ambitions, which he thought
might be forwarded by the harrying of Hayes, in a speech at
Woodstock, Conn., on the 4th of July, 1877, had gone so far as
to express a suspicion that the President was allied with the
Democrats in an enterprise to annex Mexico. In friendship for
the "rebels," for whom he had exhibited so much concern in the
withdrawal of the troops from the state houses in Columbia and
New Orleans, the overthrow of the Republican state governments in South Carolina and Louisiana and the creation of a
"solid South," he was now on the point of enlarging the area
of the country which might be controlled by the Democratic
party.[3] This unworthy and audacious foray into the realm of
partisan speculation by Blaine [4] was founded on an episode in
the foreign relations of the country marking the first year of the
new administration. For long bands of outlaws, white, Indian

[1] Diary in Williams, Life of Hayes, vol. ii, p. 97.
[2] Richardson, vol. vii, pp. 550 et seq.; Williams, Life of Hayes, vol. ii, pp.
95–7.
[3] N. Y. Nation, July 12, 1877; Williams, Life of Hayes, vol. ii, p. 210.
[4] N. Y. Nation, Dec. 20, 1877.

and of mixed blood, had crossed the Rio Grande at their pleasure to plunder our ranchmen in Texas. Valuable herds were broken up. Our citizens, now and again, were killed and their property burned. Even post offices and custom houses were entered and robbed.[1] The Mexican authorities, seeming to be unable or unwilling to adopt preventive measures, or to punish even the worst of the offenders, the feeling of resentment in this country increased.[2]

Still torn by civil war, Mexico, in 1876, had come under the control of a new leader, General Porfirio Diaz. It was that country's and the world's good fortune, but as yet his government had not been recognized by the United States. His title was contested by rivals whose armed forces were still in the field, and there was no assurance that he would concern himself with matters touching the issue with the United States, though he had been informed of their gravity.[3] The correspondence which John W. Foster, our minister at Mexico City, had carried on with Mr. Fish was continued with Mr. Evarts. Colonel Shafter, in command on the border, reported to General Ord a number of recent new incursions,[4] and the possibility of his being ordered to cross the Rio Grande in pursuit of the marauders was brought to the attention of the Mexican Foreign Office.[5] Hayes presented the case to his cabinet and, on June 1, 1877, General Ord, through General Sherman, was directed to follow Mexicans who should set foot on our soil "and overtake and punish them, as well as retake stolen property."[6] It was action reckoned to be eminently necessary for the defense of the lives and property of our citizens, and met with the approval of people and press.

To Diaz, intent upon making an initial impression of patriotic devotion to the interests of the nation, over which he had so lately assumed control,[7] such a step on our side offered an

[1] Foreign Relations for 1877–8, pp. 402, 404.
[2] See House Reports, 45th Cong. 2nd sess., no. 701, for historical account of these border outrages.
[3] Foreign Relations for 1877–8, pp. 402–3.
[4] House Ex. Doc., 45th Cong. 1st sess., no. 13, pp. 4–5, 10, 13.
[5] Ibid., p. 12; Foreign Relations for 1877–8, p. 401.
[6] House Reports, 45th Cong. 2nd sess., no. 701, p. xvi.   [7] Ibid.

opportunity for insulting retorts. Foster was told at the Mexican Foreign Office that Secretary McCrary, in the order to Sherman, had "disregarded all the rules of international law and the practices of civilized nations." If, in answer to it, Mexican territory were violated the consequences might be of the gravest character. The cabinet at Washington had sought to place Mexico "beyond the pale of civilized nations"—the people were being treated as "savages," no better than the "Kaffirs of Africa," and more of like effect.[1] Mexican pride of nationality swelled at the sound of such deliverances. The vanity of the people had been offended, and their official and semi-official press fanned the flames of public feeling. The minister of war sent a commander, General Trevino by name, to the border to execute the provisions of treaties in force between Mexico and the United States. If any invasion actually occurred he should "repel force by force." Such a movement would not be assumed to be an "act of hostility toward the United States," but merely "an exercise of the legitimate right of self-defense."[2]

That the United States had not followed the course already taken by many European nations in recognizing Diaz and his government added little to the cordiality of the tone of the diplomatic exchanges. It was intimated that General Ord was an annexationist, as were the President and his advisers at Washington, an impression which the utterances of Blaine and others in the United States had done nothing to allay. Our action was a studied attempt to precipitate war with the end of seizing the northern Mexican states.[3]

The United States had many specific cases of banditry and outlawry on the subject of the Texas border to offer in support of its policy, and Mr. Foster, with the skill of which he was a master, vigorously upheld our side of the controversy. Indeed,

[1] Foreign Relations for 1877–8, p. 411.

[2] Ibid., pp. 416–8; Am. Ann. Cyclop. for 1877, p. 513.

[3] Foreign Relations for 1877–8, pp. 412–3; House Ex. Doc., 45th Cong. 1st sess., no. 13, pp. 29–30. Minister Foster seems to have been ready, like Blaine, to accuse the administration of sinister designs.—Cf. J. W. Foster, Diplomatic Memoirs, vol. i, p. 92–3.

at this very moment revolutionary forces were pursuing their altercations with one another on American soil.[1]

Diaz, while he had been waving the Mexican flag, with braggadocios about repelling "force by force," had authorized Trevino to confer with Ord as to the capture and punishment of evil doers, though little enough was done in improving conditions on the frontier. His presence there seemed to be for the purpose of preventing us from entering the country on punitive expeditions rather than stopping the incursions of bandits across our line.[2] In January, 1878, a mob of Mexicans numbering several hundred men invaded a town in El Paso county, Texas, killed several Americans, many of them in the most brutal ways, and, pillaging their stores and houses, carried the booty in safety to the other side of the river.[3] This incident came near leading to a new and violent outburst. The tension continued for many months. The assurances of honorable purposes and the power to give effect to them, on Diaz's part,[4] remained far from satisfactory. The Mexican government, indeed, had not been in the habit of making guarantees, such as would be expected of another government, and, because of her familiar attitude on such points, we had never demanded so much of her.[5]

Finally, nearly a year after all the other principal nations had acted in the case, Diaz, in April, 1878, received the official recognition from this country which he craved,[6] though this act did not prevent him from indulging in jingoism at the expense of the United States in the message to his Congress in the following September.[7] The peace, which was enjoyed on the border, was due entirely to the continued presence of our troops in controlling positions. The House Committee on

[1] Foreign Relations for 1877–8, pp. 413–6; House Ex. Doc. 45th Cong. 1st sess., no. 13, p. 15.

[2] House Reports, 45th Cong. 2nd sess., no. 701, pp. xviii–xix.

[3] Ibid., pp. xix, 284.

[4] Ibid., p. xxxix.

[5] Ibid., p xli.

[6] Foster was also at variance with the Hayes administration on the subject of recognition. He thought it had been much too long delayed. See his Diplomatic Memoirs, vol. i, pp. 87–95.

[7] Am. Ann. Cyclop. for 1878, p. 555.

Foreign Affairs, to which the subject came, recommended that the force distributed from the mouth of the Rio Grande to El Paso should be not less than 5,000 men, of whom at least 3,000 should be mounted. Guarantees should be sought and secured by treaty, and evidence should be at hand of Diaz's ability and desire to abide by its stipulations before our watchfulness should be relaxed.[1] The fleeting imbroglio was, as it proved, the most stirring incident in the course of Mr. Evarts's conduct of the country's foreign affairs.

[1] House Reports, 45th Cong. 2nd sess., no. 701, p. xlii.

CHAPTER XXIII

ON THE PLAINS AND IN THE MOUNTAINS

THE failure of Congress to pass the enabling act for Colorado over President Johnson's veto, in 1866, at the time that favor had been extended to Nebraska, left the "Pike's Peak country," as it had been vaguely denominated when, just before the outbreak of the Civil War, the adventurers of the East took their way excitedly on horse and in prairie schooner to this new El Dorado, under territorial government. Misfortune settling upon the people, through the collapse of mining speculation, the population underwent but slow increase. In 1870 the census returns indicated that it was only 39,864. Of this number there were less than 5,000 in the city, which was to be the fair and admired metropolis of the state, while the rest were located, for the most part, on the mountain sides and in the gulches where the miners were washing out and delving for gold and silver,— gold mainly around Black Hawk, Central City, Nevada and places in Gilpin county, silver in Clear Creek county at places tributary to Georgetown. With the aid of rills, fed by the melting shows, which fell down the slopes in cascades, a few thousand persons cultivated the soil under the towering ranges which here divide the American continent.

In 1870 the territory appeared to have only 5,000 more inhabitants than in 1860. But soon other things would be seen. In June, 1870, Denver, by the completion of the Union Pacific to Cheyenne, gained railway connections, by way of Omaha, with the East, and a few weeks later the Kansas Pacific was finished, when each evening half the city crowded the streets and the hill slopes around the "Union Depot" to witness the arrival of the "Denver Express" from St. Louis and Kansas City.[1] With its coaches and Pullman "palace cars," which

[1] Blake, Handbook of Colorado, 1874, p. 24.

had been whirled across the buffalo range and through the
prairie dog "cities" of western Kansas, it gave a new impulse to
Colorado. Denver now was but 46 hours from St. Louis, 54
hours from Chicago, 83 hours from New York. Only a few more
years would pass before the Atchison, Topeka and Santa Fé,
on its way to the Pacific coast, should enter the territory, thus
affording another route to the East. In 1876 this road had
reached Pueblo.[1]

Meantime enterprising capitalists had employed dexterous
engineers to lay down a "narrow gauge" railroad, the Denver
and Rio Grande, running north and south in Colorado.[2] Thus
in 1872 were Denver, Colorado Springs and Pueblo brought
into communication, while spurs were built westwardly to serve
the miners in the mountain towns. The progress was constant.
Though in other parts of the country railway construction,
after the panic of 1873, had nearly ceased, here, in this vibrant
new land, it was actively continued.[3] There were in Colorado,
in 1874, 646 miles of railway completed and ready for use,[4]
while 671 more were in course of construction.[5]

The East had been eagerly awaiting the means of reaching
a country, the fame of whose attractions had preceded the opening of the railroads. The area of the territory was 103,658
square miles, larger by 16,000 square miles, therefore, than all
England, Scotland and Wales, larger than the whole of New
York, Pennsylvania and New Jersey, nearly as large as all New
England, plus the state of Ohio. Men who had toiled across the
plains on horse and by stage coach had returned to describe the
natural spectacle to be witnessed in this glorious land. They
told of its lofty mountains, 120 of them of a height of 13,500
feet or more, 35 of an altitude in excess of 14,000 feet, ten times
as many as in all Europe—19 more than 10,000 feet high were

[1] Frank Fossett, Colorado, 2nd ed., p. 148.
[2] Ibid., pp. 74-5; H. H. Bancroft, Nevada, Colorado and Wyoming,
p. 554.
[3] Fossett, Colorado, p. 149.
[4] Stated in the Senate in 1875 to be 735 miles.—Cong. Record, 43rd
Cong. 2nd sess., p. 1682.
[5] The Pueblo Colony, Lancaster, Pa., 1874, p. 7; Westward March of
Emigration, Lancaster, Pa., 1874, p. 41.

visible from Denver.[1] Its canyons and passes, its foaming brooks and waterfalls, its overhanging crags and dizzy precipices, its rock shapes, which looked now like weird monuments and again like massive battlements, its glittering lakes and verdant parks on high table lands, shut in by great peaks, covered even in summer with white snows, had stirred the most stolid breasts with the hope of one day visiting such a wonderland. The Alps were a great heritage from the Grand Artificer of All Things, but here in Colorado more was to be seen than had made the fame of Switzerland.

Denver itself, though placed upon a plain, stood nearly a mile above the level of the sea. Colorado's bright skies, its clear, pure, rare atmosphere, its hot and cold mineral springs invited invalids. Physicians attested to the wholesome and healing qualities of its air and its waters. In winter or in summer Colorado was a haven of health. Another resort had been found for sufferers from pulmonary ills, who continued their long and unavailing quest for a cure for their devastating malady. These were likely to direct themselves to Colorado Springs, or its environs, a place near Pike's Peak which had been established in 1871. It was estimated, in 1874, that one-third of the population of the territory was composed of "reconstructed invalids."[2] Individuals, associations of individuals, hotel keepers published the merits of the country to entice tourists and colonists. The Indians were "as subdued as little children," peace waved "her halcyon wings" over the land. Travellers could pitch their tents and form their camps on the plains as safely as in New England. The frontier settler was as secure in his hut in Colorado as any millionaire in his brown stone house on the most frequented street in New York City.[3]

Colonies were formed on the Atlantic seaboard and in the Mississippi valley, and emigrants took up land and formed communities, the most widely known being that one at Greeley, some 50 miles from Denver on the railroad to Cheyenne, at

[1] Tongue, All about Colorado, p. 88.
[2] Blake, op. cit., p. 119.
[3] Resources and Advantages of Colorado, published by Territorial Board of Immigration, p. 44.

the head of which was the agricultural editor of the New York
Tribune, who, with Horace Greeley's assistance, had promoted
the plans and gathered together a few score oddlings from the
subscribers and readers of that newspaper, willing to seek their
fortunes at the side of an irrigation ditch in the shadow of the
Rocky Mountains.[1] Colorado Springs was the outgrowth of
a settlement by the "Fountain Colony" which gave it canals,
parks, wide streets, and other improvements. None but members could purchase colony lands.[2] The old town of Pueblo
was situated on the north bank of the Arkansas River. Opposite, on the south bank, South Pueblo was platted on the
colony plan, with members drawn for the most part from
Pennsylvania.[3]

Emigration to Colorado assumed important proportions,
and many, seeking health or fortune, settled there permanently,
while the number of transient visitors who came to feast their
eyes upon the more than Alpine scenery grew in volume year
by year. Men and women, too, were bent upon climbing to
the summit of Pike's Peak, a feat, the accomplishment of which
had become a national aspiration. There were no game laws,
except for the protection of grouse, quail and prairie chickens.
Sportsmen from the Eastern cities and from England were
invited by the Kansas Pacific Railroad to come and shoot at
will the buffalo, antelope, deer, elk, bear, wild turkeys, Rocky
Mountain sheep, swan, pelican and cranes which were said to
abound on every side.[4] In 1872 Denver had a line of horse-
drawn street cars, banks, newspapers, churches, manufactories,
stores and a half dozen hotels. In the territory there were
1,018 miles of telegraph lines and seven daily papers.[5] The

[1] J. F. Willard, The Union Colony, Univ. of Col. Hist. Coll.; First Annual
Report of the Union Colony of Greeley, New York, 1871. For other
Colorado colonies see Report of Missionary Bishop of Colorado, New
Mexico and Wyoming, Oct. 1, 1871, and Westward March of Emigration,
already cited.

[2] Colorado, its Resorts and Attractions, published by Kansas Pacific
Railway, advts., p. 17.

[3] Pueblo Colony.

[4] See the company's time tables for the period.

[5] Pueblo Colony, p. 30.

value in 1873 of its mineral products—gold, silver, copper, lead and zinc,—was in excess of $4,000,000.[1]

The contest for statehood was renewed. Already, at the end of 1870, the United States marshal for the territory stated that the census returns for that year were incomplete. Instead of 40,000 Colorado had no less than 60,000 inhabitants. Instead of $20,000,000 of taxable property it had $40,000,000, not including mines of precious metals, which were not taxable. He expressed the nearly unanimous wish of the people that Congress give them a state government.[2] The House Committee on Territories, in favorably reporting an "enabling" bill in 1873, dwelt upon the mineral wealth, the timber, the pasture land, the water power of the country. The population now was stated to be 100,000. "Justice" to the people required their admission to the Union.[3] President Grant, in his message to Congress in December, 1873, championed their cause. Colorado, he said, possessed "all the elements of a prosperous state, agricultural and mineral"; he believed that it had the population "to justify" statehood.[4]

In the House of Representatives the advocates of New Mexico brought forward the claims of that territory. In area it was three times the size of Ohio. Its wealth and population were rapidly increasing.[5] It had a civilization, communicated to it by the Spaniards, two centuries old. A provision in the Treaty of Guadalupe Hidalgo, by which the country, after the Mexican War, had been transferred to the United States, was appealed to in support of a theory that an obligation had been put upon Congress to extend the inhabitants the privileges of state government. It was pointed out, on the other hand, that the people were Mexicans. They could not speak English; five-sixths of the adult residents of this broad waste of mountain and sand could not even read and write their own Spanish

---

[1] Blake, Handbook of Colorado, p. 122.
[2] Senate Mis. Doc., 41st Cong. 3rd sess., no. 40, pp. 1–2.
[3] House Reports, 42nd Cong. 3rd sess., no. 9; cf. House Reports, 43rd Cong. 1st sess., no. 619.
[4] Richardson, Messages and Papers, vol. vii, p. 255.
[5] Senate Mis. Doc., 41st Cong. 3rd sess., no. 41.

language, said George F. Hoar. They had had no public schools until some three years since, which led to the retort that the negroes in the South, of whose enfranchisement Mr. Hoar had been an advocate, were illiterates, which, in turn, induced him to distinguish, as best he could, between the business of exercising the suffrage and of forming a state for admission to the Union.[1] On May 21, 1874, the New Mexico bill passed the House by a decisive majority,[2] and a fortnight later the Colorado bill, on motion of the territorial delegate, Mr. Chaffee, drawn in similar terms, was adopted without the formality of debate.[3]

Here the subject rested until the next session, when it appeared in the Senate, where the New Mexico bill underwent amendment, which was not accepted by the House.[4] It fared otherwise with the bill dealing with Colorado. Senator Hitchcock of Nebraska espoused it. The territory, he said, had a soil which would support a population of two million, were it properly watered by irrigation canals. It was settled by "hardy, brave, enterprising, loyal and intelligent" people.[5] It was stated now that the territory had 150,000 inhabitants, nearly four times as many as the census takers had found in 1870.[6] Though the Democrats generally opposed the measure, seeing in the admission of the new state an extension of Republican power, the amendments which the Senate had tacked upon it were agreed to by the House in the closing hours of the session, on March 3, 1875.[7] Colorado now assembled a convention of delegates, who framed a constitution which, upon submission, was ratified by the people of the state, and, in conformity with the provisions of the enabling act, the President issued a proclamation declaring the fact on August 1, 1876,[8] in the midst of

[1] Cong. Record, 43rd Cong. 1st sess., pp. 4129 et seq.
[2] Cf. McPherson's Handbook for 1874, p. 220.
[3] Ibid.
[4] Ibid. for 1876, p. 46.
[5] Cong. Record, 43rd Cong. 2nd sess., p. 1671.
[6] The population of Colorado was 194,327 in 1880, according to the Census Reports of that year.
[7] McPherson's Handbook for 1876, p. 46.
[8] Richardson, vol. vii, pp. 392–4.

the celebration attending the one-hundredth anniversary of
national independence, wherefore it was generally called the
"Centennial State." The republic was now a union of 38
states.

Colorado's claims upon the attention of the rest of the country
were on the point of being extended at once in a new direction.
Much had been seen. The finding of wealth and the application
of it for the further advantage of the territory, the rapid increase of settlement and population, the loyalty and enthusiasm
of the men who had chosen this part of our American wilderness as their home had brought results which challenged general
admiration. More soon to follow would confirm the nation in
the faith which it had reposed in the people when they had been
invited to form a state that might be admitted to the Union.

Far in the heart of the great entanglement of its mountain
walls, in the high ground where the melting snows were divided,
one part to betake themselves in rivulets and cascades to the
Pacific, the other to the Atlantic Ocean, lay some half abandoned mining claims. A gash in the earth, called California
Gulch, had been explored profitably by some placer miners
in 1860. Log huts were built beside a stream and considerable excitement attended the discoveries which were made at
this place before and during the Civil War. As many as 5,000
men at one time shared in the hopes, profits and wickednesses
of the camp. But the supply of water for the diggings was
scant, the elevation was nearly two miles above sea level, the
season in which work could proceed was short, ingress and
egress were difficult, so that the production, though it may have
reached, in the period from 1860 to 1865, a total value of $3,000,-
000, had since declined.[1] The placers seeming to have been
exhausted, in 1868, a Philadelphia company found, and, erecting a stamp mill, began the development of, a gold lode. In
1877 it came to be understood that the district abounded in
what were popularly called "carbonates," i.e., formations
of carbonate of lead carrying silver. This was the signal for
a stampede which resulted in the almost magical uprising of

[1] Fossett, Colorado, pp. 404–5.

Leadville. The gulches and hills roundabout were staked by
excited miners who were arriving every day, afoot and on horseback, to see if there were truth in all or any part of what they
had heard of the riches here hidden in the earth, cabins were
hastily raised to cover the heads of the fortune hunters, stores
were opened to dispense food and supplies.[1] One discovery
followed another, and, before the winter set in, more than 1,000
men were in Leadville and the surrounding territory, and large
quantities of ore were already on the roads, behind teams of
horses and mules, for a journey of 120 miles to the nearest
accessible railroad station on the way to the smelters in Denver,
Omaha and St. Louis.[2] The opening of spring, in 1878, found
the camp in the midst of a boom rivalling any which had yet
been seen in all the history of the mining of gold and silver in
America.

Immigration from other parts of Colorado, from Montana,
Nevada and California, from the Mississippi Valley, from the
East, from Canada and Europe brought in a tide of strange
humanity. With the adventurers who would work with their
hands came men of established wealth, or their representatives,
eager to invest capital in the field, and with them, too, the
rabble of the saloon, the dance hall and the gambling house.
Claims were sold and re-sold; poor men became rich overnight.
The widespread fame of the "carbonates" made Leadville,
ere 1878 was done, a city of tents and wooden shacks extending far out over the plain. In that year the first smelting fur-
nace was blown in, so that a part of the ore could be treated
without freighting it over the mountain roads. Even the winter
brought no abatement of the "Leadville fever." No one would
jeopardize his chance of gaining riches by waiting for melting
snows under another summer's sun. The Comstock bonanzas
were outdone,[3] and the place began to assume the appearance
of a substantial city. Hotels, churches, newspapers, banks
with millions of dollars in their tills, theatres, trading houses,
furnaces, saw mills to cut lumber for the builders, comfortable
dwelling houses of brick, as well as of wood, arose on both sides

[1] Fossett, p. 410.   [2] Ibid., p. 411.   [3] Ibid., pp. 413, 422.

of busy streets. Leadville had telegraph lines, gas lights and
water works, police and fire departments. Three railroads
wildly contended for the passes and defiles leading to the town[1]
that they might carry in the immigrants and take out the
profitable freights; till these could be completed stage coaches
and wagons, employing thousands of horses, mules and oxen,
connected Leadville with the outside world. Corner lots in
1880 were selling at from $4,000 to $10,000 each; more business
was done in the Leadville post office, it was said, than in any
other office between St. Louis and San Francisco.[2]

Men whose names were widely known in trade and politics
in New York, Boston and Chicago were officers of large companies which were formed to explore the district and smelt its
rich ores. From a product valued at $500,000 in 1877 the yield
of Leadville and its vicinity in gold, silver and lead increased
in 1878 to more than $3,000,000; in 1879, to more than $11,-
000,000.[3] The first locomotive did not reach the camp until
September, 1880, when it was believed that its population was
between 25,000 and 35,000;[4] it had been increasing at the rate
of 2,000 a month.[5] At that time there were men ready to say
that Leadville had prospects which would enable it to distance
Denver in the race for honors as a great city.[6]

More than ever was Colorado seen as treasure ground, though
the state is as prominently known to-day for its cantaloupes,
sugar beets and other products of the orchard and field, for
its cattle and sheep, for its coal and iron, as for its gold and
silver.[7]

No less wild than the stampede to Leadville was the rush to
the Black Hills. Indians came into frontier posts on the upper
Missouri and the Platte carrying grains of gold which, when they
were plied with whiskey and loaded with presents, they would

[1] Am. Ann. Cyclop. for 1879, p. 159.
[2] Fossett, p. 417.
[3] Ibid., p. 422; cf. Am. Ann. Cyclop. for 1879, p. 161.
[4] Fossett, p. 417.
[5] Am. Ann. Cyclop. for 1879, p. 156.
[6] Fossett, p. 33.
[7] In 1920 its farm products had ten times the value of its manufactured
goods, eighteen times the value of its precious metals.—Census Reports.

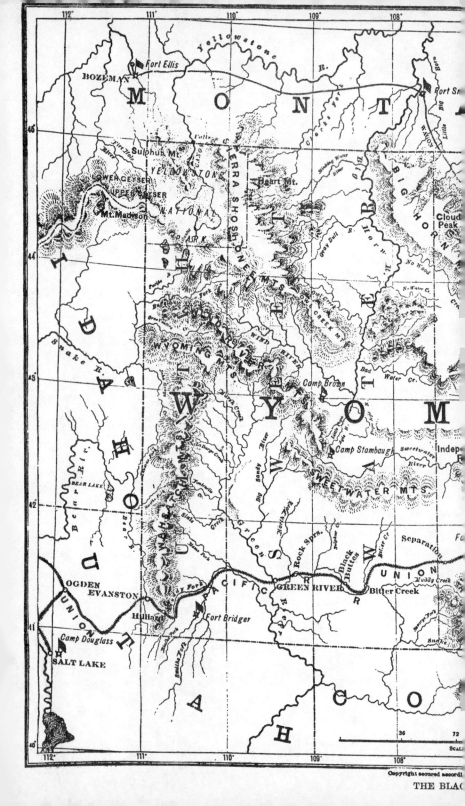

THE BLAC

K HILLS IN 1875

say came from the Black Hills.[1] For a long time explorers
had known of the existence of an elevated, wooded, well-watered
expanse of tumbled country on the buffalo plains of the northwest. It was surrounded by arms of the Cheyenne River, and
was about the size of the state of Connecticut.[2] From any
direction travellers approaching it must cross infertile, clayey
and chalky plains, weathered and wind-swept into deep gullies
and weirdly shaped hummocks, some of them so high as to be
called buttes.[3] The country was sparingly furnished with
water, which, when found, was acrid and nauseous. Here and
there were spaces covered with buffalo grass, grazed over by
the herds, which lately, however, were not seen east of the Little
Missouri River. Now the grasshoppers, each summer's recurring plague, ate what the buffaloes were not at hand to con-
sume.[4] These plains were known as the "Bad Lands." The
Black Hills were called so by the Indians,[5] because they looked,
as they were espied on the horizon, very dark, under their
covering of pine and aspen, tamerack and spruce.[6] They lay,
as Congress since the war had charted the West, in the far
southwestern part of the territory of Dakota, extending across
the boundary of that territory into Wyoming. The country,
said Colonel R. I. Dodge, after he had visited it, was a "true
oasis in a wide and dreary desert." [7]

Such a place, still veiled in mystery, presented obstacles to
the explorer who should approach its looming black mass, and
still more hazards and privations were he to penetrate it and to
attempt to remain in its strange precincts. For this very reason its name held a fascination for the adventurous man. To
pursue the water courses, to scale the mountains of which one,
Harney's Peak, rose to a height of nearly 8,000 feet, to view the
rugged scenery, to spy out, if possible, rich agricultural land,

[1] Cf. N. Y. Herald, Aug. 31, 1874.
[2] Wm. Ludlow, Report of a Reconnaisance, p. 7.
[3] Dodge, The Black Hills, pp. 46–8; Ludlow, p. 18.
[4] Ludlow, pp. 9–10.
[5] The Pah-sappa of the Dakota or Sioux nation, which, literally trans-
lated, is "Black Hills."—Dodge, The Black Hills, pp. 11, 25.
[6] Am. Ann. Cyclop. for 1874, p. 256; Ludlow, pp. 10, 13.
[7] Dodge, The Black Hills, p. 149.

pasturage for cattle and sheep, supplies of timber and building
stone, to hunt and kill wild game, were enticement enough for
the restless forces on the frontier, and the recruits which they
were constantly gaining from the ebullient youth of the East.
But when to these seductions was added the knowledge that gold
dust could be sieved up from the beds of the streams the desire
to reach the country at once became a craze.

For two or three years past General Sheridan, in command of
the Division of the Missouri, had counselled the authorities at
Washington to establish a military post in the Black Hills that
he might more effectively exercise control over the Indians.[1]
With this and other objects in view, in the summer of 1874,
a military reconnoitering expedition, under command of General
Custer, with several companies of mounted troops, supplied
with three Gatling guns, a train of wagons and a beef herd,
led by Bloody Knife and other Indian scouts and some white
plainsmen, and accompanied by several scientists and a number
of eager newspaper correspondents, in all about 1,000 men,
proceeded to the Black Hills from Fort Abraham Lincoln on
the Missouri River, near Bismarck, the railhead of the Northern
Pacific Railroad in Dakota.[2]   They were absent for two months.
The observations, hurried as they were, confirmed the popular
impression concerning the country.   It was, General Custer
said, "enchanting." Its sweet wild odors, its grasses, foliage
and flowers, so luxuriant of growth that they swept the flanks
of the horses as the soldiers rode along, its crystal waters and
its scenic prospects moved him to poetic phrase.[3]   Deer and
other wild creatures peeped out of the copse at the unexpected
visitors.   The men, begrimed and weary after their long days
upon the hot, dry plains, laved their limbs in the pure streams,
ate of the luscious berries which grew on every side, and orna-

[1] Report of Sec. of War for 1874, p. 24.
[2] Ibid., pp. 37-8; Ludlow, pp. 7, 8; Mrs. Custer, Boots and Saddles,
pp. 94 et seq.; corr. of N. Y. Tribune, July 11, Aug. 1, 4, 10, 17, 18, 20, 24
and 28, 1874.   Included in the party was the President's son, "Fred"
Grant.
[3] Senate Ex. Doc., 43rd Cong. 2nd sess., no. 32; cf. Ludlow, pp. 11, 13,
14, 43.   But Custer was restrained in his description in comparison with
the newspaper correspondents. See, e.g., N. Y. Tribune, Aug. 17, 1874.

mented the bridles of their steeds with bloom. Not one that did not think himself in a kind of Paradise.[1]

Custer's had been, primarily, a military expedition, organized for military ends. Another expedition was despatched in the following year, in 1875, by the Interior Department, under the direction of a geologist in the service of the government, Professor Walter P. Jenney, for a more careful and authoritative examination of the country. He was accompanied by several competent scientists, all well escorted and amply protected by troops assigned to the duty by the War Department.[2] This time the approach was from Fort Laramie, the old frontier post near the junction of the Laramie River with the North Platte, 90 miles from Cheyenne. Leaving that post on May 25, and, passing through "Bad Lands," not unlike those which Custer and his expedition had come over in the previous year on the way to the Hills from the north,[3] they arrived before the snows had yet melted. They remained until there were signs of winter, having in a few months made the most valuable geological, climatological and other observations concerning the region.[4]

Meanwhile the wildest anticipations were indulged in by the adventurers who were assembled in the frontier towns awaiting an opportunity for their departure to the new El Dorado. The "gold fever" was running high at Chicago. Parties were formed and advanced from Yankton, Bismarck and Sioux City.[5] The stampede began. Some of the fortune hunters reached the Black Hills soon after Custer left there in 1874, and

[1] Mrs. Custer, Boots and Saddles, chap. xx. The men returned to the Missouri veritable tatterdemalions, laden with trophies of the excursion, including a keg filled with clear water, taken from one of the mountain rills, a luxury, indeed, for the ladies in residence at the fort, whom they had left behind and who were restricted to the waters of the Missouri and its murky tributaries.
[2] House Ex. Doc., 44th Cong. 1st sess., no. 125; Report of Sec. of Int. for 1875, pp. 683–5; Dodge, The Black Hills, p. 10.
[3] Dodge, The Black Hills, pp. 16–7, 20–21, 146–8.
[4] House Ex. Doc., 44th Cong. 1st sess., no. 125; Dodge, The Black Hills, p. 10.
[5] Senate Ex. Doc., 43rd Cong. spec. sess., no. 2, p. 2; Chicago corr. N. Y. Tribune, Aug. 28, 1874.

remained during the winter,[1] and a still greater number followed in 1875. Towns were laid out and in one of them, Custer City, several log cabins were built.[2]

No one believed that the opening of the country to white settlement would be long deferred, and stage lines were soon projected from Cheyenne to Custer City, which it was held was the safest line of approach. The railroads advertised it and urged the people to leave their homes in the East in the old search for the Golden Fleece.[3] Daily the newspapers gave it renown; they "interviewed" prospective and returning emigrants; they transcribed every item of information concerning it which they could obtain.[4] Pamphlets, maps, books about the Black Hills appeared, directing attention to their wealth, and offering advice to pioneers intending to proceed into the country.[5]

[1] For the remarkable story of this experience see Mrs. A. D. Tallent, a woman who accompanied the expedition, in The First White Woman in the Black Hills; J. H. Triggs, A Reliable and Correct Guide to the Black Hills, p. 5; E. H. Saltiel, Black Hills Guide, pp. 24-32; Senate Ex. Doc., 44th Cong. 1st sess., no. 51, p. 57; Dodge, The Black Hills, pp. 57, 115-18; Report of Sec. of War for 1874, p. 33; Report of Sec. of Int. for 1874, p. 318.

[2] Dodge, The Black Hills, pp. 118-20; J. F. Finerty, Warpath and Bivouac, pp. 40-43.

[3] "From Cheyenne," said the general passenger agent of the Union Pacific, "the trip is made over good stage roads and in comparative safety from hostile Indian tribes that infest the more northern routes." (J. H. Triggs, A Reliable and Correct Guide to the Black Hills, p. 132.) Again: "By this route you avoid the Bad Lands, which are rendered utterly uninhabitable and impassable by the intense heat of summer; the roving bands of hostile Indians which infest the country, north and east of the Hills, and the discomforts and delays of Missouri River navigation." (H. N. Maguire, New Map and Guide to Dakota and the Black Hills, advt.; cf. ibid., pp. 74-5.) For advantages offered by the Missouri River route, see ibid., pp. 68-72.

[4] Newspaper correspondents accompanying the Custer expedition sent back glowing accounts of the gold fields. The N. Y. Tribune headed the letter from its correspondent: "A New Gold Country—Indications of Gold Everywhere in the Black Hills Region," etc. (Issue of Aug. 10, 1874.) The New York Herald's headline upon its "story" was "The Land of Gold—Discovery of the Precious Metal in the Black Hills." (Issue of Aug. 31, 1874). Gold abounded there, the Herald said again, in "unlimited quantities" (Issue of Sept. 1, 1874.) The Tribune said editorially that the Black Hills "summoned hopes of a new California, with visions of colossal and sudden wealth." (Issue of Aug. 10, 1874.) A correspondent of the St. Paul Daily Press in the Custer party wrote his newspaper that a miner could take out $100 a day.—Quoted in N. Y. Tribune, Aug. 24, 1874.

[5] See, e.g., "Rambler," The Black Hills, Indianapolis, 1875; J. H. Triggs, A Reliable and Correct Guide to the Black Hills, Omaha, 1876;

The stampedes to Leadville and the Black Hills were but two of the excited migrations in the Rocky Mountains. Other similar movements hither and yonder in Colorado, Montana, Idaho, Utah, Arizona, Wyoming, often upon wild rumor, engaged the minds of the restless parts of our population. If an Indian, a Chinaman, a tawny white trapper or scout, a soldier came in with an account of a find of dust or nuggets the news flew far, and instantly a crowd set off on the most perilous ways into well-nigh inaccessible places to endure insupportable hardships in the hope of bringing out their fortunes. Were enough of them located in any one spot the harpies who throve from miners' camps followed, the roads were filled with pack and wagon trains, towns rose, stage lines were established, railroads were surveyed and built.

The extension of agricultural settlement in the West and the advance of the white population out beyond the farming belt in the search for pasturage was nearly as swift as the movements of the miners. Where the buffalo had been beef herds now grazed. On the ranches, without area or limit, in the great open spaces, cattle roamed almost at will, except at the time of their general collection by "cowboys," which was called the "round up," when the owners separated their property by inspecting the animals for the private brands put upon them before they had been turned out,[1] and reaped their profits by driving the cows, bullocks and steers to a railroad station for shipment to the stockyards and packing houses of Kansas City, Omaha and Chicago. This was a business which strongly tempted enterprise and capital. On the plains and in the mountain valleys was born a great new industry, which was soon seeking the favor of Congress and the departments at Washington, and muddying the waters of government in its relations with the Indians.

It was in truth a marvelous growth. Where, in 1868, there had been millions of buffalo to be chased for their meat and sheltering skins by the Sioux, Cheyenne, Arapahoe, Comanche

E. H. Saltiel, Black Hills Guide, St. Louis, 1st ed. 1875; E. A. Curley, Glittering Gold, Chicago, 1876; R. E. Strahom, The Hand Book of Wyoming, Cheyenne, 1877.

[1] Cf. Governor of Wyoming in Report of Sec. of Int., 1878, pp. 1161–62.

and other tribes, there was now not one, said General Sherman.
Ranchmen were covering the country with their herds and
every ox and steer had an owner who would fight for his property.[1] In 1868 the white man's pasture grounds were in
Texas; now they extended over an empire from the Gulf of
Mexico to Montana. North of Texas and west of the Missouri,
where there had been no cattle in 1868, General Sheridan declared that, ten years later, the number of head fully equalled
those which were grazing in Texas.[2] In Wyoming alone, the
governor of that territory said, there were 300,000 head of
cattle,[3] and more than 200,000 sheep.[4]

And the tiller of the soil was not far behind the herdsman.
In 1877 in the new state of Minnesota 35,000,000 bushels of
wheat had been harvested. The farmers there were prospering
"beyond hope or precedent." Towns were rising on every side.[5]
Large portions of Kansas and Nebraska were under the plow,
yielding the husbandman profitable crops.[6] Farther west the
grassy valleys of Colorado, Idaho, Montana, Arizona, Washington and Oregon were being occupied by hardy colonists with
astounding rapidity. In his military department of the plains,
running up to the foot of the Rocky Mountains, and in those
mountains, Sheridan computed that there were, in 1878, not
less than two millions of people engaged in mining, grazing, and
agriculture—they were building farmhouses, founding villages,
erecting churches and schools on lands which, ten years before,
were the undisputed home of the Indian, his pony and the wild
animals which he chased.[7]

It betokened much of value to the republic in increasing
national wealth, in new commonwealths, but it meant immediate
conflict with the native peoples who had so long held sway in
this broad wilderness. They had no sooner been settled in a
part of the country which, it was surmised, would be of no use

[1] Report of Secretary of War for 1878, p. 5.
[2] Ibid., p. 38.
[3] Report of Sec. of Int. for 1878, p. 1163.
[4] Ibid., p. 1166.
[5] Phila. Inquirer, Dec. 7, 1877.
[6] Report of Sec. of War for 1878, p. 38.
[7] Ibid.

to the white man when it was found that they again stood in the pathway of progress. A treaty was no sooner made than its stipulations, it was discovered, were inconvenient, and it must be changed. The Indian "problem" was no sooner "solved" than it presented itself again in some new and more exasperating form.

At the close of Andrew Johnson's administration it was believed that the situation might be improved by a rearrangement of the reservations. Secretary Browning and Secretary Cox had such ends in view. Commissions, assigned to the duty of making recommendations on the subject, had advocated the adoption of this policy.[1] Many charitable people were calling the government to account—the Interior Department for permitting the "Indian Ring" to rob the red man, the War Department for making cruel wars upon the remnants of a weak and dwindling race instead of Christianizing it, and teaching it the arts of civilization. Religious societies were active and urgent, especially the Society of Friends. "Indian Rights," "Indian Aid" and similar associations were formed in cities and states. To meet the views of these bodies of citizens, whose devotion to the Indian's welfare was so sincere, policies, which it was confidently expected would lead to happy results, were instituted. In the first place, in 1869, by authority of Congress, a new body, a board of gentlemen, "eminent for their intelligence and philanthropy," not more than ten in number, was formed to superintend the subject.[2] Its members would be appointed by President Grant, and, while its powers, as defined by later legislation,[3] were only advisory and recommendatory, from its activities it was believed that there would come a more humane and a more responsible administration. Two millions of dollars were appropriated for use under the "joint control" of the commission and the Secretary of the Interior, to maintain peace among the tribes and promote their civilization. At any rate the complaint, which was directed at the

[1] Report of Sec. of Int. for 1869, pp. viii–ix.
[2] Act of April 10, 1869.
[3] Acts of July 15, 1870, and March 1, 1871.

Indian Bureau, and the Interior Department of which it was a part, might not be so angry, and public opinion would be appeased in some degree by the adoption of so liberal a measure.[1]

Upon the organization of the commission William Welsh of Philadelphia was elected president and Felix R. Brunot, a wealthy man of Pittsburgh,[2] secretary, Mr. Brunot, in the course of a few weeks, on Welsh's resignation, coming to the presidency. The body established an office in New York. Several of the commissioners gave generously of their time and capacities in the hope of benefitting the service.[3] Their examination of contracts, their inspection of food, clothing and other supplies for the Indians, their toilsome and perilous travels through wild parts of the West, year following year, their tedious conferences with leading savages [4] could have been in answer only to a profound conviction of the necessity for such interposition by men of charitable, if of sometimes impractical views. Their annual reports were fearful arraignments of the course of the government hitherto in its dealings with the Indian.

Furthermore it was Secretary Cox's desire, in which he had the support of President Grant, to give the appointment of a number of superintendents and agents to the Society of Friends, a religious sect which enjoyed so high and enviable a reputation in its relations with the American aborigine.[5] Soon the records of the Indian Bureau were filled with reports from Kansas, Nebraska and the Indian Territory, which, in the Quaker manner, began with an "Esteemed Friend," instead of the austerely official "Sir," ended with a "Respectfully thy friend,"

[1] Report of Sec. of Int. for 1869, pp. x–xi, 446, 485–93; Report of Indian Com. for 1869.

[2] Grandson of a Frenchman who accompanied Lafayette to this country to fight in the Revolution and who remained here. His father grew rich from the manufacture of white lead in Pittsburgh. To this fortune he added one of his own, made in the iron business, using it freely in relief work on the battle fields during the Civil War.—C. L. Slattery, Felix R. Brunot.

[3] Cf. General Cox, Report of Sec. of Int. for 1870, p. ix.

[4] For accounts of Brunot's travels see Slattery's Life of Brunot.

[5] Report of Sec. of Int. for 1869, p. x; Report of Indian Com. for 1870, p. 4.

and were written in the "Eighth Month" or the "Ninth Month," instead of August or September. The Indian commissioners recommended that the policy be extended and that other religious denominations be invited to co-operate with the government in a similar way. Thus were the Episcopalian, Presbyterian, Methodist, Baptist, Catholic and other churches invited to nominate agents, and the system, with the favor of Secretary Cox and the President, was developed rapidly.[1]

The more President Grant was complimented upon his enlightened attitude toward the Indian the greater was his feeling of pride in his "humane and peaceful" policy, and salutary progress was achieved by the philanthropists on the "Peace" or "Christian" commission, as it was called, not infrequently with irony, and by the agents selected by the religious societies, so long as the management of the Interior Department remained with General Cox.[2] The commissioners instituted several general investigations by Congress of the conduct of the Indian Department,[3] composed some differences, and averted or postponed some wars.[4] A scheme was on foot to strip the Osages of their great reservation of 8,000,000 acres in Kansas for 19 cents an acre for the advantage of a railway corporation. The commission exposed the steal and changed the form of the sale.[5] Other frauds were discovered and stopped.[6]

But in 18 months General Cox's intelligent and honest control of the subject was lost to the country, without the President's wish to make it possible for him to continue in his place, and in the hands of his successors, Columbus Delano and

[1] Report of Indian Com. for 1870, pp. 4–5, 95–8; Report of Sec. of Int. for 1870, pp. ix, 474; cf. testimony of Wm. Welsh in House Reports, 44th Cong. 1st sess., nos. 240 and 354; N. Y. Nation, Aug. 5, 1875; Slattery, Life of Brunot, pp. 144–5, particularly the map, p. 152. Accounts of the work of the agents of the churches are included in the reports of the Indian Commission year by year.
[2] Report of Sec. of Int. for 1870, pp. vi–ix.
[3] One as early as in 1871; cf. House Reports, 41st Cong. 3rd sess., no. 39.
[4] Cf. Report of Sec. of Int. for 1877, p. 405; Report of Indian Com. for 1870; House Reports, 43rd Cong. 1st sess., no. 778; ibid., 44th Cong. 1st sess., no. 354, p. 187; ibid., no. 240, p. 2.
[5] Report of Indian Com. for 1869, p. 31; ibid. for 1870, pp. 3–4.
[6] Cf. Slattery, Life of Brunot, pp. 215–6.

Zachariah Chandler, both spoilsmen, Grant's "policy," for
which it was still pleasant for him to receive praise, was not
much more useful to the Indian than was his Civil Service
Commission, from which George William Curtis had retired,
to the cause of civil service reform.[1] Each year the Secretary of
the Interior expressed to the President his satisfaction with the
course of the conduct of Indian affairs, and each year the country received his assurances that all was right with this question.
Delano, in his first report, in 1871, made a remarkable suggestion. There were, in all, he found, 321,000 Indians. Making
deductions for those residing in Alaska, and those settled in
four or five states, not maintaining tribal relations, some 242,000
were on reservations. About 60,000 were comfortably located
in the Indian Territory. Outside of this territory some 172,000
were confirmed by law in rights to 96,155,785 acres of land, or
558 acres for each Indian,—man, woman and child. He would
have them all pressed into the Indian Territory, where if the
land were partitioned among the new arrivals and the old
residents, each would find a farm of 180 acres. He would then
have the territory assume the organization of other territories,
and he would call it Oklahoma, as had been proposed at a
council at Ocmulgee in December, 1870.[2] But of this grand
plan nothing came. The dispossession of the Indians proceeded.
Commissions were appointed to hold "councils" of the chiefs,
and negotiations with the individual tribes, with which treaties
containing provisions now inconvenient to the white man had
been concluded, for piecemeal cession of their lands, in return
for more doles and presents, were begun and continued as
before.[3]

In 1873 commissioners, officially charged by the Interior
Department with the alteration of treaties and laws and the
accommodation of disputes, were in communication with 19
tribes.[4] Nearly all the questions at issue bore upon the possession and use of lands which were coveted by the whites

[1] Cf. N. Y. Tribune, June 11, 1874.
[2] Report of Sec. of Int. for 1871, pp. 5-8; cf. ibid. for 1872, pp. 6-7.
[3] Cf. ibid. for 1873, p. v.
[4] Ibid., pp. 383-7.

and had for their end a clearing of the way for our advancing Western civilization.

Red Cloud, chief of the Ogallalas, Spotted Tail, chief of the Brulés, and other Sioux chiefs visited the East in 1870, to be tendered courtesies at Washington, where they were received by the President, and at New York, where they addressed a great audience in Cooper Institute.[1] A party of Cheyennes, Arapahoes and Wichitas came in 1871 to receive similar civilities at the hands of the government.[2] As many as seven deputations of savages, each containing from ten to fifty persons, including Red Cloud and Spotted Tail and their followings again, were brought to Washington in 1872. They were escorted to view places of historical interest, shops, manufactories, wharves, harbors and navy yards in a number of the Eastern cities. Now and again they were put upon platforms to exhibit their odd figures and grunt their speeches, which were interpreted to amuse large assemblages of people. Told at the agencies and the frontier posts that the whites were as numerous as the leaves of the trees beside the streams, and the blades of grass growing upon the prairies, that their houses stood side by side for miles in every direction, these excursions were encouraged in order that the savages might come to know the power of the people, whose authority they were wont to resist. It were cheaper, our shrewd Indian administrators said, to give the chiefs "free rides" on our railroads, steamboats and Broadway omnibuses than to open their eyes through military expeditions.[3]

The conduct of any negotiation with the Indians presupposed, on their side, almost complete ignorance and credulity. The language used in communicating with them was sometimes like that of the horse trader, whose proverbial morality characterized all our conversations with them, again like that in which we address the dawning intelligences of small children. Powder Face, or Red Dog, or Crooked Nose, or Shake His Tail, whose very name was ludicrous, was spoken to and replied (by way

[1] Report of Indian Com. for 1870, pp. 38 et seq.
[2] Ibid. for 1871, pp. 21 et seq.
[3] Report of Sec. of Int. for 1872, p. 487; cf. ibid. for 1871, p. 439; Report of Indian Com. for 1872, pp. 5, 125, 127, 128.

of the interpreters) in word and phrase which was calculated,
if it were not designed, to enrich the store of our national humor.
Yet, with all their manifest benightedness of mind, and qualities generally which caused them to be fairly regarded as a
low order of mankind, they, in many instances, had marked
native shrewdness of wit; and our treaty makers and changers,
proceeding upon the theory that the savages were to be thimble-
rigged, often made serious mistakes. As a rule, however, to
cheat them seemed to be no difficult work. In 1873 the Crows
were induced to part with not less than 4,000,000 acres of land
in Montana, lying south of the Yellowstone River, which miners
were invading, and which the Northern Pacific Railroad would
cross, in exchange for a home in the Judith Basin.[1] In this
agreement Secretary Delano expressed much pride. The tribe
had been paid $130,000 a year under the terms of the old
treaty—now, after relinquishing territory of this great extent,
it would be necessary to pay them but $50,000 annually. Thus,
if Congress had ratified the scheme, $80,000 a year would have
been saved to the government.[2]

The Utes were a nuisance in Colorado. Their reservation
was of enormous size. By the treaties of 1863 and 1868 all that
part of the territory lying west of the 107th meridian, extending from New Mexico northwardly to within 50 miles of the
Wyoming line, nearly 15,000,000 acres, or 20,000 square miles,
was roving ground for this small and squalid band of savages.
It was 20 square miles, said Governor McCook, for the head of
each family, and four square miles for each individual Ute.[3]

At the head of the Rio Grande, in the so-called "San Juan
district," many claims had been staked out and machinery
had been hauled in for mining operations. The country was the
centre of "wild speculation."[4] Already, in 1872, there were

[1] Report of Sec. of Int. for 1873, pp. 391, 481–511.
[2] Ibid., pp. vii–viii; House Ex. Doc., 43rd Cong. 1st sess., no. 89. The
cessation of work on the Northern Pacific Railroad, due to the panic of
1873, made the immediate removal of the tribe unnecessary.
[3] Report of Sec. of Int. for 1870, p. 627; cf. ibid. for 1872, p. 477.
[4] House Ex. Doc., 43rd Cong. 1st sess., no. 193, p. 2. A town called Del
Norte became the centre of the district. Cf. corr. from that place in N. Y.
Tribune, July 4, 1876.

so many miners in the reserve, it was said, that "their expulsion by legal measures would be almost impracticable."[1] In the following spring, in 1873, prospectors rushed thither "from all quarters."[2] Tumult was imminent, and a commission was appointed to treat with the Utes and secure the cession, if possible, of that part of their land on which the camps had been established.[3] Meantime, the War Department, at the request of the Indian Bureau, set the troops to the task of clearing the reservation of intruders,[4] and, in order to ascertain its boundaries, its geological character and its probable wealth, despatched an engineer, with a competent staff, for a reconnaisance of the country, a work which was performed in the summer of 1873.[5]

In 1872 the Utes emphatically refused to agree to any restriction of their boundaries.[6] But in the following year they were induced to relinquish a quadrilateral block of territory, cut out of the southern half of their reservation, embracing about 4,000,000 acres.[7] They had been receiving $20,000 annually from the government. Now, after surrendering this vast amount of valuable country,[8] they were persuaded by our dexterous bargainers to accept $25,000 a year,[9] which was not more than enough, if invested in rations, to support the tribe for 16 days,[10] and which still, in 1875, remained unpaid.[11]

[1] Report of Sec. of Int. for 1872, p. 509; House Ex. Doc., 42nd Cong. 3rd sess., no. 90, p. 2.

[2] House Ex. Doc., 43rd Cong. 1st sess., no. 193, p. 2.

[3] Report of Indian Com. for 1872, pp. 15–17; House Mis. Doc., 43rd Cong. 1st sess., no. 86, pp. 6–8.

[4] House Ex. Doc., 43rd Cong. 1st sess., no. 193, pp. 2–3; Senate Ex. Doc., 46th Cong. 2nd sess., no. 29, pp. 2–5.

[5] House Ex. Doc., 43rd Cong. 1st sess., no. 193.

[6] Report of Sec. of Int. for 1872, pp. 508–9; Report of Indian Com. for 1872, pp. 17, 89–112; House Ex. Doc., 42nd Cong. 3rd sess., no. 90.

[7] They were allowed to retain a strip 20 miles wide on the southern boundary, adjacent to New Mexico, a runway 15 miles in width up the western border of the state, and Uncompagre Park which jutted down from the north into the surrendered parallelogram. The text of this and other Indian treaties may be conveniently referred to in Senate Ex. Doc., 48th Cong. 2nd sess., no. 95, a compilation of value by Alice C. Fletcher.

[8] Senate Ex. Doc., 46th Cong. 2nd sess., no. 29, p. 17.

[9] Report of Sec. of Int. for 1873, pp. viii, 384.

[10] Senate Ex. Doc., 46th Cong. 2nd sess., no. 29, p. 19.

[11] Ibid., pp. 16–18, 21.

This cession, large as it was, left these "aboriginal vagrants," as they were called by General McCook,[1] a broad and extensive reserve, which, as the excitement in Leadville and other mining camps in the mountains increased, was contemplated with envy by the whites. In the early spring of 1874, while the country was still covered with snow, ranchmen were entering the strip on the boundary line of New Mexico.[2] In 1875 white men were overrunning northern portions of the reserve,[3] and persisted in their design to occupy it and put it to their uses, in spite of the protests of the resident Indian agents, and such authorities at Washington as could be enlisted for the service, goaded to action by the entreaties of the humanitarians, that the "squatters" should be summarily removed by the troops.[4]

The Utes cultivated no land, it was said, pursued no useful occupation and were fed by the government, yet they were confirmed in their title to a reservation three times the size of Massachusetts. If it were divided, it was computed now that every individual in the tribe would receive between 3,000 and 4,000 acres. The country set aside for their occupancy was filled with rich metalliferous deposits. Contained in it, were excellent grazing grounds which amounted, indeed, so it was alleged, to nearly one-third of all the arable land in the state. Mines of great value lay beyond the reservation and could be approached only by crossing it; but this the Indians would not allow—such movements they viewed with "distrust and jealousy." The people complained, and the legislature of Colorado implored the government at Washington to open the country to exploration and settlement at once. Violent clashes, it seemed, would be unavoidable and must soon ensue.[5]

Of more urgent interest was the situation which developed as a result of the stampede to the Black Hills. The reconnoitering expedition of the government, and the invasion of pros-

[1] Report of Sec. of Int. for 1870, p. 627.
[2] Senate Ex. Doc., 46th Cong. 2nd sess., no. 29, pp. 6–8.
[3] Ibid., p. 18.
[4] Ibid., pp. 43–5. See G. W. Manypenny, Our Indian Wards, chap. xix.
[5] Am. Ann. Cyclop. for 1879, pp. 150–51.

pectors and other adventurers disturbed the Sioux Indians. This could have been certainly anticipated, since their temper, having been abundantly tried, was well known. The organization in Wyoming by some 2,000 men, in the spring of 1870, of what they called the "Big Horn Mountain Mining and Exploring Association," to proceed to the northern part of that territory, had led at Washington to so much apprehension of conflict that the subject was discussed in meetings of the cabinet, and Sherman ordered Sheridan to forbid the execution of the project.[1] Only the visit to the East of Red Cloud, Spotted Tail and other head men of the tribe in the summer of 1870 [2] had averted, it was believed, an outbreak on that question.[3] In 1872 the vanity of the chiefs had been indulged again and they were brought to Washington for another visit to the President. Once more it was believed that peace would be promoted by these Indians upon their return to their people on the northwestern plains.

But new and grave difficulties arose to disturb our relations with two bands of the tribe. They were profoundly concerned about the location of their places of abode. Red Cloud's and Spotted Tail's agencies were moved about to their great displeasure, and, as it appeared to them, to their material disadvantage, as well as in violation of faith, so that in the winter of 1873–74, it was only by the instrumentalities of a commission of discreet and experienced men, headed by Bishop W. H. Hare, and troops called from Fort Laramie, that the murmuring of the savages over this subject had been allayed.[5]

[1] Report of Sec. of War for 1870, pp. 33–4; Senate Ex. Doc., 41st Cong. 2nd sess., no. 89; N. Y. Herald, Aug. 31, 1874.

[2] For Red Cloud some of the President's friends struck a silver medal, on one side of which was the face of Grant with the motto—"Let Us Have Peace" and the words "Liberty Justice and Equality"; on the other— "On Earth Peace Good Will Toward Men."—W. K. Moorehead, The American Indian, p. 419.

[3] Report of Indian Com. for 1870, pp. 49–50; ibid. for 1872, pp. 145–6; Report of Sec. of Int. for 1870, pp. vi–vii, 468; ibid. for 1871, pp. 428–9; Report of Sec. of War for 1870, pp. 33–4.

[4] Report of Sec. of Int. for 1872, p. 85.

[5] Report of Indian Com. for 1874, p. 3; ibid. for 1875, pp. 12–13, 143; cf. Report of Sec. of War for 1874, p. 24; Howe, Life and Labors of Bishop Hare, pp. 110–21.

More impended now on the subject of the Black Hills. The
War Department was instructed to adopt measures which would,
if possible, prevent white men from entering the country for
mining and settlement until the Indians could be consulted and
the treaty could be changed.[1] Sheridan, at once, following the
return of the Custer expedition,[2] informed all who contemplated
visiting the Hills that they would not be permitted to do so.
Wagon trains directed thither were to be burned; the leaders
of the expeditions were to be arrested for confinement at the
nearest military post. Had they succeeded in already penetrating the interior they should be pursued by cavalry.[3] The daring
party which went out in 1874 and spent the winter in a stockade
were removed by the military in the spring of 1875.[4] But, in
general, such exertions on the part of the army were vain.
When Sheridan's orders could be enforced at all, and the miners
were taken into the posts for surrender to the "civil authorities," little came of it, for, these authorities being in sympathy with the white man rather than the Indian, the prisoners
were immediately released, ready to return to their placers.[5]
Colonel Dodge said, in 1875, that more than 100 men had been
arrested, though not one had received punishment beyond
what may have been incurred by the loss of time consumed in
the journey to and from the post, and his solicitude, meanwhile,
lest he might find his claim in the hands of another when he
should reach it again.[6] Such service was intensely distasteful
to the soldiers, and their activity was as perfunctory as it was
futile. As a last resort, in 1875, General Crook, in command of

[1] A design of some miners and lumbermen to invade the Black Hills
had been thwarted by the Indian Department, with the aid of the troops,
in 1872. Hancock prevented the departure of this party.—Mrs. A. D.
Tallent, The Black Hills, p. 8; Howe, Life and Labors of Bishop Hare,
pp. 127–8.
[2] August 27, 1874.
[3] Senate Ex. Doc., 43rd Cong. spec. sess., no. 2.
[4] See Mrs. Tallent, The First White Woman in the Black Hills.
[5] F. Whittaker, General G. A. Custer, p. 511.
[6] One miner declared that he had been banished four times from the
Hills; four times he had come back again. (Dodge, The Black Hills, p.
111.) Some brought suit against the military officers for false arrest.—
Report of Sec. of Int. for 1875, p. vii.

the Department of the Platte, himself visited the camp and expostulated with the miners. He issued a proclamation ordering them to depart the country. Though they generally complied with the command they withdrew to no great distance, and, as before, made their way back to their claims as soon as the troops were out of sight.[1]

The Sioux "nation," numbering perhaps 50,000, had been compressed by various processes into boundaries which were tolerably definite. Some were at the agencies in a degree of quiet, while others were entirely averse to such a life as the white man desired them to lead, and, under intractable chieftains, roamed the country at their pleasure. As they were almost entirely surrounded by Indians of tribes which were hostile to them, much of the time actively, it was shrewdly observed that this would be the solution of the "problem," and Mr. Delano, at the head of the Department of the Interior, where the instincts of humanity, it was expected, would come to expression rather than through the War Department, saw in this circumstance a possibility of great value to the government. The tribes "friendly" to us which enveloped the Sioux—the Crows, Blackfeet, Gros Ventres and Arickarees—he thought might be "liberally supplied" with "improved firearms and ammunition" for the destruction of the hostiles who were so providentially circumscribed.[2]

By the treaty of 1868, made necessary by the construction of the Union Pacific Railway,[3] which had brought the Sioux within limits then esteemed appropriate, they had been given absolute rights to all of the present state of South Dakota up to the 46th parallel, in so far as this territory lay west of the Missouri River, together with some smaller reservations located east of the river. Here was a tract of country which contained no arable land except that which might be found in the

[1] Senate Ex. Doc., 44th Cong. 1st sess., no. 51, pp. 25, 26; Dodge, The Black Hills, pp. 112–4; H. N. Maguire, New Guide to Dakota and the Black Hills, pp. 12–3; Howe, Life of Bishop Hare, pp. 122–4; J. G. Bourke, On the Border with Crook, pp. 244–5; Report of Sec. of War for 1875, pp. 69–70; G. W. Manypenny, Our Indian Wards, pp. 300–301.

[2] Report of Sec. of Int. for 1873, p. vii.

[3] Report of Sec. of War for 1876, p. 27.

unexplored Black Hills. It was deliberately bestowed upon them because of the belief in its entire want of value to the white man.[1] In addition a great tract west of Dakota, running out to the Big Horn Mountains (the range which extends north and south in the centre of Montana and Wyoming), and in Nebraska as far south as the North Platte River, was practically Sioux ground, for we had pledged ourselves not to open this country to settlement,—no one might enter it, indeed, without the Indians' consent. More than this, during the hunting season, the tribe might come farther south and visit the Republican fork of the Kansas River, in western Nebraska and Kansas and eastern Colorado, as long as buffalo should continue to range there "in such numbers as to justify the chase." It was a wide empire through which these savages might ride and forage in the spirit of their olden proprietorship.

Quite aside from complications arising out of the mining excitement in the Black Hills, the completion of the Union Pacific and the Kansas Pacific Railroads and the advancement of the lines of frontier settlement beside the tracks, made it imperative to change the provisions of the treaty in respect of the hunting rights on the Republican, and the use of the unceded territory above the North Platte in Nebraska. So much was in mind when Red Cloud, Spotted Tail and other chiefs were brought to Washington in 1872.[2] In 1873 a commission visited the various bands who had been parties to the treaty and endeavored to collect their head men in a council, but the movement met with no success.[3] The ends in view could be the more justly sought, if not demanded, it was argued, because of sundry bloody outrages perpetrated by the Sioux, while on their last excursion into Nebraska and Kansas. At that time they had massacred a party of unoffending Indians of another tribe, the Pawnees, and killed some white frontiersmen.[4] Their depredations generally and constantly were, in the sight of

[1] "The poorest [land] of all this extensive region."—Sheridan in Report of Sec. of War for 1878; cf. Howe, Life and Labors of Bishop Hare, p. 131.
[2] Report of Sec. of Int. for 1872, p. 485.
[3] Ibid. for 1873, p. 387.
[4] Ibid., p. 376.

Western men and of military officers stationed on the plains, so grossly violative of the terms of the treaty that it might well be said to be no longer in force. The Indians themselves had abrogated it.[1] Again, so few buffaloes were still to be found in the old haunts of the animal on the Republican River that the provision of the treaty, limiting the enjoyment of the privilege of chasing them there to the time when they should still range upon it, was believed to have been automatically annulled.[2]

But it was a ticklish task to deal with such a "treaty power" as the "great Sioux nation," and it were more discreet to withdraw privileges which had been distinctly granted only after new negotiations, and on a basis of purchase or exchange.[3] They had shrewd and intelligent chieftains, of whom Red Cloud was a prominent example.[4] He had lived as a boy, as he was wont to say, "where the sun rises"; his home to-day was where it set. The "white children" had surrounded him and left him "nothing but an island." He and his people had been strong; now they were "melting like snow on the hillside," while the whites were growing "like spring grass." He came to Washington—there was no blood in the land when he returned to his home. But when the whites visited his country they left behind them "a trail of blood."[5] They swindled him, said the clever chief; he was not "hard to swindle," because he did not know how to read and write. "You promise us many things," he continued, "but you never perform them." "You take away everything,"[6] leaving the Indian "poor and naked."

[1] Report of Sec. of Int. for 1873, p. vii; Report of Sec. of War for 1876, pp. 499, 500, 501; Senate Ex. Doc., 41st Cong. 2nd sess., no. 89, p. 10; H. N. Maguire, New Guide to Dakota and the Black Hills, p. 15.
[2] Report of Sec. of Int. for 1874, p. xi; ibid. for 1875, p. vi; cf. Report of Indian Com. for 1871, p. 3.
[3] Report of Sec. of Int. for 1874, pp. xi, 319.
[4] N. Y. Times, June 17, 1870; N. Y. Tribune for same date; J. K. Dixon, The Vanishing Race, pp. 118-9; Hebard and Brininstool, The Bozeman Trail, vol. ii, pp. 175-204; W. K. Moorehead, The American Indian, chap. xvii. It was Red Cloud who, by his aggressions, had compelled the government to abandon the Bozeman Trail.—C. A. Eastman, The Indian To-day, p. 30.
[5] Report of Indian Com. for 1870, p. 41.
[6] Ibid., p. 43.

The railroad came—it passed through his lands; he received no
pay for it—"not even a brass ring,"[1] and so on.

The mere advance of the Custer expedition to the Black
Hills, in the summer of 1874, though the movement should be
without portent for the future, was regarded as an infringement of the terms of the treaty.[2]   The troops, as they proceeded, met with few Indians, barring some who scampered off
as the expedition neared the boundary of Montana,[3] and a
small party in camp beside one of the pretty brooks in the
Hills.[4]   But the movements of the expedition were watched
furtively from afar. The news spread rapidly and the excitement which it awakened in the tribe was intense. As the
cavalrymen, with their long wagon train, came out of the mountains, on the return to the Missouri, they found great widths
of grass burned athwart their way and other evidences of the
displeasure of the savages. Rumors that 5,000 braves would
attack him put Custer on his guard.[5]

The parties of prospectors and settlers which started for
the Hills in the summer and autumn of 1874 were harried and,
in all but one case, driven back.[6]   The Secretary of the Interior
and the Commissioner of Indian Affairs had been at pains to
say that no valuable mineral deposits were discovered in the
country, indeed, that it was generally "undesirable for cultivation and settlement by white men,"[7] though Custer's official
report was in direct contradiction of these statements.[8]   Such

[1] Report of Indian Com. for 1870, p. 41.
[2] The government's course in authorizing and organizing it was condemned by many white men, as well as by the Indians, at the time. They
saw its dangers and plainly presented the case to the Secretary of the
Interior and President Grant.—Cf. Howe, Life and Labors of Bishop
Hare, pp. 124–9.
[3] Mrs. Custer, Boots and Saddles, pp. 300–301.
[4] Ludlow, op. cit., p. 13; Diary of Major Forsyth in H. N. Maguire,
New Guide to Dakota and the Black Hills, pp. 59–60; Letter of corr. in
N. Y. Tribune, Aug. 10, 1876.
[5] Ludlow, op. cit., pp. 12, 17.
[6] Report of Sec. of Int. for 1874, p. 318; cf. H. N. Maguire, New Guide
to Dakota and the Black Hills, p. 15.
[7] Report of Sec. of Int. for 1874, pp. xiii, 317–18.
[8] Senate Ex. Doc., 43rd Cong. 2nd sess., no. 32, p. 8; cf. Ludlow, op. cit.,
p. 14; Sheridan in Report of Sec. of War for 1874, pp. 24–5. In spite of
the fact, too, that all the newspaper correspondents who were taken along

denials had not prevented the fitting out of the government
expedition headed by Professor Jenney in the following year,
an authorized report of competent scientists that the Black Hills
were rich in mineral wealth and the frank admission of the new
Secretary of the Interior, Zachariah Chandler, that it was so.[1]
The commission to the Sioux, under the presidency of Bishop
Hare, in 1874, had convened the disaffected elements in the
tribe, and, with great peril to themselves, while endeavoring to
conciliate the Red Cloud and Spotted Tail bands on the subject
of their various grievances, reopened the question of keeping
them in future out of Nebraska and Kansas,[2] without meeting
the immediate favor of the Indians.[3] This council led to the
visit of another large delegation of chiefs to Washington in May,
1875, when, for a paltry $25,000 in hand, and the promise of
$25,000 more, to be procured from another Congress, they re-
linquished their hunting rights on the Republican fork of the
Smoky Hill, and their territorial rights in the "unceded" lands
west of their reservation, in so far as these were contained in
Nebraska, south of the south divide of the Niobrara River,[4]
but all suggestions concerning a withdrawal from the Black
Hills were emphatically repelled.

The disinterested and arduous services of Mr. Brunot, Mr.
Vincent Colyer and other commissioners met, they felt, with
little appreciation. For a while after General Cox had left the
Department of the Interior there seemed to be a wish to
adhere to high standards of administration, and, in October,
1871, Grant tendered the appointment as Commissioner of
Indian Affairs to Mr. Brunot, who was urged by his friends to
accept. He declined the responsibility,[5] and General Francis

into the Hills declared it to to be one of the richest of gold fields. The
very teamsters in Custer's train located claims in one of the valleys and
recorded their priority in a written paper for use on the first available
day.—Cf. N. Y. Tribune, Aug. 28, 1874.
  [1] Report of Sec. of Int. for 1875, p. vi.
  [2] Report of Indian Com. for 1874, pp. 60 et seq.
  [3] Howe, Life and Labors of Bishop Hare, pp. 120–22.
  [4] Report of Sec. of Int. for 1874, pp. 319, 397 et seq.; ibid. for 1875, pp.
vi, 507–508, 681.
  [5] Slattery, Life of Brunot, pp. 182–5.

A. Walker, not yet done with his tasks in connection with the taking of the census, was chosen. This was excellent,[1] but in a year, unable to cope with its corrupting vexations, he abandoned the post for a professorship in Yale University, to the regret of the reformers,[2] and no suitable successor appeared.

The advice of the citizens' board was not taken; their decisions were overruled; expenditures were made against their remonstrances;[3] they were subjected to personal indignities with the purpose of driving them from their places;[4] the department was controlled by the "Indian Ring" as before.[5] Perceiving that they were being used by the politicians merely to give a respectable appearance to the service, Mr. Colyer resigned in January, 1872;[6] and, in June, 1874, Mr. Brunot and five other members of the board retired from their posts, following a final appeal to the President which was unavailing,[7] thus making necessary an entire reorganization of the commission.[8] After a variety of efforts to find a new cover for the activities of the forces which had captured the board,[9] General Clinton B. Fisk, who had seen service with the Freedmen's Bureau, later a prominent Prohibitionist, was persuaded to become its president.

It was in the midst of these occurrences that Delano and the

[1] Cf. Wm. Welsh in J. P. Munroe, Life of F. A. Walker, p. 129.

[2] Slattery, Life of Brunot, pp. 195-7.

[3] House Ex. Doc., 43rd Cong. 1st sess., no. 123, pp. 1-5; House Reports, 43rd Cong. 1st sess., no. 778, pp. 277-9.

[4] N. Y. Tribune, July 4, 1874.

[5] Slattery, Life of Brunot, chaps. vi and vii; N. Y. Nation, June 11, 1874, and Aug. 5, 1875.

[6] Report of Indian Com. for 1872, pp. 140-41; N. Y. Tribune, July 4, 1874.

[7] Slattery, Life of Brunot, pp. 222-3.

[8] Report of Indian Com. for 1874, p. 4; Report of Sec. of Int. for 1877, p. 405; N. Y. Tribune, June 8, 1874, containing letter of resignation of the six commissioners and statement of the New York member, William E. Dodge. The Tribune said editorially: "So long as the commissioners confined themselves to moral suasion and the cardinal principles of the Christian religion they were superciliously let alone; when they attempted to enforce the law in regard to the letting of contracts there was worse than Indian howl."—Ibid., June 9, 1874; cf. ibid., June 11, June 20 and July 3, 1874.

[9] Cf. Report of Sec. of Int. for 1877, p. 405; Slattery, Life of Brunot, pp. 146, 227; N. Y. Tribune, July 4, 1874.

officers of the Indian Department fell into controversy, which
has been described, with Professor Marsh of Yale University.
In the winter of 1874–75 Red Cloud and his following had been
served uncommonly ill. They were on the verge of starvation
and Marsh had told the country of conditions, which gravely
reflected upon the Indian civil service. His charges directed
attention again to the scandalous operations of the "Indian
Ring," which led to an official investigation, and the retirement
of Delano as Secretary of the Interior.

Delano gone and Chandler in his place, another discovery
was made in the field of our Indian "diplomacy." The government had been expending about $1,250,000 a year to feed the
Sioux, or this amount of money was taken out of the Treasury of
the United States for the use, with no obligation on its part to
bestow such benefits upon them. This was five per cent, old
Mr. Chandler said, on $25,000,000, for which "no equivalent"
was received. The way was plain. In return for subsistence
now and in the future the Sioux should surrender to the white
man the gold fields of the Black Hills and the right of building
roads into that country.[1] In 1875 President Grant despatched
another commission, under the chairmanship of Senator Allison, for a meeting with the chiefs, with a view to reopening and
effecting an agreement, if possible, on this pressing question.[2]
By this time many hundreds of miners were in the Hills without the government having the means to prevent the intrusion.[3]
Though a large military force was at hand, under the command
of such officers as Sheridan, Terry and Crook, the result, the
Commissioner of Indian Affairs said sagely, proved either their
"inefficiency," or else "the utter impracticability of keeping
Americans out of a country, where gold is known to exist, by
any fear of orders, or of United States cavalry, or by any consideration of the rights of others." [4]

If, as men said, the Black Hills were of no value to the In-

[1] Report of Sec. of Int. for 1875, pp. vii, 510.
[2] Ibid., pp. 509, 538.
[3] Cf. Howe, Life and Labors of Bishop Hare, p. 130.
[4] Report of Sec. of Int. for 1875, p. 509; cf. accounts of military commanders, Report of Sec. of War for 1875, pp. 64–5, 69–70.

dians, since they visited the country only to cut lodge poles, since they were, indeed, afraid to live in it, because of the violent storms of thunder and lightning which broke over it,[1] it was plain enough now, had it not been so before, that they would resist to the uttermost the prosecution of plans to dispossess them of the land. They prized it, both as a hunting ground and as an asylum, and for many years had guarded their property in it jealously.[2] Their more astute chiefs had anticipated a time when they might here find a home, safe from the white man's molestations. Their attachment to it was a "passion," said Bishop Hare; it was "the kernel of their nut, the yelk of their egg."[3]

It was Allison's mission to convene another "grand council" in September, 1875, and secure the relinquishment of practically everything upon which the chiefs, in conversation and speech in visits to the East, placed a value. By the agreement of 1875 they had surrendered only their hunting and other rights, in so far as these were included in the state of Nebraska, south of the south divide of the Niobrara River. Now they were to be persuaded to relinquish the "Big Horn country" in Wyoming, as well as the Black Hills.[4] We wished only to take out the gold and other metals, Allison said; when this should be done the land would again be the Sioux to use as they liked.[5] But white men at the agencies, who seem to have been civil officers of the government, had filled the chiefs with the idea that the Black Hills might be worth more than a few ploughs, sulkies and milch cows, and had suggested a price of from $30,-000,000 to $50,000,000. The "Great Father" had "a house full of money"; the Indians would have some of it.[6] With

[1] H. N. Maguire, New Guide to Dakota and the Black Hills, p. 26; Report of Sec. of Int. for 1875, p. 511; Dodge, The Black Hills, pp. 177-8.
[2] Cf. Senate Ex. Doc., 41st Cong. 2nd sess., no. 89.
[3] Howe, Life and Labors of Bishop Hare, p. 122; cf. Ludlow, op. cit., p. 18. The Black Hills, Bishop Hare wrote to President Grant, were the Sioux "place of council when war parties are sent out, their retreat in times of danger and the pride of the nation." (Howe, op. cit., p. 126.) Another view in Dodge, The Black Hills, pp. 137-8, and Hinman, in Report of Indian Com. for 1875, p. 144.
[4] For Allison's report see Report of Sec. of Int. for 1875, pp. 686 et seq.
[5] Ibid., p. 689.   [6] Ibid., p. 690.

such a bargain in mind a number of the chiefs were willing to
sell the Hills for a large sum to be invested as capital—from
the interest on which they could receive annuities in goods.
But others were indisposed to part with their prized inheritance
under any conditions. So the negotiations failed again, and
the commission gave up the task to which it had been assigned,
with many an animadversion fairly directed at the Indian
administration.

Though we should agree to make a just settlement upon
the tribe for withdrawing from the country, its wise men were
authorized in entertaining the suspicion that the promise,
in all probability, would not be kept. The experience of years
had been sore—the Sioux had new and recent occasion for
their distrust. The $25,000 pledged to them during the visit
of the chiefs to Washington in May, 1875, in addition to a like
sum in hand, on condition of their retirement from thousands
of square miles in Nebraska and the surrender of their hunting
rights, had not yet been paid.[1] What assurance could they have
of fairer treatment were they to make new cessions as a result
of new negotiations?

Not with the Sioux only—with all the tribes our policy had
been vacillating and stupid, short-sighted and selfish, when not
positively knavish. That there were old men still living and
young men, who had sat at the ancients' knees, listening to
accounts of vanished liberties, in a temper to resist a course
which to an untutored, if not to the white man's better mind,
was but a continuation of one long record of faith broken and
wrong endured will seem but little strange to any one.

Nevertheless, as we have seen, the administrators of Indian
affairs each year complimented themselves and one another
upon the enlightenment of their conduct. Each year they gave
solacing accounts to the country of the state of the Indian
race. Each year they declared that there were prosperity and
peace at the points of contact with the savages on the frontiers,
that barbarian minds were being led to industry and "to Christ,"
and that never again, in spite of small raids and disorders,

[1] For Allison's report, see Report of Sec. of Int. for 1876, pp. ix, 394.

which they dismissed with a few words, could there be an Indian war. Not 500 savages could ever again be gathered together at one place for a fight.[1]

Yet it was plain to all men that the troops stationed at the posts along the lines of the Western railroads, and in key positions at other points on the plains and in the mountains, were seldom inactive. In 1872 there were six transcontinental railway enterprises to be protected by Sheridan as commander of the Military Division of the Missouri—the Northern Pacific, the Union Pacific, the Kansas Pacific, and, farther south, the Atchison, Topeka and Santa Fé, the Atlantic and Pacific and the Southern Pacific.[2] The incursions into the Indian country of miners, colonists, buffalo hunters, parties of railway surveyors, and the common rowdies and blacklegs who gravitated to the frontier were to be prevented by the armed forces of the United States. The army was occupied, too, in keeping the Indians upon their reservations. The impulse to go upon a chase, or a marauding expedition, constantly led them to cross the boundaries of lands set apart for their occupancy. Stealing from and murdering white settlers in revenge for injuries old or new, real or imaginary, or as a sport, murderous sallies into other tribes' camps employed bands of barbarians whose exploits were the subject of almost daily despatches to the newspapers.

The Piegans, a band of Blackfeet, roamed Montana. They were robbing and murdering the whites who had penetrated this wilderness, and, who goaded to activity, were savagely taking revenge upon individual Indians,[3] and demanding the right to form a volunteer organization for a general punishment of the tribe. The War Department increased its forces at the upper Missouri posts, ordered them into action and Lieutenant-Colonel Baker, on January 23, 1870, engaged a considerable number of the savages in a battle on the Matias River, in which no less than 173, including many women and children, were

[1] Cf. Report of Sec. of Int. for 1874, pp. 314–15; ibid. for 1875, pp. 506, 531.
[2] Report of Sec. of War for 1872, p. 35.
[3] House Ex. Doc., 41st Cong. 2nd sess., no. 185, p. 2; ibid., no. 197; ibid., no. 269, pp. 29–31.

killed. He was condemned in the harshest way by the agents, the Indian reformers and many of the Eastern newspapers.[1] The battle was called the "Baker Massacre." Like Chivington at Sand Creek and Custer at Washita River he had lent himself to common slaughter.

Sheridan promptly came to Baker's support. It was, he said, simply a question as to who should be killed, the whites or the Indians. Since 1862 no less than 1,200 white men, women and children within the limits of his present command, the Military Division of the Missouri, had been "murdered," many of them in the most fiendish ways, the horrible details of which he gave to Sherman in plain terms. The humanitarians were simply serving the purposes of the "Indian Ring," which he, not very generously and most unfairly, in heat of temper, concluded was the object of their protests.[2] An inquiry was begun by Congress, where again Baker was the subject of the severest strictures. The effect, nevertheless, was quieting and, for a time after the "massacre," Montana enjoyed comparative peace.[3]

The Apaches of New Mexico and Arizona were committing frightful depredations upon the white miners and ranchmen who had sought fortune in a land, long the roving ground of the various bands of that tribe of Indians.[4] Often the frontiersmen combined for their own protection. A party of American and Mexican desperadoes, with some hostile Papagoes, went out from Tucson on April 30, 1871, and attacked a body of savages, who had come in with peace on their lips, and had been interned in a compound near Camp Grant. Feeling ran so high that scores, nearly all of them women, it appears, were killed in cold blood. Children were taken and sold into slavery in Mexico.[5] Though the massacre was justified in the

[1] Cf. G. W. Manypenny, Our Indian Wards, p. 282.
[2] House Ex. Doc., 41st Cong. 2nd sess., no. 269, pp. 9–10, 70–71.
[3] Report of Sec. of Int. for 1870, p. 467; Report of Sec. of War for 1870, p. 29; Report of Indian Com. for 1870, pp. 89–93; House Ex. Doc., 41st Cong. 2nd sess., no. 485; F. A. Walker, The Indian Question, p. 27.
[4] Report of Sec. of Int. for 1871, pp. 418, 430–31.
[5] Ibid., pp. 448–9, 485–92; Report of Indian Com. for 1871, pp. 60–67 J. G. Bourke, On the Border with Crook, p. 104.

West,[1] it was a horror which shocked the sensibilities of the rest of the country.

Year by year the military were in action against Cochise, Geronimo and other defiant Apache chiefs, who, in mountain recesses, issued forth for murder and rapine.[2]   In one engagement, in 1872, Crook killed 40 savages, wounded many more, and made captive a number of women and children.   In another battle he killed 17.[3]   The campaign continued in 1873, when some of the bands surrendered, and were settled, under observation, on reservations, subject to pursuit if they left this ground to resume their predatory habits.[4]   In that year, in response to an inquiry of Congress, the Indian Bureau stated that 405 Indians had been killed and 227 captured by United States troops, nearly all of the slain, barring 17 Assinaboines and 18 Modocs, having been Apaches in Arizona;[5] in the first six months of 1874, 73, all Apaches, were taken captive and 158, all but 29 of them Apaches, were killed.[6]

By this time white settlers had established their homes in every gulch and valley of Arizona.   The failure of Congress to pass appropriation bills for the purchase of food, and the government's general mishandling of the Indian question, constantly put the frontiersmen at the mercy of the hungry and vindictive tribe.[7]   The Apaches, in 1877, were again involved in a series of engagements with the troops and were not reduced even to temporary subjugation until many had been killed and taken prisoners.[8]

In 1873 came the "Modoc War."   In Oregon there was a tribe of Indians, usually called the Snakes, which was divided into two principal branches—the Klamaths and the Modocs— who in the past twenty years had been guilty of many butcheries

[1] Report of Sec. of Int. for 1872, p. 537.
[2] Cf. W. K. Moorehead, The American Indian, chap. xxiii.
[3] Report of Sec. of Int. for 1872, p. 482.
[4] Ibid. for 1873, p. 368; House Ex. Doc., 43rd Cong. 1st sess., no. 80; ibid., 42nd Cong. 3rd sess., no. 105.
[5] Senate Ex. Doc., 43rd Cong. 2nd sess., no. 22.
[6] Ibid.
[7] Senate Mis. Doc., 44th Cong. 1st sess., no. 91.
[8] Report of Sec. of Int. for 1877, pp. 416–17.

of white emigrants, as they had been the victims, in turn, of cruelties on the part of the whites. They were now unfriendly to each other. By a treaty with the United States they were to yield possession of a large tract of land on the Pacific slope, which had long been their home, and confine their movements to a reservation. On this ground hereafter they could dwell happily together. But the Klamaths molested the Modocs, who, under the leadership of a chief called Captain Jack, sought safety, in 1870, by departing the reservation for their old camp on Lost River, which, meantime, had been occupied by the whites. The Interior Department was appealed to, and, in 1872, the troops were ordered to return the Modocs to their reserve to live again beside the Klamaths.[1]

The attempt to bring so much about was violently resisted by the Indians, and led to an attack on their camp on November 29, 1872, when a number of them, including some women and children, and, on our side, a few soldiers and citizens were killed. The savages now started out to raid the white settlements, closely pursued by the military, aided by Oregon and California volunteers,[2] who, however, could make no progress in capturing them, since they took refuge in a rough volcanic country, locally known as the "lava beds,"—rocky fastnesses which made for them a series of almost impregnable natural fortifications.[3] In 1873 a commission, of which A. B. Meacham, earlier Oregon Indian superintendent, was chairman, was appointed to effect peace by negotiation. This body acted under the direction of General E. R. S. Canby, who, as commander of the Department of the Columbia, had been in contact with the tribe in the recent military operations.

Canby held several meetings with Captain Jack and his band. There was suspicion of treachery and further negotiations had every appearance of being unsafe. But very indis-

[1] The irregularity of the proceeding, from the military standpoint, is dwelt upon by Schofield, Forty Six Years in the Army, pp. 435–6.
[2] Cf. House Reports, 43rd Cong. 2nd sess., no. 248; House Ex. Doc., 43rd Cong. 2nd sess., no. 45.
[3] House Ex. Doc. 43rd Cong. 1st sess., no. 122, p. 106. Cf. James Mc-Laughlin, My Friend the Indian, pp. 315–16, 319–20.

creetly on the morning of April 11, on the promise of a surrender,
Canby, Dr. Thomas, a clergyman, who was a member of the
commission, another commissioner named Dyar and Chairman
Meacham, with interpreters, proceeded unarmed according
to compact, to the Indian council tent in the "lava beds." It
was immediately evident that the whole party had been am-
bushed. Conversations ensued, when, suddenly, Captain
Jack pointed a revolver at Canby's head and fired.[1]   The
wound may have been mortal but before this could be ascertained Canby was shot again and stabbed. Thomas, the
preacher, was killed also, while Meacham was left for dead,
though he afterward was picked up and saved by the soldiers,
who had surveyed the bloody scene from a signal station, and
who at once came to the rescue. Dyar escaped unhurt by
flight.

There was now to be no quarter for the Modocs, but they were
a tenacious enemy and it was dangerous employment to pursue
them among the rocks in which they found shelter. A fortnight
after the murder of Canby the savages surprised and surrounded
a body of our troops, who had penetrated their refuge. Four
officers and 18 men were brutally killed, 19 were wounded in
this massacre.[2]   The campaign was doggedly continued and,
after a few weeks, General Jeff. C. Davis, who had succeeded
Canby as commander of the department, killed or captured
all but a few of the more elusive of the hostiles, thus ending a
war which General Schofield, in command of the Division of
the Pacific at San Francisco, said was "more remarkable, in
some respects, than any before known in American history."[3]

The resentment awakened within the army by the treacherous assassination of Canby, increased by the mortal shooting

<hr/>

[1] The Indian philanthropists said, by way of excusing Jack, that his
father had been slain by a white man while under a flag of truce.—Report
of Indian Com. for 1876, p. 104.

[2] Senate Ex. Doc., spec. sess. (March 5, 1877), no. 1.

[3] Report of Sec. of War for 1873, p. 52. For papers and correspondence
bearing on this campaign see House Ex. Doc, 43rd Cong. 1st sess., no.
122; Senate Ex. Doc., spec. sess. (March 5, 1877), no. 1; House Ex. Doc.,
42nd Cong. 3rd sess., no. 201; cf. James McLaughlin, My Friend the Indian,
chap. xviii.

simultaneously at another camp of Lieutenant Sherwocd, whom
the Indians had brought out in answer to a white flag,[1] was
intense. Schofield hoped to hear that the troops in Oregon had
"made an end" of the tribe.[2] Sherman also anxiously awaited
word that they had "met the doom" which they "so richly"
had earned.[3] The leaders, he said again, should be tried by
military commission and shot—the tribe should be dispersed
"so that the name of Modoc should cease."[4]

Canby's assassins were put in irons; they would have been
summarily dealt with but for orders from Washington.[5] They
were tried by court-martial, convicted and, by direction of
President Grant, Jack and three others, on October 3, 1873,
were "hanged by the neck until they were dead" in the sight
of the assembled tribe.[6] The remnants of the band were collected, conveyed to Fort McPherson in Nebraska and thence
transported, partly as a punishment and partly on grounds of
humanity—for Oregon's safety and for their own protection—
to lands in the Indian Territory, where, deprived of their tribal
relations, they might, in families and as individuals, work
out their destinies.[7]

Canby's death was sincerely mourned not only in the army,
where General Sherman declared him to be "one of the kindest
and best gentlemen of this or any other country," but throughout all circles of our national society. A Kentuckian by birth,
he was a graduate of West Point and had distinguished himself
for 34 years in the nation's military service, recently in the
great Southern rebellion, with the resultant duties which fell
to the lot of the army in the disturbed area which was being
"reconstructed." Death, suffered as it was in the cause of
peace rather than of war, was a sacrifice which our "Indian

[1] House Ex. Doc., 43rd Cong. 1st sess., no. 122, p. 82.
[2] Ibid., p. 76.
[3] Ibid., p. 77.
[4] Ibid., p. 86. In another sense were scores of appeals and petitions from
the Society of Friends, peace associations, Indian aid societies, etc., who,
as usual, exculpated the Indians and laid the blame at the white man's
door.—Ibid., pp. 309–28, passim.
[5] Ibid., p. 111; N. Y. Nation, June 12, 1873.
[6] Phila. Inquirer, Oct. 6, 1873.
[7] Report of Sec. of Int. for 1873, p. 450; ibid. for 1874, pp. 375, 391.

policy" should not have exacted of one who stood so high, as Sherman averred, in the "universal respect, honor, affection and love of his countrymen." [1]

In 1874 a determined military movement was inaugurated against hostile savages who had been settled in the western parts of the Indian Territory. Cheyennes, Arapahoes, Kiowas and Comanches found their livelihood, as well as diversion, in raiding the ranches of Texas, Kansas, New Mexico and other surrounding territory, including the areas inhabited by the Chickasaws, Choctaws and other peaceful tribes, [2] to the great exasperation of the victims of their depredations. Many of the outrages were in revenge for the aggressions of the whites. The Indians were particularly irritated by the intrusion of hunters intent upon killing buffalo within the reservations, a party of whom, in the spring of 1874, they fiercely attacked. [3] Whatever the cause, conflict between the settlers and ranchmen and the savages was frequent, and, after a clerk at an Indian agency had been assassinated, and teamsters accompanying a train of Indian supplies had been cruelly slain, [4] the troops of the United States were sent against the hostiles. The campaign was in charge of General Pope. He entrusted the expedition to General Miles, who in this war gained a high reputation for intrepidity as an Indian fighter. Even throughout the hardest months of a severe winter he gave the enemy no rest. Brushes, skirmishes and captures followed one another with staggering rapidity and, at length, early in March, 1875, the Cheyennes, completely broken down and nearly starved to death, came into their agency and surrendered. The Kiowas and Comanches in the Red River country also gave up the contest and laid down their arms at Fort Sill. The ringleaders of the Cheyennes, in accordance with orders from Washington, were being identified for conveyance to and confinement in Fort Marion at St.

[1] House Ex. Doc., 43rd Cong. 1st sess., no. 122, pp. 77–8; N. Y. Nation, April 17, 1873.
[2] Cf. House Mis. Doc., 41st Cong. 2nd sess., no. 139.
[3] Report of Sec. of War for 1874, p. 30; N. A. Miles, Serving the Republic, pp. 120–21.
[4] Report of Sec. of Int. for 1874, p. 320.

Augustine, Fla., when a stampede occurred in the camp. In the melée the prisoners, following an ugly engagement with the troops, broke away and fled to the hills. The soldiers set off to catch them and, after several desperate fights, in which many of the savages were killed, prevented all but a small party from accomplishing their design of making their way north to effect a junction with warriors of kindred blood on the upper Missouri.[1]

The self-content of the directing minds of the Indian Bureau was now to suffer a very rude disturbance in the Sioux country. The supplies for their support not arriving many Indians at the Spotted Tail and Red Cloud, as well as at other Sioux agencies,[2] faced starvation in 1876,[3] as they had in the preceding winter, a fact of which the country had learned through Professor Marsh,—as they had also in 1874,[4] and, indeed, ever since the distributing stations had been removed to distant places in the interior, inaccessible to the supply trains and out of the reach of military and other responsible control. Congress was urgently addressed in February, 1876, by the Secretary of the Interior, and President Grant; appropriations of money to be used for feeding the savages must be made immediately, else the gravest results might ensue.[5]

For a long time a band, estimated to contain 3,000 Sioux, who had never joined in the making of any treaty with the United States, and who were included in the followings of Sitting Bull[6] and some associated chiefs, roamed the plains of western Dakota, Montana and Wyoming. They lived by

[1] Report of Sec. of War for 1874, pp. 29–31; ibid. for 1875, pp. 74–5; Report of Sec. of Int. for 1874, p. 30. The army accounts state, or lead us to infer, that none escaped, (e.g., Pope in Report of Sec. of War for 1875, p. 75). The Indian Bureau, on the other hand, upon a count of arrivals at the northern agencies, gives the number who fled across Kansas and Nebraska at 400.—Report of Sec. of Int. for 1875, p. 535.

[2] For Standing Rock see House Ex. Doc., 44th Cong. 1st sess., no. 184, p. 59.

[3] Report of Sec. of Int. for 1876, pp. 382–3.

[4] House Ex. Doc., 43rd Cong. 1st sess., no. 186.

[5] Senate Ex. Doc., 44th Cong. 1st sess., no. 30.

[6] For an account of this chief see James McLaughlin, My Friend the Indian, pp. 179–82; also W. K. Moorehead, The American Indian, chap. xix.

the chase, since the remnants of the northern herd of buffalo were at their hand, made war-like incursions into the territory of other tribes, plundered white settlements, robbed wagon trains, and, in general, practiced the most repulsive and barbarous customs of their race.[1] They were reinforced by the Northern Cheyennes under Crazy Horse, like Sitting Bull's band, nomads and outlaws,[2] the renegades who had escaped the troops in the Indian Territory and many of the cheated and starving savages, who moved north and west from the Spotted Tail and Red Cloud agencies—all well supplied with arms and cartridges, which they had been accumulating in exchange at the trading posts for wild peltry and cowhides, even for material stolen in raids upon white settlements.[3]

Custer had crossed their country in 1874 with more than 1,000 troops for a reconnaisance of the Black Hills, possession of which had been pledged to them by treaty.[4] In 1875 another government expedition had entered the country. The roads were full of trains. In Cheyenne, as well as in towns on the Missouri, excited men were congregated—all eager to start away for the Indian Pactolus.[5] The number of miners settled in the Hills on July 1, 1876, was estimated by one authority at 4,000;[6] by another at 6,500.[7]

Placers yielding but indifferent returns, machinery was hauled in. Quartz mills were being built for lode mining. So rapidly were stamps being erected that in another year, in 1877, the total production of the placers would be $1,000,000—from ore, $1,500,000.[8] By this time Custer City, which had had a rapid growth, was nearly deserted, since the gulches in its neighborhood were making but meagre returns to the adven-

[1] Senate Ex. Doc., 44th Cong. 1st sess., no. 52, pp. 3–4, 10–11.
[2] Cf. G. W. Manypenny, Our Indian Wards, chap. xvi.
[3] Cf. House Ex. Doc., 44th Cong. 1st sess., no. 184, pp. 29–43; F. Whittaker, General G. A. Custer, p. 538.
[4] F. Whittaker, op. cit., p. 512.
[5] So pressing was the demand for pack trains and wagons that the army could with the greatest difficulty find conveyance for its supplies.—J. G. Bourke, On the Border with Crook, pp. 247–8, 282.
[6] Chicago Times, quoted in N. Y. Herald, July 12, 1876.
[7] H. N. Maguire, The Black Hills, p. 13.
[8] Article on Dakota in Am. Ann. Cyclop. for 1877.

turers, and a new town had sprung up, bearing the name of Deadwood.

Under such conditions the army's task of stopping the stampede might as well be abandoned. Not only was there, after a few months, no more pretense of arresting the movement, but the troops were ordered, through the influence of the politicians from the Western states and territories who visited Grant, actually to guard subsistence trains proceeding to the gold fields, and to protect from the Indians the miners and settlers on their way to, or already in, the Hills.[1]

In view of all that had befallen them in their recent relations with the government there was little wonder, perhaps, that the number of warriors in Sitting Bull's camp increased, and that they were ready for such revengeful deeds as could be nourished only in the Indian mind.

To bring the restless hostiles to order they were told to come into the agencies upon their reservation before the 31st day of January, 1876. Refusing they would be subject to the disposition of the military.[2] Couriers spread the news, and, meeting with no compliance, Sherman and Sheridan, at the request of the Department of the Interior, put the War Department in posture for an active campaign.[3] General Crook of the Department of the Platte was called from his headquarters in Omaha, and he, in the early spring of 1876, accompanied a body of troops up the old Bozeman trail. The weather was bitter. The cold sometimes was so intense that it froze the mercury in the thermometers, and the distress of the men, for this reason alone, nearly spelled the failure of the campaign. The soldiers, as they advanced, were harassed constantly by the hostiles, and, after spirited fighting in connection with the destruction of a large village on the Powder River, in which there was mismanagement on the part of a portion of the command,[4] so

[1] Cf. order of Sherman, N. Y. Herald, June 11, 1876.
[2] Report of Sec. of War for 1876, p. 28; Senate Ex. Doc., 44th Cong. 1st sess., no. 52, pp. 2, 5–6.
[3] Senate Ex. Doc., 44th Cong. 1st sess., no. 52, pp. 7–10.
[4] Report of Sec. of War for 1876, pp. 502–503.

that nothing could be achieved, the expedition returned to
Fort Fetterman.[1]

Other plans must be devised—the campaign must be more
vigorously prosecuted with a more numerous force. A large
concentric movement was organized. Three columns would
proceed simultaneously from western Montana, Dakota and
the Platte toward a common point in eastern Montana at which
the Indians were supposed to be congregated. Gibbon came
from Fort Ellis with 450 men, and early advanced as far as the
mouth of the Rosebud River in the Yellowstone valley. Crook
left Fort Fetterman at the end of May with 1,000 men, while
Custer, the most experienced and effective of all our Indian
fighters, was to have come from Fort Abraham Lincoln on the
Missouri with 1,000 more. Unfortunately for the campaign
Custer had been summoned to Washington by a Congressional
committee to give his testimony in relation to Secretary of
War Belknap. Though he obeyed very reluctantly his coming
at all gave offense to Grant, whose sympathy with the rascals
of his administration made him the spiteful enemy of any one
who was however remotely involved in the work of exposing
their iniquities. The President would not even receive Custer
when, before returning to the West he called at the White House,
and issued orders designed to deprive him of his command.
Although Grant was compelled, through the influence of others,
to modify his vindictive resolution, this result was brought
about only after delay. At length Custer could proceed at the
head of the Seventh Cavalry, with Terry, the Department
commander, accompanying him as the superior officer.[2] Terry
and Gibbon came into communication on the Yellowstone
River at the mouth of the Rosebud River on June 21.

Meanwhile, Crook, who seems at no time to have been acting in co-operation with the other columns, had reached the

[1] Report of Sec. of War for 1876, pp. 29, 441; House Ex. Doc., 44th
Cong. 1st sess., no. 184, p. 52; J. G. Bourke, On the Border with Crook,
chaps. xv and xvi; F. Whittaker, General G. A. Custer, pp. 538–43; N. Y.
Tribune, April 4, 1876.

[2] The orders bearing upon this subject are in F. Whittaker, General
G. A. Custer, pp. 551–62.

sources of the Tongue River, about 100 miles away. With his cavalry, and some infantry mounted on mules taken from the supply train, he organized a scouting expedition to the Rosebud, where, on June 17th, he was attacked by a large body of warriors, well armed and ready for battle. Severely dealt with in a rough country in which the Indians had every advantage, he withdrew and returned to his camp, to rest idly there until he could send to Fort Fetterman for, and receive, reinforcements. His action with the savages amounted to a repulse and was so regarded by the country, as it was by the Indians, who, with characteristic rites, proceeded to a celebration of their victory.[1] While awaiting an increase of his forces Crook employed himself hunting wild game in the mountains. Many of his men turned prospectors and explored the streams in search of gold.[2]

Terry about the same time had despatched Major Reno, an officer of Custer's horse, to make a circuit of the country lying south of the Yellowstone. Reno returned with the account of a trail which formed the basis of a plan of campaign. Both Gibbon's and Custer's columns were eager to start away after the savages, but Custer, since he had the greater body of cavalry, and on other accounts, was assigned to the duty. The regiment was reviewed in the wilderness by Terry, as on a parade ground, and it plunged into the mountains, on its dangerous adventure, with orders to advance to the upper Rosebud, where, it was believed, as a result of Reno's observations, that the Indians were encamped. Terry would remain on the Yellowstone to ferry Gibbon's Montana troops, still on the north side, over the river in a steamboat, which was in the service of the expedition, whereupon this column, with the forces from the east which had not gone on with Custer, including the commander of the Department of Dakota himself and a battery of Gatling guns, would proceed up the Big Horn River to a point where

[1] Report of Sec. of War for 1876, pp. 504–5; Grinnell, The Fighting Cheyennes, chap. xxv; F. Whittaker, General G. A. Custer, pp. 565–8. The "Battle of the Rosebud" is described by J. F. Finerty, a Chicago Times correspondent who was present, in Warpath and Bivouac, chap. x; also corr. from Crook's camp of N. Y. Herald in issue of June 24, 1876.

[2] J. F. Finerty, Warpath and Bivouac, pp. 151, 180, 181; corr. from Crook's camp to N. Y. Tribune, July 27, 1876.

it was joined by a tributary, which the Indians called the "Greasy Grass," but which is known to us as the Little Big Horn. There they would be on a certain day, known to Custer, and at that place the columns would resume communication.

Custer moved rapidly and soon came upon the trail of the savages which Reno had struck—the same savages who had discomfited Crook—and he followed it from the Rosebud over the "divide" to the Little Big Horn, where, on June 25, his scouts discovered their camp. It was of "almost unlimited extent." Here Sitting Bull,[1] Gall, Crazy Horse, Crow King, and other chieftains had gathered a force estimated to number from 2,500 to 3,000 warriors.[2]

Custer hastily formulated his plan of action. He had the advantage of being able to hide his movements behind a ridge of timbered bluffs, which mark the right bank of the river. In the first place Captain Benteen, with three companies, was sent off to the left to penetrate the camp as far as he could. Then Major Reno was detached with three companies more— he was to enter the valley and attack the village in the rear,[3] while Custer himself, with five companies, would continue to advance to a lower point and make a frontal charge.

Reno, who was the first to strike, succeeded in fording the river, but he was "completely overwhelmed,"[4] and was compelled to recross it, when he was joined by the three companies of Captain Benteen, who had made no progress with his task, and later by the pack train and a company which comprised its escort. The entire body, pursued by howling savages, sought protection on a hill where they hastily dug low rifle

[1] Many were more active on this occasion than this chief. He played "medicine man" in the hills out of reach of gun fire.—E. S. Godfrey, Century Magazine, Jan., 1892; McLaughlin, My Friend the Indian, pp. 140–42; cf. Report of Sec. of War for 1876, p. 447. Another version in W. K. Moorehead, The American Indian, p. 199.

[2] The village is believed to have contained about 10,000 Indians, including the women and children (McLaughlin, My Friend the Indian, p. 167). It was computed by General Terry to be three miles in length and one mile in breadth.

[3] Report of Sec. of War for 1876, pp. 479–80.

[4] "The very earth seemed to grow Indians," he said, "and they were running toward me in swarms and from all directions."—Report of Sec. of War for 1876, p. 32.

pits with the aid of a few spades and their tin cups and butcher
knives. Here the command was besieged, with no word from
Custer. The fighting around Reno, from 2.30 P. M. on the
25th until 6 P. M. of the 26th, was constant, with an intermis-
sion of but a few hours in the night—from 9 o'clock until early
daybreak—during which time the savages were holding a

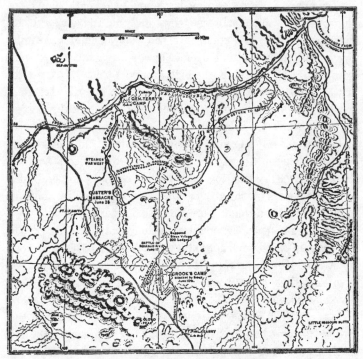

SCENE OF THE CUSTER MASSACRE

"scalp dance" underneath the eminence whereon our soldiers,
suffering distress from thirst, lay in readiness for the terrible
onslaught which was certain to be made upon them in the
morning.[1] The Indians came near enough at times to use their
bows and arrows and exhibited the greatest dexterity as marks-
men. Reno thought that he was fighting "all the Sioux nation,
and also all the desperadoes, renegades, half-breeds and squaw
men between the Missouri and the Arkansas, east of the Rocky

[1] Report of Sec. of War for 1876, p. 33.

Mountains." [1] Apprised of the approach of Gibbon and Terry, who were so close as to be able to come up on the morning of the 27th,[2] the savages, under a smoke screen, created by fire in the grass, discreetly took up their village and filed away in the direction of the Big Horn Mountains.[3]

Meanwhile, the worst fears as to the fate of Custer and his five companies were confirmed. They had kept behind the bluffs, and, while Reno was engaging the Indians with his charge, were to have come into the valley some three miles away. But they had not been allowed to reach the river and were caught while still on the high ground. Custer, in the sight of the Sioux, was a bright and coveted mark for destruction, and his entire command was obliterated by the awful processes of Indian warfare. Precisely how they met their end will never be known, for not one man survived the day. Only by conjecture, based upon a study of the position of the bodies of the slain, enforced by not too trustworthy recollections of Indian chiefs, who were on the ground, diligently collected by annalists in later years, can the account be pieced together.[4]

The news reached the country in time for late editions of the newspapers on the morning of Thursday, July 6, nearly a fortnight after the disaster. One of Gibbon's scouts had carried it to Fort Ellis, and it was telegraphed out of the wilderness by way of Bozeman and Salt Lake. The next day fuller reports were received in despatches filed at the telegraph office at Bismarck. Hayes had been nominated for President by the Republican convention at Cincinnati. Tilden had been named as the candidate of the Democrats at St. Louis. Congress was

---

[1] Report of Sec. of War for 1876, p. 33.

[2] Cf. J. K. Dixon, The Vanishing Race, p. 178.

[3] Report of Sec. of War for 1876, p. 33.

[4] The best description of the battle is that by one of Custer's troop commanders, E. S. Godfrey in Century Magazine, Jan., 1892. An excellent contemporary newspaper report is that of the correspondent of the N. Y. Tribune in the issue of the Tribune for July 13, 1876. See also Dellenbaugh, George A. Custer, chap. xix. For the Indian side see J. K. Dixon, The Vanishing Race, pp. 168–70, 174–7, 181–4; G. B. Grinnell, The Fighting Cheyennes, chap. xxvi; James McLaughlin, My Friend the Indian, chaps. viii–ix; Jesse Brown and A. M. Willard, The Black Hills Trails, chap. iv.

employed with the impeachment of Belknap. The distinguished
Fourth of July ceremonies, in connection with the Centennial
anniversary of the Declaration of Independence in all the principal cities of the country, were at an end, having reached their
highest point of brilliancy in Philadelphia, where the Centennial
exposition was being held,[1] to which place Sherman and Sheridan
had come to play their parts in the celebration. They were
taking their ease in their hotels when the reporters came to
interview them about the catastrophe. It was staggering.
Doubt at first filled the public mind. But it was soon seen to
be too true that 12 officers, including Custer, the "*beau sab-
reur* of the Army of the Potomac" and 247 men of our army,
5 civilians, one of them a New York Herald correspondent, and
3 Indian scouts had been killed, that 2 officers and 51 men had
been wounded,[2] and that the main body of the savages, at
Terry's coming, had retreated for a continuance of the war.

The response of the country to the "Custer Massacre"[3]
was instant. A thrill of horror ran through the nation. Everywhere, save in the ranks of the fanatical Indian philanthropists,
who were still governed by their charitable affinities, there was
an expression of renewed disgust for the policy of the government and a demand for prompt and severe retribution. Volunteers in great numbers offered their services for a war upon
the Sioux. Confederate General Shelby would raise troops in
Missouri, Confederate General Rosser, in Virginia. They had
fought against Custer in the Civil War; now they would avenge
his death. But all such tenders were declined. The army was
held to be large enough to cope with such an enemy.[4]

Evidence was everywhere present that the troops had been
confronted by weapons of the latest patterns which reached

[1] "Alas," wrote a correspondent of the New York Tribune on July 3
in Terry's camp, at the mouth of the Big Horn, "if the tidings of General
Custer's terrible disaster could be borne on the wings of the four winds,
dirges and not anthems would be heard in the streets of Philadelphia,
New York and San Francisco tomorrow."—N. Y. Tribune, July 13, 1876.

[2] Report of Sec. of War for 1876, p. 35.

[3] Not unfairly called this, since no quarter was given, and since the bodies
of the slain, except Custer's, which was spared, were most atrociously
beheaded, and otherwise mutilated.

[4] Cf. N. Y. Tribune, June 26, 1876.

them through the agencies and the traders licensed by the Indian Bureau.[1] A practical and useful thing was done—the agencies in the Sioux country were taken over by the War Department and put under military control, to make certain that the support in arms and rations which was reaching the savages from this source should cease.[2] Two military posts in the Yellowstone country, the establishment of which Sheridan had earlier recommended,[3] were at once, by authority of Congress, put in the way of construction.[4]

It was but natural that the causes of the disaster should be critically examined, and that mistake or neglect of duty, if it could be established, would be laid at some one's door. Aside from the division of authority between the War and the Interior Departments, which tended to frustrate all intelligent and effective control of the Indians, and the fact that the army was always too small for the duties which confronted it on so extensive a border, there were other circumstances which could well have engaged public discussion. How had it been that there was no co-operation between the commanders of the Departments of Dakota and the Platte? Crook had felt out the Indians first, but there was no courier communication with Terry. Their thirst for blood whetted on the troops from the Platte, they leapt like tigers at the troops from the Missouri. Crook, only forty miles away, was hunting elk and mountain sheep for his pleasure, his men were prospecting for gold, while one of the finest regiments in the army of the republic was being slaughtered by the hideous enemy from which he had so lately beat a hasty retreat.

[1] Cf. F. Whittaker, General G. A. Custer, pp. 531–2, 536. General Crook found that the Indian was more formidable when fighting with the bow and arrow than with a muzzle loading gun. But when he came into possession of the breechloader and the metallic cartridge, which enabled him to load and fire from a horse with perfect ease, he was "ten times more formidable." A Sioux so armed on horseback could perform feats of marksmanship impossible to a white man. The Sioux was "a cavalry soldier from the time he had intelligence enough to ride a horse or fire a gun."—Report of Sec. of War for 1876, p. 500.
[2] Report of Sec. of War for 1876, p. 445.
[3] House Ex. Doc., 44th Cong. 1st sess., no. 184, p. 54.
[4] Report of Sec. of War for 1876, p. 445.

But such stupidity of management on the part of our higher command went unnoticed. The most of what was said touched the conduct of Custer and Reno. There were many to declare that Custer was impetuous, that he should have awaited the coming of Terry and Gibbon, that he had marched his men too far and too long, and precipitated the attack while they were exhausted, that he had not obeyed Terry's instructions, though these were in such terms as to allow him great latitude of action.[1]

On the other side Custer's friends expressed the opinion that Reno had abandoned him; Reno, no too admirable a character in any relationship, had failed to move to the support of his superior officer, when he must have known that it was necessary to do so. In the absence of Custer's testimony his plan seemed to be for a double, or triple attack upon the village almost simultaneously. Either Reno charged too soon, or Custer was occupied for a longer time in reaching his objective than he supposed that he might be. Reno had retired in panic and remained inactive, while the Indians, turning from his front, surrounded Custer. Quickly annihilating Custer and his men they returned to Reno and laid siege to the bluff on which he had taken his stand. It is said that volleys were fired by Custer as a signal of distress, that these volleys were heard by Reno and his officers, but that they did not move to the support of their commander. When they resolved upon action it was too late—the Indians were again in force on all sides.

Apart from any of the other questions at issue the truth is that the troops were greatly outnumbered, and it was only by a miracle that any part of the regiment was saved from the slaughter. Without timely relief from Terry Reno's command would, to a certainty, have met Custer's fate.[2]

[1] Grant, following inclinations developed because Custer had dared to testify in hearings in the investigation of Belknap, indulged in this line of criticism.—F. Whittaker, General G. A. Custer, p. 579. Grant's interview in N. Y. Herald is quoted in Whittaker.

[2] For Custer's side of the controversy see the writings of Mrs. Custer; Nelson A. Miles, Serving the Republic, pp. 186–92, and Personal Recollections, chaps. xv and xxii; F. Whittaker, General G. A. Custer, pp. 573–608. See also J. K. Dixon, The Vanishing Race, pp. 186–7; E. S. Godfrey,

It was said, too, and justly, that if Grant had not allowed
his small and unbecoming spites to operate against Custer
because of that officer's obeying a summons to Washington
to testify against Belknap, thus delaying the departure of
the column from Dakota, that it could have effected an earlier
junction on the Yellowstone with General Gibbon who had
for some time preceded the coming of the forces from Camp
Abraham Lincoln, in which case the Indians could have been
dealt with before they had had the opportunity to concentrate
so large a body of warriors as faced the Seventh Cavalry on
the Little Horn.[1]

Terry, after burying his dead and caring for his wounded,
who were sent down the Yellowstone in a steamboat to Bismarck, regained his position on that river at the mouth of the
Big Horn, and asked for reinforcements. General Crook remained in camp, in the position which he had selected, until
his numbers could be increased.[2] The Indians, it appeared,
were stationed between Terry and Crook at a point near the
base of the Big Horn Mountains.

In August our forces were ready to resume an earnest
pursuit of the enemy in a country, which Sherman declared to
be "the most inaccessible and difficult of any east of the Rocky
Mountains."[3] The Indians sagaciously divided their bands
in the hope of escape. Sitting Bull and his followers retreated
north beyond the Yellowstone, pursued by Terry, now joined
by General Miles, brought on with his skilled forces from the
southwest, while Crazy Horse, with his body of Cheyennes
had hurried south, to be followed by Crook, who, after a spirited

Century Magazine, Jan., 1892, pp. 373, 384, 387. Reno at length, in 1879,
demanded a court of inquiry, which ended in an exculpation, which, if
rather equivocal, was attended with the statement that "no further proceedings" were necessary. (Dellenbaugh, George A. Custer, p. 179.) On
other charges, affecting his honor in his relations with women and of
drunkenness, he was the subject of courts-martial, which he did not invite,
and in 1880 he was dismissed from the service. He died in 1889.—Phila.
Evening Telegraph, April 1, 1889.
    [1] Cf. N. Y. Herald, July 7, 1876, and excerpts from many newspapers con-
cerning the disaster in ibid. for this and proximate dates.
    [2] Senate Ex. Doc., 44th Cong. 1st sess., no. 81, p. 4.
    [3] Report of Sec. of War for 1876, p. 37.

fight with American Horse at Slim Buttes,[1] desiring to re-equip, found refuge in the Black Hills.[2]

The trails of the smaller parties were difficult to follow—by separating the savages had become more mobile. In October General Miles came upon Sitting Bull's camp and, on two occasions, under a flag of truce, which the Indians presented, terms of peace were discussed. But fighting soon followed and the Indians fled for a distance of 42 miles before they were again overtaken, during which movement Sitting Bull himself, with a considerable number of companions, escaped. The main body resumed negotiations and offered five small chiefs as hostages who were taken to the Cheyenne River agency.[3] The yield in this surrender was not so large as had been expected, for, procuring buffalo meat in the period which was allowed them to come into the agency, few, except the immediate relations of the hostages, appeared.[4]

On Crook's side, a column of troops, the cavalry under command of General R. S. Mackenzie, set forth from Fort Fetterman in October, 1876. Hundreds of young braves from a number of tribes volunteered to serve as auxiliaries and accompanied the expedition, which still had for its object the capture of Crazy Horse and his band. In all, the force numbered more than 2,000 men, not counting several hundred wagon drivers, muleteers and packers, who followed with the train. Cold weather advanced before the campaign gained much progress. Mackenzie and the horse pushing on ahead, fell upon a large village, late in November, belonging to a body of Cheyennes and other hostiles under Dull Knife, near the head of the Powder River. Some of the Indians were slain, many ponies were captured. Trophies taken from the poor fellows in Cus-

[1] Finerty, Warpath and Bivouac, chap. xx.
[2] Crook entered Deadwood and the other mining camps to the great delight of the pioneers whose greedy haste had been the immediate cause of the war.—J. G. Bourke, On the Border with Crook, pp. 380–87; Finerty, Warpath and Bivouac, pp. 245–6, 275 et seq.; Report of Sec. of War for 1876, pp. 506–507.
[3] Report of Sec. of War for 1876, pp. 483–4; cf. Miles, Serving the Republic, pp. 148–52, and Personal Recollections, pp. 225–8.
[4] Report of Sec. of Int. for 1877, pp. 411–12.

ter's command were recovered. The village was sacked and a bonfire was made of everything in it which could contribute to the convenience and support of the savages.[1]

Finally in 1877, Crazy Horse and several hundred of his followers were brought in, the chief himself being killed while resisting imprisonment in a guardhouse at a fort in northern Nebraska.[2]

Miles, in further operations against Sitting Bull, succeeded in inflicting damage upon this contingent of hostiles. In a sally, in January, 1877, from his headquarters at the mouth of the Tongue River, he found a camp of 600 lodges, and had frequent skirmishes with the savages, who, again, however, were always able to escape, though, by constantly harrassing them in the depth of winter, there were unmistakable signs that he was breaking their spirit.[3]

The campaign continued through the summer of 1877 upon bands of Sioux in Montana under Lame Deer, which now again were located by their attacks on surveying parties, wagon trains, mining camps and settlers' cabins.[4] But for some time small parties had been coming into the agencies where they were dismounted and disarmed.[5] So weary of the war were the savages said to be that Spotted Tail, with a body of head men and couriers, in the spring of 1877, agreed, upon his own account, to visit the bands in the north and induce them to give up their contest against authority.[6] Miles had been pursuing them effectively. They plainly sensed their doom[7] and Spotted Tail returned, in April, with 1,100 in his train.[8] Miles, pro-

---

[1] A romantic account of this expedition is contained in Mackenzie's Last Fight with the Cheyennes, a reprint from the Journal of the Military Service Institution by John G. Bourke. Cf. the same author, On the Border with Crook, pp. 392–6; Finerty, Warpath and Bivouac, pp. 293–4.

[2] Report of Sec. of War for 1877, p. 56; J. G. Bourke, On the Border with Crook, chap. xxiv; Finerty, Warpath and Bivouac, pp. 295–6.

[3] Report of Sec. of War for 1877, p. 55; Miles, Serving the Republic, p. 153.

[4] Report of Sec. of Int. for 1877, p. 412.

[5] Ibid., p. 55.

[6] Ibid., pp. 84–5.

[7] Miles, Serving the Republic, pp. 153–60, and Personal Recollections, chap. xviii.

[8] Report of Sec. of Int. for 1877, p. 413.

ceeding against Lame Deer, killed that chief and otherwise punished the band, whereupon it dissolved. The warriors straggled into the posts in squads and gave up their arms and ponies.[1]

Sitting Bull and a considerable number of his friends had crossed the British line, where they remained, expressing their determination never to return to the United States. The Privy Council of Canada, in June, 1877, addressed the government at Washington concerning their presence in British territory, and viewed the situation with misgivings. It was desired that we should induce the fugitives to go back to their reserves, on which account the President detailed General Terry and a civilian commissioner to visit the camp and negotiate with the notorious chieftain and his leading men. The parleys took place in October, 1877, under the eye of the Northwestern Mounted Police. As before Sitting Bull declared that he would never submit to the authority of the United States. It was his and his followers' desire, as well as their intent, to remain where they now were, and, though they were informed that they could expect no aid from the Canadian government, when they should be reduced to destitution, after the extermination of the buffalo upon which they were now subsisting, their resolution was unshaken, and there the matter was allowed to rest.[2]

Even while the war proceeded a commission which had been appointed, in answer to an act of Congress appropriating $20,-000 for the use, was at work among the Sioux who had not taken up arms against the United States, to secure a further modification of the treaty of 1868. Unless they should agree to the terms laid down for them they should not in future, Congress said, receive subsistence from the government.[3] The cession of all lands, over which they had "right and claim," west of the 103rd meridian, and a triangular tract, lying between the north and south forks of the Cheyenne River, east of that

[1] Report of Sec. of War for 1877, pp. 55–6; cf. Miles, Serving the Republic, pp. 161–2, and Personal Recollections, chap. xix.
[2] Report of Sec. of Int. for 1877, pp. 410–13, 719–28.
[3] Act of Aug. 15, 1876; cf. House Ex. Doc., 44th Cong. 2nd sess., no. 10, p. 2.

meridian, which would include the Black Hills, with the privilege of crossing the reserve into the Hills by as many as three wagon roads, were the principal objects sought. It was further desired that, hereafter, the Sioux should come into the Missouri for their supplies, as they formerly had done, instead of using the agencies on the northwestern boundary of Nebraska. They had been moved to the interior because of their being brought into contact at the Missouri with the whiskey traders and with other malign influences. But, when taken to the west, they had been set upon infertile land.[1] Though they were being recommended to industry with a view to rendering themselves self-supporting, they were deprived of the means of such advancement. Furthermore the new agencies, as has been observed, were difficult and expensive to supply and, in case of tumult, were out of reach of the troops,[2] in evidence of the continued want of judgment on the part of those who were charged with the direction of Indian affairs.[3] The hope was entertained that the whole tribe might be removed to the Indian Territory.

George W. Manypenny, Commissioner of Indian Affairs under President Pierce, Bishop Whipple, A. S. Gaylord of the Attorney General's office, Newton Edmunds, an ex-governor of Dakota Territory—seven men in all—proceeded to the Red Cloud and Spotted Tail agencies in September, 1876, to attain the important ends in view.[4] Such Indians as could be communicated with were willing to accept the conditions laid down for them, though it was with much complaint, in which they were encouraged by the commissioners, whose report was a recital and denunciation of all our relations with the tribe. The war had been of our making. The causes of it were stated

[1] An "inhospitable, barren, detestable country."—Cf. Wm. Welsh in N. Y. Tribune, April 1, 1876.

[2] Report of Sec. of War for 1874, p. 32; Report of Indian Com. for 1874, p. 3; ibid. for 1875, p. 143. Bishop Hare, daring the opposition of other humanitarians, unremittingly advocated the presence of troops at the agencies.—Howe, Life and Labors of Bishop Hare, pp. 116–20, 122.

[3] Report of Sec. of Int. for 1877; W. K. Moorehead, The American Indian, pp. 182–3.

[4] Report of Sec. of Int. for 1876, p. 393; H. B. Whipple, Lights and Shadows of a Long Episcopate, chap. xxv.

in detail with evidences of the deepest sympathy for the Indian. No leader of the Sioux, however eloquent, could have framed a more severe indictment of the government and the nation. It was a shameful record, the commissioners said, and in making this new agreement, they were filled with suspicion and distrust— would its provisions be more carefully observed than similar compacts had been in the past? [1] A delegation of Sioux, accompanied by two of the commissioners, visited the Indian Territory to determine whether that might not be a suitable future home for the tribe and were favorably impressed with the prospect of the emigration.[2] The surrender of lands and the promise to keep within narrower limits hereafter, Congress had specified, should be in return for mere rations, and the furnishing of material assistance, which, it was again said, would make them, at length, self-sustaining beings, settled on separate plots of ground, and, on February 28, 1877, at the end of Grant's administration, the new agreement was ratified by Congress.[3]

Once more the difficulty of dealing with a "nation" so loosely associated and so little provided with authorized spokesmen was clearly shown. The agreement had no sooner been effected than strenuous objections to it, especially on the point of the bringing of the agencies to the Missouri, were offered by chiefs who said that they had had no part in its negotiation. They wished to talk to President Hayes and, in September, 1877, 23 of them were allowed to come to Washington to present their complaints. But the President had no alternative; Congress by its action had made the removal of the agencies imperative. The supplies were stored at the new distributing camps, or were on the way to those places, and the government faced the problem of removing no less that 14,000 Indians a distance of 300 miles, amid the storms of winter, to territory

[1] Report of Indian Com. for 1876, pp. 11–19; cf. ibid., pp. 20–23, 104–6.

[2] Report of Sec. of Int. for 1876, p. 393; ibid. for 1877, pp. 414–5; House Ex. Doc., 44th Cong. 2nd sess., no. 10, pp. 2–3; Senate Ex. Doc., 44th Cong. 2nd sess., no. 9; ibid., no. 4.

[3] Report of Sec. of Int. for 1877, p. 414. For exact boundaries of the new reservation see map accompanying Report of Indian Com. for 1877; also in W. K. Moorehead, The American Indian, p. 24.

which a few years before had been, for good reasons, abandoned.[1] Another commission was appointed to compose this difficulty, and, at length, sites for the agencies farther in the interior, which were more to the mind of the chiefs, were found.[2]

While the Sioux war still proceeded, in 1877, a tedious conflict was begun with the Nez Percés. For long this tribe had occupied a large reservation in Idaho and western Oregon. By a treaty in 1855 58 chiefs, head men and delegates ceded away a part of this territory. Contentment reigned until 1860, when gold was discovered. Then prospectors rushed in, and in April, 1861, while the Civil War was breaking upon the country, 47 chiefs entered into an agreement for a further alteration of the boundaries of the tribal reserve. But at Washington at that time everyone was so much preoccupied with questions of greater gravity to the nation that the treaty was not ratified, and trouble increased. Lewiston, a town of 1,200 inhabitants, sprang into existence on the lands of the Nez Percés. At the same time the supplies promised them by the government were not received. So little calico arrived that there were but two yards for each Indian, so few blankets that one must do for six. Another treaty, reducing the limits of the reservation, was laid before the tribe, but not all the chiefs accepted its provisions. A war party, under a leader named Joseph, who had in his band the followings of Looking Glass, Big Thunder, White Bird and Eagle from the Light, continued to roam the Wallowa and other valleys in Oregon, from which the treaty excluded them. The encroachment of white settlement led to collisions, and finally, in 1873, another commission was sent to the scene with a view to the peaceful removal of the savages. Conferences with Joseph and his band were without result, and Grant was persuaded to yield to the chief's demands. But under white frontier influences the President soon revoked his orders and trouble increased.[3] Outrages of various kinds on the part of the Indians upon white men and by white men upon

[1] Report of Sec. of Int. for 1877, pp. 414–5; cf. Report of Sec. of War for 1878, pp. 89–92.
[2] Report of Sec. of Int. for 1878, pp. vi–vii, 460–63, 652–7.
[3] Cf. article on the Nez Percé war in Galaxy, December, 1877.

Indians, raids directed at crops and herds, the burning of farm buildings and murders led, in 1876, to the appointment of another commission. This time it was made plain that, if Joseph should not meet the views of the government and occupy the reserve set aside for his people, the Wallowa valley would be occupied by United States troops, and he would be forcibly dealt with.[1] Upon the failure of the negotiations the ringleaders in the creation of the disturbance would be transported to the Indian Territory.

The subject was committed to the charge of General O. O. Howard, who convened the Indians in councils in May, and was on the point of announcing the success of his efforts. But his hopes were premature for, by reason of a Nez Percé Indian having been murdered by whites, according to one account, or for no cause, except a malicious desire for a war, the savages commenced to massacre the settlers.[2] Early in June, 1877, they slew more than a score of white men and women at various places in the region,[3] whereupon Howard prepared his troops for action. Such warriors our most experienced Indian fighters had never recently seen. In an engagement in White Bird canyon in Idaho (June 17) the army lost 34 men; in another, a fortnight later, 11 men; in still another, on July 11 and 12, when General Howard was personally in command, 15 men and 25 wounded.[4] The Indians now took flight eastwardly toward the buffalo country in Montana over the Lolo trail, which Sherman described as "one of the worst trails for man or beast on this continent,"[5] gaining a start upon their pursuers, through a part of their number making a pretense of a wish for peace.[6] On the 9th of August General Gibbon, who had been engaged in the Sioux war, came up with the fugitives at their camp in Montana, where, in a memorable battle, 3 officers and 27 men, together with 6 citizens, were killed, the commander himself, with 38 others, being wounded. The casualities were over 40 per cent of the men engaged.[7]

---

[1] Cf. Report of Sec. of War for 1877, pp. 114-8.
[2] Ibid., p. 118.
[3] Ibid., p. 120.
[4] Ibid., pp. 131-3.
[5] Ibid., p. 10.
[6] Ibid., p. 124.
[7] Ibid., pp. 57-72.

The Indians fled again and, by a number of quick turns, were nimble enough always to elude the soldiers. They made so bold at one point as to attack General Howard, stole his pack train, and, on August 27, crossed the new Yellowstone National Park.[1] Forces at various frontier posts, depleted by reason of serious riots on the railroads in the Eastern states,[2] were put in motion to catch Joseph and his band, who gave battle on September 12, and ten days later reached the Missouri River, which they crossed on their way to Sitting Bull's refuge in Canada.[3]

As they proceeded the Nez Percés were harried by the Crows, so that they lost many ponies and mules, and were burdened with wounded. They were now in the country in which General Miles had command, though Howard still followed their trail, and, on October 3, while they were in camp on Snake Creek near the Bear Paw Mountains in northern Montana, he surprised them, captured 700 of their animals and laid siege to their village. This was the severest blow they had yet received, for Joseph thought that he had lost his pursuers and was safe in British America, though, as he was to learn, he was still 30 miles from the boundary.[4] The chief now would parley, still with hope of escape, but, under Miles's attacks, on October 5, the whole band, barring a small party led by White Bird, which had slipped away to Canada,[5] surrendered, to be sent into and held at frontier forts preparatory to their transportation to the Indian Territory. No less than 31 savages were killed, including several chiefs; 46 were wounded. At the same time we lost 23 more of our soldiers, among them some excellent officers, while 40 were wounded.[6]

Military experts had observed with wonder bordering upon admiration the movements of these Indians. They had con-

---

[1] Report of Sec. of Int. for 1877, pp. 840–42.
[2] Report of Sec. of War for 1877, pp. iv–v.
[3] James McLaughlin, My Friend the Indian, p. 361.
[4] Ibid., pp. 361–3.
[5] Report of Sec. of War for 1877, pp. 74–5; Report of Sec. of Int. for 1877, pp. 405–409; McLaughlin, op. cit., pp. 364, 366; Miles, Serving the Republic, pp. 176–9, and Personal Recollections, chaps. xx and xxi.
[6] Report of Sec. of War for 1877, pp. 57, 74–5; Report of Sec. of Int. for 1878, p. 464.

ducted a noteworthy retreat for hundreds of miles across the most difficult country. It was, said General Sherman, "one of the most extraordinary Indian wars of which there is any record." The savages had fought, he said, with "almost scientific skill, using advance and rear guards, skirmish lines and field fortifications," and, to their honor, had committed none of the atrocities, such as scalping and mutilation of the slain, and the indiscriminate slaughter of civilians, usually the disgrace of Indian battle.[1] Chief Joseph achieved the distinction of being asked to write an article for the North American Review.[2]

The next year, 1878, Howard, aided by citizen volunteers, was engaged in a tedious and difficult contest with the Bannocks, Shoshones and other bands who were ravaging eastern Oregon, Idaho and northern Nevada, a campaign usually called the "Bannock War." The settlers and ranchmen were in a panic and found refuge in the towns as a result of the depredations of the hostiles, who, when driven into the mountains, issued forth for fresh outrages upon the white people. Many lives were lost, civilian as well as in the ranks of the troops, and much property was destroyed before the savages could be subdued.[3] Hostiles which crossed the range into General Miles's territory in Montana met his expert forces, who materially assisted in reducing the tribe to order.[4]

The army had been tried and pressed as never before in the entire history of our warfare upon the Indians. Sheridan said that some of the cavalry regiments, during the spring and summer of 1877, had travelled more than 4,000 miles. In that year, and, for ten years past, he alleged that no men had ever worked harder or more faithfully than the little band of soldiers who had been defending "our rapidly extending Western settlements." Always the force was inadequate for the tasks to be performed,

[1] Report of Sec. of War for 1877, p. 15; cf. Senate Ex. Doc., 45th Cong. 2d sess., no. 14; cf. Am. Ann. Cyclop. for 1877, p. 40; James McLaughlin, My Friend the Indian, chap. xix.
[2] Issue of April, 1879.
[3] Report of Sec. of War for 1878, pp. 111, 235.
[4] Miles, Personal Recollections, chap. xxiii.

and the casualties in the long series of border battles were "equal to, or greater," he said, than the ratio of loss on either side in the campaign then in progress between the armies of Russia and Turkey, or in the late American Civil War.[1] "No other army in the world," he said again, "has such a difficult line to keep in order, and no army in modern times has had such an amount of work put upon the same number of men."[2] For duties so onerous and at the same time so important the commanders should have had at least 70,000 men, but never were there more than 14,000 in the field, and nearly one-third of these were stationed on the Rio Grande to protect the Mexican frontier.[3] Always the service was thankless; the rewards, instead of citations and promotions, "unlimited abuse."[4]

By this time the direction of the Interior Department had changed, and Schurz was giving the attention of his acute mind to the Indian problem. His investigation into the conduct of the Indian Bureau had, as we have seen, brought new officers to its management. Mr. Hayt, the new commissioner, exhibited a clearer understanding of, and a more enlightened sympathy with, the great variety of questions arising out of this branch of the national service than his predecessors, and, while no administration of such a subject, with all its complications and perplexities, could hope to gain marked results immediately, there was assurance of a real improvement in the relations of the government with the native American race.

One of the principal causes of armed collision between the white man and the Indian, where they met on the frontier, was found in the system. The making of treaties presupposes independent sovereign or quasi-sovereign powers. Each of the parties to a treaty must see to the enforcement of its provisions.[5] In such a case neither, in the nature of things, could do

[1] Report of Sec. of War for 1877, p. 58.
[2] Ibid. for 1878, p. 33.
[3] Ibid., p. 36.
[4] Cf. General Charles King in Hebard and Brininstool, The Bozeman Trail, pp. 23–4.
[5] That "treaties" made after 1871 became "agreements" (Act of March 3, 1871. Cf. F. A. Walker, The Indian Question, pp. 5 et seq.; J. P. Munroe, Life of F. A. Walker, pp. 132–3; E. E. Sparks, National Development,

so. The Indian tribe had no processes for restraining or punishing its renegades who crossed a boundary and molested white men.[1] The government of the United States, with a considerable army stationed at a large number of military posts, could not prevent active borderers from invading the reserves in search of rich mines or productive soil,[2] or in crossing such territory to country lying beyond it which they wished to reach. Nor could hunters be induced to respect boundary lines and refrain from shooting game belonging to the Indians. Nor could scoundrels, bent upon maliciously attacking the savages for the sport of it, often with the deliberate purpose of fomenting strife, be put under control. Vicious and criminal white men, indeed, sought shelter on an Indian reservation, where there was no law, safe from the pursuit of civil authority in the states and the United States. The reservation became a "paradise for desperadoes."[3] Troops might be ordered upon Indian ground, but, when they crossed a boundary, that act of itself was likely to be regarded as a violation of treaty rights, and there were new possibilities of strife. As the white man's commercial interest in and on the borders of a reservation became more active and important the anomalies and failures of the treaty system were increasingly apparent.[4] Even though the best purposes might be kept in view this method of dealing

p. 266; Eastman, The Indian Today, pp. 35–6) does not much affect the underlying principle, since it was of little moment to the Indian, and of no influence upon the result, whether their relations with the "Great Father" rested with the President and two-thirds of the Senate or with the President and a majority of both branches of Congress.

[1] The treaty had not been negotiated with the entire tribe in the first instance, but with only a few chiefs who had come forward to receive the presents which our commissioners bore in their hands.—R. I. Dodge, Our Wild Indians, pp. 643–4.

[2] "The adventurous element of our people in quest of rapid gain."— Schurz in Report of Sec. of Int. for 1877, p. ix.

[3] Report of Indian Com. for 1877, p. 71. At present, said Secretary Delano in 1874, speaking particularly of the Indian Territory, "it is a resort for lawless men and criminals who take refuge thus in order to avoid the restraints incident to an efficient government, or to escape the penalties due for crimes elsewhere committed."—Report of Sec. of Int. for 1874, p. xiv.

[4] Report of Sec. of Int. for 1877, pp. ix, x.

with the Indian was wrong, as had been openly acknowledged when we so far altered the policy as to establish agencies on reserved ground for issuing doles to him, and for instructing him in the arts of civilization.[1]

Schurz, after endeavoring to make the service honest and to give it efficiency (within the bounds established by Congress in its legislation on the subject), aimed to turn the general policy of the government away from a dealing with the tribe to a dealing with the individual. Each Indian must be brought into a position where he should be subject to the law which governed the white man in a like case. In the interest of good order proper tribunals should be established and there should be a body of police composed of Indians. The head of each family must be settled on land which should be his fixed home, and his land must be good enough for tillage and pasturage. If all that was fertile should be taken from him by trickery and force, he must become a pauper and a vagabond.[2] He should be taught to be self-supporting, if not as a farmer and grazier, by some trade. The chase should be discouraged. So long as the Indian was allowed to hunt wild game for his sustenance he would be indulged in his savage propensities and rendered unfit for what must be his future place in our social and political system.[3] The policy of educating the young at schools in the East, as well as in proximity to their homes, met with Schurz's warm approval, and an army officer, who had an interest in this subject, Captain R. H. Pratt, collected a number of boys and girls and brought them to Hampton Institute in Virginia.[4] He was later to have the opportunity to make the experiment on a larger scale and in a more notable way at Carlisle, Pa., where signal success was achieved in raising the character of Indian youth, who would return to their tribes to exert a civilizing influence upon their relations and friends. Thousands were eager

[1] The treaty system was condemned by the Indian Commission in its initial statement of recommendations in 1869.—Report of Indian Com. for 1869 and Report of Sec. of Int. for 1869, p. 492.
[2] Report of Sec. of Int. for 1878, p. v.
[3] Ibid. for 1877, p. x; ibid. for 1878, p. iv.
[4] Eastman, The Indian Today, pp. 69–72.

to come to the Eastern schools, though Pratt could accept but a few score.[1]

The policy, which was followed during Grant's terms, of seeming to put the burden of Indian management upon the churches, while, as it appeared, still withholding real control of the situation from them, deserved no discussion by Schurz and received little.[2] Religious organizations had no machinery for such a work. The men, who, by divers means, were elected to go into the Indian country at niggard salaries, often gave unremitting and valuable service to the government under well-nigh intolerable conditions. But often again they were idealist, unpractical, and unable to cope with the situation which faced them at their unfamiliar posts. Liberal instincts were more prominent in them than good sense.[3] That peace would come through Quaker, Methodist or Baptist agents was disproven by new Indian wars; that corruption would be brought to an end through such influences, by the disclosures of the Red Cloud and Schurz's investigating commissions.

The experiment with the Indian Territory, where the tribes might be corralled, as it were, in one place, had afforded the country a degree of relief from its perplexities with the question. Some of the "nations" settled there had made encouraging progress toward a better civilization, in spite of the fact that it was become a kind of St. Helena for intractable chieftains taken red-handed by the military, a Botany Bay for bands which were to be penalized for insubordination, and a general discharge ground for tribes which, though unoffending, stood athwart the lines of Northern settlement, and must, for convenience, be sent to new homes. That great disorder did not arise from such a forcible mixing of elements of the Indian race, so diverse in their character, may occasion surprise. But this country was out of the course of the general movement of our population from east to west. Though the Indians in the

[1] Report of Sec. of Int. for 1878, pp. iv, 473, 669–71.
[2] Ibid., p. xiv.
[3] Cf. House Reports, 44th Cong. 1st sess., no. 240, p. 2; Slattery, Life of F. R. Brunot, p. 146; R. I. Dodge, The Plains of the Great West, pp. 431–2, 438–40.

Territory sallied forth from time to time to raid Kansas and
Texas, though a party of Cheyennes ran north through Kansas
and Nebraska to join their kin on the upper Missouri in 1874,
and another band escaped, leaving a bloody trail across the
same states on their way to their friends in the north in 1878,[1]
though white ruffians, buffalo hunters and "squatters" eluded
the troops and entered the Territory almost at will to become
disturbing factors among the Indians, the experiment, in the
main, was regarded as a success, on which account, when a
tribe elsewhere became an embarrassment to the government,
there were suggestions that it should be settled in this district.
Schurz made the observation that only those who were accustomed to a southern climate should be sent thither. The
Pawnees had suffered by the transfer. The death rate among the
Poncas and the Nez Perces, when they were taken to this
country from their homes in the north, was appalling, and, in
the interest of humanity, Schurz said, the movement of the
Indians on lines of longitude should cease.[2]

For the plan to return the Indians to the care of the War
Department Schurz had little favor; he soon became a stout
opponent of the idea.[3]   The suggestion persistently recurred,
and each time that it appeared it was to arouse the active hostility of the "friends" of the Indian in the country at large, as
well as of the official hierarchy which was called the Indian
Bureau.   The familiar arguments in proof of the impropriety
of the change were repeated.   The army's mind was murderous;
it would kill and extinguish the race.[4]   Its heartlessness had
been exhibited in many a "butchery" on the frontier, as at
Sand Creek, on the Washita and by Baker in Montana.   The
problem should not be approached in this spirit.   Instead it was
the plain duty of the nation to pursue just and kindly courses
in its dealing with the tribes with a view to civilizing them.

There were Eastern humanitarians—speakers, writers and
workers—as irrationally pro-Indian as these same men and

[1] Report of Sec. of Int. for 1878, pp. viii–ix.
[2] Ibid., p. 5; cf. Miles, Serving the Republic, p. 181.
[3] Reminiscences of Schurz, vol. iii, pp. 385–6.
[4] Cf. G. W. Manypenny, Our Indian Wards.

women, or their like, had been pro-negro in the struggle to
gain the abolition of slavery. Some were moved by religious
feeling, some by the abstract belief in human equality and the
rights of man, some again by a mere restless zeal for what they
too vaguely knew as "reform." The sympathies of many made
them quite blind, in the first place, to the ethnic place and real
character of the Indian, and also to the inevitable train of
facts and circumstances, which, whatever its apparent brutal-
ity, caused him to be an obstruction, as he had been from the
first day of the white man's contact with him on this continent,
to be removed from the path of civilization.[1]

Our treatment of this people, the Indian Commission said,
had been "unjust and iniquitous beyond the power of words
to express." The history of our connection with the whole
race was "a shameful record of broken treaties and unfulfilled
promises." [2] They were not to be raised in the human scale by
giving them over to the care of the army, which, when it was
not engaged in slaying them, debauched their morals and destroyed their souls. Its officers might be excellent persons, but
the privates were, in general, recruited from vicious classes of
the population.[3] During the Civil War the army had drawn
men to it in love of country. But it was not so now. No one
of a valuable character would enlist for a few dollars a month,
when he knew that duty would require him to live in a dirty
frontier post, hundreds of miles from the commonest con-
veniences of civilization. Nor did the officers themselves escape
the philanthropists' criticisms,—time and again had ambitious
subalterns incited strife that the military arm of the government might be used for exterminating Indian wars.[4]

---

[1] See, e.g., Report of Indian Commission for 1869, pp. 7 et seq. For two
writings of this kind expanded to book form see G. W. Manypenny, Our
Indian Wards, and Helen Hunt Jackson, A Century of Dishonor.

[2] Report of Indian Com. for 1869, pp. 7–8.

[3] Ibid. for 1875, p. 15; cf. ibid. for 1876, p. 17.

[4] Report of Sec. of Int. for 1875, pp. 520–23; Report of Indian Com. for
1875, pp. 14–5, 64 et seq.; House Reports, 44th Cong. 1st sess., no. 240, pp.
41–7. On the other hand, the army complained that the Indian Bureau
itself sometimes started wars, as in the case of the Modoc War, in which
Canby was the sacrifice.—Schofield, Forty Six Years in the Army, pp.
435–6.

The army on its side could make rejoinder. It was on the ground. Some of the officers in command were men of intelligence and high abilities, yet they were compelled to look on helplessly at the clumsy mismanagement of the subject by Congress and the Indian department. They could not be expected to view so much inefficiency without resenting it indignantly, so much dishonesty without wishing to expose it to the sight of the nation. Yet it was thought to be insubordinate and unsoldierly to make observations on matters out of the line of appointed duty. Dastards cheated the Indians and traders waxed fat under the eyes of the military officers—it was the army which must wage the wars that ensued. Appropriations of money were delayed, provisions of treaty were violated—when trouble came, it was the army which must restore peace. The Indians were required to remain on their reservations, where they were virtually prisoners of war—the army was commanded to keep them within the boundaries which had been established for them. In these confines they were left without the means of support.[1] It was "a most painful and unhappy duty," said General Pope, it was "revolting" for soldiers to watch the Indian starve, yet, he added with irony, their duty was done when they compelled him to "starve tranquilly." [2] It was alleged that the army wished to fight this unfortunate race. There was "no class of men in this country," General Pope continued, "so disinclined to war with the Indians as the army stationed among them." [3] More than this—when hostilities commenced the army must face warriors who were equipped, not with tomahawks and bows and arrows, but with improved arms which were supplied them through the agencies of the Interior Department. Nothing seemed more preposterous than that one department of the government should equip and ration a foe for rebellions which another department, at great

[1] R. I. Dodge, The Wild Indians, p. 644.

[2] Report of Sec. of War for 1877, p. 66; ibid. for 1875, pp. 76-7.

[3] Ibid. for 1875, pp. 76-7. There were two classes of people, said Sherman, one demanding the utter extinction of the Indians, and the other, "full of love for their conversion to civilization and Christianity"—the army stood between and got "the cuffs from both sides."—House Ex. Doc., 41st Cong. 2nd sess., no. 269, p. 10.

expense and peril of life, must suppress. The army had its
faults, but to stupidity such as this it was not given; filching and
thieving were not much practiced by the officer who wore his
country's uniform, and, on land and sea, served his country's
flag.

The charitable and religious sympathies of the reformers
were well known by practical men, and could be indulged and
respected. But the piety of civil officers, employed in the Indian
department, who spoke of the Indian being made in "God's
image," [1] and the duty of "Christianizing" him through churches
and Sabbath schools [2] was nauseous. Thus did these officers
seek to gain the good opinion of the country, while they continued their frauds. [3] The army, though put upon the frontier
to police it, could not do so; it must witness murders and depredations often without the power to punish the offenders. [4]
It could not enter a reservation to pursue a culprit band until
it was asked to do this by the Indian bureau, which was slow
to act. Instead of chastising the savages for their crimes, Sheridan complained, they were presented with "more blankets."
The Indian, Sheridan insisted, was "a lazy, idle vagabond,"—
he had "no profession except that of arms," to which he was
"raised from a child." Constantly a scalp was "dangled before
his eyes," and the "highest honor" to which he could aspire
was "to possess one taken by himself." [5] Few officers of the
army of any rank or influence who did not believe the administration of Indian affairs, if it were to be successful, so closely
connected with the exercise of the war power as to make their
union under one head indispensable.

In 1868 the agitation for a recommittal of the subject back
to the control of the War Department had reached a point when
it seemed likely that it might sway Congress. The question
continued to be discussed. The philanthropists who, now as
then, implacably opposed it were of opinion that the movement

[1] Report of Sec. of Int. for 1873, p. 378.
[2] Report of Sec. of War for 1877, p. iv.
[3] Cf. ibid., pp. 144–5.
[4] Cf. ibid. for 1874, p. 30; ibid. for 1875, p. 57.
[5] Ibid. for 1869, p. 38.

had been effectually stopped and ended by Baker's "massacre" of the Piegans in 1870.[1] As the evidence of the incompetency of the Interior Department to feed and control the Sioux increased the suggestion that the army should take over the whole subject was actively renewed. But it was the killing of Custer and all his men in 1876 which precipitated the issue.[2] Reno, viewing Custer and his cavalrymen as they lay mute in a horrible death in the Montana wilderness, passionately asked the question of " the good people of this country, whether a policy that sets opposing parties in the field armed, clothed and equipped by one and the same government should not be abolished." [3] Sheridan,[4] Pope, Crook,[5] Miles,[6] Schofield,[7]—all complained bitterly of the situation in which the army was placed.[8]

The subject came into Congress again. In 1876 all but two of the higher officers of the army, from Sherman downward, 60 in number, in reply to questions submitted to them by the House Committee on Military Affairs unqualifiedly approved of the transfer.[9] The Committee on Indian Affairs, after a thorough investigation, recommended it,[10] though this result was not reached without awakening violent public contention, which prevented action, and which yet for several years would not abate.

In such an era, characterized as it was by a private greed to seize and use all the country's rich natural resources, it was

[1] Report of Indian Com. for 1870, pp. 3, 89–90.
[2] Cf. N. Y. Tribune, July 7, 1876.
[3] Report of Sec. of War for 1876, p. 478; cf. ibid., pp. 443, 447; Mrs. Custer, Boots and Saddles, p. 266; F. Whittaker, General G. A. Custer, pp. 536, 538.
[4] Report of Sec. of War for 1875, p. 57.
[5] Ibid. for 1876, p. 501.
[6] Ibid. for 1875, p. 85.
[7] Ibid., pp. 122–3.
[8] Sherman said, after the Custer massacre, that the Indian was "our inveterate enemy, the enemy of cultivation, to labor of any sort and to all civilization."—Ibid. for 1877, p. 6; cf. ibid., pp. 144–5; R. I. Dodge, The Plains of the Great West, pp. 436–8.
[9] Ibid., pp. 4–6.
[10] House Reports, 44th Cong. 1st sess., no. 240, but with a strong minority report.

difficult to bring to expression any practical interest in common social rights. Miner, grazier, lumberman, farmer wanted the land, and the wealth which it might contain for instant enjoyment. No more of the public domain was to be voted away to railroad corporations,—that which remained was prize for the enterprising citizen. That he might have the more of it the Indian was to be despoiled. Game and fish, timber and minerals were to be taken, grass lands covered by herds, regardless of future, with small regard, indeed, for present consequences.

Schurz, with a well instructed, statesman-like and honest mind, came to the defense of the forests against their pillage and destruction by the lumber magnates. Many pre-empted the land and purchased it at nominal prices from the government. Others, in various parts of the country, frankly stole the trees on the public domain or the Indian reservations to feed their sawmills, as the ranchmen overran it to feed their cattle.[1] Argument unfavorable to such exhibitions of industry and enterprise was as unfamiliar as it was ungrateful to the ears of the men of the day, though a commencement in conservation had been made. In 1864 Congress had seen the fitness of setting aside and preserving some of the curiosities of nature in California. A gorge, adown which fell, with many a cataract, a narrow stream, the Yosemite, and the valleys of some of its contributing waters, together with an adjacent grove of giant redwoods, which the public knew as "Big Trees," were transferred by the United States to the state, if it would, for all time, administer the lands as a park for "public use, resort and recreation."[2]

A curative value, exaggerated in truth, was ascribed to thermal springs. These it was the wish of many to withhold from private ownership and put to common use. So long since as in 1832 Congress, knowing of the healing qualities of the waters issuing from the earth at a place in Arkansas, which on this account came to be called the Hot Springs, reserved it from sale or entry. But a town had grown up around the

[1] Report of Sec. of Int. for 1877, pp. xiv–xx; ibid. for 1878, pp. xi–xv; cf. St. Paul corr. N. Y. Tribune, Aug. 14, 1874.
[2] For long almost inaccessible. Cf. Olive Logan in Galaxy, October, 1870.

springs, private and public interests were in conflict, and, in 1877, an act was passed putting the subject in the hands of a commission. The entire area henceforward was to be included in a national reservation, and a superintendent was named to care for it. He removed the indigent invalids, many of them afflicted with loathsome diseases, who came hither from all parts of the country and lived in wagons and tents, transferred them to barracks and established regulations for the use of the baths. Likewise the sources of the springs, which were as many as 70 in number, were put under government supervision with a view to making the place one of the principal health resorts in the republic.[1]

But no action of the government was at once so eloquent of an appreciation of the wonders of nature and the need of guarding our resources from Mammonism and common vandalism as the creation of the Yellowstone National Park. "Jim" Bridger, the Rocky Mountain trapper and scout,[2] knew that there were "boiling springs" near the head of the Yellowstone River, but a United States army officer in 1859 confessed that he was unable to reach them. It remained, he said, "the most interesting unexplored district of our widely expanded country."[3]

Ten years passed; in 1869 two travellers crossed the country, making some cursory observations, which, in the next year, impelled a number of men in Montana, including N. P. Langford, formerly a governor of that territory, to organize an expedition to visit and to ascertain the true character of the wonders concerning which so much curiosity had been aroused. A cavalry lieutenant, G. C. Doane, who headed the escort, wrote a report of the trip for publication by the government,[4] while Langford directed attention in newspapers and magazines to the extraordinary objects, which he and his associates had

[1] Report of Sec. of Int. for 1877, pp. 807–18; ibid. for 1878, pp. 997–1002; Senate Ex. Doc., 46th Cong. 2nd sess., no. 21.

[2] For Bridger see Hebard and Brininstool, The Bozeman Trail, pp. 204–52.

[3] Senate Ex. Doc., 40th Cong. 2nd sess., no. 77, p. 11; House Ex. Doc., 45th Cong. 2nd sess., no. 75, pp. 6, 8.

[4] Senate Ex. Doc., 41st Cong. 3rd sess., no. 51.

witnessed.[1] Two government engineers, Captains Barlow and
Heap, at the command of General Sheridan, made a reconnais-
sance of the region in July and August, 1871.[2] But it is to
Professor Hayden, in charge of the United States Geological Survey, whose explorations of the district in the same year, were continued in 1872,[3] and Mr. Langford that we are most indebted for
the advancement of this important public project. As obviously
commendable as it might seem to be, they and its other friends
must overcome many obstructions before they could secure the
approval of Congress. Maps of the district, sketches and photo-
graphs of the geysers, craters, hot springs, waterfalls, lakes,
canyons, mountains and other natural curiosities and beauties to
be found in the confines of the proposed reserve were exhibited,
promises were made that annual appropriations for maintenance
would not be required, the aid of the Northern Pacific Railroad lobby and other powerful commercial interests was sought
and made potential, and finally, on March 1, 1872, Congress
was persuaded to withdraw from settlement, set aside and
dedicate 3,775 square miles, lying for the most part in Wyoming, though the tract extended a little way into Montana on
the north and Idaho on the west, as a "public park or pleasure
ground for the benefit and enjoyment of the people."[4]

Pledges made to members of Congress that more would not
be required of that body were not carefully kept, but all requests
addressed to it for appropriations were entirely ignored, and
soon disaster threatened the entire enterprise. A national
park was not more safe from disturbing intruders than an Indian
reservation. Sportsmen bent on the slaughter of animals,
miners, ranchmen, adventurers with the profits of commerce in
view, entered at will. Tourists, though they must come by pack
train, were already arriving; they drove their horses over and

[1] Cf. Scribner's Magazine, 1871. His Diary of the expedition was published in 1905.
[2] Senate Ex. Doc., 42nd Cong. 2nd sess., no. 66; cf. Personal Memoirs
of Sheridan, vol. ii, pp. 349–50.
[3] Report of Geological Survey of Montana and Adjacent Territory, 1871;
ibid., 1872—published in 1872 and 1873, respectively.
[4] House Ex. Doc., 45th Cong. 2nd sess., no. 75, pp. 3–4; cf. N. P. Langford, The Discovery of Yellowstone Park.

were ruining the beautiful geyser cones, some of which nature could never re-form. A hotel and baths had been built at the Mammoth Hot Springs even before the establishment of the park,[1] while explorers, writers and photographers continued to advertise its wonders to the world.[2]   Langford, the first superintendent, asked the Secretary of the Interior in 1874 for $100,000.   Delano forwarded the request to Speaker Blaine. There was no money to pay the superintendent—his was a labor of love—no money was available for any use.   For two years the park had been without protection; even its boundaries had not been defined by survey.   Langford's solicitations were enforced by statements from the territorial governors of Montana and Wyoming, Professor Hayden and many individuals at Bozeman, who, residing near the park, were witnesses of its spoliation.[3]

Now and again bills were reported by the committees of Congress; sometimes the subject reached the point of discussion by members, whose minds, however, were absorbed by questions of more immediate importance to them and the interests which they were sent to Washington to represent.[4]   When Schurz became Secretary of the Interior he appointed P. W. Norris of Michigan, an explorer of the Yellowstone country, as Langford had been, to be superintendent.   Norris, in turn, earnestly addressed Congress.   By this time six years had passed.   Bridges were to be built, roads and bridle paths laid out —nothing had been done, still no appropriation had ever been made for carrying out the purposes of the act.   Trespassers in increasing numbers invaded the district, killing bison, elk, antelope and other "beautiful and valuable animals" by thousands, "merely for their tongues and pelts," robbing the streams of their fish, burning the forests of pine and cedar.   The calcareous and silicious formations around the geysers, the pool borders,

---

[1] Report of Sec. of Int. for 1877, p. 841.
[2] Ibid. for 1878, pp. 991-2.
[3] House Ex. Doc., 43rd Cong. 2nd sess., no. 20; House Ex. Doc. 43rd Cong. 1st sess., no. 147; cf. Report of Sec. of Int. for 1873, p. xxviii.
[4] The progress of the subject in Congress is summarized in House Ex. Doc., 45th Cong. 2nd sess., no. 75, pp. 6-8.

the petrified trees and other mineral curiosities were being broken up and carried away for sale.[1]

The representations of the superintendent and the Secretary of the Interior were supported by resolutions of the American Association for the Advancement of Science at its meeting in Nashville in 1877. A committee of members of that most respectable organization memorialized Congress, commending the subject to its immediate care. The Yellowstone National Park, they said, contained within its limits "the most remarkable thermal springs and other features of interest to men of science in any part of the world." The work of devastation must be "stayed," ere it had done "irreparable injury to natural accumulations of the highest value in scientific investigation."[2]

Congress was finally moved to action and appropriated $10,000 for the park, whereupon Superintendent Norris left his home in Michigan, and in July, 1878, proceeded to the scene of his duties. The Northern Pacific Railroad, work upon which had been halted by the panic of 1873, was to have built a spur to the borders of the reserve. The only approach continued to be by stage coach, from the Union Pacific railway to Bozeman,[3] a distance of over 500 miles, though the journey was on the point of being somewhat shortened as the railhead of the Utah Northern out of Ogden advanced. At seasons when navigation into Montana was open, tourists might use a steamboat on the Missouri and up the Yellowstone River, but then, even in the best case, there was a coach ride of 160 miles to Bozeman, where wheeled vehicles must be abandoned and the trip into the park continued on horseback.[4] Norris, having used the Missouri River route in 1877, chose his way in the following year by Omaha and Ogden to Bozeman, where

[1] House Ex. Doc., 45th Cong. 2nd sess., no. 75, pp. 1–2; cf. House Ex. Doc., 43rd Cong. 1st sess., no. 147, pp. 3, 6; Report of Sec. of Int. for 1877, pp. 842–3.
[2] House Ex. Doc., 45th Cong. 2nd sess., no. 75, p. 5.
[3] Cf. Slattery, Life of F. R. Brunot, p. 189.
[4] Report of Sec. of Int. for 1878, p. 995; House Ex. Doc., 45th Cong. 2nd sess., no. 75, p. 4.

YELLOWSTONE PARK

he "outfitted," and with a party of mountaineers, well armed
to face the Indians, set off for the Mammoth Hot Springs,
70 miles away. Before winter came he had succeeded in building, under great difficulty, about 60 miles of roads. He asked for
$25,000 for the uses of the park in 1879. [1]

[1] Report of Sec. of Int. for 1878, pp. 979 et seq.

CHAPTER XXIV

LETTERS AND ART

THE war had laid a hard hand upon art and letters and they emerged from the all-absorbing sectional conflict materialized and dispirited. We had had a position in respect of these subjects which we might regard with honest satisfaction.

With our English traditions we had not gone forward in the erection of buildings, especially if these were of a public character, without a willingness to take the advice of good guides. Architects were engaged to prepare the plans for statehouses, hospitals, colleges and churches. The countryside, north and south, was dotted with graceful mansions. Many a house on a Southern plantation, on the Delaware, the Schuylkill,· the Hudson, and in New England,—on the river banks and the stage roads,—attested to an æsthetic sense in those who had built them.

Painting, especially portraiture, had yielded several worthy figures. Schools appeared for the training of artists, notably in Philadelphia, in connection with the Pennsylvania Academy of the Fine Arts. Exhibitions were arranged that the public taste in such a field might be improved. We were following western Europe at some distance, but our impulses had been sound until the slave question supervened to absorb attention, and we were thrown into the war. Toil, covering time, would be required to bring the nation back to the intellectual position which it had previously held. Power had come to be represented in the popular mind by force and numbers—Grant, Sherman, Sheridan, a million soldiers, two billions of debt. Men spoke of annexing Canada, of invading Mexico, as if these were adventures for a holiday; of cutting a canal through the isthmus of Tehuantepec, or in Nicaragua, or at Panama; of covering the country with Pacific railroads; of crossing the ocean, which

443

lay beyond our western coast, to Asia. All these things were paltry in comparison with what had just been done in the conquest of the South. Petroleum was spurting from the earth in Pennsylvania; mines of gold and silver were yielding fortunes in the Rocky Mountains; Illinois, Indiana, Iowa, Wisconsin, Minnesota, Kansas, were astir with farmers who were taking wealth in wheat and corn out of land to which men a while ago assigned no value whatever. The atmosphere was filled with the spirit of a new, and, in many respects, not a better age.[1]

Wealth could be consumed, as it had been while the war lasted—if it disappeared more would be found. So great a country held an unlimited store. The conqueror would do with the conquered at the South as he liked—soon he lost all sense of justice and confused right with advantage. The great characters of the period were not statesmen and authors, or painters and sculptors, or men in the church and the college. They were "Coal Oil Johnnies," swaggering gamblers in Wall Street, railroad and mining "kings," Southern carpetbaggers, the noisy demagogues who led the Radical party at Washington, men who would get offices from Grant that they might use the public service for their private emolument. The glories of the representative system of government had gone. The taking of advice from the elders, the feeling of respect for the school, and the men who came out of the school, made way for a democracy which was leaderless in the old sense, and in a good sense. At length we would bring order out of disorder, but it would be a new America. It would be another and a different body politic, responding to a public opinion proceeding from a popular mass, enlarged, re-mixed and thinned.

The new dwelling house, or public building, was likely to

---

[1] The "moral and intellectual elements," Bayard Taylor said, had been "shaken up," and they had not yet had the time "to settle into their new forms." (Taylor and Scudder, Life and Letters of Bayard Taylor, p. 540.) There had been a "rough overturning of old social ranks." The whole country had been materialized; now "money and leisure were in the power of people who had little intellectual training." (Ibid., p. 530.) Art and letters led a "difficult existence in the midst of the barbaric wealth of the richest millions of people in the world."—Letters of C. E. Norton, vol. i, p. 399.

be large and ugly. It was notable for nothing except its physical bulk and the generous extremity of its ornamentation. The cosy inn at which men had stopped in comfort was replaced by a great hotel with vaulted ceilings and decorated walls, suggestive of the palaces of Europe, without any of their artistic grace. Plush carpets, heavy hangings, garish papers and paints, gilt and silver, crystal and glass were introduced to dazzle eyes to which refinements of any kind hitherto had been unfamiliar. The homes of the newly enriched were planned on the same lines. No longer was value seen in the old Georgian models, simple and fine, or in the classical models which it had been a delight for the architects of the early part of the century to design. Some of these excellent edifices were razed to the ground without a qualm. Mahogany was painted over, fireplaces were blocked up, lovely mantels were put under the axe, handsome pieces of furniture were discarded for some of the ugliest which have ever appeared in the history of cabinet making as a craft. Bedchamber, drawing-room, hotel rotunda, Pullman car, steamboat—all were parts of a great vulgar spectacle prepared to open the eyes of our insolent new democracy.[1]

We were in chaos before the war had yet burst upon us in the form of an actual military struggle.[2] The "brown stone front" had appeared in New York about 1850. In the next twenty years miles upon miles of these type houses lined the streets of that city. The "Mansard roof" was introduced. This cheap and hideous form in domestic architecture, wherein the roof of the house remained only as a suggestion, to confine the uppermost story, at the top of which it was truncated, swept the country. The development of the jig saw gave us scroll work; the steam planing mill, wooden minarets and towers; the iron industry, sheathing, cornices and filagree metal work,—singly, and all together, more repulsive than anything yet seen in house making. Commercial buildings were mere walls, with

[1] Cf. Richard Grant White in Galaxy, Aug. 1, 1866, p. 650.
[2] The whole country from an architectural standpoint was "a prairie wilderness, spotted here and there with beautiful survivals of a past taste," upon which had encroached all manner of "modern disfigurements."— C. H. Caffin, Story of American Painting, p. 311.

openings at definitely assigned places for doors and windows. Shops, whether of brick, stone, wood or cast-iron, were vulgar in every line. The more elaborate, the more pretentious they were meant to be, the more objectionable they were in fact. The small town imitated the city to even worse ends. The mechanic who had been able to accomplish so much in this country in an earlier age, even without direction, had lost "the wholesome traditions of his craft." The art of architecture had "seldom sunk so low in any civilized country." [1]

The rout of the tyros, into whose charge this subject had come, was only gradual. It was begun by Richard Morris Hunt and Henry Hobson Richardson. They had studied at the École des Beaux Arts in Paris. Hunt's career was fairly started before the war. His influence grew and won acknowledgment.[2] His office in New York became one of the most valuable of schools for young men desirous of studying architecture.[3] Richardson, a native of Louisiana, was abroad during the war and came home, after a period of study covering six years, full of the spirit of southern France, as was evidenced in the Romanesque style, of which he became an exponent. He settled in New York, passing after a few years to Boston where he was glad to be—he was a graduate of Harvard—and won attention for his churches, the most notable of his achievements in this department of architecture being Trinity Church in Boston, for which he received the commission in 1872, and which he completed in 1877. This *tour de force* he accompanied and followed with townhalls, courthouses, exchanges, libraries, schools, dwelling houses, bridges, monuments, fountains—all planned in a commanding manner.[4] Each bore the impress of his personality, and he definitely raised and ennobled the standards of taste of the country.

Meanwhile architecture was coming to interest a greatly

[1] Montgomery Schuyler, article on Architecture in the United States in Sturgis, Dictionary of Architecture and Building; cf. Glenn Brown, Historical Sketch of American Institute of Architects.

[2] Cf. Galaxy, August 1, 1866, pp. 650–56.

[3] Shannon, Boston Days of William Morris Hunt, p. 95.

[4] Mrs. Schuyler Van Rensellaer, Henry H. Richardson and His Works.

increased number of educated young men as a career. They
attended courses in the schools which were established in the
United States, while many went abroad, usually to Paris, like
Richardson, bringing back with them a love of French traditions, to make these the ascendant influences during the next
few years.

The American Institute of Architects had been formed in
1857. Richard Upjohn was its first president, Hunt its secretary. Its membership increased after the war. Its first national
convention met in New York in 1867 and it began the publication of its proceedings.

The signs of a strong native modern movement in painting in
America were seen in William Morris Hunt, brother of Richard
Morris Hunt, the architect, a brilliant and forceful leader,[1]
George Inness and John La Farge. These three men were
pioneers in going abroad for an education in art, and they all
had returned home before the outbreak of the war, to find little
encouragement for their genius and talents while it proceeded.
Its troubled scenes served as a training ground, however, for
at least one master craftsman, Homer Winslow, who had found
employment in visiting the battle fronts to make illustrations
for a New York periodical. Some painting of war subjects
from his brush created a profound impression. The prosperity
of the New York magazines forwarded the interests of a number
of young men. Edwin A. Abbey and several others found
encouragement and gained experience in this field while on their
way toward larger ends.[2]

In 1875 the students who had followed the example of Inness
and La Farge, and had gone to Europe, usually to Paris and
Munich, began to arrive home in sufficient numbers to cause
their influence to be felt.[3] The Society of American Artists
was founded in 1877, under the presidency of La Farge, its

[1] Hunt, after a brief residence in Newport, settled in Boston, where he
became a vital force, by his teaching and example, in the development of
American art.—Shannon, Boston Days of Wm. Morris Hunt, pp. 21-4;
H. M. Knowlton, pp. 31-2.
[2] C. H. Caffin, American Masters of Painting, p. 84.
[3] Ibid., p. 185.

membership including practically all of the men identified with the advance movement which was now in progress throughout the country.

The Centennial Exposition of 1876 in Philadelphia, externally, for the most part, was without evidence of an art sense in the American people. Its buildings were unsightly warehouses, with decorations from the flag makers and the planing mills, but its whole effect, by reason of the exhibition of foreign products and manufactures, was to deeply stir the nation. It gave a distinct impulse to art in America, which was confirmed at once by the creation of a museum of art objects, to be housed permanently in one of the "Centennial" buildings in Fairmount Park, and the organization of a School of Industrial Art in Philadelphia, the first school in the country whose purpose it was to make industry see through art's eyes. It was under this inspiration that the school of the Pennsylvania Academy of Fine Arts was reorganized and made more serviceable. This institution now, in 1876, occupied a new building in Broad Street in Philadelphia.

The National Academy of Design in New York had gained sufficient strength to purchase a site in 1860, at the corner of 23rd Street and Fourth Avenue. The work upon a fine Gothic building for its uses proceeded during the war—the corner stone was laid with ceremonies in 1863; it was completed in 1865.[1] The Metropolitan Museum of Art in New York received its charter in 1870, an event which shortly resulted in the erection of a building in Central Park for its occupancy. In the same year the Museum of Fine Arts was established in Boston. In 1877 a school of drawing and painting was started in connection with that institution which, by this time, had completed, at a cost of $600,000, and moved into, an edifice designed for its purposes on Copley Square.[2] In 1875 Charles Eliot Norton was appointed professor of the history of art in Harvard University.[3]

[1] National Academy of Design, Ceremonies, etc., 1865.
[2] Museum of Fine Arts, Boston, 1870–1920.
[3] Letters of C. E. Norton, vol. ii, pp. 3–5.

It was a notable day when mural painting and architecture were joined through the employment of John La Farge, in 1876, to adorn the walls of Trinity Church which Mr. Richardson was erecting in Boston.[1] Two years later William Morris Hunt embellished the interior of the new capitol at Albany, a work well done but lost to the country, as was its author, by the intolerable conditions established by the politicians whom he was obliged to serve.[2]

Meanwhile wealthy Americans were developing a desire to own and exhibit objects of art in their homes. It became fashionable for a man possessed of more money than he knew what to do with to purchase paintings and sculptures. Dealers appeared to make bargains with him for what they had for sale, usually at first for European works, which in the sight of the amateurs of the day were held to be particularly estimable if they came from France.[3] But gradually support was given to American artists by the men who had spent their years in digging into the rich vitals of the country and were ending their lives in fine houses on the Fifth Avenues of our great cities. Private collections began to assume importance.[4] Yet better, affluent men were endowing communities with art collections for the free enjoyment of the people. In 1869 W. W. Corcoran, a banker in Washington, established the fine foundation which bears his name in that city.[5] George Peabody made a gift to Baltimore.[6]

For a time misfortune overtook the college also. The South no longer had young men for the Northern seats of learning. There must be economic recovery, as well as some readjustment of ideas, before the youth of Alabama, the Carolinas and Virginia would return to Harvard, Yale and Princeton; before their students in medicine could be expected to reappear in Philadelphia. The West was populated by families to which colleges

[1] Cortissoz, Life of La Farge, pp. 156–60.
[2] Cf. Shannon, Boston Days of Wm. Morris Hunt, chap. vi.
[3] C. H. Caffin, Story of American Painting, p. 167.
[4] Galaxy, July, 1870, pp. 57–8.
[5] Philadelphia Ledger, May 13, 1869.
[6] Galaxy, July, 1870, pp. 57–8.

were strange, by which they were little respected. That their instruction was "impractical," that they unfitted the young for the important tasks of life there was proof on all sides. The men who had the largest fortunes, who held the principal offices in the republic, had left school in boyhood. By going down the list of the prominent figures of the day in America it could be seen that four out of five had achieved success without the assistance of a college education. From the time when the government had been established, when many of the men of state had been graduates of distinguished European schools, we had passed to a time when there was something near to deification of those who had wrung fortune from the wilderness by early rising and the calloused hand, who had done this with a "common school education" and who were in name, as in effect, "self-made."

At best higher education in America had been and was at a low estate. It was something, said Goldwin Smith in 1868, "that has almost got to be created."[1] Conditions called imperatively for a reorganization of the system of teaching. By great good fortune the way opened at Harvard. Charles W. Eliot was the son of a merchant of Boston, who at one time had been mayor of the city. He had graduated at the university in 1853 and chose the pursuit of a teacher in his branch of knowledge, which was chemistry. During the war he was enabled to spend two years in Europe, where he familiarized himself with higher collegiate methods and improved himself in his science. He came home, as did all who enjoyed such opportunities, profoundly impressed with the inferiority of the educational system of his own country. Shortly after his return the government of Harvard University changed: the management came into the hands of the alumni, and in due time, in 1869, Eliot was elected to the presidency. He signalized this event by the most extensive reforms in an educational plant where example was a more potential factor than it could have been at any other place in the country. It was soon seen that, not only here, but in all our colleges education was to be freed of

[1] To Frederic Harrison, Goldwin Smith's Correspondence, p. 18.

the old theological influences; that it was to be given a more practical and serviceable bent, and brought into relation with the new significant movements in science; that the young man must have some measure of opportunity to elect his subjects of study and not be spoon-fed any longer, under the old system, according to rote, by teachers who were as oblivious, so it seemed, to the progress of the world around them as they were neglectful of their great duties and responsibilities.

Even the most sympathetic of Eliot's friends shook their heads in doubt and looked on in amazement at the changes which he rapidly instituted in teaching methods at the oldest of our universities.[1]   All of this came to pass while Yale was choosing "a Connecticut country minister, aet. 60, as her president,"[2] an exponent of "moral philosophy," as it was made manifest through Congregationalist eyes, and Princeton was proceeding (since 1868), under the administration of Dr. James McCosh, with a "moral philosophy" which emerged from the ratiocinative apparatus of a Presbyterian mind.

Harvard, thus reorganized, was supported in its forward movement by two wisely administered new universities, Cornell and Johns Hopkins, the one headed by Andrew D. White, the other by Daniel C. Gilman.   Ezra Cornell was a Hicksite Quaker, "raised quite from the ranks of labor,"[3] living near Ithaca, N. Y.   He had gained a fortune stringing telegraph wires on poles instead of burying them in conduits underground, the method originally followed by the promoters of telegraphy, and in other branches of business.   With a determined character, which amounted to obstinacy, a power to overcome obstacles and to face opposition, even obloquy, with forbearance, he throve, all the while nourishing an interest in higher affairs.   In the New York state senate in 1864 and 1865 he met Andrew D. White, a young man who had just come to hold a seat in the

[1] Cf. Rollo Ogden, Life of Godkin, vol. i, pp. 294–5; J. T. Morse, Life and Letters of O. W. Holmes, vol. ii, pp. 187–8, 190–91. Eliot had "turned the whole university over like a flapjack," Holmes wrote to Motley on December 2, 1871. For the effect produced upon the mind of a student see Henry Cabot Lodge, Early Memories, chap. viii.

[2] Noah Porter. Holmes to Motley, Morse, op. cit., vol. ii, p. 191.

[3] Goldwin Smith's Correspondence, p. 12.

body as a member from Syracuse. White had graduated from Yale in 1853, and, going abroad for three years for further study in France and Germany, upon his return became a professor of history in the University of Michigan, a progressive institution of learning, where he remained until the war broke up his classes.[1]

In the midst of an angry discussion as to the disposition to be made of New York's share and portion of the great land grant to the states by Congress in 1862 for industrial and technical education, Mr. Cornell offered a half million dollars of his own money and a site at Ithaca for a new university, if the legislature would endow the institution with the lands taken from the public domain which were offered it and were in danger, were something not speedily done, of reverting to the Federal government. White gave a warm welcome to the proposal, which was factiously opposed by a variety of interests. He supported Cornell throughout the stubborn parliamentary contest with the ignorant and corrupt politicians then assembled at Albany, until the result which both men had at heart was assured.

The Quaker philanthropist visited the West and South in person, and at great labor "located" the land that the college might have the largest possible endowment for its future uses. White was asked to organize the school and serve as its first president. Here was a cherished opportunity; he long had had visions of a new and better kind of university in America. He went abroad for a more particular investigation of the educational systems of Europe; he assembled books and apparatus; he built laboratories; he engaged energetic and inspiring young men whose abilities bespoke valuable service as teachers; and organized a body of non-resident professors who brought ideas to, and desirably advertised the institution, among the number Goldwin Smith, lecturer on history at Oxford, who had valiantly espoused the Northern cause in England during the war, thereby awakening much grateful feeling in this country; Louis Agassiz, James Russell Lowell, George William Curtis, Bayard Taylor

[1] Cf. Reminiscences of James B. Angell, p. 226.

and Theodore Dwight. He was ready to open the school with formal exercises on September 7, 1868, a year before Eliot was inducted into the presidential office at Harvard. Men soon saw that he had established a university completely free of sectarian influences; that he was detaching higher education in considerable degree from the classics, giving literature, history and the sciences an equal place in the courses of study; that at Cornell students were to be thrown upon their own resources and were to follow their own particular inclinations in the choice of their careers as never before; that the walks of higher learning were to be for the poor boy no less than for the rich man's son.[1]

The founding of Cornell University was followed shortly by a large gift of money from another Quaker for the establishment of a university in Baltimore. Johns Hopkins was a Maryland farmer's son who, in a wholesale grocery business in that city, had amassed a fortune which he appreciably increased in the later years of his life through his connection with banking, railroad and shipping enterprises. In 1867, he announced a plan for an educational institution and, at his death in 1873, more than $3,000,000 were left to trustees for its organization, with a like sum for a great hospital. Daniel C. Gilman had been born in Connecticut and graduated from Yale in 1852, one year before Andrew D. White. The two men were abroad together. Gilman, like White, came home to identify himself with the "new education." He was at Yale, engaged in the upbuilding of the Sheffield Scientific School, when, in 1870, he was called to the Pacific coast to assume the presidency of the University of California, which had just been founded to radiate useful and civilizing influences on that distant border of our American empire. He declined, but two years later, when it was again urged upon him, he accepted the appointment, and was in the midst of successful exertions to increase the endowment of the institution by appeals to the generosity of

[1] Autobiography of A. D. White, chapters on his life as a university president, vol. i. Goldwin Smith wrote to Max Müller that the students at Cornell were, "to a great extent, the sons of farmers and mechanics." They came to him, he said "pretty rough."—Goldwin Smith's Correspondence, p. 22.

the rich pioneers,[1] when he was drawn back east to organize
the great school which was made possible by the philanthropy
of Johns Hopkins. The trust was "without shackles of state or
political influence." [2] Like White and Eliot, Gilman gave himself to the tasks which confronted him with a full understanding of the modern requirements of a great higher school, re-
visited Europe and drew about him a group of the leading
scientists of the time. They were not to teach merely: it would
be their function, as it would be that of the university, to promote scholarship of the highest order.[3]   It would be not so
much a university of buildings as of men, and this it was in truth
when its simple halls, improvised from some old dwelling houses,
were ready for use in the autumn of 1876. Gilman threw down
the gage to those who were intent upon linking modern science
with agnosticism by inviting Professor Huxley to be the orator
on the university's opening day,[4] and it strode out upon the
open road.

Provision was made for higher teaching in postgraduate
class rooms; undergraduate work, while not neglected, was a
secondary matter; Johns Hopkins became a university in the
German sense. Through it education was raised to a rank
where results could be seen in published doctoral dissertations,
and the Ph. D., taught himself, was ready to make teaching
a vocation. Soon from this source began a flow of young men
into the teaching corps of our schools and colleges, who were to
exert the most profound influence upon the country. Journals
and transactions announced the progress and preserved the
record of achievement for other men to build upon, with a view
to further progress.

Mr. Hopkins, having made his fortune in large degree in Maryland, Virginia and North Carolina, desired that unusual advantages should be offered young men from those states, and the
institution was enabled in a short while to exercise the most

[1] Cf. Fabian Franklin, Life of D. C. Gilman, chap. iii.
[2] Ibid., p. 184.
[3] N. Y. Nation, Jan. 28, 1875; Josiah Royce, Scribner's Magazine,
Sep., 1891; D. C. Gilman in ibid., March, 1902.
[4] Fabian Franklin, op. cit., pp. 219–23.

wholesome influence upon the upper South. No university could or did play so valuable a part in putting the grace of civilization into the mind and heart of that region south of the city of Washington, which had been led astray in 1861, and now happily was restored to its allegiance to the Union.

The large sum of money which Mr. Hopkins had put into the hands of trustees for the establishment of a hospital, and a tract of land of fourteen acres in Baltimore upon which to erect the buildings for that institution, to serve as an aid to the university in the development of its medical school, did not become fruitful until 1889. This great foundation, at Mr. Hopkins's desire, was made the subject of thorough study by high authorities on hospital construction and management, and, with its clinical and other opportunities, and through the attachment to it of eminent figures in medicine, Baltimore, after Mr. Gilman succeeded in 1893 in opening the medical school, which had been so long in contemplation, assumed a position as a centre for medical teaching and research, not second to the place it had held for nigh twenty years as a result of its school of letters and science.

Once it had been created in our young men, the taste for higher education spread rapidly. Americans, since Bancroft's and Edward Everett's time, had studied in Germany. Following the war with France the German legend was written high. The development of science in the old universities of that country, with the liberal encouragement of the federal as well as the Prussian and other state governments, made them more efficient than ever before. Even the new American Ph. D.s were going abroad for further decorations, upon the recommendation of their teachers, themselves just returned, full of the German scholar's zeal. Any winter the names of from one to two hundred Americans could be found inscribed on the roll of students at the University of Berlin. Soon these numbers, coming home, found the market so thronged with young men, like themselves eager to scientificize the American mind, that, when they obtained employment at all, they were accounted not worth the wages of a teacher in a country school.

As for books, and letters generally, after the war, at least two facts were impressive. In the first place the market was crowded with books from England and Canada. In the second place there was a large new and general demand for sensational writing. The great number of foreign books in the market was ascribable to the cost of printing, binding, paper and the materials of which books are made. This was so much lower abroad that publishers in the United States declared their inability to compete with the foreign product, a condition which, however, they were not long in finding a way to correct through a revision of the tariff laws.[1]

So much had come to pass in spite of the free access which the American publisher had to the works of English authors. In the absence of an international copyright law he could appropriate to his own uses whatever he liked. Any foreign book or magazine article could be taken and reprinted for sale to the people of this Union of states without so much as a "by your leave" to the writer whose industry and genius had produced it.

The feats of rivalry of American publishers in capturing, reprinting and marketing the works of Scott, Dickens and others, whose newest novels were awaited with expectancy in this country, and for which these publishers paid nothing beyond the cost of manufacture, came to wear the aspect of comedy. The book might be set up in parts, awaiting the receipt of later sheets; expresses would race from the wharves as ships came in with material for the typesetters; the volumes printed and bound, they would be sent off on coaches, travelling often at a breakneck pace through the night from Philadelphia to New York, or from New York to Boston, as the case might be, lest some other publisher of greater activity should succeed in bringing his edition to market first. In a few days a half dozen publishers, two or three in the same city, might be advertising their reprints in the gazettes.

Occasionally a conscience was salved by sending the author, or his publisher in England, a small sum for the "advance

[1] Articles on Literature in Am. Ann. Cyclop. for 1866 and 1867.

sheets." To an increasing extent, as time went on, the larger
publishing houses bargained for the rights of American issue
and made payments which were held to stand in some relation
to the profits on sales. A kind of "gentleman's agreement"
protected the "buyer"; the announcement by a firm that it
had made such plans in reference to any forthcoming new work
would prevent others from interfering with these plans.[1] But
there were those who made no matter of this, and no method
of bringing them to account was at hand. The author in England was wholly helpless, if he so much as knew of the contention of the falcons which had plunged their talons into his work.
Following the book publishers, those who printed cheap periodicals would seize the story for serial publication, and disperse
it over the country for their advertisement and emolument.
There was limitless confusion. It was an intolerable situation,
capable of no kind of defense.[2]

Harriet Martineau had drawn attention to the injustice of such
conditions during her visit to America in 1834.[3] The subject
came forward very prominently in 1837 when Thomas Moore,
the poet laureate Southey, Disraeli, Miss Martineau, Miss
Edgeworth and all the principal authors of England, "deeply
impressed with the conviction that the only firm ground of
friendship between nations was a strict regard to simple justice,"
united in a petition to the Congress of the United States.[4] In the
Senate the subject was referred to a select committee of which
Henry Clay was the chairman. American writers came to the
support of their brothers of the pen in Great Britain; petitions
were circulated in Boston, New York and Philadelphia to be
numerously signed. Clay, in reporting a bill to the Senate,
put authors and inventors in a class together. They had,
"according to the practice among civilized nations, a property
in the respective productions of their genius," and their right
to protection was "incontestable." They were "among the

[1] J. Henry Harper, The House of Harper, pp. 110–12; Article on Literature in Am. Ann. Cyclop for 1871, pp. 455–61.
[2] Cf. article on Literature, Am. Ann. Cyclop. for 1869.
[3] Cf. Parke Godwin, Life of Bryant, vol. i, pp. 315–6.
[4] Senate Doc., 24th Cong. 2nd sess, no. 134.

greatest benefactors of mankind." This right to a protection
of their property was clear, no matter where that property
should be "situated." A bale of merchandise, owned by a
British merchant, was effectively secured to him when it
came within the jurisdiction of the United States no less than
when it lay in England. But, if the work of a British author
was brought to this country, it might be appropriated, republished and sold by anyone for his own advantage, without
possibility of the owner invoking the aid of the law.[1] The
forces which were ready to oppose such a measure soon made
themselves felt at Washington. Petitions came into Congress.

The movement rested until Dickens's visit in 1842. He was
outspoken in the expression of his opinion. The best reviews
and journals gave him their support, amazed though they were
at his temerity in denouncing an injustice which, while it was
plain, almost none had had the slightest wish to discuss or to
make a movement to abolish.[2] The principal American writers,
Washington Irving at their head, again addressed Congress.
Carlyle in a forcible statement, with the commandment "Thou
shalt not steal" as his text, came to Dickens's side in England.[3]
The enormity of the wrong done Sir Walter Scott by the theft
of his works, which had been published and republished, pur-
loined and repurloined in this country, in the face of his personal
needs, was again pointed out.[4]

Some of the publishers, led by George P. Putnam, now advocated a copyright law.[5] In 1841 John Jay, William Cullen

[1] Senate Doc., 24th Cong. 2nd sess., no. 179.
[2] An exception was found in the New York Evening Post under Bryant's
influence. Cf. Allan Nevins, The Evening Post, pp. 212–6.
[3] Forster, Life of Dickens, vol. i, pp. 235–6.
[4] Thomas Moore and the writers who had addressed Congress in 1837
had said of Scott "that, while the works of this author, dear alike to your
country and ours, were read from Maine to Georgia, from the Atlantic to
the Mississippi, he received no remuneration from the American public
for his labors"—"that an equitable remuneration might have saved his
life and would at least have relieved its closing years from the burden of
debts and destructive toils." It was necessary for Dickens to say little of
his own case, or the cases of other popular writers of the day. Their
situation was known to all who would stop to ponder it.—Senate Doc., 24th
Cong. 2nd sess., vol. ii, p. 134.
[5] Cf. Nevins, The Evening Post, p. 216.

Bryant and others again took the matter to Congress. But the yield in positive action was nothing, and the filching by publishers, both great and small, in newspaper, magazine and book, proceeded as before. Interest in the subject was reawakened during the second visit of Dickens in 1867. In 1868 an International Copyright Association was formed with Bryant as president, George William Curtis as vice president and E. C. Stedman as secretary, and new memorials were prepared.

But such demands were of no avail, because powerful interests were profiting, as they believed, by inaction. In 1867 it was stated that no less than four firms—two in Boston, one in New York and one in Philadelphia—had issued the complete works of Charles Dickens in thirty-one different editions. Three houses in the same year reprinted the Waverley novels.[1] The next year there were as many more reprints of these writers, without mention of "pirated" editions of Thackeray, Charles Reade, Bulwer Lytton and other writers, whose work was salable in the United States.[2]

The printers and typesetters, through their organizations, were made to believe that it would be to their disadvantage if British works could not be reprinted over and over again with freedom; in such a case, of course, they were told, they would be

[1] Article on Literature in Am. Ann. Cyclop. for 1867.

[2] Ibid. for 1867. In what degree American publishers remunerated English authors, under the system of paying for "advance sheets" may be inferred from Thackeray's statement in 1853 that by an international copyright law he would be "$5,000 a year richer" on his American sales. (Thackeray's Letters to an American Family, p. 26; cf. J. G. Wilson, Thackeray in the U. S., pp. 62–4.) Anthony Trollope said that he received from America but five per cent of what came to him on sales at home, though he had more readers here than in England. He did not know, indeed, that he received anything for the use of his work in this country. The sales of the sheets were made by his publishers who, so far as he could see, gave him no more for a novel than if there were no American market. The sheets of one novel, for which he was paid £1,600 in England, were sold for £20 in America, where the publishers were circulating it for fifteen cents a copy. (Autobiography of Anthony Trollope, pp. 275–80.) In twenty years Trollope made $70,000 by his pen. (Ibid., pp. 325–6.) With copyright covering the United States his returns must have been at least twice this sum. For payments which, it was alleged, had been made to Scott and earlier writers, see Senate Doc., 25th Cong. 2nd sess., no. 369; cf. J. H. Harper, The House of Harper, p. 114.

thrown out of employment. Other men pretended to fear
that with international copyright reading would be discouraged.
It would be "a tax on intellectual and moral light." Should
a dam be built "to obstruct the flow of the rivers of knowledge"?
In Europe learning might shine at a few focal points; here it
should be as "free and universal as the sunshine of Heaven."[1]
All the while an undercurrent of feeling unfavorable to copyright was stimulated in the ignorant parts of the population
by appeals to national prejudice—it would be sending money
to England which now, after the war, in return for her expressions of sympathy for the South, it was easy to see, deserved
from us even less consideration than before.[2]

It was time that the wholly commercial attitude of the country on this subject should be set forth by some one in a position to do this officially, and Senator Morrill of Maine, speaking
for the Library Committee of Congress, on February 7, 1873,
came forward for this service. He found and declared for himself and his colleagues, reversing earlier opinions of the same
committee,[3] that the adoption of any plan for international
copyright could not be urged upon Congress "upon reasons
of general equity or of constitutional law." While being of
only a "very doubtful advantage to American authors,"[4]
it would be "not only an unquestionable and permanent injury to the manufacturing interests concerned in producing
books, but also a hindrance to the diffusion of knowledge among
the people, and to the cause of universal education."[5]

[1] Senate Doc., 27th Cong. 2nd sess., no. 323.
[2] The interests in Philadelphia which held the view that protective
tariffs were good, because they harassed British industry, were in favor of
our stealing English books. See, e.g., R. R. Bowker, Copyright, its History
and its Law, pp. 347, 352.
[3] See its report of February 21, 1868, in House Reports, 40th Cong.
2nd sess., no. 16.
[4] This in spite of the obvious fact that the free use of the best English
writing tended to discourage publishers from taking the work of American
writers, for which the publishers must pay, as was repeatedly pointed out
in their memorials to Congress. Cf. article on Literature in Am. Ann.
Cyclop. for 1870.
[5] Senate Reports, 42nd Cong. 3rd sess., no. 409; cf. Cong. Globe, 42nd
Cong. 2nd sess., p. 972. Meanwhile England, which had long sought to
establish reciprocal relations with other countries on this subject, was acting

The second impressive fact concerning our books and letters in general, after the war, was the manifest cheapening of the public taste for reading. "Wishy-washy" and "sensational" writing was demanded as never before.[1] Such a tendency had been deplored in the forties and fifties. It was the reproach aimed at the so-called "Philadelphia magazines" of that period. But now what was worse was seen—"a rage for mere diversion and intellectual excitement."[2] The lecture went the way of the good book. The old lyceum, which had furnished the people a point of contact with the thoughts and graces of the world, was displaced by the new kind of newspaper, the flashy story and the trashy play.[3] Literature was a luxury, and it was the kind of a luxury which such people as had now captured the leadership in our made-over society would "give up sooner than India shawls, jewelry, suppers and fast horses."[4] If there were not a revival of interest in it men acquainted with better things predicted that it would become extinct.[5]

To supply the demand for such printed matter as this new public required the presses were employed in publishing the inconsequent and, in many instances, morally injurious[6] work of a multitude of literary hacks. For twenty-five, ten, even five cents, stories were sold in large editions. With exciting titles, which may have entirely belied their inane content, they stood on news-stands, and were cried on the trains and in the streets. One woman had written and found publishers for six such novels in 1866—in the same year each of two men had

in no retaliatory spirit with reference to our authors. They might, under conditions which were easily met, secure copyright privileges for their works in Great Britain, though we should keep to our disgraceful course yet for many years—until 1891, then acting with reservations, which called for fresh exertions on the part of honorable men in the interest of the foreign author's fair rights.—E. A. Drone, A Treatise on the Law of Property in Intellectual Productions, pp. 92–6; R. R. Bowker, Copyright, its History and its Law, Chapter xix.

[1] Taylor and Scudder, Life and Letters of Bayard Taylor, p. 527.
[2] Ibid., p. 559.
[3] Ibid., p. 530.
[4] Ibid., p. 527.
[5] Letters of C. E. Norton, vol. ii, p. 36.
[6] Cf. James T. Fields, Biographical Notes and Personal Sketches, pp. 223–6.

four to his credit. Five writers in 1867 each produced three of these works of fiction. Tales they were of the adventures of spies, trappers, scouts and guerrillas, of hermits, madmen and convicts. The very names of those who fathered and mothered this ill-begotten progeny are unrecognizable at this day.[1]

For this ignorant mass there were periodicals also, chief among them the New York Ledger, founded by Robert Bonner, an Irishman, who had graduated from the printer's "case." In the years following the war he was at the height of his profitable activities in making a weekly paper for servant girls and roustabouts. In his smudgy sheet he astutely mixed his vulgar tales[2] with better material. Noted men and women were pursued until, tempted by his great prices, they consented to send him scraps of their work. Then he announced his catches to the world in the manner that Phineas T. Barnum, the circus man of the age, advertised his bearded lady or a new elephant. Edward Everett, Dickens, Longfellow, Whittier, Tennyson and many others were offered large sums for the use of their names in connection with contributions, so large and under conditions so notorious, that they were constrained, in some cases, to assure the public that they were donating their gains to charitable objects.[3] Thus did Bonner boom his paper into a circulation which, he said, exceeded 300,000. The fortune which he accumulated was estimated in millions of dollars. He maintained a racing stable, containing some of the fastest horses in the world, which further served to advertise his periodical and the signal success of his audacity in exploiting it. He

---

[1] "Garbage," James T. Fields called it, "thrown out by infamous scribblers who pander to all the worst passions of human or inhuman nature." Wherever he went on his lecture tours he found young people reading "immoral and exciting cheap books."—Ibid.; cf. article on Literature in Am. Ann. Cyclop. for 1867.

[2] "As low and coarse an order of literature," Godkin called the Ledger, "as any publication in the world."—Rollo Ogden, Life of E. L. Godkin, vol. i, p. 179.

[3] Bonner bought the serial rights to Beecher's novel "Norwood" and Greeley's "Recollections of a Busy Life." It is said that Beecher received $30,000 for "Norwood," Edward Everett $50,000 for his writings for a year, Tennyson, $5,000 and Longfellow $3,000 for poems from their respective pens.

and a number of magazinists, drawn with pick and shovel, like the cheap book men, to the "pay ore" which had been opened to view, the crude precursors of our moving picture and "yellow" newspaper makers, did what they could—and it was a vast deal—to bring the general level of literary appreciation down to the standards of the scullery.

At the war's end the first group of large figures in American letters had all but disappeared. Cooper had died in 1851; Washington Irving in 1859; Nathaniel Hawthorne in 1864. William Cullen Bryant remained, a venerable and respected figure in public life and literary circles in New York City. He had leaped into his place as a poet upon the publication of "Thanatopsis," which he had written at the age of 18. When Lee had surrendered and Lincoln was shot he was in his seventy-first year. Younger men there were who had won honorable places for themselves before the war had yet broken upon the country. The genius of some of them had been awakened by the moral impulses which were stirred by the wrong of slavery, and the corrupting power which this gigantic evil had laid upon our national life. Emerson in 1865 was 62, Longfellow 58, Whittier 58, Holmes 56 and Lowell 46. Bancroft was 65, Motley 51 and Parkman 42. Prescott had died in 1859.

All of these were voices out of New England where the atmosphere had afforded so much encouragement to literary expression. The Middle States added little, except for Pennsylvania where there were Bayard Taylor, whose talents marked him for one of the highest places, George H. Boker, to whom greater industry would have brought enduring appreciation, Thomas Buchanan Read and Charles Godfrey Leland. In 1865 all had passed 40. Weir Mitchell was 36.

The South, busy with its slavery and the plain task of recovering from the consequences of the long indulgence in that vice, had few voices which could be heard beyond their own small neighborhoods. Two young poets in William Gilmore Simm's circle in Charleston, Henry Timrod and Paul H. Hayne, felt the cruel force of the war and died, one in 1867 and the other in 1886, as truly its victims as any slain by bullet or sword.

New figures were seen in Sidney Lanier, a poet of talent from Georgia, also a victim of its battles and prisons, and George W. Cable.

Ohio furnished William Dean Howells whom Lincoln had appointed to be consul at Venice, and who, at the end of the war, came home to make letters his profession; Illinois, John Hay, who had gone to Washington as one of Lincoln's secretaries, the author of inimitable verse, which caused his elders in literature to take notice of him. In Missouri a new and an original genius was discovered in Mark Twain, and from California came the arresting voice of Bret Harte.

In 1866 Bancroft finished the ninth volume of his "History of the United States." In that year, too, Whittier's "Snow Bound," appeared, to have instant success, the second series of Lowell's "Biglow Papers" and Bayard Taylor's poem, "The Picture of St. John." Taylor's pleasing novel of Pennsylvania country life, "The Story of Kennett" was also issued in 1866. In 1867 Dr. J. G. Holland, a popular writer of prose and verse, published "Kathrina"; 35,000 copies of this poem were sold in three months. Whitman's publishers issued the fourth edition of his "Leaves of Grass." Mark Twain appeared with a volume called "The Jumping Frog and other Sketches."

In 1868 Whittier's "Among the Hills" and "The New England Tragedies" of Longfellow, were published. John Bigelow, who had discovered Franklin's "Autobiography," while serving as United States minister in France, from which service he had just returned, brought out the first authentic version of that memorable document.

Francis Parkman, as his health would allow, was writing and revising his series of brilliant historical studies, covering the activities of the French in the settlement of America. Lowell's poem, "The Cathedral," was published in 1869. In the same year Thomas Wentworth Higginson, who essayed novel writing for the first time in "Malbone," caused men to discuss his claims to praise in his new field, and Mrs. Stowe added "Old Town Folks" to the list of works from her widely known pen. Her brother, Henry Ward Beecher, published a novel called "Nor-

wood," and Anna Dickinson, a Philadelphia woman, who had
gained remarkable transient fame as a political platform orator,
filling large halls wherever she went,[1] entered the field as a writer
of fiction with her "What Answer?" Both of these works
were numbered among the books having the largest sale in the
years in which they appeared.

Bryant's translation of the "Iliad" was soon followed by his
version of the "Odyssey." He neared eighty, and this extraordinary literary service seemed to be the "crowning work of
his life." At the same time Bayard Taylor issued his excellent
translation of "Faust."[2] Longfellow's translations of Dante
had only a little preceded the works of Bryant and Taylor.
The unsurpassed rendering into metrical English of these important works in Greek, German and Italian attested in an
unmistakable way to the vitality of our poetical scholarship.

Bret Harte awoke to find himself famous after the appearance of his book, "The Luck of Roaring Camp," an inkling of
which the world had received through the publication of some
of his work in the Overland Monthly, which he edited on the
Pacific coast, to be followed by a volume of his dialect and other
poems, including his lines about the "Heathen Chinee," soon
to be known to the very children in the streets. In 1871 a reception not much less sensational was accorded Joaquin Miller's "Songs of the Sierras," and John Hay's "Pike County
Ballads," including his "Little Breeches" and "Jim Bludso,"
which had appeared in the New York Tribune. Harte's,
Joaquin Miller's and Hay's very original additions to American
literature won attention in England, notably to increase the
esteem in which they were held in their own country.

Charles Dudley Warner enjoyed a sudden rise to notice
through "My Summer in a Garden." W. D. Howells's first
important novel, "Their Wedding Journey," with its kindly
satirizations of American life, appeared in 1871, together with
Longfellow's "The Divine Tragedy" and a collection of essays by Lowell called "My Study Windows," following "Among

[1] N. Y. Nation, Dec. 22, 1866; Ogden, Life of E. L. Godkin, vol. i, p. 288.
[2] Taylor and Scudder, Life and Letters of Bayard Taylor, p. 549.

my Books," a similar collection issued in the previous year. Horace Howard Furness in Philadelphia commenced, with "Romeo and Juliet," a new variorum edition of Shakespeare.

In 1873 came General Lew Wallace's "The Fair God," which was praised in England, and Howells's "A Chance Acquaintance," which was followed the next year by "A Foregone Conclusion." His more widely popular story, "The Rise of Silas Lapham," did not appear until 1884.

In 1874 the tenth and concluding volume of Bancroft's "History of the United States" was published. In 1875 Henry James, Jr., known as a writer of short stories, came forward with his first long novel "Roderick Hudson." "The American" was brought out in 1877; "The Europeans" and "Daisy Miller" in 1878. In 1879 George W. Cable's "Old Creole Days," short stories which had been appearing in a magazine, were collected into a volume, to be followed in 1880 by his "Grandissimes." The compelling poems of Sidney Lanier were drawing attention to his talents, which were generally acknowledged, after he had been asked, through his friend Bayard Taylor's influence, to write the cantata for the exercises attending the opening of the Centennial Exposition in Philadelphia in 1876, and had been appointed, through President Gilman's favor, to a lectureship in literature at the new Johns Hopkins University.

All the while our publishers were putting forth editions of the collected works of the New England poets, indicative of the national pride which their services continued to evoke. But they were finishing their lives. Bryant fell out at a ripe age in 1878. Bayard Taylor, while he should still have been at the height of his career, died in the same year.

A veritable outburst of literary thought, of artistic expression in prose and poetry, had suddenly brought us into honorable partnership with England herself in the creation of an intellectual heritage for our common race. That there was a spiritual depression under the influence of the materialism characteristic of the period, after the war, to which was added the economic distress in the wake of the panic of 1873, discouraging to the advancement of letters, was clear enough. The younger

writers who entered the lists from year to year, ready to break
their lances in the tourney for literary fame, made but a poor
appearance in comparison with the noble figures who had preceded them.

The publishing trade had come to be centered in New York,
though one or two firms, particularly the house of Ticknor and
Fields in Boston, played a notable and commendable part in
forwarding the interests of American literature. Philadelphia,
nearly supreme in the early part of the century as the place of
issue for books and magazines, now had a distinctly lower place.
The firm of Mathew Carey in that city had borne several names.
It and its branch-growth, known as Carey and Hart, had put
their imprints on many of the worthiest books which had appeared in America during three or four decades. But before
the war came on this old house had changed its business policies, and was confining its attention to scientific issues. The
notable Graham's Magazine had met with disaster and the
monthly visits to American homes of Godey's Lady's Book
awakened much less interest than they formerly had done.

Philadelphia's altered position was due, in a considerable degree, to the shrewd activity of four sons of a country carpenter,
who had established a large book and periodical publishing house
in New York. James and John Harper, after learning the
printing trade, opened a small shop, in 1817, in that city.
Later, joined by two younger brothers, Joseph Wesley and
Fletcher, they all together, in 1833, formed a partnership which
was known as Harper and Brothers. Out of this firm came much
of national consequence. The opening of the Mississippi
Valley, where the people were denied connection with cultural
influences, the development of the lyceum and the common
school, so indicative of an awakening interest in learning, and
the want of an international copyright law gave the Harpers
a field which they were skillful enough to occupy. They began
the issues of books in series which they called "Libraries."
These were designed both for entertainment and instruction,
and enjoyed a wide and lucrative sale.

In 1850 the firm projected a magazine. Henry J. Raymond

was engaged to edit it, under the direction of Fletcher Harper,
the youngest of the four Harper brothers. Before the first
year was out it had attained a circulation of 50,000 copies.[1]
After three years, in 1853, 130,000 copies were printed.[2]
"Harper's New Monthly Magazine" made no pretense to being
more than an eclectic publication. Unlike Graham's, whose
editor was the generous patron of American authors, it was a
mere compendium of material taken from the English periodicals, and extracts from books which Harper and Brothers were
about to put to press. Nothing in the magazine was specially
written for it except a monthly record of events, some book
reviews and a report upon the fashions in women's dress. It
was illustrated at first only sparingly, but the number of cuts
and engravings soon increased. In a short while American
writers were encouraged to send in their articles, stories and
verse. Contracts were made with the publishers of the popular
English novelists for the serial rights to their works as soon as
they were ready for the press, and the magazine became a famous
medium for "the continuous tales" of Dickens, Thackeray,
Charles Reade, Bulwer Lytton, Anthony Trollope, Miss Mu-
lock, Wilkie Collins, Charles Lever, George Eliot and other
writers of the day. Always wholesome and entertaining, clear
of polemical thought or allusion, light and relaxing, it was seen
everywhere on the library and boudoir tables of families of good
taste. It made the standards for publications of this kind, as
Graham's had done for an earlier period. Following Raymond
a number of men collaborated on the editorial staff of the magazine, under the eye of Fletcher Harper, but in 1869 it came under
the management of Henry Mills Alden, a young New England
literary man, who had entered the employ of the Harper firm
in 1863, a direction which was to continue for almost half a
century.

The house which was winning celebrity through the magazine's visits to so many American homes projected other periodicals. In 1857 the first number of Harper's Weekly appeared.

[1] Advertisement accompanying volume i of the magazine.
[2] J. H. Harper, The House of Harper, p. 86.

Established to follow the lines of the Illustrated London News it was peculiarly the creation of Fletcher Harper.[1] Correctly described as "a family newspaper," and "a journal of civilization," it soon made for itself, and held, a place which was secure against any competition in the same field. With letter press which included some of the great English novels in serial form, the use of which it shared with Harper's Magazine, and pictorial illustration, often large in size and of distinctive merit, it was issued each Saturday. For ten years George William Curtis had been a regular contributor to the Magazine; for some years, too, he had a "department" in the Weekly. After 1863 his moral weight and genial style were used in a larger way for the advantage of the Weekly of which he became the political editor. Its influence, through his prominent connection with it, increased rapidly. Drawings by artists on the ground illuminated the principal happenings of the day so that the files of the periodical are an invaluable historical record. Causes were served by cartoons, which took on great distinction and exerted an immense power in the hands of Thomas Nast, whose work began to appear in 1862. The son of a German trombone player, who had come to the United States in 1850, pupil of Sol Eytinge, whose drawings also were often seen in the publication, Nast made himself a force not in any way second to Curtis's in the direction of public thought.

During the height of the excitement over the exposures of the corruption in the New York City government in 1871 the Weekly, largely because of Nast's cartoons, reached a circulation of 300,000 copies.[2] The average number of copies issued in 1872, it was said, was 160,000.[3]

While traveling abroad Fletcher Harper saw a copy of the Berlin Bazar. Upon his return to New York he persuaded his brothers to undertake the publication in this country of a similar magazine, to be called Harper's Bazar. It was particularly designed for women. It would invade the field which Godey's

[1] J. Henry Harper, The House of Harper, p. 132.
[2] Harper's Weekly for Oct. 21 and Nov. 4, 1871.
[3] Ibid., Jan. 20, 1872.

and Peterson's in Philadelphia had profitably cultivated. Plentifully supplied with fashion plates, dress patterns, light reading and pleasant illustration, "to delight the female heart," it in a short time attained a large circulation. All three of the Harper periodicals would be sent to one address for a year for $10. Other magazines were "accumulated," so ran the advertisements, these of the Harpers were "edited." It was not until 1879 that the house began to issue Harper's Young People, a popular paper for boys and girls. By this time all of the four Harper brothers had died, James, the eldest, in 1869, Joseph Wesley in 1870, John in 1875 and Fletcher in 1877, thus committing the management of the house to younger hands.

Meanwhile another publishing firm in New York, of which George P. Putnam was the head, projected a periodical. It was the outcome of a dinner party given at Mr. Putnam's house at which Mrs. Caroline M. Kirkland, a writer favorably known at the day; George William Curtis, Parke Godwin, George Sumner, a writer and lecturer, a younger brother of Senator Sumner, and Charles F. Briggs, author, critic and intimate friend of James Russell Lowell, were present. With the co-operation of these and a few other writers Putnam's Monthly was launched in 1853 under the chief editorship of Mr. Briggs.[1] It would "combine the more various and amusing characteristics of a popular magazine with the higher and grave qualities of a quarterly review." Its interests were literature, science and art. It inherited some of the traditions of the Knickerbocker Magazine, but it felt the touch of new hands. Practically all the writers in America were named upon a list of prospective contributors, and a number of the best came to the editor's support,—Curtis with his "Potiphar Papers" and "Prue and I"; Lowell with prose and poetry; Henry D. Thoreau, Richard Grant White, Parke Godwin and many others with their contributions. The magazine would be published simultane-

[1] Putnam's Magazine, Jan. 1868—article by Briggs and letter from Curtis; Scudder, James Russell Lowell, vol. i, pp. 348-54; Cary, Life of Curtis, pp. 81-103, passim.

ously in New York and London, and the design was fine enough for a more favorable destiny. In a few months the circulation was 35,000 copies, greater, the publishers said, than had ever before been attained by "an original literary magazine either in this country or in Europe." [1]

Putnam's reached the end of its very creditable career [2] during the troubles incident to the year 1857, amid which, strangely enough, a lustier periodical, fashioned on its lines, entered the American world of letters. It was, indeed, a notable occurrence when the Atlantic Monthly appeared. If Putnam's had been the conception of Mr. Briggs, the Atlantic was peculiarly the child of Francis H. Underwood, a young literary man who had earlier had magazine editing plans which had failed to fruit, [3] and who was attached to the publishing and book jobbing house of Phillips, Sampson and Company in Boston. Though of a very cautious turn of mind Mr. Phillips was so far interested in the enterprise as to draw about him, one day in May, 1857, at a dinner at the Parker House, Emerson, Lowell, Motley, Dr. Holmes, and James Elliot Cabot. He was pleased to be one of a group of men, each of whom, as he said, was "known alike on both sides of the Atlantic and read beyond the limits of the English language," [4] and the future of the undertaking was assured. Longfellow, Whittier, Whipple, Edmund Quincy, Higginson, Thoreau, Charles Eliot Norton, Mrs. Stowe and others were soon interested in the magazine. It would start away with "the definite purpose," as Underwood declared, "of concentrating the efforts of the best writers upon literature and politics under the light of the highest morals," [5] and no other was so entirely qualified to direct a publication with such a design as James Russell Lowell, who became its editor. Though here, as in Putnam's, the names of the authors of the articles and poems were not disclosed, and they must be guessed at, the contributors to the first number,

[1] See announcement on cover of number for June, 1853.
[2] Cf. Ogden, Life of E. L. Godkin, vol. i, p. 222.
[3] Bliss Perry, Park Square Papers, pp. 205 et seq.
[4] M. A. DeWolfe Howe, The Atlantic Monthly and its Makers, p. 15.
[5] Ibid., pp. 26–7.

it is known, included Lowell himself, Motley, Longfellow, Emerson, Holmes, Whittier, Mrs. Stowe, J. T. Trowbridge and Parke Godwin. Holmes was represented by the first installment of his "Autocrat of the Breakfast Table." [1] A ship, freighted as this one was, sailed out on fortunate seas. It was the literary expression of New England in her Augustan age. There had been writing in other parts of the country, said George William Curtis, "but there had been nothing like the New England circle. It was that circle which compelled the world to acknowledge that there was an American literature." [2]

The house of Phillips, Sampson and Company fell, in 1859, at the death of Mr. Phillips, and the assignee sold the magazine for $10,000 to Mr. Ticknor of Ticknor and Fields, booksellers and publishers at the well known "Corner Book Store." At the time of the transaction Mr. Ticknor's partner, James T. Fields, was in Europe. The acquisition of the property was greatly to Mr. Fields's liking. Though a publisher of astuteness he himself was a poet not without talents. To him a book was more than a piece of merchandise. He brought feeling and sympathy into his business. The kindliest and most intimate personal relationships with authors were founded upon this quality in Mr. Fields, who, very shortly, assumed the editorship of the magazine. His own tastes inclined him to the duties of the office, the necessity for economy of management pointed in the same direction, and in 1861, after establishing "the Atlantic" on firm literary foundations, Mr. Lowell rather reluctantly retired from its direction. For ten years, or until 1871, Mr. Fields continued in the place, when William Dean Howells succeeded to the editorship, [3] to continue in it for a like period of ten years. In the meantime the publishers changed, as Ticknor and Fields became, in 1868, Fields, Osgood and Company, and, in 1871, James R. Osgood and Company. In 1874 the ownership passed to H. O. Houghton and Company, a firm which in 1880 became Houghton, Mifflin and Company.

[1] Cf. Letters of C. E. Norton, vol. i, pp. 182, 185–6, 189.
[2] James T. Fields, Biographical Notes and Personal Sketches, p. 55; cf. T. W. Higginson, Cheerful Yesterdays, p. 187.
[3] Cf. Letters of C. E. Norton, vol. ii, p. 36.

Lowell passed to the North American Review. This periodical had been founded by a number of young literary gentlemen
in Boston in 1815 on the lines of the famous quarterlies of Great
Britain. For fifty years, without interruption, it had been the
leading representative in America of dignified scholarship
and of literature as a fine art. Almost from the first day it had
been read and respected in Europe, as well as in this country,
but now, for some time under the direction of a New England
divine, it was no longer the power it had earlier been. The
publishers, in 1863, applied to Lowell to take the editorship,
and he accepted the post on the condition that he could have the
assistance of Charles Eliot Norton. Such an alliance spelled
the rebirth of this excellent magazine. Lowell himself turned
his prose work, which earlier had been given to the Atlantic,
into the Review.[1] For a number of years the co-operation of
the twain made it certain that the highest thought of the country would find expression in its pages. Following their administration Professor Gurney of Harvard University, and then
Henry Adams, aided by Henry Cabot Lodge, upheld the traditions of the magazine.[2]

The principal publisher of general literature in Philadelphia
after the war was J. B. Lippincott. He began the issue, in
January, 1868, of a magazine bearing his name. The editors,
writing in "the city of Brotherly Love," had the desire "to
occupy the historical and geographical position of Philadelphia
as the common ground, where all who love the Union (and none
others) can meet and discuss matters relating to literature,
science and education in harmony and good fellowship." The
first number contained an initial installment of Rebecca Harding Davis's popular story "Douglas Galbraith."[3]

Charles Scribner, graduate of Princeton College, later a
student at law, a young man of cultivated instincts, had entered

[1] In all, from 1867 to 1877, 34 articles and many short "notices."—
E. E. Hale, Lowell and his Friends, p. 151.
[2] Scudder, J. R. Lowell, vol. ii, pp. 45–6; Ogden, Life of E. L. Godkin,
vol. i, pp. 303–4; Letters of C. E. Norton, vol. i, pp. 265–6, 268; Motley's
Correspondence, vol. ii, p. 167; The Education of Henry Adams, pp. 293,
296, 307–8; Henry Cabot Lodge, Early Memories, pp. 240–41, 244–5.
[3] Lippincott's for January, 1868.

the publishing business in New York in 1846. His house issued a favorite periodical called Hours at Home. He made proposals to Dr. J. G. Holland, whose works in prose and verse were enjoying unusual and, at this day, not entirely understandable popularity, looking to the establishment of a new magazine. Holland was about to sail for Europe. While travelling abroad he met Roswell Smith, whose home then was in Indiana, and they together, on a bridge, at Lucerne, in Switzerland, made a compact. Holland would be editor, Smith, business manager of a Scribner's Magazine, if Mr. Scribner upon their return to New York should approve of the plan. In a short time the arrangements were completed. In 1868 Mr. Briggs had revived Putnam's Monthly. It was again making its regular appearances—still without great public appreciation. It would be merged with the new magazine; so too would Hours at Home fall into the melting pot, out of which was to come, in November, 1870, Scribner's Monthly. The new periodical was to be illustrated like Harper's, but in a better manner, and the direction made good its promises to such a degree that the Harper management was soon impelled to activity along the same lines, lest ground be lost in a contest with such a competitor.[1] Its literary material was assembled in America. The English serials, which still filled Harper's pages, Dr. Holland did not serve to his readers. The pens of Americans were employed in his service. His contributors came to include most of the younger writers of the country, who highly prized such a vehicle for their work.[2] Authors were sought for in the South and in other places and, when found, were heartily welcomed to the republic of letters.[3] Like Putnam's and the Atlantic, Scribner's was an American magazine, directed at that phalanx of readers which Harper's had gained, and bent upon entertaining them in a similar way. Beginning with a circulation of 40,000, the number of copies issued in 1881 had come to be 150,000. An English edition of the magazine found the favor

[1] J. Henry Harper, The Book of Harper, p. 202.
[2] Cf. Rebecca Harding Davis, Bits of Gossip, p. 220.
[3] Edwin Mims, Sidney Lanier, pp. 284-5.

of the British public. The circulation in that country rose from 2,000 to 18,000.

Roswell Smith, meanwhile, came into control of a young people's magazine called St. Nicholas, and by purchasing the interest of Dr. Holland, and of the Scribner firm in Scribner's Magazine he contrived, not without heartburnings, to retire Dr. Holland, and to take over the entire management of the publication, the name of which, beginning with the issue of November, 1881, became the Century Magazine.[1]

On May 15, 1866, the first number of a new fortnightly magazine called the Galaxy made its appearance in New York. It was published and edited by William Conant Church and Francis P. Church, sons of a religious editor and writer, Pharcellus Church, themselves well known in New York journalism. The periodical had high standards. Its pages contained the work of well known writers—novels in serial form, short stories, essays, criticism and verse. But after a year or two it became a monthly, bearing the imprint of Sheldon and Company. It retained a lofty tone for several years, but its publisher was under the necessity of bringing the series of issues to an end in 1878, when its list of readers were made over to the Atlantic Monthly.

The finest new fruit of this period was the New York Nation. This paper was the personal creation of Edwin Lawrence Godkin, an Irishman, born in county Wicklow, the son of a Presbyterian clergyman, who had a taste, like his son, for controversial writing. Graduating at Queen's College, Belfast, young Godkin studied law in Lincoln's Inn, but, having won a pleasant success as a war correspondent of the London Daily News in the Crimea, he determined to devote himself to journalism and literature. In 1856, at the age of 25, he came to America, where he continued his connection with the Daily News. A tour of the South on horseback in behalf of his newspaper brought him near to Frederick Law Olmsted, who is prominently identified today

---

[1] Holland died in October, 1881, while these changes were in progress. Mr. Scribner had died in 1871, shortly after the magazine was established. See Scribner's Monthly for June, 1881, and Century Magazine for November, 1881.

as the landscape architect of Central Park, the open reaches
of which so proudly adorn New York, and who earlier had
made such a journey and had written of it. Godkin's interest
still inclined him to the law, and he was admitted to the New
York bar, but his health, he believed, precluded practice, and
he continued to write. His letters to London were useful in
giving England correct views of the course of affairs in America
during the Civil War,[1] and, at its end, he put forward a plan,
which Olmsted had cherished, for a critical weekly journal.
He found a warm friend in Charles Eliot Norton, who brought
him into contact with the intellectual group in Cambridge,[2]
but he encountered difficulties which delayed the realization
of his plans. Meanwhile, a similar project was launched in
New York in the Round Table, a weekly publication containing criticism and comment by competent writers.[3] At length
a capital of $100,000 was secured, half of it in Boston, largely
through Norton's aid, and the rest in New York and Philadelphia. Godkin was made editor [4] of the new periodical, and
the first number appeared on July 6, 1865, only a few weeks
after Lee's surrender at Appomattox.

The South was in complete disorder, the position of the freedman was problematical to the last degree. One of the principal purposes of the journal, it was announced, would be "the
earnest and persistent consideration" of the condition of the
negroes with a view to their education and the improvement
of their social state. This task, the discussion of the "legal,
economical and constitutional questions," as they came forward day by day, the "sound and impartial criticism of books

[1] Cf. Ogden, Life of E. L. Godkin, vol. i, p. 220.
[2] Letters of C. E. Norton, vol. i, pp. 283-4.
[3] Cf. Mims, Sidney Lanier, pp. 75-6; Ogden, Life of E. L. Godkin, vol.
i, pp. 226, 227. The Round Table ceased publication, after a creditable
career, in 1869.
[4] The allegations that the editorship of the Nation was first offered to
George William Curtis and then to Whitelaw Reid, and that they, in turn
declined the post in no way alters the fact that the paper from the beginning was built around Mr. Godkin. Individuals among the stockholders
before the plan was crystallized seem to have made tentative proposals to
both Curtis and Reid.—Cf. Cary, Life of Curtis, pp. 189-92; Cortissoz,
Life of Whitelaw Reid, vol. i, pp. 137-8.

and works of art," and the adequate treatment of "questions
of trade and finance" gave the publication a large field for its
activities. Longfellow, Whittier, Norton, Olmsted, Francis
Lieber, Edmund Quincy, Bayard Taylor, Richard Grant White,
William Lloyd Garrison, R. H. Stoddard, Phillips Brooks and
many others were named as contributors.[1]

But no one could predicate anything about the character of
the new publication without knowing Godkin, and he, released
for a great piece of national service, exceeded every expectation
even of his warmest friends. Such a shaking up of dry bones
had not been seen before. Men looked on in wonder at such
personal courage, such learning, combined with such talent for
expression. Now, as ever afterward, Godkin impressed his own
mind upon the whole publication with indelible power. Whatever periodical came under his direction seemed to bear from
cover to cover, the individual stamp of his tenacious and indomitable personality.

The list of stockholders—there were forty—included a
variety of intractable Abolitionists, with whom the editor could
not hope long to live on friendly terms, and in a year the enterprise must be reorganized. Godkin's control was strengthened,
and, while the circulation at no time became large—it may never
have exceeded 10,000 [2]—no expectation was disappointed on this
account. It was self-supporting and made its appearance week
after week, year after year, throwing the light of knowledge
upon every subject within the range of public concern. It was
"the best weekly not only in America, but in the world," said
James Bryce.[3] "We never had such newspaper writing before," said Norton.[4] It is the "best possible journal," he said
again;[5] to Godkin there was "no second."[6] In 1868, Lowell
declared that "its discussions of politics had done more good
and influenced opinion more than any other agency, or all

[1] Ogden, Life of Godkin, vol. i, pp. 237-9.
[2] Cf. Rhodes, Historical Essays, p. 270.
[3] Studies in Contemporary Biography, p. 372.
[4] Ogden, Life of Godkin, vol. i, p. 250.
[5] Letters of C. E. Norton, vol. i, p. 398.
[6] Ibid., vol. ii, p. 86.

others combined, in the country." [1] Godkin's leaving the paper
for a professorship of history at Harvard, which was offered
him, Lowell said again, in 1870, would be a "public calamity." [2]
Men now in middle and old age, who fell under Godkin's influence in their youth, still feel the moral force of this impel-
ling mind. They know the truth of William James's words
when he said: "To my generation his [Godkin's] was certainly
the towering influence in all thought concerning public affairs,
and indirectly his influence has certainly been more pervasive
than that of any other writer of the generation, for he influenced
other writers, who never quoted him, and determined the whole
current of discussion." [3]

Here were barriers reared against the Goths and Vandals.
Harper's Magazine had come to fill the place which had been
occupied so long by the "Philadelphia magazines."   But its
value to the country was not greater than theirs had been—
indeed, its example at first was distinctly evil, since it lived by
filching, while the leading periodical publications in Philadelphia, such as Graham's and Godey's, had honestly paid for what
they set before their readers. The secret of its very great success before, during and immediately after the war was in "just
keeping pace with the popular mind." Its owners wished it
to be salable. Its policy, a critic of its methods said, was "to
bow and avoid"; it would "follow, echo and shirk." With a
"No offense I hope" it made its monthly appearance before
its readers, exerting no more influence upon them, doing no
more to forward the common weal than Godey's. [4] Harper's
Weekly had begun its career with a similar design to be opin-
ionless. When it preached at all it was of platitudes and
abstractions, [5] until the war came on, when it clearly took the
Northern side. With Curtis serving as its political editor its
course grew more definite. But his was a genial literary mind,

[1] Ogden, Life of Godkin, vol. ii, p. 78.
[2] Ibid., p. 66.
[3] Ibid., vol. i, p. 221; cf. article on Godkin in Galaxy, June, 1869.
[4] It was good naturedly called the "Buccaneer's Bag," the "Monthly
Cornplaster," the "Universal Shinsaver," the "Monthly Nurse."—See
Putnam's Monthly, vol. ix, pp. 29–36.
[5] Ibid.

he lacked the combative quality, he was prone to be deceived,[1]
and he was held to account by the heads of a very cautious
publishing firm, who owned the paper for which he wrote.[2]
Sturdier trees stood up to face the storm. Putnam's, while it
endured, the Atlantic, the North American Review and the
Nation were organs expressive of the intellectual movement of
the country. Lowell, poet, essayist, critic, publicist, scholar,
towered above all his New England contemporaries. In no
other did what was best in the American character meet in so
distinguished a combination. In establishing what Godkin,
in 1859, called "our one and only magazine" he performed a
service of inestimable importance in the history of American
letters. The moral force that Lowell and Norton together
brought to bear upon the course of thought, through their
editorship of the North American Review, during this critical
period, the encouragement that they extended to Godkin in
starting the Nation and afterward, supplied a moral background
to the country at a time when popular standards were low,
when opinion was dazed and better days seemed far away.

For their own improvement, as well as in self-defense, those
who had cultural standards, were finding comradeship in association. Never were there finer friendships between literary
men than those which are revealed by the letters and memoirs of
the writers and artists of this time. The Saturday Club in
Boston, an association of the New Englanders, the Century
Association in New York, of which Bryant was the patriarch,
were outward expressions of the fellowship which the literary
man felt for his kind. They had been formed before the war
and were still the refuge of congenial souls.

As for the newspapers, their whole tone was undergoing
change. Their fluidity, with daily issues, made them very responsive to public taste. The newspaper of Cowper, a

> "Map of the busy world—
> Its fluctuations and its vast concerns"

[1] As he was later ready to admit that he had been deceived by Grant
on the subject of civil service reform. Cf. Ogden, Life of Godkin, vol. i,
p. 293.

[2] Cf. Letters of C. E. Norton, vol. ii, pp. 67–8.

had been a good deal altered in its rightful character before the
war. The editors who had given dignified position to the press
of the country, though some of them still lingered in their
places, men like Joseph Gales and William Winston Seaton
of the National Intelligencer, Nathan Hale of the Boston
Advertiser, William Cullen Bryant of the New York Evening
Post, John Bigelow, Francis P. Blair, Robert Walsh and George
D. Prentice were not without their successors. Such journalists had sought to ascertain the truth concerning a report before
publishing it and commenting upon it. It was their aim "to
control and direct society, to teach it and to lead it," to tell it,
while informing it about what it was doing day by day, what
it ought to have done in the case and what it ought to do in
the future.[1]

Many young men had been drawn into journalism as correspondents with the armies—it is said that the New York
Herald had 63 such in the South [2]—and came home seeking
a continuance of employment in newspaper writing. Some
found places in the Washington bureaus of their newspapers,
or turned lobbyists to throng the corridors of the Capitol.[3]
The gazettes were enlarged to make places for those whose
fluent pens needed occupation, and to supply the appetite for
news which the reports from the military front had created,
and which, increased by feeding, must still be satisfied. Sunday
issues, which had been begun during the war, although their
great size is a more recent development, also gave employment
to reporters and editors.

We were coming to have journalists of a new school of manners, with new aims. Too many were busying themselves in
seeking to discover how low the desires of the people really
were and, finding out, in trying to gain profit for themselves
by pandering to these low desires. Several papers in New York,
the Public Ledger in Philadelphia said, were making almost
no distinction between what was "legitimately public" and

[1] Cf. Godwin, Life of W. C. Bryant, vol. ii, p. 415.
[2] O. G. Villard in N. Y. Nation, May 25, 1918.
[3] George F. Hoar, Autobiography of 70 Years, vol. i, p. 307.

what was "essentially private." Half of what was printed, the Public Ledger thought, were "but the impertinencies of the writer obtruding into domestic privacies" and "parading people," who do not seek such notoriety, before the world "in a ridiculous or disparaging manner" for that world to talk about.[1] Matters of the greatest moment to society and the state would be ignored entirely in favor of personalities, or dismissed in a spirit of jest.

James Gordon Bennett, of Scotch birth and parentage, arrived in New York after divers unsuccessful editorial experiences in other American cities, and in May, 1835, from a cellar in Wall Street, he issued the first number of the Herald. The old newspapers of New York at this time were all large "six penny" sheets.[2] They were conservatively edited and were sold by the year to subscribers. Not one of them seems to have had a circulation in excess of 6,000 copies.[3] The city was expanding rapidly in wealth and population as a result of the opening of the Erie Canal, and it was well started on its way toward its later primacy as a commercial and financial centre. The Sun had been established to sell for one cent in 1833,[4] and Bennett appeared now with a rival which he would issue at the same price. The competition of these two cheap gazettes in the effort to outreach each other continued for some time, the victory soon resting with Mr. Bennett. Meeting a packet with small boats many miles off the American coast, hurrying in with the European news to be printed in "extras" and cried upon the streets before the ship had yet been warped up to her dock; overland pony expresses and carrier pigeon lines, and later racing locomotive engines to beat the United States government mails, when there were yet no telegraphs—all duly advertised; the securing and publication of private and public papers by bribery, theft—no matter what means; unheard of scurrility, followed by personal encounters with the editor,

[1] Phila. Ledger, July 13, 1865.
[2] "Our bed quilt contemporaries," the smaller new penny papers called them.
[3] Frederic Hudson, History of Journalism, p. 431.
[4] Cf. Allan Nevins, The Evening Post, p. 157.

which he described with gusto and palaver for the public delight; the presentation of a ship to the Union during the war, though the paper for years had been pandering to slavery and disunion; starting subscriptions for the benefit of Mrs. Lincoln and Greeley's daughters, and to pay off the national debt; offering prizes to the winners of yacht races; the despatch of agents to far places to "interview" crowned heads and other prominent personages, and to accompany commanders on military and polar expeditions, a policy which reached its climax in the dramatic sending forth of Henry M. Stanley to "find Livingstone," an English missionary, supposed to have been "lost" in the interior of Africa—such feats made journalism into a new thing.

Some of this activity was justified in the prosecution of the business of securing the "news," though it often went forward in a conscienceless and flighty manner; the rest was undertaken as a mere advertisement of the paper and its "enterprising" owner. The development of a responsible service to report the movements of ships and to record the fluctuations in the stock and money markets was worthy of the appreciation which it received. Bennett's unexampled organization of correspondents, who lived with the armies on the field during the war, and who were stationed at focal points for the gathering of news for some years following that cataclysm, yielded returns of great advantage to the readers of his journal. But his accounts of vice and crime, which his diligent employees gathered in the police courts, greatly shocked the sensibilities of men and women who had a higher view of the functions of the newspaper.[1]

The Herald's attitude in its editorial, as well as its news columns, toward the most important questions which disturbed the nation, was a kind of "rollicking impudence."[2] Nothing

---

[1] Cf. Maverick, H. J. Raymond and the New York Press, pp. 52, 53; Allan Nevins, The Evening Post, pp. 159–60; Elmer Davis, History of the N. Y. Times, p. 8; W. A. Linn, Horace Greeley, pp. 67–8; J. M. Lee, History of Journalism, pp. 196–7; O. G. Villard, N. Y. Nation, May 25, 1918; L. D. Ingersoll, Life of Horace Greeley, pp. 109–10; !article on Bennett in Galaxy, August, 1872.

[2] Merriam, Life of Samuel Bowles, vol. i, p. 28; cf. Nevins, The Evening Post, pp. 157–9.

mattered if Bennett could make money.[1] He craved and gained
notoriety that he might make more money. It is not to be denied
that, by his restless energy and his vast resources, he instituted
many improvements in American journalism. But for the most
part these betterments were material only [2] and, though those
who have followed him have gone much farther than he can
have supposed possible, or than the times in which he lived
would have allowed, he deserves to be remembered as a pioneer
in sending our newspapers down a new and a very vulgar road.
His example was harmful because of its contagion; as soon as
it was seen how successful such methods might be others
wished to share his rich field. His profits were often a half
million dollars annually.[3] A year before his death he was said
to have been the owner of a fortune of $10,000,000. His only
son into whose hands the paper came, aimed, as nearly as his
abilities and personal convenience would allow, to follow the
course the father had taken, and the paper, under his guidance
of its destinies, assumed a no more responsible position in
reference to society or the state.

What long had been the first, if it were not really the pre-eminent newspaper of the country, the National Intelligencer, of
Washington, had fallen with the war. Two very capable men,
brothers-in-law, Joseph Gales and William Winston Seaton,
who had come to the "Federal City" from Raleigh, N. C.,
while Thomas Jefferson was yet President, took a place of
leadership as journalists. For long the daily oracle of the
Whig party, their paper attained a high reputation for ability,
fairness, courtesy, dignity and literary style. Its editors made

[1] Merriam, op. cit., vol. i, p. 28.
[2] It has been said that he was not an editor, but a journalist—more than
this that he was not even a journalist, but a mere news vender.—Nevins,
The Evening Post, p. 161.
[3] N. Y. Times, March 30, 1871, quoted in Hudson, p. 441. The returns
from advertisements for purposes of taxation were $453,122 for the nine
months ending March 31, 1865, an income from this source considerably
in excess of that of any other paper. Bennett's rates were 40 cents a line
for what Greeley in the Tribune obtained only 15 cents. Cf. Phila. Ledger,
July 13, 1865; N. Y. Tribune, July 20 and 22, 1865.

themselves "a power and a safety in the land." [1] Never was it "lent to personal predilections or antipathies"; it was conducted as "an organ of public intelligence and general discussion." [2] But the age had outrun the paper and its editors. Gales died in 1860, when Seaton took as a partner an associate for ten years, James C. Welling. Moderate counsel in polite phrase—no other could they give—was not wanted during the war and Mr. Seaton retired on January 1, 1865, after continuous service of 52 years, with opportunities for observation of the intimate movements of the government surpassing those of any surviving contemporary. He had lost two-thirds of his circulation by the secession of the South, he could expect no support from the North, and, though he preferred the "dignity of death" for his journal, he, carrying nothing away for his life of labor, gave up the property to some younger men who aimed to prolong its career as "a news and business sheet." [3] Still, during the administration of Andrew Johnson, it was listened to respectfully, but it was overwhelmed by the turmoil following the unsuccessful struggle for adherence to constitutional precedents which that President had waged with such redoubtable energy.

Among the newspapers of the country at the end of the war the New York Tribune was fairly regarded as the foremost. The services which its editor had rendered the Abolitionist cause, the leading part which it had played in bringing forward the Republican party, emphasized its prominence. Though it was patent, even to the unobserving, that he was not a man to be trusted with the solution of the large problems which the war had brought upon the nation, Greeley still was able at its end to defend his title to priority in vigorous writing and speech.

The first number of the Tribune was issued on April 10, 1841. At this time Greeley was thirty years old. He would establish a paper "removed alike from servile partisanship, on the one

[1] Atlantic Monthly, cited in W. W. Seaton, A Biographical Sketch, p. 365; cf. A. K. McClure, Recollections of a Half Century, pp. 37 et seq.
[2] W. W. Seaton, A Biographical Sketch, p. 373.
[3] Ibid., p. 372.

hand, and from gagged, mincing neutrality on the other." [1]
The inclinations of the Sun and the Herald were Jeffersonian,
those of the Tribune would be Whiggish. From this small seed
a great oak grew. Even after the war the weekly edition of the
Tribune, which for many years had enjoyed so widely national
an influence, continued to receive great popular favor. During
the campaign of 1868 its circulation was 240,000 copies; of
the weekly, semi-weekly and daily editions 300,000 copies
were printed. [2]

Much regarding Greeley and his newspaper has been related
in another place when we were concerned with the Presidential
campaign of 1872. It has been said that he was and that he
remained an uneducated man, but with all his fundamental
ignorance he had the peculiar ability of surrounding himself
with thinkers of distinction and writers of grace. Over them
all he exerted a despotic, though a kindly control. Beginning
with Margaret Fuller, George Ripley, Charles A. Dana, George
William Curtis and other refugees from Brook Farm, the list
came to include, as editors, office writers, correspondents, or contributors, Bayard Taylor, Richard Hildreth, Edmund Quincy,
Sidney Howard Gay, E. C. Stedman, William Henry Fry,
Noah Brooks, George W. Smalley, John R. G. Hassard, W. J.
Stillman, Solon Robinson, Fitz Henry Warren, William Winter,
John Hay, Mark Twain, Whitelaw Reid, Montgomery Schuyler,
—to name but a few of the host. The "great moral organ" had
a staff which was clearly the most notable that any paper has
ever had in the history of journalism in America. [3] Admission
to its columns, said Mr. Godkin, "almost gave the young writer
a patent of literary nobility." [4] The editorial page, whether the
articles came from Greeley's or other pens, were brilliant. The
book reviews, under Ripley's direction for so many years, were
written with grace and authority. The correspondence from the

[1] Horace Greeley, Recollections of a Busy Life, p. 137.
[2] N. Y. Tribune, Sep. 24, 1868.
[3] Cf. Ogden, Life of Godkin, vol. i, pp. 166–7; Harper's Weekly, Sep.
16, 1871; W. R. Thayer, Life of John Hay, vol. i, p. 334; Cortissoz, Life of
Whitelaw Reid, vol. i, p. 144; Charles T. Congdon, Reminiscences of a
Journalist.
[4] Cortissoz, Life of Whitelaw Reid, vol. i, p. 144.

West and the South, and from Europe had great informative
and often high literary value. The local news was passed
through competent hands before it was printed. In all departments; day after day during years, the paper bore the marks of
enlightened oversight and responsible management. It was a
pitiable fall, in 1872, when a group of men unhappily took
Greeley for their candidate for the Presidency, when he still
more unhappily accepted the trust; it was a tragic sacrifice, a
little later, when his death followed the disillusionment which
that year contained.

George Jones, like Greeley, a New England farm boy, was
employed after coming to New York in the business office of
the Tribune. Henry J. Raymond, son of a New York state
farmer, who had succeeded in gaining an education at the
University of Vermont, was also attached to the Tribune. He
was Greeley's first managing editor, but had had some mis-
understanding with that oracle and went his own way, as
Jones did likewise. In 1851, while Raymond was assembling
articles from the foreign periodicals for Harper's Magazine,
the two men came together again, and they formed a notable
partnership. Hearing that the Tribune had made net profits
in the previous year amounting to $50,000 they perfected their
arrangements for the publication of a newspaper to be known
as the Times. They gave it able management. Jones devoted
himself in large degree to the business side of the undertaking,
while Raymond became the editor. For eighteen years, from
1851 until his death in 1869, the Times was known, indeed, as
"Raymond's paper." He surrounded himself with good writers
and, while it had taken no advanced ground on the anti-slavery
issue,[1] and was content to seek a middle course in reference
to most subjects, it nevertheless assumed and held a dignified
place in American journalism. Like Greeley Raymond had
oratorical powers which he brought into frequent use. His
tastes led him to make excursions into politics, as a member of

[1] "A sort of via media to suit the numerous moderate or timid people
who were coming over to the Republican party from both the Whigs and
the Democrats, but were as yet unequal to the strong anti-slavery drink
of the Tribune."—Godkin in Ogden, Life of Godkin, vol. i, p. 113.

political conventions, as a chairman of the Republican National Committee, as a representative in Congress, activities which served further to advertise the paper. In 1869 a million dollars were offered and refused for the property which had represented an investment, eighteen years before, of but $69,000.[1]

Jones, at Raymond's death, increased his interest in the editorial management of the paper and soon the editorship[2] fell to Louis J. Jennings, the English journalist, reviewer and publicist, of wide experience in London and India, as well as in America, who was in place when the Times performed its notable civic service in pursuing and exposing the members of the "Tweed Ring."

Meanwhile a paper called the World entered the field. The Tribune, the Herald and the Times were pursuing their respective ways successfully. A number of men in New York, obedient to a moral impulse of protest against the general tone of the daily press, subscribed a sum of money to be used for founding a paper which would have greater regard for the religious sensibilities of the public. Half secular and half churchly it appeared in June, 1860. It promptly failed, to be merged with some older papers, and was soon in the hands of a group of Democratic politicians who made it, during the war, an organ of the New York Copperheads. It throve by its abuse of Lincoln and the Republican leaders, on crime, scandal and sensation, though it had a clever management on its literary side under Manton Marble, who was a part owner and later the sole proprietor. In 1876 he sold it to a group of capitalists headed by Thomas A. Scott, president of the Pennsylvania Railroad, who put the paper under the direction of a well known journalist and magazinist of polished wit and scholarship, William Henry Hurlbut.[3] At Scott's death it was sold to Jay Gould. Its reorganization in the hands of Joseph Pulitzer did not occur until 1883.[4]

---

[1] Elmer Davis, History of the N. Y. Times, p. 77.
[2] After negotiations with George William Curtis.—Cf. Letters of C. E. Norton, vol. i, p. 351.
[3] Galaxy, Jan., 1869.
[4] J. L. Heaton, The Story of a Page, chap. i; Henry Watterson, Marse Henry, vol. i, p. 205.

The Sun, which had been leading a quiet existence, after it
had been so soundly beaten at its own game by the Herald, was
sold.   Charles A. Dana, upon leaving Brook Farm, had, as
early as in 1846, accompanied his companion in idealism, George
Ripley, into the New York Tribune office.   He remained with
Greeley until 1862, by which time he had become a very important factor in the management of the paper.[1]   But in that
year he was dismissed by the high priest,[2] soon to become a
confidential officer, and, a little later, an assistant to Stanton,
in the War Department, which kept him in the public service
until 1865.   Then he was drawn to Chicago to take the editorship of a new Republican journal; but the plan failed and he
returned to New York where, in 1868, he, in conjunction with
a number of well known capitalists—nearly all of them leaders
of the Republican party—purchased the Sun.   He took immediate control and turned over a new leaf in the book of his life.
No one in the Brook Farm community drifted so far from his
youthful anchorages as did Dana from this time onward.[3]
Under what impulses he proceeded neither he nor any of his
friends has ever clearly explained.   To all appearances he now
set out to make money; he also had personal animosities to
ventilate, and, seeing a field in New York, which Bennett did
not quite cover for an eccentric, non-moral paper, a daily
charivari, he, with the most surprising suggestions as to public
policies and the most daring impertinences aimed at individuals,
pressed forward to occupy it.   The Herald was flippant, the
Sun became malignant and often blackguardly.[4]   Though Dana
sometimes attacked undoubted wrongs, and did this effectively,
his performances bore the appearance of being staged for the
mere amusement of his readers, when not for his own sar-
donic personal gratification.   Some good followed, but the
force of his crusades was reduced, when it was seen how many
times he would come to the defense of those whom men of good

[1] Ogden, Life of Godkin, vol. i, p. 168.
[2] Wilson, Life of Dana, pp. 171, 176.
[3] Confirmation of this may be found in Frank M. O'Brien, The Story of
the Sun.
[4] Cf. The Education of Henry Adams, p. 244.

judgment held in reproach. Rascals were selected for praise; virtue was made the subject of cavil.[1]

While its editor wrote in terse, vigorous English, and trained younger men into a command of his style, the "smart" articles in the paper, it must be believed, materially tended toward a confusion of the popular mind, already in derangement, and fed the cynical spirit of youth in other newspaper offices, too prone to follow such a master. As Dana submerged all the ideals with which his life had been commenced, and his personal feuds and commercial instincts came to control his course as a journalist, to the consternation of his friends,[2] his material prosperity increased. Of the first number of his paper 43,000 copies were printed. Soon his circulation was 100,000 a day, and he had weekly and semi-weekly editions.[3]

The Evening Post, founded in 1801, with which Bryant, the poet, had been connected since 1826, after 1829 as editor in chief, to remain there until his death in 1878, reflected the cultivated tone of his mind. His stern self-respect, amounting to something near austerity of character, his pervading sense of responsibility, the literary standards which guided his writing, gave the paper one of the highest places in the history of journalism in America.[4] His half century of service covered a period as long as the working lives of those two sterling Washington journalists, Gales and Seaton. While he was a Democrat and they were Whigs, he found it imperative, with his New England morality, to join the Free Soil movement and naturally turned his forces, like the other Democratic Free Soil leaders, into the

[1] Under a heading, "Semper Fidelis," Godkin, citing excerpts from the files of the Sun, dates being given, could furnish proof of the editor's endorsement of most of the principal knaves who had made their way into New York political life. This is said for Dana—the old readers of the Sun were mechanics and small tradesmen, nearly all Democrats; he had no intention of forfeiting their support.—O'Brien, The Story of the Sun, p. 232; Wilson, Life of Dana, p. 389; article on Dana in Galaxy, Aug., 1869.
[2] Cf. Ogden, Life of Godkin, vol. i, p. 305.
[3] The Weekly Sun at one dollar a year was put forth, in competition with the weekly editions of the Tribune and Times, as "a newspaper of the present times, intended for people now on earth, including farmers, mechanics, merchants, professional men, workers, thinkers and all manner of honest folks, and the wives, sons and daughters of all such."
[4] Letters of C. E. Norton, vol. i, p. 238.

Republican party. Social reforms and measures in the interest
of good order, the principle of free trade, of which he was an
untiring exponent, engaged his attention and that of his newspaper on every occasion. He was an attractive orator. As
age advanced upon him, finding him in full physical and mental
vigor, he became the city's Nestor. "Every movement of art
and literature, of benevolence and good citizenship," said
George William Curtis, "sought the decoration of his name.
His presence was the grace of every festival." [1] The group of
men with whom he surrounded himself culled material for the
paper and discussed public questions in his spirit, until it came
to be called the best newspaper in the world. [2] In causing it
to attain and hold its fine place as an organ of honest, intelligent and independent opinion Bryant had the aid of a number
of well known men—in the early years of William Leggett,
a political writer of vigor and distinction, [3] and later, notably,
of John Bigelow, until 1861, shortly before he was sent to France
as our consul at Paris and left the field of active journalism; [4]
Parke Godwin, who married Mr. Bryant's eldest daughter, a
publicist and a writer of respectable position, [5] who all told,
with but little interruption, served the paper for a period nearly
as long as Mr. Bryant, [6] and Charlton M. Lewis.

In Philadelphia the paper which wielded the greatest influence
was the Press under the direction of John W. Forney. Before
coming to the city he had been the editor of country Democratic
journals, and he rose to power in the retinue of James Buchanan.
Through this connection he narrowly missed high offices, including a cabinet position, a United States senatorship from
Pennsylvania and an important foreign mission. [7] After editing
another Philadelphia paper for a time, he, in 1857, established
the Press. Failing in his effort to set his party right on the

---

[1] Parke Godwin, Life of Bryant, vol. ii, p. 418.
[2] Nevins, The Evening Post, p. 341.
[3] Ibid., pp. 140–41.
[4] Cf. ibid., chap. x.
[5] Galaxy, Feb., 1869.
[6] Nevins, The Evening Post, p. 167; Godwin, Life of Bryant, vol. i, p. 339.
[7] A. K. McClure, Old Time Notes of Pennsylvania, vol. i, pp. 254–63.

slavery question,[1] he passed over to the new Republican party, becoming one of the most uncompromising of Radicals. Before the war he had been clerk of the House of Representatives at Washington—at its outbreak he was made secretary of the Senate, a position which brought him into the closest relations with the government, and which he held until 1868. After 1862 he owned and edited the Washington Chronicle, as well as the Philadelphia Press. Both reflected his impetuous zeal and his stirring personality, which in political campaigns he carried to the stump, where he was a favorite popular orator. He sold the Chronicle in 1870 to devote himself exclusively to the Press. Men who could write better than he, who possessed a literary culture that he had never acquired, were associated with him on the staff of his Philadelphia paper, which had standards higher than many contemporary publications and discussed national questions, if, with great partisan bias, at the same time, while Forney's spirit dominated it, with real ability.[2] But Forney's interest in journalism, as well as his political power, declined and, in 1875, while he was in Europe, he sold the paper to Alexander K. McClure, a well known independent politician, outside of the confidences of the dominant Cameron and pro-Grant elements of the Republican party, who, when Forney changed his mind regarding the sale, founded the Philadelphia Times.[3]

The older Public Ledger had come into possession of the Drexels, bankers in Philadelphia. They put forward to represent them George W. Childs, a publisher of "subscription books." Under his direction the paper, if dull, was a dignified and an accurate recorder of events, and it achieved notable commercial success through its well filled advertising columns.[4] Pleasing homily and abstract moral reflections, with little appearance of care for the issue of public questions—though it spoke in

---

[1] J. R. Young, Men and Memories, pp. 3, 5.
[2] See e.g., C. G. Leland's Memoirs, pp. 318–20.
[3] McClure, Old Time Notes of Pennsylvania, vol. ii, pp. 399–400.
[4] Its circulation in 1869 was said to be 70,000, larger than that of any other daily paper, except the New York Herald.—Phila. Ledger, Nov. 8, 1869.

a good undertone—or for literary ideals, led the way to fortune.
Mr. Childs was neither a writer nor an editor. As his prosperity
grew his ambitions brought him into the company of eminent
persons. He became the principal host and cicerone of "lions"
when they came to Philadelphia, while Mr. Drexel's return, barring his dividends, consisted of an enjoyed companionship with
Mr. Childs, and, prior to 1873, the attacks of the paper upon
the enterprises of Jay Cooke, a disliked rival in the banking
business,[1] with unfaltering support, in general, of the undertakings of the Drexel house.

The newspaper press of Boston exhibited little independent
force. It lived in Boston and New England to such a degree,
said Samuel Bowles, that it had "no more conception of what
was going on in the world than the South Sea Islanders." [2]
The leading journal in that city before the war was the Daily
Advertiser. It had been founded in 1813, to be edited a year
later, in 1814, and until his death in 1863, a period of nearly
fifty years, by Nathan Hale, one of the founders of the North
American Review. The Advertiser under his control, said
Robert C. Winthrop, in reviewing his career, was "second to
none in our whole land for exact information, for just criticism, for clear and candid exposition, for able and thorough
discussion." It had attained this position through his "pure,
able and accurate mind." [3] In all his writings, however volu-
minous, said Edward Everett on the same occasion there was

"Not one immoral, one corrupting thought,
One line which, dying, he could wish to blot." [4]

His sons assisted and, for a time, followed their father in the
editorial management of the journal.[5] Still after the war it
was the "respectable daily" of the city, though its opinions were

[1] Oberholtzer, Life of Jay Cooke, vol. i, pp. 546-7, and vol. ii, pp. 189
et seq.
[2] Merriam, Life of Samuel Bowles, vol. ii, p. 211; cf. ibid., vol. i, p.
211; The Education of Henry Adams, p. 241; Cortissoz, Life of Whitelaw
Reid, vol. i, p. 166.
[3] Proceedings of the Mass. Hist. Soc. for 1862-3, p. 418.
[4] Ibid., p. 423.
[5] Cf. E. E. Hale, Lowell and his Friends, p. 35.

likely to be so partisan that it wielded no great or valuable
power.

In the evening the Transcript, which had been established
in 1830, occupied an enviable field. For a time Epes Sargent
was its editor. During and after the war it was directed by
Daniel M. Haskell, under whose management and subsequently,
following his death in 1874, its aims were high and its course
creditable to those in control of it and to the community in
which it appeared.[1]

The Hartford Courant, the Providence Journal and the
Worcester Spy were journals of influence in New England whose
utterances at times merited attention beyond the local circles
which they daily served. General Joseph R. Hawley and Charles
Dudley Warner, who had been associated on an evening paper in
Hartford, called the Press, combined it in 1867 with the Courant
which under their management held a respectable position in
discussion and criticism. The Providence Journal, owned by
Henry B. Anthony, United States senator from Rhode Island,
was edited, after 1860, by James B. Angell, who had been a
professor in Brown University. He remained with the paper
until 1866 when he became president of the University of Vermont, from which he passed, in 1871, to the University of
Michigan. But, like the Spy and the Courant, it seldom broke
out of the enclosure established for those who were moving
about with the favor of, and in the hope of receiving the rewards which might come through, the Republican party.[2]

No newspaper in New England, possibly none in the country,
barring the New York Tribune, exerted so large and so salutary a public influence as the Republican in Springfield, Mass.
Greeley one time described it as "the best and ablest country
journal ever published on this continent."[3] Its power was
ascribed to the honor, courage and talents of the second Samuel
Bowles. The first Samuel Bowles printed a small weekly newspaper. His son, trained in his father's printing shop, in 1844,

[1] Cf. J. M. Lee, Hist. of American Journalism, pp. 185–6.
[2] Reminiscences of James B. Angell, pp. 110–19.
[3] Merriam, Life of Bowles, vol. i, p. 179.

when he was eighteen years of age, established a daily edition and raised it to a national position. Before the war he had enjoyed the aid for many years of Dr. J. G. Holland. Later his assistants included General Francis A. Walker, F. B. Sanborn and many other men of ability and distinction.[1] When he died, in 1878, the words of warm and sincere praise passed upon his career afforded proof of the value of a life of honorable purpose, led in a place which is the most influential in a free land, when he who holds it is gifted with the power to understand and the intelligence to discharge its high responsibilities.[2]

Joseph Medill, a Canadian by birth, had gone to Ohio in young boyhood, where he grew up on a farm. Entering country journalism he, after a while, reached Cleveland, where he founded the Leader. About 1855 he appeared in Chicago and purchased an interest in the Tribune, then at a low estate in editorial and business management. It grew as the city grew, becoming the strongest anti-slavery organ in the West. Upon Medill's election, after the war, to be mayor of Chicago the editorial direction of the paper passed to Horace White.[3]

A native of New Hampshire White, in young childhood, was taken to Wisconsin. His anti-slavery interests carried him to Kansas during the free state disturbances. Indefatigably active as a Washington correspondent and in other capacities during the war, he, all the while, was reading, translating and qualifying himself as a publicist, to which position he had attained when, little more than thirty years old, he took control of the Chicago Tribune. He at once gave the paper a greater value that it had ever had before. It became the chief among Republican journals in four cities in the West whose opinions were worthy of national attention—Charles D. Brigham's Commercial in Pittsburgh, the Gazette and the Commercial in Cincinnati, the Missouri Democrat at St. Louis, while Colonel

[1] Cf. Richard Hooker, The Story of an Independent Newspaper, chap. xvii.
[2] Cf. Letters of C. E. Norton, vol. i, p. 351; Richard Grant White, Galaxy, December, 1869.
[3] A nephew of Andrew D. White, president of Cornell University.

William M. Grosvenor was its editor,[1] being posted at the other bastions of the quadrangle. Each adopted its own course, a policy which usually brought them together—when in combination, as they so often were, their influence was immense. White's course in defense of Trumbull and the "recusant seven," who in 1868 had voted for the acquittal of Andrew Johnson, subjected him and his newspaper to that intolerant persecution which was the portion of other non-conformists at that time. As an advocate of tariff, currency and civil service reforms, and decent government, without regard for party bonds, the paper grew in respect rapidly.[2] White retired from the management in 1874, later playing a prominent part in journalism in New York City. Meanwhile Medill, acquiring by purchase a larger share in the property, resumed full control with the object, as he declared, of repairing the "mischief" which White had done and of restoring the paper to its old relations with the Republican party.[3]

Of the two Cincinnati papers deserving of respect the Gazette was the older. Charles Hammond had given it a fine independent position before 1840.[4] A number of well-known men cooperated in putting their mark upon it during and after the war. One of its battle field correspondents was Whitelaw Reid, who later became its Washington correspondent, and still later, through a loan of money made him by Jay Cooke, one of its owners.[5] General H. V. Boynton, its Washington correspondent, at a later date, continued to give the paper a wide reputation.[6] The Cincinnati Commercial was directed by Murat Halstead, who came to the journal from an Ohio farm,

[1] His connection ceased in 1871.—McDonald, Secrets of the Great Whiskey Ring, p. 40.
[2] Earl de Grey, when he was in the United States attending the conference which framed the Treaty of Washington, said that the Tribune was the ablest American journal.—Harper's Weekly, Feb. 24, 1872.
[3] Medill to E. B. Washburne, Sep. 25, 1874, in Washburne Papers in Library of Congress.
[4] Cf. Hugh McCulloch, Men and Measures, p. 492.
[5] Oberholtzer, Jay Cooke, vol. i, pp. 480–83; Harper's Weekly, July 1, 1871. He remained in Cincinnati until he passed to the New York Tribune in 1868.
[6] Cf. N. Y. Nation, Oct. 21, 1875.

and in a few years gained control of it. One of a number of muscular, self-educated men, whose writing in this period lent a picturesque character to the American press, he, by the freedom with which he criticized men and measures, and by his forcible, if at times inelegant forms of expression, won a national hearing.

In Louisville George D. Prentice, whose name was known throughout the country as a wit and a poetaster, as well as a scathing journalist, had control of the Journal, long the immediate organ of Henry Clay,[1] but age was bearing him down and he found a successor in Henry Watterson. This young man was a son of Harvey Watterson, a Democratic politician and journalist of Tennessee, well known in Washington. In that city the boy had spent his youth and at the outbreak of the war, returning to his home in Tennessee, he had given himself to the Confederate service. At the end of it he was well done with secession and ready to embark in newspaper writing in the interest of the reconciliation of the sections. He found an opportunity in Prentice's place on the Journal. At the same time Walter N. Haldeman resumed the interrupted publication of the Louisville Courier. Soon the two papers were combined, under Watterson's chief editorship, to create an independent organ to which not only the city wherein it was issued, but the country at large also, gave welcome.[2] A hearty, audacious, slangwhanging, and, at the same time, very ignorant egoist, Watterson for several decades spoke to a large audience from his acquired vantage point.

It was an event destined to have momentous consequences, when, in 1848, seven of the principal newspapers in New York formed a news association which, in a short time, came to be called the Associated Press. This organization was the natural outgrowth of some former experiments with joint action in the support of pony expresses and news boats in the collection of harbor and shipping news. The telegraph had come—now

---

[1] Cf. Hugh McCulloch, Men and Measures, pp. 491, 493.

[2] Marse Henry, vol. i, pp. 184–5; Harper's Weekly, July 6, 1872; Merriam, Life of Samuel Bowles, vol. ii, pp. 134–5.

that there was a vastly increased demand for the accounts of current happenings at the earliest possible moment, through its agencies, why should each paper have its correspondent on the ground? Manifestly it could not do so. Why should each pay telegraph tolls for an account of one and the same occurrence? After the cable was laid, and it must be used as a means of setting foreign news before the people each morning and evening, the need of a strong and efficient union of news gathering agencies became still more imperative.

The members of the group, which were making this investment for their mutual use, saw the opportunity to lease their service at a profit to subscribers in other parts of the country, as they, in turn, bought news from collecting agencies abroad. The importance of the organization increased rapidly. D. H. Craig, an enterprising pioneer in news gathering, was succeeded as general manager in 1867 [1] by James W. Simonton, who had been an associate of George Jones and Henry J. Raymond in the establishment of the New York Times, and was long a Washington correspondent of that and other newspapers. His direction continued for many years. Meantime a subsidiary of the Associated Press (the New York newspapers which had first formed the combination), the Western Associated Press, of increasing influence as the country extended into the Mississippi Valley and on to the Pacific coast, had developed an efficient executive, William Henry Smith. At the outbreak of the war he had been on the staff of the Cincinnati Gazette. He was the friend and counsellor of a number of public men including President Hayes. Historical writing claimed his attention at intervals in his life and revealed him a man of a careful habit and of creditable ideals. Early in 1883 he merged the Western Associated Press, with the New York Associated Press and reorganized the service to its great advantage. Exact in statement, impartial, incorruptible it grew in respect. [2] Utterances from this source were so responsible, as compared with the

[1] Cf. N. Y. Tribune, Nov. 30, Dec. 3 and 6, 1866.
[2] Cf. Melville E. Stone, Century Magazine, June and July, 1905, articles on "Associated Press."

despatches sent forward by most of the correspondents who
served individual newspapers, that the caption "By the Associated Press" was often inserted at the head of a telegram for
the assurance of the reader. Indeed so well did it perform its
duties that little room was left for the special correspondent,
except in adjectival and florid description, which but amplified
the facts, and for accounts of trifling and sensational occurrences
which Mr. Smith's trained body of informants saw no value
in and had designedly passed by.

By changes and transfers of membership by purchase the
number of partners in the group in New York was reduced to
six. The organization in truth was a narrow monopoly. No
journal not originally in it could enter it and reap its immense
advantages without the consent of all the members. The
lessees and franchise owners in other places acquired monopoly
rights for their respective districts.[1] The effect, as the value
of such privileges increased, was nothing short of revolutionary.
The introduction of great presses and expensive machinery
for the printing of newspapers, the development of methods
of distribution—changes which affected the journal on its
mechanical side—tended to make the conduct of such property
a complicated and an unwieldy task involving the investment
of a huge capital. But the growth of the idea of "news," the
enlargement of the issues, the extension of the circulation, and,
most of all, the conditions established by a combination of
the news gathering agencies, absolutely precluding free competition, now made journalism what it had never been before.

The field was closed. No new paper could be started with
hope of success. To enter the business meant the purchase of
a journal already in existence which held the privilege of obtaining the news despatches from this monopoly. This in a
large city was only for a rich capitalist, or a group of capitalists,
who could buy and operate the "plant," as they would an iron
mine, a railroad or a cotton mill.[2]

---

[1] M. E. Stone, Fifty Years a Journalist, pp. 212–3.
[2] Cf. ibid., pp. 369–70; Richard Hooker, The Story of an Independent
Newspaper, pp. 5–6.

Henceforth the daily press would be commercial and industrial. The man at the "case" by diligence and self-improvement, or a writer on the staff of a paper could no more rise to eminence as an editor, as Greeley and Raymond had done, than he could hope to mount the throne of some hereditary monarchy.[1]

The editors would be hired men, like those setting the type in the room overhead, who, on their side, however, would have this advantage—in that they, at the dictation of a labor union, might demand and receive an acceptable reward for their services, when this was denied the writers for the great sheet. The interests of the owner of the property would be allied, not with those who were concerned with any high public principle which it should enunciate, or the manner in which its judgments might be expressed—the most successful from a commercial standpoint, might, perhaps, have neither principles to serve nor literary form—his sympathies would lie with the solicitors of advertisements from the keepers of department stores and other patrons, without whose support the gigantic business structure would fall to the ground.

[1] Cf. O. G. Villard, Atlantic Monthly, January, 1918, p. 64.

INDEX

ABBEY, Henry A., 447.
Abbott, Josiah G., 298.
Abolitionists, denounce Hayes, 337; friends of Indians, 432-3.
Adams, Charles Francis, his opinion of Schurz, 1; appointed to adjust "Alabama" claims, 3; offered Republican nomination for Vice President, 3; supported for President at Cincinnati, 16, 17-8; Bowles urges his name, 22; strength of, as a candidate, 23; votes cast for, in convention, 24, 25; his friends support Julian for Vice President, 26; use of his name at Fifth Avenue Conference, 43; Democrats friendly to, 45; possibility of his election, 58; again proposed for the Presidency in 1876, 261; little enthusiasm for, 263; supports Tilden, 276.
Adams, Charles Francis, Jr., characterizes railroad men, 99-100, 101, 107; writes to Schurz, 252; congratulates Schurz, 253.
Adams, Henry, 473.
Adams, John Quincy, I, 339.
Adams, John Quincy, II, 52.
"Adeler, Max," 56.
Agassiz, Louis, 453.
Akerman, A. T., Attorney General, 183.
Alabama, last phases of Reconstruction in, 196-202.
"Alabama" Claims, settlement of, 3, 17, 117, 129.
Albany Regency, 140, 290.
Alcorn, James L., 143, 211, 217.
Alden, Henry Mills. 468.
Alexander, Columbus, 157, 158.
Allen, Wm., elected governor of Ohio, 130, 138; renominated, 250; popularity of, 251; menace of, 252, 269; defeat of, 253, 272; candidate for President, 270.
Allison, Wm. B., member of investigating committee, 136; Sher-

man confers with, 360; member of commission to treat with Indians, 397, 398.
Almy, Admiral, 175.
Alvord, John W., founder of Freedmen's Bank, 184.
American Association for the Advancement of Science, 441.
American Horse, fight with, 419.
American Institute of Architects, 447.
Ames, General Adelbert, governor of Mississippi, 211-2; calls for troops, 213, 216; discredited at Washington, 216; impeached, 217.
Ames, Oakes, 71, 98.
Amnesty to "rebels," 2; Republicans grant, 3; New York Tribune advocates, 9; Liberals advocate, 21; bills to grant, 256-7.
Andersonville Prison, horrors in, 257, 266.
Angell, James B., 493.
Anthony, Henry B., 493.
Anthony, Susan B., 16.
Apaches, atrocities of, 401-402.
Architecture, after Civil War, 443, 445-6.
Arkansas, last phases of Reconstruction in, 202-211.
Arthur, Chester A., befriends Babcock, 156; collector at New York, 3, 340, 349; Hayes asks, to resign, 354; declares report of Jay commission unjust, 355; Hayes suspends, 359.
Ashe, Thomas S., 142.
Associated Press, 497-9.
Atchison, Topeka and Santa Fé Railroad, 367, 400.
Atkinson, Edward, 43.
Atlantic Monthly, ridicules Greeley, 28, 35; constituency of, 58; founding of, 471-2; influence of, 479; Godkin's praise of, 479.
Attorney General's Department, investigations of, 183.

72; Cooke's loans to, 91; character of, 127; opposition leader in House, 141-2; characterizes Conkling, 255; candidate for President, 255; his attacks on the South, 256-7; "waving the bloody shirt," 257-8, 262; his opinion of Adams, 261; his railroad connections, 262-3; Bristow's friends oppose, 263; illness of, 264; Ingersoll nominates, 265-6; votes for, in convention, 267; Hayes unwilling to run on ticket with, 268; defeat of, 268; speaks for Hayes, 278; Conkling's feud with, 293; hostile to Hayes administration, 332; asks Hayes to appoint Frye to cabinet, 333; espouses cause of Kellogg, 335-6; a "Stalwart," 337; harries Hayes about Mexico, 361, 363; receives communication about Yellowstone National Park, 440.
Blair, Francis P., 480.
Blair, Francis P., Jr., and the Cincinnati convention, 23-4, 27, 29, 36.
Blair, Montgomery, 24, 162, 308.
Bloody Knife, Indian scout, 376.
Bogy, L. V., 283.
Baker, George H., 463.
Bonner, Robert, 462-3.
Booth, Newton, 272.
Booth, Wilkes, 57.
Borie, Adolph E., befriends Babcock, 156; friend of Robeson, 180; friend of Grant, 249.
Boston Advertiser, 480, 492-3.
Boston Transcript, 492.
"Bourbons," refuse to support Greeley, 52.
Boutwell, George S., United States senator, 75; pays out greenbacks, 87-8, 116, 121; defends his action, 115; his relations with Sanborn contracts, 134-5; votes to acquit Belknap, 163; conducts partisan investigation in Mississippi, 218-9; Hayes gives office to, 343.
Bowles, Samuel, in "Quadilateral," 19-20; advocate of Adams at Cincinnati, 22; accepts Greeley 30; criticizes Gratz Brown, 35; enjoins Greeley to silence, 37; characterizes Boston papers, 492; founds Springfield Republican, 493-4.
Boynton, General H. V., 343, 495.
Bradley, Joseph P., member of Electoral Commission, 298; decisions of, 304, 305-306; called "Aliunde Joe," 307.
Bragg, Braxton, 54.
Breckinridge, John C., 5, 128.
Bridger "Jim," 438.
Briggs, Charles F., editor of Putnam's Magazine, 470, 474.
Brigham, Charles D., 494.
"Brindle Tails" in Arkansas, 203.
Brinkerhoff, General, 27.
Brinkerhoff, Jacob, 42.
Bristow, Benjamin H., appointed Secretary of Treasury, 117, 136, 167; his advice on money question, 118, 122; attacks Whiskey Frauds, 144; pursues thieves, 145; supported by Grant, 147; refused Grant's support, 149; candidate for President, 150; position of, untenable, 150; his pursuit of Babcock, 151-5; Grant resolves to dismiss, 156; his activities in relation to "Safe Burglary," 157-9; resigns, 159; testifies before committee of Congress, 159; opposes Grant's Louisiana policy, 240; Independents support, for President, 263; nominated in convention, 265; votes for, 267; Hayes favors, 267; asks his friends to support Hayes, 268; his friends dismissed by Grant, 277; ignored by Hayes, 323,
Brodhead, J. O., 283.
Bromley, Isaac H., 43.
Brook Farm, 32, 485, 488.
Brooks, James, 71.
Brooks, Joseph, leader in Reconstruction politics in Arkansas, 203-210.
Brooks, Noah, 485.
Brooks, Phillips, 477.
"Brooks and Baxter War," 205-207.

INDEX

for, at Cincinnati, 24, 25; Democratic friendliness for candidacy of, 45; withdraws as a Presidential candidate, 52; marked for place on Electoral Commission, 295; elected senator, 297, 333; denounced by Democrats, 307; suggested for place on Louisiana commission, 328; independent in Senate, 351.

Davis, E. J., governor of Texas, 192–3.

Davis, Garrett, reluctantly accepts Greeley, 47.

Davis, Henry Winter, 255.

Davis, Jefferson, Greeley on bail bond of, 33; letter to, 128–9; amnesty for, 257; Blaine attacks, 258.

Davis, General Jeff. C., captures Modocs, 404

Davis, Rebecca Harding, 473.

Dawes, Henry L., leader in House, 142; votes to convict Belknap, 163.

Delano, Columbus, and the "Indian Ring," 167–8; charges brought against, by Marsh, 168–9; resigns as Secretary of Interior, 170; Indian policy of, 383, 386, 391, 396–7, 429; asks money for Yellowstone National Park, 440.

Dennison, Governor, 311.

Dent, General, 184.

Denver, railroads into, 366–7; character of, as a city, 368, 369.

Denver and Rio Grande Railroad, 367.

de Trobriand, General, 239.

Devens, Charles, Attorney General in Hayes cabinet, 322, 323.

Dewey, George, 183.

Diaz, Porfirio, President of Mexico, 362–5.

Dickens, Charles, 456, 458, 459, 462, 468.

Dickinson, Anna, 465.

"Dime Novels," 461–2.

Disraeli, 457.

District of Columbia, scandals in government of, 78–9, 136–7, 183; "safe burglary" in, 157–9.

Dix, John A., governor of New

York, 138; renomination of, 139; defeated, 140, 258; goes South for Hayes, 283.

Doane, G. C., 438.

Dodge, R. I., visits Black Hills, 375; tells of arrest of miners, 390.

Dodge, Wm. E., 396.

Dom Pedro, at Centennial, 188.

Doolittle, J. R., leaves Republican party, 2; reluctantly accepts Greeley, 47; presides over Democratic convention in 1872, 49; his successor as senator, 149; goes South for Tilden, 283.

Dorsey, Stephen W., 204, 206, 207, 209, 210.

Dorsheimer, Wm., 139.

Douglas, Beverly B., 79.

Douglas, Stephen A., 5.

Douglass, Fred., secretary of San Domingo Commission, 4; Grant "insults," 14; supports Grant, 14; head of Freedmen's Bank, 185; Hayes appoints, marshal of District of Columbia, 343.

Drew, Daniel, 104.

Drew, George F., governor of Florida, 220–21, 286.

Drexels, owners of Public Ledger, 491, 492.

Durell, Judge, midnight order of, 232, 233, 234.

Dwight, Theodore, lecturer at Cornell, 453.

Dyar, L. S., Indian commissioner, 404.

Dyer, D. P., district attorney in Whiskey Ring trials, 150, 152, 153, 159.

Early, Jubal, 48.

Eaton, Dorman B., heads Civil Service Commission, 76, 339.

Edgeworth, Miss, 457.

Edmunds, George F., opposes "Salary Grab," 73; member of committee to consider Belknap's case, 161; votes to convict Belknap, 163; "waving bloody shirt," 278; forwards bill to create Electoral Commission, 294, 297; member of commission, 298; chairman of a sub-committee, 299.

Electoral Commission, 295; member of Commission, 298; his opinion of Louisiana's returning board, 304; endorses Devens, 322; suggested as member of Hayes's Louisiana commission, 328; opposes admission of New Mexico, 370–71.
Holden, W. W., postmaster of Raleigh, 76; deposed as governor of North Carolina, 193.
Holland, J. G., 464, 474, 475, 494.
Holmes, O. W., 451, 463, 471, 472.
Hopkins, Johns, founds a university, 451, 453–5.
Hot Springs of Arkansas, 437–8.
Houghton, H. O., & Co., 472.
Houghton, Mifflin & Co., 472.
Hours at Home, 474.
Houston, George S., governor of Alabama, 199–200, 201–202.
Howard, General O. O., in Freedmen's Bureau, 183–4; his university, 184; his campaign against the Nez Percés, 425, 426; pursues the Bannocks, 427.
Howe, Senator Timothy O., chairman of sub-committee, 299; opposes Hayes, 350.
Howells, W. D., 464, 465, 466, 472.
Hoyt, Spragues & Co., 93.
Humphreys, case of, in Florida, 304, 306.
Hungerford claims, 181.
Hunt, Richard Morris, 446, 447.
Hunt, Wm. Morris, 447, 449.
Hunton, Eppa, in Congress, 79; member of Electoral Commission, 298.
Hurlbut, Wm. Henry, 487.
Huxley, Prof., at Johns Hopkins, 454.

INDIANS, scandal concerning traderships among, 165–7; charges of Marsh as to mismanagement of, 168–9, 397; Schurz's policy as to, 356–9, 428, 430–31; Grant's policy toward, 381–4; Chandler's proposal as to, 384; treaties with, 384–6; the Ute, 386–8; the Sioux, 388–95; commission to deal with, reorganized, 395–6; efforts

to buy Black Hills from, 397–9; selfish and shortsighted policy toward, 399–400; incursions of, 400; engagement with Piegan, 400–401; the Apache, 401–402; war with Modoc, 402–406; campaign against Cheyenne and other tribes of, 406–407; campaign against Sioux, ending in Custer's Massacre, 407–18; pursuit of, after the massacre, 418–21; treaty with Sioux, 421–3; difficulty of dealing with, 423–4; war with Nez Percé, 424–7; war with Bannock, 427; troubles of army in warfare with, 427–8; evils of treaty system, 428–30; control of, by agents of religious organizations, 431; in Indian Territory, 431–2; movement to return control of, to War Department, 432–6.
Indian Bureau, scandals in, under Delano, 165–70; proposed return of, to War Department, 170, 432–6; Schurz reorganizes, 356–9; mismanagement of, 415–6.
"Indian Ring," activities of, during Delano's administration, 168–9; Schurz investigates, 356–9; robberies by, 381; gets control of Indian Commission, 396.
"Inflation Bill," passage and veto of, 115–7.
Ingersoll, R. G., nominates Blaine, 265–6.
Inness, George, 447.
Interior Department, investigation of, 143; scandals in, under Delano, 165–70; plan to transfer Indians from, to War Department, 170, 416, 432–6; Schurz reorganizes, 356–9.
International Copyright, want of law as to, 456–7; efforts to secure, 457–9; opposition to, 459–60.
Interstate Commerce Commission, 111.
Irish, 39.
Irving, Washington, 458, 463.

JACKSON, Helen Hunt, 433.
James, Henry, Jr., 466.

announces election of Hayes, 281–2; founding of, 486; later course of, 487.

New York Tribune, opposes Grant in 1872, 11, 15; supports Liberal movement, 19, 22; Greeley withdraws from editorship of, 37–8; Greeley returns to, 65; contest for possession of, 67–8; opposes inflation 114; supports Hayes, 275–6; founding and influence of, 484–6, 493.

New York World, opposes Greeley, 29, 45–6; reluctantly supports Greeley, 52; founding and later course of, 487.

New Orleans Riots, 236–7.

Nez Percés, war with, 424–7; death rate among, 432.

Nichols, Commodore, 177.

Nicholls, Francis T., nominated for governor of Louisiana, 246; fate of, in balance, 300, 310; commissioners confer with, 329; in control of state government, 330.

Nordhoff, Charles, writes Schurz, 252.

Norris, P. W., superintendent of Yellowstone Park, 440; builds roads in park, 441–2.

North American Review, Chief Joseph writes for, 427; editors of, 433; influence of, 479.

North Carolina, last phases of Reconstruction in, 193–4.

Northern Pacific Railroad, Cooke's enthusiasm for, 81, 83–4, 91; failure of, 91–3; cause of collapse of, 111–2; railhead of, 376; Indians on lands of, 386; lobby of, 439; spur of, 441.

Norton, Charles Eliot, professor in Harvard, 448; his interest in Atlantic Monthly, 471; assistant editor of North American Review, 473; aids Godkin in establishing New York Nation, 476, 477; praises Nation, 477; influence of, 479.

Noyes, E. F., makes nominating speech for Hayes, 265; goes South for Hayes, 283; charge of bargain in appointment of, 344.

O'CONOR, Charles, nominated for President by Bourbons, 52; counsel for Tilden, 303.

"Ohio Idea," 4, 114.

Oklahoma, 384.

Olmsted, Frederick Law, 44, 52, 475–6, 477.

Ord, General, 362, 363, 364.

Oregon, result of election in, disputed, 284–5; scandal as to electoral vote of, 306–307, 316.

Orton, William, 67.

Osages, scheme to rob, 383.

Osgood, James R., & Co., 472.

Ottendorfer, Oswald, signs call for Fifth Avenue Conference, 42; opposes Greeley, 46; supports Tilden, 276; goes South for Tilden, 283.

Overland Monthly, 465.

PACIFIC Mail Company, lobbying for, 131–2.

Packard, S. B., carpetbagger in Louisiana, 230; supports Sheridan, 241; nominated for governor, 245–6; badgers Grant, 299–300, 325; Matthews advises, 326; protests withdrawal of troops, 329; attacks Hayes, 337; consul at Liverpool, 345.

Palmer, John M., goes South for Tilden, 283.

Panic of 1873, 79–96, 129, 137.

Parker, Cortlandt, goes South for Hayes, 283.

Parker, Joel, nominated for Vice President, 13.

Parkman, Francis, 463, 464.

Parsons, Lewis E., governor of Mississippi, 211.

Patrons of Husbandry, organization and spread of the order, 102–104.

Patterson, John J., carpetbagger in South Carolina, 223–4, 228.

Patterson, James W., of New Hampshire, 71.

Pawnees, 432.

Payne, Henry B., and the Electoral Commission, 294; member of Commission, 298.

Peabody, George, 449.

Pelton, W. T., involved in Oregon scandal, 306.

Pendleton, George H., reluctantly accepts Greeley, 47; defeated by Hayes, 251.

Penn, governor of Louisiana, 236–7.

Pennsylvania Academy of the Fine Arts, 443, 448.

Pennsylvania Railroad, 73, 86, 92, 93, 94.

Pension Bureau, scandals in, 170–71; proposed transfer of, to War Department, 170.

Peterson's Magazine, 470.

Petroleum in Pennsylvania, 444.

Pinchback, negro leader in Louisiana, 230; attempts of, to assume governorship, 232; refused a seat in Senate, 245; his nominating speech for Morton for President, 265.

Phelps, Wm. Walter, his reputed interest in New York Tribune, 67; member of Louisiana committee, 241–2, 304; favors " Wheeler Adjustment," 244.

Phelps, Dodge & Co., 133.

Philadelphia Custom House, scandals in, 353–4.

Philadelphia Press, Forney and, 12; founding of, 490–91.

Philadelphia Times, 491

Phillips, M. D., 471.

Phillips, Wendell, 337.

Phillips, Sampson & Co., 471, 472.

Pickens, Governor, of South Carolina, 221.

Piegans, atrocities of, and Baker's revenge upon, 400–401, 436.

Pierce, Franklin, 422.

Pierce, Henry L., his vote on Louisiana, 306.

Pierrepont, Edwards, Attorney General, 146; in trials of whiskey thieves, 153; witness before committee of Congress, 159; appointed minister to England, 187; sends friend to Mississippi, 216; gives opinion of Europe about Hayes, 320.

Platt, Thomas C., Conkling urges, for place in Hayes cabinet, 332; defies Hayes, 349–50.

Platt, James H., Jr., his control of navy yard at Norfolk, 175, 177.

Poland, Luke P., his course as to Arkansas, 209–10; seconds nomination of Bristow, 265.

Polo, Admiral, 124, 125, 126.

Poncas, 432.

Porter, Noah, 451.

Post Office Department, corrupt rings in, 183.

Potter, Clarkson N., on committee to study situation in Louisiana, 241–2; his committee to investigate election of 1876, 299.

"Potter Law," 109.

Pratt, Captain R. H., his efforts to educate Indians, 430–31.

Prentice, George D., 480, 496.

Prescott, Wm. H., 463.

Prince, L. Bradford, nominated to be naval officer, 354; rejected, 355.

Princeton University, Southern students at, 449; president of, 451.

Prohibitionists, form political party, 271.

Providence Journal, 493.

Public Ledger, of Philadelphia, 491–2.

Pulitzer, Joseph, 487.

Putnam, George P., 458, 470.

Putnam's Monthly, 470–71, 474, 479.

"QUADRILATERAL," 19–20, 22–3, 24–30.

Quay, M. S., goes South for Hayes, 283; active henchman of Cameron, 333.

Quincy, Edmund, 471, 477, 485.

RAILROADS, overbuilding of, 80, 83; "Farmers War" on, 98–105; Granger laws against, 106–111.

Ralston, Wm. C., failure and death of, 95–6.

Ranches in West, 379–80.

Randall, Samuel J., votes for "Salary Grab," 74; leader in House, 142; goes South for Tilden, 283; elected speaker, 291; keeps House in order as speaker, 309; pacifying influence of, 312; re-elected speaker, 351.

Tariff, Liberals oppose high, 3; Republicans reduce, 3; Greeley and the, 10; Liberal party's difficulties with, 21.

Taylor, Bayard, Greeley to, 60; minister to Germany, 343; on state of society after the war, 444; lecturer at Cornell, 452; poetry and novels of, 463, 464, 465; befriends Sidney Lanier, 466; death of, 466, 477; his connection with New York Tribune, 485.

Temperance movement, advance of, 271.

Tennessee, last phases of Reconstruction in, 191.

Tenney, A. W., 134.

Tennyson, Alfred, 462.

Terry, General, member of court to investigate Babcock, 154; inability of, to keep white men out of Indian lands, 397; commands troops in war against Sioux, 410; sends Reno on scouting expedition, 411; plans campaign, 411-2; Sioux retire at approach of, 414, 415, 417; his instructions to Custer, 417; pursues Sitting Bull, 418.

Texas, last phases of Reconstruction in, 192-3.

Texas Pacific Railroad, 86, 92-3.

Thackeray, W. M., 459, 468.

Thomas, Dr. E., killed by Modocs, 404.

Thompson, Richard W., member of Hayes cabinet, 322, 323; Stalwarts approve appointment of, 333.

Thomson, J. Edgar, 86, 92.

Thoreau, H. D., 470, 471.

Thurman, Allen G., in campaign of 1872, 6; agrees to support Greeley, 51; on committee to investigate conditions in District of Columbia, 136; defeated for governor of Ohio, 251; relationship of, with Allen, 251; Greenbacker, 269; member of Electoral Commission, 298; Tilden blames, 307; illness of, 308.

Ticknor and Fields, 467, 472.

"Tidal Wave" of 1874, 119, 137-8, 140, 141-3, 195.

Tilden, Samuel J., reluctantly accepts Greeley, 47; nominated for governor of New York, 139-40; elected governor, 258; exposes and attacks Canal Ring, 258-60; availability as a Presidential candidate, 260; pre-eminent figure in party, 269; vote for, in convention, 270; nominated for President, 270; his letter of acceptance, 273; Schurz's opinion of, 274; New York Tribune abandons, 275; some Independents support, 276; associated with ex-"rebels," 278; his income tax returns, 279; confers with his managers, 280; news of election of, 281; his election in doubt, 281-2; "visiting statesmen" to aid, 283; South Carolina claimed for, 284; Oregon claimed for, 284-5; Florida and Louisiana claimed for, 285-7; urged to fight, 289; characteristics of, 290-91; studies precedents, 292; opposes Electoral Commission, 296; downcast, 297; sacrificed by South, 299, 312; counsel for, 303, 305; his nephew and the Oregon scandal, 306; defeat of by Electoral Commission, 310; Hayes's superiority over, for tasks to be performed, 348; Stalwarts liken Hayes to, 350.

Tilton, Theodore, his scandal, 98; mentioned, 255.

Tilton, Wheelwright & Co., 182.

Timrod, Henry, 463.

Tipton, Senator, opposes Grant, 2.

Toombs, Robert, mentioned, 46; refuses to support Greeley, 48; aids in rout of carpetbaggers in Georgia, 192; Blaine attacks, 257.

Train, George Francis, 16, 35.

Trevino, General, Mexican commander, 363, 364.

Trollope, Anthony, 459, 468.

Trowbridge, J. T., 472.

Trumbull, Lyman, as a Liberal, 1; his part in the impeachment

VERMONT COLLEGE
MONTPELIER, VERMONT